Communication Yearbook 37

Communication Yearbook 37

Edited by
Elisia L. Cohen

Published Annually for the
International Communication Association

NEW YORK AND LONDON

First published 2013
by Routledge
711 Third Avenue, New York, NY 10017

Simultaneously published in the UK
by Routledge
2 Park Square, Milton Park, Abingdon, Oxon OX14 4RN

Routledge is an imprint of the Taylor & Francis Group, an informa business

© 2013 Taylor & Francis

The right of Elisia L. Cohen to be identified as the author of the editorial material, and of the authors for their individual chapters, has been asserted in accordance with sections 77 and 78 of the Copyright, Designs and Patents Act 1988.

Library of Congress Cataloging in Publication Data
A catalog record has been requested for this book

ISBN: 978-0-415-82331-9 (hbk)
ISBN: 978-0-203-55194-3 (ebk)

Typeset in Times by
EvS Communication Networx, Inc.

Printed and bound in the United States of America by Sheridan Books, Inc. (a Sheridan Group Company).

Contents

The International Communication Association

The International Communication Association (ICA) was formed in 1950, bringing together academics and other professionals whose interests focus on human communication. The Association maintains an active membership of more than 4,000 individuals, of whom some two- thirds teach and conduct research in colleges, universities, and schools around the world. Other members are in government, law, medicine, and other professions. The wide professional and geographic distribution of the membership provides the basic strength of the ICA. The Association serves as a meeting ground for sharing research and useful dialogue about communication interests.

Through its divisions and interest groups, publications, annual conferences, and relations with other associations around the world, the ICA promotes the systemic study of communication theories, processes, and skills. In addition to *Communication Yearbook*, the Association publishes the *Journal of Communication, Human Communication Research, Communication Theory, Journal of Computer-Mediated Communication, Communication, Culture & Critique, A Guide to Publishing in Scholarly Communication Journals,* and the *ICA Newsletter.*

For additional information about the ICA and its activities, visit online at www.icahdq.org or contact Michael L. Haley, Executive Director, International Communication Association, 1500 21st Ave. NW, Washington, DC 20036 USA; phone 202-955-1444; fax 202-955-1448; email ica@icahdq.org.

Editors of the *Communication Yearbook* series:

> Volumes 1 and 2, Brent D. Ruben
> Volumes 3 and 4, Dan Nimmo
> Volumes 5 and 6, Michael Burgoon
> Volumes 7 and 8, Robert N. Bostrom
> Volumes 9 and 10, Margaret L. McLaughlin
> Volumes 11, 12, 13, and 14, James A. Anderson
> Volumes 15, 16, and 17, Stanley A. Deetz
> Volumes 18, 19, and 20, Brant R. Burleson
> Volumes 21, 22, and 23, Michael E. Roloff
> Volumes 24, 25, and 26, William B. Gudykunst
> Volumes 27, 28, and 29, Pamela J. Kalbfleisch
> Volumes 30, 31, 32, and 33, Christina S. Beck
> Volumes 34, 35, and 36, Charles T. Salmon
> Volume 37, Elisia L. Cohen

Michael S. Griffin
Visual Communication Studies Div.
Chair
Macalester College

Philip Lodge
Communication History IG Chair
Edinburgh Napier U

Richard J. Doherty
Environmental Communication IG
Chair
University of Illinois – Chicago

Dmitri Williams
Game Studies IG Chair
University of Southern California

Vincent Doyle
Gay, Lesbian, Bisexual &
Transgender IG Chair
IE University

Adrienne Shaw
Gay, Lesbian, Bisexual & Transgen-
der IG Chair
Temple University

Liz Jones
Intergroup Communication IG Chair
Griffith University

Michael L. Haley
Executive Director (ex-officio)
International Communication
Association

DIVISION CHAIRS

Amy B. Jordan
Children, Adolescents & the Media
Div. Chair
University of Pennsylvania

Erica L. Scharrer
Children, Adolescents & the Media
Div. Vice-Chair
University of Massachusetts –
Amherst

Esther Rozendaal
Children, Adolescents & the Media
Div. Secretary
Radboud University Nijmegen

Kwan Min Lee
Communication & Technology Div.
Chair
University of Southern California

James A. Danowski
Communication & Technology Div.
Vice-Chair
University of Illinois at Chicago

Lee Humphreys
Communication & Technology Div.
Secretary
Cornell University

Laura Stein
Communication Law & Policy Div.
Chair
University of Texas – Austin

Seamus Simpson
Communication Law & Policy Div.
Vice-Chair
University of Salford

Roopali Mukherjee
Ethnicity & Race in Communication
Div. Chair
CUNY – Queens College

Miyase Christensen
Ethnicity & Race in Communication
Div. Vice-Chair
Karlstad U; Royal Institute of
Technology(KTH)

SPECIAL INTEREST GROUP CHAIRS

Norman C. H. Wong
Health Communication Div.
Secretary
University of Oklahoma

Philip Lodge
Communication History IG Chair
Edinburgh Napier University

Richard K. Popp
Communication History IG
Vice-Chair
University of Wisconsin-Milwaukee

Richard J. Doherty
Environmental Communication IG
Chair
University of Illinois – Chicago

Dmitri Williams
Game Studies IG Chair
University of Southern California

James D. Ivory
Game Studies IG Vice-Chair
Virginia Tech

Joyce L.D. Neys
Game Studies IG Secretary
Erasmus University – Rotterdam

Vincent Doyle
Gay, Lesbian, Bisexual & Transgen-der IG Chair
IE University

Adrienne Shaw
Gay, Lesbian, Bisexual & Transgen-der IG Chair
Temple University

Liz Jones
Intergroup Communication IG Chair
Griffith University

Howard Giles
Intergroup Communication IG
Vice-Chair
University of California – Santa Barbara

Shahira Fahmy	*University of Arizona, USA*
Edward L. Fink	*University of Maryland, USA*
Brooke Fisher Liu	*University of Maryland, USA*
Richard Fitzgerald	*University of Queensland, Australia*
Brandi N. Frisby	*University of Kentucky, USA*
Shiv Ganesh	*University of Waikato, New Zealand*
Nurit Guttman	*Tel Aviv University, Israel*
Nancy Grant Harrington	*University of Kentucky, USA*
Jenine Harris	*Washington University-St Louis, USA*
Jake Harwood	*University of Arizona, USA*
Magne Martin Haug	*Norwegian Business School, Norway*
Evelyn Y. Ho	*University of San Francisco, USA*
Thomas A. Hollihan	*University of Southern California, USA*
Liz Jones	*Griffith University, Australia*
Amy B. Jordan	*University of Pennsylvania, USA*
Joo-Young Jung	*International Christian University, Japan*
Jennifer A. Kam	*University of Illinois at Urbana-Champaign, USA*
Youna Kim	*The American University of Paris, France*
Antonio C. La Pastina	*Texas A&M University, USA*
Annie Lang	*Indiana University, USA*
Michael Latzer	*University of Zurich, Switzerland*
Chin-Chuan Lee	*City University of Hong Kong, Hong Kong*
Maria Len-Rios	*University of Missouri, USA*
Maria Löblich	*Ludwig-Maximilians-Universität, Germany*
Robin Mansell	*London School of Economics and Political Science, UK*
Caryn Medved	*Baruch College, USA*
Rebecca Meisenbach	*University of Missouri, USA*
Monique Mitchell Turner	*George Washington University, USA*
Ananda Mitra	*Wake Forest University, USA*
Seth M. Noar	*University of North Carolina at Chapel Hill, USA*
Mohammed Zin Nordin	*Universiti Pendidikan Sultan Idris, Malaysia*
Jon F. Nussbaum	*Penn State University, USA*
Amy O'Connor	*North Dakota State University, USA*
Daniel J. O'Keefe	*Northwestern University, USA*
Mary Beth Oliver	*Penn State University, USA*
Hee Sun Park	*Michigan State University, USA*
Wei Peng	*Michigan State University, USA*

Marshall Scott Poole	*University of Illinois at Urbana-Champaign, USA*
Linda L. Putnam	*University of California-Santa Barbara, USA*
Jack Linchaun Qiu	*Chinese University of Hong Kong, Hong Kong*
Brian L. Quick	*University of Illinois at Urbana-Champaign, USA*
Artemio Ramirez, Jr.	*University of South Florida, USA*
Rajiv N. Rimal	*Johns Hopkins University, USA*
Randall Rogan	*Wake Forest University, USA*
Michael Roloff	*Northwestern University, USA*
Dietram A. Scheufele	*University of Wisconsin-Madison, USA*
Allison M. Scott	*University of Kentucky, USA*
Timothy Sellnow	*University of Kentucky, USA*
Deanna Sellnow	*University of Kentucky, USA*
Michelle Shumate	*University of Illinois at Urbana-Champaign, USA*
Kami Silk	*Michigan State University, USA*
Sandi W. Smith	*Michigan State University, USA*
Jordan Soliz	*University of Nebraska-Lincoln, USA*
Krishnamurthy Sriramesh	*Purdue University, USA*
Laura Stafford	*University of Kentucky, USA*
Michael Stohl	*University of California-Santa Barbara, USA*
Jennifer Stromer-Galley	*University of Albany, SUNY, USA*
Ed Tan	*University of Amsterdam, Netherlands*
David Tewksbury	*University of Illinois at Urbana-Champaign, USA*
C. Erik Timmerman	*University of Wisconsin-Milwaukee, USA*
April R. Trees	*St. Louis University, USA*
Mina Tsay-Vogel	*Boston University, USA*
Sebastián Valenzuela	*Pontificia Universidad Católica, Chile*
Jens Vogelgesang	*University of Hohenheim, Germany*
Peter Vorderer	*University of Mannheim, Germany*
Steve R. Wilson	*Purdue University, USA*
Werner Wirth	*University of Zurich, Switzerland*
Saskia Witteborn	*Chinese University of Hong Kong, Hong Kong*
Yariv Tsfati	*University of Haifa, Israel*
Y. Connie Yuan	*Cornell University, USA*
Marc Ziegele	*Johannes Gutenberg University Mainz, Germany*

Ad Hoc Reviewers

Editor's Introduction

Elisia L. Cohen

For over a decade, communication scholarship has demonstrated how the 21st-century communication landscape will be defined by shifting patterns in media ownership and control; new developments in personalized, mobile entertainment technology; and fluid flows of people, information, and relationships as a result of globalization and economic change. Given these diverse forces creating and constraining modern communication practice, engaged communication scholars are challenged by the need to account for these emergent theories, methods, processes, and communication effects within the discipline.

Indeed, to gather a comprehensive review of what represents "excellence" in communication research for any year, for any volume, poses a challenge given the character, growth, breadth, and depth of the communication discipline. Yet, this yearbook series originated with the International Communication Association's (ICA) vision to identify a "yearbook" of research pointing to emerging trends, theories, or problems in the field. Although a single volume *Communication Yearbook* can no longer comprehensively define the field's terrain as its central goal, as editor, I hope that this volume fulfills *Communication Yearbook*'s tradition of bringing to light important controversies, questions, and programs of research that are international in scope and critical to the field's development. In examining the work of previous *Communication Yearbook* editors, I found myself guided by the writing of Charles Salmon who, in 2010, hoped the *Yearbook* might continue to "offer all-important synthesis and integration of research on a range of communication issues, help to define and articulate some of the important research questions and programs of the day, and provide a measure of the vitality of the field through its scope and breadth" (p. xvi).

As I began editing my first volume in this *Communication Yearbook* series, I did so with the goal to reflect the scholarly research and objectives of the ICA. To that end, I sent a broad call for papers to all division and interest group chairs and announcements to ICA members. I recruited a set of internationally recognized scholars to serve on the editorial board and encouraged its members to recommend authors submit manuscripts for peer review that traversed broad terrain pushing disciplinary boundaries. The results included 69 full manuscripts that were sent out for peer review on a range of communication topics. Each manuscript was sent to at least three reviewers, and the essays that were accepted for publication enormously benefited from the incisive and constructive criticism offered by reviewers. The volume of essays that resulted from the peer review process includes thirteen state-of-the-discipline reviews written to promote clearer understanding complex communication systems, information and communication technologies, entertainment, organizational, and social practices.

In many ways, the chapters in this volume defy a neat organizational scheme as they each ask unique, insightful disciplinary questions. However, each essay raises questions about our capacity as communication scholars to study complex, multileveled communication phenomena. The authors comment on how scholarship considers how new ways of organizing message production and content, social networks, and relationships affect traditional patterns of political, health and science communication. The scholarship in this volume also attends to and develops new questions regarding critical ways of engaging and studying interpersonal, organizational, and media relationships. In addition to developing multileveled, multitheoretical perspectives on problems relevant to international communication research, the volume offers one methodological essay that reviews and describes the application of latent growth modeling techniques in communication research to enhance the study of these communication phenomena over time.

The organization of this volume falls into four parts, reflecting scholars' (a) reconceptualization of organizational membership and career formation in a global information society; (b) reappraisals of communication models, methods, and paradigms; (c) reassessments of message design and persuasion scholarship; and (d) reviews of trends evaluating media engagement and exposure effects.

The first part of this volume examines organizational communication practices and constraints in the 21st-century economic environment. In Chapter 1, Patrice M. Buzzanell and Kristen Lucas examine the social construction of career choice. Lucas and Buzzanell examine the ways in which career choice is limited and contested by socio-political and economic forces. The chapter illustrates creative and constrained constructions of career path and explores how this is communicated in light of the construction of human dignity in work. They argue that choice is key to achieving dignity and that communication scholars have not paid adequate attention to the relationship between choice, dignity, and career.

Following this essay, the volume turns to Brenda Berkelaar's chapter examining the communicative forces affecting 21st-century contingencies in labor practices. Berkelaar points to the ways in which organizational socialization, often called organizational assimilation by communication scholars, is changing as a result of new information communication technologies (ICT). By examining workplace turbulence, both the entry and exit of workers from the workplaces to which they belonged, Berkelaar identifies how constructed identities constrain organizational communication practice and how additional scholarship is needed to examine organizational socialization in nontraditional organizations, especially those that do not involve paid employment and/or brick-and-mortar work places.

Part II of the volume broadly includes essays reappraising communication frameworks, models, methods, and paradigms. The first chapter in this section, written by Katherine Ognyanova and Peter Monge, provides a multi-leveled, multidimensional network assessment of the 21st-century media system. This review offers insight for interdisciplinary inquiry, as it examines the organizational aspects of media flow, and it could inspire interesting new areas of research exploring forces of media content, production, and flow across our international discipline, including the global flow of information and entertainment products and the enactment of governmental roles in facilitating and constraining media production development

The chapter in this volume that follows offers a new taxonomy of communication networks for communication research. Michelle Shumate and colleagues review the literature on network analysis developed by communication scholars and organize it to develop a taxonomy of how communication networks have been considered within the discipline. In the process, they identify the strengths of disciplinary contributions to social networks research, as well as important areas for future research and theory development.

The next chapter appraises new models of online information delivery that have the potential to enable users to participate in message production. How to conceptualize online discussion, analyze user comments, and systematically aggregate such online content production is a novel question for 21st-century research. Marc Ziegele and Oliver Quiring's chapter provides a multidimensional framework for analyzing comments on mass media websites. Ziegele and Quiring introduce the term *media-stimulated interpersonal communication* to describe communication between individuals that is the result of news media coverage. They propose a framework for analyzing the quantity and quality of online discussions that result from news media coverage.

From this chapter on media-stimulated interpersonal communication, we turn to a chapter that offers a critique of the relationship between media-stimulation and scientific enterprise. Taking a critical approach to rethinking media and science in late modern societies, Pieter Maesele provides a meta-critique of the relationship between science and the public sphere and, in doing so, points to a need for a reconsideration of science communication, the role of science journalism, and the aims and methods of science communication research.

Finally, this section reappraising disciplinary trends concludes with Flaviu A. Hodis and Georgeta M. Hodis's identification of latent growth modeling as an advance in methodological application for communication research that remains underutilized in the discipline. The chapter traces the potential opportunities offered by latent growth modeling (LGM) to enhance communication research. In addition to providing a step-by-step guide to applying this method,

Hodis and Hodis argue that LGM would expand communication scholars' theoretical knowledge by allowing communication scholars to become more adept at designing communication research studies examine change in communication practices over time.

Part III of the volume offers reassessments of message design and persuasion scholarship. The title of the first chapter in this section explains its importance and significant findings: a review of evidence from 29 meta-analysis of 2,062 effect sizes for 13 message variations shows that the relative persuasiveness of different message types does not vary as a function of the persuasive outcome assessed. Daniel J. O'Keefe offers comprehensive and exhaustive review of evidence from 939 effect sizes to explain how the relative persuasiveness of message types do not vary as a function of persuasive outcome. This research finding and cumulative study of relative persuasive message strength has profound implications for persuasive health message design in political, health, and other persuasive social contexts.

The second chapter in this section also offers an assessment of scholarship focused on message design and evaluation by reviewing the literature examining cumulative knowledge from the study of inoculation effects in political contexts. Josh Compton and Bobi Ivanov's chapter identifies how inoculation theory as a voter resistance strategy may be extended to reflect the evolving nature of political campaigns. Compton and Ivanov suggest future directions for research in political campaign scholarship, including: addressing unresolved questions about voter characteristics; inoculation message characteristics and the efficacy of booster messages; message timing; the effects resistance messages have on candidate image and political behaviors; and whether, in what contexts, and to what effects, inoculation messages function as persuasive messages.

A large number of authors contributed content related to understanding media entertainment and its effects in the 21st century, which is the subject of the final section in this volume. In reviewing trends evaluating media engagement and exposure effects, this section advances our understanding of the human need for entertainment and play. Using meta-analysis, Riva Tukachinsky and Robert S. Tokunaga examines the persuasive effects of involvement in entertainment media and, based on the results, proposes areas for scholars to consider in the future. In so doing, Tukachinsky and Tokunaga's research examines the recent history of entertainment effects to summarize the concordances of findings of the effects of homophily, empathy, parasocial relationships, and the vehicle of audience transportation on viewers.

Fundamental to the study and assumption of media effects in the 21st century is the critical question of how researchers should measure and understand exposure. In Chapter 11, authors Li and Liu identify the process of information access and media exposure in online settings, including the contexts and situations in which people choose to engage in selective exposure—or the preferring and avoiding of certain information in ways that reflects one's beliefs. The authors describe how political predisposition is a main factor that leads to selective exposure and then further delineate between intentional and unintentional media exposure to argue that selective exposure is more likely to occur when people have high Internet search self-efficacy. The chapter concludes by presenting an original model of media exposure and persuasion effects to (a) explain the factors (political predisposition, need for cognitive closure, Internet search self-efficacy) that influence media exposure type (selective, extended, and sidetracked exposure) and (b) illustrate the persuasion effects (attitude reinforcement, formation, and change) produced by different media exposure types.

The third essay in this section, by Anthony M. Limperos, Edward Downs, James D. Ivory, and Nicholas David Bowman, examines recent trends in video game research. The advent of interactive technology, advanced simulation techniques, and multiuser multigame platforms poses unique challenges to existing paradigms of entertainment effects research. The authors review the relationship between gaming and cognition, research on the positive benefits of gaming (i.e., games for health), the hypothesized negative effects of gaming, and alternative explanations for gaming influences. Finally, this chapter has the potential to guide the next generation of international video game research by depicting the ways that gaming research may consider games as a transactional medium, where what people do with games is as important as what games do to individuals.

Finally, the last chapter of this volume, written by Eric Rasmussen, argues that scholars concerned with children and media should approach the concept of active mediation from an individualized persuasion framework. Rasmussen contends that such a framework would ground this sub-area of the field theoretically, point to new opportunities for research, and provide a better understanding of the influence of media on children.

Together, the authors contributing to this volume wrestle with important contexts and problems confronting communication scholars in developing adequate communication theories, methodologies, and applications to address the changing socio-cultural, media, political, and economic environments constraining and facilitating modern communication practices in diverse environments. They also perform a service to the discipline by appraising the existing plane of knowledge in the field of communication and offering insights into its potential trajectory and room for growth.

Finally, producing this edition of *Communication Yearbook* would not have been possible without the steady assistance of the College of Communication and Information at the University of Kentucky, my colleagues in the Department of Communication, and my editorial assistants. Nicholas Iannarino and Adam Parrish provided reliable and accurate assistance by helping me manage correspondence with authors and copyediting the work published here. Sarah Vos also provided critical support with editorial correspondence, edited final drafts of manuscripts, summaries of articles and critiques, and the final production package. I am fortunate to have such talented and reliable doctoral students.

I also appreciate the willingness of supportive friends and colleagues in the discipline for acting as a sounding board, providing timely reviews and advice beyond what would typically be considered editorial service: J. Alison Bryant, Michael Cody, Lew Donahue, Brandi Frisby, Nancy Grant Harrington, Tom Hollihan, Amy Jordan, Seth Noar, Michael Roloff, Deanna Sellnow, Tim Sellnow, Michelle Shumate, Laura Stafford, Cynthia Stohl, Jeff VanCleave, Shari Veil, Peter Vorderer, and Connie Yuan. I am truly grateful.

Part I

Rethinking Organizational Membership and Career Formation in a Global Information Society

CHAPTER CONTENTS

1 Constrained and Constructed Choices in Career

An Examination of Communication Pathways to Dignity

Patrice M. Buzzanell

Purdue University

Kristen Lucas

University of Louisville

Choice is foundational to contemporary careers. Yet, it often is constrained and contested in imperceptible ways. We reposition Ciulla's (2000) four reasons for work—meaningful work, leisure, money, and security—as discursive frames whereby people make career choices, craft their choice-legitimizing stories, and overemphasize the rhetoric of individual choice. These frames attend to, as well as underplay, profound discursive and material differences and socio-political and economic forces that enable and constrain career choice across lifespans. We describe and critique communication and related literature that extends and challenges each frame. We conclude by advancing a research agenda on communication, choice, and dignity.

Organizational scholars from varied disciplines are attending to ways in which individuals experience dignity—and indignities—in their work lives. Investigations occur in contexts ranging from recruitment (Dufur & Feinberg, 2007) to terminations (Wood & Karau, 2009), and from immigrants' hardscrabble search for work on the streets (Estrada & Hondagneu-Sotelo, 2011; Purser, 2009) to professionals' identity management in healthcare and customer service organizations (Chiappetta-Swanson, 2005; Ellingson, 2011; Fleming, 2005a). In these and other contexts, scholars typically include two key components in definitions of dignity: a sense of self-worth derived from one's respective social position and basic humanity, and the experience of being treated with respect by others (Hodson, 2001; Lee, 2008).

A central thread throughout dignity research and theorizing is the essential role of autonomy. Regardless of cultural and work context differences, autonomy coincides with higher productivity and quality of life (Gagné & Bhave, 2011) at a time when, paradoxically, high employment insecurity and electronic surveillance curtail autonomy. In industrial-based work, autonomy is the "right and responsibility to make *choices*" about methods and techniques used for given tasks, prioritization of work, and determination of what constitutes satisfactory work quality (Hodson, 2001, p. 141, emphasis added). From a critical management studies perspective, autonomy is "being in control of oneself, competently and appropriately exercising one's powers" (Sayer, 2007, p. 568), evoking notions of freedom to engage in self-directed choice. From diverse philosophical and religious perspectives, autonomy is understood as self-governing capacities "to determine one's ends and make authentic *choices*" (Brennan & Lo, 2007, p. 50, emphasis added). Thus, realization of dignity aligns with material ability to make choices and exercise autonomy, perceptions that one's actions reasonably result from choices made, and the ability to discursively construct a sense of choice about one's work situation.

Autonomy functions as a core value that shapes how people make choices about their work and career. Likewise, choice can be a framework for understanding the nature and terms of one's career. Yet, scholars insufficiently challenge discourses operating at intersections of dignity, choice, and career, particularly for members of certain social identity and occupational groups. For instance, some of the most dignity-affirming occupations in contemporary U.S. society (professional athletes, surgeons) are perceived as being higher status and "chosen" if not vigorously pursued (Gilbert, 2008). In contrast, dignity-threatening careers (garbage collectors, prison guards) are those in which people assume individuals had little choice about where they worked, did not work hard enough to acquire better jobs, and/or lacked ambition to pursue more lofty career goals—thus disregarding intersecting power relations that produce and normalize such responses (Buzzanell, 2000; Buzzanell & Goldzwig, 1991; Dougherty, 2011; Winker & Degele, 2011). As Ashforth and Kreiner (1999) note, individuals directly and indirectly ask dirty workers, "How can you do it?" (p. 417). Subsumed in this question are dignity-threatening probes: Why did you *choose* this job? Did you not have other *choices*? What did you do to limit other *choices*? In short, people give little consideration to cultural discourses, structural inequities, and material forces that constrain individual freedom and human capital development needed to choose otherwise (Bühler-Niederberger & König, 2011; Buzzanell, 2000; Lareau, 2003; Williams, 2000).

How people talk about their work and position themselves vis-à-vis valued activities and motivations is implicated in and has implications for choice, dignity, and career. We define career as the themes that underlie work-related experiences and the structures that emerge from and direct such activities (Buzzanell & Lucas, 2006). We note career is political in the conditions and interests that give rise to discourse's productive capacity to (re)produce as well as change understandings (Foucault, 1972, 1977/1995). This productive capacity operates within ideological intersections among micro-, meso-, and macronarratives (Alvesson & Kärreman, 2000; Buzzanell & Goldzwig, 1991; Fairhurst & Putnam, 2004; Foucault, 1972, 1977/1995; Phillips & Oswick, 2012). Exploring the nature of choice and dignity addresses contemporary calls for engaged communication scholarship as well as research on meaningful work and careers from interdisciplinary and global perspectives (Cech &

Blair-Loy, 2010; Cheney, Zorn, Planalp, & Lair, 2008; Frey & Cissna, 2009; Gunz, Mayrhofer, & Tolbert, 2011; Putnam, 2009).

In this chapter, we examine the politics and consequences of dignity, choice, and career through discursive and material lenses. We review career and communication literature on career choice and workplace dignity from different intra- and interdisciplinary perspectives. We maintain choice is a pathway to dignity in career and, potentially, toward greater quality of life. Even as we probe discursive frames and associated materialities that produce integrated accounts of individual choice and personal and/or occupational dignity within and across communicative contexts, we also note counter-stories of constrained and contested choice. We conclude with questions directing scholars toward communication research possibilities.

Career as a Story of (Constrained) Choice

Career is an interdisciplinary research area that traditionally has focused on white-collar workers' career choices, practices, and constraints. Recent scholarship has delved into the resources to which workers turn to secure and sustain white-collar employability (Lair, Sullivan, & Cheney, 2005; Nadesan & Trethewey, 2000; Rumens & Kerfoot, 2009). In these efforts, people aim to craft productive but temporary career identities out of myriad possible selves (Ibarra, 2003). They discipline themselves to fashion enterprising selves or brands in appearance, motivation, and emotion (Lair et al., 2005; Nadesan & Trethewey, 2000; Trethewey, 2001). They search for real jobs that promise good salaries and upward mobility (Clair, 1996). They utilize organization-specific discursive resources to frame appropriate identifications and identities within particular locales (Costas & Fleming, 2009; Kuhn, 2006; Spradlin, 1998; Sveningsson & Alvesson, 2003).

This career and communication research tells one story of career. In it, white-collar professionals and managers attempt to secure their own and their children's ways of life through adherence to particular images, lifestyles, and accumulations of career capital (Lareau & Conley, 2008; Medved, 2007; Williams, 2000). This story of career is oriented toward success strategies. Much communication research can be subsumed within this career-as-choice narrative, with choice operating as the belief that one has agency to redefine situations and/or to make decisions in one's own career interests. Career-as-choice research assumes that all are able to present "ideal applicant" images for job acquisition (Buzzanell, 1999; Lamude, Scudder, & Simmons, 2003). It also includes upward mobility and reciprocal social class acceptance (Kaufman, 2003), impression management (Tal-Or, 2010), career and psychosocial support in mentoring relationships (Carr & Heiden, 2011; Høigaard & Mathisen, 2009), and handling of political issues and problematic workplace relationships (Dougherty, 2009; Jackson, Firtko, & Edenborough, 2007). The traditional tale of career as upward movement and individual choice relies on effective, efficient, and politically astute discourse and social network positioning. In the story of career as individual choice, the communicative constitution and practices of privilege and meritocracy become visible and can be problematized (e.g., Stephens, Fryberg, & Markus, 2011).

However, there is another way to tell the story of career. In this version, career actors submit to their constrained choices and stagnated movement. They temper their career aspirations through recognition of their social positioning (Bühler-Niederberger & König, 2011). They struggle in low-wage jobs in markets with few viable options (Ehrenreich, 2001; Newman, 1999). They deal with job loss and chronic underemployment (Buzzanell & Turner, 2003; Gunn, 2008; Roy, 2005). They contend with vicious cycles of abuse and destructive organizing (Lutgen-Sandvik & Sypher, 2009). They grapple with discriminatory practices and incompatible meaning systems that limit career options and quality of (work) life (Bell & Nkomo, 2001; Nicotera & Mahon, 2013; Thompson, 2010; Williams, 2000). They cope with limits of autonomy imposed on their bodies (Mears & Finlay, 2005; Zoller, 2003) and emotions (Carmack, 2008; Tracy, 2005). They make painful trade-offs between objective success and fulfilling family lives (Correll, Benard, & Paik, 2007; Hayden & O'Brien Hallstein, 2010; Hewlett, 2002; Stone, 2007; Stone & Lovejoy, 2004; Tower & Alkadry, 2008). In the story of career as constrained choice, we see processes of consent and resistance, sense making, and narratives of resilience that are constructed and constituted communicatively.

We argue choice is not simply constrained, but also contested. Contested human agency happens when choice is "actively challenged, coerced, controlled, or actually changed and even destroyed in contention with other individuals or groups as they confront a variety of geographies, ecologies, actors, and social structures" (Boudreau, 2009, p. 133). Contested choice becomes visible when individuals pursue non-normative career and life options or problematize definitions of work and career in ways that question unpaid labor or inequity regimes (Acker, 2009; Medved, 2007; Williams, 2000). Contested choice surfaces when individuals recognize ambivalences within and/or question ideological bases of their societal positioning (Lucas, 2011b). It surfaces when people usurp dominant understandings and moral and personal positionings (Broadfoot & Munshi, 2007; Medved, 2009a; Pal & Dutta, 2008).

By understanding career as a story of both unbridled choice *and* constrained/contested choice, we highlight workers' search for dignity and communication scholars' moral imperative to investigate dignity. Toward this end, our career conceptualization lessens evaluative and exclusionary dimensions of career definitions that highlight intergenerational mobility, individual advancement, and extrinsic rewards (Buzzanell & Goldzwig, 1991; Inkson, 2007). We envision career as "an expansive discourse through which work acquires coherence and meaning in individuals' lives" and across lifespans (Buzzanell & Lucas, 2006, p. 172). This definition neither distinguishes between paid and unpaid work nor work that has upward positional trajectories and that which does not. Our approach addresses material-discursive tensions in much social constructionist literature by showing how elements need to be intertwined so that ways in which they mutually hinder and enrich each other can be explored.

Communicatively Constructing Career Choice and Dignity

Individuals often assume people have equal opportunities to achieve objective career success. These assumptions subscribe to meritocratic ideologies and pay little attention to structural and contextual factors influencing traditional career processes and outcomes (Buzzanell, 2000; Buzzanell & Goldzwig, 1991; Cloud, 1996; Winn, 2003). They also minimize possibilities that some may be unwilling to subvert family and leisure priorities to those associated with career advancement. Moreover, such values and priorities have profound and long-term consequences for the form and meaning of career (Lee, Kossek, Hall, & Litrico, 2011) and individuals' (un)willingness to remove structural obstacles on others' behalf (Cech & Blair-Loy, 2010).

Current career emphases note increasing ambiguity in careers, more emphasis on self-guided processes, and greater consideration of individuals' varied career values, approaches, and interests. As Arthur, Inkson, and Pringle (1999) argued, individual action is derived increasingly from individual choice with the model for contemporary careers being more of sense-making, protean, and boundaryless processes than linear trajectories with specific benchmarks. Career specialists have moved away from viewing career choice as an early phase and have recognized career choice and attendant socialization processes occur at various points in people's lifetimes (Ashforth, 2001; Jablin, 2001; Kramer & Noland, 1999).

Yet, individuals make choices for reasons that are not always their own. Moreover, "choices" derived from involuntary job loss, corporate acquisitions, illnesses, or changes in family membership prompt transitions (Ayers, Miller-Dyce, & Carlone, 2008; Buzzanell, Shenoy, Remke, & Lucas, 2009; Buzzanell & Turner, 2003; Kramer, Dougherty, & Pierce, 2004; Maitlis, 2009; Stier, 2007). Individuals spend more than half of their lives in transition—making career transition, rather than stability, a normal part of everyday life (Arthur et al., 1999) and making choice increasingly complicated.

Individuals engaged in contemporary *choice rhetoric* attribute individuals' choices about career to personal tastes and preferences without regard to systemic constraints and/or inequity regimes that direct or shape such choices (Acker, 2009; Buzzanell, 1995, 2000; Williams, 2000). These choices can be viewed as both processes and outcomes of diverse and intersecting identity categories, as well as social and institutional negotiations (Adib & Guerrier, 2003; Holvino, 2008; Winker & Degele, 2011). However, as Williams (2000) noted, choice that coincides with marginalization in workplaces reflects discrimination.

Career choice processes differ based individuals' identities and socio-historical-economic contexts, as well as their life phases. Lapour and Heppner (2009) found young, White women raised in affluent families are exposed to important career information and value systems. Their own and others' awareness of work and career positionings began early in life and developed across their lifespans (Buzzanell, Kisselburgh, & Berkelaar, 2011; Medved, 2009b; Paugh, 2005). Yet, young and affluent White women bear social costs along with their privilege (Aisenbrey, Evertsson, & Grunow, 2009; Tower & Alkadry, 2008). They must work vigilantly to position themselves discursively and materially for career and personal life fulfillment (Medved, 2009b), even if they live within the family-friendliness of social welfare states (Aisenbrey et al., 2009). Thus, choice is both materially and discursively constrained. How people manage tensions of constraint in career choice and enactment influences realization of dignity at work.

Reasons for Work and Bases of Choice

Ciulla (2000) highlighted the central role work plays in contemporary lives. She argued society has evolved such that work has become paramount, taking on special meaning for people's overall sense of identity and self-worth. Although there is much variability in the quality of different kinds of work, it is not work itself but reasons *why* people work that are lasting. Four values are primary reasons for work. These values shape how people make choices about work and career: meaningful work, leisure, money, and security. These reasons can be considered discursive frames by which people craft their stories. In our repositioning of these reasons as discursive frames, we acknowledge the power dynamics embedded within and across Ciulla's categories. In everyday talk, such frames invoke dominant meanings associated with marginalization–privilege dialectics. These frames also provide discursive resources whereby individuals position themselves for and can be entitled to choice and dignity.

Examining these four discursive frames provides insight into career choices for several reasons. First, careers have varying degrees of each dimension. Variations depend on who does certain work, how work is done, the stability provided by jobs within particular socioeconomic contexts, and the range of economic and identity vulnerabilities (Buzzanell, 2000; Folbre, 2008; Williams, 2000). Therefore, these frames provide criteria against which career choices, their enactment, and their consequences can be judged (for occupational frames, see Meisenbach, 2008). Second, viewing these frames together calls attention to tensions surrounding the simultaneity of unencumbered individual choices, tradeoffs in career decisions, and others' ironic expectations (Tracy & Rivera, 2010). Third, privileging of any one of these discursive frames could be a pathway to self-worth and dignity. For instance, people pursuing meaningful work could be commended for following their passion; others taking jobs with little intrinsic reward, but with steady paychecks and benefits could be respected for their commitment to being providers (Lucas, 2007).

Embedded in this prioritization of work values is an assumption that there are always options. However, people rarely have the privilege of "free" choice. In fact, Ciulla (2000) argued "when it comes to work everyone has freedom of choice, but not everyone has viable options" (p. 83). Many jobs are low on all dimensions: work is devoid of meaning, leaves little time for leisure activity, and is poorly paid and insecure. Examples include low-wage service jobs that have become the mainstay of formal and informal U.S. and global economies (Godfrey, 2011). The problem is not that these careers do not fulfill *all* work values, but that no discursive frame is potent enough to provide a viable account of choice.

Another way choice can be restricted is when people cannot locate work that affirms their most meaningful value. Restricted choice could occur when available jobs lack living wages for those who prioritize money or lack intrinsic value for those who prioritize meaningfulness. Restricted choice and material consequences may occur when individuals fail to examine personal career and dignity motivations—buying into societal discourses about what makes people happy—without envisioning consequences for themselves (Christopher, 2002). In instances where choice is significantly constrained, seems "normal" or predetermined, or has no counterbalance to individuals' tradeoffs, pathways to self-worth and dignity are challenged.

In sum, it is primarily through four frames that people discursively construct dignity. We acknowledge individuals may not position these frames for dignity-enhancing communication, but for production of power, status, control, and exploitation. Although we acknowledge the potential detrimental side and structures of career, we maintain our focus on choice as a pathway to dignity. Furthermore, we celebrate the human spirit that locates opportunities to construct meaning and dignity under less than optimal conditions (Chiappetta-Swanson, 2005; Tracy & Scott, 2006; Tyler, 2011). We argue communication scholars' energies should be refocused such that greater opportunities to construct career dignity are developed and documented. Using the four discursive frames, we examine career communication. We discuss values, benefits and constraints, contestations and choice as discursively and materially constructed around each frame.

Meaningful Work

Cheney et al. (2008) described meaningful work as that which includes individuals' "dreams, hopes, and sense of fulfillment and contribution" (p. 140). Although what constitutes meaningful work can vary, meaningful work also is embedded in culturally privileged work qualities (Lair, Shenoy, McClellan, & McGuire, 2008). Therefore, individuals and group members rely on personal determinations of what are worthy expenditures of time and energy, as well as societal discourses and/or interactions with others to value or legitimize their choices as meaningful.

Meaningful work is a growing area of interest in career research (Cheney et al., 2008; Kisselburgh, Berkelaar, & Buzzanell, 2009; Lair et al., 2008; Zorn & Townsley, 2008). In this line of scholarship, meaningful work often is framed as that which benefits others or contributes to society or to specific organizations. Meaningful work can include work for organizations associated with philanthropic, spiritual, or community-based causes (Bunderson & Thompson, 2009; Kirby et al., 2006; Mize Smith, Arendt, Lahman, Settle, & Duff, 2006). It also can include work that makes contributions on more individual levels, such as instructors who consider their work especially meaningful during times of tragedy (Miller, 2002) or during sense making about the politics of their own (and others') lives (Fassett & Warren, 2007). Meaningful work also includes work that is done a certain way. For instance, post-80s generation Chinese talked about telework as meaningful, in part because of their choice in work form, their ability to disconnect from others in their workplaces, and the affordance of personal development time (Long, Kuang, & Buzzanell, in press; see also Fonner & Roloff, 2010).

Throughout this research, meanings and meaningfulness of work are associated with well-being and its implications. First, meaningful work tends to be viewed as part of careers that are chosen or to which individuals are "called." Following one's calling has been heralded as the deepest and strongest pathway to meaningful work (Hall, 2004). For example, zookeepers frequently view their careers as a calling to work with animals (Bunderson & Thompson, 2009), as do educators in Christian colleges (Scott, 2007) and leaders of non-profit organizations (Mize Smith et al., 2006). Choice is not reserved only for people with callings. High-status employees who engaged in voluntary downward career changes framed their choices as embedded in the meaning they received from their work (Tan & Kramer, 2012).

Second, meaningful work is work that individuals do freely. In this sense, meaningfulness is not only found in an individual's career choice, but the tasks that are done and how they are done. For example, low-wage home care workers (Stacey, 2005) and veterinary technicians (Sanders, 2010) found the autonomy they had to do their jobs was a key source of meaning in their work. Likewise, Shuler and Sypher (2000) described how emergency call operators use emotional labor for tension release, adrenaline rush, and fun, thus locating meaning and dignity in their work.

However, not all employees have choices regarding how work is done. Chiappetta-Swanson (2005) described incursions on nurses' dignity when their hospitals performed pregnancy terminations for genetic anomalies. Although the nurses chose their profession, many did not feel that they had any choice in whether they would assist with abortion and stillbirth procedures. The meanings (and stigma) associated with their job task were in direct conflict with the meanings of work that directed them to their chosen careers.

Studies such as these demonstrate not all career actors have choice in what careers are available or how their specific jobs are performed. Constrained choice sheds new light on how people deal with stigma associated with work (Meisenbach, 2010). Ashforth and Kreiner (1999) described different approaches to ideological reframing of work that is physically, morally, or socially stigmatized by society. One tactic was to infuse work with meaning. Continuing with our earlier examples, nurses shifted their work meanings from the consequences of medical procedures to the emotional and medical care they provided to patients (Chiappetta-Swanson, 2005). While veterinary technician's work included dirty tasks of cleaning up excrement and euthanizing animals, they found the work extremely meaningful because of their connection to and care for animals (Sanders, 2010). Home care aids found deep meaning and the source of their own dignity by bringing dignity to others through cleaning bedpans and bathing patients. Blue-collar workers found ways to infuse their work with meaning and dignity by shifting attention from job status to quality of work performed (Lucas, 2011a). Although others might consider the work to be distasteful, dirty, low status, or inexplicable, workers assign meaningfulness to what they do every day such that they construct career dignity.

Career dignity is a communicative process both constructing and con-structed by meaningful work. The search for meaningful work has prompted communication researchers to locate a story of developing new career con-nections, forging different paths amidst stigmatized occupations and work. It is a story that describes how work identities are (re)constituted and how moments of interaction help clarify what is missing and what can be built upon to construct career dignity. Because work is meaningful, its worth may provide a platform for interrogating and repositioning oneself, others, and taken-for-granted assumptions politically and materially for change (Medved, 2009a; Williams, 2000). Through critique, new communication paths for dignity can be forged.

Leisure

Leisure is more than having free time or time for which there are no prior commitments. Rather, it is the contrast between constrained and uncommitted time (Ciulla, 2000)—time allotted to goal-oriented labor and time afforded for personal pursuits that fulfill interests, curiosity, and enjoyment. Just as goal-oriented labor directs people in terms of what they should do and who they are, leisure is a quality born of not having to engage in activities for instrumental reasons in particular places and times.

Whereas leisure can be a site for escape, it also can be a site of produc-tion, such as when it provides identity authenticity in the face of self-alienating work sites (Costas & Fleming, 2009) or a site for developing expertise, build-ing confidence, and experiencing self-actualization via serious leisure pursuits (Anderson, 2011). People need leisure: "Leisure brings out what is best and most distinctive about being human—our abilities to think, feel, reflect, create, and learn. We need leisure to develop wisdom" (Ciulla, 2000, p. 193).

In Western societies, paid work pervades daily and lifetime rhythms such that leisure is lessened. Some find leisure troublesome in its lack of directed activity; others delay leisure until a time when important (economic) activi-ties are completed (Hochschild, 1997; Schor, 1992). Because the value of paid work and associated accoutrements is ingrained in Western societies, leisure can seem nebulous. Yet, leisure has been steadily increasing in importance over generations, with Millennials wanting more leisure than previous genera-tions (Twenge, Campbell, Hoffman, & Lance, 2010). This revaluing of leisure points to leisure orientations and desires for viable choices in how to spend one's time.

Defining leisure as those activities in which people engage because they enjoy the activity and for which they receive no payment or extrinsic reward, we can examine hobbies, involvement in community or church activities, or yard work as leisure. In addition, much has been written about demands of and gender inequities in duties of childcare and housework (M. K. Bolton, 2000; Hochschild, 1989). Little has been written about how such work can be viewed as leisure.

Current research on career and leisure focuses on generational work and leisure values (Jansen & Leuty, 2012), particular occupations' or national policies' effects on private lives (Nätti, Anttila, & Tammelin, 2012; Wieland, 2011), how people spend their leisure time and with what consequences (e.g., tourism), and how leisure activities might become careers (Snyder, 2012). Other research explores organizational attempts to make work feel more like play (Fleming, 2005b; Fleming & Sturdy, 2011).

In examining career choice as related to dignity, we first look at how people frame career and leisure in ways that highlight choice in their careers, as is the case with serious leisure. Second, we look at how choice is constrained. Much of leisure literature assumes a rhetoric of individual choice and does not consider how intersectionalities of difference might thwart feelings of and particular forms of leisure. Choice is constrained through overwork and incursions on work–life balance. Despite promises of autonomy and flexibility, ubiquitous technologies exacerbate overwork by rewarding tendencies to connect electronically with paid labor activities during leisure times (e.g., checking e-mail).

Leisure as a primary value for work is privileged through career choices, including both occupational choices as well as day-to-day choices about how work is enacted. For people whose formal roles do not fulfill their perceived callings ("unanswered callings"), leisure can provide an alternative (Berg, Grant, & Johnson, 2010). People strategically craft their leisure time to pursue their callings. Leisure gives individuals their sense of identity in a valued, albeit informal, role.

Furthermore, leisure has been privileged as a rationalization for career choice in the case of serious leisure. Serious leisure is "the steady pursuit of an amateur, hobbyist, or career volunteer activity that captivates its participants with its complexity and many challenges" (Stebbins, 2000, p. 54). Stebbins compared serious leisure enthusiasts (marathon runner, blogger, photographer) to serious careerists without remuneration. When it comes to serious leisure and career choice, Anderson (2011) discussed the challenges of balancing family and work expectations with his skydiving career. In response to his "leisure time crunch," he made career choices to scale back career aspirations in exchange for time for serious leisure activity.

Whereas gendered, economic, relational, societal, able-bodiedness, risk, and other discourses and associated materialities likely influenced Anderson's (2011) perceptions of choice, they probably also influenced his ability to negotiate the terms of his labor force participation. They most likely influenced the notion that he could even think about and act on his own desires and interests. Thus, leisure and career choice operate as contested and constrained sites whereby intersectionalities of difference and structures that support effects of privilege and marginalization play out.

Denials of leisure can constrain experiences of dignity and choice, particularly in cases of overwork. Hodson (2001) linked overwork with indignity at work. In addition to the physical exhaustion that comes from overwork, loss of leisure can take a toll on human dignity as it limits abilities to draw meaning from other life domains. Writing about assembly workers, Hodson observed, "Such workers must seek life satisfaction through their off-hours activities instead, although even these pursuits may be dampened by limited energy left over after a long day of continuous effort" (p. 118). Incursions on leisure time are perhaps most dramatic in the case of the migrant factory workers in China who took their lives after being exposed to undignifying conditions of extreme overwork with scant opportunities for leisure (Lucas, Kang, & Li, in press).

The crush of overwork is felt not only by blue-collar workers. Fraser (2001) described how white-collar workplaces have changed in ways that inhibit leisure time and affect workers' morale: Workdays are longer, there are fewer days off, and jobs spill into off hours. The time and energy people have for leisure activity deteriorate. Schor (1992) pointed to a bitter irony that leisure has become increasingly commodified. Leisure activities are grounded in consumption—purchase of equipment, tickets, and club memberships. The price of leisure mandates people work more hours to earn the money to be able to enjoy leisure (Hochschild, 1997).

Finally, discourses of career and related practices constrain choices both women and men make about work–life balance. Organizational, societal, and mass media messages about face time or presence in the office can impact the extent to which people choose work over leisure in attempts to present themselves as good workers (Kuhn, 2006; Perlow, 1998; Wieland, 2011). Gendered expectations combine with material conditions to affect decisions regarding opting out of the workforce altogether. Men are less likely to leave the workforce because of gendered expectations tied to ideal worker identities that position men as prioritizing work over leisure; women presumably have choice, with such positionings resulting in advantageous family structures for men (Schneer & Reitman, 2002). Further, men are stigmatized when choosing to opt-out (Petroski & Edley, 2006). When it comes to women opting out or remaining in the workforce, not only are those who opt out mostly privileged women but these decisions typically are driven by economic and instrumental imperatives rather than by what might enhance quality of life and family well-being (Williams, 2000). Buzzanell et al. (2005) found managerial women who chose to remain in the workforce admitted they had the financial resources to stay at home with their newborns. These women perceived their choice as essential to their personal well-being and vital to their family's material desires for affluent lifestyles. Such choices are channeled by rhetorics of choice and intensive mothering into diminished work and career activity (Medved, 2009a; Stone & Lovejoy, 2004; Williams, 2000).

Kirby and Krone (2002) showed how mundane interactions (re)produced the rules and resources of routine interactions and of organizational structures tied to policy formation and utilization. Their work displays how everyday micropractices inhibit choices about family leave policy use because of possible repercussions. In other research on work and personal life issues, communication researchers have critiqued caregivers' choices of maternity leaves and the ways technologies shape and are shaped by leisure and personal life interests (Hayden & O'Brien Hallstein, 2010).

In this section, we note parts of our discussion conflate middle-class values and neoliberal economic emphases on individual agency with ethics of individual choice and its rhetoric (Medved, 2009a; Stone & Lovejoy, 2004; Williams, 2000). We urge scholars to sort through moral, pragmatic, and political positionings through deconstruction of the status quo and reconstruction of leisure and dignity-affirming communication (see Medved, 2009a). In short, communicative constructions of leisure and their discursive and material associations with career afford opportunities for much needed research on intersections of national and corporate policies, communication and reproductive technologies, work–family intersections, and other life aspects.

Money

The meaningful work and leisure discursive frames privilege how one's time is *spent*; the money frame privileges what is *earned* from work. Far from being strictly material, money itself is a symbolic resource that carries a wide range of meanings (Rose & Orr, 2007). Krueger (1986) asserted, "money is probably the most emotionally meaningful object in contemporary life" (p. 3). In their examination of meanings of money, Rose and Orr (2007) identified four primary orientations: status, achievement, worry, and security. Each orientation carries consequences for crafting individual identity and motivating behaviors.

Money can contribute to achievement or denial of dignity in several ways. First, because money can be a status marker within organizations and society, it serves as an external gauge of the worthiness of career actors, with high-wage workers being more esteemed than low-wage workers. In contrast to low-wage fast food workers who are exposed to ridicule for the sheer fact they hold low-status McJobs (Gould, 2010; Newman, 1999), those in higher paid positions often are beneficiaries of occupational prestige, status shields, and status-conferring perquisites related to accumulation of money (Buzzanell & Goldzwig, 1991).

Second, money can be a pathway to dignity in that it can be an internal indicator of individuals' personal achievement (i.e., the worth others hold for job incumbents or incumbents hold for themselves). In her study of the political nature and socializing effects of the colloquialism "a real job," Clair (1996) found consensus among college students that "a real job means working for an organization and being *paid well* for one's work" (p. 263, emphasis added). Money derived from employment can be a primary indicator that someone has attained a "real job" when one leaves college. Alternatively, low wages contribute to high turnover, which in turn makes low-wage workers seem disposable (Berg & Frost, 2005). This assessment of disposability can increase others' capricious treatment of low-wage workers.

Third, money can be a pathway to dignity by enabling preferred gendered roles, such as men fulfilling roles as providers or breadwinners (Hodges & Budig, 2010). In fulfillment of this masculine role, money is valued for its instrumental purposes of providing economic security. This orientation is particularly motivating for men who find dignity in upholding gendered societal expectations of providing for their families (Lucas, 2007; Roy, 2005), but increasingly is a motivating factor for mothers (Medved, 2009a; Medved & Rawlins, 2011) and, in some cases, children (Estrada & Hondagneu-Sotelo, 2011). Finally, money can be a pathway to dignity by neutralizing or compensating for negative aspects of one's career. Ciulla (2000) explained, "money conceals many things, including how you earned it" (p. 204). An individual who may feel powerless and undervalued on the job becomes powerful, valued, and esteemed as a customer who has money to spend.

Given connections among money, choice, and dignity, literature in popular, business, and academic realms focuses on strategies for increasing earnings. Career success frequently is operationalized as the number of job promotions and raises (i.e., money) one receives. Career literature identifies traits, conditions, and variables related to objective career success (Miller Burke & Attridge, 2011a, 2011b) and offers suggestions as to how to engage in communicative practices that boost chances of career success, such as strategically building career networks (Forret & Sullivan, 2002; Seibert, Kraimer, & Liden, 2001).

In other research, money functions as a means of enacting choice and constructing dignity when people labor for funds that they use for activities they find enjoyable (e.g., prison guards using money to pursue identity-affirming interests; Tracy, 2005). Money also can be used as a rationalization for subjecting oneself to certain lines of work. Autoworkers who were exposed to repetitive strain injuries in ever-accelerating assembly lines, felt pride in their hourly wages being higher than those for other jobs (Zoller, 2003). Young call center workers in India drew upon the luxuries they could afford as ways to compensate for other identity constraints (Pal & Buzzanell, 2008). Similarly, prospective professional athletes expressed willingness to tolerate demeaning recruitment and screening practices of the National Football League, anticipating the possibility of future lucrative contracts (Dufur & Feinberg, 2007).

However, lack of money can constrain experiences of choice and dignity in career and lifestyles. Specifically, when economic insecurity is high, money can contribute to forcing unreasonable choices on workers. For instance, miners pushed themselves to the brink of exhaustion and injury and accepted positions in dangerous and toxic conditions knowing those jobs were their only viable routes to earning family paychecks (Lucas, 2007). A cultural obligation in China to contribute to the financial well-being of one's family drives many young migrant workers to seek otherwise dehumanizing work at manufacturing plants where they trade basic freedoms for money (Lucas et al., in press).

In her ethnographic study of women in welfare-to-work programs, Cleaveland (2005) addressed the lack of choice and ensuing indignities faced by these women and how they attempted to reclaim their dignity through resistance. Most of the women were forced into minimum wage jobs. In subservient positions at the bottom economic tiers, they regularly were exposed to abusive communication and incursions on their autonomy. Moreover, the low wages they received seemed to exacerbate those indignities. Instead of viewing the typically short tenure of these positions as a problem with women's work attachment, Cleaveland argued the women engaged in resistance with the only power they had: the power to quit. She concluded these acts of resistance reclaimed "some feeling of agency and dignity in the face of these structural realities" (p. 55). In the absence of occupational choices that could provide the compensation to enhance self-image and self-worth, women opted out of jobs. They chose the humiliation of welfare over workplace indignities. Money can provide tangible capital for career and lifestyle choice and pathways to dignity. However, money also can drive people to engage in unhealthy behaviors and exploitative or dignity-diminishing activities for themselves and others.

Security

Ciulla (2000) identified security as the final core value for work. Like money, security is an instrumental value and discursive career frame in that security is something earned in exchange for labor. There are three ways security can be found in career. First, security is defined as having stability in employment and predictability in one's livelihood and organizational membership, or what Bolton (2007) called secure terms of employment. Economic security is acquired from freedom from inappropriate firings, frequent layoffs, or reduction in hours (Hodson, 2001). Second, security also can mean feelings of safety in pursuit of employment without persistent concerns and conflicts about power imbalances and degradation (see Lutgen-Sandvik & Sypher, 2009; Nicotera & Mahon, 2013). Psychological security can be gained from particular occupational and organizational choices, such as when someone is free from abusive supervision (Tepper, Moss, Lockhart, & Carr, 2007) or sexual harassment (Gettman & Gelfand, 2007). Finally, security has physical bases insofar as it may indicate individuals work in environments devoid of threats to or actual physical harm.

Our three-pronged approach to security has implications for how dignity is achieved at work. The first is tied to the sense of worth gained from stable employment. When individuals possess employment security, they may feel a sense of worth and dignity that comes from an organization's long-term investment in them and benefit from investments such as job training, increased expertise, and opportunities to advance. Security also can bolster one's sense of being a good provider. Second, when people experience employment and/ or physical security, they perceive greater freedom to express voice, especially upward dissent (Kassing, 2006) when they feel mistreated (Cortina & Magley, 2003). Therefore, they may be able to fix problems that could infringe on their dignity. Third, the very freedom from power imbalances that contribute to poor treatment is dignifying in itself.

However, we live in insecure times. Changes in the global economic landscape have brought job insecurity to the forefront. Different manifestations of insecurity include the growing contingent workforce (Gossett, 2001), offshoring of jobs (Rodino-Colocino, 2012), uncertainty related to mergers and acquisitions (Kramer et al., 2004; Pepper & Larson, 2006), layoffs and job loss (Buzzanell & Turner, 2003; Gunn, 2008, 2011), downsizing (Susskind, 2007; Tourish, Paulsen, Hobman, & Bordia, 2004), and the end of lifetime employment around the globe (Buzzanell, 2000; Westwood & Lok, 2003). Consequently, career and communication research has focused on how to manage uncertainty associated with economic changes (Ayers et al., 2008; Lucas & Buzzanell, 2012; Neff, 2012; van Dam, 2004).

Whereas insecurity is high for most in the current milieu, it is particularly intense for immigrant and migrant workers. Thompson (2010) chronicled the experience of working in jobs typically reserved for immigrant workers, including lettuce cutting and poultry plant work. In one of his jobs, he discovered some employers would hire only illegal immigrants so as to retain power strongholds over them. Other insecure work includes street vending (Estrada & Hondagneu-Sotelo, 2011), day labor (Purser, 2009), housecleaning (Herod & Aguiar, 2006), and meatpacking (Apostolidis, 2005; Stuesse, 2010).

With regard to meatpacking, Stuesse (2010) detailed how economic insecurity made immigrants easy targets for indignity. In response to growing union membership among Latino workers, the company initiated aggressive immigration crackdowns as a way to limit worker autonomy. One union steward explained the constrained choices of illegal immigrants: "Well, I don't have *no choice* [emphasis added] but to put up with it…. If I make a fuss they probably gone [sic] send me back." (p. 27). In another study of meatpacking plants, supervisors described employees as "disposable objects … that you throw in the garbage" and threatened termination if employees did not consent to uncompensated overwork (Apostolidis, 2005, p. 650).

In contrast, Kim (2009) described a small restaurant where undocumented immigrant workers were targeted for employment. Rather than engaging in full worker exploitation, there was concerted effort among servers, kitchen help, and the owner to have a symbiotic relationship where dignity was preserved through a mostly benevolent relationship. In exchange for working for less than minimum wage and not complaining, employees benefitted from three meals a day and a voluntary kin network. They expressed a sense of joy, meaning, and dignity in their lives.

Not only is economic insecurity a problem, but infringements upon employee voice also are an issue (Morrison, 2011). When insecurity is high, there is more risk for voices being muted. Meares, Oetzel, Torres, Derkacs, and Ginossar (2004) explained that in cases of people mistreatment, employees with more power (and therefore greater perceived security) were more likely to respond with privileged narratives. In contrast, employees with less power and less job security were more likely to have muted mistreatment narratives. These patterns also could account for voice in defeating cycles of employee emotional abuse and bullying when more powerful organizational members target less powerful employees (Lutgen-Sandvik, 2006). Perhaps this is why employee dissatisfaction has been voiced in anonymous forums such as counter-institutional websites, rather than with direct upward dissent (Gossett & Kilker, 2006).

Toward a Research Agenda on Choice and Dignity in Career Communication

Authentic choice and autonomy are important for negotiating dignified career identities as well as for building career structures that support dignity. Although choice is tied to discursive framings whereby people engage in particular careers—meaningful work, leisure, money, and security—choice also is complex, contested, constrained, and linked to material resources and the affordances they offer for career aspiration and accomplishment. In careers from middle-class perspectives, individuals make choices about what they desire, what they believe are reasonable outcomes, and what they are willing to sacrifice for particular results. Their abilities to consider contexts as offering choices and to act upon these perceptions often are cultivated and circumscribed early in life (Buzzanell et al., 2011). Choice shapes and is shaped by what is expected, valued, and supported discursively and materially in society at large and in work situations for particular social group members. Abilities to act in accordance with one's interests and desires—agency—can be encouraged, constrained, and/or contested in complex and often paradoxical ways depending on the desired path's alignment with individualistic and/or communal values and needs, and on lines of familial decision making, ability testing results, national occupational needs, and other factors (e.g., Buzzanell, Berkelaar, & Kisselburgh, 2012; Lucas, 2011). To the extent individuals accomplish what is important to them and in ways that treat them as valued human beings, they construct dignity in their work lives.

While it is not necessary for someone's current career position to fulfill each of the core frames for dignity achievement, the relative strength of even a single reason for work can provide openings for discursively constructing a career path of choice and dignity. Therefore, we invite scholars working within and across different communication contexts to pursue and extend research agendas on communication, choice, and dignity. To assist in this pursuit, we provide key questions that can guide inquiry into this important dimension of working lives.

The first question to guide future research is, *in what ways are career and choice politicized?* To say one has choice implies that one has the power, right, or freedom to determine courses of action in given situations. Choice connotes agency, empowerment, and privilege. However, given the ways gender, race, class, sexuality, ability, and other lived experiences and identity constructions intersect with structures of inequity, even "normal" choices related to career must be examined more critically. Realistically speaking, few have total freedom of choice.

In particular, we encourage critical, poststructural, feminist, and postcolonial communication and career scholars to delve more deeply into how intersectionalities of difference impact choice and dignity. How are structural barriers and inequity regimes socially constructed and reified in ways that enable and constrain career dignity and choice? What are the particular challenges to constructing dignified identities when authentic identity expressions are discouraged? What are the discourses and material conditions that enable those at society's margins to find meaningful, challenging, and dignity-affirming work? Finally, in diverse national cultural contexts, what does career, choice, and dignity mean and how is it embodied by individuals and aligned with societal structures and policies? In other words, how does culture, structure, and history shape choice (and how is choice refashioned over time)?

The second question is, *how should dimensions of work and career be measured?* While we discourage exclusionary definitions of career and are cautious not to judge too harshly individual career paths from lenses of privilege (i.e., Western, middle class, academic), we share S. C. Bolton's (2007, 2010) position of advocating for minimum standards for evaluating the quality of dignified work. We acknowledge that what constitutes meaning (e.g., meaningful work, meaningful leisure) and materiality (e.g., enough money, enough security) varies dramatically among individuals and their structural societal locations. Yet, we also realize there are minimum standards more-or-less agreed upon by society at large. Careers are necessarily positioned within socio-political and economic contexts that have socially constructed, culturally-specific meanings of work (Cheney et al., 2008; Lair et al., 2008) and rhetoric of choice (Buzzanell, 2000; Medved, 2009a; Stone, 2007; Williams, 2000). Because individuals' ability to discursively frame their career path as *enacted choice* relies on the fidelity of their narratives within societal understandings, standards of society must be taken into account. We encourage career and communication research to identify societal standards around the globe and relationships among career, choice, dignity, and material outcomes.

Our third question to guide future research is, *how can organizations and societies create dignity-affirming conditions by which workers construct dignity?* By and large, individuals communicate intra- and interpersonally to craft identities by which they can exercise autonomy and make choices in their careers. While the extent to which organizations and society at large are responsible for workers' dignity may be debatable, applied communication scholars, in particular, are well suited to suggesting viable approaches to organizational cooperation in constructing dignity and assessing short- and long-term outcomes of dignity-affirming communication practices.

For example, how can organizations and societies encourage leisure in environments suffused by habits of (neo)capitalism—economic growth, consumption, competition—such that enjoyment of leisure leads to activities and embodiment of engagement, well-being, creativity, and spirituality? Further, in low-wage service work, how could organizations create cultures that value employees as much as customers and reduce customer abuse of employees? How might structurational divergence (SD) theory and its communicative manifestations in everyday practices correspond with choice, career, and dignity-diminishing and/or dignity-enhancing communication? How could the range and extent of choice be cultivated across the lifespan through development networks and mentoring relationships?

Our final question to guide future research is, *how do we talk about choice*? Choice plays an important role in establishing dignity in careers. If choice is classed, as our review indicates, then how might we cultivate children's capacities to question and select alternatives that suit their interests while also maintaining communal orientation toward choice? When individuals move from dignity-diminishing to dignity-affirming conditions (and vice versa), how do they productively manage and legitimize identity opportunities and/or challenges (e.g., class and occupational mobility)? The language used to talk about choice, career, and elevated or stigmatized work raises further questions and/or challenges to workers' dignity (Buzzanell & Goldzwig, 1991; Meisenbach, 2010).

Rhetorical scholars could examine ways we talk about choice in the public vernacular. Has talk about choice become more simplified and/or complicated in linguistic choices, argumentation structure, and invocation of societal discourses throughout the recent global economic recession? Moreover, how do people talk about careers and serious leisure activity that seem, to many, to be based in enjoyment or leisure? How might individuals and groups strategically engage in resistance, contestation, choice, agency, and other processes?

In closing, we envision career, choice, and dignity as intertwined discursively and materially. We focus on pathways to dignity but cannot ignore how economic and societal forces influence individuals' and collectivities' perceptions of choice, their participation in the paid work force, and the classed, gendered, and raced nature of these choices. Moreover, we cannot ignore that some conceptualizations of career have detrimental consequences insofar as they strengthen discourses of individual accountability for negative outcomes. We ask, what career discourses could encourage authentic individual choice while simultaneously questioning underlying power distributions that effectively maintain inequity? The uncritical adoption of new career ideologies and practices may replicate exclusionary practices and, by extension, dignity-diminishing communication aligned within constrained and contested choice.

Further, we note that dignity and choice often are described, researched, and perceived as all-or-nothing phenomena. Yet, there are indications that they operate dialectically and dialogically. In politics of choice and career, we note societal expectations, beliefs, and manifestations of individual choice also operate in interlocking systems of constraint and contestation. We encourage further research on choice, dignity, and career as communicatively constituted and politicized in diverse and global contexts.

References

Acker, J. (2009). From glass ceiling to inequality regimes. *Sociologie du Travail, 51*, 199–217. doi:10.1016/j.soctra.2009.03.004

Adib, A., & Guerrier, Y. (2003). The interlocking of gender with nationality, race, ethnicity and class: The narratives of women in hotel work. *Gender, Work and Organization, 10*, 413–432. doi:10.1111/1468-0432.00204

Aisenbrey, S., Evertsson, M., & Grunow, D. (2009). Is there a career penalty for mothers' time out? A comparison of Germany, Sweden and the United States. *Social Forces, 88*, 573–606. doi:10.1353/sof.0.0252

Alvesson, M., & Kärreman, D. (2000). Varieties of discourse: On the study of organizations through discourse analysis. *Human Relations, 53*, 1125–1149. doi: 10.1177/0018726700539002

Anderson, L. (2011). Time is of the essence: An analytic autoethnography of family, work, and serious leisure. *Symbolic Interaction, 34*, 133–157. doi:10.1525/si.2011.34.2.133

Apostolidis, P. (2005). Hegemony and hamburger: Migration narratives and democratic unionism among Mexican meatpackers in the U.S. west. *Political Research Quarterly, 58*, 647–658. doi:10.1177/106591290505800412

Arthur, M. B., Inkson, K., & Pringle, J. K. (1999). *The new careers: Individual action and economic change*. London, England: Sage.

Ashforth, B. E. (2001). *Role transitions in organizational life: An identity perspective*. Mahwah, NJ: Erlbaum.

Ashforth, B. E., & Kreiner, G. E. (1999). "How can you do it?": Dirty work and the challenge of constructing a positive identity. *Academy of Management Review, 24*, 413–434. doi:10.5465/AMR.1999.2202129

Ayers, D. F., Miller-Dyce, C., & Carlone, D. (2008). Security, dignity, caring relationships, and meaningful work: Needs motivating participation in a job-training program. *Community College Review, 35*, 257–276. doi:10.1177/1059601108314581

Bell, E. L. J. E., & Nkomo, S. M. (2001). *Our separate ways: Black and white women and the struggle for professional identity*. Boston, MA: Harvard Business School Press.

Berg, J. M., Grant, A. M., & Johnson, V. (2010). When callings are calling: Crafting work and leisure in pursuit of unanswered occupational callings. *Organization Science, 21*, 973–994. doi:10.1287/orsc.1090.0497

Berg, P., & Frost, A. C. (2005). Dignity at work for low wage, low skill service workers. *Industrial Relations, 60*, 657–682.

Bolton, M. K. (2000). *The third shift: Managing hard choices in our careers, homes, and lives as women*. New York, NY: Jossey-Bass.

Bolton, S. C. (2007). Dignity in and at work: Why it matters. In S. C. Bolton (Ed.), *Dimensions of dignity at work* (pp. 3–16). Oxford, England: Butterworth-Heinemann.

Bolton, S. C. (2010). Being human: Dignity of labor as the foundation for the spirit-work connection. *Journal of Management, Spirituality, and Religion, 7*, 157–172. doi:10.1080114766081003746422

Boudreau, T. E. (2009). Human agonistes: Interdisciplinary inquiry into ontological agency and human conflict. In D. Sandole, S. Byrne, I. Sandole-Staroste & J. Senehi (Eds.), *Handbook of conflict analysis and resolution* (pp. 131–143). New York, NY: Routledge.

Brennan, A., & Lo, Y. S. (2007). Two conceptions of dignity: Honour and self-determination. In J. Malapss & N. Lickiss (Eds.), *Perspectives on human dignity: A conversation* (pp. 43–58). Dordrecht, The Netherlands: Springer.

Broadfoot, K., & Munshi, D. (2007). Diverse voices and alternative rationalities: Imagining forms of postcolonial organizational communication. *Management Communication Quarterly, 21*, 249–267. doi:10.1177/0893318907306037

Bühler-Niederberger, D., & König, A. (2011). Childhood as a resource and laboratory for the self-project. *Childhood, 18*, 180–195. doi:10.1177/0907568210391490

Bunderson, J. S., & Thompson, J. A. (2009). The call of the wild: Zookeepers, callings, and the double-edged sword of deeply meaningful work. *Administrative Science Quarterly, 54*, 32–57. doi:10.2189/asqu.2009.54.1.32

Buzzanell, P. M. (1995). Reframing the glass ceiling as a socially constructed process: Implications for understanding and change. *Communication Monographs, 62*, 327–354. doi:10.1080/03637759509376366

Buzzanell, P. M. (1999). Tensions and burdens in employment interviewing processes: Perspectives of non-dominant group applicants. *Journal of Business Communication, 36*, 134–162. doi:10.1177/002194369903600202

Buzzanell, P. M. (2000). The promise and practice of the new career and social contract. In P. M. Buzzanell (Ed.), *Rethinking organizational and managerial communication from feminist perspectives* (pp. 209–235). Thousand Oaks, CA: Sage.

Buzzanell, P. M., Berkelaar, B., & Kisselburgh, L. G. (2012). Expanding understandings of mediated and human socialization agents: Chinese children talk about desirable work and career. *China Media Research, 8*, 97–110.

Buzzanell, P. M., & Goldzwig, S. R. (1991). Linear and nonlinear career models: Metaphors, paradigms, and ideologies. *Management Communication Quarterly, 4*, 466–505. doi:10.1177/0893318991004004004

Buzzanell, P. M., Kisselburgh, L. G., & Berkelaar, B. (2011). From the mouths of babes: Exploring families' career socialization of young children in China, Lebanon, Belgium, and the United States. *Journal of Family Communication, 11*, 148–164. doi:10.1080/15267431.2011.554494

Buzzanell, P. M., & Lucas, K. (2006). Gendered stories of career: Unfolding discourses of time, space, and identity. In B. J. Dow & J. T. Wood (Eds.), *Sage handbook of gender and communication* (pp. 161–178). Thousand Oaks, CA: Sage.

Buzzanell, P. M., Meisenbach, R. J., Remke, R., Liu, M., Bowers, V., & Conn, C. (2005). The good working mother: Managerial women's sensemaking and feelings about work-family issues. *Communication Studies, 56*, 261–285. doi:10.1080/10510970500181389

Buzzanell, P. M., Shenoy, S., Remke, R. V., & Lucas, K. (2009). Intersubjectively creating resilience: Responding to and rebounding from potentially destructive organizational experiences. In P. Lutgen-Sandvik & B. D. Sypher (Eds.), *The destructive side of organizational communication: Processes, consequences and constructive ways of organizing* (pp. 293–315). New York, NY: Routledge.

Buzzanell, P. M., & Turner, L. (2003). Emotion work revealed by job loss discourse: Backgrounding-foregrounding of feelings, construction of normalcy, and (re)instituting of traditional masculinities. *Journal of Applied Communication Research, 31*, 27–57. doi:10.1080/00909880305375

Carmack, H. J. (2008). "The ultimate ice cream experience": Performing passion as expression of organizational culture. *Ohio Communication Journal, 46*, 109–129.

Carr, K., & Heiden, E. P. (2011). Revealing darkness through light: Communicatively managing the dark side of mentoring relationships in organisations. *Australian Journal of Communication, 38*, 89–104.

Cech, E. A., & Blair-Loy, M. (2010). Perceiving glass ceilings? Meritocratic versus structural explanations of gender inequality among women in science and technology. *Social Problems, 57*, 371–397. doi:10.1525/sp.2010.57.3.371

Cheney, G., Zorn, T. E., Planalp, S., & Lair, D. J. (2008). Meaningful work and personal/social well-being: Organizational communication engages the meanings of work. In C. S. Beck (Ed.), *Communication yearbook 32* (pp. 137–185). New York, NY: Routledge.

Chiappetta-Swanson, C. (2005). Dignity and dirty work: Nurses' experiences in managing genetic termination for fetal anomaly. *Qualitative Sociology, 28*, 93–116. doi:10.1007/s11133-005-2632-0

Christopher, R. (2002). Rags to riches to suicide: Unhappy narratives of upward mobility. *College Literature, 29*(4), 79–108.

Ciulla, J. B. (2000). *The working life: The promise and betrayal of modern work.* New York, NY: Times Books.

Clair, R. P. (1996). The political nature of the colloquialism, "a real job": Implications for organizational socialization. *Communication Monographs, 63*, 249–267. doi:10.1080/03637759609376392

Cleaveland, C. (2005). A desperate means to dignity: Work refusal amongst Philadelphia welfare recipients. *Ethnography, 6*, 35–60. doi:10.1177/1466138105055656

Cloud, D. L. (1996). Hegemony or concordance? The rhetoric of tokenism in "Oprah" Winfrey's rags-to-riches biography. *Critical Studies in Mass Communication, 13*, 115–137. doi:10.1080/15295039609366967

Correll, S. J., Benard, S., & Paik, I. (2007). Getting a job: Is there a motherhood penalty? *American Journal of Sociology, 112*, 1297–1338. doi:10.1086/511799

Cortina, L. M., & Magley, V. J. (2003). Raising voice, risking retaliation: Events following interpersonal mistreatment in the workplace. *Journal of Occupational Health Psychology, 8*, 247–265. doi:10.1037/1076-8998.8.4.247

Costas, J., & Fleming, P. (2009). Beyond dis-identification: A discursive approach to self-alienation in contemporary organizations. *Human Relations, 62*, 353–378. doi:10.1177/0018726708101041

Doherty, E. M. (2011). Joking aside, insights to employee dignity in "Dilbert" cartoons: The value of comic art in understanding the employer–employee relationship. *Journal of Management Inquiry, 20*, 286–301. doi:10.1177/1056492610386114

Dougherty, D. S. (2009). Sexual harassment as destructive organizational process. In B. D. Sypher & P. Lutgen-Sandvik (Eds.), *Destructive organizational communication: Processes, consequences, and constructive ways of organizing* (pp. 203–225). New York, NY: Routledge.

Dougherty, D. S. (2011). *The reluctant farmer: An exploration of work, social class and the production of food.* Leics, England: Troubador.

Dufur, M. J., & Feinberg, S. L. (2007). Artificially restricted labor markets and worker dignity in professional football. *Journal of Contemporary Ethnography, 36,* 505–536. doi:10.1177/0891241606294120

Ehrenreich, B. (2001). *Nickel and dimed: On (not) getting by in America.* New York, NY: Henry Holt.

Ellingson, L. L. (2011). The poetics of professionalism among dialysis technicians. *Health Communication, 26,* 1–12. doi:10.1080/10410236.2011.527617

Estrada, E., & Hondagneu-Sotelo, P. (2011). Intersectional dignities: Latino immigrant street vendor youth in Los Angeles. *Journal of Contemporary Ethnography, 40,* 102–131. doi:10.1177/0891241610387926

Fairhurst, G. T., & Putnam, L. L. (2004). Organizations as discursive constructions. *Communication Theory, 14,* 5–26. doi:10.1111/j.1468-2885.2004.tb00301.x

Fassett, D. L., & Warren, J. T. (2007). *Critical communication pedagogy.* Thousand Oaks, CA: Sage.

Fleming, P. (2005a). "Kindergarten cop": Paternalism and resistance in a high-commitment workplace. *Journal of Management Studies, 42,* 1469–1489. doi:10.1111/j.1467-6486.2005.00551.x

Fleming, P. (2005b). Workers' playtime? Boundaries and cynicism in a "culture of fun" program. *The Journal of Applied Behavioral Science, 41,* 285–303. doi:10.1177/0021886305277033

Fleming, P., & Sturdy, A. (2011). "Being yourself" in the electronic sweatshop: New forms of normative control. *Human Relations, 64,* 177–200. doi:10.1177/0018726710375481

Folbre, N. (2008). Reforming care. *Politics & Society, 36,* 373–387. doi:10.1177/0032329208320567

Fonner, K. L., & Roloff, M. E. (2010). Why teleworkers are more satisfied with their jobs than are office-based workers: When less contact is beneficial. *Journal of Applied Communication Research, 38,* 336–361. doi:10.1080/00909882.2010.513998

Forret, M. L., & Sullivan, S. E. (2002). A balanced scorecard approach to networking: A guide to successfully navigating career changes. *Organizational Dynamics, 31,* 245–258. doi:10.1016/s0090-2616(02)00112-2

Foucault, M. (1972). *The archaeology of knowledge and the discourse on language.* New York, NY: Pantheon.

Foucault, M. (1977/1995). *Discipline and punish: The birth of the prison.* New York, NY: Vintage Books.

Fraser, J. A. (2001). White-collar sweatshop: The deterioration of work and its rewards in corporate America. New York, NY: W. W. Norton.

Frey, L. R., & Cissna, K. (2009). *Routledge handbook of applied communication research.* New York, NY: Routledge.

Gagné, M., & Bhave, D. (2011). *Human autonomy in cross-cultural context: Perspectives on the psychology of agency, freedom, and well-being.* New York, NY: Springer.

Gettman, H. J., & Gelfand, M. J. (2007). When the customer shouldn't be king: Antecedents and consequences of sexual harassment by clients and customers. *Journal of Applied Psychology, 92,* 757–770. doi:10.1037/0021-9010.92.3.757

Gilbert, D. (2008). *The American class structure in an age of growing inequality* (7th ed.). Thousand Oaks, CA: Sage.

Godfrey, P. C. (2011). Toward a theory of the informal economy. *Academy of Management Annals, 5,* 231–277. doi:10.1080/19416520.2011.585818

Gossett, L. M. (2001). The long-term impact of short-term workers: The work life concerns posed by the growth of the contingent workforce. *Management Communication Quarterly, 15,* 115–120. doi:10.1177/0893318901151007

Gossett, L. M., & Kilker, J. (2006). My job sucks: Examining counterinstitutional websites as locations for organizational member voice, dissent, and resistance. *Management Communication Quarterly, 20,* 63–90. doi:10.1177/0893318906291729

Gould, A. M. (2010). Working at McDonalds: Some redeeming features of McJobs. *Work, Employment & Society, 24,* 780–802. doi:10.1177/0950017010380644

Gunn, A. M. (2008). "People's lives are hanging here": Low wage workers share their experience of job loss. *Journal of Contemporary Ethnography, 67,* 679–693. doi:10.1177/0891241608316666

Gunn, A. M. (2011). The discursive construction of care when there is no care to be found: Organizational life (re)framed by those on the socio-economic margins facing job loss. *Culture & Organization, 17,* 65–85. doi:10.1080/14759551.2011.530745

Gunz, H., Mayrhofer, W., & Tolbert, P. (2011). Career as a social and political phenomenon in the globalized economy. *Organization Studies, 32,* 1613–1620. doi:10.1177/0170840611421239

Hall, D. T. (2004). The protean career: A quarter-century journey. *Journal of Vocational Behavior, 65,* 1–13. doi:10.1016/j.jvb.2003.10.006

Hayden, S., & O'Brien Hallstein, L. (2010). *Contemplating maternity in the era of choice: Explorations into discourses of reproduction.* Lanham, MD: Lexington.

Herod, A., & Aguiar, L. L. M. (2006). Introduction: Cleaners and the dirty work of neoliberalism. *Antipode, 38,* 425–434. doi:10.1111/j.0066-4812.2006.00587.x

Hewlett, S. A. (2002). Executive women and the myth of having it all. *Harvard Business Review, 80*(4), 66–73.

Hochschild, A. R. (1989). *The second shift.* New York, NY: Avon Books.

Hochschild, A. R. (1997). *The time bind: When work becomes home and home becomes work.* New York, NY: Metropolitan Books.

Hodges, M., & Budig, M. (2010). Who gets the daddy bonus? Organizational hegemonic masculinity and the impact of fatherhood on earnings. *Gender & Society, 24,* 717–745. doi:10.1177/0891243210386729

Hodson, R. (2001). *Dignity at work.* Cambridge, England: Cambridge University Press.

Høigaard, R., & Mathisen, P. (2009). Benefits of formal mentoring for female leaders. *International Journal of Evidence Based Coaching and Mentoring, 7*(2), 64–70.

Holvino, E. (2008). Intersections: The simultaneity of race, gender and class in organization studies. *Gender, Work & Organization, 17,* 248–277. doi:10.1111/j.1468-0432.2008.00400.x

Ibarra, H. (2003). *Working identity: Unconventional strategies for reinventing your career.* Boston, MA: Harvard Business School Press.

Inkson, K. (2007). *Understanding careers: The metaphors of working lives.* Thousand Oaks, CA: Sage.

Jablin, F. M. (2001). Organizational entry, assimilation, and disengagement/exit. In F. M. Jablin & L. L. Putnam (Eds.), *The new handbook of organizational communication: Advances in theory, research, and methods* (pp. 732–818). Thousand Oaks, CA: Sage.

Jackson, D., Firtko, A., & Edenborough, M. (2007). Personal resilience as a strategy for surviving and thriving in the face of workplace adversity: A literature review. *Journal of Advanced Nursing, 60*, 1–9. doi:10.1111/j.1365-2648.2007.04412.x

Jansen, J. I., & Leuty, M. E. (2012). Work values across generations. *Journal of Career Assessment, 20*, 34–52. doi:10.1177/1069072711417163

Kassing, J. W. (2006). Employees' expressions of upward dissent as a function of current and past work experiences. *Communication Reports, 19*, 79–88. doi:10.1080/08934210600917115

Kaufman, P. (2003). Learning to not labor: How working-class individuals construct middle-class identities. *Sociological Quarterly, 44*, 481–504. doi:10.1111/j.1533-8525.2003.tb00542.x

Kim, E. C. (2009). "Mama's family": Fictive kinship and undocumented immigrant restaurant workers. *Ethnography, 10*, 497–513. doi:10.1177/1466138109347000

Kirby, E. L., & Krone, K. J. (2002). "The policy exists but you can't really use it": Communication and the structuration of work-family policies. *Journal of Applied Communication Research, 30*, 50–77. doi:10.1080/00909880216577

Kirby, E. L., McBride, M. C., Shuler, S., Birkholt, M. J., Danielson, M. A., & Pawlowski, D. R. (2006). The Jesuit difference (?): Narratives of negotiating spiritual values and secular practices. *Communication Studies, 57*, 87–105. doi:10.1080/10510970500481771

Kisselburgh, L. G., Berkelaar, B., & Buzzanell, P. M. (2009). Discourse, gender, and the meaning of work: Rearticulating science, technology, and engineering careers through communicative lenses. In C. S. Beck (Ed.), *Communication yearbook 33* (pp. 259–299). New York, NY: Routledge.

Kramer, M. W., Dougherty, D. S., & Pierce, T. A. (2004). Managing uncertainty during a corporate acquisition: A longitudinal study of communication during an airline acquisition. *Human Communication Research, 30*, 71–101. doi:10.1111/j.1468-2958.2004.tb00725.x

Kramer, M. W., & Noland, T. L. (1999). Communication during job promotions: A case of ongoing assimilation. *Journal of Applied Communication Research, 27*, 335–355. doi:10.1080/00909889909365544

Krueger, D. W. (1986). Money, success, and success phobia. In D. W. Krueger (Ed.), *The last taboo: Money as symbol and reality in psychotherapy and psychoanalysis* (pp. 3–16). New York, NY: Brunner/Mazel.

Kuhn, T. (2006). A "demented work ethic" and a "lifestyle firm": Discourse, identity, and workplace time commitments. *Organization Studies, 27*, 1339–1358. doi:10.1177/0170840606067249

Lair, D. J., Shenoy, S., McClellan, J. G., & McGuire, T. (2008). The politics of meaning/ful work: Navigating the tensions of narcissism and condescension while finding meaning in work. *Management Communication Quarterly, 22*, 172–180. doi:10.1177/0893318908318263

Lair, D. J., Sullivan, K., & Cheney, G. (2005). Marketization and the recasting of the professional self: The rhetoric and ethics of personal branding. *Management Communication Quarterly, 18*, 307–343. doi:10.1177/0893318904270744

Lamude, K. C., Scudder, J., & Simmons, D. (2003). The influence of applicant characteristics on use of verbal impression management tactics in the employment selection interview. *Communication Research Reports, 20*, 299–307. doi:10.1080/08824090309388829

Lapour, A. S., & Heppner, M. J. (2009). Social class privilege and adolescent women's perceived career options. *Journal of Counseling Psychology, 56*, 477–494. doi:10.1037/a0017268

Lareau, A. (2003). *Unequal childhoods: Class, race, and family life.* Berkeley: University of California Press.

Lareau, A., & Conley, D. (2008). *Social class: How does it work?* New York, NY: Russell Sage Foundation.

Lee, M. D., Kossek, E. E., Hall, D. T., & Litrico, J. B. (2011). Entangled strands: A process perspective on the evolution of careers in the context of personal, family, work, and community life. *Human Relations, 64*, 1531–1553. doi:10.1177/0018726711424622

Lee, M. Y. K. (2008). Universal human dignity: Some reflections in the Asian context. *Asian Journal of Comparative Law, 3*, 283–313. doi:10.2202/1932-0205.1076

Long, Z., Kuang, K., & Buzzanell, P. M. (in press). A choice to work at home: Exploring Chinese teleworkers' strategies to legitimize their nonstandard work arrangement. *Journal of Business and Technical Communication.*

Lucas, K. (2007). Problematized providing and protecting: The occupational narrative of the working class. In W. DeGenaro (Ed.), *Who says? Working-class rhetoric, class consciousness, and community* (pp. 180–199). Pittsburgh, PA: University of Pittsburgh Press.

Lucas, K. (2011a). Blue-collar discourses of workplace dignity: Using outgroup comparisons to construct positive identities. *Management Communication Quarterly, 25*, 353–374. doi:10.1177/0893318910386445

Lucas, K. (2011b). The working class promise: A communicative account of mobility-based ambivalences. *Communication Monographs, 78*, 347–369. doi:10.1080/0363 7751.2011.589461

Lucas, K., & Buzzanell, P. M. (2012). Memorable messages of hard times: Constructing short- and long-term resiliencies through family communication. *Journal of Family Communication, 12*, 189–208. doi:10.1080/15267431.2012.687196

Lucas, K., Kang, D., & Li, Z. (in press). Workplace dignity in a total institution: Examining the experiences of Foxconn's migrant workforce. *Journal of Business Ethics.* doi:10.1007/s10551-012-1328-0

Lutgen-Sandvik, P. (2006). Take this job and...: Quitting and other forms of resistance to workplace bullying. *Communication Monographs, 73*, 406–433. doi:10.1080/03637750601024156

Lutgen-Sandvik, P., & Sypher, B. D. (2009). *The destructive side of organizational communication: Processes, consequences and constructive ways of organizing.* New York, NY: Routledge.

Maitlis, S. (2009). Who am I now? Sensemaking and identity in posttraumatic growth. In L. M. Roberts & J. E. Dutton (Eds.), *Exploring positive identities and organizations: Building a theoretical and research foundation* (pp. 47–76). New York, NY: Routledge.

Meares, M. M., Oetzel, J. G., Torres, A., Derkacs, D., & Ginossar, T. (2004). Employee mistreatment and muted voices in the culturally diverse workplace. *Journal of Applied Communication Research, 32*, 4–27. doi:10.1080/0090988042000178121

Mears, A., & Finlay, W. (2005). Not just a paper doll: How models manage bodily capital and why they perform emotional labor. *Journal of Contemporary Ethnography, 34*, 317–343. doi:10.1177/0891241605274559

Medved, C. E. (2007). Investigating family labor in communication studies: Threading across historical and contemporary discourses. *Journal of Family Communication, 7*, 225–243. doi:10.1080/15267430701392172

Medved, C. E. (2009a). Constructing breadwinning-mother identities: Moral, personal, and political positioning. *Women's Studies Quarterly, 37*, 136–152.

Medved, C. E. (2009b). Crossing and transforming occupational and household gendered divisions of labor. In C. S. Beck (Ed.), *Communication yearbook 33* (pp. 457–481). New York, NY: Routledge.

Medved, C. E., & Rawlins, W. K. (2011). At-home fathers and breadwinning mothers: Variations in constructing work and family lives. *Women & Language, 34*, 9–39.

Meisenbach, R. J. (2008). Working with tensions: Materiality, discourse, and (dis)empowerment in occupational identity negotiation among higher education fund-raisers. *Management Communication Quarterly, 22*, 258–287. doi:10.1177/0893318908323150

Meisenbach, R. J. (2010). Stigma management communication: A theory and agenda for applied research on how individuals manage moments of stigmatized identity. *Journal of Applied Communication Research, 38*, 268–292. doi:10.1080/0090988 2.2010.490841

Miller Burke, J., & Attridge, M. (2011a). Pathways to career and leadership success: Part 1—A psychosocial profile of $100k professionals. *Journal of Workplace Behavioral Health, 26*, 175–206. doi:10.1080/15555240.2011.589718

Miller Burke, J., & Attridge, M. (2011b). Pathways to career and leadership success: Part 2—Striking gender similiarities among $100k professionals. *Journal of Workplace Behavioral Health, 26*, 207–239. doi:10.1080/15555240.2011.589722

Miller, K. (2002). The experience of emotion in the workplace: Professing in the midst of tragedy. *Management Communication Quarterly, 15*, 571–600. doi:10.1177/0893318902154003

Mize Smith, J., Arendt, C., Lahman, J. B., Settle, G. N., & Duff, A. (2006). Framing the work of art: Spirituality and career discourse in the nonprofit arts sector. *Communication Studies, 57*, 25–46. doi:10.1080/10510970500481672

Morrison, E. W. (2011). Employee voice behavior: Integration and directions for future research. *Academy of Management Annals, 5*, 373–412. doi:10.1080/19416520.201 1.574506

Nadesan, M. H., & Trethewey, A. (2000). Performing the enterprising subject: Gendered strategies for success (?). *Text & Performance Quarterly, 20*, 223–250. doi:10.1080/10462930009366299

Nätti, J., Anttila, T., & Tammelin, M. (2012). Knowledge work, working time, and use of time among Finnish dual-earner families. *Journal of Family Issues, 33*, 295–315. doi:10.1177/0192513x11413875

Neff, G. (2012). *Venture labor: Work and the burden of risk in innovative industries.* Cambridge, MA: MIT Press.

Newman, K. S. (1999). *No shame in my game: The working poor in the inner city.* New York, NY: Russell Sage Foundation.

Nicotera, A. M., & Mahon, M. M. (2013). Rocks and hard places: Exploring the impact of structurational divergence in nursing. *Management Communication Quarterly, 27*, 90–120. doi:10.1177/0893318912458214

Pal, M., & Buzzanell, P. M. (2008). The Indian call center experience: A case study in changing discourses of identity, identification, and career in a global context. *Journal of Business Communication, 45*, 31–60. doi:10.1177/0021943607309348

Pal, M., & Dutta, M. J. (2008). Theorizing resistance in a global context: Processes, strategies and tactics in communication scholarship. In C. S. Beck (Ed.), *Communication yearbook 32* (pp. 41–87). New York, NY: Routledge.

Paugh, A. L. (2005). Learning about work at dinnertime: Language socialization in dual-earner American families. *Discourse and Society, 16*, 55–78. doi:10.1177/0957926505048230

Pepper, G. L., & Larson, G. S. (2006). Cultural identity tensions in a post-acquisition organization. *Journal of Applied Communication Research, 34*, 49–71. doi:10.1080/00909880500420267

Perlow, L. A. (1998). Boundary control: The social ordering of work and family time in a high-tech corporation. *Administrative Science Quarterly, 43*, 328–357.

Petroski, D. J., & Edley, P. P. (2006). Stay-at-home fathers: Masculinity, family, work, and gender stereotypes. *Electronic Journal of Communication, 16*(3/4).

Phillips, N., & Oswick, C. (2012). Organizational discourse: Domains, debates and directions. *Academy of Management Annals, 6*, 435–481. doi:10.1080/19416520.2012.681558

Purser, G. (2009). The dignity of job-seeking men: Boundary work among immigrant day laborers. *Journal of Contemporary Ethnography, 38*, 117–139. doi:10.1177/0891241607311867

Putnam, L. L. (2009, August). *The multiple faces of engaged scholarship.* Paper presented at the Aspen Conference on Engaged Communication Scholarship, Apsen, CO.

Rodino-Colocino, M. (2012). Geek jeremiads: Speaking the crisis of job loss by opposing offshored and H-1B labor. *Communication & Critical/Cultural Studies, 9*, 22–46. doi:10.1080/14791420.2011.645490

Rose, G. M., & Orr, L. M. (2007). Measuring and exploring symbolic money meanings. *Psychology & Marketing, 24*, 743–761. doi:10.1002/mar.20182

Roy, K. M. (2005). Transitions on the margins of work and family life for low-income African-American fathers. *Journal of Family and Economic Issues, 26*, 77–100. doi:10.1007/s10834-004-1413-3

Rumens, N., & Kerfoot, D. (2009). Gay men at work: (Re)constructing the self as professional. *Human Relations, 62*, 763–786. doi:10.1177/0018726709103457

Sanders, C. R. (2010). Working out back: The veterinary technician and "dirty work". *Journal of Contemporary Ethnography, 39*, 243–272. doi:10.1177/0891241610366711

Sayer, A. (2007). Dignity at work: Broadening the agenda. *Organization, 14*, 565–581. doi:10.1177/1350508407078053

Schneer, J. A., & Reitman, F. (2002). Managerial life without a wife: Family structure and managerial career success. *Journal of Business Ethics, 37*, 25–38. doi:10.1023/A:1014773917084

Schor, J. B. (1992). *The overworked American: The unexpected decline of leisure.* New York, NY: Basic Books.

Scott, J. A. (2007). Our callings, our selves: Repositioning religious and entrepreneurial discourses in career theory and practice. *Communication Studies, 58*, 261–279. doi:10.1080/10510970701518363

Seibert, S. E., Kraimer, M. L., & Liden, R. C. (2001). A social capital theory of career success. *Academy of Management Journal, 44*, 219–237. doi:10.2307/3069452

Shuler, S., & Sypher, B. D. (2000). Seeking emotional labor: When managing the heart enhances the work experience. *Management Communication Quarterly, 14*, 50–89. doi:10.1177/0893318900141003

Snyder, G. J. (2012). The city and the subculture career: Professional street skateboarding in LA. *Ethnography, 13*, 306–329. doi:10.1177/1466138111413501

Spradlin, A. L. (1998). The price of "passing": A lesbian perspective on authenticity in organizations. *Management Communication Quarterly, 11*, 598–605. doi:10.1177/0893318998114006

Stacey, C. L. (2005). Finding dignity in dirty work: The constraints and rewards of low-wage home care labour. *Sociology of Health & Illness, 27*, 831–854. doi:10.1111/j.1467-9566.2005.00476.x

Stebbins, R. A. (2000). Serious leisure. *Society, 39*, 53–57. doi:10.1007/s12115-001-1023-8

Stephens, N., Fryberg, S., & Markus, H. (2011). When choice does not equal freedom: A sociocultural analysis of agency in working-class American contexts. *Social Psychological and Personality Science, 2*, 33–41. doi:10.1177/1948550610378757

Stier, J. (2007). Game, name, and fame—Afterwards will I still be the same? A social psychological study of career, role exit, and identity. *International Review for the Sociology of Sport, 42*, 99–111. doi:10.1177/1012690207081830

Stone, P. (2007). *Opting out? Why women really quit careers and head home*. Berkeley: University of California Press.

Stone, P., & Lovejoy, M. (2004). Fast-track women and the "choice" to stay home. *Annals of the American Academy of Political and Social Science, 596*, 62–83. doi:10.1177/0002716204268552

Stuesse, A. C. (2010). What's 'justice and dignity' got to do with it?: Migrant vulnerability, corporate complicity, and the state. *Human Organization, 69*, 19–30.

Susskind, A. M. (2007). Downsizing survivors' communication networks and reactions: A longitudinal examination of information flow and turnover intentions. *Communication Research, 34*, 156–184. doi:10.1177/0093650206298068

Sveningsson, S., & Alvesson, M. (2003). Managing managerial identities: Organizational fragmentation, discourse and identity struggle. *Human Relations, 56*, 1163–1193. doi:10.1177/00187267035610001

Tal-Or, N. (2010). Indirect ingratiation: Pleasing people by associating them with successful others and by praising their associates. *Human Communication Research, 36*, 163–189. doi:10.1111/j.1468-2958.2010.01372.x

Tan, C. L., & Kramer, M. W. (2012). Communication and voluntary downward career changes. *Journal of Applied Communication Research, 40*, 87–106. doi:10.1080/00909882.2011.634429

Tepper, B. J., Moss, S. E., Lockhart, D. E., & Carr, J. C. (2007). Abusive supervision, upward maintenance communication, and subordinates' psychological distress. *Academy of Management Journal, 50*, 1169–1180. doi:10.2307/20159918

Thompson, G. (2010). *Working in the shadows: A year of doing the jobs [most] Americans won't do*. New York, NY: Nation Books.

Tourish, D., Paulsen, N., Hobman, E., & Bordia, P. (2004). The downsides of downsizing: Communication processes and information needs in the aftermath of a workforce reduction strategy. *Management Communication Quarterly, 17*, 485–516. doi:10.1177/0893318903262241

Tower, L. E., & Alkadry, M. G. (2008). The social costs of career success for women. *Review of Public Personnel Administration, 28*, 144–165. doi:10.1177/0734371X08315343

Tracy, S. J. (2005). Locking up emotion: Moving beyond dissonance for understanding emotion labor discomfort. *Communication Monographs, 72*, 261–283. doi:10.1080/03637750500206474

Tracy, S. J., & Rivera, K. (2010). Endorsing equity and applauding stay-at-home moms: How male voices on work–life reveal aversive sexism and flickers of transformation. *Management Communication Quarterly, 24*, 3–43. doi:10.1177/0893318909352248

Tracy, S. J., & Scott, C. (2006). Sexuality, masculinity, and taint management among firefighters and correctional officers. *Management Communication Quarterly, 20*, 6–38. doi:10.1177/0893318906287898

Trethewey, A. (2001). Reproducing and resisting the master narrative of decline: Midlife professional women's experiences of aging. *Management Communication Quarterly, 15*, 183–226. doi:10.1177/0893318901152002

Twenge, J. M., Campbell, S. M., Hoffman, B. J., & Lance, C. E. (2010). Generational differences in work values: Leisure and extrinsic values increasing, social and intrinsic values decreasing. *Journal of Management, 36*, 1117–1142. doi:10.1177/0149206309352246

Tyler, M. (2011). Tainted love: From dirty work to abject labour in Soho's sex shops. *Human Relations, 64*, 1477–1500. doi:10.1177/0018726711418849

van Dam, K. (2004). Antecedents and consequences of employability orientation. *European Journal of Work and Organizational Psychology, 13*, 29–51. doi:10.1080/13594320344000237

Westwood, R., & Lok, P. (2003). The meaning of work in Chinese contexts: A comparative study. *International Journal of Cross Cultural Management, 3*, 139–165. doi:10.1177/14705958030032001

Wieland, S. (2011). Struggling to manage work as a part of everyday life: Complicating control, rethinking resistance, and contextualizing work/life studies. *Communication Monographs, 78*, 162–184. doi:10.1080/03637751.2011.564642

Williams, J. (2000). *Unbending gender: Why family and work conflict and what to do about it.* Oxford, England: Oxford University Press.

Winker, G., & Degele, N. (2011). Intersectionality as multi-level analysis: Dealing with social inequality. *European Journal of Women's Studies, 118*, 51–66. doi:10.1177/1350506810386084

Winn, J. E. (2003). Every dream has its price: Personal failure and the American Dream in *Wall Street* and *The Firm*. *Southern Communication Journal, 68*, 307–318. doi:10.1080/10417940309373269

Wood, M. S., & Karau, S. J. (2009). Preserving employee dignity during the termination interview: An empirical examination. *Journal of Business Ethics, 86*, 519–534. doi:10.1007/s10551-008-9862-5

Zoller, H. M. (2003). Health on the line: Identity and disciplinary control in employee occupational health and safety discourse. *Journal of Applied Communication Research, 31*, 118–139. doi:10.1080/0090988032000064588

Zorn, T. E., & Townsley, N. (2008). Introduction to the forum on meaning/ful work studies in organizational communication. *Management Communication Quarterly, 22*, 147–151. doi:10.1177/0893318908318268

CHAPTER CONTENTS

2 Joining and Leaving Organizations in a Global Information Society

Brenda L. Berkelaar

The University of Texas at Austin

Social, political, economic, and technological changes are reshaping how people join and leave organizations, a process called organizational socialization. In light of these changes, there is a need to extend and challenge existing scholarship, while also considering the multiple organizational memberships that shape human experience (e.g., educational, healthcare, political, religious, terrorist, volunteer). Taking into account macro- through micro-level factors—globalization, new technologies, time, changing workforce conditions, family structures, political (in)stabilities, and understudied organizations/organizing—this chapter suggests research trajectories that offer opportunities for communication subdisciplines to benefit from and contribute to organizational socialization research and practice while also expanding interdisciplinary influence.

D ramatic political, economic, social, and technological changes are reshaping how individuals join and leave organizations. Current economic conditions highlight the increasingly contingent employer–employee relationships as well as growth of small businesses, the informal economy, and entrepreneurship (Ballard & Gossett, 2007; Becker, 2004; Webb, Tihanyi, Ireland, & Sirmon, 2009). Alongside recent political movements like the Occupy Movement (Kennedy, 2011), flash mobs (Wasik, 2011), and the Arab Spring (Anderson, 2011), these changes re-emphasize globalization's influence and effects. Furthermore, innovative uses of information communication technologies (ICTs) contribute to new and revised organization types, processes, structures, and lifecycles. ICTs alter perceived boundaries including time/space, work/non-work, public/private, and organization/ environment. Taken together, these changes influence how people enter into, participate in, and leave organizations—a process known as *organizational socialization* (Kramer, 2010).

Typically considered the purview of organizational scholarship, organizational socialization has wide-ranging outcomes of interest to communication, its sub-disciplines, and society more broadly. This importance results from the wide-ranging organizational contexts into which individuals may be socialized. These include employment, volunteer, activist/terrorist,[1] interpersonal, familial, religious, recreational, educational, and/or political affiliations that shape individual and collective experiences and overall quality of life. Here, I define *organization* broadly as any social group(ing) oriented around actual or perceived shared goals. Organizational members make goals visible through communication and distribution of material resources. Similarly, *organizing* refers to (re-)structuring or (re-)arranging a social group for some presumably collective purpose, even if that purpose is seemingly pointless (e.g., flash mob).

Operating from these working definitions, this chapter examines how current technological, economic, social, and political changes impact understandings, practices, and processes of organizational socialization in order to identify opportunities for future research. I begin by arguing for an expansion of organizational socialization research, followed by a brief overview of key concepts and stages. I then examine contextual changes and critical issues at macro-, meso-, and micro-levels including globalization, new ICTs, workforce conditions, multiple organizational memberships, understudied organizational forms, and changing family structures. I conclude by suggesting research trajectories that expand research contexts, emphasize contributions unique to communication scholarship, leverage new and underutilized methods, and provide opportunities for partnerships around inter-and intra-disciplinary concerns and global challenges.

Examining a Broader Range of Organizational Experiences

Organizational socialization research is relatively myopic. Although original conceptualizations considered organizational socialization to be a two-way process (Van Maanen, 1975), managerial biases persist. Furthermore, existing research privileges upward movement in paid employment contexts, emphasizing effective tactic selection by Western managers at initial entry (Kramer, 2010; Waldeck & Myers, 2007). Focusing on increased productivity and reduced turnover, recent literature reframes organizational concerns around the buzzworthy term "employee engagement" (Saks & Gruman, 2010). Research on internal promotions, lateral moves, downward movement, and/or non-Western, online, or non-employment contexts remains underdeveloped.

Communication scholars offer most exceptions. These projects include volunteer socialization (Haski-Leventhal & Bargal, 2008; Kramer, 2011a, 2011b), planned exits (Davis & Myers, 2012), and anticipatory socialization of adolescents into vocational contexts (Myers, Jahn, Gailliard, & Stoltzfus, 2011). Tan and Kramer's (2012) work on voluntary downward mobility in Singapore refreshingly moves beyond typical Western contexts, newcomer entry, and upwardly mobile assumptions, and Kramer's earlier work on job transfers and promotions (Kramer, 1989; 1993; also Kramer & Noland, 1999) is notable in its examination of peer and supervisor-subordinate communication. Additionally, Scott and Myers (2010) integrate research on member and role negotiation, applying structuration theory to examine the interactive processes of organizational socialization. Despite the potential of this research, paid-work perspectives preponderate in organizational scholarship.

Yet, organizations are more than containers for employment. Whether and how individuals enter into, affiliate with, participate in, and leave religious, political, community, volunteer, health/nursing care, terrorist, and educational organizations also matters. Socialization into different organizational contexts affects wide-ranging individual and collective outcomes: political involvement, civic engagement, terrorist activity, social support, cultural competence, personal development, educational attainment, career success, identity construction, healthcare, work productivity, work and life satisfaction, social norms, and quality of life generally (Cheney, Zorn, Planalp, & Lair, 2008; Ciulla, 2001; Jones & Volpe, 2011; Koren, 2010; Robbins, Oh, Le, & Button, 2009). Our field's commitment to recognizing and amplifying diverse perspectives can contribute to more complete, nuanced understandings of organizational socialization.

Since organizational socialization can now occur partially or fully online, scholars should compare socialization in online and offline contexts. For example, the growing popularity of distributed teams results in situations where people work with team members with whom they rarely or never interact face-to-face or synchronously (Connaughton & Shuffler, 2007). Likewise, movements toward online learning create digital classrooms where students and teachers alter the amounts of or eliminate face-to-face or synchronous communication. These examples highlight the need to understand how organizational socialization differs when online communication options are available. Although helpful, the few comparative examinations of online versus offline strategies (Flanagin & Waldeck, 2004; Hart & Miller, 2005; Waldeck, Seibold, & Flanagin, 2004) do not address social media. A somewhat artificial distinction, I define *online* behaviors as those in which an active Internet connection is essential to the initial design of the technology and the communicative practices it enables (e.g., email, social network sites, blogs, Skype™). In contrast, *offline* communication practices are those that do not involve an active Internet connection as an essential design characteristic and may include mediated (e.g., television, telephone, radio) as well as face-to face communication.

The offline/online distinction—rather than mediated/unmediated—underscores unique affordances of ICTs: invisible audiences, collapsed contexts, replicability, searchability, and persistence (boyd,[2] 2007). These affordances—and combinations thereof—create potentially different communication processes (Ramirez, Walther, Burgoon, & Sunnafrank, 2002), and therefore, outcomes. Given that offline and online communication processes are neither identical nor completely distinct (Williams, 2010), organizational socialization may differ when online behaviors supplement, replicate, or replace offline behaviors.

Opportunities to Address Technical, Socio-Political, and Economic Changes

Along with expanding the organizational and communicative contexts studied, researchers should consider how recent socio-political, economic, and technological changes shape organizational life. Recent events offer insights not considered by Jablin (2001), Waldeck and Myers (2007). Even Kramer's (2010) book—in which he makes organizational socialization research accessible and more expansive by including volunteer, part-time, downwardly and laterally mobile work—does not consider many of these trends. In part, this is because all three publications intentionally address organizational socialization as it relates to paid and unpaid work. However, it is also likely because the changes themselves and research on these contextual changes, in many cases, was—and is—not yet available.

So, how do these technological, socio-political, and economic changes affect organizational socialization scholarship? First, uses and affordances of new ICTs—as epitomized in participatory information sharing, user-centered, and identity performance practices of Web 2.0—make more and different information available in new ways from different sources (Berkelaar, 2010). Certainly researchers do consider how advanced ICTs affect socialization outcomes (Waldeck & Myers, 2007) as well as organizational structures, relationships, cultures, and practices (Kramer, 2010). Yet these researchers have not yet considered how social media (including social networking sites) might alter organizational socialization processes given distinctive information-construction and information-seeking features, uses, and outputs.

The omission is understandable. Social media technologies, despite their seeming ubiquity, are relatively new. Although social networking sites emerged in the mid-1990s, the category-defining tool, Facebook™, only entered the broader market in 2006 (boyd & Ellison, 2004). At that time, Facebook had neither the popularity nor the market dominance it has today. It was only in 2010 that social networking sites exceeded search engines as the most visited websites (Dougherty, 2010).

Information seeking is central to organizational socialization (Miller & Jablin, 1991; Waldeck & Myers, 2007). New ICTs matter because their increasing popularity, when coupled with increasingly sophisticated search algorithms, data mining, and computational abilities, provides access to information previously difficult or impossible to obtain. This extractive process is known as *cybervetting* (Berkelaar, 2010; Schott, 2007). People—workers and employers, terrorists and law enforcement officials, doctors and patients, athletes and coaches, non-profits and volunteers, politicians and voters, families and potential roommates, classmates and people seeking dates—look for information about others online before or soon after meeting. Although online surveillance research continues to grow (Kramer, 2010), most scholarship emphasizes employer surveillance using organizationally-sponsored tools. However, new social ICTs allow prospective and current organizational members to employ Miller and Jablin's (1991) information-seeking techniques in new, different, and potentially more informative—although not necessarily effective—ways (Berkelaar, 2010). Researchers do not yet know to what degree Web 2.0 tools, affordances, uses, and philosophies influence organizational socialization.

New ICTs—social media in particular—have facilitated political movements, alternative means of organizing, and different socialization timelines. For example, starting in 2010, the Arab Spring involved protests, uprisings, and overthrown governments across the Middle East and parts of Northern Africa as participants expressed growing concerns about economic unfairness, unemployment, power imbalances, and government abuses. The effective mobilization of protesters was attributed primarily to communication affordances provided by social media (Anderson, 2011). New ICTs also enable alternate forms of organizing like flash mobs, and their destructive derivative, flash robs.[3] Although perhaps not an organization *per se*, flash mobs highlight the need to consider shorter-term, anonymous, almost ephemeral organizations or organizing, constituted in and through communication. Yet, most socialization research presumes lengthier timelines. Although shorter memberships are considered as in Kramer's (2011a) study on community choirs, the overall bias is to examine socialization into longer-term organizational or occupational affiliations. Consideration of different organizational/organizing forms, types, and lifecycles would provide insight into how individuals socialize into shorter-term and non-work organizations.

Workforce changes also influence organizational socialization. Starting around 2007, the global economic downturn contributed to dramatic growth in the percentage of workers in informal economies (Webb et al., 2009) and the number of unemployed, underemployed, contingent, and part-time workers. These changes reinforced shifts in social contracts. Although Kramer (2010) argues that the long-term employment contract was "always more imaginary than real" (p. 165), recent increases in these worker categories highlights the need to understand the socialization of part-time, underemployed, and contract workers. Complicating these broad workforce changes, the increasing global mobility and changing demographics of families, students, and labor groups (Smith & Guarnizo, 2009) result in multiple sequential and/or simultaneous transitions into and out of different types of organizations.

Technological, socio-political, and economic changes influence who will or will not join, participate in, or leave which types of organizations, in which digital or physical spaces, at what times, for how long, and with what effects. Together these changes highlight key issues of concern for communication scholars including identity, agency and structure, efficacy, privacy, organizing, lifespan, technology, voice, time, and boundaries.

Opportunities to Expand the Reach and Influence of Communication Scholarship

These changes also afford opportunities to reinforce how the communication discipline can contribute to understanding organizational socialization across human experience. Communication research continues to be less visible than other disciplinary research. Visibility helps establish expertise (Treem, 2012), which in turn, influences research trajectories, funding, and practical interventions. Citations provide partial insight into disciplinary influence. Results from Google Scholar™ and Web of Science™—scholars' most-used databases (Tucci, 2010)—illustrate the low visibility of communication scholarship. A Google Scholar search of "organizational socialization" returns publications dominated by management and applied psychology (June 15, 2012). Similarly, top results from Web of Science are management (41%), applied psychology (26%), and business (20%). Communication (5%) and sociology (5%) provide similar publication counts, but communication averages fewer citations (22.28/year; 43 for top-cited) compared to sociology (27.48/year; 178 for top-cited) or any top contributors, even adjusted for subgroup size.[4] Certainly whether top search results are the most insightful or "best," is debatable; however, manuscripts leading search results are more likely to be cited (Tucci, 2010) and therefore more visible and influential.

This peripheral positioning may be the result of terminology differences. Communication scholarship often uses Jablin's (2001) term "organizational assimilation" rather than organizational socialization. A quick examination of Wikipedia™—an often-accursed, if popular source of information (Alexa, 2012)—suggests parallel conversations. The organizational socialization page is lengthy, citing 40 management, business, and psychology publications. It does not link to the much shorter organizational assimilation page which references 8 publications, all but one from communication. Furthermore, in contrast to communication publications, computer science and management results from Web of Science describe organizational assimilation as the process whereby organizations adopt technological innovations, rather than socializing people into organizations, Certainly, citations are neither a sufficient nor a complete way to measure influence, and these sources have credibility and coverage concerns. Yet, these sources provide visibility, and, therefore, presumed expertise, which implies influence.

Thus, this chapter examines organizational socialization in light of key socio-political, technical, and economic trends in order to suggest and expand particular research trajectories. In so doing, it builds on earlier reviews (Jablin, 2001; Waldeck & Myers, 2007) and responds to calls to examine communication issues across the lifespan, cultures, life spheres, over time, and in mediated and non-mediated contexts (Craig, 2005; Nussbaum, 2007).[5]

A Brief Overview of Organizational Socialization

Key Concepts

In the classic sense, organizational socialization is "the process by which a person learns the values, norms and required behaviors which permit him [sic] to participate as a member of the organization" (Van Maanen, 1975, p. 67). Although often labeled organizational assimilation by communication scholars (Jablin, 2001; Waldeck & Myers, 2007), the predominant interdisciplinary term is organizational socialization. In addition to concerns about parallel scholarly conversations, the influence of Star Trek™ with its fictional, cybernetically-enhanced Borg drones' mandate—"You will be assimilated"—has convinced me, like other scholars (Kramer, 2010), to eschew the term "organizational assimilation" in favor of "organizational socialization" for the overarching process. The Borg drones use the term "assimilate" to imply the loss of one's individual self to the interconnected collective or hive mind: "Resistance is futile. We are the Borg. We will add your biological and technological distinctiveness to our own."[6]

Although managerial perspectives dominated early scholarship (Jablin, 2001; Waldeck & Myers, 2007), organizational socialization involves interactions between competing and complementing tensions: the extent to an organization shapes an individual to meet its needs—that is, *assimilation*—and the extent to which an individual shapes an organization to meet his or her needs—that is, *personalization,* or individualization (Kramer, 2010).[7] Assimilation and personalization arise from direct, indirect, interactive, extractive, and ambient interactions experienced over time (Miller & Jablin, 1991).

Organizational perspectives often take center stage, even when newcomer perspectives are examined (for exceptions see Kramer, 2011a; 2011b; Miller & Jablin, 1991; Myers et al., 2011). Managerial perspectives focus attention on the relative effectiveness of particular assimilation strategies (formal vs. informal; sequential vs. variable; fixed vs. variable; investiture vs. divesture) for desired organizational outcomes (e.g., innovation/creativity vs. control; employee engagement; organizational identification; lower turnover; Saks & Gruman, 2010). Employers want to know which strategies encourage workers to stay (retention) and to do what employers want (control), productively (cost/benefit).

Notwithstanding a few exceptions, paid employment perspectives eclipse alternative perspectives (Ashforth, Sluss, & Harrison, 2007; for exceptions see: Miller & Jablin, 1991; Scott & Myers, 2010; Davis & Myers, 2012; Kramer, 2009, 2010, 2011a, 2011b). Individual voices and voices outside of employment contexts remain undertheorized and underexamined. For example, the unemployed and underemployed tend to be ignored. So, too, are people's non-work organizational experiences, even though early evidence suggests the type of organizational context affects socialization processes and outcomes (Kramer, 2009, 2011a, 2011b).

Researchers have addressed individual resistance to organizational control or influence (Bullis & Stout, 2000; Cheney & Cloud, 2006). However, which individual, organizational, environmental, and communication characteristics enable or constrain personalization remain understudied. When examined, personalization is primarily informed by other disciplines. For example, building on Katz and Kahn's (1978) classic role-making process, various researchers examine personalization strategies that leverage interaction and impression management for job crafting (Wrzesniewski & Dutton, 2001), career agency (Tams & Arthur, 2010), or role innovation (Katz & Kahn, 1978). Regrettably, underlying communicative practices and competencies remain unexamined. Scholars rarely consider existing message-oriented research (for exceptions see Barge & Schlueter, 2004; Hart & Miller, 2005) or draw from the expertise of interpersonal, rhetoric, and other sub-disciplines to understand how communication competencies influence organizational socialization processes, stages or outcomes.

Stages of Organizational Socialization

Organizational socialization is often conceptualized as series of interrelated communicative processes (Kramer, 2010) that occur multiple times as individuals move into, through, and out of organizations sequentially and simultaneously throughout their lives. Historically, most theorists described three stages: pre-arrival/anticipatory socialization; entry and initial participation; and active participation (metamorphosis). Increasingly, scholars include a fourth stage: organizational disengagement/exit (Jablin, 2001). Scholars have criticized stage models, arguing that communication, and therefore socialization, are recursive (Bullis & Stout, 2000). However, a stage model—loosely held—provides a useful framework for cross-disciplinary communication and focuses attention on critical moments in organizational socialization.

Anticipatory Socialization. The first stage, pre-arrival or *anticipatory socialization* is traditionally divided into two processes: *vocational anticipatory socialization* and *occupational anticipatory socialization.* Vocational anticipatory socialization is the process by which individuals select occupations, typically during the time before their first paid full-time job (Jablin, 2001). Communication scholars provide most research in this area. For example, Myers et al. (2011) developed a communicative theory of vocational anticipatory socialization by examining how message content and strategies influence adolescent occupational choice. Overall, adolescent and middle-school subjects in Western, middle-class populations continue to be the emphasis of vocational anticipatory socialization research (Kisselburgh, Berkelaar, & Buzzanell, 2009); however, some recent work examines communicative influences on occupational trajectories in early childhood across cultures (Berkelaar, Buzzanell, Kisselburgh, Tan, & Shen, 2012, Buzzanell, Berkelaar, & Kisselburgh, 2011) and socio-economic levels (Lucas, 2011).

Research on vocational anticipatory socialization typically emphasizes socialization into work roles. In part, this is because the terminology privileges paid work, rather than other forms of organizational participation. For this reason, Kramer (2010) argues for the term "role anticipatory socialization," a relabeling which helps broaden the visible scope of communicative approaches to organizational socialization. (Scholars can avoid creating parallel conversations by strategic use of key words, titling, and search engine optimization during manuscript preparation,[8] keeping role anticipatory socialization at the forefront of search results.) Since messages from family members, peers, media, educational institutions, and part-time jobs inform role anticipatory socialization (Jablin, 2001; Lucas, 2011), developmental and media scholars are uniquely positioned to contribute expertise individuals' personalization of different roles. Additionally, research into role anticipatory socialization should be expanded across the lifespan. As people change organizational affiliations more frequently as a result of (in)voluntary moves, career changes, relational changes, and other events (Smith & Guarnizo, 2009), researchers need to address potentially new—and often overlapping—role exits and entries in adulthood as well as childhood and adolescence.

As the second half of pre-arrival, *organizational anticipatory socialization* refers to the processes by which individuals anticipate and begin to join specific organizations. Most researchers emphasize paid, full-time, longer-term affiliations with brick-and-mortar "container" organizations, typical of the ideal—if not the reality—of the old social contract (Buzzanell & Goldzwig, 1991; Kramer, 2010). Yet, as reinforced in the recent economic downturn, contingent work and shorter-term affiliations increasingly supplant promises of the old social contract. This is a global phenomenon. For example, in China, even at state-owned organizations, the *iron rice bowl*—an employer-based social welfare system guaranteeing lifetime housing, income, health care, and limited work effort—is cracking under market pressures (Ding, Goodall, & Warner, 2000). Not only should workers anticipate working for multiple organizations for shorter periods of time, they might also work for multiple organizations simultaneously. These affiliative changes likely affect personalization and assimilation processes and outcomes during anticipatory socialization and the relative effectiveness of particular individual or organizational tactics.

At the same time, increased restructuring, outsourcing, mergers, and downsizing emphasize the need to examine organizational socialization for people who stay "within" an organization. Kramer's work on job transfers provides some insight into effective communicative practices for negotiating uncertainty and sensemaking processes during lateral, upward (Kramer 1989, 1993; Kramer & Noland, 1999), and voluntary downward mobility (Tan & Kramer, 2012). More work is needed. Not only does this research help adapt understandings of who constitutes a newcomer, it refocuses attention on socialization as ongoing. This emerging body of work complements movements in organizational scholarship toward more localized, and presumably flexible, processes (e.g., person-team fit versus person-organization fit; Kristof-Brown, Zimmerman, & Johnson, 2005). It also highlights opportunities for network or small group scholars to identify clusters, internal boundaries, and critical moments that might predict ongoing and transitional socialization needs.

Uses of new ICTs also influence organizational anticipatory socialization. The availability of online information about organizations and individuals, along with pressures towards organizational and personal branding (Lair, Sullivan, & Cheney, 2005), may influence when anticipatory socialization begins (Berkelaar, 2010) and which practices predominate. For example, the type and timing of knowledge influences which applicants get invited for interviews, a bridge between anticipatory socialization and entry (Jablin, 2001). ICTs provide new and different types of knowledge at different points in the process.

With social media and search engines, information-seeking practices become increasingly influential *prior to* organizational entry, expanding Miller and Jablin's (1991) timeline. Given these economic, social, and technological changes, we need to re-examine how role and organizational anticipatory processes shape which, when, how, and why people come (or are invited) to join particular organizations.

Entry and Ongoing Socialization. The second and third stages of organizational socialization address organizational entry and participation. Because of the meagerness of research on ongoing socialization, and my working assumption that ongoing changes in role conditions contribute to newcomer(-like) conditions for many organizational members, I address the two stages concurrently.

Classic organizational socialization research emphasized organizationally effective newcomer socialization, particularly the relationship between organizational tactics and outcome predictions (Bauer, Bodner, Erdogan, Truxillo, & Tucker, 2007; Waldeck & Myers, 2007). Emerging message-focused scholarship (Barge & Schleueter, 2004; Burke, Kraut, & Joyce, 2010; Hart & Miller, 2005) has highlighted how much remains unknown about how communication characteristics—content, values, norms, beliefs, skills, and knowledge—affect organizational socialization outcomes (Waldeck & Myers, 2007) even as researchers examining education, family (Munz, 2011), and online contexts (Burke et al., 2010; Neelen & Fetter, 2010) suggest that how individuals communicatively enter organizations predicts long-term outcomes including educational achievement and online social support, respectively.

Newcomer socialization is complicated by different conceptualizations of organizations. Most research—particularly outside the communication field—views organizations as *containers*, membership is traditionally seen as binary: One is or is not a member depending on whether they fulfill certain time/space conditions. New ICTs and relatively recent understandings of organizations as communicatively constituted alter traditional assumptions of what constitutes organizational boundaries and participation. This is illustrated by the previously mentioned time/space differences of distributed teams, the temporary affiliations of contingent workers, and ongoing debates about lurkers in online communities. Despite the popular devaluing of lurkers—as compared to active "participants"—researchers have started to recognize lurking as legitimate, recognized organizational activity (Burke et al., 2010) particularly when tacit learning and indirect observation are important (Neelen & Fetter, 2010). Although Miller and Jablin (1991) recognized the importance of indirect observation, ICTs further highlight strategic applications of indirect observation: ICTs create and emphasize permeable, fluctuating, and sometimes-elusive organization/environment boundaries; conceptualizations which require rethinking what it means to be a newcomer or an incumbent.

Additionally, the complex interplay of multiple organizational structures, roles, and conditions are rarely considered when examining organizational socialization. For practical reasons, researchers often focus on socialization into particular roles or occupations. Yet there is a need for more complex modeling and analysis. Consider the merger of two fire departments near my hometown: When city limits expanded, a larger, salaried department involuntarily merged with a small volunteer department with no changes in pay or benefits to either group. How do individual firefighters renegotiate roles in light of material and historical differences? Firefighting is a primary source of identity for volunteers, exceeding religious affiliation (Perkins & Metz, 1988). Additionally, highly competitive hiring into paid (professional) firefighting requires substantial pre-emptive self-socialization (Scott & Myers, 2005). Furthermore, socialization into volunteer organizations differs from paid work environments (Kramer, 2011a, 2011b). Given the high-stress nature and high-reliability requirements of firefighting, how volunteer and paid workers negotiate assimilation and personalization processes given mixed-role, multi-level situations creates a complicated problem—a problem important to resolve. In addition to considering high-reliability organizations, this example highlights the need to examine ongoing socialization in other mixed-context, mixed-role situations (e.g., refugee camps, corporate-NGO partnerships).

Even when obvious, dramatic, multi-layered organizational changes are not occurring, attention to entry as an ongoing process remains underresearched. In part, this is because researchers disagree on what constitutes a newcomer. Few longitudinal studies exist, and results are mixed (Waldeck & Myers, 2007). Recent work suggests newcomer status depends on *relative tenure* rather than calendar days, that is, the speed of organizational growth and turnover (Rollag, 2004, 2007). Practically, this creates challenges. For face-saving and other reasons, incumbents cannot easily use certain information seeking strategies (Miller & Jablin, 1991). Consequently, those in rapidly growing organizations likely receive less socialization opportunities because of reduced clock-time for information-seeking (although lurking affordances of ICTs suggest possible solutions). The challenge of defining newcomers versus incumbents highlights the need to consider relative and absolute time in empirical work (Gomez, 2009) as time further complicates or illuminates processes and outcomes.

Exit/Disengagement. The final stage is organizational exit or disengagement. Here too, researchers have emphasized paid employment, often with the goal of reducing undesirable turnover (Hom, 2010; for exceptions, see Davis & Myers, 2012; Kramer, 2011a, 2011b). Successful exits have practical importance. For example, prisoners' effective exits from prison and re-entries into society are central to avoiding recidivism. Similarly, successfully exiting college (graduation) predicts long-term quality of life (Carver, 2010). Furthermore, effectively managing organizational exits is considered central to managing stress, and increasing resilience, quality of life, and productivity for those who leave and for those who remain (Buzzanell, 2010; Ciulla, 2001; Jablin, 2001).

Research on communicative aspects of organizational exits is nascent.

Early studies have suggested that communicative reframing can help individuals manage social identity issues associated with exits (Kramer, 2011a, 2011b). Disengagement may be complicated during involuntary exits where individuals do not have access to the same decision-making processes or time for anticipatory deidentification (Davis & Myers, 2012). Additionally, most scholarship examines exits in isolation. Yet, depending on material and social conditions and the pace of individual sensemaking, people may experience multiple simultaneous exits that often overlap with (multiple) entries. Furthermore, non-employment exits such as prison release, graduation, repatriation, or deportation may be complicated further by additional material, identity, health, and interpersonal factors.

A promising research area examines voluntary versus involuntary exits. Although most research examines involuntary turnover from paid work (Kramer, 2010), Davis and Myers (2012) proposed a communicative model of planned organizational exit, using interview data to identify communicative sub-stages that helped sorority sisters first make sense of future and then present affiliations before eventually integrating past and future affiliations. Further research comparing voluntary and involuntary exits could provide additional information into how anticipatory deidentification, sensemaking, and identity (re)construction processes manifest differently or at all depending on (perceived) agency, the number of simultaneous exits, the recency of sequential exits, the history of organizational control and identification, and expectations of (im)permanence. Despite a growing, if fragmented, literature on organizational exits, factors predictive of desirable and undesirable outcomes require further examination in order to understand how exits manifest within and across different contexts and conditions.

Changing Contexts and Critical Issues for Organizational Socialization Scholarship

Organizations exist in context. Thus, changes in local or global contexts affect organizational processes, including socialization (Kramer, 2010). A defining feature of the early 21st century, globalization is central to understanding organizations and organizing (Stohl, 2005). Globalization increases global economic interdependence and interconnectedness; deepens, intensifies, and speeds-up material, political, and cultural exchanges through new ICTs, while also compressing time and space; and disembedding and allowing the realignment and restructuring of time, events, institutions, social interactions, and groups (Stohl, 2005). Globalization, thus, is an overarching process from which to understand recent macro- through micro-level changes influencing who gets socialized with (and by) whom, how fast, at what times, and into which organization(s). I begin by addressing macro-level factors including: increased intercultural contact and changing workforce conditions as globalization outcomes; understudied workplaces as conditions illuminated by globalization; and new affordances and uses of ICTs which help drive globalization and re-conceptualizations of time, even as they contribute to political (in)stabilities.

Macro-Level Factors

Increased Intercultural Contact. An outcome of globalization, increased intercultural, contact complicates assimilation and personalization of the organizational values, rules, and norms that constitute organizational socialization (Van Maanen, 1975)—since individuals being socialized possess increasingly divergent values and norms (Smith & Guarnizo, 2009). In response, scholars have called for research on sensemaking, information seeking, and socialization dynamics across cultures (Bauer & Taylor, 2001) as well as intercultural learning competencies (Ashforth et al., 2007) in order to enable effective organizational socialization into increasingly typical multinational and multicultural groups.

Despite these calls, culture remains relatively unexamined in organizational socialization, although Kramer (2010) provides an entire chapter conceptualizing culture's likely effects. When included in empirical work, culture typically operates as a descriptor for participants or contexts (Tan & Kramer, 2012) rather than a primary variable of interest. Yet, research on expatriates suggests culture differentially influences the effectiveness of socialization sources and tactics (Carraher, Sullivan, & Crocitto, 2008). Furthermore, cultural intelligence seems to operate as a proactive socialization competency predictive of successful integration into multinational work teams (Flaherty, 2008).

Increased intercultural contact highlights the need to manage tensions between assimilation and personalization, while helping individuals develop and use tactics necessary to achieve desired outcomes. For example, as post-secondary institutions promote diversity initiatives, successful admission, retention, and graduation depends in part, on how effectively students assimilate without losing personal characteristics that contribute to overall institutional diversity. Research on first-generation college students, international students, and visible minorities reveals that retention challenges often stem from information processes underlying socialization (Housel & Harvey, 2010)—such as, lack of effective information-seeking strategies, failing to obtain necessary information, or not recognizing needed information. Socialization is further complicated by the need for students to manage incongruencies between new organizational values and (perceived) familial, cultural, and/or personal values (Kisselburgh et al., 2009). Proactive information-seeking and management behaviors are predictive of organizational membership and role engagement. Therefore, students' ignorance about information targets, effective strategies, and when and how to gather information create challenges for organizational socialization and therefore retention (Housel & Harvey, 2010). An organizational socialization framework—informed by the expertise of intercultural and small group scholars—could provide insight into inter- and intra-cultural, as well as system and individually-oriented strategies that help create desirable outcomes. Conversely, this knowledge may also help dissolve or slow the development of destructive organizations or groups (terrorist cells, gangs, organized crime, cyber-gangs).

To accomplish these goals, researchers must consider the complexity of organizational socialization as manifested in layered cultural contexts that combine, compete, and complicate organizational socialization. Recognition of culture as a multi-layered construct is not new. Yet, increased global inter-connection and interdependence makes culture's multi-layered effects more salient to everyday practices and complex global challenges. For example, ref-ugee camps illustrate the need to consider multiple culture and role layers dur-ing organizational socialization. Effective assimilation is central to resilience (Doron, 2005) for the more than 42 million people who have been forcibly dis-placed (United Nations High Commission on Refugees, 2011). Refugees come from one national or regional culture to another national or regional culture hoping for repatriation. Their affiliation is conceptually temporary. Refugees are often served by a combination of organizational interests—non-profits, non-governmental organizations, alongside governmental and international aid agencies (organizational cultures)—with paid staff and volunteers (occu-pational cultures), who may come from the refugee camps themselves (insider/ outsider roles). Given different culture types and role levels intersecting in refugee camps, how do people make sense of "the values, norms, and required behaviors that permit [them to assimilate]?" (Van Maanen, 1975, p. 67). That is, how do the socialization processes, strategies, and outcomes experiences of different stakeholder or role groups interact or compete to form hybrid- or sub-cultures?

Changing Workforce Conditions.   Alongside increased interconnectedness, globalization increases economic interdependence: When one national economy struggles, the effects ripple globally. Accelerated by the global economic downturn, workforce conditions and labor pools are shifting. Free-market, planned, and transitional economies face high levels of unemployment and lack qualified workers (World Economic Forum & The Boston Consulting Group, 2012). Employers are increasingly hiring contractual, temporary, part-time, and contingent labor as a means to avoid costs and long-term risks of full-time employees, with many over-qualified senior workers taking junior positions—sometimes unpaid—in order to remain in the workforce or to retool or reskill in anticipation of occupational changes. Additionally, in Western countries, workers are often discouraged from personalizing jobs during economic downturns.

Current workforce conditions—and an increasingly interconnected global workforce—re-emphasize the need to rethink organizational socialization from lenses other than the single, upwardly mobile career. As a result of the persistence of the linear, upwardly mobile career as the archetype of workplace success (Buzzanell & Goldzwig, 1991; Kramer, 2010), little organizational socialization research addresses downward mobility, occupational transitions, or movement from full-time to part-time or contingent work. Kramer (1989) does provide insight into intra-organizational transfer and voluntary downward mobility (Tan & Kramer, 2012). However, most research emphasizes mitigating organizational consequences of turnover (Hausknecht & Trevor, 2011).

More often than not, socialization into full-time, upwardly mobile, professional work takes center stage, backgrounding intra-organizational promotions in favor of newcomer entry (for an exception, see Kramer & Noland, 1999). Certainly, Tan and Kramer's (2012) study on voluntary downward career changes offered insight into the strategic communication competencies and sensemaking necessary for managing identities and relationships during voluntary disengagement. However, given the importance of organizational affiliations to identity, relational support, and quality of life, more evidence that helps predict and describe processes and effects of organizational mobility, can encourage positive socialization processes and resilience within and outside of workplaces.

Furthermore, research is not yet clear on how and if organizational socialization of contingent workers does or should happen differently. Research suggests that contingent workers have dual identifications (George & Chattopadhyay, 2005) and differ in their organizational identifications, even as they respond to employer promises (Ashford, George, & Blatt, 2007). Increasing numbers of contingent, contractual, and multiple-part-time workers underscore potentially unique and competing socialization demands when individuals work for multiple organizations or anticipate short-term affiliations. How do individuals sequentially or simultaneously socialize with organizations whose values and norms may or may not align across organization or with each individual's values? Given assimilation demands from multiple organizations, what resources remain for personalization? The cumulative effects and relative effectiveness of strategies for managing multiple, simultaneous, and potentially competing socialization demands are not yet known. Changing work conditions also draws attention to concerns about voice and agency. Consistent with Waldeck and Myers' (2007) review, attention to changing workforce conditions requires complicating typical socialization models, moving beyond a focus on each individual's relationship with a particular organization (or the relative socialization success of a relatively homogenous group within a particular organization).

Understudied Work Contexts. Increases in informal economies and family-owned businesses underscore the need to attend to understudied organizational contexts. In response to globalization opportunities and threats, informal economies and family-owned businesses increased during recent years (Webb et al., 2009). However, they remain relatively ignored by scholars. The *informal economy* involves all economic activity not taxed, overseen, or monitored by a government or institution (Becker, 2004). Informal economies are not exclusively, or even dominantly, black market activities. Rather, this work is often legal in all aspects except failure to pay taxes. In developing countries, the informal economy accounts for an estimated 60% of economic activity (Webb et al., 2009).

Although logistically challenging, research into informal economies is not impossible, would highlight an often-ignored population, and provide insight into how motivations constrain or enable assimilation or personalization tactics. The primary motivation for participation in informal economies is often financial need—particularly for women and children who compose a large portion of these working populations (Webb et al., 2009). However, identity exploration is a common motivation for wealthier workers, at least in wealthier countries (Snyder, 2004). As with formal economies, the social norms and economic opportunities of local marketplaces enable or constrain individual agency, influencing individuals' perceived repertoire of socialization tactics, particularly for personalization. Certain groups in the informal economy often lack opportunities for personalization (e.g., domestic workers, childcare workers), yet, in response to changing regulations and enforcement activities, many informal workers also demonstrate an adaptive dynamism that suggests distinct and pervasive entrepreneurial, innovative, and resilient characteristics—desirable outcomes for work and non-work organizations (Webb et al., 2009; Snyder, 2004).

Family-owned businesses also afford productive research opportunities. Conservative estimates suggest that family-owned businesses contribute more than 20% of Western countries GDP (Astrachan & Shanker, 2004; Bjuggren, Johanssen, & Sjögren, 2011), with continued growth anticipated (Schulze & Gedajlovic, 2010). For family members, the demands, requirements, and values of family-business jobs often bleed into non-work time (Schulze & Gedajlovic, 2010). Recent research on family-owned businesses in general emphasizes leadership succession (Griffeth, Allen, & Barrett, 2006). Yet organizational socialization research, with few exceptions, fails to address unique socialization challenges and perspectives offered by family-owned businesses. Although organizational scholarship rarely addresses socialization processes for family-owned businesses directly, scholarship on family-owned businesses offers an opportunity to reconsider key aspects of organizational socialization including anticipatory socialization, role negotiation, entries, and exits. Given the blending of family and occupational roles, anticipatory socialization likely differs in content, form, and therefore outcomes. The centrality of member negotiation to organizational socialization (Scott & Myers, 2010; Katz & Kahn, 1978) suggests clear potential for conflicting family and work roles (Schulze & Gedajlovic, 2010) and a clear need for sensemaking. Pressures to identify with the family via the business may complicate organizational exit (or entry). Furthermore, family and non-family employees are likely socialized differently—in potentially destructive ways. Family scholars could help illuminate these role negotiations during socialization stages with potential extensions into other insider/outsider scenarios.

Research on changing workforce conditions and underexamined workforce contexts can provide insight into how motivations, control, and other factors influence organizational socialization. Given the salience of these two contextual changes, here I primarily attended to informal economies and family-owned businesses. However, insights could be expanded by considering different types of employment contexts (NGOs, NPOs), as well as agency with regard to organizational affiliations, time and point of exit and entry, and motivations for transitions and conditions that create or contribute to insider/outsider status offline and online.

New Affordances and Uses of ICTs.   Despite their potential influence, ICTs remain relatively understudied within organizational socialization research. Uses of ICTs—particularly the social media tools and practices of Web 2.0—alter the communicative processes and information available for socialization. Along with organizational ICTs, social media technologies are a key driver of globalization. Certainly Waldeck and Myers (2007) and Kramer (2010) have highlighted how organizational technologies—those technologies sponsored, developed, or owned by organizations—enable or undermine organizational socialization processes. Yet, this research—in part because of the recent explosion in social media use—does not address how assumptions, uses, and affordances of newer ICTs (social networking sites, search engines), change when, how, and what people learn about individuals, organizations, and organizational roles; when and how they enter organizations; how they might engage in ongoing socialization; and when and how they disengage.

   With over 1.2 billion users worldwide, social networking sites are the most popular Internet sites (Dougherty, 2010). Yet, how people use technology is as important as how much they are using it. Social networking sites are used for various purposes including broadcasting news, information, or identity claims; making (weak) connections with others; social support; performing, practicing, or playing with identity(ies); shaming or bullying; stalking; cybervetting; promoting personal brands; and reducing uncertainty (boyd, 2007; boyd & Ellison, 2007). These purposes, in combination with the habitual and popular use of social network sites, and increasingly complex search engines, make it easier to gather (potentially) greater amounts of different kinds of information that can inform socialization processes (Berkelaar, 2010). Although Jablin and Miller (1991) outlined a clear and influential typology and model of newcomers' information seeking, little research has examined the individual and contextual efficacy of these strategies given the extractive potential of social media. New ICTs provide greater potential for surveillance and indirect information seeking strategies (Ramirez et al., 2002) either through lurking or cybervetting information about organizations and their members. Whether cybervetted as a potential colleague/employee, roommate, board member, volunteer, or date—the extractive potential of ICTs potentially undermines individuals' *voices* in that they may be further limited in their entry into the organization. However, these ICTs might also provide means for destabilizing organizational power and encouraging personalization, although digital communication competencies are required (Berkelaar, 2010).

Research that examines online socialization suggests that context and goals matter for socialization success. Burke et al. (2010) found that different organizational goals alter the relative effectiveness of newcomer information seeking strategies. After analyzing 12,000 newcomer messages, researchers found that direct, linguistically specific messages, aligned with group norms, predicted successful socialization in expertise and support forums. However, although members of support forums appreciated messages that provided identity claims and group investment information, members of expertise forums ignored responses that included identity claims. Furthermore, contrary to expectations from offline research that encourage face-saving through indirect questioning, linguistically specific, direct questions received more responses from incumbents (Burke et al., 2010). How then might the characteristics of media alter appropriate information seeking strategies? In addition to highlighting the importance of contextually appropriate message strategies, this work highlighted the potential importance of visibility for organizational socialization—people who asserted that they had been lurking for a while were viewed as more organizationally invested, received more replies, and therefore were more likely to identify with the organization. Furthermore, the intensity of visible participation mattered more than longevity to organizational outcomes (Burke et al., 2010; Chang, Chang, & Jacobs, 2009). Related work suggests that online socialization through communities of practice aid role comprehension and job satisfaction (Chang et al., 2009), complementing or supplementing offline practices. From an organizational socialization perspective, there still is little insight into how, when, and why people disengage from online organizations.

Online socialization is not necessarily different from offline socialization. Similar to Moreland and Levine's (2001) group socialization model, social learning theorists Lave and Wenger (2002) provide a theoretical framework for communities of practice: Communities progress through a series of stages from potential, through coalescing, peaking at active, before dispersed and memorable stages. When combined with new organizational forms, this model could provide some insight into similarities or differences of distributed socialization, given the lack of nonverbal and other offline cues. The lack of physical boundaries online often encourages clear delineation of membership conditions (Lave & Wegner, 2002). Unfortunately, although Lave and Wenger allow for voluntary and involuntary organizational movements, they presume "full participation" as the ideal with limited options for personalization by leaders, who instead must digitally embody the community ideals. Since the visibility of one's communication and informs determinations of expertise (Treem, 2012) and presumably helps define whether or not one is a newcomer or incumbent, communicative understandings of how people move through different roles could provide further insight into online and offline organizing. Strategic visibility might allow for (perceived) assimilation even as it leaves room for hidden personalization (see Treem, 2012, on strategies for hiding unwanted expertise).

Finally, ICTs provide new data collection and analysis opportunities. Computational social science leverages increasingly available data and data mining techniques and algorithms to help researchers analyze large amounts of data from various technological and information artifacts (Lazer et al., 2009). Location-aware technologies built into most mobile devices can give scholars access to who talks to whom, when, and where; increasing understanding of communication networks and *in situ* communications informing organizational socialization. Although privacy concerns must be addressed, many participants willingly share this information given third-party researchers and anonymization (personal conversation, D. Lazer, 2010). Certainly computational analysis cannot address every research problem, yet it offers rich data into social capital, communication networks, and other ongoing communication processes of contemporary organizational socialization.

Time. Responding to technological affordances and globalization, researchers are beginning to consider different conceptualizations of time (Ballard & Gossett, 2007). Moving beyond clock or calendar time could help researchers better predict linkages between tactics and outcomes and solve a common problem in socialization research: Who counts as a newcomer? Historically, newcomer status was established by absolute time—namely, how many months that a person has been with an organization. However, recent research suggests relative time—in terms of organizational growth cycles—is more important to differentiating newcomer/incumbent status (Rollag, 2004, 2007). If relative time is more predictive of tactic effectiveness than absolute time, there are implications for understanding organizational socialization processes and outcomes. Re-conceptualizing scholarship around emerging understandings of time as relative, personal, cultural, cyclical, linear, shifting, or fixed could have striking implications for evaluating organizational socialization models, tactics, and outcomes.

Time considerations should also consider relative (a)synchronicity or time distribution during organizational socialization. The relative timing of synchronous communication can influence remote workers organizational identification, a primary concern in debates about the value of telecommuting (Connaughton & Shuffler, 2007). Time might also help expand insights into distance education, distributed families (military deployments), NGOs, and other distributed organizations/organizing, particularly as time intersects with geographic space (e.g., Are children born into generational refugee camps newcomers, incumbents, or something in between? What about if they are able to return to their "homeland"?).

Protest and Political (In)stabilities. New ICTs also contribute to political instabilities and protests. From 2007 to 2010 political instability increased in almost all of the 165 countries measured (Viewswire, 2011). Mobile ICTs helped protesters to organize the Arab Spring (Anderson, 2011) and Occupy Movements (Kennedy, 2011). The relative success of different local movements emphasizes the need to examine how different people move in and through these mediated movements and how particular socialization strategies might affect organizational resilience given structural opposition. Organizational socialization processes may help explain and enable the voluntary formation and socialization of networked resistance groups or social movements. Furthermore, attending to political instabilities foregrounds anonymity, identity, and the consideration of risk in socialization. Miller and Jablin's (2001) information-seeking model does address risk, although at a lesser scale: The risk of selecting inappropriate employment strategies pales in comparison to the risk of violent opposition faced by some social protesters.

Consideration of political (in)stabilities also highlights involuntary exits and entries of displaced persons. Socialization into refugee camps is complicated by trauma and loss from previous exits, cross-cultural and language challenges, and an ongoing sense that the situation is temporary. Besides practical values of understanding how to effectively assimilate refugees into the camps, refugee camps and other (relatively) involuntary organizations (e.g., prisons, K-12 schools) could benefit from recognizing the importance and need for personalization as well as human dignity and agency (Lucas, 2011), alongside the likely entrepreneurial, educational, and resilience outcomes that come from the necessity of crafting roles and normalcy (Buzzanell, 2010).

Meso-Level Factors

Meso-level considerations also inform organizational socialization. New global conditions and ICTs, enable and encourage different organizational forms (Fiol & Romanelli, 2011), which may result in or require different organizational socialization mechanisms. For example, new ICTs such as smart phones and social network sites allow for rapid, short-term organizing/organizations (e.g., flash mobs; Meet-up.com™). Testing organizational socialization models against shorter-term processes may challenge the established assumption that organizational socialization should aim for long-term growth and retention. Instead, new forms of organization/organizing should encourage consideration of evolutionary life-cycle approaches in communication scholarship. As organizations attempt to be increasingly nimble in the global economy, shorter—even ephemeral —organizing may offer insight into effective organizational socialization in dynamic or unstable environments—for organizations and contingent members.

The growth of multinational corporations and multi-organization partnerships complicate organizational socialization further. First, these oftentimes-networked partnerships highlight the need for transitional, internal, and ongoing socialization. Even if people do not ascend the corporate ladder, they may move over and across, under and through inter-connected groups within or across organizations, countries, time zones, and newcomer/incumbent boundaries. Career adaptability literature suggests that organizationally resilient people are proactive, engaging in effective information seeking, self-assessment, and communication skills (Fugate, Kinicki, & Ashforth, 2004), factors important to successful anticipatory socialization, assimilation, personalization, and disengagement (Kramer, 2010). New ICTs provide one means to develop career resilience as people form or join online communities in order to learn, receive support, and to connect with others outside paid employment or formal education contexts (Lave & Wegner, 2002).

At a meso-level, given the mobility of the global workforce, it is important to consider the multiple, ongoing, and changing inter- and intra-organizational socialization processes people experience at given times and across their lives. Here, research developed in one organizational context could provide beneficial insights to other contexts. For example, scholars examining career choice recognize the benefits of interventions during anticipatory socialization (Kisselburgh et al., 2009). By extending outside of occupational contexts, models such as Myers and colleagues' (2011) work on anticipatory socialization could also provide strategies to disrupt problematic role trajectories, including entry into and participation with destructive organizations.

Current scholarship also backgrounds organizational socialization into more structured contexts (e.g., planned economies, public education systems, prisons), situations outside of one's control (e.g., refugee camps, prisons), or where organizational entry/exit is a secondary effect of other choices (e.g., marriage leading to religious affiliation; job transfer leading to a new school). Predictions from Scott and Myers' (2005) structuration approach and Frankl's (1946) meaning-oriented therapy suggest that agency and sensemaking remain possible even under extreme organizational constraints (e.g., Frankl's experience in concentration camps)—although these processes might manifest differently. Much in the same way that children find ways to personalize school uniforms, understanding how individuals resist assimilation and personalize involuntary or more structured environments could provide insight into practically and theoretically desirable issues such as educational advocacy, innovation, resilience, leadership, and entrepreneurship.

An organization-level perspective also highlights grand challenges such as the global skills shortage (Kisselburgh et al., 2009). Although there is a growing body of work on entry into science, engineering, technology, and math (Berkelaar et al., 2012; Myers et al., 2011), organizational socialization researchers pay insufficient attention to educational institutions despite their importance to value formation, societal structure, organizational outcomes, and individual quality of life (Ciulla, 2001; Jablin, 2001). Greater consideration of the communicative skills, messages, frameworks, and strategies that help students socialize within and across schools or classrooms (moving between grades, transferring colleges, starting/ending new project groups or courses) could increase planned (graduation) rather than unplanned (dropping-out) exits. Furthermore, organizational socialization research could provide means of lowering the relatively (and sometimes substantially) higher incomplete rates of increasingly popular online courses—while also contributing insights into role (vocational) anticipatory socialization.

Micro-Level Factors

Changing Notions of Work and Career.   Micro-level factors must also be considered. Although influenced by macro-level changes, changing notions of work and career are salient to individuals. First, these changes highlight anticipatory socialization as a lifespan, rather than a childhood concern. Scholars increasingly recognize career processes as occurring across the lifespan, not just during adulthood (Berkelaar et al., 2012; Inkson, 2006); so, too, should organizational socialization researchers. Unfortunately, the discursive and material socialization disparities and opportunities that can result by virtue of birth alone suggest the need to better consider socio-economic, national culture, cultural, and other demographic factors in organizational socialization research and to identify unexpected agency and skills in underappreciated populations. Furthermore, increasing demands and the likelihood of occupational changes—even for those in (formerly) planned economies—suggest the need to examine how anticipatory socialization occurs during periods of (in)voluntary career reinvention (e.g., switching occupations, employers, or primary meanings of work) as well as during times of political or religious reinvention (e.g., switching political party or religious affiliation).

Individual responsibility is central to new careers (Inkson, 2006). Personal branding—a popular career development strategy (Lair et al., 2005)—provides insight into anticipatory socialization, particularly in light of cybervetting. Although branding is sold as the ultimate occupational personalization, critics argue that branding requires affiliation with a dominant White, heterosexual, middle-class male ideal (Lair et al., 2005). Scholars from rhetoric, persuasion, and marketing can offer insight into the goals, strategies, and likely outcomes of the assimilation aspects of personal branding in occupational and other contexts (e.g., "Rush" week for Greek organizations; board affiliations), even as they highlight agency-structure tensions. Relatedly, interpersonal competencies needed for personalization can be identified, described, and evaluated to help give voice to individuals without undermining opportunities afforded by collectives. In addition to understanding demographic and cultural factors, better information on how proactivity, career agency, employability, and other factors are informed by (digital) communicative competencies will provide insight into socialization outcomes.

Recent workforce changes also highlight the need to understand socialization during occupational change. Particularly in blue-collar sectors like manufacturing and mining, much attention is focused on re-skilling and re-tooling unemployed workers (Lucas, 2011). Unfortunately, less attention is given to how workers socialize into the values and norms of these new industries, roles, organizations, and occupations. Yet, emerging scholarship suggests that memorable messages from family members constructed during childhood create ambiguity, ambivalence, or identity conflict for workers who were socialized into blue-collar careers but are moving into white-collar positions (Lucas, 2011). An examination of socialization processes—alongside skills training—could provide insight into strategies for successful outcomes during necessary but unwanted individual, organizational, and community transitions.

Changing Family Structures.   Changing family structures are another micro-level consideration. The socialization of orphans, foster children, blended families, and distributed families (Smith & Guarnizo, 2009; Walsh, 2011) can inform and be informed by understandings of organizational socialization. If the family can be seen as an organization or group, de-construction and re-invention of families as a result of cultural, social, environmental, and political changes may illuminate how people interpersonally manage transitions. For example, foster children, particularly those who move between numerous homes, can provide insight into assimilation and personalization strategies that increase or decrease security, safety, and development and overall resilience (Hines, Merdinger, & Wyatt, 2005; see also, Buzzanell, 2010). The blending of two families might provide insight into the more complex situation of organizational mergers. Minimally, the family might provide a metaphor through which to view processes of anticipatory socialization. It might also complicate the ways in which anticipatory or role socialization occurs as gender role and other norms are increasingly questioned in light of alternate values accessible as a result of globalization and ICTs.

Future Research: Rearticulating and Broadening Organizational Socialization Scholarship

So, what next? By expanding the organizational and communicative contexts considered outside of paid-work, Western, offline contexts, organizational socialization research becomes increasingly relevant for individuals' myriad organizational experiences. Throughout this chapter, I highlighted research opportunities suggested by recent cultural, economic, and technological changes, limitations of existing literature, and broader understandings of organizations and organizing. In this final section, I suggest some broad themes for future research.

Expand Conceptualizations of Organizations Beyond Paid Employment. Certainly if asked, most people believe organizations serve purposes beyond employment, yet for various reasons, researchers often privilege work-oriented forms of organization and organizing—particularly for-profit organizations. A first step in expanding organizational socialization involves theorizing and studying non-employment organizational contexts and organizing, as compared to employment-oriented processes and outcomes. To question and test assumptions born from organizational socialization's long-term orientation toward paid work and ways of working, researchers should consider what organizational socialization perspectives might contribute to their subdiscipline and what their subdiscipline might offer organizational socialization theory and practice. Researchers should examine shorter, even ephemeral life-cycles; question and investigate assumptions of time, agency, identity, and boundaries; anticipate and examine unexpected uses of new ICTs; and consider the challenges of personalization and assimilation at critical stages, in different contexts, across cultures and the lifespan. Theoretically, recognition of simultaneous and competing organizational memberships that intersect across life spheres, relationships, and over time and space will help refine and test existing models and encourage new ones. Central to this broadening is an appreciation of underrepresented voices and contexts. Practically, researchers and practitioners would learn how different and multiple organizational orientations and motivations influence strategies, tactics, and the relative effectiveness of socialization outcomes for individuals, organizations, and society.

This is not a call to avoid work-related organizational socialization. Paid work matters to quality of life (Ciulla, 2001). Additionally, research on unpaid work, while nascent, offers promising insights into differences of volunteer socialization (Kramer, 2011a, 2011b). This line of research would benefit from comparisons with, and extension to, other unpaid work experiences (internships and apprenticeships) where power differences and reward structures differ from paid employment.

Specifically, I encourage scholars to build on, extend, and test existing research in organizational contexts such as schools, refugee camps, informal economies, foster families, flash mobs/flash robs, social protests, religious institutions, and terrorist/activist organizations. Schools provide opportunities to address central global challenges: educational access and achievement and workforce preparedness. Refugee camps and informal economies draw attention to underserved and oftentimes voiceless populations. Foster families highlight resilience processes, interpersonal transitions and interactions, and alternative forms of family as organization. Flash mobs and flash robs highlight anonymity as a source of voice or destruction, focus on social media capabilities for organizational mobilization, and suggest the need to consider alternative organizational (and socialization) timelines. Finally, although all organizing is ideological, religious institutions as well as terrorist and activist organizations/organizing, offer especially salient contexts within which to explore when, how, and why organizational assimilation becomes destructive or constructive.

Emphasize Uniquely Communicative Contributions. Despite wide-ranging perspectives, numerous theories, and various methods, the field of communication consistently argues that messages are central to human experience. To this end, I urge movement towards message-centered and communicatively oriented understandings of organizational socialization, building on examples set in recent empirical (Hart & Miller, 2005) and theoretical work (Scott & Myers, 2010). How do messages—whether direct, indirect, or ambient; intentional or unintentional; absent or present—influence organizational socialization processes and outcomes? This is itself not a new call, but rather one emphasized by current world state(s). As part of this process, computational power and the science of machine learning provide opportunities to gather and analyze large datasets to help uncover systemic processes and patterns over time.

Leverage New Methods. Certainly research questions should drive method selection, yet new methods may suggest previously unconsidered questions or may allow consideration of those questions that were previously too difficult to answer. The growth in computational social science alongside available and retrievable data provide new means for understanding organizational socialization in ways that help fulfill calls for research designs to address the complexity and the multi-level interactions of socialization (Waldeck & Myers, 2007). Location-aware technologies, when combined with computational science (Lazer et al., 2009) and complemented with ethnomethodology and/ or narrative research, provide big-picture perspective alongside nuanced detail into individuals' movements into and out of different roles, levels, and aspects of organizations. Imagine what we can learn by tracking and analyzing detailed daily socialization practices. Unquestionably, privacy concerns must be addressed. However, conversations with researchers starting large-scale studies using location-aware technologies (i.e., cell phones) reveal that participants are often willing to share data if the researcher is a third-party and is committed to data anonymization (personal conversation, D. Lazer, 2010). Complementary partnerships between local and global methodological foci— those that examine systems and those that are more granular—can provide rich detail, within overarching contexts, that help explain organizational socialization processes, outcomes, and recommendations.

Seeking Partnerships to Address Global Challenges. An expansive view of organizational socialization can address numerous social challenges such as educational access and attainment, repatriation and integration, workforce preparedness, integration into alternate occupations, and resistance against problematically (as opposed to creatively) destructive organizations. To address these complex challenges, intra- and inter-disciplinary partnerships are necessary. Furthermore, to be successful, we will need to publish within and outside of communication journals (which may require reframing and restructuring scholarly reward systems). As highlighted throughout this chapter, computer-mediated, family, intercultural, interpersonal, organizational, rhetoric, and other perspectives can help refine and test existing models and assumptions to address these global challenges.

Conclusion

This review illustrates how globalization, new ICTs, political instabilities, changing economic conditions, and their associated implications for orga-nizations and careers highlight important absences and opportunities in the scholarship and practices of organizational socialization. It provides opportunities to reconsider organizational socialization across the lifespan, as it occurs simultaneously, sequentially and recursively, within and across multiple organizing contexts and types, in ways that recognize diverse voices, the potential for destructive or constructive outcomes, and the complex individual/ organizational socialization processes evidenced and realized through communication. By expanding what is studied as an organization and organizing and addressing recent technological, social, and economic changes, the goal of this chapter was to re-focus and expand organizational socialization scholarship, setting an agenda for communication research that could increase the visibility and influence of communication in this globally relevant interdisciplinary arena.

Notes

1. "Terrorist" remains a contentious term. Given space constraints, I refer readers to scholarship on rhetorical constructions of terrorism (e.g., Stohl, 2008).
2. Capitalization intentional.
3. A flash rob is crowd-sourced theft. Mobilized by social media, a group descends upon targeted retail establishments, simultaneously harassing, distracting, and stealing. Approximately 10% of U.S. retail establishments report experiencing flash robs (Wasik, 2011).
4. Web of Science returned 891 results on June 16, 2012. Topic = organizational socialization. Timespan = All Years. Databases = SCI-EXPANDED, SSCI, A&HCI, CPCI-S, CPCI-SSH.
5. In this section I briefly summarized key concepts and stages. I refer readers to recent literature reviews (Jablin, 2001; Waldeck & Myers, 2007) and Kramer (2010) for additional details.
6. The phrase, "resistance is futile," has settled into the collective consciousness as an ironic mantra resisting the collective, aligned with the "resistance is useless" slogan of the Vogons, a persistently and mindlessly bureaucratic slug-like race in Douglas Adams' classic, *The Hitchhiker's Guide to the Galaxy* (Nardi & O'Day, 2000, p. 46)
7. Personalization is also labeled individualization. Given the common confusion between individualization and individuation, I use the term "personalization," introduced by Hess in 1993 and advocated by Kramer (2010).
8. Search engine optimization strategies increase visibility and ranking in search results. Generally, the earlier content appears in search results, the more likely it will be read, considered, and cited (Tucci, 2010).

References

Alexa. (2012). *The top 500 sites on the web.* Retrieved from http://www.alexa.com/topsites

Anderson, L. (2011). Demystifying the Arab Spring. *Foreign Affairs, 90*(3), 2–7.

Ashford, S. J., George, E., & Blatt, R. (2007). Old assumptions, new work. *The Academy of Management Annals, 1,* 65–117. doi:0.1080/078559807

Ashforth, B. E., Sluss, D. M., & Harrison, S. H. (2007). Socialization in organizational contexts. In G. P. Hodgkinson & J. K. Ford (Eds.), *International review of industrial and organizational psychology 2007* (Vol. 22, pp. 1–70). London, England: Wiley & Sons.

Astrachan, J. H., & Shanker, M. C. (2004). Family businesses' contribution to the U.S. economy: A closer look. *Family Business Review, 16,* 211–219. doi:10.1111/j.1741-6248.2003.tb00015.x

Ballard, D. I., & Gossett, L. M. (2007). Alternative times: Temporal perceptions, processes, and practices defining the nonstandard work relationship. In C. S. Beck (Ed.), *Communication yearbook 31* (pp. 274–321). New York, NY: Erlbaum.

Barge, J. K., & Schlueter, D. W. (2004). Memorable messages and newcomer socialization. *Western Journal of Communication, 68,* 233–256. doi:10.1080/10570310409374800

Bauer, T. N., & Taylor, M. S. (2001). A globalized conceptualization of organizational socialization. In N. Anderson, D. S. Ones, H. K. Sinangil, & C. Viswesvaran (Eds.), *International handbook of industrial, work, and organizational psychology* (Vol. 1, pp. 409–423). New York, NY: Sage.

Bauer, T. N., Bodner, T., Erdogan, B., Truxillo, D. M., & Tucker, J. S. (2007). Newcomer adjustment during organizational socialization: A meta-analytic review of antecedents, outcomes, and methods. *Journal of Applied Psychology, 92,* 707–721. doi:10.1037/0021-9010.92.3.707

Becker, K. F. (2004). *The informal economy.* Retrieved from the World Bank website: http://rru.worldbank.org/Documents/PapersLinks/Sida.pdf

Berkelaar, B. L. (2010). *Cyber-vetting: Exploring the implications of online information for career capital and human capital decisions* (doctoral dissertation). Purdue University, West Lafayette, IN.

Berkelaar, B. L., Buzzanell, P. M., Kisselburgh, L. G., Tan, W., & Shen, Y. (2012). "First, it's dirty. Second, it's dangerous. Third, it's insulting": Chinese children talk about dirty work. *Communication Monographs, 79,* 93–114. doi:10.1080/0363775 1.2011.646490

Bjuggren, C. M., Johanssen, D., & Sjögren, H. (2011). A note on employment and gross domestic product in Swedish family-owned businesses: A descriptive analysis. *Family Business Review, 24,* 362–371, doi:0.1177/0894486511420138

boyd, d. (2007). Why youth ♥ social network sites: The role of networked publics in teenage social life. In D. Buckingham (Ed.), *Youth, identity, and digital media* (pp. 119–142). Boston, MA: MIT Press.

boyd, d. m., & Ellison, N. B. (2007). Social network sites: Definitions, history, and scholarship. *Journal of Computer Mediated Communication, 13.* Article 11. Retrieved from: http://jcmc.indiana.edu/vol13/issue1/boyd.ellison.html

Bullis, C., & Stout, K. R. (2000). Organizational socialization: A feminist standpoint approach. In P. M. Buzzanell (Ed.), *Rethinking organizational and managerial communication from feminist perspectives* (pp. 47–75). Thousand Oaks, CA: Sage.

Burke, M., Kraut, R., & Joyce, E. (2010). Membership claims and requests: Conversation-level newcomer socialization strategies in online groups. *Small Group Research, 41,* 4–40. doi:10.1177/1046496409351936

Buzzanell, P. M. (2010). Resilience: Talking, resisting, and imagining new normalcies into being. *Journal of Communication, 60,* 1–14. doi:10.1111/j.1460-2466.2009.01469.x

Buzzanell, P. M., Berkelaar, B. L., & Kisselburgh, L. K. (2011). From the mouths of babes: Exploring families' career socialization of young children in China, Lebanon, Belgium, and the United States, *Journal of Family Communication, 11*, 148–164. doi:10.1080/15267431.2011.554494

Buzzanell, P. M., & Goldzwig, S. R. (1991). Linear and nonlinear career models: Metaphors, paradigms, and ideologies. *Management Communication Quarterly, 4*, 466–505. doi:10.1177/0893318991004004004

Carraher, S. M. Sullivan, S. E., & Crocitto, M. M. (2008). Mentoring across global boundaries: An empirical examination of home- and host-country mentors on expatriate career outcomes. *Journal of International Business Studies, 39*, 1310–1326, doi:10.1057/palgrave.jibs.8400407

Carver, C. (2010). *Anticipatory organizational socialization: Graduating college students' messages, information-seeking, career conceptualizations, and expectations* (doctoral dissertation). University of Kansas, Lawrence.

Chang, J., Chang, W., & Jacobs, R. (2009). Relationship between partcipation in communicaties of practice and organizational socialization in the early careers of South Korean IT employees. *Human Resource Development International, 12*, 407–427. doi:10.1080/13678860903135805

Cheney, G., & Cloud, D. (2006). Doing democracy, engaging the material: Employee participation and labor activity in an age of market globalization. *Management Communication Quarterly, 19*, 501–540. doi:10.1177/0893318905285485

Cheney, G., Zorn, T. E., Planalp, S., & Lair, D. J. (2008). Meaningful work and personal/social well-being: Organizational communication engages the meanings of work. In C. S. Beck (Ed.), *Communication yearbook 32* (pp. 137–186). New York, NY: Taylor & Francis.

Ciulla, J. B. (2001). *The working life: The promise and betrayal of modern work*. New York, NY: Random House.

Connaughton, S. L., & Shuffler, M. (2007). Multinational and multicultural distributed teams. *Small Group Research, 38*, 387–412. doi:10.1177/1046496407301970

Craig, R. T. (2005). How we talk about talk: Communciation theory in the public interest. *Journal of Communication, 66*, 659–667. doi:10.1111/j.1460-2466.2005.tb03015.x

Davis, C. W., & Myers, K. K. (2012). Communication and member disengagement in planned organizational exit. *Western Journal of Communication, 76*, 194–216. doi:10.1080/10570314.2011.651250

Ding, D. Z., Goodall, K., & Warner, M. (2000). The end of the 'iron rice-bowl': Whither Chinese human resource management? *International Journal of Human Resource Management, 11*, 217–236. doi:10.1080/095851900339837

Dougherty, H. (2010, March 15). *Facebook reaches top ranking in the U.S.* [Web log post]. Retrieved from http://www.experian.com/blogs/hitwise/2010/03/15/facebook-reaches-top-ranking-in-us/ http://weblogs.hitwise.com/heatherdougherty/2010/03/facebook_reaches_top_ranking_i.html.

Fiol, C. M. & Romanelli, E. (2011). Before identity: The emergence of new organizational forms. *Organization Science*. Advance online publication. doi:10.1287/orsc.1110.0666

Flaherty, J. E. (2008). The effects of cultural intelligence on team member acceptance and integration of multinational teams. In S. A. & L. Van Dyne (Eds.), *Handbook of cultural intelligence: Theory, measurement, and applications* (pp. 192–205). New York, NY: ME Sharpe.

Flanagin, A. J., & Waldeck, J. H. (2004). Technology use and organizational newcomer socialization. *Journal of Business Communication, 41,* 137–165. doi:10.1177/0021943604263290

Frankl, V. E. (1946). *Man's search for meaning.* Kansas City, KS: Beacon Hill Press.

Fugate, M., Kinicki, A. J., & Ashforth, B. E. (2004). Employability: A psycho-social construct, its dimensions, and applications. *Journal of Vocational Behavior, 65,* 14–38. doi:10.1016/j.jvb.2003.10.005

George, E., & Chattopadhyay, P. (2005). One foot in each camp: The dual identification of contract workers. *Administrative Science Quarterly, 50,* 68–99. doi:10.2189/asqu.2005.50.1.68

Gomez, L. F. (2009). Time to socialize organizational socialization structures and temporality. *Journal of Business Communication, 46,* 179–207. doi:10.1177/0021943608328077

Griffeth, R. W., Allen, D. G., & Barrett, R. (2006). Integration of family-owned business succession with turnover and life cycle models: Development of a successor retention process model. *Human Resource Management Review, 16,* 490–507, doi:10.1016/j.hrmr.2006.08.006

Hart, Z. P., & Miller, V. D. (2005). Context and message content during organizational socialization. *Human Communication Research, 31,* 295–309. doi:10.1111/j.1468-2958.2005.tb00873.x

Haski-Leventhal, D., & Bargal, D. (2008). The volunteer stages and transitions model: Organizational socialization of volunteers. *Human Relations, 61,* 67–102. doi:10.1177/0018726707085946

Hausknecht, J. P., & Trevor, C. O. (2011). Collective turnover at the group, unit, and organizational levels: Evidence, issues, and implications. *Journal of Management, 37,* 352–388. doi:10.1177/0149206310383910

Hess, J. A. (1993). Assimilating newcomers into an organization: A cultural perspective. *Journal of Applied Communication Research, 21,* 189–210. doi:0.1080/00909889309365366

Hines, A. M., Merdinger, J., & Wyatt, P. (2005). Former foster youth attending college: Resilience and the transition to young adulthood. *American Journal of Orthopsychiatry, 75,* 381–394. doi:10.1037/0002-9432.75.3.381

Hom, P. W. (2010). Organizational exit. In S. Zedeck (Ed.), *APA handbook of industrial and organizational psychology: Selecting and developing members for the organization* (Vol. 2, pp. 325–375). Washington, DC: American Psychological Association.

Housel, T. H., & Harvey, V. L. (2010). *The invisibility factor: Administrators and faculty reach out to first-generation college students.* Boca Raton, FL: BrownWalker Press.

Inkson, K. (2006). *Understanding careers: The metaphors of working lives.* Thousand Oaks, CA: Sage.

Jablin, F. M. (2001). Organizational entry, assimilation, and disengagement/exit. In F. M. Jablin & L. L. Putnam (Eds.), *The new handbook of organizational communication: Advances in theories, research, and methods* (pp. 732–818). Thousand Oaks, CA: Sage.

Jones, C., & Volpe, E. H. (2011). Organizational identification: Extending our understanding of social identities through social networks. *Journal of Organizational Behavior, 32,* 413–434. doi:10.1002/job.694

Katz, D., & Kahn, R. L. (1978). *The social psychology of organizing.* New York, NY: Wiley.

Kennedy, M. D. (2011, December 5). Global solidarity and the Occupy movement. *Possible Futures*. Retrieved from http://www.possible-futures.org/2011/12/05/global-solidarity-occupy-movement/

Kisselburgh, L., Berkelaar, B. L., & Buzzanell, P. M. (2009). Discourse, gender, and the meanings of work: Rearticulating science, technology, and engineering careers through communicative lenses. In C. S. Beck (Ed.), *Communication yearbook 33* (pp. 258–299). New York, NY: Routledge.

Koren, M. J. (2010). Person-centered care for nursing home residents: The culture-change movement. *Health Affairs, 29*, 312–317. doi:10.1377/hlthaff.2009.0966

Kramer, M. W. (1989). Communication during intraorganization job transfers. *Management Communication Quarterly, 3*, 219–248. doi: 10.1177/0893318989003002004

Kramer, M. W. (1993). Communication and uncertainty reduction during job transfers: Leaving and joining processes. *Communication Monographs, 60*, 178–198. doi: 10.1080/03637759309376307

Kramer, M. W. (2009). Role negotiations in a temporary organization: Making sense during role development in an educational theater production. *Management Communication Quarterly, 23*, 188–217. doi:10.1177/0893318909341410

Kramer, M. W. (2010). *Organizational socialization: Joining and leaving organizations*. Cambridge, England: Polity Press.

Kramer, M. W. (2011a). A study of voluntary organizational membership: The assimilation process in a community choir. *Western Journal of Communication, 75*, 52–74. doi:10.1080/10570314.2010.536962

Kramer, M. W. (2011b). Toward a communication model for the socialization of voluntary members. *Communication Monographs, 78*, 233–255. doi:10.1080/0363775 1.2011.564640

Kramer, M. W., & Noland, T. L. (1999). Communication during job promotions: A case of ongoing assimilation. *Journal of Applied Communication Research, 27*, 335–355. doi: 10.1080/00909889909365544

Kristof-Brown, A. L., Zimmerman, R. D., & Johnson, E. C. (2005). Consequences of individuals' fit at work: A meta-analysis of person-job, person-organization, person-group, and person-supervisor fit. *Personnel Psychology, 58*, 281–342. doi:10.1111/j.1744-6570.2005.00672.x

Lair, D. J., Sullivan, K., & Cheney, G. (2005). Marketization and the recasting of the professional self. *Management Communication Quarterly, 18*, 307–343. doi:10.1177/0893318904270744

Lave, J., & Wenger, E. (2002). Legitimate peripheral participation in communities of practice. In R. Harrison (Ed.), *Supporting lifelong learning* (Vol. 1, pp. 111–126). New York, NY: Routledge.

Lazer, D., Pentland, A. S., Adamic, L., Aral, S., Barabasi, A. L., Brewer, D., ... Gutmann, M. (2009). Life in the network: the coming age of computational social science. *Science, 323*, 721–723. doi:10.1126/science.1167742

Lucas, K. (2011). The working class promise: A communicative account of mobility-based ambivalences. *Communication Monographs, 78*, 347–369. doi:10.1080/0363 7751.2011.589461

Miller, V. D., & Jablin, F. M. (1991). Information seeking during organization entry: Influences, tactics, and a model of the process. *Academy of Management Review, 16*, 92–120. doi:10.2307/258608

Moreland, R. L., & Levine, J. M. (2001). Socialization in organizations and work groups. In M. E. Turner (Ed.), *Groups at work: Theory and research* (pp. 69–112). Mahwan, NJ: Erlbaum.

Munz, E. A. (2011). *Communication as preparation: An exploration of associations between caregiver confirmation, attachment security, and child elaboration during the transition to kindergarten* (doctoral dissertation). Purdue University, West Lafayette, IN.

Myers, K. K., Jahn, J. L. S., Gailliard, B. M., & Stoltzfus, K. (2011). Vocational anticipatory socialization (VAS): A communicative model of adolescents' interests in STEM. *Management Communication Quarterly, 25,* 87. doi:10.1177/0893318910377068

Nardi, B. A., & O'Day, V. (2000). *Information ecologies: Using technology with heart.* Boston, MA: MIT Press.

Neelen, M., & Fetter, S. (2010). Lurking: A challenge or a fruitful strategy? A comparison between lurkers and active participants in an online corporate community of practice. *International Journal of Knowledge and Learning, 6,* 269–284. doi:10.1504/IJKL.2010.038649

Nussbaum, J. F. (2007). Life span communication and quality of life. *Journal of Communication, 57,* 1–7. doi:10.1111/j.1460-2466.2006.00325.x

Perkins, K. B., & Metz, C. W. (1988). Note on commitment and community among volunteer firefighters. *Sociological Inquiry, 58,* 117–121. doi:0.1111/j.1475-682X.1988.tb00258.x

Ramirez, A., Jr., Walther, J. B., Burgoon, J. K., & Sunnafrank, M. (2002). Information—seeking strategies, uncertainty, and computer—mediated communication. *Human Communication Research, 28,* 213–228. doi:10.1111/j.1468-2958.2002.tb00804.x

Robbins, S. B., Oh, I. S., Le, H., & Button, C. (2009). Intervention effects on college performance and retention as mediated by motivational, emotional, and social control factors: Integrated meta-analytic path analyses. *Journal of Applied Psychology, 94,* 1163–1184. doi:10.1037/a0015738

Rollag, K. (2004). The impact of relative tenure on newcomer socialization dynamics. *Journal of Organizational Behavior, 25,* 853–872. doi:10.1002/job.280

Rollag, K. (2007). Defining the term new in new employee research. *Journal of Occupational and Organizational Psychology, 80,* 63–75. doi:10.1348/096317906X120420

Saks, A. M., & Gruman, J. A. (2010). Organizational socialization and newcomer engagement. In S. L. Albrecht (Ed.), *Handbook of employee engagement: Perspectives, issues, research and practice* (pp. 297–308). Northhampton, MA: Edward Elgar.

Schott, B. (2007). Schott's almanac 2008: Technology lexicon, *TimesOnline.* London, England: Times Newspapers.

Schulze, W. S., & Gedajlovic, E. R. (2010). Whither family business? *Journal of Management Studies, 47,* 191–204. doi:10.1111/j.1467-6486.2009.00887.x

Scott, C., & Myers, K. (2005). The socialization of emotion: Learning emotion management at the fire station. *Journal of Applied Communication Research, 33,* 67–92. doi: 10.1080/0090988042000318521

Scott, C., & Myers, K. (2010). Toward an integrative theoretical perspective on organizational membership negotiations: Socialization, assimilation, and the duality of structure. *Communication Theory, 20,* 79–105. doi: 0.1111/j.1468-2885.2009.01355.x

Smith, M. P., & Guarnizo, L. E. (2009). Global mobility, shifting borders and urban citizenship. *Tijdschrift voor economische en sociale geografie, 100,* 610–622. doi: 0.1111/j.1467-9663.2009.00567.x

Snyder, K. A. (2004). Routes to the informal economy in New York's East Village: Crisis, economics, and identity. *Sociological Perspectives, 47*, 215–240, doi:10.1525/sop.2004.47.2.215

Stohl, C. (2005). Globalization theory. In S. May & D. Mumby (Eds.), *Engaging organizational communication theory and research: Multiple perspectives* (pp. 223–262). Thousand Oaks, CA: Sage.

Stohl, M. (2008). The global war on terror and state terrorism. *Perspectives on Terrorism, 2*(9). Retrieved from http://terrorismanalysts.com/pt/index.php/pot/article/view/48/html

Tams, S., & Arthur, M. B. (2010). New directions for boundaryless careers: Agency and interdependence in a changing world. *Journal of Organizational Behavior, 31*, 629–646. doi:10.1002/job.712

Tan, C. L., & Kramer, M. W. (2012). Communication and voluntary downward career changes. *Journal of Applied Communication Research, 40*, 87–106. doi:10.1080/00909882.2011.634429

Treem, J. W. (2012). Communicating expertise: Knowledge performances in professional-service firms. *Communication Monographs, 79*, 23–47. doi:10.1080/03637751.2011.646487

Tucci, V. (2010). Viewpoint: Are a & i services in a death spiral? *Issues in Science and Technology Librarianship, Spring 2010*. Retrieved from http://www.istl.org/10-spring/viewpoint.html

United Nations High Commission on Refugees. (2011). *Global Trends 2011*. Retrieved from http://www.unhcr.org/4fd6f87f7.html

Van Maanen, J. (1975). Breaking in: Socialization to work. In R. Dubin (Ed.), *Handbook of work, organization, and society* (pp. 67–120). Chicago, IL: Rand-McNally.

Viewswire. (2011). *Viewswire: Social unrest*. Retrieved March 1, 2012, from http://viewswire.eiu.com/site_info.asp?info_name=social_unrest_table&page=noads&rf=0

Waldeck, J. H., Seibold, D. R., & Flanagin, A. J. (2004). Organizational assimilation and communication technology use. *Communication Monographs, 71*, 161–183. doi:10.1080/0363775042331302497

Waldeck, J. H., & Myers, K. K. (2007). Organizational assimilation theory, research, and implications for multiple areas of the discipline: A state of the art review. In C. S. Beck (Ed.), *Communication yearbook 31* (pp. 322–367). New York, NY: Routledge.

Walsh, F. (2011). *Normal family processes: Growing diversity and complexity*. New York, NY: Guilford.

Wasik, B. (2011, November). "Flash robs": Trying to stop a meme gone wrong. *Wired*. Retrieved from http://www.wired.com/threatlevel/2011/11/flash-robs/all/1

Webb, J. W., Tihanyi, L., Ireland, R. D., & Sirmon, D. G. (2009). You say illegal, I say legitimate: Entrepreneurship in the informal economy. *The Academy of Management Review ARCHIVE, 34*, 492–510. doi:10.5465/AMR.2009.40632826

Williams, D. (2010). The mapping principle, and a research framework for virtual worlds. *Communication Theory, 20*, 451–470. doi:10.1111/j.1468-2885.2010.01371.x

World Economic Forum & The Boston Consulting Group. (2012). *Global talent risk: Seven responses*. Retrieved from http://www.bcg.com/documents/file69643.pdf

Wrzesniewski, A., & Dutton, J. E. (2001). Crafting a job: Revisioning employees as active crafters of their work. *Academy of Management Review, 8*, 179–201. doi:10.2307/259118

Part II

Rethinking Communication Frameworks, Models, Methods, and Paradigms

CHAPTER CONTENTS

3 A Multitheoretical, Multilevel, Multidimensional Network Model of the Media System

Production, Content, and Audiences

Katherine Ognyanova and Peter Monge

University of Southern California

This chapter examines the network mechanisms which underlie major parts of the media system: the industry, the content, and the audience. It identifies key theoretical frameworks that can be used to explain the formation and dissolution of ties in each of those areas. The chapter presents a relational reinterpretation of classic mass communication theories and advocates the use of a multitheoretical, multilevel, and multidimensional network approach to media studies research. We examine interorganizational ties (industry sector), semantic relations (content sector), and social bonds (audience sector). Key studies and theoretical mechanisms that bridge two or three of those domains are reviewed.

The systematic study of social relationships and structures has a long tradition across disciplines including communication, media studies, sociology, social psychology, and anthropology (Freeman, 2004). Since the 1970s, the volume of published network research in particular has grown exponentially, marking a gradual shift from individualist to relational scientific explanations (Borgatti & Foster, 2003). In the last decade, technological advances have contributed to a boom in academic studies of diverse networks (Watts, 2004). Information and communication technologies have enhanced networked forms of organization, bringing to light previously implicit social relations (Castells, 2005). Technological innovations have also provided scientists with the data collection tools and computational capacity needed to develop resource-intensive network-analytical techniques.

The rapid progress of network theories and methods prompted a wave of studies offering systematic overviews of network processes and their integration in existing theoretical frameworks from a variety of academic fields (Carrington, Scott, & Wasserman, 2005). Scholars have investigated the implications of a relational approach in the areas of organizational communication (Monge & Contractor, 2003), health (Valente, 2010), economics (Schweitzer et al., 2009), management (Borgatti & Foster, 2003), warfare (Arquilla & Ronfeldt, 2001), and Web science (Turow & Tsui, 2008), among others.

Building on that foundation, this chapter examines the mechanisms and frameworks explicating communication flows and relational ties in the context of media studies. Our premises are consistent with theories of mass communication examining media effects in the context of larger social structures (Ball-Rokeach, 1985). The framework explores the dynamic relationships between audience members and news organizations. Those ties of influence are seen as grounded in the capacity of media sources to produce content serving individual information and social goals (Ball-Rokeach, Rokeach, & Grube, 1984). In view of that, we adopt a broad definition of the *media system* that comprises media organizations, the content they produce, and its consumers. We identify the relevant nodes and links underlying those three major components (see Figure 3.1). The media industry sector (or domain[1]), is characterized by links among news organizations. Media content is grounded in ties between key terms, concepts, frames, and news stories. The third part of the media system, audiences, consists of connected news consumers. Although in principle the range of available media is very broad and may encompass film, music, games, and more, for the sake of simplicity and clarity this work focuses specifically on news media.

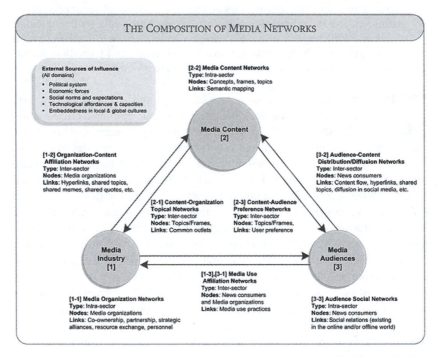

Figure 3.1 The Composition of Media Networks. *Note:* The numbers within brackets represent the three media sectors: (1) industry, (2) content, and (3) audiences. The sequence of numbers in square brackets indicates that a network is composed by nodes in the sector represented by the first number and relations/nodes from the sector represented by the second number. Intra-sector networks are represented by the same numbers: 1-1, 2-2, and 3-3. Inter-sector networks are represented by different numbers, e.g., 1-2, 3-1.

The analysis begins with a discussion of the networks within each specific media domain, called *intra-sector networks*. These networks are comprised of nodes and links belonging to a single sector, such as media organizations linked by ownership patterns (industry sector, see Figure 3.1, [1-1]) or networks of news stories linked through semantic similarities (content sector, see Figure 3.1, [2-2]). Intra-sector structures can also be multiplex. That is to say, they may include more than one type of link within a single domain. One example of this is an industry network with both ownership and partnership ties (Arsenault & Castells, 2008a).

This chapter then explores the interactions that occur between sectors. We review *inter-sector networks*—structures that involve nodes from a focal domain, and additional nodes and/or relations from one or both of the other two domains. For instance, media organizations could be connected through content-based ties, such as the hyperlinks between their websites (see Figure 3.1, [1-2]). Affiliation networks (see Figure 3.1, [1-3] [3-1]), which link individual news consumers (audience nodes) to their preferred news organizations (industry nodes) are also considered *inter-sector*. We further discuss the more complex patterns that emerge from interdependencies between different parts of the media system. Such structures may contain multiple different kinds of nodes (e.g. individuals and news organizations) and multiple kinds of relations (e.g. social and mediated). The former type of network is known as *multimodal* and the latter type is called *multiplex* (or multirelational). Inter-sector networks may also be *multidimensional* (Contractor, Monge, Leonardi, 2011). This term applies to networks that consist of both multiple kinds of nodes (multimodal) and multiple kinds of relations (multiplex).

This approach to the study of media facilitates an important shift in theoretical focus. The emphasis moves from the attributes of organizations, news stories, and consumers to the similarities, social relations, interactions, and flows of information and resources among them (Borgatti, Mehra, Brass, & Labianca, 2009). Research can thus investigate the structural determinants of social, economic and political processes, the network patterns of power and influence (Castells, 2009), as well as the impact of interpersonal ties on individual preferences and public opinion (Wasserman & Faust, 1994). This reframing of how media systems operate does not replace the examination of individual characteristics, such as political attitudes, gender, and socioeconomic status, nor does it dismiss the explanatory power of content attributes, such as news, entertainment, or opinion. Rather, it supplements and contextualizes these features by providing the web of friends, families, coworkers, neighbors, and other sources that supply the information, norms, values and motivations determining how people select and use various media.

As Castells (2009) points out, relational thinking becomes even more important in the context of a media industry moving to networked forms of content production, delivery, and consumption. We are currently seeing industry-wide trends towards consolidation, interorganizational collaborations, local and global partnerships (Arsenault & Castells, 2008b). Online formats and new technologies connect newsrooms and audience members (Cardoso, 2006), making content diffusion faster and easier to track through digital traces (Anderson, 2010). Professional and personal social ties affect individual news consumption and distribution habits (Boczkowski, 2010). News stories themselves are placed within networks of semantic relations (Diesner & Carley, 2005) and hyperlink connections (Turow & Tsui, 2008).

An early criticism of network research claimed that the field is overly descriptive: a combination of algorithms lacking a native theoretical framework (Kilduff & Tsai, 2003). More recently, scholars working in the area have argued that this claim is no longer true, suggesting that a rich network theory is now yielding new explanations in a variety of disciplines (Borgatti et al., 2009). Relational interpretations have been used to redefine key concepts, test existing theories, and develop new understanding about the structural causes and consequences of social phenomena (Marin & Wellman, 2010).

In its approach to theory, the present work draws on the multitheoretical, multilevel (MTML) analytical strategy put forward by Monge and Contractor (2003). Their proposed model incorporates a range of properties, from individual and dyadic, through more complex structural patterns, to network-level measures. Studying changes over time as well as the analysis of separate co-evolving networks are also part of the MTML approach. Monge and Contractor further argue that explaining these complex multilevel mechanisms requires the use of multiple theoretical frameworks, some independent, others competing or complementary.

Accordingly, this chapter identifies a number of theoretical mechanisms explicating the formation, dissolution and consequence of links in the media system. The theories described in the following sections come from media studies, organizational communication, economics, web science, sociology, and linguistics. Some of them (e.g., diffusion theories, communication infrastructure theory) are already framed in network terms. Others, like agenda-setting and framing, need to be adapted to a relational interpretation.

The model we propose here provides a framework organizing existing knowledge at the intersection of media studies and network science. Serving as a map of the field, it is intended to help readers think through the multiple theoretical domains, the various levels of analysis, and diverse types of linkages involved in a relational perspective on the media system. Similarly to the more comprehensive work of Monge and Contractor (2003) in the area of organizations, this study identifies layered explanations of network dynamics in mass communication. It makes explicit the structures that have remained hidden in previous works exploring the increasingly networked news media of today. In that effort, the present study aims to synthesize the core dynamics underlying a number of important works like those of Castells (2009) and McChesney (2004). As the field of mass communication undergoes a paradigm shift, adopting a relational perspective will enable scholars to integrate disparate theories, bridge separate levels, and explore multidimensional linkages, thus filling the gaps in the existing literature.

The value of multilevel network interpretations is also evident in the context of media theories explicitly employing relational explanations. The *two-step flow of communication* (Katz & Lazarsfeld, 1955; Lazarsfeld, Berelson, & Gaudet, 1944) is one classic example, as it brings together media effects and social structures. Another case in point at the macro level of analysis comes from the *media system dependency* theory (Ball-Rokeach, 1985) in its examination of power relations within and across social systems.

Monge and Contractor's (2003) work outlining their MTML approach identifies seven families of social theories that can be applied to communication networks. It explores the implications of using those theories at multiple levels, offering insights that no single framework by itself could provide. Adopting this strategy, we examine the multiplicity of theories across levels of analysis. Important to note, it is not our intention to claim that all of those theoretical frameworks need to be fused together. We do not suggest that a single empirical analysis should incorporate and test the full range of mechanisms presented here. Instead, throughout this article we identify various combinations of theoretical perspectives, analytical tools, and network definitions that could, when applied together, advance our understanding of the media system. The judicious selection and integration of theories at multiple levels and alternative types of linkages should prevent a misuse of the MTML model sometimes referred to as an eclectic approach to theorizing.

The following sections of the chapter provide a systematic overview of relevant network mechanisms and theoretical frameworks. A summary of the proposed theories is available in Table 3.1. Examples providing fruitful directions for future research are presented in the conclusion of this article.

Intra-Sector Networks

The Industry Sector: Interorganizational Networks [1-1]

From a macro-level perspective, the media industry can be seen as an intercon-nected set of corporate actors (see Figure 3.1, [1-1]), linked through economic, social, political, and cultural ties (Arsenault & Castells, 2008a). Networked forms of organization, production, and distribution, which are becoming ubiquitous across industries, are particularly prominent in the media sector (Castells, 2009). The well-studied ongoing processes of media ownership con-centration (McChesney, 2000, 2004) contribute to the complex layer of dense ownership, partnership, and cross-investment relationships between news outlets. Deregulation and digitization have further lead to convergence in the information sector as media, telecommunication, and technological compa-nies merge and expand (Chon, Choi, Barnett, Danowski, & Joo, 2003; Dan-owski & Choi, 1999).

Interorganizational networks have been a subject of inquiry in the fields of sociology and organizational theory (Baum, 2002). In this type of analysis, individual organizations constitute the network nodes, each of which may have

Table 3.1 Theories Explaining the Formation and Structural Properties of Networks within and between the Domains of Media Industry, Content and Audiences

Domains under Study	1. Media Industry	2. Media Content	3. Media Audiences
1. Media Industry	• Evolutionary Theories, Population Ecology, Theory of the Niche • Resource Dependence • Exchange Theories • Equilibrium Theories		
2. Media Content	• Evolutionary Theories, Population Ecology, Theory of the Niche • Intra and inter-media level agenda-setting • Media bias	• Semantic Networks, Cognitive Concept Mapping, Framing theories	
3. Media Audiences	• Media Ecology • Selective exposure • Uses & Gratifications • Media System Dependency • Information Seeking • Transaction cost economics	• Two Step Flow Theory • Contagion/Diffusion • Social Capital • Structural Holes • Collective Action, Public Goods	• Homophily theories • Proximity theories • Electronic Propinquity • Balance theories • CIT & Storytelling Networks

a set of properties based on the research questions posed by the study. A wide range of formal and informal relationships can be used to define the network ties. Baker and Faulkner (2002) list some of the most relevant link types: market exchanges, strategic alliances, joint participation in syndicates, joint political action, interlocking directorates, family ties, and illegal activities such as collusion. All of those are applicable to the media industry which is, in addition, characterized by frequent content/information exchange relationships.

Another set of ties between companies in the media sector can be constructed on the basis of human resources (Gulati, Dialdin, & Wang, 2002). This is especially relevant for media organizations both because the industry is known to have high turnover rates and because journalists, more so than other professionals, tend to work for multiple organizations.

Two frameworks that capture the relationships outlined above are *resource dependency* and *social exchange theory* (Blau, 1964; Emerson, 1962). These theories seek to explain interactions and relationships based on the supply, demand, and exchange of material and information resources (Monge & Contractor, 2003). Initially limited to interactions between two actors, the frameworks have expanded to explore larger structures going beyond the dyadic relationship. Participating in a network allows members to gain access to various resources: financial, institutional, and information-related among others (Gulati et al., 2002). Financial resources are linked to capital acquisition and investments, while institutional resources have to do with gaining legitimacy, credibility, and status. Both money and reputation can be accumulated based on network ties. Knowledge and information resources are particularly important in the media industry, where information dissemination is crucial and the adoption of new technologies and practices needs to happen faster than it does in many other sectors (Pew Project For Excellence in Journalism, 2010).

While network members can benefit from increased financial opportunities, improved survival chances, and enhanced learning capabilities, it is important to note that some patterns of network ties can also be detrimental (Gulati et al., 2002). A disadvantageous network position may make companies vulnerable to exclusion from valuable resources (Monge & Contractor, 2003). Furthermore, having extensive ties may prove to be a liability: over-embeddedness can prevent members from discovering new opportunities existing outside the scope of their network (Uzzi, 1997).

Monge, Heiss, and Margolin (2008) demonstrate that *evolutionary* and *ecological* theories provide a useful lens through which the dynamics of network change can be studied. Evolutionary theory, by definition a general theory of change, looks into organizational birth, development, transformation, decline, and death (Baum, 2002). The ecological approach focuses on the composition of organizational populations and the resource environments in which they are located (Aldrich & Ruef, 2006). It emphasizes the interdependencies between organizations, looking into both competitive and cooperative relations. As Monge et al. (2008) have pointed out, the combination of evolutionary and network theory can be applied to the area of mass media, providing the tools to study the changing interactions between news outlets as they compete for the scarce resource of the attention of the public. One useful analytical perspective to the investigation of dynamic interorganizational networks involves the evolutionary mechanism of V-S-R: *variation, selection* and *retention* (Campbell, 1969). *Variation* refers to the idea of exploring a range of possibilities, while *selection* involves accepting some of those options and rejecting others. *Retention* describes the persistent maintaining of a selected variation over time. The three processes can operate on a number of levels within individual organizations, populations, and communities. In the context of media industry networks, important sources of variation exist in partnership and collaboration ties, some of which are selected and retained over time (Monge et al., 2008). The ecological framework is particularly helpful in the context of one rather difficult task that empirical research on interorganizational relations presents: defining the network boundaries. The set of media outlets that need to be included in a research study is not always immediately obvious. Considering only companies which operate within a certain geographic region (such as the area where a newspaper is circulated) becomes somewhat problematic as the Web lifts territorial restrictions on content distribution. In a book taking an ecological perspective to the media sector, John Dimmick (2003) proposes using the *theory of the niche* to define the scope of populations and industries. Organizations are in the same population—or occupy the same niche—if they compete for the same set of resources. Among the resource dimensions suggested by Dimmick are consumer time and spending, advertising revenues, type of gratifications provided by the media (as described in Ball-Rokeach & DeFleur, 1976), and content.

The Content Sector: Semantic Networks [2-2]

Another sector in which networks play a fundamental role is that of content (see Figure 3.1, [2-2]). News articles, either individually or as a larger corpus of multiple texts, can be presented as maps of interrelated concepts. This allows for an exploration of the way issues and ideas are linked together in journalistic materials. It also facilitates the comparative analysis of different discourses that develop around contested social issues.

Two major frameworks come together in studies that employ concept maps to analyze news content. The theoretical background is provided by the media effects theory of *framing* (Gamson & Modigliani, 1989; Goffman, 1974). The analytical approach is that of *semantic network analysis* (SNA).

Semantic analysis is based on the premise that knowledge can be presented as networks of words and their relationships to each other in a given context (Carley, 1993). SNA software identifies the important concepts in a written work based on the frequency of their occurrence. Some types of words, such as transitive verbs, prepositions, conjunctions, etc., tend to appear often in any text but are not necessarily considered very important. Those are typically excluded from the analysis (Murphy & Maynard, 2000). A semantic network, sometimes also called a semantic map, is constructed based on a set of terms which have been identified as most relevant.

A number of methods have been developed to evaluate the strength of semantic relationships. The ties in a semantic map are typically based on related or overlapping meaning. One simple and often used way to detect a link between two words is based on the frequency of their proximate co-occurrence. If two concepts are related in the context of the framing applied to a text, they are also likely to frequently appear within several words of each other (Doerfel & Barnett, 1999). This approach has theoretic foundations grounded in cognitive processes (Scott, 2005). Words are hierarchically clustered in memory and their meaning is retrieved through associations with other words. If we assume that some patterns of those cognitive associations emerge in written text, semantic maps could be one way to capture them (Doerfel, 1998).

This type of analysis has been applied to the study of media texts, extracting important themes, central ideas, and the connections between them. Semantic studies have been used to examine journalistic representations of nicotine (Murphy, 2001), artificial sweeteners (Hellsten, Dawson, & Leydesdorff, 2009), the SARS crisis (Tian & Stewart, 2005), and political actors (Danowski & Cepela, 2009; Van Atteveldt, Kleinnijenhuis, & Ruigrok, 2008), among others. More detailed discussion of the interplay between semantic maps and media frames, as well as of their impact on audience members can be found in the inter-sector section of this article.

Once the semantic map is compiled, it can be interpreted directly based on the researcher's knowledge of the domain, or used to derive other measures and perform different types of quantitative analyses (Rice & Danowski, 1993). Clustering analysis, for example, may be used to examine groups of concepts that tend to appear together. Different frames emerge as different clusters of the focal concepts. Another type of analysis takes separate bodies of texts and constructs a semantic network for each one of them. Network correlations can be used to assess the level of similarity between different semantic maps over the same concepts (Doerfel & Barnett, 1999).

Although it has its disadvantages (e.g., problems with precision and flexibility), automated semantic mapping is likely to produce more consistent results across texts than human coders (Vlieger & Leydesdorff, 2011). It is, furthermore, particularly well-suited for analysis of large corpora of media content which would present some challenge to manual coding.

The Audience Sector: Social Networks [3-3]

The third type of network-centric research studies media distribution and consumption. The focus is on audience members and the connections between them. Those connections may be social ties of friendship, common affiliations and media preferences, as well as links based on information exchange (see Figure 3.1, [3-3], [3-2], [3-1]).

In the context of media research, communication connections between audience members are crucial as they provide an infrastructure allowing the spread of media preferences and the diffusion of content. This is especially visible online: social consumption of news is both easy to track and ubiquitous on the Web (Purcell, Rainie, Mitchell, Rosenstiel, & Olmstead, 2010).

The pattern of ties between individuals is a well-studied research area. In the field of social networks, a host of mechanisms underlying the structure of interpersonal relationships has been identified. Those include, among others, balance, homophily, and proximity theories (Monge & Contractor, 2003). Balance models suggest that two people are more likely to be connected if they have friends in common. In a network context, this manifests in a tendency towards triadic transitivity. The premise of balance theory is borrowed from cognitive consistency frameworks (Cartwright & Harary, 1956; Heider, 1946) which propose that friends will evaluate objects in a similar fashion and, as a corollary, will have similar attitudes towards the people they meet.

Homophily is colloquially known as the "birds of a feather flock together" principle: individuals have a preference for social ties with those who are similar to them (Monge & Contractor, 2003). Associating with like-minded others makes interactions more predictable, reducing the potential stress or discomfort associated with encountering diversity (Brass, 1995). As a result, personal networks are often homogenous with regard to multiple socio-demographic characteristics including age, gender, race, religion, and occupation (McPherson, Smith-Lovin, & Cook, 2001).

Another closely related theory proposes geographic proximity as an important factor predicting interpersonal relationships. Occupying the same physical space gives people opportunities for interaction, thus facilitating closer relationships. Spatial propinquity has been found to foster the formation and maintenance of ties between similar individuals (Preciado, Snijders, Burk, Stattin, & Kerr, 2011).

Studying the impact of communication technologies on relationship patterns, scholars have investigated the principles affecting online tie formation. Internet interactions may be expected to relax somewhat the constraints of proximity and homophily, as they allow for diverse and long-distance relations (Cairncross, 1997). Yet geography and similarity remain crucial for social structures. In one example, a recent study of social ties on Twitter demonstrates that a substantial portion of ties on the platform were formed between users in the same metropolitan region (Takhteyev, Gruzd, & Wellman, 2011). Ties connecting individuals across regional clusters, furthermore, were predicted by distance, nationality and language. Research further indicates that online social networks tend to mirror close personal relationships from the offline world (Hampton, Goulet, Rainie, & Purcell, 2011).

Inter-Sector Networks

In this section we review inter-sector networks: structures that involve nodes from a focal domain, but have additional nodes and relations from one or more of the other two domains. For instance, the following two sections discuss adding content elements (Industry-Content) or audience-defined nodes and links (Industry-Audience) to interorganizational networks of media venues.

Industry-Content Networks: News Organizations and Content Production [1-2]

Organizational ecology suggests that the content produced by media outlets is bound to be influenced by some of their organizational characteristics. Larger, generalist companies have broad content niches in that they provide a wide variety of materials in an attempt to appeal to large audiences. Smaller, specialized news enterprises have narrow niches in that they focus on a limited number and type of stories (Dimmick, 2003). At an institutional level, selection of stories depends on established internal routines. Those routines are subject to the *variation-selection-retention* mechanisms discussed earlier.

Media outlets vary in type, location, projected identity, social context, target audiences, political orientation, production technologies, available resources, and ties to other organizations. All of those characteristics—and many more—affect content production (Allern, 2002; McManus, 2008). It is only to be expected that the properties of an individual outlet will affect the type, volume, and diversity of its content. What is more interesting is that content is also influenced by the *links* between organizations. The network relationships described in the previous section—financial, corporate, interpersonal—have considerable bearing on the production process and output.

Ownership and partnership ties are particularly important in that they influence the homogenization and diversification of media content. Research has found that the corporate policies of parent companies affect the news agenda of their subsidiaries, as do ties with advertisers and sponsors (Duplessis & Li, 2004). The impact is not only due to the adoption of formal policies. As corporations seek economies of scale, they share organizational knowledge and resources, including information and staff, between the media outlets they own. As a result, journalistic and editorial practices are transferred between different news sources. Studies in this area have confirmed the impact of ownership structure on news quality (Dunaway, 2008) and diversity (Huber, 2006).

In addition to being affected by links between organizations, media content can also constitute a link in itself. One potential tie of that kind is created through the exchange of stories between partnering news outlets. Another possibility, suggested by Ognyanova (2010), involves defining links based on the overlap of issue coverage between media outlets. Researchers studying the interdependencies between the topics covered by different news providers often employ the mass communication paradigm of *intermedia agenda-setting*. Theory suggests that elite media like the *New York Times* have the ability to influence the topic selection of other outlets (Rogers, Dearing, & Bregman, 1993). The current dominant approach in agenda setting research involves computing correlations between rank-ordered lists of media issue priorities (Coleman & McCombs, 2007). While useful in demonstrating similarities, this method is problematic when trying to answer more specific questions about directions of influence, centrality of outlets and external factors affecting the agenda overlap. Moreover, it does not provide a particularly helpful description of the global patterns of shared issue priorities. A network approach, on the other hand, allows for a more sophisticated exploration of the social influence between media organizations and content selection.

Industry-Audience Networks: Media Companies and Online Audiences [1-3]

As media outlets increasingly offer their content on the Web, researchers have developed online methods to trace patterns of influence. News websites, like nytimes.com, can be seen as online representations of their respective media organizations, in this case, the *New York Times*. Hyperlinks embedded in the content constitute the network connections. While the analysis of online link structures may present methodological challenges (Barnett, Chung, & Park, 2011), this approach provides a rare opportunity for longitudinal studies of online patterns, tracking Web configurations over time (Park, Barnett, & Chung, 2011).

A number of scholars have used the hyperlink perspective to explore the ties that exist between mainstream news sites and blogs (Kelly, 2008; Meraz, 2009; Tremayne, 2006; Turow & Tsui, 2008). For the purposes of those studies, blogs are often implicitly regarded as a special, more opinionated, individualized online form that gives voice to audience members. Online presence of this kind allows news consumers to interact with professional journalists, potentially engaging them in a productive conversation. In some prominent cases, bloggers have succeeded in influencing the U.S. media industry agenda and focusing public attention on previously ignored issues (Ward, Cahill, & Petelin, 2007).

Three major approaches to deriving meaning from hyperlinks can be identified in existing research. The distinctions stem from viewing online links as signifying *affiliation, similarity,* or *value.* The first two approaches posit that more linking is likely to occur between the websites of companies or people who share some common ground. The *affiliation* frame regards hyperlinks as a proxy for social and organizational relationships (Mika, 2007; Park & Thelwall, 2003). This may refer to existing relations such as those between people who know each other, between organizations that work together or between subsidiaries of the same parent company (Ali-Hasan & Adamic, 2007; Weber, 2012; Weber & Monge, 2011). The *similarity* frame views the existence of online links as an indicator of a different type of commonality based on shared properties. Elite news venues may, for instance, only post links to other outlets of the same type (Meraz, 2009). Political bloggers may overwhelmingly link to people with similar political ideology (Adamic & Glance, 2005; Nahon & Hemsley, in press; Park & Thelwall, 2008).

Network methods, which take into account individual attributes, dyadic connections, and the dependencies between the two, are particularly well-suited to study these processes. Network clustering provides one way to explore the tendency of similar online actors to link to each other. Another method that has been used to examine the social patterns of linking in blogs employs community detection algorithms (Chin & Chignell, 2006).

The *value* frame, the third view on the significance of online connections, sees the hyperlink as an information exchange tie. Links are expected to point to content or organizations that are considered relevant, credible, and authoritative (Park, Barnett, & Nam, 2002). Similar to citations in scientometric research, hyperlinks are treated as indicators of quality and as markers for reputation (Park & Thelwall, 2003; Thelwall, 2009). In its simplest version, this approach can assess the influence of a media website based on its *in-degree centrality*, calculated in this case as the number of hyperlinks point-ing to the site. More sophisticated network algorithms have also been devel-oped to explore the relevance of online content within a specific knowledge domain (Easley & Kleinberg, 2010). One framework suggests distinguishing between sites containing valuable new material, called *sources*, aggregation sites that filter information and add value, called *authorities*, and sites which "collect links and direct users to the most relevant or appropriate information for a given topic," called *hubs* (Kleinberg, Kumar, Raghavan, Rajagopalan, & Tomkins, 1999; Weber & Monge, 2011).

Researchers looking into patterns of online influence have found that mech-anisms of preferential attachment are shaping the structure of the Web. "The rich get richer" mechanism leads to a power law distribution[2] of links to main-stream media and blog sites (Drezner & Farrell, 2004). Studies have associ-ated those findings with the existence of an *elite bias*. There is evidence that a small number of high-profile news venues have a major impact over the rest of the media and the public opinion (Pew Project For Excellence in Journalism, 2010, 2011).

Link analysis has thus emerged as a useful new method in the area of *agenda-setting* research. The ability of prominent news sources to set the issue coverage priorities of other outlets and audience members is assessed through patterns of hyperlinking. In one study of that kind, Meraz (2009) looks at links to examine the power of the *New York Times* and the *Washington Post* to set the political news agenda. Her results suggest that mainstream media outlets, while not the sole source of influence online, remain dominant agenda-setters on the web.

While most of the articles referenced in this section do not employ multi-plex designs in their study of ties between news sources and individuals, this approach can provide a useful analytical framework for future investigations in the area. In addition to looking into organizational ties, for example, schol-ars may explore a second type of connection between online media that is con-structed through web co-link analysis (Zuccala, 2006). This technique allows researchers to evaluate the relationship between two news sites based on the number of cases in which individual audience members have linked to both.

In the context of a media interorganizational network, co-link relationships provide a new set of ties determined by co-occurrence of hyperlinks generated by the general public. Using analytical tools similar to those of bibliomet-rics, researchers can further identify clusters of news sources that typically get "cited" together by consumers (Thelwall & Wilkinson, 2004).

Another key application of hyperlink analysis emerges from *world sys-tem theory* studies investigating international flows of information (Park et al., 2011). Works in that line of research explore the structure of online and telecommunication networks among countries, identifying a core-periphery structure with central positions reserved for first-world rich economies (Bar-nett, Jacobson, Choi, & Sun-Miller, 1996). One relevant aspect of *world sys-tems theory* lies in its capacity to predict the prominence of nations in foreign affairs news (Chang, 1998). While international networks are beyond of the scope of this work, as nations do not fall into the core node types examined by mass communication research (e.g., audience members, media organizations, and content), this application of link analysis deserves to be mentioned as a fruitful direction for further research.

Content-Audience Networks: Framing Research and Public Opinion [2-1]

One important aspect of the interaction between content networks and audience members is captured by the classic theory of framing. The main idea behind it is that media can affect the way we think about an issue by making some of its aspects more salient while ignoring others. Framing is not necessarily limited to a media "spin" on controversial issues. Rather it serves as a parsing mechanism, a collective sense-making tool aiding the understanding of everyday events and social interactions (Goffman, 1974). Recognizing the significance of frames as socially shared, persistent organizing principles that structure meaning (Reese, 2007), scholars in media and political studies began looking for ways to access those structures. Developing a practical definition of framing that can be used in empirical research is recognized as a notoriously difficult task (Koenig, 2004). One attempt to do that comes from Entman (1993), who suggested looking for the presence or absence of certain "keywords, stock phrases, stereotyped images, sources of information and sentences that provide thematically reinforcing clusters of facts or judgments" (p. 52). Semantic network analysis provides a useful set of methods allowing scholars to identify central concepts, evaluate the relationships between them, and uncover the constellations of terms or ideas that tend to cluster together.

Most of the research on framing confirms the assumption that media frames have a powerful impact on public opinion (Castells, 2009; Shen & Edwards, 2005). Pan and Kosicki (2001) go as far as to suggest that it is an essential part of public deliberation. Semantic links established in the news should then have an observable impact on its consumers.

Guo and McCombs (2011) further developed this line of research, testing empirically the capability of semantic relationships present in media content to influence the cognitive concept maps held by audience members. Their study found similarities between media-generated and public-opinion semantic networks of attributes about Texas gubernatorial candidates. Analysis of this type provides a good example of multiplex thinking about the media system. Guo and McCombs in effect study a media content network with an additional set of semantic links generated by audience members.

Content-Industry Networks: Framing Research and Media Organizations [2-3]

Researchers have applied semantic analysis in a wide diversity of contexts to explore the implications of media framing. SNA research has examined political debates, organizational literature, media framing of genetic testing, health crises, nicotine, artificial sweeteners, and other topics (Hellsten et al., 2009; Murphy, 2001; Murphy & Maynard, 2000; Samkin & Schneider, 2008; Tian & Stewart, 2005). These studies analyze clusters of terms frequently used within a thematic domain in order to identify implicit frames employed by media outlets or political factions.

Semantic mapping can be particularly helpful in studies that bridge the content and organizational levels of analysis. Research may, for instance, explore the theoretically predicted similarity between the frames employed by news outlets which are part of the same media conglomerate (Allern, 2002; McManus, 2008). Scholars have already used SNA to compare the framing strategies of different media companies (L. Kim, 2011; Tian & Stewart, 2005). Work in this area of content research can be further advanced through a multiplex network perspective. One direction for future research in this field involves analyzing news stories produced by different media organizations and testing whether interorganizational links are associated with semantically similar structures of content.

In addition to providing an instrument for the analysis of news content, a semantic approach can be applied to study the internal discourse of media companies. As Monge and Poole (2008) suggest, the texts and conversations generated by an organizational discourse can be viewed as networks of intertextual and reflexive links. Constructing those links as semantic relationships allows for the study of discourse structure and evolution over time, giving a network interpretation to the symbolic and rhetorical dynamics involved in the process.

SNA is expected to become more methodically sophisticated and more popular as a research technique with the advent of the Semantic Web (O'Hara, Berners-Lee, Hall, & Shadbolt, 2010). The key driving force behind that new strategy of information representation is the use of formal languages that computers can process to describe the meaning of online content (Mika, 2007). Embedded metadata will allow machines to understand the context of information, combining facts from multiple sources to perform an ever more intelligent knowledge analysis. Media outlets like the *New York Times* have already begun releasing their stories under a new *linked open data* format (*New York Times*, 2009). This makes it possible for computers to automatically determine which names in the text refer to people, organizations or places, and retrieve background information about those entities.

Audience-Industry Networks: Explaining Media Preferences [3-1]

In the realm of media studies, multiple paradigms provide insight into audience relationships with news organizations. *Media system dependency* suggests that individuals rely on media for their information needs such as understanding the environment, learning social norms, and escaping from everyday pressures through entertainment (Ball-Rokeach, 1985; Ball-Rokeach & DeFleur, 1976). The *uses and gratifications* approach (Katz, Blumler, & Gurevitch, 1973) similarly emphasizes the role of the consumer in selecting the appropriate media to meet their needs.

One perspective which explicitly focuses on both social ties and news organizations is *communication infrastructure theory* or CIT (Ball-Rokeach, Kim, & Matei, 2001; Y. C. Kim & Ball-Rokeach, 2006). The framework builds on media system dependency (Ball-Rokeach, 1998), investigating interpersonal and mediated interactions along with their civic outcomes (Ball-Rokeach et al., 2001). It proposes a holistic, multi-method approach to studying the community *storytelling network,* an integrated system encompassing local residents, organizations, and media outlets. CIT emphasizes the importance of both interpersonal ties and engagement with media as factors contributing to civic engagement. The social networks connecting residents, as well as the affiliation links between residents and their preferred media outlets, are among the important aspects of the local storytelling system. Higher level multiplex structures are implied here as we can envision an additional set of ties between individuals constructed on the basis of their shared news source preferences.

In the ideal case, CIT suggests that micro-level agents (residents) and meso-level agents (organizations and news media) should form a single, well-integrated network (Matei & Ball-Rokeach, 2002). As the Internet becomes an increasingly important part of local communication infrastructures, ties between audience members and online news organizations become another relevant set of connections linking micro- and meso-level actors (Matei & Ball-Rokeach, 2001).

Research in this area has already identified a number of individual properties affecting the patterns of ties between audience members and local news providers. Generational differences, socio-economic status and ethnicity may have an impact on both interpersonal contacts and individual links to media organizations (Y. C. Kim & Ball-Rokeach, 2006).

Audience-Content Networks: Diffusion of News Stories [3-2]

In the context of media studies, social structures can be seen as a part of a larger system. Online and offline connections between audience members form the infrastructure over which media content can be propagated.

A classic media effects theory, the two-step flow of communication, provides the basis for network studies of media content diffusion. The model suggests that instead of reaching the public directly, the ideas broadcasted by media outlets are channeled through a particularly active segment of audience members: the opinion leaders (Katz, 1957; Katz & Lazarsfeld, 1955). Translating the two-step flow into network terms, we can see the mechanism it describes as a diffusion process (Valente, 1996). Certain central, well-connected nodes in the network, known as the opinion leaders, pick up ideas or other information from the media. That information is then disseminated further through their interpersonal network connections.

The diffusion of media content has been particularly well-studied in an online context. In the past few years, Web platforms have started providing multiple tools that allow users to reconstruct their real life social networks in an online space (Kleinberg, 2008). Sites like Facebook and Twitter give audience members the option to forward media content to their connections with the click of a button. A recent Pew report suggests that that's exactly what 37% of U.S. Internet users are doing (Purcell et al., 2010). More than half of the people using social networking sites, furthermore, receive and follow links to news items on a daily basis.

Blogs are another medium in which news content is propagated. As it is an accepted norm for bloggers to link to their sources (Chin & Chignell, 2006; Ferdig & Trammell, 2004), information diffusion in the blogosphere can be tracked based on hyperlink patterns and time stamps.

Taking into account these new trends, scholars have started studying the spread of topics through both social networking platforms (Oh, Susarla, & Tan, 2008) and blogs (Leskovec, Backstrom, & Kleinberg, 2009; Leskovec, McGlohon, Faloutsos, Glance, & Hurst, 2007). The two analytical approaches used to explore the online diffusion of media content involve threshold models (Valente, 1996) and cascade models (Cointet & Roth, 2009). In threshold models, an actor's decision to disseminate a topic is based on the proportion of their connections who have already started discussing the subject. In a cascade model, each time an actor is "infected" with a new topic, there is a certain probability that the infection will spread to neighboring nodes.

Epidemic models of diffusion are often used for online content as their robustness has been well established through long use in other scientific fields. Much of the research looking into the network flow of information is based on methods initially developed to model the spread of disease through interpersonal connections. Clinical research in epidemiology often uses the *SIR* (*susceptible - infected - recovered*) cycle to describe the stages through which a node may pass (Easley & Kleinberg, 2010; Lewis, 2009). The same model has been adapted to study audience members and their exposure to media content (Leskovec et al., 2007). In the online-diffusion version of SIR, users may become *susceptible* to a topic when it is suggested to them by a friend (either through a blog post or via a service like Twitter or Facebook). The person may then be *infected* with the topic (i.e., they write a post about it or publish it on a social networking platform). With this, the individual is considered to have *recovered* from the topic, although a relapse is possible when something new appears on the subject.

Modeling the spread of media content through social networks has allowed researchers to understand topic life-cycles, spikes and declines (Cointet, Faure, & Roth, 2007; Gruhl, Guha, Liben-Nowell, & Tomkins, 2004; Leskovec et al., 2007). It has also provided a way to explore patterns of influence and identify opinion leaders (Java, 2006; Nakajima, Tatemura, Hara, Tanaka, & Uemura, 2006).

Conclusion, Limitations, and Future Research

This chapter has presented a multilevel, multitheoretical, and multidimensional network model of the media system. Three major sectors were described: the media industry, content, and audiences. The role of networks linking nodes within these three sectors, called *intra-sector networks,* was examined. *Inter-sector* networks were further introduced as a way to tie together entities from different domains, creating macro-level networks among different components of the media system. *Intra-* and *inter-sector* network interactions, including multiplex and multidimensional structures, were shown to influence media production, output, and consumption. Existing studies and theories that bridge two or all three media domains were briefly discussed. Grounded in Monge and Contractor's (2003) multilevel, multitheoretical network model, expanded to include multidimensional links, we suggested that complementary theoretical mechanisms and analytical tools are needed to explain network phenomena in the increasingly interconnected media system (Castells, 2009).

Several of those combinations deserve to be highlighted here as they provide particularly promising directions for future research:

- *Ecological theory and organizational networks.* This group of theoretical tools allows for the construction of networks between media outlets based on resource exchange, competition, ownership, partnership, or strategic alliances. A study taking this approach may explore the effects of strategic content and audience resources (Dimmick, 2003) on organizational networks.
- *Agenda-setting theory and hyperlink networks.* As media organizations and audience members coexist on the Web and link to each other's content, patterns of influence can be detected from existing hyperlink networks. Studies in that area can identify prominent news outlets, but they can also look for bottom-up effects of topics crossing from audience members to mainstream media.
- *Framing theory and semantic networks.* This type of analysis is set to become widely used in the social sciences as the Semantic Web and open linked data format allow an intelligent automated parsing of media content. Semantic maps are already used to identify the dominant frames of media texts. While this approach focuses on content, it has potential applications bridging the levels of media organizations and consumers. Semantic tools may, for example, be used to compare the framing of issues between different news outlets.
- *Communication infrastructure theory (CIT) and social networks.* CIT is explicitly formulated in network terms, as it emphasizes the importance of links between residents, media and community organizations. The storytelling system described by the theory incorporates social relations based on local information exchange. Research using this framework may investigate the structure, density and clustering patterns of the sto-

rytelling network. Central actors, as well as actors serving as bridges between different groups can be identified.

- *Diffusion theories and semantic or hyperlink networks.* Social contagion and diffusion theories are used to track the online spread of topics or specific stories between media outlets and consumers. Extracting the underlying topics from text requires the use of semantic parsing (Leskovec et al., 2009). Tracking the spread of specific media stories can also be done based on hyperlink structure. Studies in the area model the diffusion, trying to identify cyclical patterns, influential nodes, and mechanisms guiding the dissemination.

While this work focuses on the promise of relational approaches to media studies, we recognize a number of limitations that also need to be taken into consideration. Network data is, by its nature, relatively difficult to collect (Hanneman & Riddle, 2005). Studying full networks may be an expensive and lengthy exercise. Moreover, because of the relational focus, sampling strategies may be difficult to design. Network researchers frequently encounter boundary specification problems (Marin & Wellman, 2010). While it is usually easy to identify all members of a particular group, the same is not true of networks (Marsden, 2005). Deciding where a network "ends" can be challenging, as networks often have no natural boundaries (Borgatti & Halgin, 2011).

As with other statistical techniques, establishing causality is a major challenge in network research (Fowler, Heaney, Nickerson, Padgett, & Sinclair, 2011). This is particularly problematic in studies which need to determine whether social ties are the cause or consequence of individual attributes (Shalizi & Thomas, 2011).

While the challenges in data collection and analysis are serious, it is our belief that most of them are far from permanent. The parallel advancement of network theories and methods is living up to its early promise in the social as well as the physical sciences (Borgatti et al., 2009). In a new media landscape characterized by networked production, networked distribution and networked consumption, relational thinking should be an essential aspect of theorizing and research.

Notes

The preparation of this article was supported by a grant from the National Science Foundation (IIS-0838548) and by funding to the Annenberg Networks Network from the Annenberg School for Communication and Journalism. The authors would like to express their appreciation to Amanda Beacom, Janet Fulk, Nina O'Brien, Peter Knaack, and the *Communication Yearbook* reviewers for their helpful comments on earlier drafts of the chapter.

1. Throughout this text we use the terms *sector* and *domain* interchangeably to refer to the three components of the media system: industry, content, and audience.

2. That is to say, the probability that a web page will have k incoming links is inversely proportional to a power of k. In particular, k is roughly proportional to 1/k2 (Easley & Kleinberg, 2010).

References

Adamic, L., & Glance, N. (2005, August). *The political blogosphere and the 2004 U.S. election: Divided they blog.* Paper presented at the 3rd International Workshop on Link discovery, Chicago, IL.

Aldrich, H., & Ruef, M. (2006). *Organizations evolving* (2nd ed.). Thousand Oaks, CA: Sage.

Ali-Hasan, N., & Adamic, L. (2007, March). *Expressing social relationships on the blog through links and comments.* Paper presented at the International Conference on Weblogs and Social Media, Boulder, Colorado.

Allern, S. (2002). Journalistic and commercial news values. News organizations as patrons of an institution and market actors. *Nordicom Review, 23*(1/2), 137–152.

Anderson, C. W. (2010). Journalistic networks and the diffusion of local news: The brief, happy news Life of the "Francisville Four." *Political Communication, 27*(3), 289–309. doi:10.1080/10584609.2010.496710

Arquilla, J., & Ronfeldt, D. F. (2001). *Networks and netwars: The future of terror, crime, and militancy.* Santa Monica, CA: Rand Corporation.

Arsenault, A., & Castells, M. (2008a). Switching power: Rupert Murdoch and the global business of media politics: A sociological analysis. *International Sociology, 23*(4), 488. doi:10.1177/0268580908090725

Arsenault, A., & Castells, M. (2008b). The structure and dynamics of global multimedia Business Networks. *International Journal of Communication, 2*, 707–748.

Baker, W. E., & Faulkner, R. R. (2002). Interorganizational networks. In J. A. C. Baum (Ed.), *The Blackwell companion to organizations* (pp. 520–540). Oxford, England: Blackwell.

Ball-Rokeach, S. J. (1985). The Origins of Individual Media-System Dependency: A sociological framework. *Communication Research, 12*(4), 485. doi:10.1177/009365085012004003

Ball-Rokeach, S. J. (1998). A theory of media power and a theory of media use: Different stories, questions, and ways of thinking. *Mass Communication and Society, 1*(1), 5–40. doi:10.1080/15205436.1998.9676398

Ball-Rokeach, S. J., & DeFleur, M. L. (1976). A dependency model of mass-media effects. *Communication Research, 3*(1), 3. doi:10.1177/009365027600300101

Ball-Rokeach, S. J., Kim, Y. C., & Matei, S. (2001). Storytelling neighborhood: Paths to belonging in diverse urban environments. *Communication Research, 28*(4), 392–428. doi:10.1177/009365001028004003

Ball-Rokeach, S. J., Rokeach, M., & Grube, J. W. (1984). *The great American values test: Influencing behavior and belief through television.* New York, NY: The Free Press.

Barnett, G. A., Chung, C. J., & Park, H. W. (2011). Uncovering transnational hyperlink patterns and web-mediated contents: A new approach based on cracking. com domain. *Social Science Computer Review, 29*(3), 369–384. doi:10.1177/0894439310382519

Barnett, G. A., Jacobson, T. L., Choi, Y., & Sun-Miller, S. L. (1996). An examination of the international telecommunication network. *Journal of International Communication, 3*(2), 19–43. doi:10.1080/13216597.1996.9751833

Baum, J. A. C. (Ed.). (2002). *The Blackwell companion to organizations*. Oxford, England: Blackwell.

Blau, P. M. (1964). *Exchange and power in social life*. New York, NY: John Wiley.

Boczkowski, P. J. (2010). *News at work: Imitation in an age of information abundance*. Chicago, IL: University Of Chicago Press.

Borgatti, S. P., & Foster, P. C. (2003). The network paradigm in organizational research: A review and typology. *Journal of management, 29*(6), 991. doi:10.1016/S0149-2063_03_00087-4

Borgatti, S. P., & Halgin, D. S. (2011). On Network Theory. *Organization Science, 22*(5), 1168–1180. doi:10.1287/orsc.1100.0641

Borgatti, S. P., Mehra, A., Brass, D. J., & Labianca, G. (2009). Network analysis in the social sciences. *Science, 323*(5916), 892. doi:10.1126/science.1165821

Brass, D. J. (1995). A social network perspective on human resources management. *Research in Personnel and Human Resources Management, 13*, 39–79.

Cairncross, F. (1997). *The death of distance: how the communications revolution will change our lives*. Cambridge, MA: Harvard Business Press.

Campbell, D. T. (1969). Variation and selective retention in socio-cultural evolution. *General Systems, 14*(1), 69–85.

Cardoso, G. (2006). *The media in the network society: Browsing, news, filters and citizenship*. Liboa, Portugal: CIES-ISCTE.

Carley, K. M. (1993). Coding choices for textual analysis: A comparison of content analysis and map analysis. *Sociological methodology*, 75–126. doi:10.2307/271007

Carrington, P. J., Scott, J., & Wasserman, S. (Eds.). (2005). *Models and methods in social network analysis*. New York, NY: Cambridge University Press.

Cartwright, D., & Harary, F. (1956). Structural balance: a generalization of Heider's theory. *Psychological Review, 63*(5), 277. doi:10.1037/h0046049

Castells, M. (2005). Informationalism, networks, and the network society: A theoretical blueprint. In M. Castells (Ed.), *The network society: A cross-cultural perspective* (pp. 3–45). London, England: Edward Elgar.

Castells, M. (2009). *Communication power*. Oxford, England: Oxford University Press.

Chang, T. (1998). All countries not created equal to be news: World system and international communication. *Communication Research, 25*(5), 528.

Chin, A., & Chignell, M. (2006). A social hypertext model for finding community in blogs. *Proceedings of the seventeenth conference on Hypertext and hypermedia* (pp. 11–22). New York, NY: ACM Press.

Chon, B. S., Choi, J. H., Barnett, G. A., Danowski, J. A., & Joo, S. H. (2003). A structural analysis of media convergence: Cross-industry mergers and acquisitions in the information industries. *The Journal of Media Economics, 16*(3), 141–157. doi:10.1207/S15327736ME1603_1

Cointet, J. P., Faure, E., & Roth, C. (2007. March). *Intertemporal topic correlations in online bedia*. Paper presented at the International Conference on Weblogs and Social Media, Boulder, Colorado.

Cointet, J. P., & Roth, C. (2009, August). *Socio-semantic dynamics in a blog network*. Paper presented at the IEEE SocialCom 09 International Conference Social Computing, Vancouver, Canada.

Coleman, R., & McCombs, M. (2007). The young and agendaless? Exploring age-related differences in agenda setting on the youngest generation, baby boomers, and the civic generation. *Journalism and Mass Communication Quarterly, 84*(3), 495. doi:10.1177/107769900708400306

Contractor, N., Monge, P., & Leonardi, P. (2011). Multidimensional networks and the dynamics of sociomateriality: Bringing technology inside the network. *International Journal of Communication, 5*, 682–720.

Danowski, J. A., & Cepela, N. T. (2009). Automatic mapping of social networks of actors from text corpora: Time series analysis. *Advances in Social Network Analysis and Mining, 12*, 137–142. doi:10.1109/ASONAM.2009.71

Danowski, J. A., & Choi, J. H. (1999). Convergence in the information industries: Telecommunications, broadcasting, and data processing—1981–1996. In H. Sawhney & G. A. Barnett (Eds.), *Progress in communication sciences* (Vol. 15, pp. 125–150). Stamford, CT: Ablex.

Diesner, J., & Carley, K. M. (2005). Revealing social structure from texts: Meta-matrix text analysis as a novel method for network text analysis. In V. K. Narayanan & D. J. Armstrong (Eds.), *Causal mapping for research in information yechnology* (pp. 81–108). Hershey, PA: IGI Global.

Dimmick, J. W. (2003). *Media competition and coexistence: The theory of the niche.* Mahwah, NJ: Erlbaum.

Doerfel, M. L. (1998). What constitutes semantic network analysis? A comparison of research and methodologies. *Connections, 21*(2), 16–26.

Doerfel, M. L., & Barnett, G. A. (1999). A semantic network analysis of the International Communication Association. *Human Communication Research, 25*(4), 589–603. doi:10.1111/j.1468-2958.1999.tb00463.x

Drezner, D., & Farrell, H. (2004). Web of influence. *Foreign Policy,* 32–41. doi:10.2307/4152942

Dunaway, J. (2008). Markets, ownership, and the quality of campaign news coverage. *The Journal of Politics, 70*(04), 1193–1202. doi:10.1017/S0022381608081140

Duplessis, R., & Li, X. (2004, May). *Cross-media ownership and its effect on technological convergence of online news content — A content analysis of 100 Internet newspapers.* Paper presented at the Annual Meeting of the International Communication Association (ICA), New Orleans, LA.

Easley, D., & Kleinberg, J. (2010). *Networks, srowds, and markets: Reasoning about a highly connected world.* New York, NY: Cambridge University Press.

Emerson, R. M. (1962). Power-dependence relations. *American Sociological Review, 27*(1), 31–41. doi:10.2307/2089716

Entman, R. M. (1993). Framing: Toward clarification of a fractured paradigm. *Journal of Communication, 43*(4), 51–58. doi:10.1111/j.1460-2466.1993.tb01304.x

Ferdig, R. E., & Trammell, K. D. (2004). Content delivery in the 'blogosphere'. *Technological Horizons In Education Journal, 31*(7), 12–16.

Fowler, J. H., Heaney, M. T., Nickerson, D. W., Padgett, J. F., & Sinclair, B. (2011). Causality in political networks. *American Politics Research, 39*(2), 437. doi:10.1177/1532673X10396310

Freeman, L. C. (2004). *The development of social network analysis: A study in the sociology of science.* Vancouver, BC: Empirical Press.

Gamson, W. A., & Modigliani, A. (1989). Media discourse and public opinion on nuclear oower: A constructionist approach. *The American Journal of Sociology, 95*(1), 1–37. doi:10.1086/229213

Goffman, E. (1974). *Frame analysis: An essay on the organization of experience.* Cambridge, MA: Harvard University Press.

Gruhl, D., Guha, R., Liben-Nowell, D., & Tomkins, A. (2004, May). *Information diffusion through blogspace*. Paper presented at the 13th international conference on World Wide Web New York, NY.

Gulati, R., Dialdin, D. A., & Wang, L. (2002). Organizational networks. In J. A. C. Baum (Ed.), *The Blackwell companion to organizations* (pp. 281–303). Oxford, England: Blackwell.

Guo, L., & McCombs, M. (2011, May). *Network agenda setting: A third level of media effects*. Paper presented at the Annual Meeting of the International Communication Association (ICA), Boston, MA.

Hampton, K., Goulet, L., Rainie, L., & Purcell, K. (2011). Social networking sites and our lives. Pew Internet & American Life Project. Retrieved November 1, 2011, from www.pewinternet.org/Reports/2011/Technology-and-social-networks.aspx

Hanneman, R. A., & Riddle, M. (2005). *Introduction to social network methods*. Riverside, CA: University of California.

Heider, F. (1946). Attitudes and cognitive organization. *Journal of psychology, 21*(1), 107–112. doi:10.1080/00223980.1946.9917275

Hellsten, I., Dawson, J., & Leydesdorff, L. (2009). Implicit media frames: Automated analysis of public debate on artificial sweeteners. *Public Understanding of Science, 19*(5), 590–608. doi:10.1177/0963662509343136

Huber, S. (2006). Media markets in Central and Eastern Europe. A network analytic investigation. In S. Huber (Ed.), *Media markets in Central and Eastern Europe. An analysis on media ownership in Bulgaria, Czech Republic, Estonia, Hungary, Latvia, Lithuania, Poland, Romania, Slovakia and Slovenia* (pp. 9–48). London, England; LIT Verlag.

Java, A. (2006). *Tracking influence and opinions in social media* (doctoral dissertation). University of Maryland Baltimore County.

Katz, E. (1957). The two-step flow of communication: An up-to-date report on an hypothesis. *Public Opinion Quarterly*, 61–78. doi:10.1086/266687

Katz, E., Blumler, J. G., & Gurevitch, M. (1973). Uses and gratifications research. *Public Opinion Quarterly, 37*(4), 509–523. doi:10.1086/268109

Katz, E., & Lazarsfeld, P. F. (1955). *Personal influence: The part played by people in the flow of mass communication*. Glencoe, IL: The Free Press.

Kelly, J. (2008). *Pride of place: Mainstream media and the networked public sphere Media Re:public*. Cambridge, MA: Berkman Center for Internet & Society.

Kilduff, M., & Tsai, W. (2003). *Social networks and organizations*. Thousand Oaks, CA: Sage.

Kim, L. (2011). Media framing of stem cell research: a cross-national analysis of political representation of science between the UK and South Korea. *Journal of Science Communication, 10* (3), 1–16..

Kim, Y. C., & Ball-Rokeach, S. J. (2006). Civic engagement from a communication infrastructure perspective. *Communication Theory, 16*(2), 173. doi:10.1111/j.1468-2885.2006.00267.x

Kleinberg, J. (2008). The convergence of social and technological networks. *Communications of the ACM, 51*, 66–72. doi:10.1145/1400214.1400232

Kleinberg, J., Kumar, R., Raghavan, P., Rajagopalan, S., & Tomkins, A. (1999). The web as a graph: Measurements, models, and methods. *Computing and Combinatorics*, 1–17.

Koenig, T. (2004, July). *On frames and framing: Anti-Semitism as free speech*. Paper presented at the Annual Meeting of the International Association of Media and Communication Research (IAMCR), Porto Alegre, Brazil.

Lazarsfeld, P. F., Berelson, B., & Gaudet, H. (1944). *The people's choice: How the voter makes up his mind in a presidential campaign.* New York, NY: Columbia University Press.

Leskovec, J., Backstrom, L., & Kleinberg, J. (2009, June). *Meme-tracking and the dynamics of the news cycle.* Paper presented at the The 15th ACM SIGKDD International Conference on Knowledge Discovery and Data Mining, Paris, France.

Leskovec, J., McGlohon, M., Faloutsos, C., Glance, N., & Hurst, M. (2007, April). *Cascading behavior in large blog graphs: Patterns and a model.* Paper presented at the Society of Applied and Industrial Mathematics: Data Mining, Minneapolis, MN.

Lewis, T. G. (2009). *Network Science: Theory and practice.* Hoboken, NJ: Wiley.

Marin, A., & Wellman, B. (2010). Social network analysis: An introduction. In P. Carrington & J. Scott (Eds.), *Handbook of social network analysis* (pp. 11–26). Thousand Oaks, CA: Sage.

Marsden, P. (2005). Recent developments in network measurement. In P. J. Carrington, J. Scott, & S. Wasserman (Eds.), *Models and methods in social network analysis* (pp. 8–30). New York, NY: Cambridge University Press.

Matei, S., & Ball-Rokeach, S. J. (2001). Real and virtual social ties: Connections in the everyday lives of seven ethnic neighborhoods. *American Behavioral Scientist, 45*(3), 550. doi:10.1177/0002764201045003012

Matei, S., & Ball-Rokeach, S. J. (2002). Belonging in geographic, ethnic, and Internet spaces. In B. Wellman & C. A. Haythornthwaite (Eds.), *The Internet in everyday life* (pp. 404–427). Oxford, England: Wiley-Blackwell.

McChesney, R. W. (2000). *Rich media, poor democracy: Communication politics in dubious times.* New York, NY: The New Press.

McChesney, R. W. (2004). *The problem of the media: US communication politics in the 21st century.* New York, NY: Monthly Review Press.

McManus, J. H. (2008). The commercialization of news. In W.-J. K. & T. Hanitzsch (Eds.), *Handbook of journalism studies* (pp. 218–233). New York, NY: Routledge.

McPherson, M., Smith-Lovin, L., & Cook, J. M. (2001). Birds of a feather: Homophily in social networks. *Annual Review of Sociology*, 415-444. doi:10.1146/annurev.soc.27.1.415

Meraz, S. M. (2009). Is there an elite hold? Traditional media to social media agenda setting influence in blog networks. *Journal of Computer-Mediated Communication, 14*(3), 682-707. doi:10.1111/j.1083-6101.2009.01458.x

Mika, P. (2007). *Social networks and the semantic web.* New York, NY: Springer.

Monge, P., & Contractor, N. (2003). *Theories of communication networks.* New York, NY: Oxford University Press.

Monge, P., Heiss, B. M., & Margolin, D. B. (2008). Communication network evolution in organizational communities. *Communication Theory, 18*(4), 449-477. doi:10.1111/j.1468-2885.2008.00330.x

Monge, P., & Poole, M. S. (2008). The evolution of organizational communication. *Journal of Communication, 58*(4), 679-692. doi:10.1111/j.1460-2466.2008.00408.x

Murphy, P. (2001). Framing the nicotine debate: A cultural approach to risk. *Health Communication, 13*(2), 119–140. doi:10.1207/S15327027HC1302_1

Murphy, P., & Maynard, M. (2000). Framing the genetic testing issue. *Science Communication, 22*(2), 133–153. doi:10.1177/1075547000022002002

Nahon, K., & Hemsley, J. (in press). Political blogs and content: Homophily in the guise of cross-linking. *Journal of Computer-Mediated Communication.*

Nakajima, S., Tatemura, J., Hara, Y., Tanaka, K., & Uemura, S. (2006). Identifying agitators as important blogger based on analyzing blog threads. *Lecture Notes in Computer Science, 3841*, 285–296.

New York Times. (2009). Linked open data. Retrieved April 12, 2010, from data. nytimes.com

O'Hara, K., Berners-Lee, T., Hall, W., & Shadbolt, N. (2010). Use of the semantic web in e-research. In W. H. Dutton & P. W. Jeffreys (Eds.), *World wide research: Reshaping the sciences and humanities* (pp. 130). Cambridge, MA: The MIT Press.

Ognyanova, K. (2010). News ties: A network study of media-level agenda-setting. *Journal of Social Structure, JoSS Visualization Symposium 2010, 11.* Retrieved from http://www.cmu.edu/joss/content/issues/vizsymposium.html

Oh, J., Susarla, A., & Tan, Y. (2008). Examining the diffusion of user-generated content in online social networks. *SSRN.* Retrieved from http://ssrn.com/abstract=1182631

Pan, Z., & Kosicki, G. M. (2001). Framing as a strategic action in public deliberation. In S. D. Reese, O. H. Gandy, & A. E. Grant (Eds.), *Framing public life: Perspectives on media and our understanding of the social world* (pp. 35–65). Mahwah, NJ: Erlbaum.

Park, H. W., Barnett, G. A., & Chung, C. J. (2011). Structural changes in the 2003–2009 global hyperlink network. *Global networks, 11*(4), 522–542. doi:10.1111/j.1471-0374.2011.00336.x

Park, H. W., Barnett, G. A., & Nam, I. Y. (2002). Hyperlink–affiliation network structure of top web sites: Examining affiliates with hyperlink in Korea. *Journal of the American Society for Information Science and Technology, 53*(7), 592–601. doi:10.1002/asi.10072

Park, H. W., & Thelwall, M. (2003). Hyperlink analyses of the World Wide Web: A review. *Journal of Computer-Mediated Communication, 8*(4). doi:10.1111/j.1083-6101.2003.tb00223.x

Park, H. W., & Thelwall, M. (2008). Link analysis: Hyperlink patterns and social structure on politicians' web sites in South Korea. *Quality & Quantity, 42*(5), 687–697. doi:10.1007/s11135-007-9109-z

Pew Project For Excellence in Journalism. (2010). *The state of the news media 2010: An annual report on American journalism.* Washington, DC: Author.

Pew Project For Excellence in Journalism. (2011). *The state of the news media 2011: An annual report on American journalism.* Washington, DC: Author.

Preciado, P., Snijders, T. A. B., Burk, W. J., Stattin, H., & Kerr, M. (2011). Does proximity matter? Distance dependence of adolescent friendships. *Social Networks.* doi:10.1016/j.socnet.2011.01.002

Purcell, K., Rainie, L., Mitchell, A., Rosenstiel, T., & Olmstead, K. (2010). *Understanding the participatory news consumer: How internet and cell phone users have turned news into a social experience.* Pew Internet & American Life Project. Retrieved November 1, 2011, from http://www.journalism.org/analysis_report/understanding_participatory_news_consumer

Reese, S. D. (2007). The framing project: A bridging model for media research revisited. *Journal of Communication, 57*(1), 148–154. doi:10.1111/j.1460-2466.2006.00334.x

Rice, R. E., & Danowski, J. A. (1993). Is it really just like a fancy answering machine? Comparing semantic networks of different types of voice mail users. *Journal of Business Communication, 30*(4), 369. doi:10.1177/002194369303000401

Rogers, E. M., Dearing, J. W., & Bregman, D. (1993). The anatomy of agenda-setting research. *Journal of Communication, 43*(2), 68–84. doi:10.1111/j.1460-2466.1993.tb01263.x

Samkin, G., & Schneider, A. (2008). Adding scientific rigour to qualitative data analysis: an illustrative example. *Qualitative Research in Accounting & Management, 5*(3), 207–238. doi:10.1108/11766090810910227

Schweitzer, F., Fagiolo, G., Sornette, D., Vega-Redondo, F., Vespignani, A., & White, D. R. (2009). Economic networks: The new challenges. *Science, 325*(5939), 422. doi:10.1126/science.1173644

Scott, P. (2005). Knowledge workers: Social, task and semantic network analysis. *Corporate Communications: An International Journal, 10*(3), 257–277.

Shalizi, C. R., & Thomas, A. C. (2011). Homophily and contagion are generically confounded in observational social network studies. *Sociological Methods & Research 40*(2), 211–239. doi:10.1177/0049124111404820

Shen, F., & Edwards, H. H. (2005). Economic individualism, humanitarianism, and welfare reform: A value-based account of framing effects. *Journal of Communication, 55*(4), 795–809. doi:10.1093/joc/55.4.795

Takhteyev, Y., Gruzd, A., & Wellman, B. (2011). Geography of Twitter networks. *Social Networks.* doi:10.1016/j.socnet.2011.05.006

Thelwall, M. (2009). *Introduction to webometrics: Quantitative Web research for the social sciences* (Vol. 1). San Rafael, CA: Morgan & Claypool.

Thelwall, M., & Wilkinson, D. (2004). Finding similar academic web sites with links, bibliometric couplings and colinks. *Information Processing & Management, 40*(3), 515–526. doi:10.1016/S0306-4573(03)00042-6

Tian, Y., & Stewart, C. (2005). Framing the SARS crisis: A computer-assisted text analysis of CNN and BBC online news reports of SARS. *Asian Journal of Communication, 15*(3), 289–301. doi:10.1080/01292980500261605

Tremayne, M. (2006). Applying network theory to the use of external links on news web sites. In X. Li (Ed.), *Internet newspapers: The making of a mainstream medium* (pp. 49–64). Mahwah, NJ: Erlbaum.

Turow, J., & Tsui, L. (Eds.). (2008). *The hyperlinked society: Questioning connections in the digital age.* Ann Arbor: University of Michigan Press.

Uzzi, B. (1997). Social structure and competition in interfirm networks: The paradox of embeddedness. *Administrative Science Quarterly, 42*(1), 35–67. doi:10.2307/2393808

Valente, T. W. (1996). Social network thresholds in the diffusion of innovations. *Social Networks, 18*(1), 69–89. doi:10.1016/0378-8733(95)00256-1

Valente, T. W. (2010). *Social networks and health: Models, methods, and applications.* New York, NY: Oxford University Press.

Van Atteveldt, W., Kleinnijenhuis, J., & Ruigrok, N. (2008). Parsing, semantic networks, and political authority using syntactic analysis to extract semantic relations from dutch newspaper articles. *Political Analysis, 16*(4), 428–446. doi:10.1093/pan/mpn006

Vlieger, E., & Leydesdorff, L. (2011). Content analysis and the measurement of meaning: The visualization of frames in collections of messages. *The Public Journal of Semiotics, 1*(28), 28–50

Ward, I., Cahill, J., & Petelin, R. (2007). Old and new media: Blogs in the third age of political communication. *Australian Journal of Communication, 34*(3), 1–21.

Wasserman, S., & Faust, K. (1994). *Social network analysis: Methods and applications*. New York, NY: Cambridge University Press.

Watts, D. J. (2004). The "new" science of networks. *Annual Review of Sociology.* doi:10.1146/annurev.soc.30.020404.104342

Weber, M. (2012). Newspapers and the long-term implications of hyperlinking. *Journal of Computer-Mediated Communication, 17*(2), 187–201. doi:10.1111/j.1083-6101.2011.01563.x

Weber, M., & Monge, P. (2011). The flow of digital news in a network of authorities, hubs and providers. *Journal of Communication, 61*(6), 1062–1081. doi:10.1111/j.1460-2466.2011.01596.x

Zuccala, A. (2006). Author cocitation analysis is to intellectual structure as web colink analysis is to...? *Journal of the American Society for Information Science and Technology, 57*(11), 1487–1502. doi:10.1002/asi.20468

CHAPTER CONTENTS

4   A Taxonomy of Communication Networks

Michelle Shumate

Northwestern University

*Andrew Pilny, Yannick C. Atouba,
Jinseok Kim, Macarena Peña-y-Lillo,
Katherine R. Cooper, Ariann Sahagun*

University of Illinois at Urbana-Champaign

Sijia Yang

University of Pennsylvania

Communication network research is increasingly being used across the communication discipline. However, most social network research is limited in its generalizability because it focuses on either a single network case or ego-centric network data. In order to generate knowledge across network studies, a mechanism is needed to synthesize. This chapter presents a taxonomy of communication relations, differentiating between communication flow, affinity, representational, and semantic networks. Then, it demonstrates the utility of the taxonomy for synthesizing network research by reviewing 139 studies in communication journals, focusing on the antecedents, outcomes, and processes of each type of network.

Although social media, like Facebook and LinkedIn, and networked organizational forms, like the Network Society (Castells, 1996), have only recently made social networks part of the everyday vernacular, the network perspective has shaped communication thinking since the 1970s. The adoption of the network perspective and its increasing popularity in communication research (see Figure 4.1) is in part due to a general shift in the social sciences away from individualist, atomistic, and essentialist explanations toward more relational, systemic, and contextual explanations of social phenomena (Borgatti & Foster, 2003; Monge & Contractor, 2003). Despite the popularity of the network perspective, most social network research that extends beyond ego-networks may best be described as quantitative case analysis (Faust & Skvoretz, 2002). That is, most network research focuses either on a single network or uses ego-centric network data, where data only about a node's immediate connections is gathered. In order to draw conclusions across multiple cases, communication researchers need a network taxonomy.

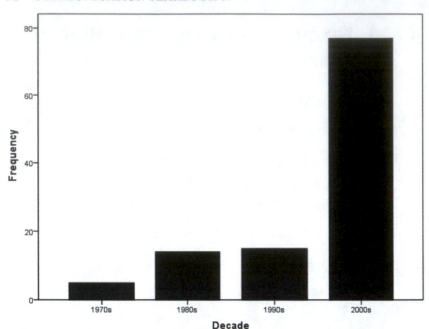

Figure 4.1 Frequency of communication articles using network analysis per decades (*N* = 111). Articles from 2010 and 2011 (*N* = 28) are not included in the chart.

In this chapter, we present a recently developed taxonomy of the multiple types of communication relations (Shumate & Contractor, 2014). We use this taxonomy to synthesize communication network research in communication journals across interpersonal, organizations, mass, health, political, and computer-mediated communication. In doing so, we present a case for what is known about particular communication relations based upon their type—specifically, flow, affinity, representational, and semantic relations—rather than synthesizing across either the node types (e.g., individual, group, organization) or contexts of the study. We review 41 years of research (1970–2011) research that focuses on the antecedents, outcomes, and processes of communication networks, highlighting results for each relation type. This differs from the purposes of previous reviews of social network research (Farace, Monge, & Russell, 1977; Monge & Eisenberg, 1987; Shumate & Contractor, 2014) in two important ways. First, this review is more expansive than previous reviews, focusing on communication as a field rather than organizational communication network research. Second, this review aims to synthesize results across sub-fields, based upon relation type, suggesting ways for communication network research to move forward together.

This chapter makes three contributions to communication research. First, it utilizes a relatively new network taxonomy (Shumate & Contractor, 2014) that will allow for the synthesis of disparate communication research. In doing so, we demonstrate promising ways for communication network research, across sub-field divides, to be informative and generative of cumulative knowledge. As a field, communication research can and should be able to make a cumulative statement about the nature of various communication network types. Without a taxonomy or mechanism for synthesis, communication network research provides an interesting method for the study of disparate phenomenon but does not contribute to cumulative knowledge. Second, the chapter highlights the importance of multiplex communication ties across relation types. Although previous research has addressed multiplexity, the current review suggests that flow, affinity, representational, and semantic networks are mutually influential; however, little research has examined the ways in which these networks interact. Finally, beyond the call for research on multiplexity across relation types, we present a call for future research based upon relation types that have received scant attention in communication journals. We find that more research is needed on the (a) outcomes of semantic networks, (b) the outcomes of representational networks, and (c) the processes of communication networks across types.

Communication Networks

Communication networks are relations among various types of nodes that illustrate the ways in which messages are transmitted or interpreted. This definition is more expansive than that put forward by previous reviews of communication networks (e.g., Monge & Contractor, 2001; Monge & Eisenberg, 1987), because it includes research that examines semantic networks based on the interpretation of particular words or concepts and hyperlink research in which no message is exchanged between the actors directly. A network perspective on communication processes emphasizes structural patterns but is not necessarily a functional perspective. Although many think about communication networks as the exchange of messages among individuals, communication research across sub-fields have examined a variety of nodes and relations. Nodes that have been examined are as diverse as newsgroups (e.g., Choi & Danowski, 2002; Kang & Choi, 1999), organizations (e.g., Doerfel & Taylor, 2004; Shumate, Fulk, & Monge, 2005), and characters on television shows (e.g., Fine, 1981; Livingstone, 1987). Relations have included agreement (e.g., Stohl, 1993), membership (e.g., Barnett & Danowski, 1992), cooperation (Doerfel & Taylor, 2004), and telecommunications traffic (e.g., Monge & Matei, 2004).

Following Shumate and Contractor (2014) this chapter suggests that relation types, not actor types, are the best way to synthesize findings about communication networks. This presupposition is supported by two distinct studies. First, Faust and Skvoretz's (2002) comparison of the structural characteristics of 43 networks, ranging from advice networks among managers to licking behavior among cows, found that actor type did not explain the patterns of networks as well as relations did. Second, Leskovec, Kleinberg, and Faloutsos's (2007) study of positive link growth rates (i.e., the relationship between the rate in which links and nodes are added to a network) across 12 networks of 7 types found that the relationship between the addition of nodes and the addition of relations was much stronger for the citation networks than for the communication networks (e.g., communication via e-mail). Monge, Heiss, and Margolin (2008) suggested that Leskovec and colleagues' findings indicated that various types of relations have different carrying capacities, or limitations. This contention falls in line with one of the hallmark tenets of social network analysis, that researchers should shift the focus of their analysis from attributes to relations (Marin & Wellman, 2011).

Communication Network Relation Types

Shumate and Contractor (2014) argued that communication network relations can be classified into four categories: flow, affinity, representational, and semantic. Each of these relation types describe a way in which communication may be represented in a network. In the original work, Shumate and Contractor organized organizational communication research using the taxonomy, inclusive of interdisciplinary work in management journals. The purpose of presenting this taxonomy here is to enable researchers to cumulatively draw conclusions across communication network research that appears in communication journals.

Flow.   Communication flow relations describe ties that indicate sending and receiving messages, information, or data (Shumate & Contractor, 2014). In other words, communication flow relations refer to the exchange or transmission of messages, information, and data among nodes. Communication flow can take place among individuals, as in information seeking (Palazzolo, 2005), or between individuals and other types of nodes, including technologies, documents, and other artifacts. For example, when individuals exchange messages or when a person retrieves information from a website, these relations demonstrate communication flow.

Affinity.   In contrast, affinity relations refer to socially constructed relationships that have either a positive or negative valence (Shumate & Contractor, 2014). These relations do not explicitly indicate the exchange or transmission of messages, information, or data among actors; rather, they describe more enduring relationships among them. Individual affinity relations include friendship and marriage, whereas organizational affinity relations include collaboration and alliances. In each case, the type of relationship is symbolically constructed by one or both parties, and communication is assumed to be implicit in the relation. Thus, although it is difficult to conceive of friends or interorganizational partners that do not exchange messages or information, friendships or interorganizational partnerships do not represent flow relations as they do not explicitly refer to the transmission or exchange of messages, information, or data.

Representational.   Representational relations involve messages about an association among actors communicated to a third party or the public (Shumate & Contractor, 2014). In other words, these relations describe messages about one node's affiliation with other nodes. Representational ties including hyperlink networks[1] (e.g., Tateo, 2005), bibliometric networks[2] (e.g., So, 1988), a network of USENET responses (Himelboim, 2008), and a network of name mentions on websites (Shumate & O'Connor, 2010). These relations are distinguished from flow relations because no messages are exchanged between nodes. Additionally, they are distinguished from affinity relations because they do not necessarily entail enduring relationships among actors. Consider, for example, the contrast between conversing with a friend, a flow relation, having a friend, an affinity relation, and name-dropping, a representational relation. In the representational relation, the person whose name is dropped does not receive a message. Additionally, the person whose name is dropped may not even have a friendship or an enduring relationship with the person dropping his or her name. Unlike flow and affinity relations, there is no cost to receiving additional ties in representational networks. For example, a website being the recipient of an increasing number of hyperlinks bears no direct cost burden,[3] whereas being flooded with an increasing number of emails may result in costly information overload. As such, preferential attachment effects may drive the formation of representation networks (e.g., exponential growth in links to a popular site).

Semantic.   Semantic relations focus on shared meaning or symbol use (Shumate & Contractor, 2014). Semantic relations are examined on two levels: (a) the shared meanings as indicated by the patterns of word usage in text or discourse and (b) individuals' cognitive maps of shared meanings. An example of the first type is Doerfel and Barnett's (1999) analysis of the paper titles of the 1991 International Communication Association Conference. Word frequencies, combinations, and differences across divisions were compared to a prior affiliation analysis, based upon membership. In general, when members were jointly affiliated with two divisions, the authors of papers in those two divisions used similar words in their titles. Stohl (1993) provided an example of the second type of semantic network research. In her study, managers' ties to one another were based upon the number of common interpretations they had of the term *participation*. A semantic relation between the actors in this case indicated that they had similar perceptions of the same concept; it did not indicate a transmission or exchange of information (i.e., a flow relation), an enduring relationship (i.e., an affinity relation), or a message to a third party or the public about an association among actors (i.e., a representational relation).

The four types of relations have different types of logical network patterns. For example, flow relations have constrained degree distributions. The constraint arises from the capacity of an actor to process or send messages. In contrast, representational relations are relatively unconstrained because there is not a corresponding cost to receiving this type of tie. As such, we would expect that representational networks would tend to have highly skewed in-degree distributions.[4] For example, hyperlink networks composed of representational relations often have power-law degree distributions (Barabási, Albert, & Jeong, 2000), in which a small number of actors receive a significant number of ties and many actors receive very few ties. Affinity relations, especially if they are positively valenced, are expected to result in networks that have a greater number of clusters, based upon balance theory (Heider, 1958; Holland & Leinhardt, 1972). Balance theory suggests that triangles of positively valenced ties are more likely to exist in networks (Monge & Contractor, 2003), which are the building blocks of clusters in a network. Representational network relations, in contrast, should have less clustering because they are not sentiment-based networks. Representational networks rely on impression management as their foundational mechanism, and, as such, cognitive dissonance plays a lesser role in these networks. Consider the research of Shumate and O'Connor (2010) on corporate-NGO networks. In these representational networks, corporations seek to set themselves apart from other corporations by presenting unique relations with NGOs. As such, triangles of relationships are less likely in representational relations than in affinity relations. Finally, Carley and Kaufer (1993) suggested concepts that have the most meaning will have higher connectivity and that semantic networks at the individual level tend to converge among actors who are similar to one another. In other words, similar individuals will think about the relationships among concepts in more similar ways than individuals with fewer similarities.

In addition to the four types of communication network relations defined earlier, Shumate and Contractor (2014) identified other networks that enable and constrain the configuration of various types of communication networks, infrastructure networks. Infrastructure networks include technology networks, physical networks, and affiliation networks. Technology networks describe the supporting paths along which communication flow, affinity, representational, and semantic communication networks are made manifest. For example, consider the potential for mobile communication in a country where individuals must pay for "talk time" in order to use their phones. The technology network in any given point in time would be a network of those individuals who have "talk time" available, because only those individuals would be able to communicate with one another via mobile phone at that moment. Physical networks describe the proximity of actors to one another. Research on communication and affinity networks has consistently shown that physical proximity plays an important role in network structuring. For example, Sykes (1983) found that physical proximity explained much of the frequency of interaction among individuals. Finally, affiliation networks are two-mode networks (i.e., networks of two different types of actors in which connections are only permitted among actors of different types), where actors are affiliated with organizational entities (e.g., organizations, groups, social movements, online communities). Infrastructure networks do not explicitly or implicitly involve communication or shared meaning, but they affect flow, affinity, representational, and semantic network relations among actors.

In summary, communication research has been at the forefront of social network analysis, leading researchers to analyze an eclectic range of contexts, node types, and relationships. Despite this diversity, however, there have been few attempts to classify the state of the communication network field across sub-disciplines (e.g., organizational, interpersonal, health, mass, computer-mediated, and political communication). In doing so, we submit that researchers across sub-disciplinary divides can be informed by one another's research and nuanced findings can be generated. Using a relation-driven approach, we offer a framework that synthesizes the field and identifies areas for future research.

Method

In the following section, we present a review of communication research articles in communication journals that use social network analysis. Employing the four relations defined above, and following Monge and Eisenberg's (1987) lead, we examine the antecedents, outcomes, and processes of each type of network. Antecedents to networks describe research in which the communication network is the dependent variable, analyzing a variety of factors that predict particular network structural properties. Outcomes of networks describe research in which the communication network or some property of the communication network is the independent variable and predicts specific consequences. Processes of networks describe longitudinal communication research that explores the dynamic rewiring of the network over time.

In order to conduct this review of communication research, we explored all journals in the Communication Institute for Online Scholarship (CIOS) database from 1970 to 2011. We did not examine books, book chapters, or journal articles published by communication scholars in interdisciplinary journals; as such, our review is limited in its generalization to an examination of communication research in communication journals. We searched indices contained in these journals for network terms including *social network, network analysis, UCINET, density, centrality,* and *network data.* We discarded any article that did not conduct an empirical analysis or did not operationalize a communication network (i.e., any article that developed a scale or attitudinal measure of networking). We identified a total of 159 articles. Of these, 18 were interpersonal communication articles, 8 were health communication articles, 53 were organizational communication articles, 49 articles were computer-mediated communication articles, 14 were mass communication articles, and 17 were political communication articles. We excluded articles that simply visualized or described networks from our review ($n = 7$), because they did not examine antecedents, outcomes, or processes. Additionally, we excluded articles whose primary focus was infrastructure networks ($n = 13$). We then classified the remaining articles ($n = 139$) based upon relation type and whether the network was a dependent, independent, or longitudinal variable. The results of this classification are presented in Table 4.1. In addition, an online supplement, which identifies each article included, the type of network examined, and a brief description of the results of that study is available at www.michelleshu-mate.com/resources.

Table 4.1 Taxonomy of Network Studies in Communication Journals

	Antecedents	*Outcomes*	*Process*
Affinity	Atouba and Shumate (2010) Magdol (2000) Mueller, Kuerbis, and Pagé (2007) Neal (2010) Reese, Grant, and Danielian (1994) Roberts and O'Reilly (1978) Sykes (1983) Taylor and Doerfel (2003) Widmer (2006) Yuan and Gay (2006)	Beinstein (1977) Breidenstein-Cutspec and Georing (1989) Feeley and Barnett (1997) Lewis, Kaufman, and Christakis (2008) Parks (1977) Raile, Kim, Choi, Serota, Park, and Lee (2008) Sanders and Nauta (2004) Smith and Fink (2010) Sohn (2009) Taylor-Clark, Viswanath, and Blendon (2010) Wakabayashi, Yamashita, and Yamada (2009)	Bryant and Monge (2008) Chon, Choi, Barnett, Danowski, and Joo (2003) Doerfel and Taylor (2004) Shumate, Fulk, and Monge (2005) Terhell, van Groenous, and van Tilburg (2004)
Flow	Ang and Zaphiris (2010) Boase (2008) Cho and Lee (2008) Cho, Trier, and Kim (2005) Choi and Danowski (2002) Corman (1990) Ersig, Hadley, and Koehly (2011) Himelboim, Chang, and McCreery (2010) Hurt and Preiss (1978) Kim and Barnett (1996) Kim, Kim, Park, and Rice (2007) Ksiazek (2011) Mohammed (2001) Moon, Barnett, and Lim (2010) Nonaka (2005) Palazzolo (2005) Tardy and Hale (1998)	Balkundi, Barsness, and Michael (2009) Cho (2005) Danowski (1980) Dorsey, Scherer, and Real (1999) Eisenberg, Monge, and Miller (1983) Eveland and Hively (2009) Feeley (2000) Fink and Chen (1995) Gil de Zúñiga and Valenzuela (2011) Hartman and Johnson (1989) Huffaker (2010) Ikeda and Boase (2011) Ishii (2006) Kuhn and Nelson (2002) Leonardi (2009) MacDonald (1976) Papa (1990) Parks and Adelman (1983) Postmes, Spears, and Lea (2000)	Boulay and Valente (2005) Chung (2011) Danowski and Edison-Swift (1985) Lee, Monge, Bar, and Matei, (2007) Monge and Matei (2004) Palazzolo, Serb, She, Su, and Contractor (2006) Paollio (1999) Sinnreich, Chib, and Gilbert (2008) Susskind (2007) Yuan and Ksiazek (2011)

	Antecedents	Outcomes	Process
	Weber and Monge (2011) Yuan, Fulk, Monge, and Contractor (2010) Yum (1982)	Prell (2003) Rice (1993) Rice and Love (1987) Rojas, Shah, and Friedland (2011) Russo and Koesten (2005) Schmitz and Fulk (1991) Vergeer and Pelzer (2009) Wing and More (2005) Yuan, Cosley, Welser, Ling, and Gay (2009) Yuan, Fulk, Shumate, Monge, Matsaganis, and Bryant (2005)	
Representational	Barnett and Sung (2005) Bennett, Foot, and Xenos (2011) Brooks, Welser, Hogan, and Titsworth (2011) Caiani and Wagemann (2009) Feeley (2008) Himelboim (2008) Johnson (2011) Kropczynski and Nah (2011) Park (2010) Park and Jankowski (2008) Park and Thelwall (2006) Park and Thelwall (2008) Reeves and Borgman (1983) Rice, Borgman, and Reeves (1988) Shumate and Dewitt (2008) Shumate and Lipp (2008) Shumate and O'Connor (2010) So (1988)	Biddix and Park (2008)	**None**

(*continued*)

Table 4.1 Continued

	Antecedents	Outcomes	Process
	Tai (2009) Tateo (2005) Tremayne, Zheng, Lee, and Jeong (2006)		
Semantic	Adam (2008) Becker-Beck, Wintermantel, and Borg (2005) Chow-White (2006) Danowski (2008) Doerfel and Barnett (1999) Doerfel and Marsh (2003) Eveland, Cortese, Park, and Dunwoody (2004) Gilpin (2010) Kim, Su, and Hong (2007) Kwon, Barnett, and Chen (2009) Maynard (1997) Murphy (2001) Murphy and Maynard (2000) Reese, Rutigliano, Hyun, and Jeong (2007) Rice and Danowski (1993) Stohl (1993) Zywica and Danowski (2008)	**None**	Murphy (2010)
Multiplex	Albrecht and Ropp (1984) Birnie and Horvath (2002) Bryant, Sanders-Jackson, and Smallwood (2006) Goering and Breidenstein-Cutspec (1989) Haythornthwaite (2003) Haythornthwaite (2005)	Campbell and Kwak (2011) Colon-Ramos, Atienza, Weber, Taylor, Uy, and Yaroch (2009) Feeley, Hwang, and Barnett (2008) Hampton (2011) Pollock, Whitbred, and Contractor (2000) Xia, Yuan, and Gay (2009)	Igarashi, Takai, and Yoshida (2005) Whitbred Fonti, Steglich, and Contractor (2011)

Flow

Communication network research has traditionally focused on flow relations exclusively. For example, Monge and Contractor (2001) defined communication networks as: "the patterns of contact between communication partners that are created by transmitting and exchanging messages through time and space" (p. 440), or communication flow relations. For our purposes, any work that examines the transmission of messages or frequency of communication between individuals, organizations, or media outlets focuses on communication flow. Indeed, communication flow relations are the most commonly studied type of communication relation in communication journals ($n = 59, 42.4\%$).

There are 20 studies of **antecedents** to communication flow networks. Together, research on antecedents to communication flow networks suggests that a combination of a node's resources, motivations, and perceptions of others in the network influence the pattern of communication ties. Examples of node-level resources include lack of communication apprehension (Hurt & Preiss, 1978), time to make contacts (Yum, 1982), and economic development (Kim & Barnett, 1996). A few examples of motivational factors include special interest in a topic (Ersig, Hadley, & Koehly, 2011), similar department tasks (Cho, Trier, & Kim, 2005), and shared task interdependence (Yuan, Fulk, Monge, & Contractor, 2010). Examples of perceptions include others' expertise (Palazzolo, 2005; Tardy & Hale, 1998; Yuan et al., 2010), similar demographics (Mohammed, 2001), perceptions of technology utility (Kim, Kim, Park & Rice, 2007), and partner's social role (Kim et al., 2007). However, no study examined all three of these factors together, suggesting the need for greater synthesis across sub-fields and studies in this area. One prescription from this review is for future research on antecedents to communication flow networks to include node resources, motivational factors, and perceptions of others to determine their relative effects.

There were 29 articles that focused on the **outcomes** of communication flow networks. The most common theme evident in results across cases is that social influence occurs via communication networks. For example, consider the work of Schmitz and Fulk (1991). In their study of e-mail use, a relatively new technology at the time, both the richness of the media and individual's social networks influenced perceptions of the technology. Thus, social influence plays an important role in attitude formation. In examining the results across studies in communication networks, however, a more nuanced conclusion can be drawn. Attitude change appears to occur through weak ties, whereas dense communication networks tend to support and reinforce uniform opinions. For example, consider the work on political knowledge and civic engagement. Eveland and Hively (2009) and Gil de Zúñiga and Valenzuela (2011) suggested that political knowledge is positively related to a diversity of ties. Papa (1990) found that network diversity increased the likelihood of adoption of a new technology. In all three of these studies, new information came from a diverse set of communication interactions. In contrast, consider the work of health communication scholars on engaging in risky health behavior.

For example, binge drinking (Dorsey, Scherer, & Real, 1999) is reinforced by dense communication with a network of others also engaging in the same behavior. In sum, the diversity of communication contacts creates the opportunity to learn more and brings opportunities for attitude and behavior change, whereas dense communication with similar nodes reinforces both attitudes and behavior. Social influence, to a large extent, depends on the configuration of communication networks. Specifically, networks that emphasize diverse connections and weak ties create opportunities for new information to shape attitudes and behavior. In contrast, cohesive, dense networks of like others reinforce existing attitudes and behaviors.

Research on the **processes** of communication flow networks has examined the ways in which changes in network positions or structures (i.e., relative centrality, mutuality, transitivity) are related to attributes and outcomes for individual actors ($n = 10$). In many ways, these studies are extensions of the two logics already identified in the examination of the antecedents and outcomes of flow networks; node-level resources, motivations, and perceptions of others are antecedents to and differential access to information results from the configuration of social networks. However, current research on the process of communication flow examines *increases* in network ties/properties and the impact of *changes* in communication networks on outcomes.

As an example of the first logic, consider the article by Lee, Monge, Bar, and Matei (2007). They examined the ways in which economic and telecommunications development *increases* the tendency to connect and reciprocate ties among nations. The primary difference between the logic in this article and that of the antecedents' articles is the examination of changes in these network properties. Similarly, Danowski and Edison-Swift (1985), Monge and Matei (2004), and Palazzolo, Serb, She, Su, and Contractor (2006) examined the antecedents to changes in communication networks. In general, the researchers concluded that nodes that have greater resources are likely to *continue to increase* their centrality and mutuality in communication networks. Resource types in these studies include economic, knowledge, and development resources.

In contrast, four studies examined the outcomes of dynamic communication flow networks. Researchers involved in these studies generally found that communication centrality and connectedness matter. For example, Susskind (2007) examined a network of employees at an international hotel company across three time periods. He found that increased centrality was related to increased perceptions of information adequacy during downsizing and was negatively related to turnover intentions. In these studies in general, greater connectedness led to better information, which is an important resource.

In summary, network research in communication journals has focused largely on flow relations. Research on antecedents to these networks and some process research has focused on node resources, motivations, and perceptions as determinants. However, these related findings have not been well synthesized, and much of the research to date has examined only one of these factors. In contrast, most of the research on outcomes of communication flow networks and some process research has focused on the ways by which information flows transform nodes, by either giving them better information resources or by changing their attitudes over time.

Affinity

A second type of communication network research has focused on socially constructed relationships among actors in a network, affinity relations. Examples of such relations include friendships, alliances, and various types of cooperation. In communication journals, affinity relations are often assumed to imply communication flow relations between actors without examining such flows. However, such research also has tended to examine enduring states rather than message flow.

Together, the 10 studies that have considered **antecedents** suggest that two factors play a significant role in the social construction of affinity relations across node types: interdependent network structures (e.g., mutuality, transitivity) and node homophily. Although not exclusively (see Weber & Monge, 2011), research on affinity relations has a greater tendency to focus on network structures than research on communication flows. Interdependent network structures describe the ways in which the social construction of relationships is a coordinated effort among actors. For example, if two individuals are friends with a third person, they are more likely to report that they are friends with each other; maintaining a dislike would result in significant psychological discomfort for the individuals (Heider, 1958). Similarly, communication researchers have found that reciprocating ties and transitivity (Atouba & Shumate, 2010), bridges and liaisons (Roberts & O'Reilly, 1978), and centrality (Reese, Grant, & Danielian, 1994) influence the configuration of the affinity network. Because affinity relations focus on states rather than dynamic flows of information among participants, affinity networks are better suited for the study of network structures of these types.

Second, communication researchers have examined homophily as a powerful predictor of the presence of affinity ties. Atouba and Shumate (2010), Mueller, Kuerbis, and Pagé (2007), Neal (2010), Widmer (2006), and Yuan and Gay (2006) found evidence of homophily, or at least a type of similarity that makes relations more likely, across affinity networks. However, the node characteristic examined varies across studies and, as illustrated by the Yuan and Gay study, homophily effects differ by attribute type (e.g., gender, location, and job specialization). As such, more efforts are needed to discern which attributes influence the configuration of affinity networks.

Eleven articles focused on the **outcomes** of affinity networks. All but one of these studies (Wakabayashi, Yamashita, & Yamada, 2009) were concerned with friendship networks. Intriguingly, these studies had tremendously varied outcomes. Perhaps because friendship is a socially constructed affinity relation that varies a great deal across cultures (Adams & Plautt, 2003), the effects of friendship networks may be relative across cultural populations. More theoretical work is needed to understand the ways in which differently understood friendship networks influence both individual and systemic outcomes. For example, would Granovetter's (1973) classic work on the outcomes of weak ties in finding employment in the US differ across cultural understandings of friendship?

To date, researchers interested in the **processes** of affinity networks have examined only the antecedents of network ties ($n = 5$). However, in contrast to the communication flow research, affinity researchers have studied the influence of past network ties on future network ties. For example, Doerfel and Taylor (2004) found that occupying structural holes[5] in a network at one time was related to the level of cooperativeness at a later time. Again, the durability of affinity ties, by their very nature, makes such an inclusion more logical than with communication flow ties.

Affinity ties are more durable, socially constructed relations between actors in a network. Their antecedents include network interdependencies and homophilous attributes. Over time, future relations build on past relations. The outcomes of these networks, however, are poorly understood. A stronger, cumulative line of research on the outcomes of affinity relations is needed to better understand their implications.

Representational Communication

Research on representational communication has significantly increased in the last decade in communication journals. Before 2000, there were 3 articles that focused on representational networks, all of them focusing on bibliometric networks (Reeves & Borgman, 1983; Rice, Borgman, & Reeves, 1988; So, 1988). Since 2000, there have been 19 articles, mostly focusing on hyperlink networks. Almost all the studies of representational relations have focused on the antecedents to these networks ($n = 21$).

Two conclusions about the **antecedents** to representational networks can be drawn. One overarching finding of this research is that clusters are prevalent based upon socially constructed groupings of actors. These clusters can vary from external characteristics outside the network (e.g., Caiani & Wagemann, 2009) to properties of the nodes themselves (e.g., Park & Jankowski, 2008). For example, framing of the fair trade issue has influenced the hyperlink network among websites in two countries (Bennett, Foot, & Xenos, 2011). Similarly, the framing of some research as mass communication and other research as interpersonal communication has influenced citations patterns in communication journals (Rice et al., 1988; So, 1988). The second finding is that representational networks tend to have highly skewed indegree distributions (Barnett & Sung, 2005; Himelboim, 2008; Shumate & O'Connor, 2010). Unlike other relation types, there is no cost of receiving additional ties, making such distributions more likely.

Only one article to date has considered the **outcomes** of representational networks. Biddix and Park (2008) used an innovative combination of interviews and hyperlink analysis in studying the living wage campaign. Using interviews, they described the ways in which hyperlinks helped to support the geographically distributed movement.

Representational networks differ significantly from both communication flow and affinity relations. There is little cost to "receiving" a representational link, and, as such, these networks tend to have highly skewed or power-law degree distributions. Further, because these networks are about messages communicated to a third party, they tend to be influenced by the framing of messages about the nature of the social issue or node sets. Through 2011, there has been little research on either the outcomes or processes of these networks, suggesting an area for future research. However, more theorizing is needed to understand the implications of these networks for publics.

Semantic Networks

Semantic network research focuses on the ways that words are used or interpreted by publics. Research to date on semantic networks, much like representational networks, has focused on its antecedents ($n = 17$); no research to date has focused on the outcomes associated with these networks.[6] In addition, one article (Murphy, 2010) examined the process of semantic network transformation, but like research on antecedents, focused on network structure.

Scholars have examined semantic relations on two levels: (a) the shared meanings as indicated by the patterns of word usage in text or discourse and (b) cognitive maps of shared meanings. Research on the **antecedents and processes** of semantic networks has tended to focus on the first type (for the one notable exception, see Stohl, 1993). Unfortunately, there has been relatively little theory driving most of this research. Instead, researchers have identified general word clusters or themes (e.g., Chow-White, 2006) and have noted differences across outlets or channels in the frequency of words (e.g., Adam, 2008; Doerfel & Marsh, 2003; Gilpin, 2010). However, they have not adequately examined the reasons driving these patterns.

Becker-Beck, Wintermantel, and Borg (2005) suggested a useful direction for semantic network research. They used an experimental design to understand the differences between face-to-face and computer-mediated teams. Using an innovative combination of sequential and semantic networks analysis, they demonstrate that uttered concepts are more specific in the computer-mediated condition than those uttered in the face-to-face condition. This conclusion is both consistent with and furthers theory and research in group communication. This study is unique in that it combined semantic network analysis with another research design.

Multiplexity Across Relation Types

Sixteen articles included multiplex ties across relation types. Multiplexity, or the inclusion of multiple relation types with the same set of nodes, is a relatively old concept in social network research (e.g., Hartman & Johnson, 1989). What is unique about this category is the focus on multiplexity across relation types (i.e., flow, affinity, representational, and semantic). In other words, rather than considering multiplexity within relation type (e.g., three different communication flow networks about different topics), multiplex relations across different network relation types is the focus (e.g., considering both friendship and communication frequency). Since we argue that the essential way to organize communication network research across studies is to focus on relation types, the next logical step is to consider how these various types of relations are related to one another.

All of the articles examining the antecedents, outcomes, or processes of multiplex networks focus on the relationship between flow and affinity networks. Research on the **antecedents** to multiplex networks ($n = 6$) and one article focusing on the **process** of communication networks (Whitbred, Fonti, Steglich, & Contractor, 2011) have tested the implicit assumption of much of affinity network research, that communication flow relations are necessary for the formation and maintenance of affinity networks. Research on the **outcomes** of affinity and flow relations ($n = 6$) and one article on the processes of communication networks (Igarashi, Takai, & Yoshida, 2005) compared their effects, hinting that communication networks of different types (i.e., flow, affinity, representational, and semantic) have different outcomes.

Discussion

The purpose of this chapter is to use a network taxonomy of communication networks based upon relations (Shumate & Contractor, 2014) to synthesize network research in communication journals. By examining network research findings in communication journals across node types, we are able to point to areas where conclusions across the field can be drawn. Such a synthesis is important for the future of network research as generative of new knowledge beyond case studies and single contexts. Based upon this review, researchers can justify new hypotheses and compare findings with what is known about certain network relation types to those types in other contexts.

We were able to draw conclusions about the antecedents to and outcomes of communication flow networks, the antecedents to affinity networks, and the antecedents to representational networks. In particular, communication flow networks were influenced by node resources, motivations, and perceptions. They resulted in information resource benefits for individuals with greater centrality. Weak ties were sources of new information leading to attitude change, but strong ties reinforced already held attitudes. Affinity networks were influenced by network interdependencies and homophily. Representational networks were influenced by popularity effects, as evidenced by skewed distributions and the framing of issues or sets of actors.

When synthesizing the results, comparisons across network types can also be drawn. In examining the antecedents to flow, affinity, and representational networks, different variables dominated. The nature of the relation explains why. Communication flow relations are about the creation of messages. As such, node resources, motivations, and perceptions of audiences are critical. However, affinity relations are socially constructed. As such, network interdependencies can take shape because these relations are more enduring. Further, other ways in which individuals socially construct the world make a difference, including through dominant categories (Turner, 1987). Representational relations do not bear the same cost as either affinity or flow relations; as such, they are more likely to have unconstrained degree distributions. Further, since they are communicated to third parties, they are more likely to be shaped by the framing of social issues than other types of relations that are about the parties in the network.

Moreover, through an examination of the four types of relations, we are able to identify uncharted areas of communication network research for future exploration. These include (a) the examination of the outcomes of semantic networks, (b) the examination of the outcomes of representational networks, (c) further examination of the processes of communication networks, and (d) the examination of multiplex relations across relation types. Each of these opportunities for future work is discussed in turn.

Although communication scholars were among the first to introduce semantic network analysis (Danowski, 1988; Monge & Eisenberg, 1987), most of the studies about these networks are inductive, concluding about prominent themes, or clusters. As such, a model of the types of outcomes expected from different semantic network configurations, especially derived from textual analysis alone, is difficult. Although the prevalence and ease of computer-generated content analysis software makes generating semantic networks relatively easy, in order to gain theoretical insight into these texts, research is needed that combines this analysis with other research designs. By integrating semantic network analysis into a larger design, more robust research on antecedents and new research on outcomes are within reach.

Second, communication scholars have readily embraced the study of the antecedents of representational relations, including hyperlink and bibliometric networks. However, to date, this research in communication journals has not examined the expected outcomes of such networks as frequently (for a notable exception, see Biddix & Park, 2008). This presents a puzzle: Why are communication researchers so interested in the structure of these networks, but not interested in the outcomes of these very same structures? Research questions that might be advanced in this area include: Are there advantages to being central in a hyperlink or bibliometric network? Are there consequences to clustering in these networks? Such inquiries need both research and theorizing.

Third, comparatively few studies have examined the processes of communication networks, regardless of relation types ($n = 18$, 13%). Almost all of these studies focus on the processes of communication flow networks ($n = 10$). By examining networks at only one point in time, researchers miss the dynamics that may have led to a particular network configuration or a particular outcome. In short, examining a network at one point in time represents only a snapshot of a stream of activity that may or may not be representational of the processes that led to that moment in time. Further, current communication research on processes typically examines changes in networks across a single period ($n = 7$), neglecting the potential for variations in rates of change and effects across multiple time periods. Finally, to date, communication research has focused on individual-level outcomes of network processes. Research on sub-group and whole network outcomes is necessary to understand the impact of network rewiring; examples of such outcomes include whole network effectiveness, sub-group efficiency, and community-level health (e.g., levels of obesity for the whole network).

Monge, Farace, Eisenberg, Miller, and White (1984) offered three explanations for the paucity of research on communication processes that, in our view, still hold today. They traced the lack of process research in communication studies to three factors: "methodological determinism, the inaccessibility of process techniques, and the perceived scope of effort required from the researcher" (p. 28). They suggested that the survey and experimental methods that dominated empirical communication research in the 1980s were not suitable for the study of processes, techniques like Markov analysis and time series analysis were seen as arcane and difficult, and that collecting longitudinal data was too time-consuming and difficult. According to Poole (2007), the scarcity of research on communication processes may also be due to a submersion of process under other constructs. Poole suggested this is due to the lack of methods for the study of process and the adoption of approaches from other disciplines, such as psychology, that do not emphasize process as much as communication.

Fourth, more research is needed on multiplex networks across the relation types. In our review of research, there were 16 studies that addressed multiplexity in communication networks. Each of these studies focused on affinity and flow relations. Future researchers should seek to examine other types of relation multiplexity, including semantic and representational relations. Such research has the potential to highlight the interrelatedness of different facets of communication including message flow, social construction, impression management, and linguistic variation.

The current chapter makes three contributions. First, it demonstrates the utility of a taxonomy that allows for the synthesis of disparate communication research. We presented four types of communication networks—flow, affinity, representational, and semantic—and three types of infrastructure networks—technology, physical proximity, and affiliation. We reviewed network research across communication journals, demonstrating the utility of this approach for identifying common findings across traditional communication discipline divides and types of nodes. For example, consider the review of the outcomes of communication flow networks. In order to draw our conclusion about social influence, we drew upon organizational communication, political communication, and health communication research. Studies in each of these sub-fields aided us in understanding the ways in which communication flow relations lead to social influence as an outcome. In addition, this approach assisted us in identifying areas for future research and theorizing.

Second, the chapter highlights the importance of multiplex communication ties. To date, relatively few communication studies have examined the intersections and overlaps between the four types of communication relations, and all of that research has examined the relationship between affinity and communication flow relations. Further, infrastructure networks that support communication networks represent an important covariate in communication networks. Multiplexity is foundational to the relational perspective of network studies (Lee & Monge, 2011); as such, this chapter serves as a call for more communication research to fill this gap.

Finally, we present a call for future research based upon relation types and questions that have received scant attention from communication scholars. These areas include any research examining semantic networks, outcomes of representational relations, and processes of all types of communication networks. Each of these areas of research suggests opportunities for both innovative theory and new empirical projects.

In sum, this chapter uses a taxonomy of communication networks based upon relations to examine the state of network research in communication journals. Although communication research has been examining networks for almost 40 years, the sub-field remains in its adolescence in many ways. Synthesizing findings and drawing conclusions across studies is the next important steps to transform this body of research into a more mature field.

Notes

1. Hyperlink networks describe the hypertext relationships that exist between websites.
2. Bibliometric networks describe the citation and authorship relationships that exist, often in academic papers.
3. However, there may be an indirect cost resulting from increased visibility in search engine results. This cost burden is imposed by a third party, as opposed to flow or affinity relations where the other actors doing the linking impose the cost.
4. An indegree distribution describes the spread of indegree centrality scores—or the number of links coming into a node.
5. Structural holes are gaps between two groups in a network. Nodes that occupy structural holes have brokerage benefits (see Burt, 1982).
6. Outside of communication journals, some research on semantic network outcomes does exist. For example, Doerfel and Connaughton (2010) find an association between the overall centrality in a semantic network in presidential debates and election outcomes. Although they stop short of suggesting causality, such research shows a promising association with outcomes.

References

Adam, S. (2008). Do mass media portray Europe as a community? German and French debates on EU enlargement and a common constitution. *Javnost-The Public, 15*(1), 91–112.

Adams, G., & Plautt, V. C. (2003). The cultural grounding of personal relationship: Friendship in North American and West African worlds. *Personal Relationships, 10*, 333–347. doi:10.1111/1475-6811.00053

Albrecht, T. L., & Ropp, V. A. (1984). Communicating about innovation in networks of 3 United-States organizations. *Journal of Communication, 34*, 78–91. doi:10.1111/j.1460-2466.1984.tb02175.x

Ang, C. S., & Zaphiris, P. (2010). Social roles of players in MMORPG guilds: A social network analytic perspective. *Information, Communication & Society, 13*, 592–614. doi:10.1080/13691180903266952

Atouba, Y., & Shumate, M. (2010). Interorganizational networking patterns among development organizations. *Journal of Communication, 60*, 293–317. doi:10.1111/j.1460-2466.2010.01483.x

Balkundi, P., Barsness, Z., & Michael, J. H. (2009). Unlocking the influence of leadership network structures on team conflict and viability. *Small Group Research, 40*, 301–322. doi:10.1177/1046496409333404

Barabási, A.-L., Albert, R., & Jeong, H. (2000). Scale-free characteristics of random networks: The topology of the world-wide web. *Physica A: Statistical Mechanics and its Applications, 281*(1-4), 69–77.

Barnett, G. A., & Danowski, J. A. (1992). The structure of communication: A network analysis of the international communication association. *Human Communication Research, 19*, 264–285. doi:10.1111/j.1468-2958.1992.tb00302.x

Barnett, G. A., & Sung, E. (2005). Culture and the structure of the international hyperlink network. *Journal of Computer-Mediated Communication, 11*, 217–238. doi:10.1111/j.1083-6101.2006.tb00311.x

Becker-Beck, U., Wintermantel, M., & Borg, A. (2005). Principles of regulating interaction in teams practicing face-to-face communication versus teams practicing computer-mediated communication. *Small Group Research, 36*, 499–536. doi:10.1177/1046496405277182

Beinstein, J. (1977). Friends, media, and opinion formation. *Journal of Communication, 27*, 30–39. doi:10.1111/j.1460-2466.1977.tb01853.x

Bennett, W. L., Foot, K., & Xenos, M. (2011). Narratives and network organization: A comparison of fair trade systems in two nations. *Journal of Communication, 61*, 219–245. doi:10.1111/j.1460-2466.2011.01538.x

Biddix, J. P., & Park, H. W. (2008). Online networks of student protest: The case of the living wage campaign. *New Media & Society, 10*, 871–891. doi:10.1177/1461444808096249

Birnie, S. A., & Horvath, P. (2002). Psychological predictors of Internet social communication. *Journal of Computer-Mediated Communication, 7*(4). Retrieved from http://jcmc.indiana.edu/vol7/issue4/horvath.html

Boase, J. (2008). Personal networks and the personal communication system. *Information, Communication & Society, 11*, 490–508. doi:10.1080/13691180801999001

Borgatti, S. P., & Foster, P. C. (2003). The network paradigm in organizational research: A review and typology. *Journal of Management, 29*, 991–1013. doi:10.1016/s0149-2063(03)00087-4

Boulay, M., & Valente, T. W. (2005). The selection of family planning discussion partners in Nepal. *Journal of Health Communication, 10*, 519–536. doi:10.1080/10810730500228789

Breidenstein-Cutspec, P., & Goering, E. (1989). Exploring cultural diversity: A network analysis of the communicative correlates of shyness within the black culture. *Communication Research Reports, 6*, 37–46.

Brooks, B., Welser, H. T., Hogan, B., & Titsworth, S. (2011). Socioeconomic status updates: Family SES and emergent social capital in college student Facebook networks. *Information, Communication & Society, 14*, 529–549. doi:10.1080/13691 18x.2011.562221

Bryant, J. A., & Monge, P. R. (2008). The evolution of the children's television community, 1953–2003. *International Journal of Communication, 2,* 160–192.

Bryant, J. A., Sanders-Jackson, A., & Smallwood, A. M. K. (2006). IMing, text messaging, and adolescent social networks. *Journal of Computer-Mediated Communication, 11,* 577–592.

Burt, R. S. (1982). *Toward a structural theory of action: Network models of social structure, perception, and action.* New York, NY: Academic Press.

Buzzanell, P. M. (1994). Gaining a voice: Feminist organizational communication theorizing. *Management Communication Quarterly, 7,* 339–383. doi:10.1177/0893318994007004001

Caiani, M., & Wagemann, C. (2009). Online networks of the Italian and German extreme right: An explorative study with social network analysis. *Information, Communication & Society, 12,* 66–109. doi:10.1080/13691180802158482

Campbell, S. W., & Kwak, N. (2011). Political involvement in "mobilized" society: The interactive relationships among mobile communication, network characteristics, and political participation. *Journal of Communication, 61,* 984–1004. doi:10.1111/j.1460-2466.2011.01601.x

Carley, K. M., & Kaufer, D. S. (1993). Semantic connectivity: An approach for analyzing symbols in semantic networks. *Communication Theory, 3,* 183–213. doi:10.1111/j.1468-2885.1993.tb00070.x

Castells, M. (1996). *The rise of the network society.* Boston, MA: Blackwell.

Cho, H., & Lee, J. S. (2008). Collaborative information seeking in intercultural computer-mediated communication groups: Testing the influence of social context using social network analysis. *Communication Research, 35,* 548–573. doi:10.1177/0093650208315982

Cho, H. K., Trier, M., & Kim, E. (2005). The use of instant messaging in working relationship development: A case study. *Journal of Computer-Mediated Communication, 10*(4), article 17. Retrieved from http://jcmc.indiana.edu/vol10/issue4/cho.html.

Cho, J. (2005). Media, interpersonal discussion, and electoral choice. *Communication Research, 32,* 295–322. doi:10.1177/0093650205275382

Choi, J. H., & Danowski, J. A. (2002). Making a global community on the Net-global village or global metropolis?: A network analysis of Usenet newsgroups. *Journal of Computer-Mediated Communication, 7*(3). Retrieved from http://jcmc.indiana.edu/vol7/issue3/choi.html

Chon, B. S., Choi, J. H., Barnett, G. A., Danowski, J. A., & Joo, S. H. (2003). A structural analysis of media convergence: Cross-industry mergers and acquisitions in the information industries. *Journal of Media Economics, 16,* 141–157. doi:10.1207/s15327736me1603_1

Chow-White, P. A. (2006). Race, gender and sex on the net: Semantic networks of selling and storytelling sex tourism. *Media Culture & Society, 28,* 883–905. doi:10.1177/0163443706068922

Chung, J. E. (2011). Mapping international film trade: Network analysis of international film trade Between 1996 and 2004. *Journal of Communication, 61,* 618–640. doi:10.1111/j.1460-2466.2011.01567.x

Colon-Ramos, U., Atienza, A. A., Weber, D., Taylor, M., Uy, C., & Yaroch, A. (2009). Practicing what they preach: Health behaviors of those who provide health advice to extensive social networks. *Journal of Health Communication, 14,* 119–130. doi:10.1080/10810730802659111

Contractor, N. (2009). The emergence of multidimensional networks. *Journal of Computer-Mediated Communication, 14*, 743-747. doi:10.1111/j.1083-6101.2009.01465.x

Corman, S. R. (1990). A model of perceived communication in collective networks. *Human Communication Research, 16*, 582–602. doi:10.1111/j.1468-2958.1990. tb00223.x

Danowski, J. A. (1980). Group attitude uniformity and connectivity of organizational communication networks for production, innovation, and maintenance content. *Human Communication Research, 6*, 299–308.

Danowski, J. A. (1988). Organizational infographics and automated auditing: Using computers to unobtrusively gather as well as analyze communication. In G. M. Goldhaber & G. A. Barnett (Eds.), *Hanbook of Organizational Communication* (pp. 385–434). Norwood, NJ: Ablex.

Danowski, J. A. (2008). Short-term and long-term effects of a public relations campaign on semantic networks of newspaper content: Priming or framing? *Public Relations Review, 38*, 288–290.

Danowski, J. A., & Edison-Swift, P. (1985). Crisis effects on intraorganizational computer-based communication. *Communication Research, 12*, 251–270. doi:10.1177/009365085012002005

Doerfel, M. L., & Barnett, G. A. (1999). A semantic network analysis of the International Communication Association. *Human Communication Research, 25*, 589–603. doi:10.1111/j.1468-2958.1999.tb00463.x

Doerfel, M. L. & Connaughton, S. L. (2010). Semantic networks and competition: Election year winners and losers in U. S. televised presidential debates, 1960-2004. *Journal of the American Society for Information Science and Technology, 60*, 201–218. doi:10.1002/asi.20950.

Doerfel, M. L., & Marsh, P. S. (2003). Candidate-issue positioning in the context of presidential debates. *Journal of Applied Communication Research, 31*, 212–237. doi:10.1080/00909880032000103449

Doerfel, M. L., & Taylor, M. (2004). Network dynamics of interorganizational cooperation: The Croatian civil society movement. *Communication Monographs, 71*, 373–394.

Dorsey, A. M., Scherer, C. W., & Real, K. (1999). The college tradition of "drink 'til you drop": The relation between students' social networks and engaging in risky behaviors. *Health Communication, 11*, 313–334. doi:10.1207/s15327027hc1104_1

Eisenberg, E. M., Monge, P. R., & Miller, K. I. (1983). Involvement in communication: Networks as a predictor of organizational commitment. *Human Communication Research, 10*, 179–201. doi:10.1111/j.1468-2958.1983.tb00010.x

Ersig, A. L., Hadley, D. W., & Koehly, L. M. (2011). Understanding patterns of health communication in families at risk for hereditary nonpolyposis colorectal cancer: Examining the effect of conclusive versus indeterminate genetic test results. *Health Communication, 26*, 587–594. doi:10.1080/10410236.2011.558338

Eveland, W. P., Cortese, J., Park, H., & Dunwoody, S. (2004). How Web site organization influences free recall, factual knowledge, and knowledge structure density. *Human Communication Research, 30*, 208-233. doi: 10.1111/j.1468-2958.2004. tb00731.x

Eveland, W. P., & Hively, M. H. (2009). Political discussion frequency, network size, and "heterogeneity" of discussion as predictors of political knowledge and participation. *Journal of Communication, 59*, 205–224. doi: 10.1111/j.1460-2466.2009.01412.x

Farace, R. V., Monge, P. R., & Russell, H. M. (1977). *Communicating and organizing.* Reading, MA: Addision-Wesley.

Faust, K., & Skvoretz, J. (2002). Comparing networks across space and time, size and species. *Sociological Methodology, 32*, 267–299. doi:10.1111/1467-9531.00118

Feeley, T. H. (2000). Testing a communication network model of employee turnover based on centrality. *Journal of Applied Communication Research, 28*, 262–277.

Feeley, T. H. (2008). A bibliometric analysis of communication journals from 2002 to 2005. *Human Communication Research, 34*, 505–520. doi:10.1111/j.1468-2958.2008.00330.x

Feeley, T. H., & Barnett, G. A. (1997). Predicting employee turnover from communication networks.. *Human Communication Research, 23*, 370–387. doi:10.1111/j.1468-2958.1997.tb00401.x

Feeley, T. H., Hwang, J., & Barnett, G. A. (2008). Predicting employee turnover from friendship networks. *Journal of Applied Communication Research, 36*, 56–73.

Fine, M. G. (1981). Soap opera conversations: The talk that binds. *Journal of Communication, 31*, 97–115. doi:10.1111/j.1460-2466.1981.tb00432.x

Fink, E. L., & Chen, S.-S. (1995). A Galileo analysis of organizational climate. *Human Communication Research, 21*, 494–521. doi:10.1111/j.1468-2958.1995.tb00356.x

Gil de Zúñiga, H., & Valenzuela, S. (2011). The mediating path to a stronger citizenship: Online and offline networks, weak ties, and civic engagement. *Communication Research, 38*, 397–421. doi:10.1177/0093650210384984

Gilpin, D. (2010). Organizational image construction in a fragmented online media environment. *Journal of Public Relations Research, 22*, 265–287. doi:10.1080/10627261003614393

Goering, E., & Breidenstein-Cutspec, P. (1989). The web of shyness: A network analysis of communicative correlates. *Communication Research Reports, 6*, 111–118. doi:10.1080/08824098909359843

Granovetter, M. S. (1973). The strength of weak ties. *American Journal of Sociology, 78*, 1360–1380.

Hampton, K. N. (2011). Comparing bonding and bridging ties for democratic engagement: Everyday use of communication technologies within social networks for civic and civil behaviors. *Information, Communication & Society, 14*, 510–528.

Hartman, R. L., & Johnson, J. D. (1989). Social contagion and multiplexity: Communication networks as predictors of commitment and role ambiguity. *Human Communication Research, 15*, 523–548. doi:10.1111/j.1468-2958.1989.tb00198.x

Haythornthwaite, C. (2003). Supporting distributed relationships: Relationship development and media use in two classes of internet-based learners. *Electronic Journal of Communication, 13*(1). Retrieved from http://www.cios.org/EJCPUBLIC/013/1/01313.HTML

Haythornthwaite, C. (2005). Social networks and Internet connectivity effects. *Information, Communication & Society, 8*, 125–147.

Heider, F. (1958). *The psychology of interpersonal relations*. New York, NY: Wiley.

Himelboim, I. (2008). Reply distribution in online discussions: A comparative network analysis of political and health newsgroups. *Journal of Computer-Mediated Communication, 14*, 156–177. doi:10.1111/j.1083-6101.2008.01435.x

Himelboim, I., Chang, T.-K., & McCreery, S. (2010). International network of foreign news coverage: Old global hierarchies in a new online world. *Journalism & Mass Communication Quarterly, 87*, 297–314.

Holland, P. W., & Leinhardt, S. (1972). Some evidence on the transitivity of positive interpersonal sentiment. *American Journal of Sociology, 72*, 1205–1209.

Huffaker, D. (2010). Dimensions of leadership and social influence in online communities. *Human Communication Research, 36,* 593–617. doi:10.1111/j.1468-2958.2010.01390.x

Hurt, H. T., & Preiss, R. (1978). Silence isn't necessarily golden: Communication apprehension, desired social choice, and academic success among middle-school students. *Human Communication Research, 4,* 315–328.

Igarashi, T., Takai, J., & Yoshida, T. (2005). Gender differences in social network development via mobile phone text messages: A longitudinal study. *Journal of Social and Personal Relationships, 22,* 691–713. doi:10.1177/0265407505056492

Ikeda, K. i., & Boase, J. (2011). Multiple discussion networks and their consequence for political participation. *Communication Research, 38,* 660–683. doi:10.1177/0093650210395063

Ishii, K. (2006). Implications of mobility: The uses of personal communication media in everyday life. *Journal of Communication, 56,* 346–365. doi:10.1111/j.1460-2466.2006.00023.x

Johnson, J. A. (2011). Mapping the feminist political economy of the online commercial pornography industry: A network approach. *International Journal of Media and Cultural Politics, 7,* 189–208.

Kang, N. W., & Choi, J. H. (1999). Structural implications of the crossposting network of international news in cyberspace. *Communication Research, 26,* 454–481. doi:10.1177/009365099026004005

Kim, H., Kim, G. J., Park, H. W., & Rice, R. E. (2007). Configurations of relationships in different media: FtF, email, instant messenger, mobile phone, and SMS. *Journal of Computer-Mediated Communication, 12,* 1183–1207. doi:10.1111/j.1083-6101.2007.00369.x

Kim, J. H., Su, T.-Y., & Hong, J. (2007). The influence of geopolitics and foreign policy on the US and Canadian media: An analysis of newspaper coverage of Sudan's Darfur conflict. *Harvard International Journal of Press-Politics, 12,* 87–95. doi:10.1177/1081180x07302972

Kim, K., & Barnett, G. A. (1996). The determinants of international news flow: A network analysis. *Communication Research, 23,* 323–352. doi:10.1177/009365096023003004

Kropczynski, J., & Nah, S. (2011). Virtually networked housing movement: Hyperlink network structure of housing social movement organizations. *New Media & Society, 13,* 689–703. doi:10.1177/1461444810372786

Ksiazek, T. B. (2011). A network analytic approach to understanding cross-platform audience behavior. *Journal of Media Economics, 24,* 237–251. doi:10.1080/08997 764.2011.626985

Kuhn, T., & Nelson, N. (2002). Reengineering identity. *Management Communication Quarterly, 16,* 5–38. doi:10.1177/0893318902161001

Kwon, K., Barnett, G. A., & Chen, H. (2009). Assessing cultural differences in translations: A semantic network analysis of the universal declaration of human rights. *Journal of International and Intercultural Communications, 2,* 107–138.

Lee, S., & Monge, P. R. (2011). The coevolution of multiplex communication networks in organizational communities. *Journal of Communication, 61,* 758–779. doi:10.1111/j.1460-2466.2011.01566.x

Lee, S., Monge, P. R., Bar, F., & Matei, S. A. (2007). The emergence of clusters in the global telecommunications network. *Journal of Communication, 57,* 415–434.

Leonardi, P. M. (2009). Why do people reject new technologies and stymie organizational changes of which they are in favor?: Exploring misalignments between social interactions and materiality. *Human Communication Research, 35,* 407–441.

Leskovec, J., Kleinberg, J., & Faloutsos, C. (2007). Graph evolution: Densification and shrinking diameters. *ACM Transactions on Knowledge Discovery from Data, 1*, 1–41.

Lewis, K., Kaufman, J., & Christakis, N. (2008). The taste for privacy: An analysis of college student privacy settings in an online social network. *Journal of Computer-Mediated Communication, 14*, 79–100. doi:10.1111/j.1083-6101.2008.01432.x

Livingstone, S. M. (1987). The implicit representation of characters in Dallas: A multidimensional-scaling approach. *Human Communication Research, 13*, 399–420. doi:10.1111/j.1468-2958.1987.tb00112.x

MacDonald, D. (1976). Communication roles and communication networks in a formal organization. *Human Communication Research, 2*, 365–375.

Magdol, L. (2000). The people you know: The impact of residential mobility on mothers' social network ties. *Journal of Social and Personal Relationships, 17*, 183–204. doi:10.1177/0265407500172002

Marin, A., & Wellman, B. (2011). Social network analysis: An introduction. In P. Carrington & J. Scott (Eds.), *The SAGE handbook of social network analysis* (pp. 11–25). Thousand Oaks, CA: Sage.

Maynard, M. L. (1997). Opportunity in paid vs. unpaid public relations internships: A semantic network analysis. *Public Relations Review, 23*, 377–390. doi:10.1016/s0363-8111(97)90052-7

Mohammed, S. (2001). Personal communication networks and the effects of an entertainment-education radio soap opera in Tanzania. *Journal of Health Communication, 6*, 137–154. doi:10.1080/108107301750254475

Monge, P. R., & Contractor, N. (2001). Emergence of communication networks. In F. M. Jablin & L. Putnam (Eds.), *New handbook of organizational communication* (pp. 440–502). Newbury Park, CA: Sage.

Monge, P. R., & Contractor, N. (2003). *Theories of communication networks.* New York, NY: Oxford University Press.

Monge, P. R., & Eisenberg, E. M. (1987). Emergent communication networks. In F. M. Jablin, L. L. Putnam, K. H. Roberts, & L. W. Porter (Eds.), *Handbook of organizational communication: An interdisciplinary perspective* (pp. 304–342). Newbury Park, CA: Sage.

Monge, P. R., Farace, R. V., Eisenberg, E. M., Miller, K. I., & White, L. L. (1984). The process of studying process in organizational communication. *Journal of Communication, 34*, 22–43. doi:10.1111/j.1460-2466.1984.tb02983.x

Monge, P. R., Heiss, B. M., & Margolin, D. (2008). Communication network evolution in organizational communities. *Communication Theory, 18*, 449-477. doi:10.1111/j.1468–2885.2008.00330.x

Monge, P. R., & Matei, S. A. (2004). The role of the global telecommunications network in bridging economic and political divides, 1989 to 1999. *Journal of Communication, 54*, 511–531.

Moon, S.-I., Barnett, G. A., & Lim, Y. S. (2010). The structure of international music flows using network analysis. *New Media & Society, 12*, 379–399. doi:10.1177/1461444809346720

Mueller, M. L., Kuerbis, B. N., & Pagé, C. (2007). Democratizing global communication? Global civil society and the campaign for communication rights in the information society. *International Journal of Communication, 1*, 267–296.

Murphy, P. (2001). Framing the nicotine debate: A cultural approach to risk. *Health Communication, 13*, 119–140. doi:10.1207/s15327027hc1302_1

Murphy, P. (2010). The intractability of reputation: Media coverage as a complex system in the case of Martha Stewart. *Journal of Public Relations Research, 22*, 209–237. doi:10.1080/10627261003601648

Murphy, P., & Maynard, M. (2000). Framing the genetic testing issue: Discourse and cultural clashes among policy communities. *Science Communication, 22*, 133–153. doi:10.1177/1075547000022002002

Neal, J. W. (2010). Hanging out: Features of urban children's peer social networks. *Journal of Social and Personal Relationships, 27*, 982–1000. doi 10.1177/0265407510378124

Nonaka, A. M. (2009). Estimating size, scope, and membership of the speech/sign communities of undocumented indigenous/village sign languages: The Ban Khor case study. *Language & Communication, 29*, 210–229. doi:10.1016/j.langcom.2009.02.004

Palazzolo, E. T. (2005). Organizing for information retrieval in transactive memory systems. *Communication Research, 32*, 726–761.

Palazzolo, E. T., Serb, D. A., She, Y., Su, C., & Contractor, N. S. (2006). Coevolution of communication and knowledge networks in transactive memory systems: Using computational models for theoretical development. *Communication Theory, 16*, 223–250.

Paollio, J. (1999). The virtual speech community: Social network and language variation on IRC. *Journal of Computer-Mediated Communication, 4*(4). Retrieved from http://jcmc.indiana.edu/vol4/issue4/paolillo.html

Papa, M. J. (1990). Communication network patterns and employee performance with new technology. *Communication Research, 17*, 344–368. doi:10.1177/009365090017003004

Park, H. W. (2010). Mapping the e-science landscape in South Korea using the webometrics method. *Journal of Computer-Mediated Communication, 15*, 211–229. doi:10.1111/j.1083-6101.2010.01517.x

Park, H. W., & Jankowski, N. W. (2008). A hyperlink network analysis of citizen blogs in South Korean politics. *Javnost-The Public, 15*, 57–74.

Park, H. W., & Thelwall, M. (2006). Web-science communication in the age of globalization. *New Media & Society, 8*, 629–650. doi:10.1177/1461444806065660

Park, H. W., & Thelwall, M. (2008). Developing network indicators for ideological landscapes from the political blogosphere in South Korea. *Journal of Computer-Mediated Communication, 13*, 856–879. doi:10.1111/j.1083-6101.2008.00422.x

Parks, M. R. (1977). Anomia and close friendship communication networks. *Human Communication Research, 4*, 48–57.

Parks, M. R., & Adelman, M. B. (1983). Communication networks and the development of romantic relationships: An expansion of uncertainty reduction theory. *Human Communication Research, 10*, 55–79. doi:10.1111/j.1468-2958.1983.tb00004.x

Pollock, T. C., Whitbred, R. C., & Contractor, N. (2000). Social information processing and job characteristics: A simultaneous test of two theories with implications for job satisfaction. *Human Communication Research, 26*, 292–310.

Poole, M. S. (2007). Generalization in process theories of communication. *Communication Methods and Measures, 1*, 1–10.

Postmes, T., Spears, R., & Lea, M. (2000). The formation of group norms in computer-mediated communication. *Human Communication Research, 26*, 341–371. doi:10.1111/j.1468-2958.2000.tb00761.x

Prell, C. L. (2003). Community networking and social capital: Early investigations.

Journal of Computer-Mediated Communication, 8(3). Retrieved from http://jcmc.indiana.edu/vol8/issue3/prell.html

Raile, A. N. W., Kim, R. K., Choi, J., Serota, K. B., Park, H. S., & Lee, D. W. (2008). Connections at work: How friendship networks relate to job satisfaction. *Communication Research Reports, 25,* 168–178.

Reese, S. D., Grant, A., & Danielian, L. H. (1994). The structure of new sources on television: A network analysis of CBS-News, Nightline, MacNeil/Lehrer, and This-Week-With-David-Brinkley. *Journal of Communication, 44,* 84–107. doi:10.1111/j.1460-2466.1994.tb00678.x

Reese, S. D., Rutigliano, L., Hyun, K., & Jeong, J. (2007). Mapping the blogosphere: Professional and citizen-based media in the global news arena. *Journalism, 8,* 235–261. doi:10.1177/1464884907076459

Reeves, B., & Borgman, C. L. (1983). A bibliometric evaluation of core journals in communication research. *Human Communication Research, 10,* 119–136. doi:10.1111/j.1468-2958.1983.tb00007.x

Rice, R. E. (1993). Media appropriateness: Using social presence theory to compare traditional and new organizational media. *Human Communication Research, 19,* 451–484.

Rice, R. E., Borgman, C. L., & Reeves, B. (1988). Citation networks of communication journals, 1977–1985: Cliques and positions, citations made and citations received. *Human Communication Research, 15,* 256–283. doi: 10.1111/j.1468-2958.1988.tb00184.x

Rice, R. E., & Danowski, J. A. (1993). Is it really just like a fancy answering machine? comparing semantic networks of different types of voice mail users. *Journal of Business Communication, 30,* 369–397.

Rice, R. E., & Love, G. (1987). Electronic emotion: Socioemotional content in a computer-mediated communication network. *Communication Research, 14,* 85–108. doi:10.1177/009365087014001005

Roberts, K. H., & O'Reilly, C. (1978). Organizations as communication structures: An empirical approach. *Human Communication Research, 4,* 283–293.

Rogers, E. M., & Antola, L. (1985). Telenovelas: A Latin American success story. *Journal of Communication, 35,* 24–35. doi:10.1111/j.1460-2466.1985.tb02970.x

Rogers, E. M., & Kincaid, D. L. (1981). *Communication networks: Toward a new paradigm for research.* New York, NY: Free Press.

Rojas, H., Shah, D. V., & Friedland, L. A. (2011). A communicative approach to social capital. *Journal of Communication, 61,* 689–712. doi:10.1111/j.1460-2466.2011.01571.x

Russo, T. C., & Koesten, J. (2005). Prestige, centrality, and learning: A social network analysis of an online class. *Communication Education, 54,* 254–261.

Sanders, K., & Nauta, A. (2004). Social cohesiveness and absenteeism: The relationship between characteristics of employees and short-term absenteeism within an organization. *Small Group Research, 35,* 724–741. doi:10.1177/1046496404267186

Schmitz, J., & Fulk, J. (1991). Organizational colleagues, media richness, and electronic mail: A test of the social influence model of technology use. *Communication Research, 18,* 487–523.

Shumate, M., & Contractor, N. (2014). Organizational communication and social networks. In L. Putnam & D. K. Mumby (Eds.), *Sage handbook of organizational communication* (3rd ed.). Thousand Oaks, CA: Sage.

Shumate, M., & Dewitt, L. (2008). The North/South divide in NGO hyperlink networks. *Journal of Computer-Mediated Communication, 13,* 405–428. doi:10.1111/j.1083-6101.2008.00402.x

Shumate, M., Fulk, J., & Monge, P. R. (2005). Predictors of the international HIV/AIDS INGO network over time. *Human Communication Research, 31*, 482–510. doi:10.1111/j.1468-2958.2005.tb00880.x

Shumate, M., & Lipp, J. (2008). Connective collective action online: An examination of the hyperlink network structure of an NGO issue network. *Journal of Computer-Mediated Communication, 14*, 178–201. doi:10.1111/j.1083-6101.2008.01436.x

Shumate, M., & O'Connor, A. (2010). Corporate reporting of cross-sector alliances: The portfolio of NGO partners communicated on corporate websites. *Communication Monographs, 77*, 238–261. doi:10.1080/03637751003758201

Sinnreich, A., Chib, A., & Gilbert, J. (2008). Modeling information equality: Social and media latency effects on information diffusion. *International Journal of Communication, 2*, 132–159.

Smith, R. A., & Fink, E. L. (2010). Compliance dynamics within a simulated friendship network I: The effects of agency, tactic, and node centrality. *Human Communication Research, 36*, 232–260. doi:10.1111/j.1468-2958.2010.01375.x

So, C. Y. K. (1988). Citation patterns of core communication journals: An assessment of the developmental status of communication. *Human Communication Research, 15*, 236–255. doi:10.1111/j.1468-2958.1988.tb00183.x

Sohn, D. (2009). Disentangling the effects of social network density on electronic word-of-mouth (eWOM) Intention. *Journal of Computer-Mediated Communication, 14*, 352–367. doi:10.1111/j.1083-6101.2009.01444.x

Stohl, C. (1993). European managers' interpretations of participation: "A semantic network analysis". *Human Communication Research, 20*, 97–117.

Susskind, A. M. (2007). Downsizing survivors' communication networks and reactions: A longitudinal examination of information flow and turnover intentions. *Communication Research, 34*, 156–184. doi:10.1177/0093650206298068

Sykes, R. E. (1983). Initial interaction between strangers and acquaintances: A multivariate analysis of factors affecting choice of communication partners. *Human Communication Research, 10*, 27–53. doi:10.1111/j.1468-2958.1983.tb00003.x

Tai, Z. (2009). The structure of knowledge and dynamics of scholarly communication in agenda setting research, 1996-2005. *Journal of Communication, 59*, 481–513. doi:10.1111/j.1460-2466.2009.01425.x

Tardy, R. W., & Hale, C. L. (1998). Getting "plugged in": A network analysis of health-information seeking among "stay-at-home moms". *Communication Monographs, 65*, 336–357.

Tateo, L. (2005). The Italian extreme right on-line network: An exploratory study using an integrated social network analysis and content analysis approach. *Journal of Computer-Mediated Communication, 10*(2), article 10. Retrieved from http://jcmc.indiana.edu/vol10/issue2/tateo.html

Taylor-Clark, K. A., Viswanath, K., & Blendon, R. J. (2010). Communication inequalities during public health disasters: Katrina's wake. *Health Communication, 25*, 221–229. doi:10.1080/10410231003698895

Taylor, M., & Doerfel, M. L. (2003). Building interorganizational relationships that build nations. *Human Communication Research, 29*, 153–181.

Terhell, E. L., van Groenou, M. I. B., & van Tilburg, T. (2004). Network dynamics in the long-term period after divorce. *Journal of Social and Personal Relationships, 21*, 719–738. doi:10.1177/0265407504047833

Tremayne, M., Zheng, N., Lee, J. K., & Jeong, J. (2006). Issue publics on the web: Applying network theory to the war blogosphere. *Journal of Computer-Mediated Communication, 12*, 290–310. doi:10.1111/j.1083-6101.2006.00326.x

Turner, J. C. (1987). *Rediscovering the social group: A self-categorization theory.* Oxford, England: Blackwell.

Vergeer, M., & Pelzer, B. (2009). Consequences of media and Internet use for offline and online network capital and well-being. A causal model approach. *Journal of Computer-Mediated Communication, 15*, 189–210. doi:10.1111/j.1083-6101.2009.01499.x

Wakabayashi, N., Yamashita, M., & Yamada, J. (2009). Japanese networks for top-performing films: Repeated teams preserve uniqueness. *Journal of Media Business Studies, 6*(4), 31–48.

Weber, M. S., & Monge, P. R. (2011). The flow of digital news in a network of sources, authorities, and hubs. *Journal of Communication, 61*, 1062–1081. doi:10.1111/j.1460-2466.2011.01596.x

Whitbred, R., Fonti, F., Steglich, C., & Contractor, N. (2011). From microactions to macrostructure and back: A structurational approach to the evolution of organizational networks. *Human Communication Research, 37.* doi:10.1111/j.1468-2958.2011.01404.x

Widmer, E. D. (2006). Who are my family members? Bridging and binding social capital in family configurations. *Journal of Social and Personal Relationships, 23*, 979–998. doi:10.1177/0265407506070482

Wing, P., & More, E. (2005). Understanding business-transformation success: A new communication-centric model. *Australian Journal of Communication, 32*, 13–31.

Xia, L., Yuan, Y. C., & Gay, G. (2009). Exploring negative group dynamics: Adversarial network, personality, and performance in project groups. *Management Communication Quarterly, 23*, 32–62. doi:10.1177/0893318909335416

Yuan, E. J., & Ksiazek, T. B. (2011). The duality of structure in China's national television market: A network analysis of audience behavior. *Journal of Broadcasting & Electronic Media, 55*, 180–197. doi:10.1080/08838151.2011.570825

Yuan, Y. C., Cosley, D., Welser, H. T., Ling, X., & Gay, G. (2009). The diffusion of a task recommendation system to facilitate contributions to an online community. *Journal of Computer-Mediated Communication, 15*, 32–59. doi:10.1111/j.1083-6101.2009.01491.x

Yuan, Y. C., Fulk, J., Monge, P. R., & Contractor, N. (2010). Expertise directory development, shared task interdependence, and strength of communication network ties as multilevel predictors of expertise exchange in transactive memory work groups. *Communication Research, 37*, 20–47. doi:10.1177/009365020351469

Yuan, Y. C., Fulk, J., Shumate, M., Monge, P. R., Matsaganis, M., & Bryant, J. A. (2005). Individual participation in organizational information commons: The impact of team level social influence and technology-specific competence. *Human Communication Research, 31*, 212–240.

Yuan, Y. C., & Gay, G. (2006). Homophily of network ties and bonding and bridging social capital in computer-mediated distributed teams. *Journal of Computer-Mediated Communication, 11*, 1062–1084. doi:10.1111/j.1083-6101.2006.00308.x

Yum, J. O. (1982). Communication diversity and information acquisition among Korean immigrants in Hawaii. *Human Communication Research, 8*, 154–169. doi:10.1111/j.1468-2958.1982.tb00662.x

Zywica, J., & Danowski, J. A. (2008). The faces of Facebookers: Investigating social enhancement and social compensation hypotheses; Predicting Facebook™ and offline popularity from sociability and self-esteem, and mapping the meanings of popularity with semantic networks. *Journal of Computer-Mediated Communication, 14*, 1–34. doi:10.1111/j.1083-6101.2008.01429

CHAPTER CONTENTS

5 Conceptualizing Online Discussion Value

A Multidimensional Framework for Analyzing User Comments on Mass-Media Websites

Marc Ziegele and Oliver Quiring

Johannes Gutenberg-University of Mainz

This chapter provides a micro-framework for analyzing the quantity and quality of online user comments on mass-media websites. On one dimension, news factors of news items and discussion factors of existing user comments are assumed to indicate the relevance of participating in online discussions. On a second dimension, specific motivational, social, and design factors are influential when reconstructing users' decisions to participate in online discussions and when analyzing the content of online user comments. The two dimensions in combination describe the discussion value of news items. Potential applications of this framework on other forms of interpersonal communication are discussed.

Much has changed since the advent of writing letters to the editor of a newspaper over 200 years ago (Nielsen, 2010). Today, many news-media organizations allow their users to publish online comments in the immediate context of the related news items, and audiences take advantage of this feature (Reich, 2011; Singer, 2009). In addition to providing journalists with direct and potentially real-time feedback, the user comments indicate interest in an article, constitute unique discussion chains within their environment, and potentially reach large audiences (Daughtery, Eastin, & Bright, 2008; Lee & Jang, 2010; Singer, 2009). Moreover, both offline and online, the social, political, and journalistic relevance of media users talking about and discussing the news is widely acknowledged (e.g., Graham & Witschge, 2003; Scheufele, 2000; Walsh, 2004).

When Internet users comment on and discuss the news online, the interpersonal communication and mass communication processes become structurally integrated. Leung (2009) describes this situation as a power shift in the relationship between media companies and their users, in that publicly accessible user postings in the immediate context of mass-media content provide an "independent voice to viewpoints previously disenfranchised by the corporate media" (p. 1328). These independent voices can affect how a large proportion of both the (inter)active and the inactive audience perceive and use mass-media content (Daughtery et al., 2008; Lee & Jang, 2010; Walther, DeAndrea, Kim, & Anthony, 2010).

However, little is known about how, why, and under what conditions users comment on news items online and about how these activities can be scientifically described (Reich, 2011; Southwell & Yzer, 2009). Anecdotal observations suggest that both the quantity and the quality of online user comments vary between and within news websites. Even on the same website, an online discussion about a particular political news story can be polite and well-grounded, while another story on the same issue might be discussed in a heated and emotional manner (Tsagkias, Weerkamp, & de Rijke, 2009). These observations raise the question of whether the news items and/or the user comments can have specific characteristics that stimulate or inhibit further discussion. In addition, these message-inherent characteristics are likely to interact with the users' individual motives and their perception of the computer-mediated communication settings. However, most current research concentrates on analyzing either the users' motives for publishing content on different Internet communication platforms (e.g., Guadagno, Okdie, & Eno, 2008; Leung, 2009) or on the specific characteristics of the messages that users remember better than others (e.g., Eilders, 2006). To our knowledge, no scholarly work has attempted to interpret the quantities and qualities of online user discussions of different news items as a product of the message-inherent characteristics, the users' personal involvement and the particular design factors of online discussion spaces. This chapter aims to provide this type of multidimensional theoretical micro-framework for the case of online user comments on news items.

In the first part of the chapter, we review the previous research about media users' discussions of the news and/or public affairs offline and online. We then suggest the term *media-stimulated interpersonal communication* (MSIC) to describe the basic social activity behind the offline and the online discussions about mass-media content and to overcome the still existing dichotomy between offline and online communication. We continue by defining online user comments on mass-media websites as a particular, yet representative subcategory of MSIC, and we discuss their social, political and journalistic relevance.

In the second part, we delineate and discuss the message-inherent, motivational, social, and design factors that might account for the different quantities and qualities of online user comments. Finally, we integrate our arguments into a multidimensional micro-framework of the discussion value of online news items and discuss its adequacy for analyzing other forms of offline and online MSIC.

Conversations and Discussions about Mass-Media Content

Past and Current Research

Interpersonal communication about mass-media content is a permanent part of peoples' everyday social interactions (e.g., Katz & Lazarsfeld, 1955;

Lazarsfeld, Berelson, & Gaudet, 1944; Price & Roberts, 1987; Wyatt, Katz, & Kim, 2000). As early as the late 19th century, French sociologist Gabriel Tarde theorized about citizens discussing topics from the news media (Tarde, 1901/1910). Kim, Wyatt, and Katz (1999) summarize Tarde's idea of "the news media as the universal trigger of conversation providing the public with conversational topics of the day" (p. 364).

More than a century later, the functions and effects of interpersonal communications about mass-media content have been analyzed in a variety of contexts. With regard to the functions, it has been stated that individuals introduce topics from the mass media as common topics for discussion and that they use arguments from the mass media to persuade others and to support their own points of view (Berelson, 1949; Greenberg, 1964). As to the effects, interpersonal communication about mass-media content has been found to assist media users to better understand what they have heard or seen (de Boer & Velthuijsen, 2001; Hardy & Scheufele, 2005). This interpersonal communication can also increase the reach of the mass-media messages (Rogers, 2000). On a more general level, interpersonal communication about mass-media content is an important aspect in theories and concepts such as the two-step flow of communication, news diffusion research, the uses-and-gratifications approach and agenda-setting (Lazarsfeld et al., 1944; Deutschmann & Danielson, 1960; Katz & Gurevitch, 1976; McCombs & Shaw, 1972).

In the field of political communication, analyses of how people talk about and discuss politics and public affairs have received a great deal of attention because these conversations and discussions are perceived to be crucial to effective democracies (Eveland, Morey, & Hutchens, 2011). As "[t]he world that we have to deal with politically is out of reach [...]" (Lippmann, 1922, p. 7), the conversations and discussions between citizens about public affairs often rest upon stories and reports from the mass media. With regard to the quality of political talk, some authors have argued that political conversations and discussions are of democratic value only if they proceed as a critical civic discourse that is strictly organized, discursive and appears apart from informal conversations (e.g., Eliasoph, 1998; Schudson, 1997; Scheufele, 2000). However, others emphasize the positive political consequences of informal talks and discussions about public affairs, for example, with regard to opinion quality, political understanding, efficacy, and participation (e.g., Eveland, 2004; Kim et al., 1999; Wyatt et al., 2000). This perspective considers that people often do not discuss political issues apart from other activities (Wyatt et al., 2000).

While political communication research intensely debates the normative aspects of interpersonal conversations about public affairs, the influence of specific mass-media content on the processes and effects of interpersonal conversations and discussions has only been infrequently analyzed. Qualitative research has primarily investigated the mechanisms of interpersonal discussions about public affairs. Gamson (1992) and Walsh (2004), for example, emphasize the complexity of these discussions: people do not only discuss facts and statements from the news media, but they also transform issues by integrating their own experience and by "applying their identity-based perspectives to supplement the information provided by the news stories" (Walsh, 2004, p. 16). Quantitative research, in contrast, focuses on describing the more general links between media consumption on the one hand and the frequency of discussions about public affairs on the other hand. For example, Kim et al. (1999) and Scheufele (2000) show significant positive correlations between the frequency of newspaper reading and the frequency of political talk. In addition, Kim et al. (1999) report significant positive correlations between the frequency of newspaper reading and measures of opinion quality as defined by, for example, the respondents' ability to express an opinion regarding given public issues or their ability to consider both sides of these issues. In this context, it can be assumed that newspaper reading also has an effect on the media consumer's opinion quality in news discussions. However, it should be considered that social dynamics can reduce the individual's willingness to engage in discussions. Among these social dynamics are politeness, group pressure, and the feeling of embarrassment (Brown & Levinson, 1987; Eliasoph, 1998; Goffman, 1959; Mutz, 2002; Walsh, 2004).

People do not confine themselves to discussing the news and/or public affairs offline. With the advent of the social web, interpersonal communication about mass-media content has increasingly emerged in public or semipublic spheres: among other venues, this communication takes place on blogs (Wallsten, 2007), in the comments sections of news websites (Lee & Jang, 2010; Ruiz et al., 2011; Singer, 2009), on Twitter and YouTube (Kwak, Lee, Park, & Moon, 2010; Walther et al., 2010), in political discussion groups (Price, 2009; Stromer-Galley, 2002; Wojcieszak & Mutz, 2009), and on a variety of other social network sites (SNSs; Glynn, Huge, & Hoffman, 2012). "These conversations—easily observable, readily joinable for anyone interested in doing so —offer researchers an intriguing opportunity to watch unstructured [...] conversations to see who participates [and] what the content of the conversation consists of [...]" (Stromer-Galley, 2002, p. 24).

Along with this optimistic view on online discussions, many scholars expected the Internet to serve as some type of an ideal public sphere for deliberation (Papacharissi, 2002; Price, 2009). Other scholars doubt this perspective and criticize online discussions for being impersonal, uncivil, and superficial (Davis & Owen, 1998; Sunstein, 2002). A third perspective argues that it is not the Internet per se that accounts for the discussion quality; rather, the design and usability of the online communication services are held to be responsible for the different discussion qualities within the respective spaces (e.g., Wright & Street, 2007).

The debate on online deliberation has generated a considerable amount of research that has investigated the characteristics of people discussing public issues in different online spaces, their aims, the contents of these discussions and the effects on subsequent behavior (e.g., Baek, Wojcieszak, & Delli

Carpini, 2012; Price, 2009; Price, Nir, & Cappella, 2005). We will revisit some of this research in a later chapter. With regard to particular news items as antecedents of online discussions, however, little research has been conducted. For the case of synchronous chat communication, Stromer-Galley and Martinson (2009) find that the chat topic (e.g., politics, auto racing) influence the degree of topic relevance and coherence in the subsequent user discussions. A study by Price et al. (2005) reports interaction effects between the discussion group type (i.e., conservative, moderate and liberal) and the moderator's framing of the discussion on the number of arguments and valenced statements in user postings. These frames, although introduced by a moderator, can also be interpreted in terms of a standardized media input. Again, such findings show that neither the message-centered aspects (e.g., interpretation frames) nor the social or ideological orientations of the group members alone can comprehensively explain the quality of the online discussions.

User conversations and discussions about mass-media content have also been analyzed in light of a potential democratization of online journalism. With the Internet reducing the barriers for user participation, there has been speculation about a radical change in the (professional) public sphere (Bowman & Willis, 2003; Glasser, 1999). It was thought that citizens would obtain a prominent role in the production process of professional news and that the communication paradigm of journalists would evolve into a dialogue with participating users (cf., Bakker & Schoenbach, 2011; Singer et al., 2011). However, despite manifold theoretical arguments and empirical analyses of the diverse forms of participatory journalism, this potential does not appear to be entirely realistic. For example, journalists remain skeptical about the potential of public user participation (Reich, 2011; Thurman, 2008), and it appears that only a minority of online users participate regularly (Ruiz et al., 2011; Singer et al., 2011).

Looking back on the previous sections, we can again conclude that users' offline and online conversations and discussions about mass-media content, public affairs, and/or politics are interdisciplinary and important objects of study. Both informal conversations and deliberative talks about public affairs can be meaningful from a social, political, and journalistic perspective. Scholars have only infrequently analyzed the antecedents of these conversations and discussions, the discussion processes per se and their effects, but these analyses have occurred in a wide variety of theoretical and methodological contexts. However, there is still much that we do not know about these communicative practices. In the following sections, we will therefore (a) suggest a new term that covers different forms of offline and online user conversations about mass-media content and (b) explicate the need for research on what makes news worth discussing. In this context, we describe why we believe that online user comments on mass-media websites are suitable for use in developing a systematic research framework to analyze the discussion value of online news items.

Terminology: Media-Stimulated Interpersonal Communication

As noted above, there is no comprehensive term that covers both offline and online conversations and discussions about mass-media content. In the offline context, these conversations and discussions have been labeled *interpersonal communication about topics in the news* (Lazarsfeld et al., 1944), *conversations about public affairs* (Beinstein, 1975), or *conversations about the news* (de Boer & Velthuijsen, 2001), for example. In reference specifically to online environments, the conversations and discussions about mass-media content have often been described as *user-generated content* (UGC) (Daughtery et al., 2008; Reich, 2011; Ruiz et al., 2011; Thurman, 2008). Other terms that have been suggested are *human interactions* (Stromer-Galley, 2000) or *user-to-user interactivity* (e.g., McMillan, 2002). However, we do not see the rationale in preserving those various terms to describe media users' offline and online discussions about mass-media content. Rather, we suggest using one common umbrella term that considers the common social activity behind the different communication contexts (offline and online). Additionally, terms such as *UGC* are more generic and encompass online user actions that are not necessarily stimulated by the mass-media content. For example, UGC has been used to describe customer reviews on e-commerce websites (Schweiger & Quiring, 2005) and Wikipedia articles (Vickery & Wunsch-Vincent, 2007).

We therefore suggest the term *media-stimulated interpersonal communication* (MSIC; Rogers, 2000) to describe offline and online conversations and discussions about mass-media content for two reasons. First, these types of communication should be labeled *interpersonal* communication to emphasize their social and potentially interactive character (for discussions of the characteristics of interpersonal communication, see, e.g., Reardon & Rogers, 1988; Southwell & Yzer, 2007). Second, the aforementioned manifestations of both offline and online communication are media-stimulated in that any type of mass-media content can serve as their inspiration and their primary subject. If we used terms such as *UGC* or user-to-user interactivity, we would neglect this particular characteristic. However, media-stimulated does not mean that the mass-media content is necessarily the exclusive subject of the subsequent interpersonal communication. During discussions, topic shifts are likely to occur that can lead the discussants away from the original news item's content (e.g., Schank, 1977). However, as long as there is an identifiable reference to the original mass-media content, we define the interpersonal communication as media-stimulated. In other words, any discussion can be conceptualized as MSIC as long as the communication was initiated by a particular mass-media stimulus and as long as a neutral observer can identify the mass-media stimulus in the conversation or discussion.

Online User Comments as Media-Stimulated Interpersonal Communication

Earlier in this chapter, we argued that we do not yet have a comprehensive understanding of what constitutes the discussion value of a news item. Are there specific aspects of news items that are more likely to be picked up in discussions than others? Under what conditions will apolitical news become political in MSIC? To what extent do different news items provoke different content, tones or direction for discussions? Under what conditions will these discussions digress from the original topic of a news item and when will they stay close to it? Last, how are these aspects connected with any motivational factors on the individual level?

In the following, we will investigate some of these questions in the case of online user comments on mass-media websites. Our main arguments for investigating online user comments are their spatial proximity to mass-media stimuli, their particular functions, their popularity, and their thematic diversity.

We define an online user comment as a computer-mediated, written, public, and asynchronous subcategory of MSIC that is published in the immediate context of a news item on the websites of mass-media organizations (such as NYtimes.com) or on their respective presences within other online communication services (such as facebook.com/NYtimes). A sequence of online user comments in the immediate context of a particular news item is defined as an online discussion. In this context, the indicators for the discussion value of an online news item are the number of user comments (quantitative criterion) and their attributes (qualitative criterion, for example, the number of realized interactions between the user comments).

Per this definition, it should become clear that the online user comments and the interactions between them complement the mass-media content. Thereby, they shape the professionally constructed public spheres with (inter) personal contributions (e.g., De Keyser & Raeymaeckers, 2011; Reich, 2011). There are manifold strategies that news-media organizations apply to integrate user comments into their platforms and into their daily routines (e.g., Domingo, 2008; Hermida & Thurman, 2008; Reich, 2011; Singer & Ashman, 2009; Thurman, 2008). Journalists can, for example, control user comments before or after their publication. In addition, users are sometimes required to register before being able to publish comments.

Although statistical data are still rare, commenting on news items and reading other users' online comments are by no means marginal phenomena; according to a recent study by Purcell, Rainie, Mitchell, Rosenstiel, and Olmstead (2010), 25% of adult U.S. Internet users have commented on online news or blogs. More specifically, 37% of online news users perceive that the opportunity to comment on the stories is important. For the Netherlands, Bakker and Schoenbach (2011) show that 36% of the Dutch population aged 13 years and older read online user comments at least once a month. During an equal time span, however, only approximately 11% of the population actively participates by publishing their own comments. For South Korea, Lee and Jang (2010) report that 84% of the Internet news users read other users' online comments at least once a week. Reich (2011), although arguing that only a minority of online users write and read user comments, acknowledges their "great popularity" (Reich, 2011, p. 9).

These studies certainly do not provide a complete picture. Nevertheless, we can conclude that even if there are relatively few participating users, a considerable audience reads their contributions. Do other online discussion spaces, such as political forums or chats that are not associated with news-media organizations, attract equally large audiences? According to recent analyses, these discussion spaces reach participation rates between 6% and 11% of U.S. Internet users (Smith, 2011; Pew Research Center, 2005; Wojcieszak & Mutz, 2009). Data on passive usage (i.e., users observing the conversations in other discussion spaces) are not available, as far as we know. However, we assume that this audience is not as large as the audience that regularly visits the comments section of mass-media websites (e.g., Reich, 2011; Schultz, 2000).

Online user comments, although controlled by news-media organizations to some extent, appear to resemble other manifestations of offline MSIC. Similar to offline news discussions, online users integrate their personal experience into their comments, criticize and reframe news items, distance themselves from journalistic arguments, help other users understand particular aspects of an issue, and begin discussions with other users (Gamson, 1992; De Keyser & Raeymaeckers, 2011; Ruiz et al., 2011; Singer, 2009; Walsh, 2004). However, regarding their potential function of providing information, persuasion, deliberation, and (journalistic) feedback, the online user comments can differ from the traditional forms of MSIC. In the following, we will first describe these extended functions of online user comments and then confront them with empirical research.

- *Information/persuasion*: Online user comments can provide other users of mass-media websites with alternative perspectives on issues raised by journalists. While most offline MSIC and some forms of online MSIC remain private, online user comments are published in the immediate context of online news item and thus become structurally integrated in the process of mass communication (Lee & Jang, 2010). Comments can include personal experiences, additional arguments, and links to other websites and other information, which are not perceived to be news-worthy enough to be integrated into journalistic articles (e.g., Thurman, 2008). This information might support the other media users in critically addressing the information that journalists provide and might even persuade them to change their attitude. Ultimately, this information might influence the formation of public opinion regarding an issue (Lee & Jang, 2010) or might be carried back into offline discussions.
- *Deliberation*: Contrary to traditional mass-media feedback tools, such as letters to the editor, online user comments enable interactivity between the discussants (Singer, 2009; De Keyser & Raeymaeckers, 2011; for the concept of interactivity see, e.g., McMillan, 2002; Rafaeli & Sudweeks, 1997; Stromer-Galley, 2000; Sundar, 2004). For example, users can actively discuss political-related attitudes and behaviors with other

online users. In combination with the perceived anonymity of many of these situations, users might find it easier to express different opinions or to disagree with other discussants than they would when using traditional interpersonal communication (e.g., Stromer-Galley & Muhlberger, 2009). During the latter, nonconforming opinions or disagreement can easily evoke feelings of rudeness or embarrassment, which individuals try to avoid (Brown & Levinson, 1987; Eliasoph, 1998; Goffman, 1959, 1981; Mutz, 2002). However, in online discussions, the condition of interactivity and the facilitated expression of disagreement can foster a greater diversity of opinions, which is supposed to be essential to an effective democracy (e.g., Eveland et al., 2011; Schudson, 1997). In terms of opinion diversity and cross-cutting political views, Wojcieszak and Mutz (2009) find that "the potential for deliberation occurs primarily in online groups where politics comes up only incidentally [...]" (p. 40). This statement largely applies to mass-media websites, where a wide variety of political and apolitical news items can be discussed. Moreover, the mass-media websites usually reach more people than the other (political) online discussion spaces (Schultz, 2000). Thus, more people can observe and join discussions on these websites.

• *Feedback*: From an economic point of view, mass-media organizations that allow users to comment on their stories might experience a positive image shift. Both active and inactive users can perceive these organizations to be transparent, credible and tolerant regarding other opinions (Schweiger & Quiring, 2005). In contrast, online news sites without comments "are becoming rare and starting to look [...] even suspicious" (Reich, 2011, p. 9). User comments may contain hints or corrections that the journalists can use to improve their articles (De Keyser & Raeymaeckers, 2011; Domingo, 2008). User comments might also be featured in professional news coverage (Thurman, 2008). Finally, the journalists might perceive the amount of user comments on a news story to be an indicator for their readers' interest in the reported story or topic (Reich, 2011).

Findings on whether the online user comments actually accomplish these ideal functions are mixed. As to the information value, De Keyser & Raeymaeckers (2011) find that only a low share of user comments contain information of "immediate journalistic value" (p. 11). However, over one-third of their 1,074 user comments analyzed offer new perspectives on the news stories. In a similar manner, by comparing the quality of user comments on six German news websites, Lolies (2012) finds a high share of user comments that provide new viewpoints on the issues raised by journalists. However, the users predominantly report these viewpoints in an emotional manner.

Boczkowski, Pablo, and Mitchelstein (2012) examine three U.S. news websites and show that users prefer to comment on public affairs stories rather than on stories of low public interest. In a case study, Singer (2009) finds that over half of the 2,527 comments analyzed reference remarks from other users, indicating some type of interactivity that is necessary during deliberation. Due to the factual and organized character of the discussions analyzed, Singer (2009) suggests that there is "the presence of some elements of a public sphere as originally proposed by Habermas [...]" (p. 490). However, other explanatory studies report less interactivity in the online user comments (De Keyser & Raeymaeckers, 2011; Lolies, 2012). In one of the few available quantitative cross-media studies, Ruiz et al. (2011) show that the interactivity, the opinion diversity, the topic focus, and the argument quality of online user comments fluctuate on the five analyzed news websites from Spain, the United States, the United Kingdom, Italy, and France.

With regard to the feedback function, studies have found that online mass-media organizations sometimes appreciate user comments (Domingo, 2008; Reich, 2011; Thurman, 2008). However, instead of thoroughly stressing their journalistic value, the online journalists surveyed also emphasize the additional effort that is necessary to moderate online user comments (Reich, 2011; Thurman, 2008) and the possible threat that these comments pose for the quality, relevance, and credibility of journalistic products (Hermida & Thurman, 2008).

To summarize, the news stories published on news-media websites reach large audiences every day. These news items are often complemented by a particular form of MSIC, i.e., online user comments. To some extent, these online user comments resemble traditional formal and informal (political) conversations and discussions about the news. However, they are much more visible than private conversations, thus reaching more people, and they can have interesting effects on both active and passive users. Furthermore, the quantity and quality of the online user comments appears to vary. Some news items receive thousands of comments, while others do not—although the latter news items might be of equal importance (Tsagkias et al., 2009). The study by Ruiz et al. (2009) indicates that the same phenomenon can be observed with regard to the quality of the user discussions.

While several studies suggest that both the passive and active use of the comment sections on online news websites is increasing, current research cannot offer a coherent clue as to what stimulates the users' needs to comment on news items. The studies agree in emphasizing the social, political, and/or journalistic relevance of online user comments. Although these studies have incontestable empirical value because they explore online user comments, they are limited either in their theoretical or their methodological focus. Therefore, the following sections describe the components of an integrated and multidimensional approach to analyzing online users' media-stimulated commenting and discussion behavior. We start by theorizing why particular characteristics of news items stimulate, to a different extent, the users' need to initiate or join the online discussion.

A Multidimensional Micro-Framework of the Discussion Value

First Dimension: Message-Inherent Factors

A Brief Overview of News Value Theory.   Communication science provides numerous approaches to explaining users' selection and consumption of offline and online media content, including the uses-and-gratifications and selective-exposure approaches (e.g., Bennett & Iyengar, 2008; Katz & Gurevitch, 1976; Yoo, 2011). However, these approaches do not comprehensively explain why the users produce content (in terms of commenting on or discussing news items). In contrast with these frameworks, news value theory originally focused on explaining the journalists' perception, selection, and production of news items. The roots of news value research can therefore be found in journalism studies and handbooks (e.g., Lippmann, 1922; Warren, 1934). A systematic theoretical framework was developed by Galtung and Ruge (1965). Their theoretical approach attempts to describe news events in terms of their inherent and largely stable attributes, their so-called news factors. For example, these event attributes include proximity, negativity, controversy, and personalization (Galtung & Ruge, 1965). News value theory's central hypothesis is that journalists select events according to their news value, which is an effect of the number, the intensity, and the relative weight of the individual news factors (Galtung & Ruge, 1965; Kepplinger & Ehmig, 2006). For example, all else being equal, a journalist writing for a newspaper would rather headline a national political scandal than an equivalent foreign scandal because the latter event does not have the news factor of geographical proximity. After perceiving an event as newsworthy, it is hypothesized that journalists then emphasize its news factors within their stories (Galtung & Ruge, 1965; Staab, 1990). Thus, the news factors also have an effect on the production of news items.

The claimed scope of news value theory is not limited to the journalists' selection and production behavior; the founders of both the American (e.g., Lippmann, 1922) and the European (Galtung & Ruge, 1965) traditions of news value research have described the theory as universally applicable to journalists and media users. In subsequent research, Shoemaker (1996) provides arguments for the anthropological validity of (some) news factors (i.e., deviance and related sub-factors such as scarcity, conflict and controversy) from an evolutionary and cultural standpoint (see also Shoemaker & Cohen, 2006; Shoemaker & Reese, 1996). Eilders (1997) provides a principal theoretical and empirical adaption of news value theory to the analysis of media users (see also Eilders, 2006). This author's empirical findings suggest that specific news factors (i.e., reach, conflict, controversy, prominence, continuity and unexpectedness) influence both the selection and the retention of news items by media users. Although media users differ in the extent to which they perceive each of these news factors as important, they are conceptualized as collective (rather than individual) relevance indicators (Eilders, 2006). That is, the factors indicate a basic level of overall relevance. However, do media users comment on, for example, deviant news more intensively than they comment on news that is not deviant? To answer this and similar questions, an extension of news value theory is needed.

News Factors and Online User Comments.   News value theory's current scope is limited to the news-selection and news-production behavior of journalists and, in its broader application, to the media users' selection, consumption, and retention of news. However, as we have emphasized, media users do not only passively receive news; rather, they discuss the news regularly and they can accentuate or distort a news item's news factors in this process, just as journalists can disproportionately distort an event's news factors when communicating the event to their audience. By returning to some of the theory's original assumptions (Galtung & Ruge, 1965), we can thus adapt it to the communicative behavior of media users and hypothesize that the news factors should influence both (a) the quantity and (b) the quality of the online user comments.

The first assumption that could be derived from the theory is that the more news factors a news item contains, the more it will be discussed online (for more on the additivity hypothesis, see Galtung & Ruge, 1965). News-diffusion research has repeatedly shown that high news values can lead to higher rates of news diffusion via interpersonal channels. That is, people tell others about high-news-value news more quickly and more frequently (for an overview, see Rogers, 2000). However, in traditional user-focused news value research, there has been, at best, mixed empirical evidence for the simplistic form of the additivity hypothesis (cf. Eilders, 2006). In either case, analyzing the influence of different news factors (and combinations of factors) on the quantity of online user comments can only be a first step toward an understanding of the discussion value of news items; news factors might also have an impact on the quality of the online user comments. However, most of the aforementioned studies neglect questions about whether and how the news is actually discussed after it has been received via the various channels.

A second assumption could be arrived about the quality of the online user discussions from news value theory. When people's retention of informative mass-media content is determined by the news factors, these factors should also emerge as significant when people actively discuss the mass-media content in offline and online MSIC. In an analysis of offline MSIC, Sommer (2010) shows that media users are particularly likely to emphasize the personalized, established, controversial, and exceptional aspects of the news. Gamson (1992) argues that the personalization of news stories in combination with "injustice frames" can guide subsequent discussions in that these stories "offer potential hooks to which people can attach their anger" (p. 36). An analysis of how these factors affect online user comments, in particular, merits empirical investigation. Additionally, there might be online-specific news factors that account for the different qualities of online user comments. For example, some news-media organizations actively moderate the news items that they publish on SNSs such as Facebook. Moderation as a news factor has repeatedly been found to significantly influence the users' intent to participate in discussions and their discussion behavior (e.g., Wise, Hamman, & Thorson, 2006; Wright & Street, 2007).

It is also important to assess the tone and intensity of the news factors in online user comments in both theoretical and empirical research. As we noted above, news value theory would predict that users disproportionately distort the news factors in their communicative actions. This distortion can happen either unconsciously or deliberately. Users might intend to generate additional discussion value, for example, by overemphasizing the controversial aspects of a news item in their comment so that they will receive feedback (for similar arguments related to journalists, see Staab, 1990).

The theoretical arguments that we have made so far suggest that news value theory can provide considerable help in explaining the quantity and quality of online user comments. At the same time, it has become apparent that the original theory alone does not sufficiently explain the discussion value of news in general and of online news in particular. We therefore suggest two more extensions. First, we must differentiate the news factors (event factors) from the secondary (formal) message factors (e.g., Eilders, 2006). The latter can include the length or the dramaturgy of news items, their credibility or the rhetorical devices used. These secondary factors are likely to influence the media users' communicative behavior (e.g., Hoeken, Swanepoel, Saal, & Jansen, 2009; Southwell & Yzer, 2007). For example, extensive use of metaphors can result in a lack of comprehension (Hoeken et al., 2009) and can thereby also prevent users from commenting on a news item. Source credibility (e.g., Hovland & Weiss, 1951; Metzger, Flangain, Eyal, Lemus, & McCann, 2003) can be conceptualized as another important secondary factor that is likely to influence the quantity of the online user comments: Chung (2008), for example, reports significant positive correlations between the trustworthiness of the online news sources and the individuals' engagement with the human interactive features such as online comments. Moreover, it appears plausible that the quality of the online discussions will differ depending on the source credibility, for example, in terms of the extent to which the users criticize the communicating mass-media organization. Second, to further transform the news value of the online news items into their discussion value, we must (a) conceptualize the specific characteristics of the existing user comments that influence subsequent user behavior and (b) examine both the behavioral consequences of the users' expectations and motives and the influence of the computer-mediated communication settings in shaping the user's discussions about online news items.

Discussion Factors and Online User Comments.   So far, we have not considered the nature and causes of one of the inherent factors of online discussions, namely interactivity. Although interactivity can be seen as an attribute of technological systems, user perceptions or communication processes (e.g., McMillan, 2002; Stromer-Galley, 2004), our argument here focuses on the interactivity of the communication processes (Rafaeli & Sudweeks, 1997). Therefore, we can classify the user comments by the degree to which they are interconnected with other comments. A rough distinction can be made between the user comments that refer to the original news items and those that address the other users' comments. As we have argued in the previous sections, exploratory content analyses have shown that between 20% and 50% of all user comments refer to other user comments (Lolies, 2012; De Keyser & Raeymaeckers, 2011; Ruiz et al., 2011; Singer, 2009). These results raise the question, why do some user comments stimulate feedback from other users while others do not? By adapting the logic of news value theory, feedback comments have specific factors that provoke reactions from subsequent users. These factors distinguish feedback comments from comments that do not stimulate feedback. Therefore, from a theoretical perspective, we suggest integrating discussion factors as a characteristic of online user comments into our framework for the discussion value of online news items.

Before we describe the nature of these factors more fully, a short illustration might be helpful. Imagine a neutral, descriptive online news report in a Western news website about an upcoming cultural event in Asia. A user posts a comment comparing that event to a similar one in the user's home country. A subsequent user contributes to the discussion with a complaint about a particular national-level politician in the first user's home country, who, on the second user's opinion, does not care about culture. The discussion becomes increasingly centered on different politicians and their willingness to invest in national cultural events. Later, another user of the site forms an intention to comment on the reported event but ultimately decides not to because of the thematic distance of the current discussion.

This fictive scenario offers a glimpse of the potential feedback dynamics involved in online user comments. Even when they are initiated by a media stimulus, discussions can quickly digress from the original issue when specific discussion factors occur. In the scenario above, news factors that are missing from the original news item (such as geographical proximity and personalization) are added and maintained in the publicly visible user comments. In addition, these comments can involve factors that provoke (or prevent) the subsequent users' reactions, though they may not be included in the current catalogues of news factors. It remains an open question as to what degree the users base their decision on whether to post comments on the aggregate characteristics of the ongoing discussions, such as thematic distance or interactivity, or to what degree they base their decision on the existence of individual comments that agree or disagree with the users' own attitudes. For an analysis of genuine discussion factors, we suggest integrating different types of provocation (Donath, 1999; Herring, Job-Sluder, Scheckler, & Barab, 2002), such as exaggeration, fatalism, and simplification, into exploratory studies as well as indicators of credibility such as expertise, neutrality, and humor.

From an abstract perspective, these and similar discussion factors constitute an additional source of relevance (in addition to the basic relevance stemming from the news factors of the news items) that can cause the subsequent users to join the online discussion or to refrain from joining it. In offline MSIC, the competition of the relevance indicators related to the news items and to the users' communicative actions is moderated by particular conversational rules (e.g., Kim, Wyatt, & Katz, 1999; Schank, 1977) such as sequential coherence (Schank, 1977). In other words, in offline MSIC, it can be impolite to ignore a conversational partner's proposal to continue a discussion with a non-media-related topic. In interactive online environments, however, discussions appear to violate these conversational rules; they are often perceived as "fragmented [...] and interactionally disjointed" (Herring, 1999; Rafaeli & Sudweeks, 1997). A proposal such as that mentioned above could incur fewer obligations in potential communication partners when it is made publicly in an online discussion space (e.g., Herring, 2010).

For the case of online user comments, however, their particular qualities or their sheer volume can be conceptualized as constituting additional relevance indicators for the subsequent users. These later users can decide whether to enter the discussion by commenting on the news item or on a previous user posting. Consequently, given that the user comments contribute dynamically to the total discussion value, even low-interest news items can be discussed intensively if the initial user comments indicate to the subsequent users a high relevance. Conversely, the low quality of an initial discussion can indicate a low discussion value to the subsequent users and therefore discourage them from posting comments.

Second Dimension: Personal Involvement and Design Factors

It is maintained throughout the user-focused news value research tradition that news characteristics alone are not sufficient to explain people's selection and consumption behavior. It appears that it is essential to also consider the stimulating (or discouraging) influence of individual motivations (Eilders, 2006; Shoemaker, 1996; Southwell, 2005; Southwell & Yzer, 2009). This is also true in a multidimensional analysis of online user comments. Having discussed the potential collective relevance indicators in the previous sections, we now move to a more individual dimension and analyze the influence of personal involvement and its related sub-factors on the users' intentions to discuss news items online.

Personal Involvement and Online User Comments.   Among the factors that are likely to indicate personal relevance is a user's involvement in the issue (e.g., Leippe & Elkin, 1987; Petty & Cacioppo, 1979). Although it might appear to be self-evident that users tend to discuss the news topics that they are interested in, this assumption can also be substantiated and extended using a behavioral approach. The users who are involved in the topic of a particular news item are not only likely to process the information given at a deeper level but can also think more about that news item (Brickner, Harkins, & Ostrom, 1986; Leippe & Elkin, 1987). This reflection can, in turn "boost [their] sense of topical understanding and conversational competency" (Southwell, 2005, p. 436) and lead to high perceived efficacy (Ajzen, 1985; Bandura, 1977). High perceived efficacy, in addition to the specific influences of perceived social norms or an individual's attitude toward a specific behavior, can ultimately result in characteristic behavioral consequences for the news exposure, such as the decision to engage in an online discussion.

In this view, news and discussion factors are likely to interact with the users' issue involvement; these factors might be able to explain the different degrees of involvement within particular topics. For example, suppose a news item headlines unemployment rates in general. This headline could motivate a fictive user who works for a car manufacturer to read the article but not to comment on the issue. However, if another user publishes a comment that blames the automobile industry for the high unemployment rates, the relevance to the first user of discussing this issue could be increased. In addition, news and discussion factors can influence the users' perceived efficacy by boosting or reducing their confidence in their ability to comment on specific postings (e.g., simplified or biased news items or user postings).

The uses-and-gratifications approach provides an established framework that we can use to analyze the influence of situational needs or goals on the individuals' online discussion behavior. The findings of recent studies on user activity on the social web (Chung & Yoo, 2008; Leung, 2009; Springer, 2011; Yoo, 2011) suggest that users seek specific gratifications, such as discussing issues or meeting people with the same interests, which should be considered when analyzing the user's social web activity in general and particularly when analyzing the quantity and quality of online user comments. Situational needs can further moderate the impact of news and discussion factors on user comments; for example, the users with a strong need to seek information or to conduct surveillance might pay more attention to the characteristics of the original news item when posting a comment. In contrast, the users seeking opportunities to socialize might concentrate on addressing user comments that include specific discussion factors (e.g., questions).

In the first sections of this article, we illustrated that ritualized behavioral patterns, such as a user's general level of media consumption (e.g., Kim et al., 1999; Scheufele, 2000), are likely to influence individual engagement in offline MSIC and therefore should also be considered when analyzing the quantity and quality of online user comments. The same argument holds true for political participation and civic engagement; scholars have repeatedly analyzed changes in these ritualized behavioral patterns as possible outcomes of offline and online discussions (e.g., McClurg, 2003; Price, 2009). However, it appears to be legitimate to assume that existing attitudes toward political participation and the ensuing behaviors and civic engagement also influence the individuals' willingness to participate in online discussions. For example, Chung (2008) reports that political engagement predicts the use of "human interactive" features on mass-media websites that enable interpersonal communication. Similar results are shown by Baek et al. (2012). Individuals with characteristic ritualized behavioral patterns thus might perceive online user comments on mass-media websites to be an additional opportunity to express their general interest in the news or their political and/or civic engagement. In this context, an interesting, yet unanswered, question is if and how the ritualized behavioral patterns discussed are reflected in different qualities within the published user comments.

On a high level of stability, the users' personality attributes (traits) should be considered to be an additional source of individual motivation. Studies have identified the influence of traits such as the need for cognition (Amichai-Hamburger, 2007; Lee & Jang, 2010) on users' perception and use of different online communication services. Similar influences can be found in adapting these findings to elucidate the differences between individuals' perceptions of online discussions and their participation in these discussions. For example, the sensation-seeking personality trait has repeatedly been found to correlate with media users' conversational tendencies and styles (Alonzo & Aiken, 2004; David, Cappella, & Fishbein, 2006; Hwang & Southwell, 2007). These findings suggest that individuals who are willing to accept risk for the sake of having intense experiences are likely to talk more than others in a variety of social situations (David et al., 2006; Hwang & Southwell, 2007). In their analysis of communicative styles, Alonzo and Aiken (2004) observe that individuals with sensation-seeking personalities are more likely to publish hostile and insulting postings.

In addition, the Big Five personality inventory (Costa & McCrae, 1992) is frequently used to evaluate different levels of social web activity (Amichai-Hamburger & Vinitzky, 2010; Correa, Hinsley, & de Zúñiga, 2010; Guadagno et al., 2008). One repeated finding is that extraversion is a significant predictor of the frequency and the intensity of social media use (Amichai-Hamburger & Vinitzky, 2010; Correa et al., 2010). For other personality variables, such as agreeableness and conscientiousness, the findings are more mixed. Although most of these results have been limited to describing the use of instant messaging and SNSs, the concept of personality variables certainly provides some additional insights for research on online user comments in regards to what the users actually communicate (or do not communicate) and to what degree they depend on different news and discussion factors.

Design Factors and Online User Comments.   The influence of technology and its social shaping on the process, content, and outcome of social interactions has been the subject of some controversial scientific debates (e.g., Herring, 1999; Papacharissi, 2005; Walther, 1996). There is little doubt that both face-to-face and computer-mediated communication fulfill some common, basic social needs (Papacharissi, 2005), but other factors, such as the willingness to express one's opinion, have been found to vary between mediated and non-mediated contexts (e.g., Ho & McLeod, 2008). Concerning the relationships among technology, its social shaping and online user comments, we hypothesize that two influences are particularly important: service architecture/design and perceived social context. Computer-mediated environments provide characteristic interactive architectures that resemble natural communicative settings, though some bear more resemblance than others (Quiring & Schweiger, 2008; Ho & McLeod, 2008; Papacharissi, 2009).

The number and structure of the (sub)services that allow participation in online discussions on a given platform codetermine the way that users interact on that platform (Herring, 1999). For example, platforms that require registration demand a higher degree of user motivation than those allowing unregistered discussion. To some extent, different registration rules can explain different quantities of online user comments (Ruiz et al., 2011). It might further be the case that a lower number of positive user comments will generally be found on websites that provide a standardized means to appreciate the other users' comments. In addition, there may be less interactivity in user discussions if the platforms either set a low default limit on the number of comments shown per news item or do not provide functionality for explicitly replying to or citing the postings of other discussants. On an administrative level, platform providers can stimulate or restrict online discussions by providing incentives or by moderating user comments (Reich, 2011; Ruiz et al., 2011). The discourse architecture (Sack, 2005) of online communication services can therefore influence the users' general participation levels, their perceptions of news and discussion factors and the overall quality of the online discussions.

Although we have explained that user comments are likely to be influenced by the previous user comments, we have not yet discussed social influences on user behavior as a whole. As people orient their own behavior relative to their affiliation with specific social groups (Reicher, Spears, & Postmes, 1995; Taylor, Peplau, & Sears, 2003), it is important to analyze the influence of perceived social context on an individual's decision for or against online communicative action (e.g., Ho & McLeod, 2008). As mass-media websites vary in their degree of community orientation (Reich, 2011), the perceived social context should depend heavily on which platform users choose for online MSIC. Consequently, a user's online comments are likely to be differentially affected by the (perceived) size of the group and by the individual's commitment to the group (Cialdini & Trost, 1998).

There are at least three different situations that can be distinguished for our purposes. First, in situations of *perceived anonymity*, the users are neither conscious that their comments might be visible to particular sectors of the public, nor do they expect other users to read the posting. The opinions in these comments should be the most socially unbiased. Second, in situations of *perceived low-binding publicness*, the users are conscious that their posting will be visible to an unspecified population of readers. They might therefore show more group-compliant behavior in their posting, for example, by carefully pondering the pros and cons of an issue to avoid negative feedback. Third, in situations of *perceived high-binding publicness*, the users are conscious that their posting will be visible to their primary network of colleagues, friends, and family members. This situation is likely to primarily be relevant on SNSs or in highly transitive communities. In such situations, the user comments are likely to be strongly influenced by specific pressure to conform to the group.

It is likely that the importance of different news factors in an individual's decision regarding whether to engage in online discussions or not differs among those three perceived social contexts. The same holds true for how individuals perceive the discussion factors of other comments and which discussion factors they are more likely to emphasize when posting a comment. These influences should be thoroughly examined in future research.

The Integrated Model

We have shown that attempts to understand online user comments without addressing individual factors cannot be comprehensive. Conversely, users' motivation for engaging in online discussions on mass-media websites also cannot be comprehensively understood without considering the characteristics of the news items and the existing user postings as collective relevance indicators of some sort. Therefore, our multidimensional micro-framework for analyzing the discussion value of online news items first integrates the message-inherent characteristics of online news items and existing user comments. On a second dimension, our framework includes motivational factors, the influences of the (perceived) design of online communication settings and their social constraints. Finally, it is likely that most of the factors mentioned interact with other factors, so our framework considers the possible interactions within and between the dimensions. Figure 5.1 shows the basic model that integrates the two dimensions.

As we described above, the news factors (e.g., the level of controversy about an issue or the degree of personalization of the story) make up the specific news value of news items. In addition, news items can be described in terms of diverse secondary message factors such as their length or source credibility. Assuming that news items do not have any user comments associated with them at the time of their publication, it is at first solely the news and the secondary factors that contribute to the item's discussion value and that determine the specific degree of relevance of posting a comment for a given online user. The quality of this relevance is codetermined by the user's issue involvement, perceived efficacy, situational needs, ritualized behavioral patterns, and personality attributes.

The service architecture/design and the perceived social context within a given CMC setting are expected to further stimulate or reduce the user's

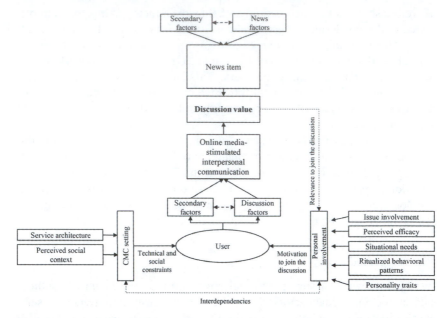

Figure 5.1 A multidimensional micro-framework for analyzing the discussion value of online news items.

motivation to initiate or join a discussion. Given sufficient motivation, the user will post a comment. Similar to news items, each posted comment has its own secondary factors and discussion factors that might match or accentuate the news factors of the original news item. Additionally, the comment can introduce new discussion factors, which can be attributed in part to the user's individual motivations, such as specific issue involvement. Insofar as the posted comment is directly visible, it should affect the total discussion value because the subsequent users perceive the relevance indicators stemming from both the original news item and the published comments. As the discussion value is (incrementally) modified with each added comment, it is important to emphasize the iterative and dynamic character of this process.

Because of the current lack of empirical research, it is likely to be challenging to quantify the different influences on a user's decision to join an online discussion and on the interactions between users. However, our framework does provide some ideas for a multi-method research program. For example, content analyses can be applied to analyze the correlations between the characteristics of news items and the user comments or to extract the discussion factors of user comments that shape particular discussion qualities. Subsequent experiments can then systematically vary the news factors of news items and test their influence on the users' decision about whether to post comments. News factors in news items can also be changed with the discussion factors in the user comments (and vice versa), and the consequences for the users' communicative intentions and behaviors can then be investigated. The users' personalities, for example, should be considered as a possible moderating variable in these experiments. Finally, surveys can be designed as conjoint analyses, for example, to assess the specific influences of individual motivations on a user's participation behavior as well as the consequences of (specific combinations of) message-inherent relevance indicators. Naturally, these ideas only offer a starting point for empirical research; they will need to be refined in terms of specific research questions, hypotheses, and methodologies.

It is important to mention that although our framework might appear to be designed for the analysis of online user comments, its variables can likely be modified or adapted to fit the conditions of other manifestations of MSIC. For example, in online political discussion groups, a moderator's activities can be conceptualized as a media stimulus that frames the subsequent discussion (e.g., Price et al., 2005). Knowing the effects of the discussed message factors on user behaviors might help the moderators or other professional communicators increase the topic relevance and coherence of the discussion. For analyses of chat discussions, a topic variable might replace the news item variable (Stromer-Galley & Martinson, 2009). In offline MSIC, the service architecture variable might be replaced by a particular conversational rules variable. This variable, in turn, might interact with the media user's perception of news and discussion factors. Finally, while it has been stated that offline MSIC occurs in different social contexts (e.g., Wyatt et al., 2000), our framework provides ideas for analyzing whether different aspects of mass-media content are discussed in these different situations.

Conclusion

In this chapter, we have provided a theoretical analysis of media-stimulated interpersonal communication and have suggested a research framework for the analysis of the discussion value of online news items. Thus, our contributions are twofold. First, the concept of MSIC shows the basic social activity behind offline and online discussions about mass-media content and could help us breach some barriers still existing between interpersonal and mass communication research, on the one hand, and offline and online communication research, on the other hand. In this context, we have theorized that online user comments are a particular manifestation of MSIC and have discussed their suitability for investigating the question of what makes the news worth discussing.

Second, by conceptualizing the discussion value of online news as a function of message-inherent, motivational, social and design factors, we have suggested an answer to the aforementioned question. We have argued that news value theory provides a promising starting point for analyzing the aspects of news items that stimulate the users' need to comment on them. In addition, we have suggested extending the news-factor logic to an analysis of discussion factors for the existing user comments. These discussion factors, although largely neglected in previous research on offline and online MSIC, could help us to quantify the impact of the existing online user comments on the subsequent discussion processes. However, only by adding the constraints of online communication settings and users' individual needs, goals, and characteristics will we be able to shed a brighter light on the different quantities and qualities of users' online discussions about the news. A comprehensive analysis such as we have proposed here can therefore provide genuine insights into how and why users interactively negotiate the relevance and attractiveness of news items. Because the variables in our suggested model are highly modifiable, the model can also be adapted to other manifestations of offline and online MSIC. Our suggested micro-framework therefore promises to provide an integrated approach to assessing the discussion value of online news items in particular and, more generally, the nature of offline and online MSIC and the differences between them.

References

Ajzen, I. (1985). From intentions to actions: A theory of planned behavior. In J. Kuhl (Ed.), *Springer series in social psychology. Action control. From cognition to behavior* (pp. 11–39). Berlin, Germany: Springer.

Alonzo, M., & Aiken, M. (2004). Flaming in electronic communication. *Decision Support Systems, 36*, 205–213.

Amichai-Hamburger, Y. (2007). Personality, individual differences and Internet use. In A. N. Joinson, K. Y. A. McKenna, T. Postmes, & U.-D. Reips (Eds.), *The Oxford handbook of Internet psychology* (pp. 187–204). Oxford, England: Oxford University Press.

Amichai-Hamburger, Y., & Vinitzky, G. (2010). Social network use and personality. *Computers in Human Behavior, 26*, 1289–1295.

Baek, Y. M., Wojcieszak, M., & Delli Carpini, M. X. (2012). Online versus face-to-face deliberation: Who? Why? What? With what effects? *New Media and Society, 14*, 363–383.

Bakker, T., & Schoenbach, K. (2011, May). *Active Audiences and An Inclusive Online Public Sphere: Truths About Internet Myths.* Paper presented at the 61st Annual Conference of the International Communication Association, Boston, MA.

Bandura, A. (1977). Self-efficacy: Toward a unifying theory of behavioral change. *Psychological Review, 84*, 191–215.

Beinstein, J. (1975). Conversations in public places. *Journal of Communication, 25*, 85–95.

Berelson, B. (1949). What "missing the newspaper" means. In P. F. Lazarsfeld & F. N. Stanton (Eds.), *Communications Research 1948–1949* (pp. 111–129). New York, NY: Arno Press.

Boczkowski, P. J., Pablo, J., & Mitchelstein, E. (2012). How users take advantage of different forms of interactivity on online news sites: Clicking, e-mailing, and commenting. *Human Communication Research, 38*, 1–22.

Boer, C. de, & Velthuijsen, A. S. (2001). Participation in conversations about the news. *International Journal of Public Opinion Research, 13,* 140–158.

Bowman, S., & Willis, C. (2003). *We media: How audiences are shaping the future of news and information.* Reston, VA: The Media Center at the American Press Institute.

Brickner, M. A., Harkins, S. G., & Ostrom, T. M. (1986). Effects of personal involvement: Thought provoking implications for social loafing. *Journal of Personality and Social Psychology, 51,* 763–769.

Brown, P., & Levinson, S. C. (1987). *Politeness: Some universals in language usage. Studies in Interactional Sociolinguistics: Vol. 4.* Cambridge, England: Cambridge University Press.

Chung, D., & Yoo, C. (2008). Audience motivations for using interactive features: Distinguishing use of different types of interactivity on an online newspaper. *Mass Communication & Society, 11,* 375–397.

Chung, D. S. (2008). Interactive features of online newspapers: Identifying patterns and predicting use of engaged readers. *Journal of Computer-Mediated Communication, 13,* 658–679.

Cialdini, R. B., & Trost, M. R. (1998). Social influence: Social norms, conformity, and compliance. In D. T. Gilbert, S. T. Fiske, & G. Lindzey (Eds.), *Handbook of social psychology* (2nd ed., pp. 151–192). Boston, MA: McGraw-Hill.

Correa, T., Hinsley, A. W., & de Zúñiga, H. G. (2010). Who interacts on the Web?: The intersection of users' personality and social media use. *Computers in Human Behavior, 26,* 247–253.

Costa, P. T., Jr., & McCrae, R. R. (1992). *Revised NEO Personality Inventory (NEO PI-R) and NEO Five-Factor Inventory (NEO-FFI): Professional manual.* Odessa, FL: Psychological Assessment Resources.

Daughtery, T., Eastin, M. S., & Bright, L. (2008). Exploring consumer motivations for creating user-generated content. *Journal of Interactive Advertising, 8,* 16–25.

David, C., Cappella, J. N., & Fishbein, M. (2006). The social diffusion of influence among adolescents: Group interaction in a chat room environment about anti-drug advertisements. *Communication Theory, 16,* 118–140.

Davis, R., & Owen, D. (1998). *New media and American politics.* Oxford, England: Oxford University Press.

Deutschmann, P. J., & Danielson, W. A. (1960). Diffusion of knowledge of the major news story. *Journalism Quarterly, 37,* 345–355.

De Keyser, J., & Raeymaeckers, K. (2011, May). *Content or complaining? A study on the added value of online feedback features for journalism and democracy.* Paper presented at the 61st Annual Conference of the International Communication Association, Boston, MA.

Donath, J. S. (1999). Identity and deception in the virtual community. In M. A. Smith & P. Kollock (Eds.), *Communities in cyberspace* (pp. 29–59). London, England: Routledge.

Domingo, D. (2008). Interactivity in the daily routines of online newsrooms: dealing with an uncomfortable myth. *Journal of Computer-Mediated Communication, 13,* 680–704.

Eliasoph, N. (1998). *Avoiding politics: How Americans produce apathy in everyday life.* Cambridge, England: Cambridge University Press.

Eilders, C. (1997). *Nachrichtenfaktoren und Rezeption: Eine empirische Analyse zur Auswahl und Verarbeitung politischer Information* [News factors and reception:

An empirical analysis of the selection and processing of political information]. *Studien zur Kommunikationswissenschaft: Vol. 20.* Opladen, Germany: Westdeutscher Verlag.

Eilders, C. (2006). News factors and news decisions. Theoretical and methodological advances in Germany. *Communications, 31,* 5–24.

Eveland, W. P., Jr. (2004). The effect of political discussion in producing informed citizens: The roles of information, motivation, and elaboration. *Political Communication,* 21, 177–193.

Eveland, W. P., Jr., Morey, A. C., & Hutchens, M. J. (2011). Beyond deliberation: New directions for the study of informal political conversation from a communication perspective. *Journal of Communication,* 61, 1082–1103.

Galtung, J., & Ruge, M. H. (1965). The structure of foreign news. *Journal of Peace Research,* 2, 64–91.

Gamson, W. A. (1992). *Talking politics.* Cambridge, MA: Cambridge University Press.

Glasser, T. L. (Ed.). (1999). *The idea of public journalism.* New York, NY: Guilford Press.

Glynn, C. J., Huge, M. E., & Hoffman, L. H. (2012). All the news that's fit to post: A profile of news use on social networking sites. *Computers in Human Behavior, 28,* 113–119.

Goffman, E. (1959). *The presentation of self in everyday life.* New York, NY: Doubleday.

Goffman, E. (1981). *Forms of talk.* Philadelphia: University of Pennsylvania Press.

Graham, T., & Witschge, T. (2003). In search of online deliberation: Towards a new method for examining the quality of online discussions. *Communications,* 28, 173–204.

Greenberg, B. S. (1964). Person-to-person communication in the diffusion of news events. *Journalism Quarterly,* 41, 489–494.

Guadagno, R. E., Okdie, B. M., & Eno, C. A. (2008). Who blogs? Personality predictors of blogging. *Computers in Human Behavior, 24,* 1993–2004.

Hardy, B. W., & Scheufele, D. A. (2005). Examining differential gains from Internet use: Comparing the moderating role of talk and online interactions. *Journal of Communication, 55,* 71–83.

Hermida, A., & Thurman, N. (2008). A clash of cultures: The integration of user-generated content within professional journalistic frameworks at British newspaper websites. *Journalism Practice,* 2, 343–356.

Herring, S. C. (1999). Interactional coherence in CMC. *Journal of Computer-Mediated Communication, 4.* Retrieved from http://jcmc.indiana.edu/vol4/issue4/herring.html

Herring, S. C. (2001). Computer-mediated discourse. In D. Schiffrin, D. Tannen, & H. Hamilton (Eds.), *The handbook of discourse analysis* (pp. 612–634). Oxford, England: Blackwell.

Herring, S. C. (2010). Who's got the floor in computer-mediated conversation? Edelsky's gender patterns revisited. *Language@Internet, 7.* Retrieved from http://www.languageatinternet.com/articles/2010/2857

Herring, S. C., Job-Sluder, K., Scheckler, R., & Barab, S. A. (2002). Searching for safety online: Managing "trolling" in a feminist forum. *The Information Society, 18,* 371–383.

Ho, S. S., & McLeod, D. M. (2008). Social-psychological influences on opinion expression in face-to-face and computer-mediated communication. *Communication Research*, *35*, 190–207.

Hoeken, H., Swanepoel, P., Saal, E., & Jansen, C. (2009). Using message form to stimulate conversations: The case of tropes. *Communication Theory*, *19*, 49–65.

Hovland, C. I., & Weiss, W. (1951). The influence of source credibility on communication effectiveness. *The Public Opinion Quarterly*, *15*, 635–650.

Hwang, Y., & Southwell, B. G. (2007). Can a personality trait predict talk about science?: Sensation seeking as a science communication targeting variable. *Science Communication*, *29*, 198–216.

Katz, E., & Lazarsfeld, P. F. (1955). *Personal influence: The part played by people in the flow of mass communication*. New York, NY: Free Press.

Katz, E., & Gurevitch, M. (1976). *The secularization of leisure: Culture and communication in Israel*. London, England: Faber & Faber.

Kepplinger, H. M., & Ehmig, S. (2006). Predicting news decisions: An empirical test of the two component theory of news selection. *Communications*, *31*, 25–43.

Kim, J., Wyatt, R. O., & Katz, E. (1999). News, talk, opinion, participation: The part played by conversation in deliberative democracy. *Political Communication*, *16*, 361–385.

Kwak, H., Lee, C., Park, H., & Moon, S. (2010). What is Twitter, a social network or a news media? In *Proceedings of the nineteenth international WWW conference (WWW2010)* (pp. 591–600). Raleigh, NC: ACM Press.

Lazarsfeld, P. F., Berelson, B., & Gaudet, H. (1944). *The people's choice: How the voter makes up his mind in a presidential campaign*. New York, NY: Columbia University Press.

Lee, E. J., & Jang, Y. J. (2010). What do others' reactions to news on Internet portal sites tell us? Effects of presentation format and readers' need for cognition on reality perception. *Communication Research*, *37*, 825–846.

Leippe, M. R., & Elkin, R. A. (1987). When motives clash: Issue involvement and response involvement as determinants of persuasion. *Journal of Personality and Social Psychology*, *52*, 269–278.

Leung, L. (2009). User-generated content on the internet: An examination of gratifications, civic engagement and psychological empowerment. *New Media and Society*, *11*, 1327–1347.

Lippmann, W. (1922). *Public opinion*. New York, NY: Free Press.

Lolies, I. (2012). Leserbriefe 2.0? Nutzer-Partizipation durch Online-Kommentare [Letters to the editor 2.0? User participation through online comments]. *Journalistik Journal*, 1/2012, 28–29.

McClurg, S. D. (2003). Social networks and political participation: The role of social interaction in explaining political participation. *Political Research Quarterly*, *56*, 448–464.

McCombs, M., & Shaw, D. L. (1972). The agenda-setting function of mass media. *The Public Opinion Quarterly*, *36*, 176–187.

McMillan, S. J. (2002). Exploring models of interactivity from multiple research traditions: User, documents and systems. In L. A. Lievrouw & S. Livingstone (Eds.), *Handbook of new media: Social shaping and consequences of ICTs* (pp. 161–183). London, England: Sage.

Metzger, M. J., Flangain, A. J., Eyal, K., Lemus, D. R., & McCann, R. (2003). Credibility for the 21st century: Integrating perspectives on source, message, and media credibility in the contemporary media environment. In P. J. Kalbfleisch (Ed.), *Communication yearbook 27* (pp. 293–335). Mahwah, NJ: Erlbaum.

Mutz, D. C. (2002). The consequences of cross-cutting networks for political participation. *American Journal of Political Science, 46*, 838–855.

Nielsen, R. K. (2010). Participation through letters to the editor: Circulation, considerations, and genres in the letters institution. *Journalism, 11*(1), 21–35.

Papacharissi, Z. (2002). The virtual sphere: The internet as a public sphere. *New Media and Society,* 4, 9–27.

Papacharissi, Z. (2005). The real-virtual dichotomy in online interaction: New media uses and consequences revisited. In P. J. Kalbfleisch (Ed.), *Communication yearbook 29* (Vol. 29; pp. 215–237). Mahwah, NJ: Erlbaum.

Papacharissi, Z. (2009). The virtual geographies of social networks: A comparative analysis of Facebook, LinkedIn and ASmallWorld. *New Media and Society, 11*, 199–220.

Petty, R. E., & Cacioppo, J. T. (1979). Issue involvement can increase or decrease persuasion by enhancing message-relevant cognitive responses. *Journal of Personality and Social Psychology, 37*, 1915–1926.

Pew Research Center (2005). *Trends 2005.* Washington, DC: Author.

Price, V., & Roberts, D. F. (1987). Public opinion processes. In C. R. Berger & S. H. Chaffee (Eds.), *Handbook of communication science* (pp. 781–816). Newbury Park, CA: Sage.

Price, V. (2009). Citizens deliberating online: Theory and some evidence. In T. Davies & S. P. Gangadharan (Eds.), *Online deliberation. Design, research, and practice* (pp. 37–58). Chicago, IL: CSLI Publications.

Price, V., Nir, L., & Cappella, J. N. (2005). Framing Public Discussion of Gay Civil Unions. *Public Opinion Quarterly, 69,* 179–212.

Purcell, K., Rainie, L., Mitchell, A., Rosenstiel, T., & Olmstead, K. (2010). *Understanding the participatory news consumer: How internet and cell phone users have turned news into a social experience.* Retrieved from http://www.pewinternet.org/~/media//Files/Reports/2010/PIP_Understanding_the_Participatory_News_Consumer.pdf

Quiring, O., & Schweiger, W. (2008). Interactivity — a review of the concept and a framework for analysis. *Communications — the European Journal of Communication Research, 33*, 147–167.

Rafaeli, S., & Sudweeks, F. (1997). Networked interactivity. *Journal of Computer-Mediated Communication, 2.* Retrieved from http://jcmc.indiana.edu/vol2/issue4/rafaeli.sudweeks.html

Reardon, K. K., & Rogers, E. M. (1988). Interpersonal versus mass media communication: A false dichotomy. *Human Communication Research, 15*, 284–303.

Reich, Z. (2011). User comments: The transformation of participatory space. In J. B. Singer, A. Hermida, D. Domingo, A. Heinonen, S. Paulussen, T. Quandt, … M. Vujnovic (Eds.), *Participatory journalism: Guarding open gates at online newspapers* (pp. 96–117). Malden, MA: Wiley-Blackwell.

Reicher, S. D., Spears, R., & Postmes, T. (1995). A social identity model of deindividuation phenomena. *European Review of Social Psychology, 6*, 161–198.

Rogers, E. M. (2000). Reflections on news event diffusion research. *Journalism & Mass Communication Quarterly, 77*, 561–576.

Ruiz, C., Domingo, D., Micó, J. L., Díaz-Noci, J., Meso, K., & Masip, P. (2011). Public sphere 2.0? The democratic qualities of citizen debates in online newspapers. *The International Journal of Press/Politics, 22*, 463–487.

Sack, W. (2005). Discourse architecture and very large-scale conversation. In R. Latham & S. Sassen (Eds.), *Digital formations: IT and new architectures in the global realm* (pp. 242–282). Princeton, NJ: Princeton University Press.

Schank, R. C. (1977). Rules and topics in conversation. *Cognitive Science, 1*, 421–441.

Scheufele, D. A. (2000). Talk or conversation? Dimensions of interpersonal discussion and their implications for participatory democracy. *Journalism & Mass Communication Quarterly, 77*, 727–743.

Schudson, M. (1997). Why conversation is not the soul of democracy. *Critical Studies in Mass Communication, 14*, 297–309.

Schultz, T. (2000). Mass media and the concept of interactivity: an exploratory study of online forums and reader email. *Media Culture Society, 22*(2), 205–221.

Schweiger, W., & Quiring, O. (2005, May). *User-generated content on mass media web sites - just a variety of interactivity or something completely different?* Paper presented at the 55th Annual Conference of the International Communication Association, New York, NY.

Shoemaker, P. J. (1996). Hardwired for news: Using biological and cultural evolution to explain the surveillance function. *Journal of Communication, 46*, 32–47.

Shoemaker, P. J., & Cohen, A. (2006). *News around the world: Content, practitioners, and the public.* New York, NY: Routledge.

Shoemaker, P. J., & Reese, S. D. (1996). *Mediating the message: Theories of influences on mass media content.* White Plains, NY: Longman.

Singer, J. B. (2009). Separate spaces: Discourse about the 2007 Scottish elections on a national newspaper web site. *The International Journal of Press/Politics, 14*, 477–496.

Singer, J. B., Hermida, A., Domingo, D., Heinonen, A., Paulussen, S., Quandt, T., ... Vujnovic, M. (Eds.). (2011). *Participatory Journalism: Guarding Open Gates at Online Newspapers.* Malden, MA: Wiley-Blackwell.

Singer, J. B., & Ashman, I. (2009). "Comments is free, but facts are sacred". User-generated content and ethical constructs at the Guardian. *Journal of Mass Media Ethics: Exploring Questions of Media Morality, 24*, 3–21.

Smith, A. (2011). *The Internet and campaign 2010.* Retrieved from http://pewresearch.org/pubs/1931/online-political-use-2010-over-half-us-adults

Sommer, D. (2010, May). *News values in conversations about single news events.* Paper presented at the 60th annual conference of the International Communication Association, Singapore, Malaysia.

Southwell, B. G. (2005). Between messages and people: A multilevel model of memory for television content. *Communication Education, 32*, 112–140.

Southwell, B. G., & Yzer, M. (2007). The roles of interpersonal communication in mass media campaigns. In C. Beck (Ed.), *Communication yearbook 31* (pp. 420–462). New York, NY: Erlbaum.

Southwell, B. G., & Yzer, M. (2009). When (and why) interpersonal talk matters for campaigns. *Communication Theory, 19*, 1–8.

Springer, N. (2011). Suche Meinung, biete Dialog? Warum Leser die Kommentarfunktion auf Nachrichtenportalen nutzen [Looking for opinion, offering dialogue? Why readers use the comment function on news-media websites]. In J. Wolling, A. Will, & C. Schumann (Eds.), *Medieninnovationen. Wie Medienentwicklungen die*

Kommunikation in der Gesellschaft verändern (pp. 247–264). Konstanz, Germany: UVK.

Staab, J. F. (1990). The role of news factors in news selection: A theoretical reconsideration. *European Journal of Communication*, 5, 423–443.

Stromer-Galley, J. (2000). On-line interaction and why candidates avoid it. *Journal of Communication*, 50, 111–132.

Stromer-Galley, J. (2002). New voices in the public sphere: A comparative analysis of interpersonal and online political talk. *Javnost — The Public*, 9, 23–42.

Stromer-Galley, J. (2004). Interactivity-as-product and interactivity-as-process. *The Information Society*, 20, 391–394.

Stromer-Galley, J., & Martinson, A. M. (2009). Coherence in political computer-mediated communication: analyzing topic relevance and drift in chat. *Discourse & Communication*, 3, 195–216.

Stromer-Galley, J., & Muhlberger, P. (2009). Agreement and disagreement in group deliberation: Effects on deliberation satisfaction, future engagement, and decision legitimacy. *Political Communication*, 26, 173–192.

Sundar, S. S. (2004). Theorizing interactivity's effects. *The Information Society*, 20, 385–389.

Sunstein, C. (2002). *Republic.com*. Princeton, NJ: Princeton University Press.

Tarde, G. (1901/1910). *L'opinion et la foule* [Opinion and the crowd] (3rd ed.). Paris, France: Alcan.

Taylor, S. E., Peplau, L. A., & Sears, D. O. (2003). *Social psychology* (11th ed.). Upper Saddle River, NJ: Pearson Education.

Thurman, N. (2008). Forums for citizen journalists? Adoption of user generated content initiatives by online news media. *New Media and Society*, 10, 139–157.

Tsagkias, M., Weerkamp, W., & de Rijke, M. (2009, November). News comments: Exploring, modeling, and online prediction. In D. Cheung (Ed.), *Proceedings of the ACM eighteenth international conference on information and knowledge management* (pp. 1765–1768). New York, NY: ACM.

Vickery, G., & Wunsch-Vincent, S. (2007). *Participative web and user-created content: Web 2.0, wikis and social networking*. OECD, 2007. Retrieved from http://www.oecd.org/document/40/0,3343,en_2649_201185_39428648_1_1_1_1,00.html

Wallsten, K. (2007). Agenda setting and the blogosphere: An analysis of the relationship between mainstream media and political blogs. *Review of Policy Research*, 24, 567–587.

Walsh, K. C. (2004). *Talking about politics: Informal groups and social identity in American life*. Chicago, IL: University of Chicago Press.

Walther, J. B. (1996). Computer-mediated communication: Impersonal, interpersonal, and hyperpersonal communication. *Communication Research*, 23, 3–43.

Walther, J. B., DeAndrea, D., Kim, J., & Anthony, J. C. (2010). The influence of online comments on perceptions of antimarijuana public service announcements on YouTube. *Human Communication Research*, 36, 469–492.

Warren, C. N. (1934). *Modern news reporting*. Madison, WI: Harper & Brothers.

Wise, K., Hamman, B., & Thorson, K. (2006). Moderation, response rate, and message interactivity: Features of online communities and their effects on intent to participate. *Journal of Computer-Mediated Communication*, 12, 24–41.

Wojcieszak, M. E., & Mutz, D. C. (2009). Online groups and political discourse: Do online discussion spaces facilitate exposure to political disagreement? *Journal of Communication*, 59, 40–56.

Wright, S., & Street, J. (2007). Democracy, deliberation and design: the case of online discussion forums. *New Media and Society, 9*, 849–869.

Wyatt, R. O., Katz, E., & Kim, J. (2000). Bridging the spheres: Political and personal conversation in public and private spaces. *Journal of Communication, 50*, 71–92.

Yoo, C. Y. (2011). Modeling audience interactivity as the gratification-seeking process in online newspapers. *Communication Theory, 21*, 67–89.

CHAPTER CONTENTS

6 On Media and Science in Late Modern Societies

Pieter Maeseele

University of Antwerp

This literature review of the media-and-science field identifies a traditional and alternative media-sociological approach and reflects on how two structural developments in late modern societies—reflexive scientization and commercialization of science—influence their performance and strategic use. As the literature review reveals how successfully the institution of science has adapted to the *mediatisation* of society in terms of a relatively effective control of its public image, this chapter concludes by calling for a rethinking of (a) the paradigm of science communication, (b) the role of science journalism, and (c) the aims and methods of (science) communication research.

S cience and technology have not only pervaded our daily lives through the many technological products and services whose comfort we enjoy, but they have also taken center stage in many of today's social and political debates: Climate change has achieved celebrity status as an international social problem, the debate on nuclear energy has resurfaced worldwide after Fukushima, and, on a national level, Belgium has witnessed how the attack on a field trial of genetically manipulated (GM) potatoes led to a fierce social debate on freedom of expression and academic research in the context of an ever increasing commercialization of science. The latter was further intensified by the Catholic University of Leuven's dismissal of a post-doctoral researcher who declared her sympathy for the action to a television reporter. The many rapid advances in science and technology confront us with tremendous democratic challenges. As the previous examples demonstrate, these scientific and technological developments offer many potential benefits to health, quality of life, and economic development and simultaneously introduce known and unknown risks to health, the environment, and social justice. Increasingly, the development and introduction of new technologies precedes public debate and political regulation, thereby intensifying the weight placed upon public credulity and legitimation.

Starting from this context, this chapter explores how the relationship between media and science has been approached—conceptually as well as empirically—in academic literature and how the latter has accounted for the myriad ways in which scientific findings and research circulate in mediated and public discourses. It contains a critical reappraisal of large bodies of literature without any predefined geographical or historical limits,[1] covering a wide area, since the relationship between media and science has been of interest not only to communication scholars. Many conceptual and empirical papers have been published in journals covering disparate fields, including medicine, sociology, and biotechnology; in multi- and interdisciplinary journals such as *Nature, Science* and *Risk Analysis*; and in journals covering science, technology, and society. The first aim of this literature review, then, is to distinguish the underlying assumptions and implicit communication models within this disparate literature, after which the results of empirical case studies starting from a specific approach are discussed.

Furthermore, taking up the call of Hesmondhalgh and Toynbee (2008) for media scholars to engage with social theory by introducing a metatheoretical dimension to their work, a second aim is to relate this literature to two structural developments in late modern societies with important consequences for understanding the relationship between science and the public sphere, and, by extension, science and the media: reflexive scientization and the commercialization of science. This chapter will argue that although two basic approaches can be distinguished in terms of conflicting underlying communication models, we need to account for their position with regard to these processes within science to adequately understand their performance and strategic use in academic research and public discourse as well as their precise relationships.

This dual objective is reflected in the structure of this chapter. The two approaches, which were identified through the literature review, are discussed first: The traditional science- and media-centered science communication or science popularization model with its later adaptations and a second, more loosely defined, alternative media-sociological perspective generally focusing on the meaning-making processes underlying the definition of science in public and media discourses. Subsequently, this chapter reflects on how the performance and strategic use of the traditional model is related to processes of reflexive scientization and commercialization of science by explaining how this model is capable of simultaneously failing in some respects and working in others. This exercise further demonstrates how both approaches differ on both a social-theoretical and political-ideological level. Finally, as the literature review reveals how successfully the institution of science has adapted to the *mediatisation* of society in terms of a relatively effective control of its public image, this chapter concludes, in light of the tremendous democratic challenges discussed above, by calling for a rethinking of (a) the paradigm of science communication, (b) the role of science journalism, and (c) the aims and methods of (science) communication research.

Science and Technology in Late Modern Societies

Reflexive Scientization

According to social theorists Beck (1992) and Giddens (1990), Western societies are confronted today with the social consequences of processes involving the *modernization* of industrial society or late/reflexive modernity. Industrial society then is considered as the result of the modernization of traditional (feudal) society or simple modernity. The categories of primary and reflexive scientization are used for explaining the consequences of these processes for the relationship between science and the public sphere. In the model of primary scientization (during the 19th and first half of the 20th centuries), science was applied to an external world in which there was "a clear demarcation between solutions of problems and causes of problems" (Beck, 1992, p. 159) and possible shortcomings could be attributed to the unfinished degree of *intra*disciplinary scientific development, which subsequently shielded the scientific monopoly on rationality from outside critique. Scientific findings could be advanced in an authoritarian fashion in the public sphere under the conditions of a sharp distinction between tradition and modernity and lay person and expert and an unbroken faith in scientific progress. These conditions are undermined once modernization risks occur, and science needs to account for the definition and distribution of its own negative by-products (i.e., reflexive scientization). Furthermore, modernization risks such as climate, genetic engineering, or radiation risks are ontologically and epistemologically complex: They are global, imperceptible except in terms of physical and chemical formulas, and incalculable in terms of spatial and temporal consequences. Scientific research becomes not only a necessary but also an insufficient condition for making sense of these risks as *inter*disciplinary scientific developments result into a variety of hypothetical scientific findings (either contradictory, complementary, or incomparable). These often conflicting findings are subsequently selectively adopted by various social actors to pursue broader social, economic, or political agendas (Böschen, Kastenhofer, Rust, Soentgen, & Wehling, 2010; Carvalho, 2005; Maeseele, 2010b). The antagonisms originating in these processes produce a new type of social conflict in late modern societies, risk conflicts, involving contestation over competing risk definitions, which are based on competing (a) rationality claims, (b) values, and (c) interests (Maeseele, 2010a, 2011). Furthermore, the im/materiality and in/visibility of these risks not only theoretically privileges science as a key site in late modernity but also mass media: not only in terms of the social definition and revelation of these risks to society at large but also in terms of their social contestation and social criticism (Cottle, 1998).

Commercialization of Science

Universities, science organizations, and individual scientists have increasingly become players in the commercial arena during the past decades (Baskaran & Boden, 2004; Bauer & Gregory, 2007). Whereas the successes of World War II had originally secured the production of scientific knowledge largely within the public sector, helping to establish the ideal of science as a common good, a shift has taken place since the late 1970s and early 1980s from public to private patronage of science research, as Western governments framed the privatization of scientific research as another interesting condition for stimulating economic growth within a context of global economic competitiveness. Programs were set up to reduce public expenditure, while scientific research was relocated within either the private commercial sphere or a marketized public sector. Second, legislation has been passed worldwide related to university patenting, allowing the private exploitation of publicly funded research, which has led to university researchers licensing patents to industry and starting companies themselves. Scientific research and knowledge have increasingly become private goods with the commercialization and marketization of science as an inevitable consequence. The ideal of the independent scientist that serves the public interest and provides disinterested knowledge has become less credible, further weakening the claim—already under pressure through the increasing emergence of modernization risks and risk conflicts—that science provides a universal authority (Levidow, 1999; Maeseele, 2009; Meyer, 2006). This context creates multiple possibilities for conflicts of interest, which could either deliberately or unintentionally, lead to biased conduct: Researchers are increasingly found to hold a financial interest in the research being published in scientific journals with biased conduct being identified particularly in the fields of biomedicine, GM crops, and food (Andersson, 2008; Krimsky, Rothenberg, Stott, & Kyle, 1996; Ruse & Castle, 2002). In addition to specific cases of biased conduct, a more general problem is the trend in which tools such as hyperbole or sensationalism—standard tools for marketing products— easily (and deliberately) find their way into the public communication of science and technology as researchers become actors on the market looking for ways to benefit from their accomplishments (Caulfield, 2004). In some cases science and global capital have been found to blend together into a science-industrial complex united by powerful economic interests in the promotion of certain technologies, such as GM crops and food, while enjoying high levels of institutionalization and state support (Jasanoff, 2005; West, 2007).

The Traditional Model

The field of media and science has traditionally been influenced by adjacent fields of science communication, science popularization, and risk communication. Based on the influence of early communication theory and early sociology of science,[2] the overarching idea has always been and largely continues to be (certainly with natural scientists and policy makers) that scientific knowledge is produced by scientists and experts in a realm separate from the realm of non-scientists to whom it must subsequently be transmitted. By putting science outside of society, the relationship between science and society is characterized as primarily a problem of communication and information. Bucchi (1996, 1998, 2002) has emphasized how this characterization necessarily involves the intervention of a category of professionals and institutions performing this mediation task (e.g., science journalists and communicators, science museums and centers), which is conceived in terms of a metaphor of linguistic translation, reducing the problem of communicating science to the public to a matter of linguistic competence. As illustrated in Figure 6.1, the media in this model only function as "a 'dirty mirror' held up to science" (Bucchi, 2002, p. 109).

By making scientists extraneous to the process and establishing them as hierarchically dominant, this model is clearly science-centered: It problematizes the media and the public but not science. Therefore, its research agenda is reduced to how well the transmission process functions, either in terms of adequate media coverage or adequate public understanding. Furthermore, its attribution of any dislocation in the relationship between science and society (or science and the public) to an inadequate transmission of information, which in our media-saturated societies primarily comes down to targeting media coverage, also makes it a media-centered model. Finally, it regards public acceptance of science and technology as simply a matter of overcoming resistance, from special interest groups, professional mediators such as journalists, or the lay public, by more and better (a) science diffusion, (b) media coverage, and (c) public understanding.

The assumptions underlying this model have strongly affected the research literature on science in the media. In general, the core argument of early reports such as *The Public Impact of Science in the Mass Media* (Davis, 1958) or books such as *Science and the Mass Media* (Krieghbaum, 1967), *Science and the Media* (Farago, 1976), etc., is that the media ignore, misunderstand, and/or misrepresent science. Therefore, what is needed is (a) enhanced science writing and (b) a subsequent redoubling of science journalism. After reviewing the literature on science in the media between 1967 and 1987, Dornan (1990) criticized its normative point of departure and concluded that the popular representation of science had apparently been designated as "a special problem within the field of communication studies" (p. 48). The focus of these studies was the level of accuracy in science reporting, which was often determined by comparing newspaper articles with the original scientific source, meaning the scientists as the scientist sources were frequently asked to quantify the journalists' success. These studies appeared in *Journalism Quarterly* (Tankard &

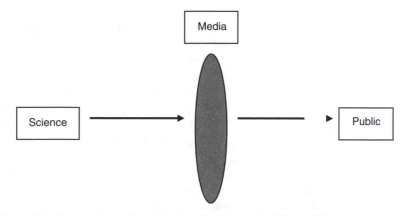

Figure 6.1 The Traditional Model (taken from Bucchi, 2002, p. 108).

Ryan, 1974), *IEEE Transaction of Professional Communication* (Dunwoody, 1982; but also more recently, Carsten & Illman, 2002), and in medical journals (Basu & Hogard, 2008). In general, these studies concluded the scientists' dissatisfaction with science reporting, not only in terms of its factual errors, incompleteness, or lack of essential details, but also in terms of style (sensationalization, misleading headlines, etc.). By blaming the noise in science writing on the press, the strategies advocated to remedy the problem of science in the media were aimed at minimizing journalistic interference by calling for more specialized science writers, by encouraging scientists to handle the press themselves, or to bypass journalists completely and publish their work themselves (Dornan, 1990; Weingart, 1998). The ideal science journalist in this model should act as a subservient spokesperson and marketing agent for science by only transporting scientific knowledge from scientists to the public while identifying with the scientific profession instead of with the public (Lewenstein, 1995b; Meyer, 2006; Nelkin, 1995). Furthermore, the following assumptions have been found to be common within the scientific community related to risk reporting, subsequently coloring research on media coverage and public perceptions (Hornig Priest, 1995): (i) a strong and direct influence of media on public risk perceptions, (ii) a systematic and excessive focus on 'extremist' activists and possible risks, and (iii) a tendency to raise questionable risk issues the public never would raise from itself.[3]

This model has been given many names, primarily by authors criticizing its assumptions: the canonical account (Bucchi, 1996), transfer model (Bucchi, 2004), traditional model (Lewenstein, 1995b, 1995b; Weingart, 1998) or paradigm (Väliverronen, 1993), dominant concern (Dornan, 1990), culturally-dominant view (Hilgartner, 1990; Myers, 2003; van Dijck, 1998), traditional notion of scientific popularization (Shinn & Whitley, 1985b), technocratic approach (Peters, 1994), rationalist position (Hornig, 1993; Hornig Priest, 1995), and risk communication paradigm (Otway & Wynne, 1989).

... And Its Critics

The conception of two separate realms of science and society has primarily been criticized by historians and sociologists of science working in the domains of the sociology of scientific knowledge (SSK) or science and technology studies (STS), both of which resulted from a turn in the sociology of science in the 1970s (Barnes, 1972; Latour & Woolgar, 1979). These authors have questioned (a) the assumption that public discourse only begins where scientific discourse ends, (b) the linearity of the communication process, (c) the neglect of feedback on the core scientific practice, and (d) of interactivity between different forms of media, scientists, and the public.

A seminal edited volume by Shinn and Whitley (1985a) was devoted entirely to questioning the separation of scientific popularization from the communication of science within purely professional contexts. The alternative concept of *scientific exposition* was first proposed here, defined as "a sort of continuum

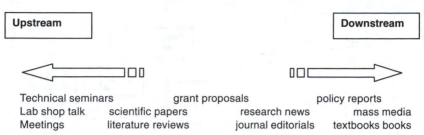

Upstream

Downstream

Technical seminars	grant proposals	policy reports
Lab shop talk scientific papers	research news	mass media
Meetings literature reviews	journal editorials	textbooks books

Figure 6.2 Contexts in which scientific knowledge is communicated (Hilgartner, 1990, p. 528).

of methods and practices utilized both within research and far beyond, for purposes of conveying science-based information, whether as pure cognition, pedagogy or in terms of social and economic problems" (p. viii). The authors also took aim at the idea that the transmission of scientific knowledge served only these purposes and was further unrelated to the process of knowledge production and validation itself, arguing that the social sciences and humanities draw on everyday discourses and concerns, while the research strategies of the natural and life sciences are inevitably affected by the need for resources from external agencies. Hilgartner (1990) further criticized the conceptual and empirical problems relating to the underappreciation of the flexibility and ambiguity of concepts such as "genuine scientific knowledge" and "popularized representations," or "appropriate simplification," and "distortion." Unless in rare cases such as with a scientific journal article and a newspaper article, a clear boundary is often impossible to draw as scientific knowledge is communicated in many different contexts. This implies that comparing representations between contexts will inevitably reveal differences, for instance in terms of the degree of technical information (see Figure 6.2).

Further elaborating the idea of popularization as matter of degree in which the exposition of scientific knowledge occurs in many contexts with different forms and functions, Bucchi (1996, 1998, 2002) subsequently argued that this continuity model should be a multilevel, multivariate model that acknowledges the specific roles of science communication at the level of popular media. A continuity model with four main levels was first proposed in the 1985 volume (Cloître & Shinn, 1985), with an (a) intraspecialist level (e.g., a specialized scientific journal article), (b) interspecialist level (e.g., interdisciplinary journals), (c) pedagogic level (e.g., so-called textbook science), and (d) popular level (e.g., mass media coverage). Bucchi (1996) further distinguished a consensual, non-problematic trajectory from an alternative trajectory for particular conflict situations. When perceived as impossible to solve at the specialist levels, these are deviated to the popular, mass media level, with the aim of in- or excluding certain actors or theories, or launching new interpretations. Once the direction is reversed, core scientific practice is potentially influenced.

Finally, Lewenstein (1995a) emphasized the interactivity between different forms of media, scientists, and the public in science communication. In his

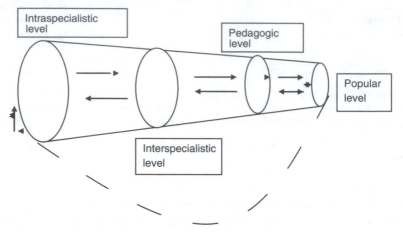

Figure 6.3 A Continuity Model (Bucchi, 2002, p. 115).

landmark study of the cold fusion controversy, which included new media and information communication technologies (ICTs) in the research design, Lewenstein found how people not only make use of a mix of communication channels that continuously interact in the exchange of information but also how the main effect of mass media coverage is the temporary intensification of the complexity of information contexts. Instead of a continuum, he launched the idea of an interactional model in the shape of a circle or a web (see Figure 6.4) in which the focus is not reduced to one communication channel, but in which multiple science communication contexts interact. In an interesting follow-up, Brossard found how in some cases of crisis situations the media and scientific journals are found to switch attributes (Brossard, 2009).

Despite these adaptations, we are referring to the basic assumptions of the traditional model when it is discussed in the remainder of this chapter, as

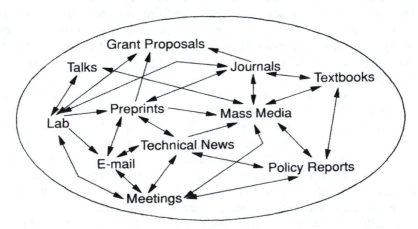

Figure 6.4 The Web of Science Communication Contexts (Lewenstein, 1995a, p. 426).

policy makers, scientific institutes and societies, advocacy organizations, etc., keep reinventing the original model in response to crises in public trust.

A Media-Sociological Perspective

The literature review also revealed a different more loosely defined approach to the relationship between media and science, generally focusing on the meaning-making processes underlying public and media discourses on science. Studies starting from this approach exceed the science- and media-centeredness of the traditional model by abandoning a conception of the scientific establishment as the ultimate arbiter of the accuracy and adequacy of popular media representations and also allowing a distinct and independent role for mass media in general and journalism in particular. The traditional model, on the other hand, systematically ignores the distinct selection criteria and operational independence of media and journalism. Second, exceeding media-centeredness implies not only abandoning a conception in which the relationship between science and society is explained exclusively in terms of an inadequate information transmission, it assumes public representations of science and technology to be part of wider cultural frameworks from which journalists draw and to which media discourse simultaneously contributes. This means that although media discourse reflects and shapes these images, the latter are not completely reducible to the former:

> The interpretive packages in media discourse are one part of a larger issue culture, both reflecting it and contributing to its creation. Journalists draw their ideas and language from other forums, frequently using the language and frames of their sources. At the same time, they contribute their own metaphors, drawing on a popular culture that they share with the audience. (Gamson, 1988, p. 166)

Social psychologists, for instance, studying social representations of science and technology not only find contrasting representations being contested and negotiated in public discourse, but in doing so almost inevitably end up discussing the role of media in these processes (Bauer, 2003; Flynn, Slovic, & Kunreuther, 2001; Gaskell, 2001; Wagner & Kronberger, 2001). Unlike the traditional model, science and scientific legitimacy then are not assumed to be constituted a priori public distribution. They are assumed to be achieved within the communication process itself. Science is not located outside of society, it is defined within society. This creates a discursive, theoretical, and empirical space for focusing on the meaning-making processes underlying definitions of science (communication) in public and media discourses. Popularization then is interpreted as a multi-layered process in which different social actors (heterogeneous and unequal in power), such as science organizations, industry associations, consultants, policy makers, independent (dissenting) scientists, citizen groups, and political and social movements/NGOs are involved in defining the hegemonic meanings of science and technology, and in which the media constitute a site of contestation not only over different representations but also over science's representations of science and technology (Schlesinger & Silverstone, 1995; van Dijck, 1998). The research questions in this approach focus on understanding (a) how scientific rationality and scientific claims are represented in the media and by whom, (b) how this relates to issues of access to the media and social debate, and (c) how these media products are interpreted and used by their various audiences. This requires an examination of not only the production, (re)presentation(s), and reception[4] of science and technology in the media, but also the consequences of the mediatisation of society in terms of the mediatisation of science.

The Mediatisation of Science

When societies and cultures undergo processes of mediatisation,[5] the struggle for mediated visibility assumes central importance, as public legitimacy and power increasingly relate to the management of visibility and self-presentation and an orientation towards media practices (Hjarvard, 2008; Thompson, 1995). The extent to which a social institution is both affected by and adapts to mediatisation is an empirical matter, and studies have explored whether and to what extent the mediatisation of society also stimulates a mediatisation of science, in terms of changes in (a) presentation mode and (b) the inner workings of the scientific profession itself (see also Väliverronen, 2001[6]). The professionalization of marketing practices, public relations, and image management has been found to increasingly turn science communication into science public relations or science PR. In the context of reflexive scientization and the commercialization of science, the problem of popularization has partly become a problem of selling science. Besides changes in presentation modes, several authors have also indicated changes in the content and workings of the institution of science in what has been called the science-media coupling.

Public Relations.   A dominant feature of developments in the relationship between science and the media has been an increasing market orientation of universities and science organizations. The art of managing visibility and self-promotion has become a new institutional practice, not only for fund raising, but also for student recruitment, career competition, grading, and academic publishing. (Borcholt, 2008; Gregory & Miller, 1998; Hansen, 1994; Nelkin, 1995; Peters, Heinrichs, Jung, Kallfass, & Petersen, 2008c; Väliverronen, 1993; van Dijck, 1998). The aim of professionalizing public communication and moderating the exchange of information between scientists, journalists, and society has brought the advent of PR-departments and public information and press offices. In a study of interviews with heads of PR-departments and public information offices, Peters et al. (2008c) conclude there is a significant influence from scientific institutes on how media cover their organization and activities. This happens by exercising central control over their public communication by fine tuning the self-presentation of the organization, and by successfully adapting to media practices. This influence is present not only in terms of anticipated media expectations being the key selection criteria for managing any contacts between journalists and scientists but also in terms of disseminating their own content by means of press releases, press conferences, and exclusive information. Furthermore, the interviewees pointed out that they have found science reporting to be not only predominantly affirmative but also indicated an eager readiness on the part of media organizations to accept PR-material "relatively uncritically and sometimes even without reference to its source" (Peters et al., 2008c, p. 82). The authors conclude that in addition to an increased media presence, the success of the professionalization of science PR leads to an increased usage of non-scientific frames of reference, constructing scientific research through meaning patterns such as a competitive sport frame or a guild or hubris frame.

The Science-Media Coupling. Weingart (1998; Weingart & Pansegrau, 1999) in particular has shown how mediatisation not only influences the public presentation of science, but also decisions in the research process and the knowledge it produces, especially in terms of shifting funding priorities. He explicitly deals with the mediatisation of science in three respects. The first is the detour of scientists directly to the media in terms of the pre-publication of scientific results. In very competitive scientific domains, symbolized by prizes and patents, the media are often instrumentalized for securing priority and/or attaining public attention. Seminal examples of science by press conference are the cold fusion case in 1989 (Bucchi, 1998; Lewenstein, 1995a; Välliverronen, 1993; Weingart, 1998), the publication of the first draft of the human genome in 2000 (Ho, 2000; Rödder, 2008), and the Pusztai-interview in 1998 on the health risks of GM potatoes (Smith, 2003). Second is the competition between media prominence and scientific reputation, relating to how media criteria of relevance and validation can lead to an increase in symbolic capital that is potentially converted into financial resources, while being unrelated to a scientist's scientific reputation (Weingart, 1998; Weingart & Pansegrau, 1999). Third is the competition for public attention in terms of overbidding discourses: Scientists are found to either adapt their discourses to catastrophic scenarios, triggering media attention, calls for political action, and an eventual re-allocation of funding priorities (Weingart, 1998), or to hyperbolic scenarios, proclaiming the next big breakthrough with over-optimistic predictions, mostly related to potentially commercial products (Bubela & Caulfield, 2004; Caulfield, 2004, 2005; Caulfield & Bubela, 2004). Regarding the former, Weingart (1998) details how the pressure for political action following widely mediated catastrophic climate predictions in 1986 by German physicists led to the establishment of two new climate research institutions, even though the physicists' original objective was the rehabilitation of nuclear energy following Chernobyl. The use of hyperbolic scenarios has especially been found in the case of recent advances in biotechnology, a phenomenon labeled "genohype."

Caulfield (2004, 2005) has found this hyping to be part of a more systemic problem following the commercialization of the research environment, as the increasing pressure placed on researchers and research institutions to justify their work in economic terms creates a particular spin in terms of an optimistic picture that minimizes risks and limitations and leads to research portrayals that emphasize near-future economic benefits and potential therapies. Driven by researchers casting their work in ways attractive to private investors as well as research funded and published by the private sector itself, a media arms race arises in which neither researcher, science organization, biotechnology corporation nor reporter has anything to gain by mediating the hyperbolic rhetoric which becomes part of the way these actors speak about biotechnology. When public expectations about genetic research are subsequently raised, this further stimulates researchers for another round of over-optimistic messages, thereby creating a cycle of hype. With the traditional model's main tenets in mind, it is ironic that in both cases it is the accurate media portrayal of messages created by the scientific community that makes this possible.

The Science-Media Interface

Science News Production.   Starting from the premises of the traditional model, the literature on science-media interactions in the past suggested a deficient scientist-journalist interaction, even assuming unbridgeable gaps between media and science (Dunwoody & Ryan, 1985; Peters, 1995). Although many science organizations and public institutions (e.g., Royal Society, 2006), advocacy groups (e.g., Hartz & Chapell, 1997), and scholars (Willems, 2003) still start from these premises, recent studies have concluded interactions to be widespread and appreciative, even revealing a symbiotic relationship between journalists and their scientific sources (Geller, Bernhardt, Gardner, Rodgers, & Holtzman, 2005; Peters et al., 2008a, 2008b, 2008c), especially in the case of biomedical researchers. Although these studies observe consistent discrepancies in terms of the underlying communication model and consequent normative expectations (e.g., scientists prefer a purely instrumental role for the media and almost unanimously call for proof-reading stories) as well as respective professional cultures and styles, the reporting is found to serve the surveyed scientists' pragmatic communication goals: Its affirmative nature enjoys a high degree of acceptance. Peters et al. (2008b) relate an increasing use and success of science PR and a shift in which strategic PR-oriented criteria supersede accuracy-oriented criteria to a more positive perception of science-media interactions and attribute these developments to a search for public legitimacy in a late modern context.

    In addition to studies on scientist-journalist interactions, media scholars have also shown an interest in the journalistic practices, routines, and news values related to science in the media. In general, these were found to differ little from media coverage of other topics in terms of training and skills, conventional news values and source-orientation. Although science reporters seemed to experience more pressure from the mass of promotional material, press releases, and information demands from a variety of organizations, including universities, government agencies, corporations, NGOs, PR agencies, and scientific journals (Allan, 2002; Gregory & Miller, 1998; Hansen, 1994). Studies on the selection of scientific studies for newspaper coverage, for example, have shown that there is a correlation between whether a press release was issued from the scientific journal in which that study had appeared and its subsequent publication in a newspaper (Bartlett, Sterne, & Egger, 2002; de Semir, Ribas, & Revuela, 1998; Kitzinger & Reilly, 1997). This could be problematic as press releases not only use formats that exaggerate the importance of findings but, more importantly, frequently leave out study limitations as well as the role of industry funding (Woloshin & Schwartz, 2002). Similar results have been found concerning video news releases for television news (Machill, Beiler, & Schmutz, 2006). Similar to journalism in general, news coverage of environmental risks has systematically been found to prefer the spectacular and often visually sensational events over everyday hazards, such as a pesticide-driven agriculture, in addition to being event-sensitive as opposed to issue-sensitive (Allan, 2002; Allan, Adam, & Carter, 2000; Hansen, 1993). The implication of both of these elements is that the one-in-a-million accident provides the explicit discursive tool for the implicit normalization of the safety of the status quo of modernization risks such as nuclear energy, GM food, etc.

Meyer (2006) and Priest (2001) have also stressed how the norm of objectivity leads journalists to uncritically accept the authority of science, evoking an uncritical reproduction by journalists. Whenever there appear to be diverging scientific opinions, the larger-institution stakeholder position will mostly preside over other positions. This adjoins the institutional reality of how journalists rarely transcend the hegemony of contemporary market-centered news production to challenge powerful institutions, leading to repeated episodes of scientific hype in science reporting, with the Hwang Woo-Suk episode[7] as an exemplary case (Jensen, 2010). Furthermore, this conclusion is problematic in a context of reflexive scientization in which citizen groups and environmental movements are found to publicize the existence of modernization risks, to make claims about them, often in the face of a scientific consensus that denies their existence. These pressure groups are vying for media attention (Allan et al., 2000; Anderson, 2000; Hansen, 1993; Miller & Riechert, 2000; Mormont & Dasnoy, 1995), along with companies and industry associations that increasingly promote their technological products using the prestige of science and technology to enhance their claims as well as their credibility in general (Bauer, 2008; Fennel, 2009; Nelkin, 1995). Scientific images and scientists are increasingly brought forward in advertising and PR-efforts to instill confidence in commercial products.

In addition to the former social-organizational elements, some authors have also pleaded for taking into consideration the discursive landscape which influences how certain discourses facilitate and constrain the elaboration and coverage of particular topics (Allan, 2002; Gamson & Modigliani, 1989; Hansen, 1991, 1994). These discourses are embedded within dominant ideologies of a political culture and resonate with these existing and widely held cultural concepts that privilege the advancement of some issues, perspectives, and sources above others in public and media debates. Technological progressivism, scientism, and neo-liberal discourses make it much harder for critical stories to gain prominence or for critical sources to be accredited with legitimacy (Carvalho, 2007; Hansen, 1991; Maeseele, 2010a, 2011).

Media Representations of Science.   Influential studies on science coverage in newspapers have consistently concluded that the typical science story focuses on medicine and health, is a hard news story (event-oriented, time-bound reports), has an international focus, originates from a wire service, and contains one scientist source and a predominantly positive tone, heralding an advancement and highlighting positive consequences (Bauer, Durant, & Ragnarsdottir, 1995; Bauer & Gregory, 2007; Bucchi & Mazzolini, 2003; Einsiedel, 1992). Particularly significant are the findings in these studies that almost three in four articles come from wire services and that stories in general tend to rely on uncontested scientific expertise, thereby preserving the dominance of scientific authority. In the last decade, numerous representation studies have been published on emerging technologies such as biotechnology or nanotechnology, or on complex environmental problems such as climate change. In general, these studies have confirmed a predominant source-generated, pro-technology bias, except in those cases where social movements or non-governmental organizations have succeeded in politicizing scientific or economic progress[8] (Anderson, Allan, Petersen, & Wilkinson, 2005; Gaskell & Bauer, 2001; Maeseele, 2011; Nisbet & Lewenstein, 2002; Väliverronen, 2004; van Dijck, 1998).

Why the Traditional Model Fails (and Works)

The traditional model is clearly an exponent of the characterization of the relationship between science and society in the model of primary scientization, whose impetus was provided by (a) the demarcation between modernity and tradition, and expert and lay person, (b) an unbroken faith in science and progress, and (c) the subsequent authoritarian enforcement of scientific knowledge in external relations (Beck, 1992). In conditions of reflexive scientization, however, these concepts and hierarchical relations come under pressure as modernization risks increasingly become center stage, render the instrumental control of science and the institutionalized rationality of risk control inadequate, and strong scientific disagreements are publicly displayed in terms of competing and conflicting claims of knowledge. Moreover, scientific knowledge is increasingly demonopolized and other actors than the scientific community enter the public arena armed with scientific results, not only corporations and consultants, but also environmental movements and consumer organizations (e.g., the issues of nuclear energy, GM food, climate change, etc.). The traditional model, therefore, fails in conditions of reflexive scientization, as it does not allow the limits of expertise to be acknowledged or uncertainties and alternative understandings to be discussed.

Nevertheless, following the publication of a report in 1985 by the Royal Society of London (Bodmer, 1985), the concept of the Public Understanding of Science (or PUS) has come to symbolize the tenacity and enduring strength of the traditional model for policy-makers and scientific societies and institutes. Widely interpreted as a legitimation for popularization (often considered the prerogative of lesser scientists until then), it encouraged the scientific community to regard the active promotion of the public understanding of science as its duty (Bauer & Gregory, 2007) and has been found to serve as "a clarion call to action ... [it] galvanized a series of practical initiatives ... [and] grew from a small, evangelical crusade into something like a mass movement" (Durant, 1999, p. 314). This science-centered and science-led movement emphasizes the educational role of the scientist in a context of technological competition and frames its task as "one of combating public hostility and resistance to new technology" (Elam & Bertilsson, 2003, p. 239). Seminal authors such as Durant (1999) and Wynne (1995) have explained the rise of the PUS-movement since the mid-1980s by relating it to that second structural development identified earlier: the commercialization of science. They consider this inflation of the traditional model in the guise of PUS as a response of the scientific establishment to a widely perceived legitimation vacuum and crisis in public trust in a period in which the commercialization of science took off in leading areas of biotechnology. This commercialization did not intensify only the weight placed upon public credulity and legitimation, but it also raised the stakes for the scientific community, policy-makers, and industry. Economic concerns have thus been found to be important underlying motivations for the PUS agenda. For the past two decades, the problem of the public understanding of science has been a part of government policies around the industrial world with the necessary funds reserved for addressing the issue through science museums, science festivals, and science weeks.

The question then comes forward how to explain the apparently strong relationship between the intensity of processes of reflexive scientization and commercialization and the strategic usefulness of the traditional model? A likely explanation is that the traditional model not only fails in some respects, but simultaneously works in others: In public discourse the traditional model serves to deny a framing of risk debates as opposing responses to uncertainty by (a) using rhetorical devices such as discourses of sound science, (b) emphasizing an unproblematic notion of scientific consensus to de-politicize and suppress democratic debate, and (c) having the media validate dominant institutional risk definitions. Hilgartner (1990) warned how the traditional model serves as a powerful tool in public discourse for anyone who derives his or her authority from scientific expertise, because it provides a repertoire of conceptual and rhetorical devices for sustaining the social hierarchy of expertise, for instance, by using the appropriate simplification label for influencing down-stream audiences when it comes to their support, while using the distortion label for delegitimizing unfavorable media representations. In each case, the authority of genuine scientific knowledge is (re)affirmed as extra-scientific factors or actors such as the mass media or the public are blamed for flawed information. In other words, the traditional model succeeds in dividing society into those who accept and promote science and technology and those who resist (van Dijck, 1998). Its function is clearly ideological and political: By throwing the spotlight on public cognitions, motivations, and capabilities as well as on communication patterns and the media, the dominant PUS agenda naturalizes the existing institutionalized culture of science in terms of its representation, organization, patronage, control, and social relations, while systematically deleting the institutional and epistemic characteristics of dominant forms of science (Wynne, 1995).

Eventually, what we find is a complicated dialectic manifesting itself between the invalidity of the traditional model and its strategic usefulness: The traditional model's conceptual and rhetorical devices are used most fiercely where the conditions invalidating the traditional model are most intense, for instance, in the context of a risk conflict such as the GM food controversy in which the science establishment and biotech-industry unite in the promotion of GM food against critical scientists and civil society (Maeseele, 2010a). Furthermore, amplifying the PUS agenda in these conditions further stifles any democratic space between science and society and inadvertently encourages more public ambivalence and alienation. The PUS agenda creates the context which is subsequently used as a pretext for its necessity.

Finally, this demonstrates that the relationship between media and science is an essential political-ideologically contested relationship, which implies that we find an intricate process of in- and exclusion, of defining the boundaries, of science in science communication or science in the media. Both the traditional model and the proposed media-sociological perspective take a radically different position when it comes to interpreting this relationship. If we were to make a distinction between a minimalist and maximalist interpretation of this relationship, the former would refer to a strategy of safeguarding dominant forms of science communication by distinguishing these from false manifestations instead of alternative ones, while the latter would refer to a strategy of focusing on the meaning-making processes underlying definitions of science communication as part of a political-ideological struggle. While both interpretations represent a struggle between two political-ideological models for interpreting the relationship between media and science, only one of these creates the discursive space for approaching public and media discourse as a site of struggle between political-ideological projects. The traditional model then represents the minimalist interpretation (of which the aim is exactly to delegitimize the acknowledgment of a political-ideological struggle), while the media-sociological perspective represents the maximalist interpretation.

Discussion: From PUS Inc. to Risk Journalism

Seminal figures such as Bauer and Bucchi (2007) conclude that today there is a new regime of science communication in which a logic of public relations, marketing, and corporate communication has displaced a logic of journalistic reportage. Underlying this evolution, according to the authors, is the increasingly privatized production of scientific knowledge during the last decades of the 20th century. They refer to it as PUS Inc., as they consider it to be an offshoot of the Public Understanding of Science movement initiated by the Bodmer-report in 1985. Despite the tenets of the traditional model, the results of the many recent empirical studies that were discussed starting from a media-sociological perspective indeed reveal how successfully the institution of science has adapted to the mediatisation of society in terms of a relatively effective control of its public image: We have found (a) a largely affirmative character of science reporting, even in terms of hyperbolic rhetoric in the case of heavily commercialized fields of research, (b) relatively effective science PR in terms of a determinative effect of press releases on science reporting and an uncritical reproduction by journalists of PR material, (c) indications of a symbiotic relationship between scientists and their media-contacts with recent cross-national surveys indicating that media reporting enjoys a high degree of satisfaction among scientists, (d) a coverage largely reliant on uncontested scientific expertise by drawing from only one institutional source, and (e) cultural resonances and the dominant ideologies in which these are embedded that make it harder for critical stories to gain prominence or for critical sources to be accredited with legitimacy.

This conclusion of a relatively effective control of science's public image has troublesome implications in a late modern context of modernization risks and the commercialization of science, leading to an array of democratic challenges as discussed in the introduction of this chapter, and calls for a rethinking of (a) the paradigm of science communication, (b) the role of science journalism, and (c) the aims and methods of (science) communication research.

First, many authors have called for replacing the delivery of public acceptance at the core of the paradigm of science communication and science in the media by the encouragement of the public scrutiny of often privatized scientific developments (Bauer, 2008; Bauer & Bucchi, 2007; Meyer, 2006; Mormont & Dasnoy, 1995; Salleh, 2004, 2008). These authors have argued that it is impossible to save the idea of knowledge as a common good without breaking with the convention of PUS Inc. and its associated marketing practices, in order to promote and facilitate public scrutiny, discussion, and reflection on questions of knowledge and technological innovation.

Second, science journalism has traditionally been conceptualized as an extension of institutional science communication, with science journalists seen as transporting scientific knowledge from scientists to the public while relying on an unproblematic notion of scientific consensus. As a result, a clear lack of skepticism has been found to be common in the practice of science journalism

(Jensen, 2010). The most elaborate attempt at a reformulation of science jour-nalism in a late modern context has been made by Salleh (2004, 2008), who pleads for a journalism in which risk debates are framed as conflicts between opposing responses to the unforeseen consequences of any risk technology. The strategy of powerful scientific elites is exactly to suppress such a debate by using the rhetorical devices of sound science and the tenets of the traditional model to control public discourse. The task of the journalist here is to show how different responses to uncertainty have legitimate standing in the debate by examining their underlying assumptions and interests, as to publicly con-trast their different underlying rationalities (see also Peters et al., 2008b, pp. 274–275).

Third, this context brings forward important questions concerning the social role of media in democratic societies and the relationship between media, power, and democracy. What is at stake in contemporary risk conflicts is an ideological struggle between alternative technological futures based on competing analyses of the current and ideal state of affairs. Therefore, from a perspective of democratic debate, these controversies should be approached from a framework of political conflict, entailing ideological discussion and collective debate and choice (Mouffe, 2005; Swyngedouw, 2010). Avoiding the trap of the post-political and post-democratic condition implies making a conceptual and empirical choice for politicization and conflict in a specific research design. Therefore, in future research, studies from a media-sociolog-ical perspective should exceed a narrow focus on the meaning-making pro-cesses underlying media discourses on science and ask whether and to what extent media are found to facilitate or impede democratic debate and demo-cratic citizenship by contributing to a framing of risk conflicts as political choices between alternative technological futures, or to the contrary, as mat-ters best left to technocratic decision-making and/or market forces, or between processes of politicization and de-politicization (see Carvalho, 2007; Hansen, 2011; Maeseele, 2010a, 2011). This agenda will not only require a method-ological framework focusing simultaneously on the three levels of the reflexive circuit between frame sponsors, media discourses, and audience discourses, but also critical qualitative methods, such as framing and critical discourse analysis which allow to register the extent and nature of ideological discussion in public and media discourses on science.

Conclusion

This literature review has revealed how the disparate academic literature on science and the media can be subdivided in two broad approaches in terms of underlying assumptions and communication models. Similar to trends within Communication Studies in general, there has been a shift from an instru-mental, linear perspective on how to communicate science more effectively, starting from the assumption of an undefined notion of information, to a soci-ological perspective focusing on the meaning-making practices underlying definitions of science in the media, starting from an assumption of communication practices as indefinite articulations of meaning. At the same time, many sociologists and historians of science developed a multilevel and interactive perspective as an alternative to the traditional model, without engaging cultural frameworks and meaning-creation.

Finally, there has been growing academic interest in the consequences of a converging, digital media environment for science journalism with special issues in *Journalism* (Allen, 2011) and the *Journal of Science Communication* (Pitrelli, 2011). A new interactive and informational environment with countless new websites and tools such as blogs, podcasts, Twitter, Skype, Facebook, and Youtube, is changing the forms and practices of science journalism. The changing media landscape however does not affect the arguments of this chapter. Not only is the pace of the structural developments of reflexive scientization and the commercialization of science (i.e., the social context in which these changes take place) left unaltered, but the fundamental question remains the underlying communication models and assumptions informing academic research of these new forms of communication and the conclusions which these allow to draw. For instance, do we find a focus on the extent to which these new information channels misrepresent true science or recast scientist-source interactions in terms of allowing science bloggers to publicly scrutinize the accuracy of science stories or to bypass the journalistic level by undertaking journalistic activity themselves (traditional model)? Or is the focus put on the ever-increasing potential for complex, interactive communication mechanisms involving diverse actors in understanding controversies (adaptation of the traditional model)? Or, are these studies focusing on the extent to which alternative discourses and representations are available to counter the successful PUS Inc. practices in the promotion of new technologies by supplementing their coverage online or on the extent to which the increasing deskbound nature of science journalistic work is likely to reduce investigative newsgathering even more (the media-sociological model)? Only future literature reviews will tell.

Notes

1. The selected papers, reports, and books in this literature review have not been collected in a specific moment in time using a specific method and specific selection criteria which would allow the use of a quantitative approach in making statements on the existing relevant literature. The selection, analysis, and synthesis of literature in this chapter is the result of a process spanning eight years of scholarship on media and science, in which relevant literature was collected and analyzed until a point of saturation was reached regarding the general aim of distinguishing underlying communication models and assumptions in a disparate literature (as well as understanding their specific recurrences and adaptations over time). This involved repeated instances of occasional focused searches through academic databases or journal archives as well as the retrieval of potentially relevant publications from specific article reference lists or citation lists. There was a specific sequence involved in developing my argumentation: the

underlying communication models and assumptions were identified first using exclusively literature published on the relationship between media and science in general. Only subsequently, specific case studies were collected with the aim of explaining how research is conducted within the identified approaches and with what results. During this process, no specific geographical or historical limitations were set forward from the start, although the eventual selection has turned out to be limited to post-war English-language publications, focusing primarily on authors and case studies from the Western world. It is unlikely however that this significantly limits the analyses and conclusions of this chapter, not only because its main aim is to distinguish the underlying communication models and assumptions informing academic research in the field of media and science and not to understand specific case studies in specific time-bound locales, but more importantly, because the structural developments of reflexive scientization and the commercialization of science to which the analyzed literature is related in this chapter, are primarily Western developments.

2. Starting from an objectivist concept of science, a positivist view of scientific knowledge and the assumption that there is always one "correct" interpretation of any risk controversy, in other words, an unproblematic notion of scientific consensus.

3. However, these have shown to be false by numerous studies (e.g., respectively by Bucchi, 2004, Nisbet & Lewenstein, 2002, and Hornig, 1995).

4. Reception analyses of science in the media however have been found to be quite rare during the process of this review, which serves as an important observation for much-needed future research. For example, the few studies to have been found were Lowe et al. (2006), on a climate change film, Peters (2000), on genetic engineering stories, and Davin (2003), on medical narratives in television entertainment.

5. The concept of mediatisation has been used to explain different things by different authors who have used slightly different terms: *medialization* (Peters et al., 2008c; Rödder, 2008; Weingart, 1998), *mediazation* (Thompson, 1995), *mediatization* (Fornäs, 1995; Hellsten, 2002; Hjarvard, 2008; Krotz, 2007; Schulz, 2004; Väliverronen, 2001), for example. I draw from the work of John Thompson (1995, 2005) and Stig Hjarvard (2008) who emphasize how the public sphere has transformed from a non-mediated agora for dialogue and debate to a new kind of publicness: mediated visibility. Freed from the constraints of the spatial and temporal properties of the here and now, mediated visibility is shaped instead by the distinctive properties of the media, whether by their social or technical considerations or the new types of interaction they make possible. Amongst others, this implies that new modes of exercising power are created, which are no longer related to the sharing of a common physical locale and which are shaped by the differential quantities of power and resources of those with an interest in managing their visibility and public image.

6. Mediatisation therefore is reserved for how the science institute adapts and orients itself to the increasing significance of the media (see also Hellsten, 2002; Weingart, 1998). Some authors (Rödder, 2008; Schäfer, 2009) use mediatisation also to refer to an increasing (and changing) media attention for scientific issues. The former regard the process solely from the perspective of science, the latter regard the process also from the perspective of the media.

7. The South-Korean Professor Hwang-Woo Suk received international stardom

after authoring two articles in *Science* which appeared to establish the technical feasibility of therapeutic cloning. Several months after the second article, however, Hwang's articles appeared fraudulent and eventually both were retracted. This episode serves an exemplary case of the lack of journalistic scepticism in science journalism (Jensen, 2010).

8. Other exceptions to this general trend are those examples in which we find corporate and other special interests manufacturing doubt about scientific findings that threaten their interests (or values), which has happened in cases such as acid rain, the ozone hole, smoking, global warming, evolution theory, etc. (Oreskes & Conway, 2010).

References

Allan, S. (2002). *Media, risk and science*. Buckingham, England: Open University Press.

Allan, S., Adam, B., & Carter, C. (Eds.). (2000). *Environmental risks and the media*. London, England: Routledge.

Allen, S. (Ed.). (2011). Science journalism in a digital age [Special issue]. *Journalism, 12*(7).

Anderson, A. (2000). Environmental pressure politics and the 'risk society.' In S. Allan, B. Adam, & C. Carter (Eds.), *Environmental risks and the media* (pp. 93–104). London, England: Routledge.

Anderson, A., Allan, S., Petersen, A., & Wilkinson, C. (2005). The framing of nano-technologies in the British newspaper press. *Science Communication, 27*, 200–220. doi:10.1177/1075547005281472

Andersson, K. (2008). *Transparency and accountability in science and politics. The awareness principle*. Houndsmills, England: Palgrave MacMillan.

Bartlett, C., Sterne, J., & Egger, M. (2002). What is newsworthy? Longitudinal study of the reporting of medical research in two British newspapers. *British Medical Journal, 325*(7355), 81–84. doi:10.1136/bmj.325.7355.81

Barnes, B. (Ed.). (1972). *Sociology of science*. Middlesex, England: Penguin Books.

Baskaran, A., & Boden, R. (2004). Science: A controversial commodity. *Science, Technology & Society, 9*, 1–26. doi:10.1177/097172180400900101

Basu, A., & Hogard, E. (2008). Fit for public consumption? An exploratory study of the reporting of nutrition research in UK tabloids with regard to its accuracy, and a preliminary investigation of public attitudes towards it. *Public Health Nutrition, 11*(11), 1124–1131.

Bauer, M. W. (2003). 'Science in the media' as a cultural indicator: Contextualizing surveys with media analysis. In M. Dierkes & C. van Grote (Eds.), *Between understanding and trust. The public, science and technology* (pp. 157–178). London, England: Routledge.

Bauer, M. W. (2008). Paradigm change for science communication: Commercial science needs a critical public. In D. Cheng, M. Claessens, T. Gascoigne, J. Metcalfe, B. Schiele, & S. Shi (Eds.), *Communicating science in social contexts. New models, new practices* (pp. 7–25). Dordrecht, Holland: Springer.

Bauer, M. W., & Bucchi, M. (Eds.). (2007). *Journalism, science and society. Science communication between news and public relations*. New York, NY: Routledge.

Bauer, M. W., Durant, J., & Ragnarsdottir, A. (1995). *Science and technology in the British press (1946–1990)*. London, England: The Science Museum.

Bauer, M. W., & Gregory, J. (2007). From journalism to corporate communication in post-war Britain. In M. W. Bauer & M. Bucchi (Eds.), *Journalism, science and society. Science communication between news and public relations* (pp. 33–52). New York, NY: Routledge.

Beck, U. (1992). *Risk society. Towards a new modernity.* London, England: Sage.

Bodmer, W. (1985). *The public understanding of science.* London, England: Royal Society.

Borcholt, R. E. (2008). Public relations in science. In M. Bucchi & B. Trench (Eds.), *Handbook of public communication of science and technology* (pp. 147–157). London, England: Routledge.

Böschen S., Kastenhofer, K., Rust, I., Soentgen, J., & Wehling, P. (2010). Scientific nonknowledge and its political dynamics: The cases of agri-biotechnology and mobile phoning. *Science, Technology & Human Values, 35,* 783–811. doi:10.1177/0162243909357911

Brossard, D. (2009). Media, scientific journals and science communication: Examining the construction of scientific controversies. *Public Understanding of Science, 18,* 258–274. doi:10.1177/0963662507084398

Bubela, T., & Caulfield, T. (2004). Do the print media 'hype' genetic research? A comparison of newspaper stories and peer-reviewed research papers. *Canadian Medical Association Journal, 170,* 1399–1407. doi:10.1503/cmaj.1030762

Bucchi, M. (1996). When scientists turn to the public: Alternative routes in science communication. *Public Understanding of Science, 5,* 375–394. doi:10.1088/0963-6625/5/4/005

Bucchi, M. (1998). *Science and the media. Alternative routes in scientific communication.* London, England: Routledge.

Bucchi, M. (2002). *Science in society: An introduction to social studies of science.* London, England: outledge.

Bucchi, M. (2004). Can genetics help us rethink communication? Public communication of science as a 'double helix.' *New Genetics and Society, 23,* 269–283. doi:10.1080/1463677042000305048

Bucchi, M., & Mazzolini, R. G. (2003). Big science, little news: Science coverage in the Italian daily press, 1946–1997. *Public Understanding of Science, 12,* 7–24. doi:10.1177/0963662503012001413

Carsten, L. D., & Illman, D. L. (2002). Perceptions of accuracy in science writing. *IEEE Transactions on Professional Communication, 45,* 153–156. doi:10.1109/TPC.2002.801632

Caulfield, T. (2004). Biotechnology and the popular press: Hype and the selling of science. *Trends in Biotechnology, 22,* 337–339. doi:10.1016/j.tibtech.2004.03.014

Caulfield, T. (2005). Popular media, biotechnology and the 'cycle of hype.' *Journal of Health Law and Policy, 5,* 213–233.

Caulfield, T., & Bubela, T. (2004). Media representations of genetic discoveries: Hype in the headlines? *Health Law Review, 12*(3), 53–61.

Carvalho, A. (2005). Cultural circuits of climate change in U.K. broadsheet newspapers, 1985–2003. *Risk Analysis, 25,* 1457–1469.

Carvalho, A. (2007). Ideological cultures and media discourses on scientific knowledge: Re-reading news on climate change. *Public Understanding of Science, 16,* 223–243. doi:10.1177/0963662506066775

Cloître, M., & Shinn, T. (1985). Expository practice. Social, cognitive and epistemological linkages. In T. Shinn & R. Whitley (Eds.), *Expository science: Forms and functions of popularisation* (pp. 31–60). Dordrecht, Holland: D. Riedel.

Cottle, S. (1998). Ulrich Beck, 'risk society' and the media: A catastrophic view? *European Journal of Communication, 13*, 5–32. doi:10.1177/0267323198013001001

Davin, S. (2003). Healthy viewing: The reception of medical narratives. *Sociology of Health and Illness, 25*, 662–679. doi:10.1111/1467-9566.00364

Davis, R. C. (1958). *The public impact of science in the mass media*. Ann Arbor: University of Michigan Institute for Social Research.

De Semir, V., Ribas, C., & Revuela, G. (1998). Press releases of science journal articles and subsequent newspaper stories on the same topic. *The Journal of the American Medical Association, 280*, 294–295. doi:10.1001/jama.280.3.294

Dornan, C. (1990). Some problems in conceptualizing the issue of "science and the media." *Critical Studies in Mass Communication, 7*, 48–71. doi:10.1080/15295039009360163

Dunwoody, S. (1982). A question of accuracy. *IEEE Transactions on Professional Communication, 25*, 196–199.

Dunwoody, S., & Ryan, M. (1985). Scientific barriers to the popularization of science in the mass media. *Journal of Communication, 35*, 26–42. doi:10.1111/j.1460-2466.1985.tb01882.x

Durant, J. (1999). Participatory technology assessment and the democratic model of the public understanding of science. *Science and Public Policy, 26*, 313–319. doi:10.3152/147154399781782329

Einsiedel, E. (1992). Framing science and technology in the Canadian press. *Public Understanding of Science, 1*, 89–101. doi:10.1088/0963-6625/1/1/011

Elam, M., & Bertilsson, M. (2003). Consuming, engaging and confronting science. The emerging dimensions of scientific citizenship. *European Journal of Social Theory, 6*, 233–251. doi: 10.1177/1368431003006002005

Farago, P. (1976). *Science and the media*. Oxford, England: Oxford University Press.

Fennel, D. (2009). Marketing science. The corporate faces of genetic engineering. *Journal of Communication Inquiry, 33*, 5–26. doi:10.1177/0196859908325144

Flynn, J., Slovic, P., & Kunreuther, H. (2001). *Risk, media and stigma. Understanding public challenges to modern science and technology*. London, England: Earthscan.

Fornäs, J. (1995). *Cultural theory and late modernity*. London, England: Sage.

Gamson, W. A. (1988). The 1987 distinguished lecture: A constructionist approach to mass media and public opinion. *Symbolic Interaction, 11*, 161–174. doi:10.1525/si.1988.11.2.161

Gamson, W. A., & Modigliani, A. (1989). Media discourse and public opinion on nuclear power: A constructionist approach. *American Journal of Sociology, 95*, 1–37. doi:10.1086/229213

Gaskell, G. (2001). Attitudes, social representations, and beyond. In K. Deaux & G. Philogène (Eds.), *Representations of the social. Bridging theoretical traditions* (pp. 228–241). Oxford, England: Blackwell.

Gaskell, G., & Bauer, M. W. (Eds.). (2001). *Biotechnology 1996–2000: The years of controversy*. London, England: Science Museum.

Geller, G., Bernhardt, B. A., Gardner, M., Rodgers, J., & Holtzman, N. A. (2005). Scientists' and science writers' experiences reporting genetic discoveries: Toward an ethic of trust in science journalism. *Genetics in Medicine, 7*, 198–205.

Giddens, A. (1990). *The consequences of modernity*. Cambridge, England: Polity Press.

Gregory, J., & Miller, S. (1998). *Science in public. Communication, culture, and credibility*. Oxford, England: Basic Books.

Hansen, A. (1991). The media and the social construction of the environment. *Media, Culture & Society, 13*, 443–458. doi:10.1177/016344391013004002

Hansen, A. (1994). Journalistic practices and science reporting in the British Press. *Public Understanding of Science, 3*, 111–134. doi:10.1088/0963-6625/3/2/001

Hansen, A. (Ed.). (1993). *The mass media and environmental issues*. Leicester, England: Leicester University Press.

Hansen, A. (2011). Communication, media and environment: Towards reconnecting research on the production, content and social implications of environmental communication. *The International Communication Gazette, 73*, 7–25. doi:10.1177/1748048510386739

Hartz, J., & Chapell, R. (1997). *Worlds apart: How the distance between science and journalism threatens America's future*. Nashville, TN: First Amendment Center. Retrieved from http://www.firstamendmentcenter.org/PDF/worldsapart.PDF

Hellsten, I. (2002). *The politics of metaphor. Biotechnology and biodiversity in the media*. Tampere, Finland: Tampere University Press.

Hjarvard, S. (2008). The mediatization of society. A theory of the media as agents of social and cultural change. *Nordicom Review, 29*(2), 105–134.

Hesmondhalgh, D., & Toynbee, J. (Eds.). (2008). *The media and social theory*. London, England: Routledge.

Hilgartner, S. (1990). The dominant view of popularization: Conceptual problems, political uses. *Social Studies of Science, 20*, 519–539. doi:10.1177/030631290020003006

Ho, M. -W. (2000). *Human Genome — The biggest sellout in human history*. Retrieved from   http://www.ratical.org/co-globalize/MaeWanHo/humangenome.pdf

Hornig, S. (1993). Reading risk: Public response to print media accounts of technological risk. *Public Understanding of Science, 2*, 95–109. doi:10.1088/0963-6625/2/2/001

Hornig Priest, S. (1995). Information equity, public understanding of science and the biotechnology debate. *Journal of Communication, 45*, 39–53. doi:10.1111/j.1460-2466.1995.tb00713.x

Jasanoff, S. (2005). *Designs on nature. Science and democracy in Europe and the United States*. Princeton, NJ: Princeton University Press.

Jensen, E. (2010). Between credulity and scepticism: Envisaging the fourth estate in 21st-century science journalism. *Media, Culture & Society, 32*, 615–630. doi:10.1177/0163443710367695

Kitzinger, J., & Reilly, J. (1997). The rise and fall of risk reporting. Media coverage of human genetics research, 'false memory syndrome' and 'Mad Cow Disease'. *European Journal of Communication, 12*, 319–350. doi:10.1177/0267323197012003002

Krieghbaum, H. (1967). *Science and the mass media*. New York, NY: New York University Press.

Krimsky, S., Rothenberg, L. S., Stott, P., & Kyle, G. (1996). Financial interests of authors in scientific journals: A pilot study of 14 publications. *Science and Engineering Ethics, 2*, 395–410.

Krotz, F. (2007). The meta-process of 'mediatization' as a conceptual frame. *Global Media and Communication, 3*, 256–260. doi:10.1177/17427665070030030103

Latour, B., & Woolgar, S. (1979). *Laboratory life. The social construction of scientific facts*. London, England: Sage.

Levidow, L. (1999). Britain's biotechnology controversy: Elusive science, contested expertise. *New Genetics and Society, 18*, 47–64. doi:10.1080/14636779908656889

Lewenstein, B. V. (1995a). From fax to facts: Communication in the cold fusion saga. *Social Studies of Science, 25*, 403–436. doi:10.1177/030631295025003001

Lewenstein, B. V. (1995b). Science and the media. In S. Jasanoff, G. E. Markle, J. C. Petersen, & T Pinch (Eds.), *Handbook of Science and Technology Studies* (pp. 343–360). Thousand Oaks, CA: Sage.

Lowe, T., Brown, K., Dessai, S., de França Doria, M., Haynes, K., & Vincent, K. (2006). Does tomorrow ever come? Disaster narrative and public perceptions of climate change. *Public Understanding of Science, 15*, 435–457. doi:10.1177/0963662506063796

Machill, M., Beiler, M., & Schmutz, J. (2006). The influence of video news releases on the topics reported in science journalism. *Journalism Studies, 7*, 869–888. doi:10.1080/14616700600980637

Maeseele, P. (2009). NGOs and GMOs: A Case Study in Alternative Science Communication. *Javnost-The Public, 16*, 55–72.

Maeseele, P. (2010a). On neo-luddites led by ayatollahs. The frame matrix of the GM food debate in Northern Belgium. *Environmental Communication: A Journal of Nature and Culture, 4*, 277–300. doi:10.1080/17524032.2010.499211

Maeseele, P. (2010b) Science journalism and social debate on modernization risks. *Journal of Science Communication, 9*, C02.

Maeseele, P. (2011). On news media and democratic debate: framing agricultural biotechnology in Northern Belgium. *The International Communication Gazette, 73*, 83–105. doi: 10.1177/1748048510386743

Meyer, G. (2006). Journalism and science: How to erode the idea of knowledge. *Journal of Agricultural nd Environmental Ethics, 19*, 239–252. doi:10.1007/s10806-005-6163-1

Miller, M. M., & Riechert, B. P. (2000). Interest groups strategies and journalistic norms: News media framing of environmental issues. In S. Allan, B. Adam, & C. Carter (Eds.), *Environmental risks and the media* (pp. 45–54). London, England: Routledge.

Mormont, M., & Dasnoy, C. (1995). Source strategies and the mediatization of climate change. *Media, Culture & Society, 17*, 49–65. doi:10.1177/016344395017001004

Mouffe, C. (2005). *On the political: Thinking in action.* London: Routledge.

Myers, G. (2003). Discourse studies of scientific popularization: Questioning the boundaries. *Discourse Studies, 5*, 265–295. doi:10.1177/1461445603005002006

Nelkin, D. (1995). *Selling science: How the press covers science and technology.* New York, NY: W.H. Freeman.

Nisbet, M. C., & Lewenstein, B. V. (2002). Biotechnology and the American media. The policy process and the elite press, 1970 to 1999. *Science Communication, 23*, 359–391. doi:10.1177/107554700202300401

Oreskes, N., & Conway, E. M. (2010). *Merchants of doubt. How a handful of scientists obscured the truth on issues from tobacco smoke to global warming.* New York, NY: Bloomsbury Press.

Otway, H., & Wynne, B. (1989). Risk communication: Paradigm and paradox. Guest editorial. *Risk Analysis, 9*, 141–145. doi:10.1111/j.1539-6924.1989.tb01232.x

Peters, H. P. (1994). Mass media as an information channel and public arena. *Risk: Health, Safety & Environment, 5*, 241–250.

Peters, H. P. (1995). The interaction of journalists and scientific experts: Co-operation and conflict between two professional cultures. *Media, Culture & Society, 17*, 31–48. doi:10.1177/016344395017001003

Peters, H. P. (2000). The committed are hard to persuade. Recipients' thoughts during exposure to newspaper and TV stories on genetic engineering and their effect on attitudes. *New Genetics & Society, 19*, 365–381. doi:10.1080/713687608

Peters, H. P., Brossard, D., de Cheveigné, S., Dunwoody, S., Kallfass, M., Miller, S., & Tsuchida, S. (2008a). Interactions with the mass media. *Science, 321*, 204–205. doi:10.1126/science.1157780

Peters, H. P., Brossard, D., de Cheveigné, S., Dunwoody, S., Kallfass, M., Miller, S., & Tsuchida, S. (2008b). Science-media interface: It's time to reconsider. *Science Communication, 30*, 266–276. doi:10.1177/1075547008324809

Peters, H. P., Heinrichs, H., Jung, A., Kallfass, M., & Petersen, I. (2008c). Medialization of science as a prerequisite of its legitimization and political relevance. In D. Cheng, M. Claessens, T. Gascoigne, J. Metcalfe, B. Schiele, & S. Shi (Eds.), *Communicating science in social contexts. New models, new practices* (pp. 71–92). Dordrecht, Holland: Springer.

Pitrelli, N. (Ed.). (2011). Comments: Science journalism and digital storytelling [Special issue]. *Journal of Science Communication, 4*(December).

Priest, S. H. (2001). *A grain of truth: The media, the public, and biotechnology.* Lanham, MD: Rowman and Littlefield.

Rödder, S. (2008). Reassessing the concept of a medialization of science: A story from the "book of life". *Public Understanding of Science, 18*, 452–463. doi:10.1177/0963662507081168

Royal Society. (2006). *Science communication: Survey of factors affecting science communication by scientists and engineers.* London, England: Author. Retrieved from http://royalsociety.org/downloaddoc.asp?id=3052

Ruse, M., & Castle, D. (Eds.). (2002). *Genetically modified foods. Debating biotechnology.* Amherst, NY: Prometheus Books.

Salleh, A. (2004). *Journalism at risk: Factors influencing journalistic coverage of the GM food and crops debate (Australia, 1999–2001) and prospects for critical journalism* (doctoral dissertation). University of Wollongong, New South Wales, Australia.

Salleh, A. (2008). The fourth estate and the fifth branch: The news media, GM risk, and democracy in Australia. *New Genetics and Society, 27*, 233–250. doi:10.1080/14636770802326919

Schäfer, M. S. (2009). From public understanding to public engagement. An empirical assessment of changes in science coverage. *Science Communication, 30*, 475–505. doi:10.1177/1075547008326943

Schlesinger, P., & Silverstone, R. (1995). Editorial. *Media, Culture & Society, 17*, 5–11. doi:10.1177/016344395017001001

Shinn, T., & Whitley, R. (1985a). Editorial preface. In T. Shinn & R. Whitley (Eds.), *Expository science: Forms and functions of popularisation* (pp. vii–xi). Dordrecht, Holland: D. Riedel.

Shinn, T., & Whitley, R. (Eds.). (1985b). *Expository science: Forms and functions of popularisation. Sociology of the sciences, Volume IX.* Dordrecht, Holland: D. Riedel.

Smith, J. M. (2003). *Seeds of deception. Exposing industry and government lies about the safety of the genetically engineered foods you're eating.* Fairfield, IA: Yes Books!

Schulz, W. (2004). Reconstructing mediatization as an analytical concept. *European Journal of Communication, 19*, 87–101. doi:10.1177/0267323104040696

Swyhgedouw, E. (2010). Apocalypse forever?: Post political populism and the spectre of climate change. *Theory, Culture & Society, 27*, 213–232.

Tankard, J. W., & Ryan, M. (1974). News source perceptions of accuracy of science coverage. *Journalism Quarterly, 51*, 219–225. doi:10.1177/107769907405100204

Thompson, J. B. (1995). *The media and modernity. A social theory of the media.* Cambridge, England: Polity Press.

Thompson, J. B. (2005). The new visibility. *Theory, Culture & Society, 22*(6), 31–51. doi:10.1177/0263276405059413

Väliverronen, E. (1993). Science and the media: Changing relations. *Science Studies, 6*(2), 23–34.

Väliverronen, E. (2001). From mediation to mediatization. The new politics of communicating science and biotechnology. In U. Kivikuru & T. Savolainen (Eds.), *The politics of public issues* (pp. 157–178). Helsinki, Finland: University of Helsinki, Department of Communication.

Väliverronen, E. (2004). Stories of the 'medicine cow': Representations of future promises in media discourse. *Public Understanding of Science, 13*, 363–377. doi:10.1177/0963662504046635

van Dijck, J. (1998). *Imagenation: Popular images of genetics.* New York, NY: New York University Press.

Wagner, W., & Kronberger, N. (2001). Killer tomatoes! Collective symbolic coping with biotechnology. In K. Deaux & G. Philogène (Eds.), *Representations of the social. Bridging theoretical traditions* (pp. 147–164). Oxford, England: Blackwell.

Weingart, P. (1998). Science and the media. *Research Policy, 27*, 869–879.

Weingart, P., & Pansegrau, P. (1999). Reputation in science and prominence in the media: The Goldhagen debate. *Public Understanding of Science, 8*, 1–16. doi:10.1088/0963-6625/8/1/001

West, D. M. (2007). *Biotechnology policy across national boundaries. The science-industrial complex.* New York, NY: Palgrave Macmillan.

Willems, J. (2003). Bringing down the barriers. *Nature, 422*(6931), 470.

Woloshin, S., & Schwartz, L. M. (2002). Press releases: Translating research into news. *The Journal of the American Medical Association, 287*, 2856–2858. doi:10.1001/jama.287.21.2856

Wynne, B. (1995). Public understanding of science. In S. Jasanoff, G. E. Markle, J. C. Petersen, & T. Pinch (Eds.), *Handbook of science and technology studies* (pp. 361–388). Thousand Oaks, CA: Sage.

CHAPTER CONTENTS

7 Latent Growth Modeling for Communication Research
Opportunities and Perspectives

Flaviu A. Hodis

Victoria University of Wellington, New Zealand

Georgeta M. Hodis

Massey University

Latent growth modeling (LGM) is a powerful, flexible, and versatile methodology for studying time-related change. Employing LGM in the communication field can make important contributions to advancing communication research, theory, and pedagogy. This chapter presents the specific advantages of conceptualizing and analyzing change in a LGM framework and offers a methodologically sound and useful presentation of the procedure from a structural equation modeling perspective. In addition, the chapter illustrates the benefits of studying change at the construct (latent variable) level, offers a comprehensive example of testing for longitudinal invariance, and introduces the unconditional and conditional second-order LGMs.

Communication processes and their impact on individuals and communities are dynamic and develop over time (Henry & Slater, 2008). Thus, an in-depth understanding of change processes is essential "to properly study the mechanisms of communication influence on human behavior, as well as the influence of human dispositional, experiential, and environmental differences on choices regarding communication behavior" (Henry & Slater, 2008, p. 55). Research in communication has targeted a number of important change processes, including developmental change in communication skills, change in attitudes and/or behaviors associated with exposure to media, political or health campaigns, as well as change in interpersonal communication patterns (Henry & Slater, 2008). Change cannot be investigated effectively without extending theoretical frameworks beyond pre–post designs (Nesselroade, Stigler, & Baltes, 1980; see also Hecht, Graham, & Elek, 2006). In the communication field, a longitudinal framework of inquiry is needed for answering salient research questions such as "Does participation in a communication-based substance-use prevention program lead to decreases in adolescents' substance use over time?" (Hecht et al., 2006). Although the importance of studying change appropriately has been recognized in communication research (Imahori & Cupach, 2005; Henry & Slater, 2008), cross-sectional designs remain most common. However, employing cross-sectional data to draw inferences about change is problematic, as cross-sectional investigations cannot capture the information needed to analyze change and can lead to biased estimates of relationships across time (Maxwell & Cole, 2007).

The introduction of new longitudinal data analytic techniques, such as latent growth modeling (LGM), has produced major shifts in the way change is being conceptualized and analyzed (Duncan & Duncan, 2004a, 2009). These advances have been catalyzed by continuous developments in dedicated software, which facilitate a relatively straightforward employment of these modern techniques in applied research. Although LGM is considered to be among the most important recent statistical developments in the social sciences (Duncan & Duncan, 2009), the procedure has yet to be used extensively by communication researchers (for notable exceptions see Caughlin, 2002; Eggermont, 2006; Hecht et al., 2006; Henry & Slater, 2008; Hodis, Bardhan, & Hodis, 2010; Hodis & Hodis, 2012; Jeong, Hwang, & Fishbein, 2010; Schemer, 2012; Schemer, Matthes, & Wirth, 2009; Slater & Hayes, 2010; Slater, Henry, Swaim, & Anderson, 2003). This is potentially a problematic drawback of current longitudinal research in communication because analyzing repeated measures data with traditional techniques has serious limitations. This lack of enthusiasm for embracing advanced longitudinal data analytic techniques aside, the investigation of time-related change patterns has been on the agenda of applied communication researchers. For instance, employing classical longitudinal techniques such as repeated measures MANOVA and paired-samples z-tests, Dwyer and Fus (2002) and Rubin and colleagues (Rubin, Graham, & Mignerey, 1990; Rubin, Rubin, & Jordan, 1997) analyzed developments in self-perceptions of communication competence. Similarly, Zorn and associates investigated increases in communicative self-efficacy associated with participation in focus group discussions (Zorn, Roper, Broadfoot, & Weaver, 2006), as well as small-group and online dialogues (Zorn, Roper, Weaver, & Rigby, 2010).

Given the potential applications for LGM to advance communication research, this chapter has two overarching aims. The first is to outline the important contributions that employment of LGM can make to communication research, theory, and pedagogy. The second is to provide a comprehensive overview of LGM that will enable readers to understand the tenets of this technique as well as to evaluate the advantages of employing it. Using an example centered around a well-known communication construct, willingness to communicate (WTC; McCroskey, 1986), this chapter makes a case for how the application of LGM can broaden knowledge of time-related development in a communication construct. Investigating change by means of LGM presents numerous advantages. In particular, LGM fits a unique trajectory of change for each participant and, as a result, the focus switches from imperfect individual observations to the estimated values of corresponding intercepts and slopes. Mean estimates of individual intercepts and slopes describe a group-level trajectory, whereas variances of these two factors quantify the variability in individual intercepts/slopes around the average population trend. Thus, LGM is able to provide information on both mean change and individual deviation from average trends (Duncan & Duncan, 2009; Henry & Slater, 2008).

To facilitate a thorough understanding of LGM and further enhance its relevance for applied communication research, this chapter offers a detailed account of how to conduct an LGM analysis using a popular software package. Although LGM can also be used in a multilevel framework (Kaplan, 2002; Raudenbush & Bryk, 2002), this presentation introduces LGM from a structural equation modeling (SEM) perspective. This choice is grounded on the fact that the SEM framework has several important advantages compared to its multilevel counterpart (Kaplan, 2002).

In this chapter, we discuss: (a) the advantages associated with employing LGM in the communication field; (b) the benefits of using LGM compared to traditional methods of analyzing longitudinal data; (c) the opportunities associated with studying change in a SEM rather than in a multilevel framework; (d) the theoretical tenets underlying the first-order LGM (1LGM) and its essential characteristics; (e) the limitations of the 1LGM compared to the benefits of studying change at the latent variable level in a second-order LGM (2LGM); (f) a detailed, practical illustration of how to examine longitudinal invariance of, and growth in, constructs defined by multiple indicators; (g) an example of a 1LGM using the same data, and the results associated with this model, are compared to those obtained for the 2LGM case; (h) additional applications and possible extensions of the proposed methodology that are relevant for communication research; and (i) a summary of the findings and the associated conclusions. Throughout the discussion, we assume that the reader has a basic understanding of linear models and of structural equation modeling (or multilevel modeling).

Advantages of Using LGM in Communication Research

To detail how employing LGM can be beneficial to facilitate important advances in the communication field, first we overview the pivotal role LGM can play in advancing extant communication theory. Second, we discuss how using LGM can contribute to better assessments of and practical utility for assessing the effectiveness of communication interventions. Third, we review the usefulness of LGM for communication pedagogy.

LGM's Contribution to Communication Theory

The power and flexibility of LGM (Voelkle, 2007) enables researchers employing it to make pivotal contributions to advancing communication theory. Although these contributions span a wide range of communication paradigms, they are grounded on LGM's ability to: (a) offer accurate representations of complex communication processes and (b) assess simultaneously the cross-sectional and longitudinal relationships among variables/constructs of interest. An important illustration of the contributions that LGM can make in expanding communication theory is provided by the work of Slater and colleagues (Slater & Hayes, 2010) on the salience of incorporating change in theoretical models of adolescent social identity development. Slater and Hayes employed

LGM to weigh the merits of competing theoretical frameworks (reinforcing spirals model; Slater, 2007; and social cognitive theory; Bandura, 2002). They showed that the influence of music channel viewing on smoking behavior was mediated by the role that usage of media has on the development of adolescent social identity and not by means of affecting social cognitive processes. Similarly, Slater et al. (2003) successfully used LGM to test the tenets of the downward spiral model (Slater, 2003), positing that a dynamic and reciprocal association exists over time between aggressive tendencies of youth and their patterns of watching violent media content.

As these examples illustrate, using LGM in communication research can facilitate access to fresh information that is essential for (a) broadening theoretical frameworks to incorporate change processes along with cross-sectional relationships and (b) proposing more realistic paradigms that can account for the fact that, over time, relationships among variables may change. For example, Hodis and colleagues (2010) found that in a public speaking context a well-known cross-sectional relationship, the negative association between communication apprehension (CA) and willingness to communicate (WTC), was not consistent with corresponding longitudinal trends. Specifically, the study showed that although at a given point in time the more apprehensive one is, the less willing she/he is to engage in communication, the relationship between CA and *change* in WTC is positive. Along similar lines, Slater and Hayes (2010) found that longitudinal associations can be markedly different from their cross-sectional counterparts. Employing LGM, they showed that although early exposure to MTV and VH-1 music channels predicted increases in both adolescent smoking and association with smoking peers, *change* in the frequency of viewing these channels was not associated with *changes* in the other two outcomes. These examples demonstrate that access to fresh information, enabled by the employment of LGM, is invaluable in informing subsequent theory developments in given areas. More precisely, grounded on results from LGM analyses, competing hypotheses can be generated to account for the putative causes of the divergence between cross-sectional and longitudinal associations. In turn, testing these hypotheses can highlight plausible explanations for observed trends and, thus, shed more light on the determinants of change in the given communication processes.

Another example of how LGM can contribute to theory testing and development is associated with the reinforcing spirals model (Slater, 2007), which posits that a reciprocal relationship exists between media effects and selectivity. Employing LGM, Schemer (2012) found support for this theory and concluded that attention to political advertising was reciprocally related over time to the negative affective reactions elicited in response to given political advertising. In particular, by employing LGM to model concomitant changes in both the effects of political advertising and selection dynamics, the author showed that attention to political advertisements depicting a negative view of asylum seekers was associated with stronger anxiety and fear, which, in turn, contributed to increasing attention toward subsequent campaign cues.

Primary socialization theory (PST; Oetting & Donnermeyer, 1998), which posits that the main agents shaping adolescents' beliefs regarding what constitutes normative (vs. deviant) behavior are parents, peers, and school, provides a good example of how LGM can help advance communication theory. During the developmental transition spanning the adolescence years, changes in the rank-order of the importance of each socialization agent may occur (Oetting & Donnermeyer, 1998). Thus, investigations employing LGM can advance PST by exploring how the influence of these socialization agents changes over time.

Research in health and managerial communication provides additional examples of how employing LGM could further the development of communication theory. Specifically, Hong (2012) found that the persuasive effect of health-related communication can be enhanced when given messages are framed to fit with people's regulatory focus orientations: *promotion*, which relates to the extent to which people are motivated by ideals, aspirations, and personal growth; and *prevention*, which pertains to the extent to which individuals are motivated by duty and responsibility (Higgins, 1997, 2012). These promising cross-sectional results can be augmented in a longitudinal framework, where LGM could be used to explore how changes in promotion and prevention are linked to changes in the magnitude of persuasive effects (attitude toward the given behavior or behavioral intentions; see Hong (2012) for an account of the corresponding cross-sectional results). Similarly, in a cross-sectional design, Fransen and ter Hoeven (2011) found that framing negative managerial communications (refusing an employee's request for promotion or time off) in ways that fit employees' regulatory focus orientations lead to employees experiencing more empowerment compared to situations in which the given communication was not aligned to their regulatory focus. With respect to this research, in longitudinal settings, LGM could help advance extant theories by evaluating the extent to which these cross-sectional results are in line with their longitudinal counterparts. For example, two salient questions that need to be answered to advance understanding of the effects of negative managerial communication are: (a) Do increases in promotion and prevention lead to increases in empowerment in the workplace whenever negative managerial communication fits people's underlying regulatory focus orientations? or (2) Is it more likely that longitudinal relations between regulatory focus and empowerment in the workplace are moderated by other psychological constructs that influence the communication encounter (e.g., psychological distance; Liberman, Trope, & Stephan, 2007)?

LGM's Contribution to the Evaluation of the Effectiveness of Communication Intervention Studies

Among the important features of LGM is that it enables the empirical assessment of whether changes in given constructs/variables of interest differ across groups. Thus, LGM can be used effectively to tease out the effects of the intervention. Hecht and colleagues (2006) employed LGM to evaluate a communication-based intervention aimed at reducing adolescents' substance use. By using LGM, the authors were able to test for differential effects of communication interventions. They compared rates of change across both groups and focal criteria and found that intervention effects were not uniformly positive across the spectrum of substance abuse considered. Overall, the intervention seemed effective in reducing alcohol consumption but showed less promise with regards to cigarette smoking and marijuana use. Furthermore, by having the ability to compare and contrast the effectiveness of different types of communicative messages, findings from LGM analyses offered support for a particular model of constructing culturally grounded health messages (Gosin, Marsiglia, & Hecht, 2003).

LGM's Contribution to Communication Pedagogy

Information unearthed in LGM analyses can inform pedagogical practice. Hodis and Hodis (2012) employed LGM to demonstrate that changes in student communicative self-efficacy beliefs during a basic communication course were more accentuated in communication contexts emphasizing persuasion (contexts reflecting primarily a rhetorical or masculine orientation toward communication) than in contexts emphasizing relationship building and maintenance (reflecting a relational or feminine) orientation toward communication (McCroskey & Richmond, 1996; Shepherd, 1992). These findings have significant pedagogical implications as they pinpoint that different types of teaching and learning settings (structure of class instruction, format of assignments, etc.) are conducive to enhancing communicative self-efficacy beliefs in specific communication contexts but not in others. Thus, by using LGM, scholars can investigate how individuals' chronic predispositions to emphasize one type of communication orientation versus the other interact across time with the specific contextual constraints (type of instruction and the nature of assignments) to shape the evolution of people's communicative self-efficacy beliefs. Additionally, the ability of LGM to provide evidence that in certain instructional settings and for particular communication contexts, cross-sectional relationships are not consistent with their longitudinal counterparts has important pedagogical consequences: These findings underline that in enhancing students' willingness to communicate, "past history need not dictate future achievement and that all students can benefit from systematic and appropriately targeted instruction" (Hodis et al., 2010, pp. 261–262).

Benefits of Employing LGM when Studying Time-Related Change

LGM is a comprehensive system for the analysis of longitudinal data, which includes as particular cases traditional techniques such as paired *t*-tests, repeated measures ANOVA, and MANOVA (Voelkle, 2007). Employing LGM in applied research presents numerous benefits compared to using more traditional techniques. These benefits are grounded on three pivotal characteristics of the procedure: (a) LGM makes less restrictive assumptions than its traditional counterparts (Curran & Muthen, 1999; Voelkle, 2007) and, thus, can be appropriately used in situations in which traditional techniques cannot be trusted to produce unbiased findings; (b) LGM is flexible (Curran, Obeidat, & Losardo, 2010; Duncan & Duncan, 2004b, 2009) and can be employed to study change in various experimental and non-experimental research designs; and (c) LGM facilitates the testing of hypotheses that could not be studied with traditional techniques such as multiple regression, dependent *t*-tests, and repeated measures ANOVA (RANOVA) (Byrne, Lam, & Fielding, 2008).

First, LGM uses simultaneously "data on all individuals at every time point to concurrently investigate within—and between—individual change" (Lenzenweger, Johnson, & Willett, 2004, p. 1017). In particular, LGM can be used to analyze intraindividual change (how individuals develop over time with respect to some characteristics of interest such as communicative self-efficacy, willingness to communicate, etc.) as well as interindividual differences in intraindividual change (the extent to which individual developments are similar/different for people in a given population; Henry & Slater, 2008; Willett & Sayer, 1994). Thus, LGM facilitates access to salient information about the heterogeneity of people's patterns of intraindividual variability (Chan, 1998; Curran, 2000; Ram & Grimm, 2007). As a consequence of this versatility, in LGM the estimation of effects is more powerful and precise than in RANOVA, which focuses exclusively on average trends and relegates interindividual (between-subjects) variability to the error term (Hess, 2000; Hodis et al., 2010; Lenzenweger et al., 2004). Because LGM uses all available information from participants who have incomplete data, the technique facilitates researchers' access to both unbiased parameter estimates and increased levels of power for testing statistical hypotheses (Willett, 1997).

Second, LGM enables investigators to gauge true change that underlies fallible observable developments in a set of variables measuring a construct (Willett, 1997; Yuan & Bentler, 2001). Taking into account that large measurement errors generate biased parameter estimates and contribute to inaccurate inferences regarding the functional form of change (Chan, 1998), this is an important benefit of LGM that is unmatched by either traditional techniques or multilevel approaches. Moreover, procedures that account for measurement errors, such as LGM, generate more theoretically meaningful and stable parameter estimates than techniques that do not correct for the unreliability of the observed measures (ANOVA, regression, etc.; Yuan & Bentler, 2001).

Third, by employing LGM, researchers are able to model the covariance structure of uniquenesses (error terms) to test the plausibility of competing structures (e.g., homoscedastic covariance matrix with uncorrelated uniquenesses vs. heteroscedastic structure with correlated disturbances), and to choose the one that best fits the empirical data (Henry & Slater, 2008; Ployhart & Hakel, 1998; Willett & Sayer, 1994). Thus, unlike RANOVA, LGM does not assume a restrictive and often unrealistic structure of the error terms (e.g., sphericity, which posits that error variances are homogeneous and uncorrelated across time) (Curran & Muthen, 1999; Voelkle, 2007). This is an invaluable feature of LGM. In longitudinal studies, it is quite possible that errors are heterogeneous and correlated for adjacent times, especially when the same instrument is used in all waves and successive measurements are separated by relatively short periods of time (Chan, 1998; Martin, 2008).

Fourth, unlike more traditional procedures, LGM can easily accommodate unequal time lengths between various waves of data collection (Lenzenweger et al., 2004). From a practical standpoint this is an extremely valuable feature of LGM, especially for long-term studies in which logistic issues may force researchers to "skip" one or more waves of data collection.

The flexibility of LGM allows it to be used in many different experimental and non-experimental types of longitudinal investigations in which three or more waves of data are available. It is important to note that although latent change can be studied in a 2-wave design, this setting is limited in its ability to assess the tenability of even the simplest functional form of change: because two data points determine a line perfectly, in a 2-wave design it is not possible to test linear hypotheses of development. Increasing the number of measurement waves enlarges not only the range of functional forms of change that can be tested (quadratic, etc.), but also the precision of the estimation and the reliability of assessing change (Willett & Sayer, 1994). However, practical constraints pertaining to data collection (budget, time, respondent availability, etc.) may limit researchers' ability to test complex non-linear models that require numerous waves of data.

Opportunities of Studying Change in a SEM Rather than in a Multilevel Framework

Under some conditions, studying change in a SEM framework is equivalent to analyzing change from a multilevel perspective (Curran, 2003). However, in other situations, the employment of the SEM approach to growth modeling (i.e., LGM) offers several advantages over its multilevel counterpart (Curran, 2003; Willett, 2004). First, in the LGM approach, but not in the multilevel one, change can be assessed at the latent (factor) level (Willett, 2004). Thus, on the grounds that in the multilevel framework one is constrained to analyze development in one variable at a time, when the outcome of interest is a construct measured by multiple indicators, the usage of LGM is preferable (Bauer, 2003; Holt, 2008). Second, a pivotal strength of the LGM framework is that it is able to use multiple indicators of latent constructs and, thus, to explicitly model measurement error in predictors as well as outcomes (Curran, 2003). In contrast, in a multilevel framework, only directly measured predictors can be included in the model (MacCallum, Kim, Malarkey, & Kiecolt-Glaser, 1997), a characteristic that forces these models to make a restrictive assumption, namely that predictors are measured without errors (Curran, 2003). Violations of this assumption, which are common in practice, are associated with biased results. Third, the LGM approach is better suited than its multilevel counterpart to investigate simultaneous change processes as well as to "model change as part of an extended network of hypothesized relations" (Willett, 2004, p. 40). As Ghisletta and Lindenberger (2004) noted, LGM may also be favored over the multilevel approach when "relations among the variables' level and change components cannot be represented by covariances (e.g., dynamic condition)" (p. 13). Fourth, in LGM a wide range of fit indices is available for assessing model fit. This offers LGM an important advantage over the multilevel framework, which offers only a limited range of measures of model fit (Holt, 2008; MacCallum et al., 1997) and requires "complete data (or the use of imputation techniques) at higher-levels of the analysis" (Holt, 2008, p. 133). Finally, unlike its multilevel counterparts, the SEM framework (through its multiple-groups approach) can be employed to examine group differences when growth patterns exhibit amplitude variance (when growth patterns have inverted U shapes, some groups may exhibit more abrupt growth and subsequently more accentuated decline than others), phase variance (some groups peak earlier than others), or both (K. J. Grimm, personal communication, 22 June, 2011).

Although this discussion highlighted the advantages of employing a SEM framework over a multilevel one (when studying change processes), there are situations in which it is advantageous to use a multilevel approach rather than a SEM framework to study change processes (Bauer, 2003; Curran, 2003; Ghisletta & Lindenberger, 2004). The multilevel paradigm is better suited for situations in which participants are measured at individually-varying time points and the data are highly unbalanced (Bollen & Curran, 2006; Ghisletta & Lindenberger, 2004). Moreover, the multilevel approach is preferable to the SEM one when more than three levels of the analysis are required (Bollen & Curran, 2006; Preacher, Wichman, MacCallum, & Briggs, 2008). Furthermore, the multilevel framework may provide a better approximation of complex nonlinear patterns of growth than the SEM one (Preacher et al., 2008). Additionally, some models are easier to implement in multilevel programs than in SEM ones (Bauer, 2003; Curran, 2003). Finally, for time-series with a large number of repeated measures, multilevel models may be more advantageous than their SEM counterparts (Jones, 2012).

Methodological Presentation of the Procedure

In the following, the first-order latent growth model (1LGM) is presented. The procedure is introduced for the case of a linear model because extensions to other functional forms of growth (quadratic, cubic, etc.) follow from the linear case. In addition, parameters of linear 1LGM (intercept and slope) are straightforward to interpret, demonstrating the wealth of hypotheses that can be tested using this approach. To facilitate links between the theoretical foundation of the technique and the analysis of the data), this presentation makes use of the WTC construct previously mentioned. For all subsequent discussions, WTC denotes the average of the 12 scored items of the willingness to communicate scale. To begin, let us assume that individual plots of the evolution of WTC suggest that, in general, students' WTC levels increase linearly over time. Suppose also that t waves of data (where $t = 1, 2, 3$) were collected for a number of N subjects on the focal variable (WTC) and two time-invariant predictors, gender (categorical) and communication apprehension measured at Time 1 (continuous) are available.

Following, an overview of the unconditional model (Bollen & Curran, 2006), which employs the repeated measures of WTC and includes no predictor of change, is provided. Let WTC_{it} denote the value of WTC for participant i at time t ($i = 1, 2, ..., N; t = 1, 2, 3$). Drawing from Flora (2008), Hancock and Lawrence (2006), and Slater and Hayes (2010), the functional form of growth at the individual level can be expressed as:

$$WTC_{it} = (Latent\_Baseline)_i + (Latent\_Change\_per\_unit\_of\_time)_i$$
$$* \lambda_t + Error_{it} \qquad (1)$$

where λ_t includes "a set of factor loadings that are constrained to represent the passage of time" (Flora, 2008, p. 515). Equation 1 can describe both growth and decline (Hertzog & Nesselroade, 2003), for individuals exhibiting decreases in WTC show negative change scores per unit of time. In addition, the model in Equation 1 makes no assumption about the linearity of the time-related change (Raykov, 2007) in WTC: It is only when λ_t values are chosen in a way that takes into account the time elapsed between measurement waves that Equation 1 defines a linear latent trajectory model.

For the linear case, the $(Latent\_Baseline)_i$ term in Equation 1 represents the model predicted value of WTC for individual i when $\lambda_t = 0$ (Flora, 2008). Quite common in applied studies, the time t that is associated with a null value of λ_t (the reference time) is set to be the initial measurement. In this case, the $(Latent\_Baseline)_i$ becomes an intercept $(Intercept_i)$. The approach of setting $\lambda_t = 0$ at the first measurement wave is used here to facilitate inferences about true WTC levels at the beginning of the study. The second term in Equation 1 is simply a rate of change per unit of time (a slope), whereas $Error_{it}$ represents the unique part of WTC_{it} that cannot be predicted from knowing the corresponding values of the latent baseline and rate of change. Equation 1 shows that the WTC score for participant i at each of the three time points ($t = 1, 2, 3$) is a function of her/his own intercept, slope, and error term. The interpretation of intercept and slope in 1LGM is the same as in a linear regression (Hancock & Lawrence, 2006). Furthermore, from Equation 1, it is also apparent that the intercept and slope are constant across time (Duncan, Duncan, & Hops, 1996) but can vary among respondents.

Using the notation in Bollen and Curran (2006), Equation 1 can be rewritten as

$$WTC_{it} = \alpha_i + \lambda_t \beta_i + \varepsilon_{it} \qquad (2)$$

where α_i and, respectively, β_i are the random intercept and, respectively, random slope for participant i, ε_{it} is the error for respondent i at time t, and $\lambda_t = \{0,$

0.5, 1} is a constant. More formally, Equation 2 is called the Level 1 equation of the LGM (Curran, 2000; Willett, 1997; Willett & Sayer, 1994) or the equation for the within-person change (Curran, 2000; Willett, 1994).

In conjunction with equally-spaced measurement occasions, the chosen values in λ_t reflect the hypothesis of linear growth because change from Time 1 ($\lambda_t = 0$) to Time 3 ($\lambda_t = 1$) is hypothesized to be twice as large as change from Time 1 to Time 2 ($\lambda_t = 0.5$). This particular set of values ($\lambda_t = \{0, 0.5, 1\}$) was chosen because data were collected from students enrolled in a semester-long course and, thus, change in WTC across the entire semester is of major interest. This choice, which operationalizes the unit of time as the interval between the first and the third wave of measurement, also enables us to make inferences about students' levels of WTC at the beginning of the given semester.

The core assumption of LGM, for both first- and second-order models, is that all members of the population of interest share the same functional form of change over time. In other words, in the linear growth framework, for all participants change in true WTC is assumed to be linear. However, this assumption should not be interpreted as saying that all members of a population have the same intercept and the same slope. On the contrary, some respondents may start at lower levels of WTC and increase abruptly, whereas others may have a descending trajectory starting from high levels of WTC; but for all of them change in WTC unfolds linearly over time. Other assumptions of LGM are similar to assumptions from regression analysis: The errors ε_{it} have a mean of zero and are uncorrelated with both intercepts (α_i) and slopes (β_i), and "the random intercepts and slopes for one case are assumed to be uncorrelated with those of another" (Bollen & Curran, 2006, p. 20). More detailed accounts of the LGM assumptions can be found in Bollen and Curran (2006) and Preacher et al. (2008).

In light of this discussion, it follows that individual intercepts/slopes can be expressed as functions of their corresponding mean levels and individual disturbances. Using the notations in Bollen and Curran (2006), the Level 2 (or between-person) change equations can be written as

$$\alpha_i = \mu_\alpha + \xi_{\alpha i} \tag{3}$$

$$\beta_i = \mu_\beta + \xi_{\beta i} \tag{4}$$

In Equations 3 and 4, μ_α and μ_β are the average intercept and slope, whereas $\xi_{\alpha i}$ and $\xi_{\beta i}$ are the corresponding disturbances (assumed to have a mean of zero and null correlations with the measurement errors ε_{it}). The variance of intercept disturbances ($\xi_{\alpha i}$) is denoted $\Psi_{\alpha\alpha}$, the variance of slope disturbances ($\xi_{\beta i}$) is denoted $\Psi_{\beta\beta}$, and their covariance is denoted $\Psi_{\alpha\beta}$. It is important to note that μ_α, μ_β, $\Psi_{\alpha\alpha}$, $\Psi_{\beta\beta}$, and $\Psi_{\alpha\beta}$ are parameters that are estimated when fitting the LGM to the observed data (Bollen & Curran, 2006). As Equations 3 and 4 illustrate, it is the individual intercept (α_i) and slope (β_i) values that are "of most interest to the model, and not the individual observed repeated observations" (Curran, 2000, p. 16) of WTC over time.

Many indices can be used to evaluate whether a proposed model receives support from empirical data, but only some of them are independent of sample size and perform well in identifying model misspecifications (Jackson, Gillaspy, & Purc-Stephenson, 2009). Among the overall fit measures having these desirable features are the Comparative Fit Index (CFI; Bentler, 1990), the Tucker-Lewis index (TLI; Tucker & Lewis, 1973), and the Root Mean Square Error of Approximation (RMSEA; Steiger, 1990). Guidelines concerning these indices have changed over time, and currently there is no consensus about cutoff values (Jackson et al., 2009). The more stringent criteria for evaluating fit were used here. Following Hu and Bentler (1999), a cutoff value of .95 was used for CFI and TLI to indicate a good fit. For RMSEA, values smaller than .05 indicated a good model fit, those between .05 and .10 a moderate fit, and values greater than .10 a poor fit (Bollen & Curran, 2006). For a detailed discussion of definitions and properties of fit indices used in SEM research, see Raykov and Marcoulides (2006) and Brown (2006).

A graphical representation of the single-group unconditional linear 1LGM is presented in Figure 7.1. The conventional symbols of SEM are employed in depicting the model: Latent constructs are represented in circles (ovals), observed variables in rectangles, straight lines with arrows at one end represent directional effects toward the variable at the arrow's end, and curved lines with arrows at both ends represent either variances (if both arrows are attached to the same variable/construct) or covariances (if the arrows are attached to different variables/constructs). For instance, $V(E_3)$ represents the variance of the error term associated with the third wave of measurement and Cov(Int, Slp) represents the covariance between the intercept and slope factors. The triangle that hosts the Digit 1 is used to introduce the mean structure of the LGM besides the covariance structure. The symbol represents a unit constant (thus having variance of zero) and the paths leading from it depict the means of the intercept and, respectively, slope factors. As the diagram in Figure 7.1 illustrates, the observed scores are not completely determined by the two latent growth factors. As the presence of error terms in Figure 7.1 indicates, there is a certain difference between observed WTC scores and the values "we would expect from the latent growth portion of the model" (Hancock & Lawrence, 2006, p. 176).

Assessing Change in a Second-Order LGM (2LGM) Framework and the Issue of Longitudinal Invariance

Although studying change in a 1LGM framework has numerous advantages, it is not without limitations. 1LGM cannot assess the tenability of the hypothesis that the same construct is being measured at all data collection waves (Ferrer, Balluerka, & Widaman, 2008). Most commonly, in a 1LGM, the average/total score of all items in a scale is calculated at each wave of measurement, and the resulting index is taken without further testing to represent a valid realization of the construct of interest at successive points in time. However, in a 2LGM framework, items/parcels of items are used as indicators of the construct at

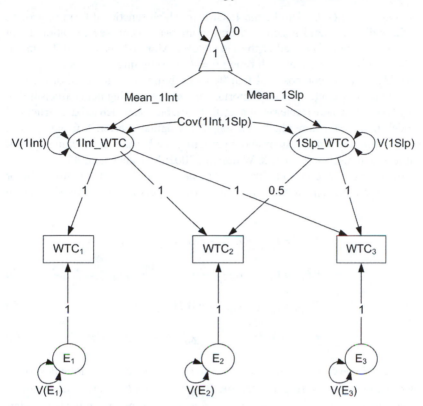

Figure 7.1 Graphical representation of the single-group unconditional first-order model, 1LGM. 1Int = intercept of the first-order model; 1Slp = slope of the first-order model; V() = variance; Cov(,) = covariance; WTC_i = willingness to communicate score at the i-th wave of measurement (i=1,2,3); E_i = uniqueness (residual) of the i-th wave of measurement.

each time of measurement. In this way, the construct of interest is defined as a first-order common factor measured by the given items/parcels, and "change is modeled through the repeated latent factors, rather than through the manifest variables" (Ferrer et al., 2008, p. 22).

The 2LGM brings together (a) the confirmatory factor analytic model linking the items/parcels to one or more common factors and (b) the LGM assessing change in factor scores over time (Duncan et al., 2006). As a result, the main benefit of adopting a 2LGM framework of inquiry is that it raises researchers' awareness that longitudinal invariance of the given construct(s) is a testable hypothesis that needs to be addressed before analyses of growth patterns can begin. Another important advantage of the 2LGM over the 1LGM approach is that the former provides separate estimates for construct variance(s) as well as unique (measurement error) and time-specific variances (Ferrer et al., 2008; Sayer & Cumsille, 2001). By studying change at the latent rather than manifest level, 2LGM enables researchers to make inferences at the (error-free) construct level (Hancock, Kuo, & Lawrence, 2001).

Defining the 2LGM.   Unlike the 1LGM, in which functional form of growth at the individual level is centered on a composite score (see Equation 1), in a 2LGM growth is defined at the latent level. More precisely, a WTC factor ($FWTC_{(t)}$) is measured, at each time t ($t = 1, 2, 3$) by three parcels ($P1_{(t)}$, $P2_{(t)}$, and $P3_{(t)}$) that are composed of four items each (one item for each of the four communication contexts). One important advantage of using item parcels is that they "provide a more stable set of manifest variables on which to base structural models than do the individual scale items" (Widaman, Ferrer, & Conger, 2010, p. 13; for in-depth discussions about parceling see Kishton & Widaman, 1994; Little, Cunningham, Shahar, & Widaman, 2002; Matsunaga, 2008).

Following the conceptualization of the first-order confirmatory factor model, the equation for these indicators (for a person i, at a time t) can be written

$$P1_{(t)i} = \tau_{(P1_t)} + \lambda_{(P1_t)} * FWTC_{(t)i} + e_{(P1_t)i} \tag{5}$$

$$P2_{(t)i} = \tau_{(P2_t)} + \lambda_{(P2_t)} * FWTC_{(t)i} + e_{(P2_t)i} \tag{6}$$

$$P3_{(t)i} = \tau_{(P3_t)} + \lambda_{(P3_t)} * FWTC_{(t)i} + e_{(P3_t)i} \tag{7}$$

$$\text{where } FWTC_{(t)i} = \alpha_i + \lambda_{(t)} * \beta_i + \varepsilon_{(t)i} \tag{8}$$

In the above equations α_i and β_i are the mean intercept and slope described by Equations 3 and 4, respectively; the $P1_{(t)}$, $P2_{(t)}$, and $P3_{(t)}$ terms are the three indicators of $FWTC_{(t)}$; the $\tau_{(P1_t)}$, $\tau_{(P2_t)}$, and $\tau_{(P3_t)}$ terms are indicators' intercepts; the $\lambda_{(P1_t)}$, $\lambda_{(P2_t)}$, $\lambda_{(P3_t)}$ terms are the first, second, and third factor loadings of the $FWTC_{(t)}$ factor; the $e_{(P1_t)}$, $e_{(P2_t)}$, $e_{(P3_t)}$ terms represent that part of an indicator score that is independent of $FWTC_{(t)}$.

Once the first-order common factor model is conceptualized, change can be analyzed at the theoretically error-free latent level. More specifically, as illustrated by Equations 5–8, time-related change in the FWTC factor is analyzed in this 2LGM. However, one additional step needs to be taken before the analysis of change patterns can begin.

Longitudinal Invariance.   Meaningful investigations of change and/or development cannot be conducted unless researchers "measure the same thing in the same metric at each occasion" (Widaman et al., 2010, p. 11). Whenever, multiple indicators of a construct are available, this hypothesis can be formally tested (Ferrer et al., 2008; Widaman et al., 2010). Following, the process of testing longitudinal invariance is briefly described (for a more detailed discussion, see Ferrer et al., 2008; Widaman et al., 2010; Widaman & Reise, 1997).

Testing longitudinal invariance involves fitting an increasingly restrictive sequence of nested models (Widaman et al., 2010). In the first step, configural invariance is assessed by evaluating whether the common factors (in this case, $FWTC_{(t)}$) exhibit an identical pattern of fixed and free factor loadings across time. More specifically, in the configured invariance step, it is tested whether given items measure given factors, but no restrictions are imposed in terms of the magnitudes of item-factor, interfactor, or inter-item relations. In the case that this configural invariance model fits the data well, weak factorial invariance (configural invariance plus across-time equality of $FWTC_{(t)}$ factor loadings) is assessed by restricting corresponding factor loadings to being equal across time. Assuming that weak factorial invariance holds, in the next step an additional restriction (the equality of corresponding intercepts over time) is added to the previous model and the strong factorial invariance is tested. Finally, if strong invariance holds, the strict invariance is tested by additionally restricting the corresponding unique variances to be equal over time. To compare the fit of these nested models, likelihood ratio chi-square difference tests are used (Widaman et al., 2010).

Importantly, SEM literature suggests that model evaluation and comparison is a subject of controversy. Specifically, the value and use of the chi-square test statistic is heavily questioned. Some authors argue that the information provided by the chi-square test is compromised when the sample size is large (e.g. Byrne & Crombie, 2003; Schumacker & Lomax, 2010). Other authors, however, emphasize that for correctly specified models the chi-square test statistic is not correlated with sample size (Hayduk, Cummings, Boadu, Pazderka-Robinson, & Boulianne, 2007; McIntosh, 2007). From a strict statistical perspective, the chi-square difference test provides valid inference when the baseline model fits the data (Yuan & Bentler, 2004). However, common practice in communication research is to neglect significant chi-square values when approximate goodness of fit indices suggests good model fit. The chi-square difference test procedures are simple and involve, at every step, estimating two nested models: a *parent model*, which has comparatively less restrictions imposed on its parameters (factor loadings, factor variances, and covariances, etc.), and a *restricted model*, which is obtained from the parent model by restricting some of the free parameters in the parent model (Brown, 2006). Using the empirical data, both models are fit separately. Assuming that the parent model offers a good approximation for the empirical relations depicted by the data, the chi-square difference test evaluates the extent to which the set of constraints imposed is associated with a significant deterioration of the fit. If this is the case, the parent model is retained; otherwise the restricted model is adopted. The procedure then continues with the next pair of nested models, which includes the retained model from the previous step (now playing the role of the next parent model) and a new restricted model (Brown, 2006). Conducting meaningful tests of mean differences on latent variables requires strong but not strict invariance constraints (Widaman & Reise, 1997). Additionally, strong factorial invariance ensures that in 2LGM relations among first-order factors and second-order intercept and slope are independent of the choice of the reference indicator (Ferrer et al., 2008).

Example of Assessing Longitudinal Invariance and Fitting the 2LGM

To illustrate how 2LGM can be used in applied research settings, a detailed example is provided. First, the sequence of steps needed to establish longitudinal invariance is presented. Following, unconditional and conditional 2LGM models are fitted and their results are discussed. This section begins with a brief overview of the construct studied, the instruments used to collect data, and the sample.

Brief Overview of WTC. WTC (McCroskey, 1986) is strongly linked to people's well-being for it "permeates every facet of an individual's life and contributes significantly to the social, educational, and organizational achievements of the individual" (Richmond & Roach, 1992, p. 104). Although people's WTC levels are correlated across communication contexts and types of interlocutors, situational constraints also affect this construct (McCroskey & Richmond, 1987). Among the aspects that influence one's WTC are one's mood and recent communicational experiences, specific characteristics of the interlocutor (who is she/he, what's her/his look, etc.), and one's beliefs regarding the advantages/drawbacks of communicating in a given situation (McCroskey & Richmond, 1987).

Description of Instruments and Sample.   Data used in this example came from a large research study conducted at a midwestern U.S. university. For this study, students' WTC scores (measured in the first, eighth, and fifteenth week of a semester) along with initial (Time 1) communication apprehension scores and a demographic variable (gender) are used. The WTC scale (McCroskey, 1986) contains 20 items (12 scored and eight filler) related to four communication contexts (talking in dyads, small groups, large meetings, and public speaking) and three types of interlocutors (friends, acquaintances, and strangers). The instrument prompts respondents to indicate the percentage of time they would choose to communicate in various settings, with certain types of interlocutors ("talk in a large meeting of friends") assuming they had completely free choice to communicate or not. Individual items are measured on a scale of 0–100 where 0 means never and 100 means always. Whenever composite WTC scores are used, these are obtained by averaging each student's answers to the 12 scored items. The PRCA-24B (McCroskey, 1986) was employed to measure students' communication apprehension at the beginning of the semester. Participants' answers to the 24 items were averaged to form the CA_1 index.

Participants in the study were undergraduate students enrolled in a core curriculum communication course at the given university. After the Institutional Review Board approval was secured, all 1,187 students enrolled in all sections of the course in the given semester were asked to participate. Every instructor assigned to teach the course was contacted, informed, and asked to administer the questionnaires during class periods of the respective week. Researchers were not directly involved in any phase of data collection.

Of 706 students participating in the research (response rate 59.48%), 398 provided data for all measurement waves, 62 for only the first two waves, 81 for the first and third waves only, and 67 for the second and third waves only. The remaining students had data available on only one measure of WTC. From the total number of participants, 319 (45.18%) were female and 387 (54.82%) were male. Because two students did not provide any information about WTC, the sample size used in these analyses was $N = 704$. Table 7.1 summarizes the characteristics of the sample and includes the means, standard deviations, correlations, covariances, skew, kurtosis, and reliabilities of the variables.

To investigate the potentially biasing effect of missing data several analyses were undertaken. First, a one-way ANOVA was conducted to assess whether average WTC levels at Time 1 had differed across students who participated in all three, or respectively only in one or two waves(s) of data collection. The results of this test were not statistically-significant, $F(2, 600) = 1.43$, $p = .24$, indicating that in terms of initial average WTC scores students who had complete data did not differ significantly from those who had incomplete data. A similar test was conducted for age, $F(2, 703) = 3.73$, $p = .32$, indicating that the average age of participants who had complete data did not differ significantly from that of students who participated only in one or two measurements. To further investigate the effect of missing data, two additional chi-square tests were conducted for gender and class rank (first-year students vs. all other students). These tests were also non-significant ($p = .95$ for gender; $p = .46$ for class rank), showing that no significant associations were detected between gender and respectively, class rank and the pattern of missing data. Results from all these analyses suggest that it is unlikely that missing data have any biasing effect in this study. This conclusion is further supported by our knowledge of the data collection process. More specifically, we believe that most missing observations can be attributed to instructors failing to administer

Table 7.1 Full Information Maximum Likelihood Estimates of Observed Sample Statistics

Variable	WTC_1	WTC_2	WTC_3	Gender
1.WTC_1	**289.93**	.66	.61	−.01
2.WTC_2	197.01	**309.51**	.69	.02
3.WTC_3	179.41	209.51	**301.51**	.06
4. Gender	−0.08	0.16	0.50	**0.25**
Mean	66.92	69.31	71.61	0.55
Skew	−0.34	−0.46	−0.44	−0.19
Kurtosis	−0.22	−0.03	−0.10	−1.97
Reliability	0.87	0.89	0.88	1.00

Note: Variances are denoted in bold, covariances are included in the lower triangular part, and correlations are in the upper triangular part of the table. WTC_1, WTC_2, WTC_3 = average WTC scores at times 1–3; Gender (0 = female; 1 = male); Reliabilities reported in this table are the α coefficient of internal consistency.

questionnaires in all data collection waves and to students missing class on the data collection days.

An examination of Table 7.1 reveals that at all time points WTC scores had excellent reliabilities and very small absolute values of skewness and kurtosis. Taking into account that multivariate normality (MVN) violations are suspected only when absolute values of univariate skewness and/or kurtosis are greater than 2.00 and, respectively, 7.00 (Curran, West, & Finch, 1996), it can be concluded that the MVN assumption is tenable. As an additional precaution, this study made use of maximum-likelihood estimation, a procedure that has been found to be robust to small and medium violations of MVN (Fan & Wang, 1998). All analyses were conducted in Mplus version 6.1 (Muthen & Muthen, 1998–2010). To estimate model parameters, full information maximum likelihood (FIML) was used. Employment of this estimation method is particularly recommended in longitudinal studies where people's answers to a questionnaire are correlated across waves of measurement. In such situations, FIML "estimation is the most appropriate method of handling missing data because it uses all available data from earlier and later waves to estimate parameters and standard errors" (Dogan, Stockdale, Widaman, & Conger, 2010, p. 1753).

Test of Longitudinal Invariance.   Following recommendations in Widaman et al. (2010), "a longitudinal factor analysis model with configural invariance and minimal identification constraints" (p. 12) was employed to test across-time configural invariance of first-order factor scores. This model hypothesized that at all three waves of measurement the WTC factor has an identical pattern of zero and non-zero loadings. To identify the model, the mean and variance of FWTC at Time 1 ($FWTC_{(1)}$) were fixed to 0 and 1, respectively, whereas the factor loading and the intercept associated with the first parcel were estimated (but constrained to be invariant across time). All other parameters (other loadings and intercepts, variances of uniqueness, means and variances of FWTC at Times 2 and 3) were freely estimated (for more details on this identification method, see Widaman et al., 2010). In addition, because the same people were measured with the same instrument at relatively short intervals of time (seven weeks), lag-one correlations between corresponding parcels over time (correlation between $Pl_{(1)}$ and $Pl_{(2)}$, $Pl_{(2)}$ and $Pl_{(3)}$, etc.) were specified (see Ferrer et al., 2008; Hancock et al., 2001; Widaman et al., 2010 for examples using the same approach). It is noteworthy that although this approach has been widely used, a different approach to model lag-one correlations recently has been introduced by Geiser and Lockhart (2012). Correlating unique factors across time is important for longitudinal research: "Because the uniquenesses contain non-random variance in each item that is not shared with other indicators of the same construct, they contain reliable variance and may covary over time" (Sayer & Cumsille, 2001, p. 188). On a similar note, Millsap and Everson (1991) argue that "in longitudinal data, it may be unreasonable to assume that unique factors are mutually uncorrelated" (p. 492).

This configural invariance model (denoted CFA1) had a good fit to the data (see Table 7.2), indicating that the pattern of restricted and unrestricted loadings was invariant across time for the WTC factor. In the next step, the model imposing the across-time equality of corresponding factor loadings (CFA2) was fit to test for weak longitudinal invariance. An analysis of the results for CFA2 and CFA1 indicates that despite constraining factor loadings to be equal across time, the fit of the model did not worsen significantly: $\Delta\chi^2 = 5.89$, $\Delta df = 4, p = .21$. This result is strengthened by the fact that the AIC and BIC associated with the CFA2 model were smaller in magnitude than their corresponding counterparts in CFA1 (see Table 7.2). (In general, models that have smaller AIC and BIC values provide a more accurate description of empirical data than models with higher values of these information criteria; Raykov & Marcoulides, 2006.) Thus, it can be concluded that the relations between the WTC factor and its three indicators did not change significantly over time.

Following, a more restricted model (CFA3) imposing the restriction of equal corresponding intercepts across time in addition to the equality of factor loadings was employed to test the hypothesis of strong longitudinal invariance. This model also had a good fit (see Table 7.2), and the restrictions did not worsen significantly the fit compared to the model for weak longitudinal invariance: $\Delta\chi^2 = 4.23, \Delta df = 4, p = .38$. Once again, this result is strengthened by the fact that AIC and BIC corresponding to the restricted model (CFA3) are smaller in magnitude than their counterparts from the less restricted model (CFA2; see Table 7.2). As a result, it can be concluded that the data offered support for the hypothesis of strong longitudinal invariance. In practical terms, these results indicated that the WTC factors were measured in the same ways at each of the three times, and that any change recorded in WTC can be meaningfully interpreted as change in construct over time (as opposed to change in the yardstick employed to gauge WTC).

Finally, a last model (CFA4) was fit to the data to test for strict longitudinal invariance. This model imposed the additional constraints of equal (corresponding) unique variances and had a good fit to the data (see Table 7.2). The chi-square difference test was statistically significant, $\Delta\chi^2 = 22.82, \Delta df = 6, p < .01$, indicating that strict factorial invariance is not tenable for WTC. The AIC for model CFA4 is larger than AIC for model CFA3, pointing to the same conclusion. However, a different picture emerges when considering the BIC criterion: Because BIC for CFA4 is smaller than BIC for CFA3, it can be concluded that there is some support favoring the strict invariance model (for arguing that the three parcels measured the WTC factor with similar precision at each wave of measurement). All in all, because strong (and not strict) longitudinal invariance is needed for a meaningful comparison of mean differences as well as for employing a second-order growth model (Ferrer et al., 2008; Widaman & Reise, 1997), the 2LGM used in this research is grounded on the CFA3 model and only imposes strong (but not strict) longitudinal invariance restrictions.

After establishing the tenability of the strong longitudinal invariance hypothesis, the CFA3 model was employed to assess factorial invariance across gender. Following the sequence of steps described for longitudinal invariance,

Table 7.2 Goodness-of-fit Indices of the Models Used to Test Longitudinal and Multiple-Group Invariance

Model	χ^2	df	RMSEA	(90% CI)	CFI	TLI	AIC	BIC	$\Delta\chi^2/\Delta df$
CFA1- configural L-invar.	112.82	18	.09	(.07–10)	.97	.95	41346.99	41511.04	—
CFA2- weak L-invar. ($\lambda_=$)	118.71	22	.08	(.06–09)	.97	.96	41344.88	41490.70	5.89/4; $p = .21$
CFA3- strong L-invar. ($\lambda_= + \tau_=$)	122.94	26	.07	(.06–09)	.97	.96	41341.11	41468.70	4.23/4; $p = .38$
CFA4- strict L-invar. ($\lambda_= + \tau_= + \theta_=$)	145.76	32	.07	(.06–08)	.97	.96	41351.93	41452.18	22.82/6; $p < .01$
2LGMU- unconditional 2LGM	128.45	29	.07	(.06–08)	.97	.97	41340.61	41454.53	—
2LGMC- conditional 2LGM	182.86	36	.08	(.07–09)	.96	.95	37158.89	37277.88	—
CFA5- configural MG-invar.	159.00	54	.07	(.06–09)	.97	.96	41298.68	41544.75	—
CFA6- weak MG-invar. ($\lambda_=$)	165.66	56	.08	(.06–09)	.97	.96	41301.34	41538.29	6.66/2; $p = .04$
CFA7- strong MG-invar. ($\lambda_= + \tau_=$)	168.72	59	.07	(.06–09)	.97	.97	41298.40	41521.69	3.06/2; $p = .38$
CFA8- strict MG-invar. ($\lambda_= + \tau_= + \theta_=$)	243.79	68	.09	(.07–10)	.95	.95	41355.48	41537.75	75.07/9; $p < .01$

Note: RMSEA = Root Mean Square Error of Approximation; CI = confidence interval; CFI = Comparative Fit Index; TLI = Tucker and Lewis non-normed fit index; AIC = Akaike Information Criterion; BIC = Bayesian Information Criterion; L-invar = longitudinal invariance; MG-invar = multiple group invariance across gender; 2LGM = second order latent growth model; $\lambda_=$ = equal corresponding factor loadings across time; $\lambda_= + \tau_=$ = equal corresponding factor loadings and intercepts across time; $\lambda_= + \tau_= + \theta_=$ = equal corresponding factor loadings, intercepts, and variance of uniquenesses across time.

a set of four nested models (see Models CFA5, CFA6, CFA7, and CFA8 in Table 7.2) was used to test whether the structure of the 3-factor WTC model (including factors measured at Times 1, 2, and 3) was invariant for male and female participants. Fitting these models provided empirical support (see the BIC values associated with the increasingly restrictive sequence of models) for the fact that the factorial structure exhibited strong (but not strict) invariance across these two groups. In other words, the models for females and males had identical configurations, as well as equal factor loadings and intercepts, but different unique variances. Thus, changes in WTC factor scores for these two populations were on the same metric and can be meaningfully compared.

The Unconditional 2LGM.   Grounded on the results of the longitudinal invariance testing, a 2LGM was employed to model the mean and covariance structure of the WTC factors at the three measurement occasions. As illustrated in Table 7.2, the 2LGMU had a good fit to the data, demonstrating that change in WTC was linear across the given semester. The parameters that are of most interest for the 2LGM are the mean initial level ($\mu_{Int\_2LGM} = 65.95$, $p < .01$; variance=135.15) and mean rate of change ($\mu_{S2pt\_2LGM} = 4.07, p < .01$; variance=12.59), and, to a lesser extent, the correlation between initial levels and rates of change ($\rho_{I-S\_2LGM} = .03, p < .91$). The findings associated with 2LGM indicate that students began the semester with average levels of WTC factor of about 66 points and exhibited a linear increase of about 4 points.

To obtain a precise indication of the magnitude of the average change in the latent WTC factor across the given semester (in a Cohen's d metric as opposed to the initial metric discussed previously), an alternative specification of the 2LGM was employed following the steps in Ferrer et al. (2008). This model, which has an identical fit with 2LGMU in Table 7.2, indicates that in the given semester WTC factor scores increased moderately, with 0.30 units in a Cohen's d metric.

The Conditional 2LGM.   Using a 2LGM makes it possible to study important aspects regarding both common and specific effects of predictor(s) on latent change patterns (Duncan, Duncan, & Strycker, 2006). Common effects refer to the influence of predictor(s) on the higher-order growth factors (intercept and slope) whereas specific effects are those effects of the predictor(s) that are unique to a particular point in time (Duncan et al., 2006). The ability of 2LGM to analyze these effects is particularly salient for it allows the examination of predictor influences that cannot be accounted for by the relations among predictor(s) and the growth factors. Moreover, it is important to assess whether specific effects exist because their presence would indicate that the second-order growth model cannot entirely account for the relations among predictor(s) and lower order factors ($FWTC_{(t)}$). By analyzing both common and specific effects in the 2LGM framework, researchers can test whether or not predictor(s) influences are adequately modeled by the incorporation of direct paths to the second-order growth factors. If significant specific effects are identified, it can be concluded that predictor(s) effects are time-dependent (predictors exert a non-linear influence on the growth trajectories) and need to be modeled accordingly (Duncan et al., 2006).

To evaluate common effects, a conditional 2LGM model (2LGMC in Table 7.2) was employed, in which the student communication apprehension score recorded at time 1 (CA_1) was employed as a sole predictor of intercept and slope. This model, which is schematically represented in Figure 7.2, included no direct effects of CA_1 on the first-order WTC factors and had a good fit to the data. Analyzing the results of 2LGMC indicates that apprehension had a significant negative effect on the initial latent WTC score but a significant positive effect on the rate of change in factor WTC. These results can be interpreted as suggesting that students who had higher apprehension scores at Time 1 than their peers were likely to exhibit lower WTC levels at Time 1. However, students who were initially more apprehensive than their colleagues were likely to exhibit sharper increases in WTC over the course of the semester.

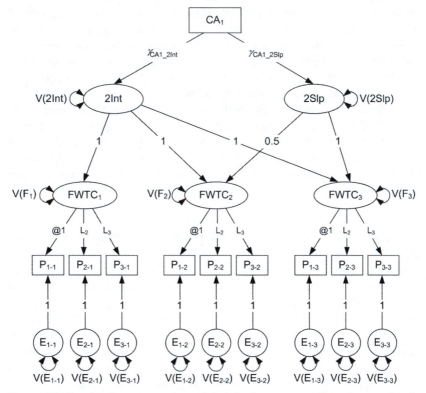

Figure 7.2 Graphical representation of the single-group conditional second-order model, 2LGM. CA_1 = communication apprehension measured at Time 1; 2Int = intercept of the second-order model; 2Slp = slope of the second-order model; γ_{CA1_2Int} = regression coefficient for regressing 2Int on CA_1 ; γ_{CA1_2Slp} = regression coefficient for regressing 2Slp on CA_1. V() = variance; Cov(,) = covariance; WTC_i = willingness to communicate score at the *i*-th wave of measurement (*i* = 1,2,3); E_i = uniqueness (residual) of the *i*-th wave of measurement.

These results show that in longitudinal studies the effects of predictors on various growth factors need not have the same direction (for similar findings, see Hodis et al., 2010). CA_1 alone accounted for over 46.5% of variability in initial WTC factor scores ($p < .01$). The value of the corresponding R^2 for slope was not statistically significant.

Three additional models were run to assess whether specific effects of CA_1 on WTC factors were apparent. All these models included, in addition to the common effects discussed previously (effects of CA_1 on the latent intercept and slope), direct influences of CA_1 on the first order factor at Time 1 (Model 1), and, respectively, at Time 2 and Time 3 (Models 2 and 3). Successive fitting of these three models to the data indicated that none of the specific effects was statistically significant. Therefore, it can be concluded that the hypothesis of non-linear effect of CA_1 on WTC did not receive support from the data and that the effect of CA_1 on the WTC change trajectories was accounted for by the influence of the predictor on the second-order latent intercept and slope.

Under certain conditions, findings from the second- and first-order latent growth models can be similar. Results from Ferrer and colleagues (2008) demonstrate that "when the hypothesis of factorial invariance over time is tenable in the data, the estimates from a 1st-order latent model and a 2nd-order latent model lead to roughly equal expected trajectories" (p. 34). As the WTC factor analyzed in this research exhibited strong (and possibly strict) longitudinal invariance, it is important to compare the results from the unconditional 1LGM and 2LGM models. This is a pivotal step of the analysis. If the two solutions are similar, simplicity and interpretability considerations would recommend employing the simpler model (1LGM) when conducting further investigations (e.g., multiple-group analyses).

Unconditional First Order Linear Latent Growth Model (1LGM)

Single-Group 1LGM. The 1LGM uses the average WTC score as its focal variable. The model had good fit to the data: χ^2 (1, N = 704) = 0.004, $p = .95$, CFI = 1.00, TLI = 1.00, RMSEA = .00 with the 90% confidence interval for RMSEA being 90% C.I. = (.00, .01). Once it was found that the model exhibits an adequate overall fit, it is meaningful to discuss the model parameters that are of interest (Curran, 2000). The estimated means of the intercept and slope latent factors were $\mu_{Int} = 66.94$ and $\mu_{Slp} = 4.68$, respectively, both of which were significantly different from zero ($p < .01$ for both). These findings indicate that at the beginning of the semester the estimated true WTC population mean was 66.94 points whereas the estimated true average rate of change was 4.68 points. The fact that the mean of the slope factor was significantly different from zero indicates that students' WTC (composite) scores exhibited a systematic (non-random) increase from the beginning to the end of the semester. These results are similar to those obtained in the 2LGM analysis. Moreover, when expressing the average rate of change in WTC in standardized terms, the result (0.32 Cohen's *d* units) is also very similar to the value obtained in 2LGM.

Thus, it can be concluded that in the interest of simplicity and to facilitate an easier interpretation of the findings, the 1LGM model offers a good substitute for the more complex 2LGM.

The variance estimates for intercept ($\sigma^2_{Int} = \Psi_{\alpha\alpha} = 215.17$) and slope ($\sigma^2_{Slp} = \Psi_{\beta\beta} = 97.10$) factors were significantly different from zero ($p < .01$, for both intercept and slope), suggesting that a substantial interindividual variability in intraindividual change was apparent for WTC. In other words, students exhibited substantial variability (around the corresponding mean values) with respect to both true initial levels and true rates of change in WTC. The estimate of the covariance between the intercept and slope factors was non-significant ($\sigma_{Int-Slp} = \Psi_{\alpha\beta} = -36.31$, $p = .09$). The R^2 values associated with the observed WTC scores were high (.74 at the first measurement, .66 at the second, and .80 at the third), indicating that most variability in WTC was attributable to the latent growth factors. In this light, and following the rationale delineated in Chan, Ramey, Ramey, and Schmitt (2000), it can be concluded that most of the change in WTC scores was time related.

Single- vs. Multiple-Group Approaches in LGM.   Grounded on the fact that "sex differences in communication do exist" (Canary & Hause, 1993, p. 130), it is quite often of interest to analyze whether male and female students exhibit different patterns of change with respect to focal variable (here WTC). In 1LGM this test can be approached from two different standpoints. First, gender can be included as a predictor of latent intercept and slope factors and, thus, slight modifications in Equations 3 and 4 will now describe a conditional linear LGM. Second, a multiple-groups LGM can be conducted to test the effect of gender on WTC trajectories. While the first alternative is more commonly employed in applied research, it has certain drawbacks that will be discussed next. Although this presentation uses a two-group scenario, the multiple-groups 1LGM is applicable to practically any number of groups (Preacher et al., 2008).

When a single-group model, regardless of whether it is a 1LGM or 2LGM, is estimated in a sample including both males and females, the researcher assumes that all parameters of the model are equivalent for people in the sample (Curran et al., 2010). When gender is used to predict systematic variability in the latent factors, an additional implicit assumption is being made: Gender's only role is to "shift the conditional means of the intercept and slope to higher or lower values" (Curran et al., 2010, p. 130). In our example, this is equivalent to assuming that although on average, males and females could start the semester with different WTC levels and/or increase more or less abruptly, all other LGM parameters (variances of latent growth factors, their covariance, and the three error variances) are identical for the two groups. To the extent that this assumption is untenable, biased parameter estimates are likely to occur (Curran et al., 2010). In a multiple-groups LGM frame of inquiry, this limiting assumption is not needed because researchers can test the tenability of all equality constraints across the given groups and retain only those restrictions that do not worsen the fit significantly. Thus, employment of multiple-groups LGM has important advantages over including the grouping variable as a predictor in the model, as the former approach "provides yet another option for maximally understanding growth processes both within and across groups" (Curran et al., 2010, p. 131).

Multiple-Groups 1LGM.   Multiple-groups 1LGM is employed next to assess whether the linear growth model is tenable for both females and males, as well as to evaluate whether patterns of change in WTC composite are different across gender. To this end, an increasingly restrictive sequence of multiple-groups LGMs was fit to the data. In the first step, a base multiple-groups (1BMG) model was employed. This model imposed no restriction whatsoever (it estimated separate parameters of growth for female and male subsamples) and was evaluated simultaneously for both groups. The model fitted the data very well (see Table 7.3) indicating that WTC scores increased linearly in the given semester for both females and males. In the next step, a more restricted model was employed to test whether female and male subsamples began the semester at similar WTC levels. This intercept multiple-groups (1IMG) model, which posited as its unique restriction that the mean of the latent intercept factor is the same for the female and male subsamples, also fitted the data well (see Table 7.3). Because these two models are nested, the difference in fit between the two models can be formally evaluated. The chi-square difference test evaluating the tenability of this equality constraint was not statistically significant: $\Delta\chi^2 = 0.12 - 0.04 = 0.08$, $\Delta df = 1$, p = .78, indicating that, on average, the two groups did not differ significantly in their initial WTC levels.

In the last step, the equality of the mean rates of change across the two groups was imposed and tested. This intercept and slope multiple-groups model (1ISMG) additionally restricts the two groups to having identical average increases in WTC. 1ISMG had a good fit to the data (see Table 7.3), and the chi-square difference test was not significant: $\Delta\chi^2 = 3.37 - 0.02 = 3.25$, $\Delta df = 1$, p = .07. If this were a substantive study, as opposed to a methodological one, we would cautiously point to male and female subgroups exhibiting similar patterns of evolution with respect to WTC. To this conclusion also contributed the close alignment between average intercepts and rates of change in the single-group model (66.94; 4.68) versus the multiple-groups one (67.05; 4.54). However, because we want to exemplify how effect sizes can be easily calculated in the multiple-groups LGM context, we will revert back to the 1IMG model. Findings from this model are summarized in Table 7.4, the rows denoted with 1F for the female subsample and with 1M for the male. An annotated Mplus code for running the single- and multiple-groups LGM is included in the appendix.

To illustrate the magnitude of the difference between average rates of change for males and females, a latent standardized effect size (Δ) was estimated following the procedure described in Hancock et al. (2001). Specifically, Δ was defined as the ratio of the absolute value of the difference between estimated

Table 7.3 Values of the Chi-Squared Tests and Goodness-of-Fit Indices for First- and Second-Order LGMs

Model	$\chi^2(df, N); p$	CFI	TLI	RMSEA (90% CI)
1BMG	$\chi^2(2, N = 704) = 0.04; p = .98$	1.00	1.00	.00 (.00, .00)
1IMG	$\chi^2(3, N = 704) = 0.12; p = .99$	1.00	1.00	.00 (.00, .00)
1ISMG	$\chi^2(4, N = 704) = 3.37; p = .50$	1.00	1.00	.00 (.00, .08)
1O	$\chi^2(1, N = 704) = 0.00; p = .95$	1.00	1.00	.00 (.00, .01)
2BMG	$\chi^2(64, N = 704) = 168.23; p < .01$	.97	.97	.07 (.06, .08)
2IMG	$\chi^2(65, N = 704) = 168.34; p < .01$	.97	.97	.07 (.06, .08)
2ISMG	$\chi^2(66, N = 704) =172.94; p < .01$	.97	.97	.07 (.06, .08)
2O	$\chi^2(29, N = 704) = 128.45; p < .01$	.97	.97	.07 (.06, .08)

Note: CFI = Comparative Fit Index; TLI = Tucker and Lewis non-normed fit index; RMSEA = Root Mean Square Error of Approximation; CI = confidence interval; BMG = base multiple-groups LGM (a model that is fitted simultaneously to the female and male subsamples but imposes no equality constraints across these two groups); IMG = intercept multiple-groups LGM (a model that is fitted simultaneously to the female and male subsamples and posits equal average initial levels for female and male subsamples); ISMG = intercept and slope multiple-groups LGM (a model that is fitted simultaneously to the female and male subsamples and posits equal average initial levels and rates of change for female and male subsamples); O = overall single-group model; 1- denotes the first-order (1LGM) model; 2- denotes the second-order (2LGM) model; the 2O model is identical to the model denoted 2LGMU in Table 2 and is included here for the sake of completeness.

average rates of change for male and female subgroups and the square root of the pooled variance of the two groups' rates of change (employing the sample sizes as weights). Using the results in the first two rows of Table 7.4, Δ can be easily obtained:

$$\Delta = \frac{|5.58 - 3.46|}{\sqrt{\dfrac{386 \cdot 148.98 + 318 \cdot 32.72}{386 + 318}}} = 0.22.$$

The value of this estimated latent standardized effect indicates that, on average, the increase in male students' WTC scores was about one-fourth of a standard deviation steeper than that of their female counterparts. The multiple-group LGM analyses can also be conducted in the 2LGM framework. Specifically, taking into account the strong invariance of the measurement model for gender was previously supported (see Table 7.2), at this stage, a sequence of increasingly restrictive models was employed. This sequence is identical in scope with the one discussed for the 1LGM case. The results of fitting the 2BMG, 2IMG, and 2ISMG models are summarized in Table 7.3.

It is worth noting that the flexibility of the multiple-groups LGM framework allows testing of a wide range of theoretically justifiable hypotheses. For instance, to assess whether males and females differ in terms of *variability* around the respective average rates of change in WTC, one can impose

Table 7.4 Unstandardized Parameter Estimates for First- and Second-Order LGMs

Sample (N)	Average TIS			Average TRC			Variance TIS			Variance TRC			Cov (Corr) of TIS and TRC		
	Est	SE	p	Est	SE	p	Est	SE	p	Est	SE	p	Est	SE	p
1F(318)	66.95**[a]	0.66[a]	<.01	3.46**	0.89	<.01	202.72**	22.34	<.01	32.72	57.69	.57	0.14 (.00)	33.01	.99
1M(386)	66.95**[a]	0.66[a]	<.01	5.58**	0.87	<.01	226.52**	29.02	<.01	148.98**	47.24	<.01	-67.66* (-.37)	28.76	.02
1O (705)	66.94**	0.66	<.01	4.68**	0.66	<.01	215.17**	21.61	<.01	97.10**	36.60	<.01	-36.31 (-.25)	21.68	.09
2F(318)	65.98**[b]	0.58[b]	<.01	2.89**	0.75	<.01	148.22**	24.50	<.01	25.36	41.00	.54	-0.79 (-.01)	24.11	.97
2M(386)	65.98**[b]	0.58[b]	<.01	5.00**	0.72	<.01	151.09**	21.24	<.01	92.41**	33.67	<.01	-38.15 (-.32)	20.30	.01
2O (705)	65.95**	0.58	<.01	4.07**	0.55	<.01	135.15**	12.76	<.01	12.59	13.72	.36	1.19 (.03)	9.76	.91

Note: Est = Estimate; TIS = true initial status; TRC = true rate of change; Cov = covariance; Corr = correlation; N = sample size; SE = standard error; F = female; M = male; O = overall single-group; 1- denotes the first-order (i.e., 1LGM) model; 2- denotes the second-order (2LGM) model; All p values are two-tailed.
* p < .05. ** p < .01. [a,b] denotes parameters held equal across groups.

constraints on the two slope variances and then conduct a chi-square difference of fit between the restricted and unrestricted models (see Preacher et al.,
2008, for an example involving slope-intercept covariances). Another interesting finding that can be unearthed in multiple-groups LGM investigations is
that the variance in rates of change was statistically significant for the male
subgroup but not for the female subgroup (in both 1LGM and 2LGM settings).
Thus, it appears that females were characterized by homogeneous increases in
WTC, whereas males exhibited more heterogeneous patterns of growth. This
information is valuable for it points to the benefits of instruction being more
evenly shared in the female subpopulation than in the male one (assuming that
the increase in WTC is a worthwhile aim of a core communication course). In
turn, this knowledge raises interesting and important questions: What aspects
of the pedagogical practice could account for greater variability of outcomes for
males? Is it the case that instruction, examples, and assignments were generally
more relevant for female than for male students? If so, was this differential relevance associated with the fact that, as a group, females were more uniformly
engaged with the course but for males engagement varied significantly? Alternatively, can the variability (vs. homogeneity) in males' versus females' patterns
of growth be attributed to variability (vs. homogeneity) in the goals with which
they entered the given communication course? Pondering on these questions
could be very beneficial, as putative answers can be used to make beneficial
adjustments to given aspects of the learning and teaching process.

Additional Applications and Extensions of Latent Growth Curve Modeling

The versatility of LGM makes it an attractive option for many research
scenarios that can be encountered in applied communication investigations.
Latent growth curve models "are most easily and usefully applied when data
are collected on *at least four* waves of measurement, although meaningful
analyses can be conducted sometimes with less than four waves" (Jones,
2012, p. 273; emphasis in original). Following, some extensions of LGM that
communication scholars might find useful in their work are briefly overviewed.
First, if four or more measurement waves are available, non-linear models of
change can be hypothesized and tested (Grimm & Ram, 2009, 2012; Grimm,
Ram, & Hamagami, 2011). Moreover, because a linear model is nested within a
non-linear one, the difference in fit between competing models can be assessed
using the chi-square difference test.

Comparisons between the fit of linear and non-linear latent change models
are essential for assessing whether a given model provides the most accurate
representation of growth/decline in the empirical data. Hence, these types
of comparisons need to be conducted whenever four or more measurement
waves are available for the communication variables/constructs of interest. For
example, if a researcher wants to assess whether students' WTC scores reach
a plateau and then decrease after the end of the semester, LGM can readily
answer this question, provided that enough waves of data are available. Second, although this presentation included discussions of some conditional LGM

models, further extensions are certainly possible (using 1LGM or 2LGM as a part of nomological network of relations including both predictors and distal outcomes). Third, if researchers are interested in analyzing how two or more change processes interact, they can employ parallel growth modeling and look at substantively meaningful relations among growth factors (Henry & Slater, 2008; Slater & Hayes, 2010). Fourth, more specialized extensions of LGM are also available (piecewise growth models, accelerated designs, growth mixture models; Duncan & Duncan, 2009; Preacher et al., 2008). Finally, the strengths of LGM enable the procedure to play an important role in the process of comparing the effectiveness and efficiency of competing instructional strategies. In particular, if multiple strategies (targeting the development of one or more salient communication competencies) are implemented, by means of LGM they can be evaluated both in terms of average gains and homogeneity/heterogeneity of given gains. The flexibility of LGM makes it feasible to assess the extent to which certain subgroups of students benefit more or less from exposure to a certain instructional strategy across one dimension versus the other dimension. All in all, it is clear that "growth modeling analysis provides a promising methodological approach to assessing communication development" (Hecht et al., 2006, p. 275), and we hope that communication researchers will increasingly include it in their methodological toolkits.

Conclusion

This chapter provides a methodological overview of both 1- and 2LGM. The presentation underlines important features of this procedure that recommends its use in applied longitudinal communication research. By using the example of a well-known communication construct, the discussion highlights salient linkages between theoretical aspects of LGM and their practical implementation. To this end, the chapter provides in-depth discussions of results and offers a detailed explanation of the computer code needed to implement single- and multiple-groups LGMs. In addition, this work illustrates how employment of a powerful and versatile methodology such as LGM can help researchers find answers to questions that cannot be properly addressed with more traditional data analytical techniques such as multiple regression, repeated measures *t*-tests, and ANOVA (Byrne et al., 2008; Lance, Meade, & Williamson, 2000), or in a multilevel framework (Curran, 2003). To conclude, important advances in communication research can be achieved by placing change processes at the core of theory development and testing (Henry & Slater, 2008). To do so, communication scholars need to add modern longitudinal techniques such as LGM to their preferred analytical tools.

References

Bandura, A. (2002). Social cognitive theory of mass communication. In J. Bryant & D. Zillmann (Eds.), *Media effects: Advances in theory and research* (2nd ed., pp. 121–154). Hillsdale, NJ: Erlbaum.

Bauer, D. J. (2003). Estimating multilevel linear models as structural equation models. *Journal of Educational and Behavioral Statistics, 28*, 135–167. doi:10.3102/10769986028002135

Bentler, P. M. (1990). Comparative fit indexes in structural models. *Psychological Bulletin, 107*, 238–246. doi:10.1037/0033-2909.107.2.238

Bollen, K. A., & Curran, P. J. (2006). *Latent curve models: A structural equation perspective*. Hoboken, NJ: Wiley.

Brown, T. A. (2006). *Confirmatory factor analysis for applied research*. New York, NY: Guilford.

Byrne, B. M., Lam, W. T., & Fielding, R. (2008). Measuring patterns of change in personality assessments: An annotated application of latent growth curve modelling. *Journal of Personality Assessment, 90*, 536–546. doi:10.1080/00223890802388350

Byrne, B. M., & Crombie, G. (2003). Modeling and testing change: An introduction to the latent growth curve model. *Understanding Statistics, 2*, 177–203.

Canary, D. J., & Hause, K. S. (1993). Is there any reason to research sex differences in communication? *Communication Quarterly, 41*, 129–144. doi:10.1080/01463379309369874

Caughlin, J. P. (2002). The demand/withdraw pattern of communication as a predictor of marital satisfaction over time. *Human Communication Research, 28*, 49–85. doi:10.1111/j.1468-2958.2002.tb00798.x

Chan, D. (1998). The conceptualization and analysis of change over time: An integrative approach incorporating longitudinal mean and covariance structures analysis (LMACS) and multiple indicator latent growth modeling (MLGM). *Organizational Research Methods, 1*, 421–483. doi:10.1177/109442819814004

Chan, D., Ramey, S., Ramey, C., & Schmitt, N. (2000). Modeling intraindividual changes in children's social skills at home and at school: A multivariate latent growth approach to understanding between-settings differences in children's social skills development. *Multivariate Behavioral Research, 35*, 365–396. doi:10.1207/S15327906MBR3503_04

Curran, P. J. (2000). A latent curve framework for the study of developmental trajectories in adolescent substance use. In J. S. Rose, L. Chassin, C. C. Presson, & S. J. Sherman (Eds.), *Multivariate applications in substance use research: New methods for new questions* (pp. 1–42). Mahwah, NJ: Erlbaum.

Curran, P. J. (2003). Have multilevel models been structural equation models all along? *Multivariate Behavioral Research, 38*, 529–569. doi:10.1207/s15327906mbr3804_5

Curran, P. J., & Muthen, B. O. (1999). The application of latent curve analysis to testing developmental theories in intervention research. *American Journal of Community Psychology, 27*, 567–595.

Curran, P. J., Obeidat, K., & Losardo, D. (2010). Twelve frequently asked questions about growth curve modeling. *Journal of Cognition and Development, 11*, 121–136. doi:10.1080/15248371003699969

Curran, P. J., West, S. G., & Finch, J. F. (1996). The robustness of test statistics to nonnormality and specification error in confirmatory factor analysis. *Psychological Methods, 1*, 16–29. doi:10.1037//1082-989X.1.1.16

Dogan, S. J., Stockdale, G. D., Widaman, K. F., & Conger, R. D. (2010). Developmental relations and patterns of change between alcohol use and number of sexual partners from adolescence through adulthood. *Developmental Psychology, 46*, 1747–1759. doi:10.1037/a0019655

Duncan, S. C., Duncan, T. E., & Hops, H. (1996). Analysis of longitudinal data within accelerated longitudinal designs. *Psychological Methods, 1,* 236–248. doi:10.1037/1082-989X.1.3.236

Duncan, T. E., & Duncan, S. C. (2004a). A latent growth curve modeling approach to pooled interrupted time series analyses. *Journal of Psychopathology and Behavioral Assessment, 26,* 271–278. doi:10.1023/B:JOBA.0000045342.32739.2f

Duncan, T. E., & Duncan, S. C. (2004b). An introduction to latent growth curve modeling. *Behavior Therapy, 35,* 333–363. doi:10.1016/S0005-7894(04)80042-X

Duncan, T. E., & Duncan, S. C. (2009). The ABC's of LGM: An introductory guide to latent variable growth curve modeling. *Social and Personality Psychology Compass, 3,* 979–991. doi:10.1111/j.1751-9004.2009.00224.x

Duncan, T. E., Duncan, S. C., & Strycker, L. A. (2006). *An introduction to latent variable growth curve modeling: Concepts, issues, and applications* (2nd ed.). Mahwah, NJ: Erlbaum.

Dwyer, K. K., & Fus, D. A. (2002). Perceptions of communication competence, self-efficacy, and trait communication apprehension: Is there an impact on basic course success? *Communication Research Reports, 19,* 29–37.

Eggermont, S. (2006). Television viewing and adolescents' judgment of sexual request scripts: A latent growth curve analysis in early and middle adolescence. *Sex Roles, 55,* 457–468. doi:10.1007/s11199-006-9099-7

Fan, X., & Wang, L. (1998). Effects of potential confounding factors on fit indices and parameter estimates on true and misspecified SEM models. *Educational and Psychological Measurement, 58,* 701–735. doi:10.1177/0013164498058005001

Ferrer, E., Balluerka, N., & Widaman, K. F. (2008). Factorial invariance and the specification of second-order latent growth models. *Methodology, 4,* 22–36. doi:10.1027/16142241.4.1.22

Flora, D. B. (2008). Specifying piecewise latent trajectory models for longitudinal data. *Structural Equation Modeling: A Multidisiplinary Journal, 15,* 513–533. doi:10.1080/10705510802154349

Fransen, M. L., & ter Hoeven, C. L. (2011). Matching the message: The role of regulatory fit in negative managerial communication. *Communication Research.* Advance online publication. doi:10.1177/0093650211427140

Ghisletta, P., & Lindenberger, U. (2004). Static and dynamic longitudinal structural analyses of cognitive changes in old age. *Gerontology, 50,* 12–16. doi:10.1159/000074383

Gosin, M., Marsiglia, F. F., & Hecht, M. L. (2003). *keepin' it REAL:* A drug resistance curriculum tailored to the strengths and needs of pre-adolescents of the Southwest. *The Journal of Drug Education, 33,* 119–142. doi:10.2190/DXB9-1V2P-C27J-V69V

Grimm, K. J., & Ram, N. (2009). Nonlinear growth models in Mplus and SAS. *Structural Equation Modeling: A Multidisciplinary Journal, 16,* 671–701. doi:10.1080/10705510903206055

Grimm, K. J., & Ram, N. (2012). Growth curve modeling from a structural equation modeling perspective. In B. Laursen, T. D. Little, & N. A. Card (Eds.), *Handbook of developmental research methods* (pp. 411–431). New York, NY: Guilford Press.

Grimm, K. J., Ram, N., & Hamagami, F. (2011). Nonlinear growth curves in developmental research. *Child Development, 82,* 1357–1371. doi:10.1111/j.1467-8624.2011.01630.x

Geiser, C. & Lockhart, G. (2012). A comparison of four approaches to account for method effects in latent state-trait analyses. *Psychological Methods, 17,* 255–283. doi:10.1037/a0026977

Hancock, G. R., Kuo, W., & Lawrence, F. R. (2001). An illustration of second-order latent growth models. *Structural Equation Modeling: A Multidisciplinary Journal, 8,* 470–489. doi:10.1207/S15328007SEM0803_7

Hancock, G. R., & Lawrence, F. R. (2006). Using latent growth models to evaluate longitudinal change. In G. R. Hancock & R. O. Mueller (Eds.), *Structural equation modeling: A second course* (pp. 171–186). Greenwich, CT: Information Age.

Hayduk, L. A., Cummings, G., Boadu, K., Pazderka-Robinson, H., & Boulianne, S. (2007). Testing! Testing! one, two, three testing the theory in structural equation models! *Personality and Individual Differences, 42,* 841–850.

Hecht, M. L., Graham, J. W., & Elek, E. (2006). The drug resistance strategies intervention: Program effects on substance use. *Health Communication, 20,* 267–276. doi:10.1207/s15327027hc2003_6

Henry, K. L., & Slater, M. D. (2008). Assessing change and intraindividual variation: Longitudinal multilevel and structural equation modeling. In A. F. Hayes, M. D. Slater, & L. B. Snyder (Eds.), *The Sage sourcebook of advanced data analysis methods for communication research* (pp. 55–87). Thousand Oaks, CA: Sage.

Hertzog, C., & Nesselroade, J. R. (2003). Assessing psychological change in adulthood: An overview of methodological issues. *Psychology and Aging, 18,* 639–657. doi:10.1037/0882-7974.18.4.639

Hess, B. (2000). Assessing program impact using latent growth modeling: A primer for the evaluator. *Evaluation and Program Planning, 23,* 419–428. doi:10.1016/S0149-7189(00)00032-X

Higgins, E. T. (1997). Beyond pleasure and pain. *American Psychologist, 52,* 1280–1300. doi:10.1037//0003-066X.52.12.1280

Higgins, E. T. (2012). *Beyond pleasure and pain: How motivation works.* New York, NY: Oxford University Press.

Hodis, G. M., Bardhan, N. R., & Hodis, F. A. (2010). Patterns of change in willingness to communicate in public speaking contexts: A latent growth modeling analysis. *Journal of Applied Communication Research, 38,* 248–267. doi:10.1080/0090988 2.2010.490840

Hodis, G. M., & Hodis, F. A. (2012). Trends in communicative self-efficacy: A comparative analysis. *Basic Communication Course Annual, 24,* 40–80.

Holt, J. K. (2008). Modeling growth using multilevel and alternative approaches. In A. A. O'Connell & D. B. McCoach (Eds.), *Multilevel modeling of educational data* (pp. 111–159). Charlotte, NC: Information Age.

Hong, T. (2012). Examining the role of exposure to incongruent messages on the effect of message framing in an internet health search. *Communication Research.* Advance online publication. doi:10.1177/0093650212439710

Hu, L. T., & Bentler, P. M. (1999). Cutoff criteria for fit indexes in covariance structure analysis: Conventional criteria versus new alternatives. *Structural Equation Modeling, 6*(1), 1–55. doi:10.1080/10705519909540118

Imahori, T. T., & Cupach, W. R. (2005). Identity management theory: Facework in intercultural relationships. In W. B. Gudykunst (Ed.), *Theorizing about intercultural communication* (pp. 195–210). Thousand Oaks, CA: Sage.

Jackson, D. L., Gillaspy, J. A., Jr., & Purc-Stephenson, R. (2009). Reporting practices in confirmatory factor analysis: An overview and some recommendations. *Psychological Methods, 14,* 6–23. doi:10.1037/a0014694

Jeong, S.-H., Hwang, Y., & Fishbein, M. (2010). Effects of exposure to sexual content in the media on adolescent sexual behaviors: The moderating role of multitasking with media. *Media Psychology, 13,* 222–242. doi: 10.1080/15213269.2010.502872

Jones, R. N. (2012). Latent growth curve models. In J. T. Newsom, R. N. Jones, & S. M. Hofer (Eds.), *Longitudinal data analysis: A practical guide for researchers in aging, health, and social sciences* (pp. 271–290). New York, NY: Routledge.

Kaplan, D. (2002). Methodological advances in the analysis of individual growth with relevance education policy. *Peabody Journal of Education, 77*, 189–215. doi:10.1207/S15327930PJE7704_9

Kishton, J. M., & Widaman, K. F. (1994). Unidimensional versus domain representative parceling of questionnaire items: An empirical example. *Educational and Psychological Measurement, 54*, 757–765. doi:10.1177/0013164494054003022

Lance, C. E., Meade, A. W., & Williamson, G. M. (2000). We *should* measure change — and here's how. In G. M. Williamson, D. R. Shaffer, & P. A. Parmelee (Eds.), *Physical illness and depression in older adults: A handbook of theory, research, and practice* (pp. 201–235). New York, NY: Kluwer Academic.

Lenzenweger, M. F., Johnson, M. D., & Willett, J. B. (2004). Individual growth curve analysis illuminates stability and change in personality disorder features. *Archives of General Psychiatry, 61*, 1015–1024. doi:10.1001/archpsyc.61.10.1015

Liberman, N., Trope, Y., & Stephan, E. (2007). Psychological distance. In A. W. Kruglanski & E. T. Higgins (Eds.), *Social psychology: A handbook of basic principles* (pp. 353–381). New York, NY: Guilford Press.

Little, T. D., Cunningham, W. A., Shahar, G., & Widaman, K. F. (2002). To parcel or not to parcel: Exploring the question, weighting the merits. *Structural Equation Modeling: A Multidisciplinary Journal, 9*, 151–173. doi:10.1207/S15328007SEM0902_1

MacCallum, R. C., Kim, C., Malarkey, W. B., & Kiecolt-Glaser, J. K. (1997). Studying multivariate change using multilevel models and latent curve models. *Multivariate Behavioral Research, 32*, 215–253. doi:10.1207/s15327906mbr3203_1

Martin, A. J. (2008). How domain specific is motivation and engagement across school, sport, and music? A substantive-methodological synergy assessing young sportspeople and musicians. *Contemporary Educational Psychology, 33*, 785–813. doi:10.1016/j.cedpsych.2008.01.002

Matsunaga, M. (2008). Item parceling in structural equation modeling: A primer. *Communication Methods and Measures, 2*, 260–293. doi:10.1080/19312450802458935

Maxwell, S. E., & Cole, D. A. (2007). Bias in cross-sectional analyses of longitudinal data. *Psychological Methods, 12*, 23–44. doi:10.1037/1082-989X.12.1.23

McCroskey, J. C. (1986). *An introduction to rhetorical communication.* Eaglewood Cliff, NJ: Prentice-Hall.

McCroskey, J. C., & Richmond, V. P. (1987). Willingness to communicate. In J. C. McCroskey & J. A. Daly (Eds.), *Personality and interpersonal communication* (pp. 129–156). Newbury Park, CA: Sage.

McCroskey, J. C., & Richmond, V. P. (1996). Human communication theory and research: Traditions and models. In M. B. Salwen & D. W. Stacks (Eds.), *An integrated approach to communication theory and research* (pp. 233–242). Mahwah, NJ: Erlbaum.

McIntosh, C. N. (2007). Rethinking fit assessment in structural equation modeling: A commentary and elaboration on Barrett. *Personality and Individual Differences, 42*, 859–867.

Millsap, R. E., & Everson, H. (1991). Confirmatory measurement model comparisons using latent means. *Multivariate Behavioral Research, 26*, 479–497. doi:10.1207/s15327906mbr2603_6

Muthen, L. K., & Muthen, B. O. (1998–2010). *Mplus user's guide* (6th ed.). Los Angeles, CA: Muthen & Muthen.

Nesselroade, J. R., Stigler, S. M., & Baltes, P. B. (1980). Regression toward the mean and the study of change. *Psychological Bulletin, 88,* 622–637. doi:0033-2909/80/88030622

Oetting, E., & Donnermeyer, J. F. (1998). Primary socialization theory: The etiology of drug use and deviance. *Etiology of Substance Use, 33,* 995–1026. doi:10.3109/10826089809056252

Ployhart, R. E., & Hakel, M. D. (1998). The substantive nature of performance variability: Predicting interindividual differences in intraindividual performance. *Personnel Psychology, 51,* 859–901. doi:10.1111/j.1744-6570.1998.tb00744.x

Preacher, K. J., Wichman, A. L., MacCallum, R. C., & Briggs, N. E. (2008). *Latent growth curve modeling.* Los Angeles, CA: Sage.

Ram, N., & Grimm, K. (2007). Using simple and complex growth models to articulate developmental change: Matching theory to method. *International Journal of Behavioral Development, 31,* 303–316. doi:10.1177/0165025407077751

Raudenbush, S. W., & Bryk, A. S. (2002). *Hierarchical linear models: Applications and data analysis methods* (2nd ed.). Thousands Oaks, CA: Sage.

Raykov, T. (2007). Longitudinal analysis with regressions among random effects: A latent variable modeling approach. *Structural Equation Modeling: A Multidisciplinary Journal, 14,* 146–169. doi:10.1207/s15328007sem1401_8

Raykov, T., & Marcoulides, G. A. (2006). *A first course in structural equation modeling* (2nd ed.). Mahwah, NJ: Erlbaum.

Richmond, V. P., & Roach, K. D. (1992). Willingness to communicate and employee success in US organizations. *Journal of Applied Communication Research, 20,* 95–115. doi:10.1080/00909889209365321

Rubin, R. B., Graham, E. E., & Mignerey, J. T. (1990). A longitudinal study of college students' communication competence. *Communication Education, 39,* 1–14. doi:10.1080/03634529009378783

Rubin, R. B., Rubin, A. M., & Jordan, F. F. (1997). Effects of instruction on communication apprehension and communication competence. *Communication Education, 46,* 104–114. doi:10.1080/03634529709379080

Sayer, A. G., & Cumsille, P. E. (2001). Second-order latent growth models. In L. M. Collins & A. G. Sayer (Eds.), *New methods for the analysis of change* (pp. 177–200). Washington, DC: American Psychological Association.

Schemer, C. (2012). Reinforcing spirals of negative affects and selective attention to advertising in a political campaign. *Communication Research, 39,* 413–434. doi:10.1177/0093650211427141

Schemer, C., Matthes, J., & Wirth, W. (2009). Applying latent growth models to the analysis of media effects. *Journal of Media Psychology, 21,* 85–89. doi:10.1027/18641105.21.2.85

Schumacker, R. E., & Lomax, R. G. (2010). *A beginner's guide to structural equation modeling* (3rd ed.). New York, NY: Routledge.

Shepherd, G. J. (1992). Communication as influence: Definitional exclusion. *Communication Studies, 43,* 203–219. doi:10.1080/10510979209368373

Slater, M. D. (2003). Alienation, aggression, and sensation-seeking as predictors of adolescent use of violent film, computer and website content. *Journal of Communication, 53,* 105–121. doi:10.1093/joc/53.1.105

Slater, M. D. (2007). Reinforcing spirals: The mutual influence of media selectivity and media effects and their impact on individual behavior and social identity. *Communication Theory, 17,* 281–303. doi:10.1111/j.1468-2885.2007.00296.x

Slater, M. D., & Hayes, A. F. (2010). The influence of youth music television viewership on changes in cigarette use and association with smoking peers: A social identity, reinforcing spirals perspective. *Communication Research, 37*, 751–773. doi:10.1177/0093650210375953

Slater, M. D., Henry, K. L., Swaim, R. C., & Anderson, L. L. (2003). Violent media content and aggressiveness in adolescents: A downward spiral model. *Communication Research, 30*, 713–736. doi: 10.1177/0093650203258281

Steiger, J. H. (1990). Structural model evaluation and modification: An interval estimation approach. *Multivariate Behavioral Research, 25*, 173–180. doi:10.1207/s15327906mbr2502_4

Tucker, L. R., & Lewis, C. (1973). A reliability coefficient for maximum likelihood factor analysis. *Psychometrika, 38*, 1–10. doi:10.1007/BF02291170

Voelkle, M. C. (2007). Latent growth curve modeling as an integrative approach to the analysis of change. *Psychology Science, 49*, 375–414.

Widaman, K. F., Ferrer, E., & Conger, R. D. (2010). Factorial invariance within longitudinal structural equation models: Measuring the same construct across time. *Child Development Perspectives, 4*(1), 10–18. doi:10.1111/j.1750-8606.2009.00110.x

Widaman, K. F., & Reise, S. P. (1997). Exploring the measurement invariance of psychological instruments: Applications in the substance use domain. In K. J. Bryant, M. Windle, & S. G. West (Eds.), *The science of prevention: Methodological advances from alcohol and substance abuse research* (pp. 281–324). Washington, DC: American Psychological Association.

Willett, J. B. (1994). Measuring change more effectively by modeling individual change over time. In T. Husen & T. N. Postlethwaite (Eds.), *The international encyclopedia of education* (2nd ed., pp. 671–678). Oxford, England: Pergamon Press.

Willett, J. B. (1997). Measuring change: What individual growth modeling buys you. In E. Amsel & K. A. Renninger (Eds.), *Change and development: Issues of theory, method, and application* (pp. 213–243). Mahwah, NJ: Erlbaum.

Willett, J. B. (2004). Investigating individual change and development: The multilevel model for change and the method of latent growth modeling. *Research in Human Development, 1*(1&2), 31–57. doi:10.1207/s15427617rhd0101&2_4

Willett, J. B., & Sayer, A. G. (1994). Using covariance structure analysis to detect correlates and predictors of individual change over time. *Psychological Bulletin, 116*, 363–381. doi:10.1037/0033-2909.116.2.363

Yuan, K. H., & Bentler, P. M. (2001). A unified approach to multigroup structural equation modeling with nonstandard samples. In G. A. Marcoulides & R. E. Schumacker (Eds.), *New developments and techniques in structural equation modeling* (pp. 35–56). Mahwah, NJ: Erlbaum.

Yuan, K.-H., & Bentler, P. M. (2004). On Chi-square difference and z-tests in mean and covariance structure analysis when the base model is misspecified. *Educational and Psychological Measurement, 64*, 737–757.

Zorn, T. E., Roper, J., Broadfoot, K., & Weaver, C. K. (2006). Focus groups as sites of influential interaction: Building communicative self-efficacy and effecting attitudinal change in discussing controversial topics. *Journal of Applied Communication Research, 34*, 115–140. doi:10.1080/00909880600573965

Zorn, T. E., Roper, J., Weaver, C. K., & Rigby, C. (2012). Influence in science dialogue: Individual attitude changes as a result of dialogue between laypersons and scientists. *Public Understanding of Science, 21*, 848–864. doi:10.1177/0963662510386292

Appendix

! This is the Mplus code for the first-order single- and multiple-groups unconditional LGM. In any Mplus code, statements following an exclamation mark are comments and are ignored by the program. Every comment line should begin with the ! symbol but for ease of reading here only one ! symbol will be used per comment.

! You can store your data as either tab- or comma-delimited in a .dat type of file. For the examples discussed in this chapter, all information from one subject was stored on a single row.

TITLE: your title here

DATA: FILE IS ! include the exact path to yourdata.dat;

VARIABLE: NAMES ARE wtc1 wtc2 wtc3 gender; ! Here you include the name of the variables in your data set;

USEVARIABLES ARE wtc1 wtc2 wtc3; ! For the single-group unconditional model you need to use only the repeated measures of the focal variables;

!GROUPING IS GENDER (1= MALE 0 = FEMALE); ! You need this command only for multiple-groups LGM. The values in parenthesis (1 and 0) are the same values you used to code gender in your data set.

MISSING = ALL (–99); ! In this data set missing values are denoted by –99

MODEL: i s | wtc1@0 wtc2@0.5 wtc3@1; ! This is the statement that defines a linear growth model. The time scores for the latent slope factor are fixed at 0, 0.5 and 1.

! Following are the additional lines of code that need to be included when fitting multiple-groups LGMs.

! [I] (1); ! This command is used for IMG model and instructs the program to restrict the mean of the intercept factor to be equal across the two groups.

! [S] (2); ! This command instructs the program to restrict the mean of the slope factor to be equal across the two groups. Together with the previous command, this will prompt the computer to run the ISMG model.

OUTPUT: SAMPSTAT STANDARDIZED;

! This command requests sample statistics and standardized results

PLOT: TYPE IS PLOT 3;

SERIES = wtc1(0) wtc2(0.5) wtc3(1);

! The last two commands instruct the program to produce specific plots of the LGM.

These plots can be found in a separately generated graphic file.

Part III

Reassessments of Message Design and Persuasion Scholarship

CHAPTER CONTENTS

8 The Relative Persuasiveness of Different Message Types Does Not Vary as a Function of the Persuasive Outcome Assessed

Evidence from 29 Meta-Analyses of 2,062 Effect Sizes for 13 Message Variations

Daniel J. O'Keefe

Northwestern University

Experiments that compare the persuasiveness of two message types (e.g., strong vs. weak fear appeals) characteristically examine persuasive impact using attitudinal, intention, or behavioral outcomes. The equivalence of these three outcomes as indices of relative persuasiveness is assessed by re-analyzing data from 2,062 effect sizes in 29 meta-analyses of 13 different message variations, including one-sided and two-sided messages, negative political advertising, and several fear appeal variations. The relative persuasiveness of alternative message types is found to be largely invariant across these different outcomes: If message type A is more persuasive than message type B with attitudinal outcomes, it is also—and equally—more persuasive with intention and behavioral outcomes. Methodological and theoretical implications are discussed.

One recurring question in communication research concerns the relative persuasiveness of alternative message types, in general or under specified conditions. For instance: Are stronger fear appeals more persuasive than weaker ones? Are examples more persuasive than statistics? Are implicit conclusions more persuasive than explicit conclusions for audiences initially opposed to the advocated view? And so forth.

Such questions are commonly addressed through randomized trials (experiments) in which participants are exposed to one or another message condition, with persuasive outcome variables assessed subsequently. The most commonly-studied persuasive outcome variables are attitude (overall evaluation: attitude toward the advocated policy, the advertised product, and so forth), intention (e.g., purchase intention or voting intention), and behavior (either self-reported or observed). These are not the only possible indicators of persuasive effect, but attitudinal, intention, and behavioral outcomes are the most frequently employed outcome variables in persuasion effects research.

A potential problem arises, however, because different studies of a given message variation can employ different indices of persuasive effect. One study might examine attitudinal outcomes, another intention outcomes, a third behavioral outcomes. In comparing or synthesizing findings across a set of such studies, one might naturally wonder whether studies assessing one index of persuasiveness ought to be unproblematically lumped with studies using other assessments.

This problem arises especially acutely in the context of meta-analysis, that is, quantitative research synthesis aimed at providing (inter alia) an estimate of the size of the effect associated with the message variation. When the primary research being summarized contains more than one of these persuasive outcomes, a question naturally arises as to how to proceed. Meta-analytic summaries of persuasion research have followed three different general approaches with respect to this issue. One has been to report results (mean effect sizes, etc.) separately for attitudinal, intention, and behavioral outcomes (e.g., Witte & Allen, 2000). A second is to review only studies using a single kind of outcome; for example, Sopory and Dillard (2002) examined only attitudinal outcomes, Keller and Lehman (2008) examined only effects on intentions, and Noar, Benac, and Harris (2007) examined only behavioral outcomes. A third is to combine results indiscriminately across the three outcomes (e.g., O'Keefe & Jensen, 2006).

These different approaches to persuasion meta-analysis will have different weaknesses depending on whether effect sizes (ESs) vary across persuasive outcomes. If ESs do not vary across outcomes, then the first two approaches— reporting results separately for different outcomes or restricting the review to one kind of outcome—will suffer needlessly diminished statistical power and needless vulnerability to outlier effects (e.g., false positives). By contrast, if ESs do vary across outcomes, then the last approach—combining ESs across the different outcomes—will be entirely inappropriate.

Several commentators have suggested that persuasion ESs should be expected to vary depending on which outcome variable is assessed (e.g., Floyd, Prentice-Dunn, & Rogers, 2000, p. 421; Reinhart, 2006, pp. 17–18). Two related rationales suggest themselves. One is the differential ease of influencing these outcomes; attitudes are presumably easier to change than are intentions, and intentions in turn easier to change than behaviors. The other is the presumable causal sequence in which messages influence attitudes, which influence intentions, which influence behaviors. Taken together, these two considerations might suggest that ESs are likely to vary across persuasive outcomes, progressively weakening as one moves from attitude to intention to behavior.

Thus the broad question addressed in the present project is whether, in assessing the relative persuasiveness of alternative message types, effect sizes vary across attitudinal, intention, and behavioral outcomes. This is a question of considerable importance when it comes to establishing sound generalizations about the persuasive effects of message variations. If, on the one hand, the relative persuasiveness of two message types is roughly similar across attitudinal, intention, and behavioral indicators, then (for example) two studies that use different outcome variables may nevertheless be appropriately compared.

On the other hand, if the relative persuasiveness of two message forms varies considerably across these different indicators, then one will want different generalizations about effects on attitude, on intention, and on behavior.

Plainly, no individual experiment can provide very decisive evidence on this question. For example, even if the ES associated with a given message variable was, in a given study, identical across attitudinal, intention, and behavioral outcomes, that would not provide evidence that the same pattern would occur in other studies of that message variable or in studies of other message variables.

Hence to address this question, data from existing meta-analyses were re-analyzed. By way of brief overview, suitable meta-analyses of message variables studied for their effects on persuasive outcomes were identified. Each meta-analysis's ESs were separated on the basis of the outcome variable assessed (attitude, intention, and behavior), and the resulting mean ESs (for the different outcomes for that message variable) were compared. This analysis permits one to see whether, for the purposes of assessing the relative persuasiveness of two message types, attitudinal outcomes, intention outcomes, and behavioral outcomes yield similar ESs and so are functionally equivalent or yield different ESs and so are functionally distinct.

Methods

Literature Search and Inclusion Criteria

Potential meta-analyses of interest were initially identified by searches through January 2012 of ERIC, Medline, ProQuest Dissertations and Theses, PsycEXTRA, PsycINFO, and Web of Science combining *meta-analysis* with such terms as *persuasion*, *message*, and *attitude*. Additional candidates were located through examination of textbooks and through personal knowledge of the literature.

The analysis was restricted to meta-analyses of the effects of a persuasive message variation on attitudinal, intention, or behavioral outcomes, where at least two of those outcomes were assessed (across the studies reviewed) and where appropriate information was available to permit the necessary re-analyses (information about the ES, sample size, and outcome variable for the cases included in the meta-analysis). These criteria thus excluded meta-analyses that did not examine message-variation effects (e.g., Milne, Sheeran, & Orbell, 2000), meta-analyses involving only one kind of persuasive outcome (e.g., Argo & Main, 2004; Cruz, 1998; Hamilton & Hunter, 1998; Reinard, 1998), and meta-analyses for which necessary additional information was not available (Allen & Preiss, 1997; Boster & Mongeau, 1984; Floyd et al., 2000; Grewal, Kavanoor, Fern, Costley, & Barnes, 1997; Mongeau, 1998). Additionally, to provide a modicum of statistical power, in each meta-analysis, analyses involving a given outcome variable were excluded unless at least five ESs were available for that outcome for both initial and any follow-up analyses (described below); all or part of several meta-analyses were excluded for this reason (Burrell & Koper, 1998; Eisend, 2009; Gayle, Preiss, & Allen, 1998; Hale, 1998; Hornikx and O'Keefe, 2009; O'Keefe, 1998, 1999, 2000, 2002; Reinhart, 2006). If multiple suitable meta-analytic datasets were available for a given message variable, each such dataset was analyzed.

Included Meta-Analyses

These inclusion criteria yielded a total of 29 meta-analyses, with 2,062 ESs in all, concerning the effects of 13 diverse persuasive message variations: gain-loss framing, message sidedness, threat severity, fear appeal strength, threat vulnerability, cultural value adaptation, humor in advertising, response efficacy, negative political advertising, self-efficacy, conclusion explicitness, legitimizing paltry contributions, and recommendation specificity. Details about each message variation and its corresponding meta-analytic data follow.

Gain-Loss Framing.   This message variation contrasts gain-framed messages, which emphasize the advantages of compliance with the recommended action, and loss-framed messages, which emphasize the disadvantages of not complying with the recommended action. Meta-analyses of this message variation have often been less interested in framing effects across all topics (public policy issues, consumer advertising, health-related topics, and so forth) than in framing effects concerning specifically disease detection topics (e.g., mammography) and disease prevention topics (e.g., using sunscreen). Correspondingly, re-analyses of these datasets were conducted for all topics, for detection topics only, and for prevention topics only. The datasets of Akl et al. (2011), Gallagher and Updegraff (2012), and Kyriakaki (2007) contributed to all three analyses.[1] The datasets of O'Keefe and Jensen (2006, 2007, 2009) contributed to, respectively, the all-topics analysis, the prevention-topic analysis, and the detection-topic analysis. For the all-topics analysis, across all datasets, a total of 526 ESs were available; for the prevention-topic and detection-topic analyses, 294 and 187 ESs were available, respectively. Positive ESs indicated a persuasive advantage for gain-framed appeals.

Message Sidedness.   This message variation contrasts one-sided messages, which present only supporting arguments, and two-sided messages, which both present supporting arguments and discuss opposing arguments. The datasets of Eisend (2006, 2007) and O'Keefe (1999) were analyzed. Across the two datasets, a total of 222 ESs were available. Positive ESs indicated a persuasive advantage for two-sided messages.

Threat Severity.   This fear appeal-related message variation contrasts messages varying in the depicted severity of a potential threat; the contrast is thus between messages suggesting that the threat is relatively more severe (high threat severity) and messages suggesting that the threat is relatively less severe (low threat severity). The datasets of de Hoog, Stroebe, and de Wit

(2007) and Witte and Allen (2000) were analyzed. Across the two datasets, a total of 192 ESs were available. Positive ESs indicated a persuasive advantage for high depicted threat severity.

Fear Appeal Strength.   This message variation contrasts messages varying in the explicitness and vividness of the depictions of the threatened consequences; the contrast is thus between strong (relatively more explicit and vivid) and weak (relatively less explicit and vivid) fear appeals. The datasets of Sutton (1982) and Witte and Allen (2000) were analyzed. Across the two datasets, a total of 126 ESs were available. Positive ESs indicated a persuasive advantage for strong fear appeals.

Threat Vulnerability.   This fear appeal-related message variation contrasts messages varying in the depicted vulnerability (susceptibility) of the message recipient to the potential threat; the contrast thus is between messages that depict the receiver as relatively more vulnerable to the threat (high threat vulnerability) and messages that depict the receiver as relatively less vulnerable to the threat (low threat vulnerability). The datasets of de Hoog et al. (2007) and Witte and Allen (2000) were analyzed. Across the two datasets, a total of 118 ESs were available. Positive ESs indicated a persuasive advantage for messages with high depicted threat vulnerability.

Cultural Value Adaptation.   This message variation contrasts consumer advertisements varying in the degree to which the appeals are adapted to the audience's cultural values, as when Chinese and American audiences receive either collectivistic appeals (adapted to Chinese audiences) or individualistic appeals (adapted to American audiences); the contrast is thus between culturally-adapted and culturally-unadapted appeals. The dataset of Hornikx and O'Keefe (2009), providing a total of 96 ESs, was analyzed. Positive ESs indicated a persuasive advantage for messages with culturally-adapted appeals.

Humor in Advertising.   This message variation contrasts humorous and non-humorous consumer advertisements. The dataset of Eisend (2009), providing a total of 95 ESs, was analyzed. Positive ESs indicated a persuasive advantage for humorous advertisements.

Response Efficacy.   This fear appeal-related message variation contrasts messages with differing depictions of the efficaciousness (effectiveness) of the recommended course of action; the contrast thus is between messages that depict the recommended action as relatively more effective (high response efficacy) and messages that depict the recommended action as relatively less effective (low response efficacy). The datasets of de Hoog et al. (2007) and Witte and Allen (2000) were analyzed. Across the two datasets, a total of 65 ESs were available. Positive ESs indicated a persuasive advantage for messages with high depicted response efficacy.

Negative Political Advertising.   This message variation contrasts political messages varying in evaluative tone; the contrast thus is between negative and positive political advertising. Lau, Sigelman, and Rovner's (2007) data for net affect (attitude), vote intention, and actual vote choice (behavior), providing a total of 53 ESs, were analyzed. Positive ESs indicated a persuasive advantage for negative campaigning.

Self-Efficacy.   This fear appeal-related message variation contrasts messages with differing depictions of the message recipient's ability to adopt or engage in the advocated action; the contrast thus is between messages that depict the action as one that is relatively easy to adopt (high self-efficacy) and messages that depict the action as one that is relatively difficult to adopt (low self-efficacy). The dataset of Witte and Allen (2000), providing a total of 40 ESs, was analyzed. Positive ESs indicated a persuasive advantage for messages with high depicted self-efficacy.

Conclusion Explicitness.   This message variation contrasts messages varying in the explicitness of the message's overall conclusion; the contrast thus is between messages in which the conclusion is stated overtly (explicit conclusion) and messages in which that conclusion is left unstated (implicit conclusion). The dataset of O'Keefe (2002), providing a total of 18 ESs, was analyzed. Positive ESs indicated a persuasive advantage for messages with explicit conclusions.

Legitimizing Paltry Contributions.   This research examines the effectiveness of a donation-request strategy that explicitly legitimizes making a small contribution, as compared to a control-condition request without such legitimization. These studies examined either intention outcomes (pledges to donate) or behavioral outcomes (actual donations). Andrews, Carpenter, Shaw, and Boster's (2008) data for face-to-face implementations, providing a total of 18 ESs, were analyzed. Positive ESs indicated a persuasive advantage for the experimental condition (legitimizing paltry contributions).

Recommendation Specificity.   This message variation contrasts messages on the basis of the specificity of the description of the recommended action; the contrast thus is between messages that provide only a general description of the recommended action and messages that provide a more detailed recommendation. The dataset of O'Keefe (2002), providing a total of 12 ESs, was analyzed. Positive ESs indicated a persuasive advantage for messages with more specific recommendations.

Effect Sizes and Analyses

Effect Size.   Correlation (r) was used as the ES metric. Many of the meta-analyses recorded ESs in terms of r; for those that did not, ESs were converted to r using widely available formulas (e.g., Borenstein, Hedges, Higgins, & Rothstein, 2009, pp. 45–49; Card, 2012, pp. 118–119).

Outcome Variables. For each meta-analysis, for each ES, the outcome variable involved (attitude, intention, behavior) was identified. Where composite ESs (based on more than one outcome) were originally reported, information was acquired to obtain a separate ES for each different outcome variable. Thus, each included meta-analysis yielded a list of cases, where each case provided an ES (with some associated sample size) for one of the three outcome variables. The ESs were accepted as given in each meta-analytic dataset; that is, ESs were not recomputed, adjusted, deleted, or otherwise altered (save, as indicated above, where a composite ES was replaced by separate ESs for different outcomes). (Thanks to Mike Allen, Kyle Andrews, Natascha de Hoog, Martin Eisend, Kristel Gallagher, Rick Lau, and Kim Witte for providing additional information about their meta-analytic datasets.)

Analysis. For each meta-analysis's list of cases, a meta-analytic re-analysis was undertaken that separated cases on the basis of the outcome variable involved (attitude, intention, behavior). This yielded two or three groups of cases for each meta-analysis, depending on how many different outcomes were available. The average ES in each group of cases was computed. Random-effects meta-analytic procedures were used to produce the means and confidence intervals of interest and to test the significance of differences between mean effect sizes (with a separate estimate of τ^2, the variance of true effect sizes across studies, for each group: Borenstein et al., 2009, pp. 164–171; Borenstein & Rothstein, 2005). Random-effects analyses were used because generalization beyond the cases in hand is of interest (Borenstein, Hedges, Higgins, & Rothstein, 2010; Card, 2012, pp. 233–234; Hedges & Vevea, 1998).

For any comparison that yielded a significant difference between the mean ESs for two outcome variables within a meta-analysis, a follow-up analysis was conducted to consider between-studies differences as a possible explanation. If a given message variable's mean effect on (for example) behavioral outcomes was significantly different from the mean effect on attitudinal outcomes, one possible explanation would be that studies that assessed behavioral outcomes differed in some way from studies that assessed attitudinal outcomes; this between-studies difference could be responsible for the observed variation of ESs across different outcomes. Hence, when such significant differences appeared in the initial analysis, a follow-up analysis was undertaken that was limited to studies that obtained data on both outcomes of interest (provided at least five ESs were available for each outcome); analysis of data from such within-study comparisons permits one to assess extraneous between-studies differences as a possible explanation for overall differences.

Results

Table 8.1 provides a summary of the mean effect sizes. Across the 29 meta-analyses of the 13 message variations, the data afforded a total of 63 comparisons between mean effects. Of these, 59 were nonsignificant. Of the four significant differences, only two remained significant in follow-up analyses restricted to within-study comparisons.

Table 8.1 Mean Effect Sizes (*r*) and 95% Confidence Intervals for Message Variations across Different Outcomes

Message Variation	Attitude	Intention	Behavior
Gain-Loss Framing: All Topics			
Akl et al. (2011)		$-.027$ (*k* = 23) [$-.103, .048$]	$-.058$ (*k* = 16) [$-.126, .011$]
Gallagher & Updegraff (2012)	.024 (*k* = 59) [$-.026, .075$]	.004 (*k* = 78) [$-.036, .043$]	.030 (*k* = 52) [$-.001, .062$]
Kyriakaki (2007)	$-.014$ (*k* = 19) [$-.062, .034$]	$-.000$ (*k* = 35) [$-.038, .037$]	.028 (*k* = 19) [$-.027, .083$]
O'Keefe & Jensen (2006)	$.040_a$ (*k* = 82) [$.004, .075$]	$.027_b$ (*k* = 101) [$-.006, .061$]	$-.022_{ab}$ (*k* = 42) [$-.050, .006$]
Gain-Loss Framing: Prevention			
Akl et al. (2011)		.027 (*k* = 13) [$-.073, .126$]	$-.092$ (*k* = 5) [$-.296, .121$]
Gallagher & Updegraff (2012)	.037 (*k* = 46) [$-.016, .090$]	.022 (*k* = 47) [$-.024, .067$]	.078 (*k* = 32) [$.036, .121$]
Kyriakaki (2007)	.018 (*k* = 14) [$-.025, .062$]	.020 (*k* = 24) [$-.027, .067$]	.087 (*k* = 10) [$.008, .165$]
O'Keefe & Jensen (2007)	.088 (*k* = 30) [$.024, .152$]	.032 (*k* = 58) [$-.004, .068$]	.021 (*k* = 15) [$-.046, .088$]
Gain-Loss Framing: Detection			
Akl et al. (2011)		.016 (*k* = 6) [$-.128, .159$]	$-.039$ (*k* = 10) [$-.088, .009$]
Gallagher & Updegraff (2012)	$-.040$ (*k* = 14) [$-.174, .096$]	$-.024$ (*k* = 30) [$-.102, .055$]	$-.038$ (*k* = 20) [$-.081, .004$]
Kyriakaki (2007)	$-.122$ (*k* = 5) [$-.256, .018$]	$-.041$ (*k* = 11) [$-.098, .017$]	$-.025$ (*k* = 9) [$-.098, .048$]
O'Keefe & Jensen (2009)	$-.027$ (*k* = 33) [$-.078, .024$]	$-.051$ (*k* = 34) [$-.107, .004$]	$-.039$ (*k* = 15) [$-.080, .003$]
Message Sidedness			
Eisend (2006)	.117 (*k* = 65) [$.067, .166$]	.082 (*k* = 37) [$-.027, .190$]	
O'Keefe (1999)	$-.010$ (*k* = 94) [$-.049, .028$]	$-.012$ (*k* = 26) [$-.081, .057$]	
Threat Severity			
de Hoog et al. (2007)	.128 (*k* = 40) [$.074, .182$]	.116 (*k* = 55) [$.079, .152$]	.094 (*k* = 41) [$.044, .143$]
Witte & Allen (2000)	.152 (*k* = 14) [$.064, .238$]	.147 (*k* = 26) [$.085, .207$]	.120 (*k* = 16) [$.057, .183$]

Message Variation	Attitude	Intention	Behavior
Fear appeal strength			
Sutton (1982)		.154 (k = 13) [.110, .196]	.149 (k = 8) [.031, .262]
Witte & Allen (2000)	.144 (k = 34) [.104, .183]	.147 (k = 43) [.095, .198]	.159 (k = 28) [.081, .236]
Threat vulnerability			
de Hoog et al. (2007)	−.041$_{ab}$ (k = 19) [−.138, .057]	.162$_a$ (k = 31) [.085, .236]	.188$_b$ (k = 19) [.089, .284]
Witte & Allen (2000)	.104 (k = 11) [−.017, .222]	.167 (k = 27) [.096, .235]	.132 (k = 11) [.058, .205]
Cultural value adaptation			
Hornikx & O'Keefe (2009)	.067 (k = 65) [.021, .113]	.096 (k = 31) [.022, .170]	
Humor in advertising			
Eisend (2009)	.189 (k = 49) [.086, .288]	.192 (k = 46) [.110, .272]	
Response efficacy			
de Hoog et al. (2007)		.119 (k = 12) [.071, .166]	.123 (k = 6) [.045, .199]
Witte & Allen (2000)	.178 (k = 11) [.074, .277]	.198 (k = 24) [.126, .268]	.137 (k = 12) [.073, .200]
Negative political ads			
Lau et al. (2007)	−.073 (k = 10) [−.216, .073]	−.010 (k = 27) [−.093, .074]	−.036 (k = 16) [−.073, .001]
Self-efficacy			
Witte & Allen (2000)	.188 (k = 8) [.036, .332]	.199 (k = 21) [.124, .272]	.145 (k = 11) [.066, .222]
Conclusion explicitness			
O'Keefe (2002)	.102 (k = 13) [−.002, .203]		.137 (k = 5) [−.060, .323]
Legitimizing paltry contributions			
Andrews et al. (2008)		.157 (k = 5) [−.011, .316]	.179 (k = 13) [.125, .232]
Recommendation specificity			
O'Keefe (2002)	.001 (k = 5) [−.087, .089]	−.041 (k = 7) [−.119, .038]	

Note: Within a row, means with a common subscript are significantly different ($p < .05$).

Gain-Loss Framing: All Topics

In studies of gain-loss framing across all topics, in Akl et al.'s (2011) dataset, the mean ES for intention outcomes (–.027) did not differ significantly from the mean ES for behavior outcomes (–.058; $Q(1)$ = .349, p = .555).

In Gallagher and Updegraff's (2012) dataset, the mean ES for attitude outcomes (.024) did not differ significantly from the mean ES for intention outcomes (.004; $Q(1)$ = .405, p = .525) or from the mean ES for behavior outcomes (.030; $Q(1)$ = .041, p = .839). The mean ESs for intention outcomes and for behavior outcomes did not differ significantly ($Q(1)$ = 1.105, p = .293).

In Kyriakaki's (2007) dataset, the mean ES for attitude outcomes (–.014) did not differ significantly from the mean ES for intention outcomes –.000; $Q(1)$ = .187, p = .666) or from the mean ES for behavior outcomes (.028; $Q(1)$ = 1.256, p = .262). The mean ESs for intention outcomes and for behavior outcomes did not differ significantly ($Q(1)$ = .698, p = .404).

In O'Keefe and Jensen's (2006) dataset, the mean ESs for attitudinal outcomes (mean r = .040) and intention outcomes (.027) did not significantly differ ($Q(1)$ = .259, p = .611). The mean ESs for attitudinal outcomes (.040) and behavioral outcomes (–.022) were significantly different ($Q(1)$ = 7.260, p = .007); however, in a follow-up analysis restricted to studies affording the relevant within-study comparison (k = 11), the mean ESs (for attitude, mean r = –.030, 95% C [–.113, .052]; for behavior, mean r = –.017, 95% C [–094, .060]) did not significantly differ ($Q(1)$ = .052, p = .819). The mean ESs for intention outcomes (.027) and behavioral outcomes (–.022) were significantly different ($Q(1)$ = 4.910, p = .027); however, in a follow-up analysis restricted to studies reporting both intention and behavioral outcomes (k = 15), the mean ESs (for intention, mean r = –.015, 95% C [–.075, .045]; for behavior, mean r = –.002, 95% C [–.084, .079]) did not significantly differ ($Q(1)$ = .060, p = .806).

Gain-Loss Framing: Prevention

In studies of gain-loss framing in disease prevention messages, in Akl et al.'s (2011) dataset, the mean ES for intention outcomes (.027) did not differ significantly from the mean ES for behavior outcomes (–.092; $Q(1)$ = .974, p = .324).

In Gallagher and Updegraff's (2012) dataset, the mean ES for attitude outcomes (.037) did not differ significantly from the mean ES for intention outcomes (.022; $Q(1)$ = .187, p = .665) or from the mean ES for behavior outcomes (.078; $Q(1)$ = 1.430, p = .232). The mean ES for intention outcomes (.022) did not differ significantly from the mean ES for behavior outcomes (.078; $Q(1)$ = 3.191, p = .074).

In Kyriakaki's (2007) dataset, the mean ES for attitude outcomes (.018) did not differ significantly from the mean ES for intention outcomes (.020; $Q(1)$ = .002, p = .962) or from the mean ES for behavior outcomes (.087; $Q(1)$ = 2.252, p = .133). The mean ES for intention outcomes (.020) did not differ significantly from the mean ES for behavior outcomes (.087; $Q(1)$ = 2.071, p = .150).

In O'Keefe and Jensen's (2007) dataset, the mean ES for attitude outcomes (.088) did not differ significantly from the mean ES for intention outcomes (.032; $Q(1) = 2.234$, $p = .135$) or from the mean ES for behavior outcomes (.021; $Q(1) = 2.003$, $p = .157$). The mean ES for intention outcomes (.032) did not differ significantly from the mean ES for behavior outcomes (.021; $Q(1) = .080$, $p = .777$).

Gain-Loss Framing: Detection

In studies of gain-loss framing in disease detection messages, in Akl et al.'s (2011) dataset, the mean ES for intention outcomes (.016) did not differ significantly from the mean ES for behavior outcomes (−.039; $Q(1) = .502$, $p = .479$).

In Gallagher and Updegraff's (2012) dataset, the mean ES for attitude outcomes (−.040) did not differ significantly from the mean ES for intention outcomes (−.024; $Q(1) = .040$, $p = .841$) or from the mean ES for behavior outcomes (−.038; $Q(1) = .000$, $p = .985$). The mean ES for intention outcomes (−.024) did not differ significantly from the mean ES for behavior outcomes (−.038; $Q(1) = .104$, $p = .747$).

In Kyriakaki's (2007) dataset, the mean ES for attitude outcomes (−.122) did not differ significantly from the mean ES for intention outcomes (−.041; $Q(1) = 1.114$, $p = .291$) or from the mean ES for behavior outcomes (−.025; $Q(1) = 1.447$, $p = .229$). The mean ES for intention outcomes (−.041) did not differ significantly from the mean ES for behavior outcomes (−.025; $Q(1) = .105$, $p = .746$).

In O'Keefe and Jensen's (2009) dataset, the mean ES for attitude outcomes (−.027) did not differ significantly from the mean ES for intention outcomes (−.051; $Q(1) = .401$, $p = .527$) or from the mean ES for behavior outcomes (−.039; $Q(1) = .120$, $p = .729$). The mean ES for intention outcomes (−.051) did not differ significantly from the mean ES for behavior outcomes (−.039; $Q(1) = .130$, $p = .718$).

Message Sidedness

In studies of message sidedness, in Eisend's (2006, 2007) dataset, the mean ESs for attitude outcomes (.117) and intention outcomes (.082) did not significantly differ ($Q(1) = .318$, $p = .573$).

In O'Keefe's (1999) dataset, the mean ESs for attitudinal outcomes (−.010) and intention outcomes (−.012) did not significantly differ ($Q(1) = .002$, $p = .966$).

Threat Severity

In studies of threat severity, in de Hoog et al.'s (2007) dataset, the mean ES for attitudinal outcomes (.128) did not significantly differ from the mean ES for intention outcomes (.116; $Q(1) = .135$, $p = .714$) or from the mean ES for behavioral outcomes (.094; $Q(1) = .844$, $p = .358$). The mean ESs for intention outcomes and behavioral outcomes did not significantly differ ($Q(1) = .496$, $p = .481$).

In Witte and Allen's (2000) dataset, the mean ES for attitudinal outcomes (.152) did not significantly differ from the mean ES for intention outcomes (.147; $Q(1) = .011$, $p = .917$) or from the mean ES for behavioral outcomes (.120; $Q(1) = .342$, $p = .559$). The mean ESs for intention outcomes and behavioral outcomes did not significantly differ ($Q(1) = .348$, $p = .555$).

Fear Appeal Strength

In studies of fear appeal strength, in Sutton's (1982) dataset, the mean ES for intention outcomes (.154) and the mean ES for behavior outcomes (.149) did not differ significantly ($Q(1) = .006$, $p = .941$.

In Witte and Allen's (2000) dataset, the mean ES for attitudinal outcomes (.144) did not significantly differ from the mean ES for intention outcomes (.147; $Q(1) = .009$, $p = .923$) or from the mean ES for behavioral outcomes (.159; $Q(1) = .124$, $p = .725$). The mean ESs for intention outcomes and behavioral outcomes did not significantly differ ($Q(1) = .069$, $p = .793$).

Threat Vulnerability

In studies of threat vulnerability, in de Hoog et al.'s (2007) dataset, the mean ES for intention outcomes (.162) did not differ significantly ($Q(1) = .177$, $p = .674$) from that for behavioral outcomes (.188), but each differed (for intention, $Q(1) = 10.159$, $p = .001$; for behavior, $Q(1) = 10.315$, $p = .001$) from the mean ES for attitudinal outcomes (−.041). In an analysis restricted to studies affording the relevant within-study comparison, when studies had both attitudinal and intention outcomes ($k = 12$), the mean effects (for attitude, mean $r = −.004$, 95% C [−.093, .085]; for intention, mean $r = .270$, 95% CI [.160, .374]) significantly differed ($Q(1) = 14.152$, $p < .001$). When studies had both attitudinal and behavioral outcomes ($k = 8$), the mean effects (for attitude, mean $r = .013$, 95% C [−.059, .084]; for behavior, mean $r = .250$, 95% CI [.123, .368]) significantly differed ($Q(1) = 10.080$, $p = .001$).

In Witte and Allen's (2000) dataset, the mean ES for attitudinal outcomes (.104) did not significantly differ from the mean ES for intention outcomes (.167; $Q(1) = .781$, $p = .377$) or from the mean ES for behavioral outcomes (.132; $Q(1) = .153$, $p = .696$). The mean ESs for intention outcomes and behavioral outcomes did not significantly differ ($Q(1) = .443$, $p = .506$).

Cultural Value Adaptation

In studies of cultural value adaptation, in Hornikx and O'Keefe's (2009) dataset, the mean ESs for attitudinal outcomes (.067) and intention outcomes (.096) did not significantly differ ($Q(1) = .424$, $p = .515$).

Humor in Advertising

In studies of humor in advertising, in Eisend's (2009) dataset, the mean ESs for attitudinal outcomes (.189) and intention outcomes (.192) did not significantly differ ($Q(1) = .002, p = .963$).

Response Efficacy

In studies of depicted response efficacy variations, in de Hoog et al.'s (2007) database, the mean ES for intention outcomes (.119) and the mean ES for behavior outcomes (.123) did not differ significantly ($Q(1) = .007, p = .933$).

In Witte and Allen's (2000) dataset, the mean ES for attitudinal outcomes (.178) did not significantly differ from the mean ES for intention outcomes (.198; $Q(1) = .103, p = .748$) or from the mean ES for behavioral outcomes (.137; $Q(1) = .435, p = .509$). The mean ESs for intention outcomes and behavioral outcomes did not significantly differ ($Q(1) = 1.552, p = .213$).

Negative Political Advertising

In studies of negative political advertising, in Lau et al.'s (2007) dataset, the mean ES for attitudinal outcomes (−.073) did not significantly differ from the mean ES for intention outcomes (−.010; ($Q(1) = .544, p = .461$) or from the mean ES for behavioral outcomes (−.036; ($Q(1) = .232, p = .630$). The mean ESs for intention outcomes and behavioral outcomes did not significantly differ ($Q(1) = .315, p = .575$).

Self-Efficacy

In studies of depicted self-efficacy variations, in Witte and Allen's (2000) dataset, the mean ESs for attitudinal outcomes (.188) did not significantly differ from the mean ES for intention outcomes (.199; $Q(1) = .017, p = .898$) or from the mean ES for behavioral outcomes (.145; $Q(1) = .254, p = .614$). The mean ESs for intention outcomes and behavioral outcomes did not significantly differ ($Q(1) = .982, p = .322$).

Conclusion Explicitness

In studies of conclusion explicitness, in O'Keefe's (2002) dataset, the mean ESs for attitudinal outcomes (.102) and behavioral outcomes (.137) did not significantly differ ($Q(1) = .096, p = .757$).

Legitimizing Paltry Contributions

In studies of legitimizing paltry contributions, in Andrews et al.'s (2008) dataset, the mean ESs for intention outcomes (.157) and behavioral outcomes (.179) did not significantly differ ($Q(1) = .061, p = .805$).

Recommendation Specificity

In studies of recommendation specificity, in O'Keefe's (2002) dataset, the mean ESs for attitudinal outcomes (.001) and intention outcome (–.041) did not significantly differ ($Q(1) = .494, p = .482$).

Discussion

The General Pattern

The general picture that emerges from these data is that the relative persuasiveness of alternative message forms does not vary much as a function of whether attitudinal, intention, or behavioral outcomes are assessed. A glance across each row in Table 8.1 makes it plain that, in general, these different persuasive outcomes yield quite similar conclusions concerning the relative persuasiveness of the message variations reviewed here. For 11 of the 13 message variables, none of the mean effects is statistically significantly different from another.

One apparent exception emerged in one aspect of the analyses of gain-loss message framing effects. No significant differences were found between message framing mean ESs based on different outcomes for studies of disease prevention messages (across four meta-analyses) or studies of disease detection messages (again, across four meta-analyses). And in analyses across all topics, three of the four meta-analytic reviews also found no significant differences (Akl et al., 2011; Gallagher & Updegraff, 2012; Kyriakaki, 2007). But in one meta-analysis (O'Keefe & Jensen, 2006), the behavioral-outcome mean ES was significantly different from the mean ESs for attitudinal and intention outcomes. However, those differences evaporated when other between-studies differences were removed.

The other apparent exception emerged in the analyses of threat vulnerability effects. One meta-analytic database yielded significant differences that persisted in the follow-up analysis (de Hoog et al., 2007), but a second meta-analytic database produced no such differences (Witte & Allen, 2000). This result is discussed in more detail below.

In all other analyses, no significant differences were found. In general, then, these results are strikingly consistent. The available meta-analytic databases afforded 63 comparisons between mean ESs involving different outcome variables, and only two such comparisons were statistically significant in a follow-up analysis (in the threat vulnerability data of de Hoog et al., 2007)—and even those two differences did not appear in another meta-analysis of that same message variable (by Witte & Allen, 2000).

The general consistency of this pattern is especially notable given the diversity of the evidentiary base. A range of message variables was represented in this analysis; some consist of substantive variation in the appeals advanced (as in the contrast between one-sided and two-sided messages, which present different arguments), as opposed to what might seem to be more superficial variations (such as gain-loss framing, where the same argument is framed differently). And the meta-analytic databases that were re-analyzed arose from a variety of procedural decisions about which studies to include, how to compute effect sizes, and so forth. The present analysis did not, for example, recompute effect sizes, or alter the inclusion criteria, or re-do the literature retrieval procedures of the individual meta-analyses; whatever procedures yielded the original meta-analytic databases were accepted at face value, even when these differed from one meta-analysis to another. The consistency of the obtained results thus suggests a certain robustness of effect, in the sense of being impervious to these various substantive and methodological dissimilarities.

To be sure, when multiple meta-analyses have been conducted concerning a given message variable—with at least some of the same studies contributing to each meta-analytic dataset—a finding of consistent results across those meta-analyses may not be entirely surprising. But even those meta-analyses can and do have procedural differences (different search procedures, different inclusion criteria, different procedures for computing effect sizes, and so forth), which means that the observed consistency of results was not guaranteed. In such circumstances, the replication of the result in multiple meta-analyses of a given message variation only strengthens the conclusion that attitudinal, intention, and behavioral assessments generally provide functionally equivalent indices of relative persuasiveness.

A compelling example is provided by the two meta-analyses of message sidedness. Eisend's (2006, 2007) review was restricted to studies of consumer advertising, and the dataset included multiple ESs from a given study for a given type of outcome (e.g., if a study had two assessments of intention, two separate ESs were entered in the dataset).[2] O'Keefe's (1999) review included studies of both advertising and other topics (public policy questions, health behaviors, and so forth), and the dataset collapsed ESs from a given study for a given type of outcome (so that if two intention assessments were available in a study, the ESs were averaged to create a single intention ES). Despite these procedural differences, and despite mean ESs that look rather different (e.g., a mean ES for attitudinal outcomes of .12 in one meta-analysis and -.01 in the other), within each meta-analysis there were no significant differences between the mean ESs for different outcomes.

Persuasiveness and Relative Persuasiveness

It is important to be clear about what the present results do and do not show. These results do not show that attitudinal, intention, and behavioral assessments are equivalent indices of *persuasiveness*. They show that in experiments comparing two messages, attitudinal, intention, and behavioral assessments are equivalent indices of *relative persuasiveness*.

This distinction can be embodied in two questions. The first is: How persuasive is a given message? Examination of attitudinal, intention, and behavioral outcomes might yield different answers to such a question. For example, a given message might appear quite persuasive when attitudes are assessed, but produce little persuasion when behavioral outcomes are examined.

The second question is: What is the difference in persuasiveness between two messages? That is, what is the relative persuasiveness of two messages? The present results indicate that examination of attitudinal, intention, and behavioral outcomes will yield substantively identical answers to such a question. If message A is more persuasive than message B when attitudes are assessed, then message A will also be more persuasive than message B—and more persuasive to the same degree—if either intentions or behaviors are assessed.

So, although the *persuasiveness* of a single message might vary across attitudinal, intention, and behavioral outcomes, the present results indicate that the *relative persuasiveness* of two messages does not vary across those outcomes.

Implications

These results have implications for primary persuasion research, for research synthesis in persuasion, and for practical message pretesting. First, in primary research concerning specifically questions of the relative persuasiveness of two message forms, these results suggest that a research design need not assess all three kinds of outcome discussed here. The present results give considerable confidence that, in general, the same conclusion (both about the direction of effect and about the magnitude of effect) will be given by attitudinal outcomes, intention outcomes, and behavioral outcomes. In that sense, these three outcomes are functionally equivalent with respect to the assessment of relative persuasiveness.

To be clear: The claim advanced here is not that the difference between the population effects for any two kinds of outcome is literally zero (the statistical "null hypothesis"). The claim is simply that these different outcome measures are functionally interchangeable with respect to research questions concerning relative message persuasiveness. And these results do not show that attitude, intention, and behavior are functionally equivalent variables for all research questions (i.e., do not show that these variables will always give the same answer to any question whatever—such as questions about the persuasiveness of a single message). These results indicate that when the research question concerns specifically the relative persuasiveness of two message types, the same answer to that question will be given by any of these kinds of outcome.

Second, research synthesis (e.g., meta-analysis) aimed at assessing the relative persuasiveness of two message forms should be conducted in ways that recognize this functional equivalence. For example, when two studies with different outcome assessments yield different conclusions about the persuasive effects of a given message variable, those conflicting results should presumably not be ascribed to the different outcome assessments, but rather to other causes. In meta-analytic research, when more than one of these three kinds of outcome are available, a meta-analyst appropriately can and should combine

ESs across outcomes. Analyzing these three outcomes separately or restricting a meta-analysis to one kind of outcome incurs all the costs associated with smaller-sample studies, such as enhanced vulnerability to false positives and reduced ability to detect either main effects (simple differences between the two message types) or moderator-variable effects (differences between subsets of studies).

Third, these results have implications for practical persuasive-message pretesting, as when formative persuasive campaign research compares two or more possible messages with the purpose of identifying the most effective one. For the specific goal of pinpointing which message is likely to be most persuasive, campaign planners need not collect attitudinal, intentional, and behavioral outcome data. Any one of these three kinds of assessment will suffice to identify the most persuasive message.

Inconsistent with Previous Findings?

One might suspect that the present results must somehow be inaccurate because they appear to be inconsistent with various well-established findings and theoretical frameworks. In particular, these results might seem inconsistent with (a) the differential ease of influencing these three outcomes, (b) the causal sequence of the three outcome variables, and (c) Gallagher and Updegraff's (2012) meta-analytic results. Each of these is discussed in turn.

Differential Ease of Influence.   Attitudes are presumably easier to change than are intentions, and intentions in turn easier to change than behaviors. Thus (one might reason) effect sizes should be largest for attitudes, smaller for intentions, and smaller still for behaviors—but the present results are inconsistent with this expectation. So one might think that something must be amiss with the present results.

But this reasoning is not sound. Even if these three outcomes are differentially easy to change, effect sizes could still be constant across them. This mistake in reasoning may arise from a confusion concerning what effect sizes represent in the meta-analyses reviewed here—and specifically a confusion between persuasiveness (of a single message) and relative persuasiveness (of two messages).

In these meta-analyses, the effect size (ES) for a given study represents the difference in persuasive effect between the two message conditions being compared (the relative persuasiveness of the two messages), not the persuasive effect (persuasiveness) of any one message in that study or the overall persuasive effect across message conditions in that study. For instance, an ES of zero in these meta-analyses indicates that there was no difference in persuasiveness between the two message conditions—but this does not necessarily mean that the messages were not individually persuasive. In fact, both of a study's two messages could be highly persuasive, but if the messages were *equally* highly persuasive then the ES would be zero.

So even if the absolute amount of persuasion varies by outcome (with some outcomes more easily influenced than others), the difference in persuasiveness between the two message conditions—the effect size—could be identical for the three outcomes. To see this concretely, imagine having an index of message persuasiveness ranging from zero (no persuasion) to 10 (complete persuasion). Suppose that in a given experiment, message A produces mean persuasion scores of 9.0 on attitude, 6.0 on intention, and 3.0 on behavior; message B produces mean persuasion scores of 8.0, 5.0, and 2.0, respectively. Each message is progressively less persuasive as one moves from attitudinal to intention to behavioral outcomes, but the *relative* persuasiveness of the two messages is the same no matter which outcome is examined.[3]

Hence, for example, the apparent equivalency of the ESs for response efficacy variations across the different persuasive outcomes in Witte and Allen's (2000) meta-analysis (mean rs of .18, .20, and .14, for attitude, intention, and behavior, respectively) does not mean that the three outcomes were equally affected by message exposure (does not mean that attitudes, intentions, and behaviors were equally influenced by the messages). Rather, it means that the size of the persuasive advantage enjoyed by the high-efficacy message over the low-efficacy message was the same (more carefully: statistically indistinguishable) across the three outcomes.

Thus the present results are not inconsistent with a belief that attitudes, intentions, and behaviors are differentially easy to influence. That belief has implications for expectations about how the persuasiveness of a single message might differ for different outcomes (e.g., an expectation that a given message will affect attitudes more than it will affect behaviors), but it does not underwrite expectations about whether the relative persuasiveness of two messages—the effect size—will differ for different outcomes.

Causal Sequence.   There is a clear presumable causal sequence among attitudes, intentions, and behavior. As depicted in theoretical approaches such as the theory of planned behavior (TPB; Ajzen, 1991) and the theory of reasoned action (TRA; Fishbein & Ajzen, 1975, 2010), attitudes influence intention, and intentions influence behavior. These theoretical frameworks have appeared to receive extensive empirical confirmation, in the form of the expected positive correlations between these variables. (For a review of several relevant meta-analyses, see Hale, Householder, & Greene, 2002. For other relevant meta-analyses, see Albarracin, Johnson, Fishbein, & Muellerleile, 2001; Armitage & Conner, 2001; Cooke & French, 2008; Hagger, Chatzisarantis, & Biddle, 2002. For complexities, see Weinstein, 2007.) The correlations are far from perfect and can vary considerably depending on a number of moderating variables (e.g., Cooke & Sheeran, 2004; Glasman & Albarracin, 2006; Wallace, Paulson, Lord, & Bond, 2005), but the general pattern of relationship is that of positive correlations.

This causal chain implies that effects will progressively weaken as one moves from attitude to intention to behavior. If V1-V2-V3-V4 is a chain of imperfectly-causally-related variables, variations in V1 will generally be manifest in relatively large effects on V2, smaller effects on V3, and still smaller effects on V4. That is, the relationship of an earlier variable in the chain to later variables weakens as one moves down the chain. If message-attitude-intention-behavior is such a chain, then the effect of a message variation on attitude should presumably be larger than its effect on intention, which in turn should be larger than the message variation's effect on behavior. Because the present results seem to indicate no such weakening of effect, these data seem inconsistent with the presumed causal chain—and so one might think there must be something amiss with the present results.

In fact, however, these data can be completely consistent with the presumed causal sequence. The reason is that the transmission of causal effect through the chain occurs for both messages in an experimental design. That is, message A would produce some given effect transmitted through the chain of outcome variables, and message B would similarly transmit its effect through the chain. But even if the *effect* of a given message weakens as it is transmitted down the chain, the *effect sizes* associated with each outcome variable (i.e., the differences between the effect of message A and the effect of message B) can be similar provided that the relationships between the outcome variables were identical for the two message conditions. Concretely: If attitudes are imperfectly correlated with intentions, and intentions are imperfectly correlated with behaviors, then the effect of message A on attitudes would be larger than its effect on behaviors by virtues of the imperfect causal relationships along the chain. But for the same reason, the effect of message B on attitudes would also be larger—and larger to the same degree—than its effect on behaviors. This process thus can produce identical differences between message A and message B in effectiveness at each point in the causal sequence (i.e., for each different outcome variable).

Gallagher and Updegraff's (2012) Results.   Several readers have pointed to Gallagher and Updegraff's (2012) message framing meta-analytic results as a potential counterexample to the present conclusion. Gallagher and Updegraff reviewed published studies of prevention messages (messages urging actions to prevent disease or illness) and detection messages (e.g., messages concerning cancer screening), and they distinguished cases on the basis of whether attitudes, intentions, or behaviors were assessed. They found no significant framing effect (i.e., no significant differences between gain-framed and loss-framed appeals) for detection messages no matter which outcome was assessed. For prevention messages, however, they reported finding a statistically significant framing effect when behavioral outcomes were assessed but not when attitudinal or intention outcomes were assessed. This might be taken to be evidence that, contrary to the results reported above, distinguishing attitudinal, intention, and behavioral outcomes is important for assessing questions of relative persuasiveness.

But in fact, Gallagher and Updegraff's (2012) data are completely consistent with the general conclusion offered earlier. As indicated in the re-analysis reported earlier, in Gallagher and Updegraff's data, there are no differences (in mean ESs) between attitudinal outcomes, intention outcomes, and behavioral outcomes, either for detection messages or for prevention messages.[4]

Gallagher and Updegraff's (2012) discussion of their results obscures this fact. For example, that discussion appears to contemplate various alternative possible explanations for why, among prevention messages, the mean ES for behavioral outcomes is larger than the mean ESs for attitudinal and intention outcomes (see p. 111)—but those mean ESs in fact are statistically indistinguishable. That is, the mean effect for prevention behaviors is not actually significantly larger than the mean effect for prevention attitudes or intentions, so there is no difference to explain. Gallagher and Updegraff's discussion of such explanations was thus inappropriate—and potentially quite confusing.

It is important not to be misled by Gallagher and Updegraff's (2012) finding of a statistically significant mean framing effect for prevention messages with behavior outcomes but non-significant mean framing effects for prevention messages with attitude or intention outcomes. The fact that one mean effect is significantly different from zero, while another mean effect is not significantly different from zero, does not show or imply that the two mean effects are significantly different from each other.[5] In fact, in this case, the mean effects for attitude, intention, and behavior are *not* significantly different from each other—replicating the general pattern observed earlier.

One might somehow have nagging doubts on this point. After all, in Gallagher and Updegraff's (2012) prevention-message dataset, there was a difference between outcomes in whether a statistically significant effect was observed: The mean ES for behavioral outcomes was statistically significant and those for attitudinal and intention outcomes were not. So, one might think that somehow this shows some consequential difference between outcomes, despite the lack of any statistically significant difference between the mean ESs.

To quell such doubts, consider the 95% confidence intervals for the mean ESs in question (see Table 8.1). The 95% CI for behavioral outcomes excludes zero (hence that effect is statistically significant); the 95% CIs for attitudinal and intention outcomes do not exclude zero (those mean ESs were not statistically significantly different from zero). However, those three 95% CIs overlap such that a common population effect could underlie all three. For example, a population effect of .04 falls within the 95% CI for each of the three outcomes. So even though (on the basis of the sample data in hand) one outcome's population effect can confidently be said to be nonzero and the other two cannot, it is nevertheless possible that all three have an identical population effect.[6]

In short, properly analyzed and interpreted, Gallagher and Updegraff's (2012) data concerning gain-loss framing effects in prevention messages display a pattern exactly like those of other meta-analytic reviews of message-variation persuasion effect sizes: Attitudinal, intention, and behavioral outcomes yield functionally equivalent assessments of the relative persuasiveness of message types.

Summary.   The present results are not inconsistent with a belief that attitudes, intentions, and behaviors are differentially easy to influence; they are not inconsistent with a belief that attitudes, intentions, and behaviors form a causal sequence; and they are not inconsistent with Gallagher and Updegraff's (2012) meta-analytic results.

Artifactual Results?

One might worry that the similarity of the behavioral-outcome ESs to the attitude-outcome and intention-outcome ESs has been artificially inflated by the use of self-report data for behavioral assessments. Self-report behavioral data might be subject to processes that incline respondents to offer reports more consistent with their attitudes and intentions than would be revealed by direct behavioral observation. Thus it might be suspected that the use of self-report behavioral data artificially influences the observed results.

This suggested artifact cannot account for all of the observed consistency, of course, because it cannot explain the consistency between attitude-outcome ESs and intention-outcome ESs. At most, it suggests that the consistency of behavior-outcome ESs with those based on the other two outcomes might be artificial.

But, more fundamentally, this concern is based on a misunderstanding. The present results do not address the consistency of attitudinal measures and behavioral measures (consistency that indeed might be artificially increased by the use of self-report behavioral measures) or the consistency of intention measures and behavioral measures (which also might be increased by the use of self-report behavioral data). The present results concern the consistency of message-variation effect sizes across attitudinal, intention, and behavioral measures—and that sort of consistency is not straightforwardly affected by the use of self-report behavioral data.

To concretize this matter: Imagine an experimental message-variable persuasion study that has both self-reported behavioral data and direct-observation behavioral data. Suppose that participants exaggerate the consistency of their behaviors with their attitudes. If participants in the two message conditions exaggerate equally, then (*ceteris paribus*) the effect size—the comparison between message A and message B—will be similar for self-reported behavioral data and for direct-observation behavioral data. The absolute values of the two behavioral indices will be different (such that the self-reported data will make people look more consistent with their attitudes than the direct-observation data do), but if all the participants are distorting their self-reported behavioral data in the same way, then the difference between the two message conditions will be similar for the two kinds of behavioral data.

So even if participants' behavioral self-reports exaggerate the consistency of their behaviors with their attitudes and intentions, such distortion could not explain the consistency of effect sizes (differences between message conditions) across these three outcomes.

The Anomalous Result

For the message variable of threat vulnerability, one meta-analysis, but not a second, yielded anomalous effects in both the overall analysis and the follow-up (within-studies) analyses. In de Hoog et al.'s (2007) review, ESs were significantly smaller with attitudinal outcomes than with either intention or behavioral outcomes (with these latter two not differing significantly from each other). However, this pattern of results did not appear in Witte and Allen's (2000) meta-analysis of threat vulnerability effects.

The locus of the difference between these two meta-analytic results is the mean ES concerning attitudinal outcomes. Similar mean effects were obtained by the two reviews for intention outcomes (Witte and Allen's was .167, de Hoog et al.'s was .162) and for behavioral outcomes (Witte and Allen's was .132, de Hoog et al.'s was .188). But quite different mean effects appeared for attitudinal outcomes: Witte and Allen (2000) reported a mean r of .104, whereas de Hoog et al. (2007) had a mean r of −.041.

The mystery deepens if one compares the attitude-outcome studies included in the two meta-analyses. Some differences are to be expected by virtue of the later review's being able to include studies appearing subsequent to the earlier review. But of Witte and Allen's (2000) 11 attitude-outcome cases, de Hoog et al. (2007) included only one (Dziokonski & Weber, 1977). And of de Hoog et al.'s eight attitude-outcome cases with a publication date of 1999 or earlier, only one—Dziokonski and Weber (1977)—was included in Witte and Allen's (2000) analysis.

One hypothesis might be that differing inclusion criteria gave rise to the divergent results. Witte and Allen's (2000) review included both published and unpublished studies, whereas de Hoog et al.'s (2007) review was limited to published studies. Given that published and unpublished studies may differ in some ways (e.g., because of the familiar bias toward publication of statistically significant effects: Gerber & Malhotra, 2008a, 2008b; Levine, Asada, & Carpenter, 2009), one might suspect that some publication-bias-related mechanism could be at work.

However, for other message variables, such differences in inclusion criteria did not produce divergent results. For example, O'Keefe and Jensen's (2009) review of gain-loss message framing variations in disease detection messages included both published and unpublished studies, whereas Gallagher and Updegraff's (2012) review of that same research area was restricted to published studies—but neither dataset contained any significant differences between mean ESs based on different outcomes. As another example, Witte and Allen's (2000) review of fear appeal strength variations included both published and unpublished studies, whereas Sutton's (1982) review included only published studies—but neither dataset had any significant differences between mean ESs for different outcomes. Indeed, with respect to threat severity variations, both de Hoog et al.'s (2007) review and Witte and Allen's (2000) review yielded no significant differences between mean ESs based on different outcomes, despite the difference in inclusion criteria. In short, the difference in whether unpublished studies were included does not seem like a plausible account of the observed divergence.

This is not the place to attempt to sort out the details of how and why these two meta-analyses came to yield such different results for the effects of variations in depicted threat vulnerability on attitudes.[7] For present purposes, the appropriate conclusion would seem to be that it is not entirely clear whether variations in depicted threat vulnerability produce ESs for attitudinal outcomes that are different from the ESs produced for intention and behavioral outcomes. If such differences are indeed genuine, they would have considerable interest, precisely because such differences would represent a singular departure from the general pattern of effects for other message variables. But the evidence in hand is unhappily ambiguous on this score.

Limitations and Cautions

Limitations. As with any secondary data analysis, the present report's conclusions are circumscribed by the available research literature. One cannot know how the results might have been different if, for example, additional meta-analytic databases had been available or if additional meta-analytic reviews had been performed. And some of the meta-analytic comparisons were based on relatively small numbers of studies; for example, O'Keefe's (2002) dataset for the effects of variations in recommendation specificity had only 12 ESs. But other datasets were substantially larger (e.g., the 225 ESs for gain-loss framing variations in the dataset of O'Keefe & Jensen, 2006). And, as noted earlier, the datasets in hand provide a strikingly consistent picture—consistent across different kinds of message variables and across different meta-analytic procedures (different inclusion criteria, different ways of computing effect sizes, and so on).

Cautions. Some readers have been alarmed by the apparent implications of the present results. In particular, concerns have been raised that these results might be taken to underwrite avoidance of collection of behavioral outcome data in persuasion research (and collection of such data is taken to be an unquestionable good).

Such concerns are partly, but not entirely, misplaced. They are partly misplaced in the following way: Given the present results, collecting behavioral outcome assessments is indeed unnecessary for answering research questions concerning *specifically* the relative persuasiveness of message types. If a message designer wants to know whether message A or message B will be more persuasive in influencing behavioral outcomes and so conducts a randomized trial as part of pre-campaign message testing, the designer does not need to collect behavioral outcome data. The question of relative persuasiveness can be confidently answered by collecting attitude or intention assessments.

But such concerns are not entirely misplaced, because behavioral outcome assessments can be useful—indeed, crucial—for answering *other* questions. Two general kinds of such questions can be identified.

First, questions about the persuasiveness of a given message in influencing behavior will require behavioral assessments. The present results indicate that a campaign planner can learn that message A is more persuasive than message B with respect to behavioral outcomes without having to assess behavioral outcomes themselves. But a campaign planner might well want to know just how large the absolute effect of message A will be on behaviors—and for answering that question, assessment of behavioral outcomes is essential.

Second, theoretical questions concerning the relationships—and especially the causal relationships—of message variations, attitudes, intentions, and behaviors will require behavioral assessments. As noted above, attitude, intentions, and behaviors are commonly taken to form a causal sequence, as in theoretical perspectives such as TRA and TPB. The evidence that is often adduced to support such theories is based on cross-sectional correlational analyses (e.g., indicating that attitude and intention are strongly correlated at a given point in time). However, as Weinstein (2007) has pointed out, such analyses can produce misleading tests of the causal claims embedded in such theories. Better evidence would be provided by experimental studies of the longitudinal effects of interventions (such as alternative persuasive messages) on all three persuasive outcomes. For example, appropriate longitudinal data would permit cross-lagged correlations (to help clarify the causal relationship of two variables that are positively correlated in cross-sectional data) and would provide information about both relative and absolute amounts of persuasion at different points in time with different outcomes. Hence even though, as indicated earlier, a researcher might need to assess only one of the three outcomes in order to answer specific questions about the relative persuasiveness of two message forms, assessing all three outcomes—and assessing them longitudinally—will provide richer information.

Conclusion

These results underwrite a general presumption that the relative persuasiveness of message types will be substantively identical if compared using attitudinal, intention, or behavioral outcomes. Where research questions are specifically focused on the relative persuasiveness of alternative message types, these three outcome variables are functionally equivalent, in the sense of giving the same answer to that research question. If message type A is more persuasive than message type B with attitudinal outcomes, it is also—and equally—more persuasive with intention and behavioral outcomes.

Notes

1. The dataset in Gallagher and Updegraff's Table 1 had two errors (K. M. Gallagher, personal communication, April 4, 2012), which were corrected for this

analysis. The two effect sizes for Block and Keller's (1995) Study 2 high-efficacy condition were recoded as prevention (not detection) cases, and the effect size for Rothman, Salovey, Antone, Keough, and Martin's (1993) Study 2 was entered as .09 (not .28).

2. Readers with concerns about this procedure can put them aside in the present context. As with the other meta-analytic datasets re-analyzed here, Eisend's (2006, 2007) dataset was accepted at face value.

3. These imaginary numbers are potentially misleading. For each outcome, the raw difference between the two means is the same (1.0), but whether the ES for each outcome is the same depends on the various standard deviations. If one adds the simplifying assumption that the standard deviation is the same for each outcome, then the three ESs would be identical.

4. The mean ESs reported here differ slightly from those in Gallagher and Updegraff's (2012) Table 2, in part because of the two corrections described in footnote 1, and in part because the ESs in Gallagher and Updegraff's (2012) Table 1—the ones re-analyzed here—may have been rounded for reporting purposes.

5. As a parallel illustrative case, imagine a study that found that variables X and Y were statistically significantly correlated in male participants ($r = .198$, $N = 100$; $p < .05$, two-tailed), but were not statistically significantly correlated in female participants ($r = .196$, $N = 100$; *ns*). This would not mean that the correlations for men and women were statistically significantly different. (In fact, these two correlations are not significantly different.)

6. To put this more abstractly: If, in a persuasion meta-analysis that (contrary to the present recommendation) reports a separate mean ES for each outcome, the results are such that the various mean ESs are not significantly different from each other even though some—but not all—of them are significantly different from zero, then such results should be interpreted by remembering that (a) the research goal is presumably estimation of the population effect, (b) the CI associated with each mean ES specifies the range of plausible population effects, and (c) the overlap of the CIs can suggest a possible common population effect.

7. One notices that each meta-analytic result is especially congenial with the theoretical framework associated with its authors. The extended parallel process model (EPPM; Witte, 1992, 1994) provides a basis for expecting that variations in depicted threat vulnerability will influence attitudes (e.g., Witte & Allen, 2000, p. 603). The stage model of fear appeal messages (de Hoog, Stroebe, & de Wit, 2005) makes many of the same predictions as does the EPPM, but—quite distinctively—hypothesizes that "attitudes toward a protective action ... should be unaffected by feelings of vulnerability" (de Hoog et al., 2007, p. 264). Perhaps a disinterested review would be helpful.

References

Ajzen, I. (1991). The theory of planned behavior. *Organizational Behavior and Human Decision Processes, 50*, 179–211. doi:10.1016/0749-5978(91)90020-T

Akl, E. A., Oxman, A. D., Herrin, J., Vist, G. E., Terrenato, I., Sperati, F., … Schünemann, H. (2011). Framing of health information messages. *Cochrane Database of Systematic Reviews*, Issue 12 (article no. CD006777). doi:10.1002/14651858. CD006777.pub2

Albarracin, D., Johnson, B. T., Fishbein, M., & Muellerleile, P. A. (2001). Theories of reasoned action and planned behavior as models of condom use: A meta-analysis. *Psychological Bulletin, 127*, 142–161. doi:10.1037//0033-2909.127.1.142

Allen, M., & Preiss, R. W. (1997). Comparing the persuasiveness of narrative and statistical evidence using meta-analysis. *Communication Research Reports, 14*,125–131.

Andrews, K. R., Carpenter, C. J., Shaw, A. S., & Boster, F. J. (2008). The legitimization of paltry favors effect: A review and meta-analysis. *Communication Reports, 21*, 59–69. doi:10.1080/08934210802305028

Argo, J. J., & Main, K. J. (2004). Meta-analyses of the effectiveness of warning labels. *Journal of Public Policy and Marketing, 23*, 193–208.

Armitage, C. J., & Conner, M. (2001). Efficacy of the theory of planned behaviour: A meta-analytic review. *British Journal of Social Psychology, 40*, 471–499. doi:10.1348/014466601164939

Block, L. G., & Keller, P. A. (1995). When to accentuate the negative: The effects of perceived efficacy and message framing on intentions to perform a health-related behavior. *Journal of Marketing Research, 32*, 192–203.

Borenstein, M., Hedges, L. V., Higgins, J. P. T., & Rothstein, H. R. (2009). *Introduction to meta-analysis*. Chichester, West Sussex, England: Wiley.

Borenstein, M., Hedges, L. V., Higgins, J. P. T., & Rothstein, H. R. (2010). A basic introduction to fixed-effect and random-effects models for meta-analysis. *Research Synthesis Methods, 1*, 97–111. doi:10.1002/jrsm.12

Borenstein, M., & Rothstein, H. (2005). Comprehensive meta-analysis (Version 2.2.023) [Computer software]. Englewood, NJ: Biostat.

Boster, F. J., & Mongeau, P. (1984). Fear-arousing persuasive messages. *Communication Yearbook, 8*, 330–375.

Burrell, N. A., & Koper, R. J. (1998). The efficacy of powerful/powerless language on attitudes and source credibility. In M. Allen & R. W. Preiss (Eds.), *Persuasion: Advances through meta-analysis* (pp. 203–215). Cresskill, NJ: Hampton Press.

Card, N. A. (2012). *Applied meta-analysis for social science research*. New York, NY: Guilford Press.

Cooke, R., & French, D. P. (2008). How well do the theory of reasoned action and theory of planned behaviour predict intentions and attendance at screening programmes? A meta-analysis. *Psychology & Health, 23*, 745–765. doi:10.1080/08870440701544437

Cooke, R., & Sheeran, P. (2004). Moderation of cognition-intention and cognition-behaviour relations: A meta-analysis of properties of variables from the theory of planned behaviour. *British Journal of Social Psychology, 43*, 159–186. doi:10.1348/0144666041501688

Cruz, M. G. (1998). Explicit and implicit conclusions in persuasive messages. In M. Allen & R. W. Preiss (Eds.), *Persuasion: Advances through meta-analysis* (pp. 217–230). Cresskill, NJ: Hampton Press.

de Hoog, N., Stroebe, W., & de Wit, J. B. F. (2005). The impact of fear appeals on the processing and acceptance of action recommendations. *Personality and Social Psychology Bulletin, 31*, 24–33. doi:10.1177/0146167204271321

de Hoog, N., Stroebe, W., & de Wit, J. (2007). The impact of vulnerability to and severity of a health risk on processing and acceptance of fear-arousing communications: A meta-analysis. *Review of General Psychology, 11*, 258–285. doi:10.1037/1089-2680.11.3.258

Dziokonski, W., & Weber, S. J. (1977). Repression-sensitization, perceived vulnerability, and the fear appeal communication. *Journal of Social Psychology, 102*, 105–112.

Eisend, M. (2006). Two-sided advertising: A meta-analysis. *International Journal of Research in Marketing, 23*, 187–198. doi:10.1016/j.ijresmar.2005.11.001

Eisend, M. (2007). Understanding two-sided persuasion: An empirical assessment of theoretical approaches. *Psychology and Marketing, 24*, 615–640. doi:10.1002/mar.20176

Eisend, M. (2009). A meta-analysis of humor in advertising. *Journal of the Academy of Marketing Science, 37*, 191–203. doi:10.1007/s11747-008-0096-y

Fishbein, M., & Ajzen, I. (1975). *Belief, attitude, intention, and behavior.* Reading, MA: Addison-Wesley.

Fishbein, M., & Ajzen, I. (2010). *Predicting and changing behavior: The reasoned action approach.* New York, NY: Psychology Press.

Floyd, D. L., Prentice-Dunn, S., & Rogers, R. W. (2000). A meta-analysis of research on protection motivation theory. *Journal of Applied Social Psychology, 30*, 407–429. doi: 10.1111/j.1559-1816.2000.tb02323.x

Gallagher, K. M., & Updegraff, J. A. (2012). Health message framing effects on attitudes, intentions, and behavior: A meta-analytic review. *Annals of Behavioral Medicine, 43*, 101–116. doi:10.1007/s12160-011-9308-7

Gayle, B. M., Preiss, R. W., & Allen, M. (1998). Another look at the use of rhetorical questions. In M. Allen & R. W. Preiss (Eds.), *Persuasion: Advances through meta-analysis* (pp. 189–201). Cresskill, NJ: Hampton Press.

Gerber, A., & Malhotra, N. (2008a). Do statistical reporting standards affect what is published? Publication bias in two leading political science journals. *Quarterly Journal of Political Science, 3*, 313–326. doi:10.1561/100.00008024

Gerber, A. S., & Malhotra, N. (2008b). Publication bias in empirical sociological research: Do arbitrary significance levels distort published reports? *Sociological Methods & Research, 37*, 3–30. doi:10.1177/0049124108318973

Glasman, L. R., & Albarracín, D. (2006). Forming attitudes that predict future behavior: A meta-analysis of the attitude–behavior relation. *Psychological Bulletin, 132*, 778–822. doi:10.1037/0033-2909.132.5.778

Grewal, D., Kavanoor, S., Fern, E. F., Costley, C., & Barnes, J. (1997). Comparative versus noncomparative advertising: A meta-analysis. *Journal of Marketing, 61*(4), 1–15.

Hagger, M. S., Chatzisarantis, N. L. D., & Biddle, S. J. H. (2002). A meta-analytic review of the theories of reasoned action and planned behavior in physical activity: Predictive validity and the contribution of additional variables. *Journal of Sport and Exercise Psychology, 24*, 3–32.

Hale, S. L. (1998, April). *Attack messages and their effects on judgments of political candidates: A random-effects meta-analytic review.* Paper presented at the annual meeting of the Midwest Political Science Association, Chicago, IL.

Hale, J. L., Householder, B. J., & Greene, K. L. (2002). The theory of reasoned action. In J. P. Dillard & M. Pfau (Eds.), *The persuasion handbook: Developments in theory and practice* (pp. 259–286). Thousand Oaks, CA: Sage.

Hamilton, M. A., & Hunter, J. E. (1998). The effect of language intensity on receiver evaluations of message, source, and topic. In M. Allen & R. W. Preiss (Eds.), *Persuasion: Advances through meta-analysis* (pp 99–138). Cresskill, NJ: Hampton Press.

Hedges, L. V., & Vevea, J. L. (1998). Fixed- and random-effects models in meta-analysis. *Psychological Methods, 3*, 486–504. doi:10.1037/1082-989X.3.4.486

Hornikx, J., & O'Keefe, D. J. (2009). Adapting consumer advertising appeals to cultural values: A meta-analytic review of effects on persuasiveness and ad liking. *Communication Yearbook, 33,* 39–71.

Keller, P. A., & Lehman, D. R. (2008). Designing effective health communications: A meta-analysis. *Journal of Public Policy and Marketing, 27,* 117–130. doi:10.1509/jppm.27.2.117

Kyriakaki, M. (2007). *Promotion of physical health behaviours: "Framing" the persuasive message* (Unpublished doctoral dissertation). University of Essex, Colchester, England.

Lau, R. R., Sigelman, L., & Rovner, I. B. (2007). The effects of negative political campaigns: A meta-analytic reassessment. *Journal of Politics, 69,* 1176–1209. doi:10.1111/j.1468-2508.2007.00618.x

Levine, T., Asada, K. J., & Carpenter, C. (2009). Sample sizes and effect sizes are negatively correlated in meta-analyses: Evidence and implications of a publication bias against non-significant findings. *Communication Monographs, 76,* 286–302. doi:10.1080/03637750903074685

Milne, S., Sheeran, P., & Orbell, S. (2000). Prediction and intervention in health-related behavior: A meta-analytic review of protection motivation theory. *Journal of Applied Social Psychology, 30,* 106–143. doi:10.1111/j.1559-1816.2000.tb02308.x

Mongeau, P. A. (1998). Another look at fear-arousing persuasive appeals. In M. Allen & R. W. Preiss (Eds.), *Persuasion: Advances through meta-analysis* (pp. 53–68). Cresskill, NJ: Hampton Press.

Noar, S. M., Benac, C. N., & Harris, M. S. (2007). Does tailoring matter? Meta-analytic review of tailored print health behavior change interventions. *Psychological Bulletin, 133,* 673–693. doi:10.1037/0033-2909.133.4.673

O'Keefe, D. J. (1998). Justification explicitness and persuasive effect: A meta-analytic review of the effects of varying support articulation in persuasive messages. *Argumentation and Advocacy, 35,* 61–75.

O'Keefe, D. J. (1999). How to handle opposing arguments in persuasive messages: A meta-analytic review of the effects of one-sided and two-sided messages. *Communication Yearbook, 22,* 209–249.

O'Keefe, D. J. (2000). Guilt and social influence. *Communication Yearbook, 23,* 67–101.

O'Keefe, D. J. (2002). The persuasive effects of variation in standpoint articulation. In F. H. van Eemeren (Ed.), *Advances in pragma-dialectics* (pp. 65–82). Amsterdam, The Netherlands: Sic Sat.

O'Keefe, D. J., & Jensen, J. D. (2006). The advantages of compliance or the disadvantages of noncompliance? A meta-analytic review of the relative persuasive effectiveness of gain-framed and loss-framed messages. *Communication Yearbook, 30,* 1–43.

O'Keefe, D. J., & Jensen, J. D. (2007). The relative persuasiveness of gain-framed and loss-framed messages for encouraging disease prevention behaviors: A meta-analytic review. *Journal of Health Communication, 12,* 623–644. doi:10.1080/10810730701615198

O'Keefe, D. J., & Jensen, J. D. (2009). The relative persuasiveness of gain-framed and loss-framed messages for encouraging disease detection behaviors: A meta-analytic review. *Journal of Communication, 59,* 296–316. doi:10.1111/j.1460-2466.2009.01417.x

Reinard, J. C. (1998). The persuasive effects of testimonial assertion evidence. In M.

Allen & R. W. Preiss (Eds.), *Persuasion: Advances through meta-analysis* (pp. 69–86). Cresskill, NJ: Hampton Press.

Reinhart, A. M. (2006). *Comparing the persuasive effects of narrative versus statistical messages: A meta-analytic reviw* (Doctoral dissertation). Retrieved from ProQuest. (UMI No. AAT 3213634)

Rothman, A. J., Salovey, P., Antone, C., Keough, K., & Martin, C. D. (1993). The influence of message framing on intentions to perform health behaviors. *Journal of Experimental Social Psychology, 29,* 408–433. doi:10.1006/jesp.1993.1019

Sopory, P., & Dillard, J. P. (2002). The persuasive effects of metaphor: A meta-analysis. *Human Communication Research, 28,* 382–419. doi:10.1111/j.1468-2958.2002.tb00813.x

Sutton, S. R. (1982). Fear-arousing communications: A critical examination of theory and research. In J. R. Eiser (Ed.), *Social psychology and behavioral medicine* (pp. 303–337). New York, NY: Wiley.

Wallace, D. S., Paulson, R. M., Lord, C. G., & Bond, C. F., Jr. (2005). Which behaviors do attitudes predict? Meta-analyzing the effects of social pressure and perceived difficulty. *Review of General Psychology, 9,* 214–227. doi:10.1037/1089-2680.9.3.214

Weinstein, N. D. (2007). Misleading tests of health behavior theories. *Annals of Behavioral Medicine, 33,* 1–10. doi:10.1207/s15324796abm3301_1

Witte, K. (1992). Putting the fear back into fear appeals: The extended parallel process model. *Communication Monographs, 59,* 329–349.

Witte, K. (1994). Fear control and danger control: A test of the extended parallel process model (EPPM). *Communication Monographs, 61,* 113–134.

Witte, K., & Allen, M. (2000). A meta-analysis of fear appeals: Implications for effective public health programs. *Health Education and Behavior, 27,* 591–615. doi:10.1177/109019810002700506.

CHAPTER CONTENTS

9 Vaccinating Voters
Surveying Political Campaign Inoculation Scholarship

Josh Compton

Dartmouth College

Bobi Ivanov

University of Kentucky

Inoculation theory has seen dramatic theoretical development since it was first introduced in the early 1960s, and applied research has explored its efficacy in such domains as politics, health, and commerce. This chapter notes a dearth in political campaign inoculation scholarship in recent years and calls for renewed interest. A survey of inoculation research offers a nuanced portrait of how inoculation has functioned in campaigns, yet several findings remain unexplained by the theory. The chapter concludes with proposals for future political campaign inoculation research, exploring new campaign technologies and new insights into how inoculation functions in political campaigns.

Romney ad preempts Bain attacks in Florida

—*Blog title in Politico (Schultheis, 2012)*

Inoculation and pre-emption are what win campaigns.

—*Jim Innocenzi, political consultant (cited in Ehrenhalt, 1985, p. 2E)*

Michael Pfau and Michael Burgoon's 1988 political campaign inoculation study is a milestone in the chronicle of resistance to influence research. That their study found inoculation works as a campaign strategy is not particularly noteworthy; a slate of studies going back to the early 1960s had already supported inoculation's efficacy in conferring resistance to subsequent persuasion attempts. Instead, the Pfau and Burgoon study is noteworthy because it confirms that inoculation functions as an effective political campaign strategy *during an actual campaign* in the way that inoculation researchers had theorized: resistance as the product of threat and refutational preemption. During campaigns, politicians can acclaim, attack, defend (see, for example, Benoit, 1999), or inoculate (Pfau & Burgoon, 1988; Pfau & Kenski, 1990).

Of course, politicians had inoculated prior to the 1988 study. The strategy is ancient. In *Rhetoric*, Aristotle (1960) advised refuting oppositional arguments before the opposition has its chance. But the 1988 study offered empirical support for inoculation's mechanisms and efficacy as "the first scientific effort to apply inoculation in a political context" (Pfau & Kenski, 1990, p. 99). A combination of threat and refutational preemption derogated perceptions of sources of political attacks, made people skeptical of attack content, and bolstered supporters' commitment to vote for the candidate under attack (Pfau & Burgoon, 1988). Following this study, Pfau and Kenski (1990) offered their book-length treatment of attack messages and inoculation's potential, *Attack Politics*, and a handful of follow-up studies in the next few years extended the analysis and application of inoculation to political campaigning. Since then, a number of political campaign and persuasion texts have pointed to inoculation as a potentially effective strategy in political campaigning (e.g., Newman & Perloff, 2004; Perloff, 2010). Yet, perhaps because of limited recent political campaign inoculation scholarship, many contemporary political campaign texts give inoculation only passing mention (e.g., Trent, Friedenberg, & Denton, 2011).

Twenty-five years after Pfau and Burgoon's (1988) study, we have a more developed understanding of inoculation's efficacy as a resistance strategy. Recent inoculation scholarship reveals a complex relationship between resistance and intricate attitudinal components (e.g., Pfau et al., 2005) and intriguing potential with considering inoculation theory with other theories, including psychological reactance (Miller et al., 2013) and cognitive dissonance (Ivanov, Parker, & Compton, 2011). New findings of the role of affect paint a broader portrait of what is going on when people inoculate and are inoculated (e.g., Pfau et al., 2009). Surveys of developments in inoculation theory reflect the leaps forward in understanding inoculation as a process of resistance (Compton, 2013; Compton & Pfau, 2005), even as some results give us pause when considering conventional explanations for how inoculation works (e.g., Banas & Rains, 2010).

Inoculation scholarship in general has taken off in new and exciting directions, but applied political campaign inoculation scholarship in particular has not had the same level of dynamic development. Of course, progress in inoculation scholarship informs political campaign inoculation. Inoculation theory is not bound by context: "Inoculation is appropriate for any context where strongly held attitudes are vulnerable to challenge" (Szabo & Pfau, 2002, p. 252). Nevertheless, inoculation does have boundary conditions, and some contexts—including politics—make some of these boundary conditions all the more salient. Applied political campaign inoculation scholarship is the most informative resource for theorizing, studying, and putting inoculation theory into practice in a political context, and we have not seen much development of applied political campaign inoculation scholarship in recent years.

We think new development in this line of research is long overdue. Political campaigning has changed. Our understanding of inoculation theory has changed. What findings we do have from political campaign inoculation scholarship are informative, but are also often inconsistent. Confirming inoculation's efficacy as a political campaign strategy was an important first step;

what we need now are advances in inoculation's application to political campaigns. Such work would do more than improve political campaign strategies; it could also expand our thinking about persuasive campaigns in other contexts, including health and marketing, while at the same time clarify the processes of and boundary conditions for inoculation theory.

Before we review and organize the inoculation literature in the context of candidates' political campaigns, we define inoculation and establish its confirmed efficacy and application. Then, with consideration of unique political campaign contexts and new developments in inoculation scholarship, we turn to opportunities for future directions for applications of inoculation theory to candidates' political campaigns.

Inoculation Theory: Established Efficacy and Application

Inoculation is a theory and a message strategy. The theory, first articulated by McGuire (1964), was derived from a medical or biological analogy and extended the two-sided persuasive message research of Lumsdaine and Janis (1953) and others. Just as a medical inoculation triggers a process of resistance by introducing weakened offending agents, like viruses, McGuire reasoned that we can trigger a process of persuasion resistance by introducing weakened attempts at persuasion, like counterarguments. Overcoming weakened viruses protects the body; for example, the body produces antibodies to fight that virus and wards off future illness. Overcoming weakened counterarguments protects an attitude or position; for example, the mind produces refutations to counterarguments and wards off future persuasive attacks (see Compton, 2013; McGuire, 1964).

Before taking a closer look at the specific mechanisms of inoculation, it is important to note two characteristics of inoculation. First, inoculation is preemptive. The "right" position must be in place before that position can be strengthened against future attacks (see Compton, 2013; McGuire, 1964). Second, inoculation against persuasion benefits from a delay between the inoculation treatment and the actual attack, much the way inoculation against future viruses requires time for the body to build up its defenses (see Compton, 2013; McGuire, 1964; but see Banas & Rains, 2010).

Resistance conferred by inoculation has been confirmed by decades of scholarship in laboratory (e.g., Bernard, Maio, & Olson, 2003; Ivanov, Miller, et al., 2012) and field research (e.g., Pfau & Van Bockern, 1994), with primary foci in three contexts: health (e.g., Banerjee & Greene, 2007; Parker, Ivanov, & Compton, 2012), commerce (e.g., Bechwati & Siegal, 2005; Ivanov, Pfau, & Parker, 2009b), and politics (e.g., Pfau & Burgoon, 1988). Recently scholars have extended inoculation into new domains, exploring issues of culture (e.g., Ivanov, Parker, Miller, & Pfau, 2012), education (e.g., Compton, 2011a), interpersonal communication (e.g., Sutton, 2011), organizational communication (e.g., Haigh & Pfau, 2006), and crisis management (e.g., Wan & Pfau, 2004; Wigley & Pfau, 2010).

254 COMMUNICATION YEARBOOK 37

Although politics has received comparably more attention than other applied inoculation contexts, much of this research took place more than 20 years ago. We reconsider the political campaign potential of inoculation in this essay, with specific attention paid to how contextual dimensions of political campaigning correspond with unique features of inoculation theory, creating a powerful form of campaign rhetoric.

We can illuminate the unique connections between inoculation and politics by turning to the conventional explanation for how inoculation works: *threat* and *refutational preemption*. Threat is a recognition that an existing belief (or attitude or position) may be at risk, or vulnerable to future influence. According to the conventional explanation of how inoculation confers resistance, threat is what motivates processes (e.g., continued counterarguing) that lead to resistance (Compton, 2013; McGuire, 1964). To elicit threat, a typical inoculation message begins with an explicit forewarning that a position held by its reader (or, with a video or audio message, its viewer or listener) may be confronted in the future by persuasive arguments that could change an existing belief (or attitude or position). Again, this perception of vulnerability is called *threat*. Although most inoculation messages in inoculation studies use a forewarning as part of the inoculation message treatment, a forewarning is not required for inoculation; threat is (but see Banas & Rains, 2010). Because forewarnings have been found to enhance inoculation (McGuire & Papageorgis, 1962) and elicit threat (Compton & Ivanov, 2012), forewarnings continue to be used as a part of an inoculation treatment message. Consider this generic forewarning that could be used in a political campaign message:

> I appreciate your current support, and be assured, you are supporting the best candidate in this contest. But there's a good chance you'll encounter some strong attacks on me in the coming days, and some of these arguments might make you question your support of my candidacy.

No specific counterarguments are mentioned. Instead, the reader is warned that arguments exist—somewhere out there—and these arguments could sway positions. Again, the purpose of a forewarning is to generate threat, to make salient the possibility of future attitude change, and threat motivates continuing processes of resistance (e.g., counterarguing). Threat is a key factor in the conventional explanation for inoculation's efficacy (Compton, 2013; Compton & Pfau, 2005; but see Banas & Rains, 2010).

Threat is also generated by the next part of a typical inoculation message: refutational preemption. Refutational preemption is the raising and refuting of counterarguments, serving as preparation for the types of challenges mentioned in the forewarning (Compton, 2013; McGuire, 1964). To return to our generic example, a refutational preemption could begin in the following manner:

> My opponent may tell you that I lack the experience to lead. But my opponent is wrong. Just look at how my record reflects my experience.

In a typical inoculation treatment message, two or three sets of counterarguments and refutations are raised (Ivanov, 2011). In each pair, a challenge to an existing position is first raised, and then the challenge is refuted.

Thus, refutational preemption—the raising and refuting of counterarguments—is another core component of inoculation theory. It likely elicits threat (although not as much as the forewarning: Compton & Ivanov, 2012) and also provides a sort of training for continued counterarguing on the part of those inoculated (e.g., Ivanov, 2011; Ivanov, Pfau, & Parker, 2009a). Indeed, more recent theorizing (Compton & Pfau, 2009) and empirical research (Ivanov, Miller, et al., 2012) suggests that the continued counterarguing is more than an intrapersonal process; counterarguing also manifests after inoculation treatments in the conversations of those inoculated.

Inoculation and political campaigning seem to be a particularly good match. Persuasive attempts are ubiquitous, with politicians attempting to build and then protect positive images, communicate policy positions and priorities, advocate comparative advantages over competitors, and frame decisions as wise. Forewarnings of impending attacks are believable, and campaign materials offer plenty of options for counterarguments and refutations to use in refutational preemption. The two core components of inoculation, threat and refutational preemption, are part of political campaign communication (see Pfau & Kenski, 1990).

Inoculation's efficacy in political communication is more than consistent with theory and concepts; it has been supported by a number of empirical studies. No finding is more important or applicable to inoculation in political campaigns than the confirmation that inoculation could protect against counterarguments not even mentioned in the inoculation treatment message. McGuire confirmed this potential of inoculation in some of the earliest inoculation research (e.g., McGuire, 1961). He and his colleagues found that in refutational-same (when the same counterarguments in the treatment message are launched in a later attack message) and in refutational-different (when new counterarguments are launched in a later attack message) scenarios, inoculation treatment messages conferred resistance. A meta-analysis confirms this (Banas & Rains, 2010). Pfau and Burgoon (1988) found support for this finding through field research during a contested political campaign. This feature of inoculation—to protect against attacks that have not yet been launched—makes it a particularly attractive strategy for political campaign practitioners to preempt attacks that come late in a campaign (Pfau & Kenski, 1990). For example, when news of presidential candidate George W. Bush's past drunk driving incident broke only five days before the 2000 presidential election, some voters questioned Bush's judgment (Shepard, 2000). The Bush campaign team had little time to prepare and deliver a response. But what if the story had run on the day before or the day of the election? Could a strong response be mounted and disseminated in time, before voters cast their ballots? According to Compton and Pfau (2005), inoculation may be the "only strategy for preempting attacks initiated late in a campaign" (p. 117; also, see Pfau & Kenski, 1990).

Inoculation and Political Campaigns

In some ways, political campaign practitioners were quicker to realize the potential of inoculation in political campaign settings than inoculation and political campaign scholars were. Predating Pfau and Burgoon's (1988) seminal piece on inoculation and political campaigns, Jim Innocenzi, a political consultant, concluded, "Inoculation and pre-emption are what win campaigns" (cited in Ehrenhalt, 1985, p. 2E). Charlie Black, a Republican political consultant, added: "If you know what your negatives are, and you know where you're vulnerable, you can pre-empt [challenges]" (as cited in Ehrenhalt, 1985, p. 2E). Since then, more political strategists and consultants have shared similar sentiments. A strategy of preemption has been said to be "a Morris trademark" (Lewis, 1995, p. 11A), a label referencing Dick Morris, campaign advisor to President Clinton. An example of Morris's reliance on preemption comes from President Clinton's reelection campaign. President Clinton's camp, with Morris' advice, developed an advertisement considered by many as an effort to "preempt any attempt [in the following election] year to paint Clinton as soft on crime" (Lewis, 1995, p. 11A).

Perloff (2010) detailed a more recent example of inoculation as a preemptive political campaign strategy. Noting inoculation's potential as "a potent weapon in politics" (p. 132), Perloff (2010) provided the following example of inoculation at work:

> Barack Obama used [inoculation] in the 2008 election, trying to build voter resistance to Republican opponent John McCain. Obama first acknowledged McCain's service to the country. "Now let there be no doubt. The Republican nominee, John McCain, has worn the uniform of our country with bravery and distinction, and for that we owe him our gratitude and respect. And we'll also hear about those occasions when he's broken with his party as evidence that he can deliver the change that we need." He then proffered the counterargument. "But the record's clear: John McCain has voted with George Bush 90 percent of the time. Senator McCain likes to talk about judgment, but, really, what does it say about your judgment when you think George Bush was right more than 90 percent of the time? I don't know about you, but I'm not ready to take a 10 percent [chance] on change." ... Obama staffers undoubtedly hoped that their candidate had successfully inoculated Americans. (p. 132)

In the 2012 Republican Party presidential election primary in Florida, Mitt Romney's camp purchased an advertisement targeting any potential attacks on his tenure at Bain Capital, an investing and venture capital corporation for which he had worked (Schultheis, 2012). In other primaries, political opponents had claimed that Bain Capital engaged in exploitative practices (Haberman, 2012) with decisions that resulted in lost jobs (King & Yadron, 2012). Acknowledging in the advertisement the likelihood of such attacks in press in the Florida primary, Romney countered by presenting the successes of the companies in which Bain Capital had invested during his tenure (Schultheis, 2012).

Although we have evidence of a growing recognition of inoculation as a potent strategy among political campaign strategists and consultants, the effectiveness of an inoculation strategy in political campaigning remains largely unknown from their work. We see two reasons for this. First, political campaign strategists and consultants are guarded about their strategies. Second, because inoculation is often just one of many strategies used in a political campaign, its effectiveness cannot be linked to a single strategy, like inoculation. Did President Clinton win his re-election bid solely as a result of inoculation? Did President Obama win his presidential election largely due to relying on inoculation? Probably not. The more pertinent questions are: How much of a role did inoculation play in their effective presidential bids? And, if inoculation played a role, how did it work to confer resistance to future attacks?

To answer these questions we need to turn to the systematic experimental work of inoculation researchers who have tested this strategy in the context of political campaigns. In the next section, we survey published studies on inoculation in political campaigns and synthesize their general findings, with specific attention paid to effects and message design.

Political Campaign Inoculation Scholarship: Review and Analysis

Since 1988, inoculation scholars have demonstrated inoculation's efficacy in a number of United States political campaigns, including races for the presidency (Pfau & Kenski, 1990; Pfau, Kenski, Nitz, & Sorenson, 1990; Pfau, Park, Holbert, & Cho, 2001); U.S. Senate (An & Pfau, 2004; Pfau & Burgoon, 1988, 1990; Pfau & Kenski, 1990); State House of Representatives (Wisconsin; Pfau, Park, et al., 2001); and State Senate (Wisconsin; An & Pfau, 2004; Pfau, Park, et al., 2001). Specific campaigns include: James Abnor versus Tom Daschle for U.S. Senator from South Dakota in 1986 (Pfau & Burgoon, 1988, 1990; Pfau & Kenski, 1990); George Bush versus Michael Dukakis for president in 1988 (Pfau & Kenski, 1990; Pfau et al., 1990); the 2000 Second District of Wisconsin seat for U.S. representative (Pfau, Park, et al., 2001); the District 16 seat for Wisconsin State Senate (Pfau, Park, et al., 2001); and James Inhofe versus David Walters for U.S. Senator in 2002 (An & Pfau, 2004). A few of these campaign studies took place during the last weeks of the campaign: October (Pfau & Burgoon, 1988, 1990; Pfau & Kenski, 1990) and September-October (Pfau & Kenski, 1990; Pfau et al., 1990).

Effect sizes in political campaign inoculation studies are often small, with reported effect size in the following ranges: $\omega^2 = .01–.29$; $\eta^2 = .04–.19$ (see An & Pfau, 2004; Pfau & Burgoon, 1988, 1990; Pfau & Kenski, 1990; Pfau et al., 1990; Pfau, Park, et al., 2001). We want to echo three points offered by Pfau and Burgoon (1988) about the meaningfulness of smaller effect sizes in political campaign inoculation research. First, to find an inoculation effect in inoculation research, the attack message used in the study must be persuasive, and "even the most successful attempts to influence the attitudes of receivers who already support the opposing candidate in a political campaign will account for only a small proportion of the total variance ..." (Pfau & Burgoon, 1988, p. 108). Second, many political campaign studies use one inoculation message, and that single message must compete with the many messages launched in an ongoing campaign (Pfau & Burgoon, 1988). Third, as Pfau and Burgoon (1988) point out in the discussion of their results, small proportions of variance could be enough to make a difference in close elections (Jeffries, 1986).

Inoculation and political campaign studies are diverse in scope (e.g., district vs. presidential) and place (e.g., state vs. national). What unifies these experimental studies is the unique contribution of inoculation to the success of each campaign strategy. By comparing experimental groups, such research could better isolate the unique effects of inoculation components on potential voters. Although we will look more closely at the specific contributions of inoculation to the above campaigns in the sections that follow, a general conclusion about the effectiveness of inoculation as a political campaign strategy can be drawn at this point: Inoculation works in political campaigns.

That inoculation works is an unsurprising finding for many political campaign strategists, consultants, and successful candidates; nevertheless, it is a welcome confirmation of inoculation's efficacy for inoculation and political communication scholars. But how do voter characteristics affect inoculation's efficacy? Does inoculation work better with some voters than others? Scholarship has explored these questions and others, and we survey these findings next.

Voter Characteristics

The first political campaign studies involved adult voters in the field (Pfau & Burgoon, 1988, 1990; Pfau & Kenski, 1990; Pfau et al., 1990), and the most recent campaign studies used a pool of undergraduate students (An & Pfau, 2004; Pfau, Park, et al., 2001). In terms of voter demographics, researchers have examined party identification and strength of political party identification (Pfau & Burgoon, 1988; Pfau & Kenski, 1990; Pfau et al., 1990; Pfau, Park, et al., 2001), political involvement (An & Pfau, 2004), gender (Pfau & Burgoon, 1990; Pfau & Kenski, 1990), and age (Pfau & Kenski, 1990).

Evidence suggests that political campaign inoculation works best with strong political party identifiers. Less resistance is conferred when attempting to inoculate weak political party identifiers, nonidentifiers, and crossovers (Pfau & Burgoon, 1988; Pfau & Kenski, 1990; Pfau et al., 1990).

We also have a more nuanced understanding of inoculation's efficacy in the context of party identification. Pfau and Burgoon (1988) noted:

[S]ame inoculation pretreatments were significantly more effective in deflecting attack messages among strong identifiers as opposed to nonidentifiers, weak identifiers, or crossovers. By contrast, novel inoculation pretreatments were more effective with weak identifiers, strong identifiers, and crossovers than with nonidentifiers. (p. 104)

Pfau and colleagues (1990) revealed a complicated portrait of inoculation effects and party identification. With weak identifiers, post hoc refutations and inoculation-plus-reinforcement protected against issue attacks, whereas conventional inoculation failed to confer resistance. But with character attacks, the post hoc refutation did not confer resistance, whereas the inoculation and inoculation-plus-reinforcement did. With strong identifiers, inoculation, inoculation-plus-reinforcement, and post hoc refutations protected voter support in the face of an attack message, with inoculation-plus-reinforcement working better than post-hoc refutation. With nonidentifiers, inoculation and inoculation-plus-reinforcement worked; post hoc refutation did not (Pfau et al., 1990). These effects seem conditional and complicated, and as the researchers noted, extant theory does not fully explain the differences. As with the inoculation laboratory studies that would follow, Pfau and his colleagues revealed effects of applied inoculation that complicate the conventional model. Clearly, more research exploring potential effects of political identification is needed so that we can better understand these and similar findings.

Voter demographics usually show modest relationships with inoculation's efficacy. With gender, Pfau and Kenski (1990) concluded "inoculation strengthens resistance among both male and female receivers, but leaves male receivers more resistant overall" (p. 146). Pfau and Burgoon (1990) found "strong support for a gender effect based on receiver ratings of the source credibility of the candidate supported in the attack message" (p. 12), but no differences in terms of attitude toward the candidate supported in the attack message or attitude toward the position supported in the attack message. Pfau and Burgoon (1990) explained that "it *may require more specific information to alter women's than men's judgments about candidate credibility*" (p. 14; emphasis in original).

In terms of age and education, researchers have concluded that "age plays a minor role in the process of inoculation" (Pfau & Kenski, 1990, p. 151), and with regard to education, voters with higher education levels were more resistant after inoculation than those with lower education levels. Inoculation-different messages (messages that raised and refuted arguments that were not included in the attack message) were more effective with low education voters, and inoculation-same messages (messages that raised and refuted the same arguments as were used in the attack message) were more effective with moderate education voters (Pfau & Kenski, 1990).

Even a brief survey of findings about inoculation and voter characteristics reveals complex relationships, with subtle differences that should not be ignored when designing and assessing inoculation-based political campaigns. Consequently, as illustrated in the next section, designing inoculation messages must be done carefully and deliberately.

Political Campaign Inoculation Messages

Drawing from political campaign inoculation research, we have insight into a number of message variables, including inoculation pretreatment messages and attack messages. Investigators have prepared inoculation messages to protect against issue and character attacks (An & Pfau, 2004; Pfau & Burgoon, 1988, 1990; Pfau & Kenski, 1990; Pfau et al., 1990), using material from candidate advertisements (Pfau & Burgoon, 1988, 1990; Pfau & Kenski, 1990) and other candidate communications, such as position papers, advertisements, and campaign speeches (An & Pfau, 2004; Pfau & Kenski, 1990; Pfau et al., 1990). In selecting arguments, researchers have relied on polling data to identify the most important issues and character concerns (An & Pfau, 2004; Pfau & Kenski, 1990; Pfau et al., 1990). Although most messages presented counterarguments (arguments that challenged existing positions) and refutations of those counterarguments (An & Pfau, 2004; Pfau & Burgoon, 1988, 1990; Pfau & Kenski, 1990; Pfau et al., 1990), one study used inoculation messages that offered strategies for careful scrutiny of future attack messages in general instead of specific counterarguments and refutations (Pfau, Park, et al., 2001). Some treatment messages were attributed to a fictitious interest group, the Center for the Study of Political Argument (An & Pfau, 2004; Pfau & Burgoon, 1988, 1990; Pfau & Kenski, 1990). Most studies used multiple messages (An & Pfau, 2004; Pfau & Burgoon, 1988, 1990; Pfau & Kenski, 1990; Pfau et al., 1990). Inoculation messages in political campaign research were 228–256 words (Pfau & Burgoon, 1988, 1990); 245–249 words (Pfau & Kenski, 1990; Pfau et al., 1990); and 300–303 words (An & Pfau, 2004) in length.

In published inoculation scholarship, inoculation messages began with a forewarning that a candidate would be attacked (An & Pfau, 2004; Pfau & Burgoon, 1988, 1990; Pfau & Kenski, 1990; Pfau et al., 1990). As for message modality, inoculation treatment messages were written (An & Pfau, 2004; Pfau & Burgoon, 1988, 1990; Pfau & Kenski, 1990; Pfau et al., 1990; Pfau, Park, et al., 2001). In one study, participants received inoculation via postal mail (Pfau & Kenski, 1990; Pfau et al., 1990), and in another, via e-mail (Pfau, Park, et al., 2001).

Attack messages included the same counterarguments refuted in the inoculation messages or different counterarguments (Pfau & Burgoon, 1988, 1990; Pfau & Kenski, 1990; Pfau et al., 1990), and attack messages launched issue or character attacks (Pfau & Burgoon, 1988, 1990; Pfau & Kenski, 1990; Pfau et al., 1990). As with inoculation messages, most attack messages were written and created by researchers based on polling data (Pfau & Burgoon, 1988, 1990; Pfau & Kenski, 1990; Pfau et al., 1990). Some attack messages were purportedly sponsored by a fictitious interest group, Citizens for an Informed Electorate (Pfau & Burgoon, 1988, 1990; Pfau & Kenski, 1990; Pfau et al., 1990). Attack messages were administered by trained researchers in participants' homes (Pfau & Burgoon, 1988, 1990; Pfau & Kenski, 1990; Pfau et al., 1990), mailed (Pfau & Kenski, 1990; Pfau et al., 1990), or shown in laboratory settings (An & Pfau, 2004). Attack messages ranged from 231–254 words (Pfau & Burgoon, 1988; Pfau & Kenski, 1990) and 244–247 words (Pfau & Kenski, 1990; Pfau et al., 1990) in length. Reflecting changing campaign technologies, a couple of inoculation campaign studies used videos as attack messages. One used television political advertisements during game shows and sitcoms (Pfau, Park, et al., 2001), and another employed a televised debate as an attack (An & Pfau, 2004).

Regardless of inoculation message structure (e.g., same or different counterarguments from those in the attack), length (e.g., 228 or 303 words), focus (e.g., issue or character attacks), or delivery (e.g., postal mail, e-mail, or in person), results indicated that inoculation conferred resistance to political attacks. Inoculation's success is even more impressive when we consider the diversity of attack messages to which inoculated individuals were exposed in the campaign studies, including attacks on the message source (e.g., general or interest groups), and modality (e.g., print or television). All the more remarkable is that studies found effects of inoculation during ongoing campaigns (Pfau & Kenski, 1990).

At this point in our survey of findings, we can expand our general conclusion that inoculation works. We have explored not only that it works, but also with whom, through what types of messages, and against what types of attacks. What we have not yet explored is timing, a central issue for inoculation theory-conferred resistance.

Inoculation and Timing

Inoculation's effects do not last forever: "It makes intuitive sense that the effect of inoculation pretreatments decays over time" (Pfau & Kenski, 1990, p. 102). A meta-analysis by Banas and Rains (2010) failed to reveal differences in resistance when comparing no delay (immediate attack after the inoculation treatment) to a moderate delay, and resistance seems to drop off after about two weeks (Banas & Rains, 2010).

Political campaign inoculation research has compared one-, two-, and three-week delays between treatment and attack, finding inoculation-conferred resistance decays over time (Pfau & Burgoon, 1988). Shorter intervals (one week) between inoculation and attack work best in terms of voters' attitudes toward candidates and attitudes toward the position of the attack message, as compared to moderate intervals (two weeks) or longer intervals (three weeks) (Pfau & Burgoon, 1988). There is a difference between moderate and longer intervals in terms of voters' attitudes toward positions advocated in attack messages, with moderate intervals being more effective (Pfau & Burgoon, 1988). Inoculation's decay does not seem linked to whether the treatment messages address the same or novel counterarguments (Pfau & Burgoon, 1988). Evidence for decay is limited to attitudinal measures of resistance (attitude toward source of the attack message and attitude toward the position of the attack message) (see Pfau & Burgoon, 1988).

The timing of the inoculation message presentation may play a key role, as some of its effectiveness dissipates. Of course, this finding is not unique to inoculation messages used in political campaigns; it is a limitation of most persuasion and resistance messages (Stiff & Mongeau, 2003). Even so, inoculation messages have been demonstrated to be more effective than some other types of resistance messages (e.g., supportive and restoration) in terms of decay (Ivanov et al., 2009a). To combat decay, scholars have explored potential methods to boost the effectiveness of inoculation over time and slow the rate of message and effectiveness decay. A prime candidate to do this is booster sessions. Boosters are frequently used to prolong the protection of medical inoculations. With the right form and timing, they might also work with persuasion inoculations (see Compton & Pfau, 2005; McGuire, 1964).

One political inoculation study looked at whether inoculation's effects could be bolstered with booster sessions. The researchers found that booster (or reinforcement) messages did not enhance inoculation (Pfau et al., 1990), a finding consistent with other inoculation booster research outside of the political campaign context (e.g., Pfau, Compton, et al., 2006). Research should continue to examine the potential role of timing in inoculation (Banas & Rains, 2010) and ways of crafting and administering booster treatments (Compton & Pfau, 2005).

At this point, we turn back to our general conclusion—that inoculation works—for a better idea of what we mean by "works." What are the effects of inoculation treatments? When inoculation "works," what happens to voters?

Effects of Inoculation

Inoculation messages are designed to confer resistance, and in campaign inoculation research, we have evidence that inoculation works (An & Pfau, 2004; Pfau & Burgoon, 1988, 1990; Pfau & Kenski, 1990; Pfau et al., 1990; Pfau, Park, et al., 2001), conferring resistance to the same arguments raised and refuted in the pretreatment message *and* conferring resistance to different or novel arguments (Pfau & Burgoon, 1988, 1990; Pfau et al., 1990). We have no evidence of overall differences between refutational-same and refutational-different approaches (Pfau & Burgoon, 1988). Inoculation works somewhat better than post-hoc refutation, affecting the image of the source of the attack but not affecting support for the position in the attack (Pfau et al., 1990). But how does this influence manifest itself?

We have some evidence from campaign inoculation scholarship that inoculation pretreatments lead individuals to derogate sources of attack messages (Pfau & Burgoon, 1988; Pfau & Kenski, 1990; Pfau et al., 1990), elicit disagreement with positions advanced in attack messages against candidates (Pfau & Burgoon, 1988; Pfau & Kenski, 1990; Pfau et al., 1990), enhance interest in campaigns (Pfau, Park, et al., 2001), increase knowledge about candidates and their positions (Pfau, Park, et al., 2001), increase the likelihood of voting (Pfau, Park, et al., 2001), decrease the likelihood of voting for sources of attack messages (Pfau & Burgoon, 1988; Pfau & Kenski, 1990; Pfau et al., 1990), enhance global attitudes toward candidates (An & Pfau, 2004), enhance perceptions of candidates' competency (An & Pfau, 2004), and enhance perceptions of candidates' character (An & Pfau, 2004).

Most of these effects benefit the candidate favored by the inoculation pretreatment message. Reviewing some of the early findings (e.g., Pfau & Burgoon, 1988), Allen and Burrell (2002) noted that, at least from the perspective of the candidate under attack, inoculation "may offer a potential solution to the problem of negative political advertising" (p. 93). Other effects (e.g., increasing political participation) suggest benefits that reach beyond helping the individual candidates who employ inoculation-guided strategies during campaigns.

A closer look at these effects suggests some interesting differences. In terms of image effects, Pfau and Burgoon (1988) found that inoculation messages derogate sources of attack messages on one credibility dimension—extroversion. In the face of attacks launched in political debates, inoculation confers resistance in terms of general attitudes toward candidates and perception of candidate competence and character (An & Pfau, 2004). A study by An and Pfau (2004) failed to find any significant effects on behavioral outcomes, including on activities such as donating to campaigns and voting, but the researchers noted that power for the test was low. Pfau, Park, and colleagues (2001) found that behavioral effects depend on the type of attack advertisement. In the face of party-sponsored political advertisements, inoculation enhances interest in campaigns, knowledge about candidates and positions, and likelihood of voting. With PAC-sponsored political advertisements, inoculation leads to more awareness, more interest, greater likelihood of seeking more information, and greater likelihood of voting. But with PAC-sponsored political advertisements, these effects were only found with Republicans (Pfau, Park, et al., 2001).

What can be deduced from the above review is that political campaign inoculation research, although limited, has revealed powerful processes and effects of inoculation during political campaigns. Although inoculation research in general has seen resurgence in recent years, and modern inoculation research has explored political issues independent of candidates' campaigns (e.g., Lin, 2005; Lin & Pfau, 2007; Lim & Ki, 2007; Pfau, Haigh, et al. 2006, 2008), there has been a dearth in candidates' political campaign inoculation research. We think this is unfortunate. Next we turn to suggested future directions for such research.

Directions for Future Political Campaign Inoculation Research

Our summary of literature on inoculation and political campaigns highlights important strengths of this strategy (e.g., offering protection against attacks launched late in a campaign), and a few weaknesses (e.g., decay of message effectiveness over time). The findings as a whole attest to the robustness of inoculation and its effectiveness in the context of political campaigns.

However, many issues remain under- or unexplored. We address a number of these issues next.

Campaigns

Field research in political campaign inoculation research is limited to the earliest studies (Pfau & Burgoon, 1988; Pfau & Kenski, 1990; Pfau et al., 1990). With changes in modern political campaigning and the shifting demographics of likely voters, a return to theory-guided field research in political campaign inoculation scholarship is long overdue.

Political campaign inoculation research has assessed inoculation's efficacy mostly in U. S. political campaigns (An & Pfau, 2004; Pfau & Burgoon, 1988; Pfau & Kenski, 1990; Pfau et al., 1990; Pfau, Park, et al., 2001), and of the studies with identifiable campaign phases, most took place in the later months of the campaign (e.g., Pfau & Burgoon, 1988; Pfau & Kenski, 1990; Pfau et al., 1990). Future research should explore inoculation's efficacy beyond the United States and at different phases of campaigns to assess whether such contextual dimensions affect inoculation's efficacy or processes of resistance.

Lin (2005) and Lin and Pfau (2007) explored inoculation's efficacy with political issues outside of the United States. Unlike the studies surveyed previously in this essay, they were not studying political candidates' campaigns. Instead, they studied a political issue (e.g., Pfau, Haigh, et al., 2006, 2008) prior to an election. Lin and Pfau investigated Taiwanese citizen's attitudes concerning Taiwan's future relationship with China: "independence, unification with the People's Republic of China (PRC), or maintaining the status quo" (2007, p. 160). Lin and Pfau (2007) explored whether inoculation could allay the stifling effects of the spiral of silence—a process through which minority perspectives are discouraged (see Noelle-Neumann, 1984). Inoculation strengthened attitudes, making people more confident and more likely to talk with others about their positions. In another analysis of Taiwanese citizens' attitudes regarding Taiwan's political future, Lin (2005) found that inoculation worked best for those with stronger party identification, consistent with findings from previous political campaign inoculation research (Pfau & Burgoon, 1988; Pfau & Kenski, 1990; Pfau et al., 1990). Lin and Pfau's research should be a springboard for future inoculation studies outside of the United States, including candidates' strategies during election campaigns.

Much of the political campaign inoculation research has assessed inoculation's efficacy during late phases of campaigns. Yet, Pfau and Burgoon (1988) surmised that "inoculation should prove most effective *early* in a political campaign, prior to the saturation of political campaign messages ..." (p. 106, emphasis added). Inoculation is a preemptive strategy, and consistent with the medical analogy of the theory, treatments need precede the attacks for optimum inoculation efficacy (McGuire, 1964). Researchers should turn more attention to primary phases of campaigns; as Pfau, Diedrich, Larson, and Van Winkle (1993) observed, it is during primaries "that most voters initially form attitudes about candidates" (p. 287). Additionally, Wlezien and Erikson (2002) have found that "polls can move quite a lot during campaigns, especially during the late summer, in the period surrounding the conventions" (p. 988). Inoculation research has largely ignored the campaign phases when theory suggests its effects could be the strongest.

Further, evaluation criteria change during the course of a campaign. "[V]oters initially judge candidates in terms of whether they seem personable, enthusiastic, warm, similar, friendly, interested, caring, receptive, honest, and sincere" (Pfau et al., 1993, p. 287). Later in the campaign, the researchers found, perceptions of competence trump these relational variables (Pfau et al., 1993). Would an optimal inoculation strategy adapt to the changing ways voters assess candidates, or is inoculation theory's "blanket of protection" (Pfau & Kenski, 1990, p. 75) sufficiently large enough to account for these changes during campaigns? The most recent findings about the scope of inoculation's protection suggest that inoculation's protection is robust, stretching not only across arguments but even across issue domains (Parker et al., 2012). It may well be that an inoculation treatment is able to confer resistance during a campaign without requiring major adjustments as voters' criteria change. Future research should investigate this issue and related issues.

Voters and Issues of Involvement

Party identification and strength of party identification seem to affect inoculation's efficacy (Pfau & Burgoon, 1988; Pfau et al., 1990; Pfau, Park, et al., 2001). But many more questions about voter demographics remain unanswered. For example, why were refutational-different messages more effective with weak and strong political party identifiers and crossovers when compared to nonidentifiers? The finding "cannot be explained by extant theory" (Pfau & Burgoon, 1988, p. 107). Also, why does inoculation protect against some negative effects of PAC-sponsored advertisements with Republicans, but not with Democratic or unaffiliated voters (Pfau, Park, et al., 2001)? Was this unique to the campaign (Pfau, Park, et al., 2001), or does this finding unearth a yet-to-be-explained boundary condition for inoculation as a political campaign strategy?

Perhaps the answer to some of these questions includes involvement (but see Banas & Rains, 2010). The first campaign inoculation study to control for involvement was conducted by An and Pfau (2004), and they treated political involvement as a covariate. More recent inoculation scholarship suggests that enhanced perceptions of involvement may also be a product of inoculation (e.g., Pfau, Compton, et al., 2004). That is, an inoculation treatment boosts perceptions of involvement with an issue. Scholars should assess whether inoculation treatments enhance voters' perceived involvement during specific campaigns and reveal any behavioral or attitudinal implications of enhanced involvement. Furthermore, future research can follow the lead of Pfau and his colleagues (2010) who looked not only at involvement and inoculation, but also at different types of involvement.

Gender

Inoculation scholars have found few differences in terms of gender (e.g., Pfau & Burgoon, 1990; Pfau & Kenski, 1990), but Pfau, Haigh, and colleagues (2006) found that gender does matter when inoculating against visual images (in their study, print news photographs of war casualties on support for United States involvement in the war in Iraq). Inoculation treatments conferred resistance to the influence of visual messages with women, but not with men (Pfau, Haigh, et al., 2006). Future political campaign inoculation research should assess not just whether gender matters, but also, under what conditions (e.g., against visuals employed during candidates' campaign advertising).

Messages

During the late 1980s, direct mail was an innovative mode of campaign communication. Pfau and colleagues' (1990) confirmation of inoculation's efficacy in the context of direct mail advertising was forward-looking. But political campaign inoculation research has fallen behind in exploring the newest campaign technologies. Haynes and Pitts (2009) reminded us: "While the same basic goals for campaigns apply, the tools to accomplish these goals have expanded" (p. 53).

The content of treatment messages needs further exploration. Nearly every political campaign inoculation study has used treatment messages that raise and refute specific counterarguments against a candidate. However, more recent inoculation research has used unconventional argumentation approaches. For example, Pfau, Haigh, and colleagues (2006, 2008) warned against visuals as a persuasive medium, an inoculation strategy they called "generic preemption of the influence of visual images" (2006, p. 154). That is, instead of raising actual counterarguments and refutations about the issue (e.g., support for the war in Iraq), they warned about the influence of war visuals on support for U.S. involvement. Another political campaign inoculation study used a generic pre-emption approach (Pfau, Park, et al., 2001), but instead of warning about attack message modality (Pfau, Haigh, et al., 2006, 2008), the researchers encouraged careful scrutiny of attack messages *in general*. Future research should continue to tweak inoculation treatment message strategies to assess its protection against specific types of arguments as well as general strategies.

Some of the inoculation messages employed in political campaign scholarship have been between 228 (Pfau & Burgoon, 1988; Pfau & Kenski, 1990) and 303 (An & Pfau, 2004) words in length, about one double-spaced typed page. Future research should explore whether inoculation messages could be more concise—perhaps even within the parameters of Twitter messages (or "tweets"), 140 characters. The Obama campaign frequently used Twitter leading up to the 2008 election (see Abroms & Lefebvre, 2009). Romero, Meeder, and Kleinberg found "hashtags on politically controversial topics are particularly persistent, with repeated exposures continuing to have unusually large marginal effects on adoption" (2011, p. 1). Could a message inoculate in 140 or fewer characters? For comparison, one inoculation message in a study had 2,695 characters (Ivanov, Miller, et al., 2012). Tweeted inoculation treatments would look much different than conventional inoculation messages used in previous studies, perhaps more along the lines of "My opponents are about to attack, but stay strong. They say I'm not ready to lead. They are wrong. I am. Look at my record" (123 characters). One study by the first author of this chapter is already in progress to assess whether inoculation messages can function in Twitter-length messages. We expect that it will. McGuire's (1964) original theorizing and subsequent empirical testing suggests inoculation's efficacy is linked to the active processes that occur after an inoculation treatment message (e.g., counterarguing). As long as the treatment message triggers this active process, the message's length, or number of characters, should not matter.

Our understanding of attack messages in political campaign inoculation research also remains limited. Future research should examine the content of attacks, the modality of attacks, and the frequency of attacks. Political campaign inoculation scholarship has treated attacks as explicit arguments—written messages (e.g., Pfau & Burgoon, 1988), television advertisements (e.g., Pfau, Park, et al., 2001), and debates (An & Pfau, 2004). However, political attacks use many strategies. Consider, for example, findings that subliminal priming (using verbal or visual primes) can affect political attitudes (e.g., Weinberger & Westen, 2008). Could inoculation protect against subliminal attacks? What would such an inoculation pretreatment look like, in content and in modality? One theoretical issue that should guide research in this area is threat. Threat is a product of external forewarnings in inoculation messages (Compton & Ivanov, 2012), and an inoculation message could forewarn of impending subliminal influence. But, if the eventual attack message were not recognized as an attack, would inoculation still protect? Perhaps the treatment message would need to not only warn of the future attack, but also, provide ways of identifying the attack when it occurs. Protecting against more subtle and perhaps even subliminal influence is consistent with inoculation theory's domain, but some adaptations to the treatment message (e.g., forewarnings) might be necessary.

Most political campaign inoculation research has examined written attack messages. However, An and Pfau (2004) confirmed that inoculation can protect viewers' support of candidates prior to watching candidates in televised debates. Nevertheless, the visuals in a debate are not particularly evocative. Inoculation scholarship suggests that inoculation may not be as successful against stronger images, such as images of violence in war (Pfau, Haigh, et al., 2008). Nabi (2003) also found the impact that evocative visuals have on the inoculation process. Her work (exploring the issue of animal testing) used inoculation treatment videos against video attacks to find that the affect intensity of the counterargument and refutation components of a treatment message should be consistent (e.g., high-high) for optimum resistance. How would inoculation fare against evocative visuals used during campaign advertising?

Would affect intensity affect the efficacy of video-based inoculation treatments? What types of affect would be most effective? Nabi (2003) studied collective negative affect, a combination of anxiety, anger, fear, disgust, pity, guilt, hate, and surprise. Would we find unique effects for any of these discrete emotions? Furthermore, what would be the effect of positive affect (e.g., pride, hope) generated by visual messages during political campaigns? Inoculation messages using positive affect have been successful in conferring resistance (e.g., Pfau, Szabo, et al., 2001), but negative affect seems to trigger a more active process of resistance (Pfau et al., 2009). More research in the domain of political campaigns could contribute to a resurgence of interest in affect and inoculation (e.g., Pfau et al., 2009).

As we continue exploring more multimodal forms of attack messages, we should consider how technology affects more conventional written approaches. Consider, for example, blogs. Blogs are an increasingly common component of the modern campaign and one with historic roots. Davis (2009) noted that "[t]he use of writing to make political points to a broader audience is an ancient practice, but this particular form—'blogs,' short for 'weblogs'—is a wholly new medium" (p. 3). Blogs often contain the type of political attacks inoculation strategies seek to deflect. One investigation found that 83.6% of the political statements on the official campaign blogs of John Kerry and George W. Bush during the 2004 presidential campaign contained attacks on an opponent or on an issue (Trammell, 2006). Wicks, Bradley, Blackburn, & Field (2011) found that candidates during the 2008 presidential election used blogs for self-promotion (to acclaim) and political parties used blogs to attack opponents. They found few instances of rebuttals in political blogs. A preemptive strategy may be particularly warranted using this new political messaging technology.

Political campaign inoculation research has not yet explored messages in blogs—either for inoculating or to inoculate against. Of course, there is an argument to be made that blogs function as a message mode in inoculation just as other written messages have. But it is an argument that needs to be made and supported through scholarship. Blogs are often products of collaboration, with authors and readers posting arguments, which stands in contrast to single-authored writings (Zhou & Hovy, 2006). Further, blogs often contain links (URL) to additional material (Zhou & Hovy, 2006), and this feature adds an interesting interactive possibility with inoculation's requisite counterarguments and refutations.

In addition to considering different modes of attack messages, we should continue to explore the number of attack messages. Ivanov and colleagues' (2009a) study of consumer attitudes suggests that inoculation can protect against two attack messages, with the second occurring, on average, two weeks after the first. Although resistance decays a bit, inoculation is more effective than bolstering, post-hoc restoration, or no message at all. Their findings should be assessed in the context of an actual political campaign, when multiple attacks are common (Ivanov et al., 2009a). Further, scholars should assess inoculation's efficacy after more than two attacks. Theory, including the explanatory analogy of medical inoculations, suggests that protection can endure, but for precisely how long is currently unknown.

Timing

Timing is critical in campaign communication, however our understanding of timing during inoculation remains limited (see Pfau & Burgoon, 1988). Although political campaign inoculation research has mostly followed a one-shot approach, inoculation in practice would probably use a number of inoculation messages at various points during a campaign (Pfau & Burgoon, 1988). What is the optimum timing for inoculation strategies during political campaigns? We can turn to nonpolitical inoculation research for some guidance. Pfau, Compton, and colleagues (2006) found that the recipient's counterarguing continues much longer after an inoculation treatment than originally thought—and even longer when reinforcement messages were used in conjunction with inoculation treatments. The issue of timing and inoculation should continue to be explored in candidates' political campaigns (see also Banas & Rains, 2010).

Effects

Future political campaign inoculation scholarship should explore how resistance manifests itself, looking beyond attitudes toward candidates and more into political behaviors (Pfau, Park, et al., 2001), political interest (Pfau, Park, et al., 2001), political knowledge (Pfau, Park, et al., 2001), willingness to speak up (Lin & Pfau, 2007), and other effects. In their review of inoculation scholarship, Compton and Pfau (2005) highlighted how "inoculation also protects participatory attitudes and behaviors, which underpin democracy" (p. 119).

Future scholarship should explore any incidental effects of inoculation. For example, one finding suggests that inoculation treatments bolster perceptions of self-efficacy (Pfau et al., 2009). Efficacy can be derogated by negative political advertising (Lau, Sigelman, & Rovner, 2009). Might inoculation not only protect attitudes toward specific candidates but also bolster voters' confidence in their political roles? Limited evidence suggests that it might (e.g., Pfau et al., 2009).

Scholars should also explore whether voters learn from inoculation-based campaign strategies. Analyses of political advertisements suggest that political ads, in general, are mostly persuasive: "Advertising does a little to inform, next to nothing to mobilize, and a great deal to persuade potential voters" (Huber & Arceneaux, 2007, p. 979). Might inoculation, with its focus on careful scrutiny of arguments, promote learning where other campaign strategies fail? One study by the first author of this chapter is currently underway to examine learning effects of inoculation treatment messages. If inoculation triggers an active process of counterarguing, as suggested by McGuire (1964) and empirically supported by subsequent research (e.g., Pfau et al., 2009), those inoculated may be learning new information as they accumulate material for counterarguments and refutations.

Image

We need a more nuanced understanding of effects of inoculation on candidate image (Ivanov & Parker, 2011). Inoculation protects candidate image in the face of political attacks, including bolstering general attitudes toward candidates, perceptions of candidates' competence, and perceptions of candidates' character (An & Pfau, 2004). Scholars should follow Pfau and Wan's (2006) recommendation to combine inoculation with image boosting strategies. One study by the authors of this chapter is in progress to explore inoculation theory in conjunction with W. Benoit's (1995, 2000) typology of image repair and P. Benoit's (1997) typology of acclamation strategies. We expect to find that most image repair and acclamation strategies can preemptively confer resistance, as inoculation's efficacy does not seem restricted to specific argument types.

Humor

Humor is an underexplored area of inoculation research in general. Compton (2004) looked at humor and political campaign messages during the Democratic presidential primaries in 2004, using experimental research to assess effects of late night political comedy on viewers and the influence of inoculation. At this stage of the campaign, results suggested that late night humor effects were minimal (e.g., monologue jokes lead to more negative feelings of viewers toward the candidates, but did not affect perceptions of candidates' competence, character, or sociability). Effects of late-night television variety shows (and specifically, *Saturday Night Live*) were more surprising and counter to predictions: Instead of hurting candidates' images, caricatures seemed to help candidates, boosting general perceptions of them and improving perceptions of the candidates' competence, character, and sociability.

Compton's (2004) study also found that using inoculation treatments prior to late night humor actually did more harm to candidate images than good. When inoculation treatments preceded late-night comedy "attacks," the treatments boomeranged on several image dimensions, leaving politicians with worse images than if they would have only been mocked by the late-night comedians (e.g., lower perceptions of candidate competence, character, and sociability). Viewers also became less likely to vote for the candidate and tell other people positive things about the candidate if they had read inoculation messages prior to watching the parody (Compton, 2004). Compton (2004) also explored whether appearing on late-night comedy shows could serve an inoculation function, with hosts' questions functioning as counterarguments and candidates' responses as refutations. Candidate appearances had limited inoculative effects, but appearances did boost the effectiveness of conventional inoculation treatments. When college students read an inoculation message and then later watched candidates' appearances on the late-night programs, inoculation effects were stronger (Compton, 2004).

A number of issues remain unresolved with humor, political campaigns, and inoculation, and contemporary campaign practices give us a number of artifacts to study. For example, on March 19, 2009, President Obama appeared on *The Tonight Show with Jay Leno* (Leno, Medeiros, & Vickers, 2009). Did his appearance inoculate against subsequent criticism? Were requisite features of inoculation present (e.g., threat, refutational preemption) in the exchange between President Obama and Jay Leno? Research indicates that political humor affects voters (Compton, 2008, 2011b), and inoculation is a promising theoretical framework from which to study political humor effects (Compton, 2008). Lim and Ki's (2007) success in inoculating against the influence of online parody videos suggests the potential success of using inoculation in a political campaign context, but other findings (e.g., Compton, 2004) suggest that we are far from a thorough understanding of inoculation and humor.

Narratives

Narratives can be powerful strategies during political persuasion, although some have challenged their importance (Ghoshal, 2009; Mazzocco, Green, Sasota, & Jones, 2010). President Ronald Reagan effectively used narratives during his presidency (Lewis, 1987). According to Slater (2002), "Use of narratives … may be one of the only strategies available for influencing the beliefs of those who are predisposed to disagree with the position espoused in the persuasive message" (p. 175). The success of narratives may be attributed to their ability to increase identification with the characters in the story and to reduce the effectiveness of message counterarguing and logical scrutiny (Dal Cin, Zanna, & Fong, 2004). "In a narrative, beliefs are often implied as opposed to stated explicitly. This may inhibit counterarguing because it leaves the reader with no specific arguments to refute" (Dal Cin et al., 2004, p. 178) and because "the structure of narratives may impede forewarning of a counterattitudinal message" (p. 177). In addition, processing narratives depletes the cognitive resources necessary for counterarguing (Green & Brock, 2000). The desire to remain engaged in the narrative further decreases the motivation to engage in counterarguing, thus rendering potential counterarguments more inaccessible (Dal Cin et al., 2004). Kim, Moon, and Feeley (2011) reported a negative relationship between transportation, or the ability to be absorbed by the story, and counterarguing.

If narratives indeed suppress threat (in the form of forewarning) as well as counterarguing ability and motivation—the two conventional theoretical explanations for how inoculation confers resistance—then political campaign messages delivered in the form of a narrative might nullify or reduce the effects of inoculation messages. Could this be the case? Can inoculation be successful when narratives challenge attitudes? Future inoculation political campaign studies should explore answers to these questions.

Additionally, what would be the effect of an inoculation message that forewarns individuals about the covert persuasiveness of political narratives? Would an inoculation message that sensitizes individuals to recognize and resist the transportation effect of a political narrative be more effective than a traditional inoculation message? These are questions that future studies should consider.

Cross-Protection

Scholars have long noted that inoculation's efficacy is not limited to specific counterarguments refuted in a treatment message (McGuire, 1964). Inoculation's protection extends to counterarguments not mentioned or refuted. This potential has been touted as one of inoculation's greatest strengths as a campaign strategy (Pfau & Kenski, 1990). More recent research suggests that this "umbrella of protection" (Pfau et al., 1997, p. 188) or "blanket of protection" (Pfau & Kenski, 1990, p. 75) is even larger than we once thought. Parker and colleagues (2012) found that inoculation confers resistance not only to novel counterarguments but even to novel (unmentioned) issues: Inoculating against challenges to condom-use attitudes also conferred protection against challenges to binge-drinking attitudes. These findings raise intriguing possibilities for future political campaign inoculation scholarship. Inoculation offers cross-protection with health issues. Would we find similar results for political issues? Theory and limited empirical evidence suggest this possibility.

Parker and colleagues (2012) attributed the effects of cross-protection to the relatively high relatedness of the two issues. By pointing to the literature on multiple theoretical concepts (e.g., consistency theories), they reasoned that inoculation-induced threat motivates individuals to not only protect the attitude toward the inoculated issue, but also the attitudes toward any related issues (e.g., Nelson, 1968; Holt, 1970; Holt & Watts, 1969; Watts & Holt, 1970). More specifically, by citing examples in the literature of alcohol negatively affecting safer sex practices, Parker and colleagues reasoned that binge drinking could increase the likelihood of engaging in unprotected sex through attitudes linkages (see Dinauer & Fink, 2006). Consequently, they concluded, individuals motivated to prevent instances of engaging in unprotected sex would also be motivated to monitor their alcohol intake, which may have a direct effect on their judgment when making sex-related decisions.

The prospect of cross-protection is indeed intriguing and highly relevant in the context of political campaigns, where issue consistency is valued. For example, social conservatives might expect the candidate they support to espouse certain beliefs about specific issues (e.g., abortion, gay marriage, embryonic stem-cell research, gun control). If beliefs about specific issues are closely linked, a voter's shift in how the candidate is perceived on one of these beliefs (e.g., abortion) may lead to a perceptual shift in another (e.g., embryonic stem-cell research). Hence, an effective attack on a candidate's stance (or belief) on abortion may also affect the perception of the candidate's stance (or belief) on embryonic stem-cell research. The candidate may even face separate attacks on the two issues. Should cross-protection effects be confirmed in inoculation political campaigns, inoculating against challenges of one issue may offer the candidate additional protection on related issues.

Further, inoculation scholars should assess whether inoculation can protect a more general belief about a candidate's ideology. For example, in the 2012 Republican presidential primary races, candidate Mitt Romney was repeatedly criticized by his political opponents for not being a strong conservative on social issues (Peoples, 2012). Some attacks included challenges to his stances on gay marriage, freedom of religion, and abortion (Peoples, 2012). Could a general inoculation message protect Romney's stance as a social conservative and preempt specific attacks on his beliefs about specific social conservative values (e.g., abortion, freedom of religion, gay marriage)? Future inoculation political campaign research should test such possibilities across political ideologies and with different specific issues.

Perhaps more intriguing is this: Could inoculation offer cross-protection across candidates? During elections and primaries, candidates are often perceived to hold similar positions on issues and ideas. Consider the following excerpt from an editorial about the 2012 Florida Republican presidential primary: "While today's Florida Republican presidential primary will be remembered for many things, it won't be recalled as a contest of ideas. The four remaining candidates agreed on a host of issues" ("GOP," 2012, para. 1–2). Should inoculation generate cross-protection in the context of political campaigns, the resulting effect of the cross-protection could be positive or mixed. Some of the positive effects of cross-protection have already been addressed. In addition, given a perceived similarity among candidates on a host of ideas, inoculating against attacks on specific issues may create protection not only for the specific candidate who is the target of the preemption message, but it may also create protection for all candidates who are perceived to hold similar stances on the same issue. This potential outcome could be seen as beneficial by a political party in general, because it could ensure that all of its candidates who share similar positions on important issues would find those positions strengthened. However, the potential cross-protection outcome for the individual candidate may be mixed. Although the candidate stands to benefit from the inoculation message and its cross-protection effects that protect the candidate's inoculated or related positions on specific issues, the cross-protection may also provide equivalent protection to the competitors, a potentially unwelcome byproduct of inoculation's cross-protection. Inoculation scholarship should investigate these potential outcomes in future political campaign research.

Boosters

Inoculation scholars have assessed the efficacy of inoculation booster sessions since the early years of the theory (e.g., McGuire, 1961). The concept of boosters is consistent with the medical analogy (McGuire, 1964); however, evidence fails to confirm much of an effect, if any, of boosters on resistance to influence (e.g., Pfau, Compton, et al., 2004). Compton and Pfau (2005) suggested the problem with boosters is either form or timing. Studies are using the wrong types of boosters or not administering boosters at the ideal time. Pfau and colleagues (1990) wondered if boosters failed because there were not enough boosters. Future political inoculation scholarship should experiment with different types and numbers of booster messages. For example, inoculation scholars have used intact inoculation messages repeatedly to serve as a booster (Compton & Pfau, 2005). Compton and Pfau (2005) wondered if the use of forewarnings would be better alternatives as boosters. Future investigations of inoculation in the context of political campaigns should manipulate the type and timing of booster messages.

Threat

Although threat is a critical component of the explanation for how inoculation confers resistance (Compton, 2013; Compton & Pfau, 2005), threat remains a mysterious variable in the process of inoculation (Compton, 2009). Pfau and Kenski (1990) noted that "it may be necessary to rethink the notion of threat in a political campaign context" (p. 97). Nearly 20 years later, Compton (2009) called for a rethinking of threat in general. A meta-analysis (Banas & Rains, 2010) calls into question our conventional understanding of how threat functions in resistance, with results failing to connect greater levels of threat to greater levels of resistance. Scholars should continue to assess such issues as optimal threat levels, when and how threat affects the process of resistance, and how to best elicit threat during inoculation-based campaigns (Compton, 2009; Compton & Pfau, 2005). Threat has been one of the core elements of inoculation theory since its inception (see McGuire, 1964), but many unanswered questions remain.

In one experiment, Compton and Ivanov (2012) discovered that a forewarning (explicit threat) placed in the opening paragraph of an inoculation message generates as much threat as the entire inoculation message, which includes both the explicit forewarning (explicit threat) and refutational preemption (implicit threat). Future political campaign research using inoculation should test this possibility. If confirmed, the forewarning may be used in conjunction with the refutational preemption but also in addition to it, whether as a booster or as a separate message that precedes the inoculation message.

As previously mentioned, the use of forewarning as a potential booster has been suggested (Compton & Pfau, 2005). If this forewarning has the ability to generate levels of threat equal to that of the entire inoculation message (Compton & Ivanov, 2012), it should have the ability to generate the necessary motivation for inoculation to endure for longer periods of time. Earlier we discussed the threat of message decay to inoculation or any other type of persuasive and resistance message. What is also significant is that motivation to protect the attitude can decay with time (Insko, 1967). A forewarning used as a booster may provide the necessary threat to the attitude, which should boost motivation to protect it, potentially warding off motivation decay. In this respect, the shorter length of a forewarning compared to that of an entire inoculation message has its advantages. For example, earlier in this chapter we discussed the potential benefit of Twitter as an inoculation treatment delivery vehicle. However, we also acknowledged its shortcoming given the 140-character limitation. Although 140 characters may not allow for presentation of a conventional inoculation message, the character limit should not have as strong of an effect on presenting the opening paragraph (forewarning) of the inoculation message. Tweets—which have been used previously in political campaigns (see Abroms & Lefebvre, 2009)—structured as forewarnings could be used intermittently to boost the potency of inoculation by fending off motivation decay. Of course, although forewarnings are much shorter than complete conventional inoculation messages, revisions for length would still be necessary. Consider that the forewarning component alone in three recent inoculation studies has far exceeded 140 characters (397 characters in Ivanov, Miller, et al., 2012; 1,439 characters in Parker et al., 2012; and 446 characters in Ivanov et al., 2009b).

Explicit threat in the form of forewarning could also be effective as a forerunner to an inoculation message. For example, in a multimodal political campaign, a tweet could be used to disseminate the forewarning message in order to increase the salience toward the threat, thus increasing the likelihood of a person being in the right frame of mind for an inoculation message distributed via more traditional media vehicles. In addition, the forewarning message may be coupled with a website and distributed via Twitter. The forewarning message could deliver an explicit threat to the attitude, which could motivate the individual to visit the site or blog hyperlink included in the tweet to read (or watch) the entire inoculation message. Given advances in computer, cell phone, and tablet technology, many of those individuals receiving the tweeted message should have the ability to directly click on the hyperlink, which would open the URL or blog hosting the inoculation message. Future political campaign studies testing inoculation strategies should explore these and other possibilities.

Risks of Using Inoculation

If an inoculation message warns against an attack, and the attack never comes, what happens? Pfau and colleagues (1990) put it this way: "[I]f an attack does not occur, the strategy could undermine the candidate's standing" (p. 41). Research outside of a political context suggests that inoculation can negatively affect attitudes when attacks are not raised (Wan & Pfau, 2004); other research has not found this negative effect (Wigley & Pfau, 2010). When and under what conditions inoculation negatively affects attitudes is an area that warrants much more investigation, and a political campaign context seems appropriate for these questions.

Using Inoculation as Persuasion

When those without the "right" attitude receive an inoculation treatment message, their attitudes can be influenced in the direction of the treatment message (e.g., Wood, 2007). In other words, an inoculation message can function as a persuasive message. These findings, if supported in the context of political campaigns, could further increase the heuristic value of an inoculation strategy by rendering inoculation relevant not only for those with "right" attitudes, but those with neutral and opposed positions as well. In essence, inoculation could be used as a single strategy to create resistance in individuals who hold the "right" attitude and at the same time persuade those with neutral and opposed positions to move in the "right" attitudinal direction. Consequently, we join Wood (2007) in calling for the testing of this effect in a political context. As inoculation theory does not seem to be context-dependent, we expect that similar findings will be found in a political context.

Post-Inoculation Talk

Inoculation's reach might extend well beyond what we have assumed (Compton & Pfau, 2009; Southwell & Yzer, 2009). Compton and Pfau (2009) laid out a theoretical case, based largely on threat's influence during inoculation, to argue that inoculation treatments motivate people to talk about the focal issue with their friends and family, perhaps spreading inoculation content along social networks. Some empirical evidence supports their claim (e.g., Compton & Pfau, 2004), with the most recent investigation confirming that inoculation motivates talk about the issue, and that this talk strengthens resistance to influence (Ivanov, Miller, et al., 2012). Compton and Pfau (2009) specifically pointed to politics as a context ripe for continuing post-inoculation talk research. Political campaign inoculation research has only skimmed the surface of what may be going on with post-inoculation talk (PIT), or more specifically, political post-inoculation talk (PPIT). Theory suggests that inoculation treatments trigger an active process of counterarguing, and PIT research suggests that some of this counterarguing may be vocal.

Conclusion

The past few decades have been exciting for inoculation scholarship. Inoculation scholarship entered new applied domains in the late 1980s (e.g., Pfau & Burgoon, 1988) and early 1990s, then examined complementary theoretical explorations in the late 1990s (e.g., Pfau, Tusing, et al., 1997). In the 2000s, inoculation entered even more applied contexts (e.g., Compton & Pfau, 2004) and explored more theoretical issues (e.g., Ivanov, Miller, et al., 2012). Although inoculation scholarship in general has been cutting-edge and forward-thinking, political campaign inoculation has received less attention in recent years. This chapter outlined some future directions for political campaign inoculation research to help address this unfortunate dearth in political campaign inoculation scholarship.

It is worth noting again that the developments in inoculation theory from laboratory studies and other applied contexts can and should inform political campaign inoculation scholarship. But it is also worth noting that applied communication research has its unique strengths. It assesses theory in actual situations, with current issues, and among current contextual influences. Field research has the advantage of producing results that "can be generalized more easily than those obtained in laboratory settings" (Malhotra, 2012, p. 233). Additionally, we can extend inoculation scholarship to political campaigning while continuing to explore theoretical and conceptual developments in the theory. Applied research can and should confront theoretical issues, including the areas of humor and narrative.

A few years after Pfau and his colleagues conducted the first empirical investigations of inoculation's efficacy in a political campaign, Pfau and Kenski (1990) noted that "[t]he results of both studies indicate that inoculation is a viable and promising strategy of resistance to the influence of political attack messages" (p. 99). Subsequent findings have confirmed their conclusion. Next, we need to return to the field and examine specific campaign factors that further explore this "viable and promising strategy of resistance" (Pfau & Kenski, 1990, p. 99).

References

Abroms, L. C., & Lefebvre, R. C. (2009). Obama's wired campaign: Lessons for public health communication. *Journal of Health Communication, 14*, 415–423. doi:10.1080/10810730903033000

Allen, M., & Burrell, N. (2002). The negativity effect in political advertising: A meta-analysis. In J. P. Dillard & M. Pfau (Eds.), *The persuasion handbook: Developments in theory and practice* (pp. 83–98). Thousand Oaks, CA: Sage.

An, C., & Pfau, M. (2004). The efficacy of inoculation in televised political debates. *Journal of Communication, 54*(3), 421–436. doi:10.1111/j.1460-2466.2004.tb02637.x

Aristotle. (1960). *Rhetoric.* (L. Cooper, trans.). New York, NY: Appleton-Century-Crofts.

Banas, J. A., & Rains, S. A. (2010). A meta-analysis of research on inoculation theory. *Communication Monographs, 77*(3), 281–311. doi:10.1080/03637751003758193

Banerjee, S. C., & Greene, K. (2007). Antismoking initiatives: Effects of analysis versus production media literacy interventions on smoking-related attitude, norm, and behavioral intention. *Health Communication, 22*, 37–48. doi:10.1080/10410230701310281

Bechwati, N. N., & Siegal, W. S. (2005). The impact of prechoice process on product returns. *Journal of Marketing Research, 42*, 358–367. doi:10.1509/jmkr.2005.42.3.358

Benoit, P. J. (1997). *Telling the success story: Acclaiming and disclaiming discourse.* Albany, NY: State University of New York Press.

Benoit, W. L. (1995). *Accounts, excuses, apologies: A theory of image restoration strategies.* Albany, NY: State University of New York Press.

Benoit, W. L. (1999). *Seeing spots: A functional analysis of presidential television advertisements.* Westport, CT: Praeger.

Benoit, W. L. (2000). Another visit to the theory of image restoration strategies. *Communication Quarterly, 48*(1), 40–44. doi:10.1080/01463370009385578

Bernard, M. M., Maio, G. R., & Olson, J. M. (2003). The vulnerability of values to attack: Inoculation of values and value-relevant attitudes. *Personality and Social Psychology Bulletin, 29*(1), 63–75. doi:10.1177/0146167202238372

Compton, J. A. (2004). *Late night political comedy, candidate image, and inoculation: A unique test of inoculation theory* (doctoral dissertation). University of Oklahoma. Norman.

Compton, J. (2008). More than laughing? Survey of political humor effects research. In J. C. Baumgartner & J. S. Morris (Eds.), *Laughing matters: Humor and American politics in the media age* (pp. 39–63). New York, NY: Routledge.

Compton, J. (2009). Threat explication: What we know and don't yet know about a key component of inoculation theory. *Journal of the Speech and Theatre Association of Missouri, 39*, 1–18.

Compton, J. (2011a). Frustration vaccination? Inoculation theory and digital learning. In S. P. Ferris (Ed.), *Teaching, learning and the net generation: Concepts and tools for reaching digital learners* (pp. 61–73). Hershey, PA: IGI Global.

Compton, J. (2011b). Surveying scholarship on *The Daily Show* and *The Colbert Report.* In A. Amarasingam (Ed.), *The Colbert/Stewart effect: Essays on the real impacts of fake news* (pp. 9–33). Jefferson, NC: McFarland and Company.

Compton, J. (2013). Inoculation theory. In J. P. Dillard & L. Shen (Eds.), *The Sage handbook of persuasion: Developments in theory and practice* (2nd ed., pp. 220–237). Los Angeles, CA: Sage.

Compton, J., & Ivanov, B. (2012). Untangling threat during inoculation-conferred resistance to influence. *Communication Reports, 25*, 1–13. doi:10.1080/08934215.2012.661018

Compton, J. A., & Pfau, M. (2004). Use of inoculation to foster resistance to credit card marketing targeting college students. *Journal of Applied Communication Research, 32*(4), 343–364. doi:10.1080/0090988042000276014

Compton, J., & Pfau, M. (2005). Inoculation theory of resistance to influence at maturity: Recent progress in theory development and application and suggestions for future research. In P. J. Kalbfleisch (Ed.), *Communication Yearbook 29* (pp. 97–146). Mahwah, NJ: Erlbaum.

Compton, J., & Pfau, M. (2009). Spreading inoculation: Inoculation, resistance to influence, and word-of-mouth communication. *Communication Theory, 19*(1), 9–28. doi: 10.1111/j.1468-2885.2008.01330.x

Dal Cin, S., Zanna, M. P., & Fong, G. T. (2004). Narrative persuasion and overcoming resistance. In E. S. Knowles & J. A. Linn (Eds.), *Resistance and persuasion* (pp. 175–191). Mahwah, NJ: Lawrence.

Davis, R. (2009). *Typing politics: The role of blogs in American politics.* New York, NY: Oxford University Press.

Dinauer, L. D., & Fink, E. L. (2006). Interattitude structure and attitude dynamics. *Human Communication Research, 31*(1), 1–32. doi:10.1111/j.1468-2958.2005.tb00863.x

Ehrenhalt, A. (1985, December 22). Like it or not, negative political ads work. *Sunday Start-News*, p. 2E.

Ghoshal, R. (2009). Augment forms, frames, and value conflict: Persuasion in the case of same-sex marriage. *Cultural Sociology, 3*, 76–101. doi:10.1177/1749975508100672

GOP primary revealed few differences on issues [Editorial]. (2012, January, 31). *The Daytona Beach News-Journal*. Retrieved from http://www.news-journalonline.com/opinion/editorials/n-j-editorials/2012/01/31/gop-primary-revealed-few-differences-on-issues.html

Green, M. C., & Brock, T. C. (2000). The role of transportation in the persuasiveness of public narratives. *Journal of Personality and Social Psychology, 79*(5), 701–721. doi:10.1037//0022-3514.79.5.701

Haberman, M. (2012, January 17). Gingrich calls Bain's model "exploitative." *Politico* [Web log message]. Retrieved from http://www.politico.com/blogs/burns-haberman/2012/01/gingrich-calls-bains-model-exploitative-111217.html

Haigh, M. M., & Pfau, M. (2006). Bolstering organizational identity, commitment, and citizenship behaviors through the process of inoculation. *International Journal of Organizational Analysis, 14*(4), 295–316. doi:10.1108/19348830610849718

Haynes, A. A., & Pitts, B. (2009). Making an impression: New media in the 2008 presidential nomination campaigns. *PS: Political Science & Politics, 42*, 53–58. doi:10.1017/S1049096509090052

Holt, L. E. (1970). Resistance to persuasion on explicit beliefs as a function of commitment to and desirability of logically related beliefs. *Journal of Personality and Social Psychology, 16*(4), 583–591. doi:10.1037/h0030060

Holt, L. E., & Watts, W. A. (1969). Salience of logical relationships among beliefs as a factor in persuasion. *Journal of Personality and Social Psychology, 11*, 193–203. doi:10.1037/h0027023

Huber, G. A., & Arceneaux, K. (2007). Identifying the persuasive effects of presidential advertising. *American Journal of Political Science, 51*(4), 961–981. doi:10.1111/j.1540-5907.2007.00291.x

Insko, C. A. (1967). *Theories of attitude change*. New York, NY: Appleton-Century-Crofts.

Ivanov, B. (2011). Designing inoculation messages for health communication campaigns. In H. Cho (Ed.), *Health communication message design: Theory and practice* (pp. 73–93). Thousand Oaks, CA: Sage.

Ivanov, B., Miller, C. H., Compton, J., Averbeck, J. M., Harrison, K. J., Sims, J. D., & Parker, J. L. (2012). Effects of post-inoculation talk on resistance to influence. *Journal of Communication, 62*, 701–718 . doi:10.1111/j.1460-2466.2012.01658.x

Ivanov, B., & Parker, K. A. (2011). Protecting images with inoculation: A look at brand, country, individual, and corporate images. *International Journal of the Image, 1*(1), 1–12.

Ivanov, B., Parker, K. A,, & Compton, J. (2011). The potential of inoculation in reducing post-purchase dissonance: Reinforcement of purchase behavior. *Central Business Review, 30*, 10–16.

Ivanov, B., Parker K. A., Miller, C. H., & Pfau, M. (2012). Culture as a moderator of inoculation success: The effectiveness of a mainstream inoculation message on a subculture population. *The Global Studies Journal, 4*(3), 1–22.

Ivanov, B., Pfau, M., & Parker, K. A. (2009a). Can inoculation withstand multiple attacks?: An examination of the effectiveness of the inoculation strategy compared to the supportive and restoration strategies. *Communication Research, 36*(5), 655–676. doi:10.1177/0093650209338909

Ivanov, B., Pfau, M., & Parker, K. A. (2009b). The potential of inoculation in protecting the country of origin image. *Central Business Review, 28,* 9–16.

Jeffries, L. W. (1986). *Mass media: Processes and effects.* Prospect Heights, IL: Waveland.

Kim, K., Moon, S., & Feeley, T. H. (2011, May). *Transportation lowers resistance to narrative persuasion messages: Testing three explanations.* Paper presented at the annual meeting of the International Communication Association, Boston, MA.

King, N., & Yadron, D. (2012, January 10). Rivals attack Romney on Bain: Debate sparked within GOP over free enterprise; Romney defends his record. *The Wall Street Journal.* Retrieved from http://online.wsj.com/article/SB1000142405297020 3436904577151211420780338.html

Lau, R. R., Sigelman, L., & Rovner, I. B. (2009). The effects of negative political campaigns: A meta-analytic reassessment. *The Journal of Politics, 69*(4), 1176–1209. doi:10.1111/j.1468-2508.2007.00618.x

Leno, J., Medeiros, J., & Vickers, D. (2009, March 19). *The Tonight Show with Jay Leno* [Television series]. Episode No. 17.50. Hollywood: NBC.

Lewis, K. (1995, July 5). Clinton tries to claim political center. *Ocala-Star Banner,* p. 11A.

Lewis, W. F. (1987). Telling America's story: Narrative form and the Reagan presidency. *Quarterly Journal of Speech, 73*(3), 280–302. doi:10.1080/00335638709383809

Lim, J. S., & Ki, E.-J. (2007). Resistance to ethically suspicious parody video on YouTube: A test of inoculation theory. *Journalism and Mass Communication Quarterly, 84*(4), 713–728.

Lin, W.-K. (2005). Inoculation to resist attacks. *Asian Journal of Communication, 15*(1), 85–103. doi:10.1080/0129298042000329810

Lin, W.-K., & Pfau, M. (2007). Can inoculation work against the spiral of silence? A study of public opinion on the future of Taiwan. *International Journal of Public Opinion Research, 19*(2), 155–172. doi:10.1093/ijpor/edl030

Lumsdaine, A. A., & Janis, I. L. (1953). Resistance to "counterpropaganda" produced by one-sided and two-sided "propaganda" presentations. *Public Opinion Quarterly, 17*(3), 311–318. doi:10.1086/266464

Malhotra, N. K. (2012). *Basic marketing research: Integration of social media* (4th ed.). Upper Saddle River, NJ: Pearson.

Mazzocco, P. J., Green, M. C., Sasota, J. A., & Jones, N. W. (2010). This story is not for everyone: Transportability and narrative persuasion. *Social Psychological and Personality Science, 1*(4), 361–368. doi:10.1177/1948550610376600

McGuire, W. J. (1961). Resistance to persuasion conferred by active and passive prior refutation of the same and alternative counterarguments. *Journal of Abnormal and Social Psychology, 63*(2), 326–332. doi:10.1037/h0048344

McGuire, W. J. (1964). Inducing resistance to persuasion: Some contemporary approaches. In L. Berkowitz (Ed.), *Advances in experimental social psychology* (Vol. 1, pp. 191–229). New York, NY: Academic Press.

McGuire, W. J., & Papageorgis, D. (1962). Effectiveness of forewarning in developing resistance to persuasion. *Public Opinion Quarterly, 26*(1), 24–34. doi:10.1086/267068

Miller, C. H., Ivanov, B., Sims, J. D., Compton, J., Harrison, K. J., Parker, K. A. ... Parker, J. L. (2013). Boosting the potency of resistance: Combining the motivational forces of inoculation and psychological reactance. *Human Communication Research*, 39, 127–155.

Nabi, R. (2003). "Feeling" resistance: Exploring the role of emotionally evocative visuals in inducing inoculation. *Media Psychology, 5*(2), 199–223. doi:10.1207/S1532785XMEP0502_4

Nelson, C. E. (1968). Anchoring to accepted values as a technique for immunizing beliefs against persuasion. *Journal of Personality and Social Psychology, 9*, 329–334. doi:10.1037/h0021255

Newman, B., & Perloff, R. (2004). Political marketing: Theory, research, and applications. In L. Kaid (Ed.), *Handbook of political communication research* (pp. 17–34). Mahwah, NJ: Erlbaum.

Noelle-Neumann, E. (1984). *The spiral of silence*. Chicago, IL: University of Chicago Press.

Parker, K. A., Ivanov, B., & Compton, J. (2012). Inoculation's efficacy with young adults' risky behaviors: Can inoculation confer cross-protection over related but untreated issues? *Health Communication, 27*, 223–233. doi:10.1080/10410236.2011.575541

Peoples, S. (2012, February 7). Mitt Romney intensifies fight for social conservatives. *The Huffington Post*. Retreived from http://www.huffingtonpost.com/2012/02/07/mitt-romney-social-conservatives_n_1261283.html

Perloff, R. P. (2010). *The dynamics of persuasion: Communication and attitudes in the 21st century* (4th ed.). New York, NY: Routledge.

Pfau, M., Banas, J., Semmler, S. M., Deatrick, L., Lane, L., Mason, A. ... Underhill, J. (2010). Role and impact of involvement and enhanced threat in resistance. *Communication Quarterly, 58*(1), 1–18. doi:10.1080/01463370903520307

Pfau, M., & Burgoon, M. (1988). Inoculation in political campaign communication. *Human Communication Research, 15*(1), 91–111. doi:10.1111/j.1468-2958.1988.tb00172.x

Pfau, M., & Burgoon, M. (1990). Inoculation in political campaigns and gender. *Women's Studies in Communication, 13*(1), 1–16.

Pfau, M., Compton, J., Parker, K. A., An, C., Wittenberg, E. M., Ferguson, M. ... Malyshev, Y. (2004). The traditional explanation for resistance versus attitude accessibility: Do they trigger distinct or overlapping processes of resistance? *Human Communication Research, 30*(3), 329–360. doi:10.1111/j.1468-2958.2004.tb00735.x

Pfau, M., Compton, J., Parker, K. A., An, C., Wittenberg, E. M., Ferguson, M. ... Malyshev, Y. (2006). The conundrum of the timing of counterarguing effects in resistance: Strategies to boost the persistence of counterarguing output. *Communication Quarterly, 54*(2), 143–156. doi:10.1080/01463370600650845

Pfau, M., Diedrich, T., Larson, K. M., & Van Winkle, K. M. (1993). Relational and competence perceptions of presidential candidates during primary election campaigns. *Journal of Broadcasting & Electronic Media, 37*(3), 275–292. doi:10.1080/08838159309364222

Pfau, M., Haigh, M., Fifrick, A., Holl, D., Tedesco, A., Cope, J., ... Martin, M. (2006). The effects of print news photographs of the casualties of war. *Journalism and Mass Communication Quarterly, 83*(1), 150–168. doi:10.1177/107769900608300110

Pfau, M., Haigh, M. M., Shannon, T., Tones, T., Mercurio, D., Williams, R., ... Melendez, J. (2008). The influence of television news depictions of the images of war on viewers. *Journal of Broadcasting & Electronic Media, 52*(2), 303–322. doi:10.1080/08838150801992128

Pfau, M., Ivanov, B., Houston, B., Haigh, M., Sims, J., Gilchrist, E., ... Richert, N. (2005). Inoculation and mental processing: The instrumental role of associative networks in the process of resistance to counterattitudinal influence. *Communication Monographs, 72*(4), 414–441. doi:10.1080/03637750500322578

Pfau, M., & Kenski, H. C. (1990). *Attack politics: Strategy and defense.* New York, NY: Praeger.

Pfau, M., Kenski, H. C., Nitz, M., & Sorenson, J. (1990). Efficacy of inoculation strategies in promoting resistance to political attack messages: Application to direct mail. *Communication Monographs, 57*(1), 25–43. doi:10.1080/03637759009376183

Pfau, M., Park, D., Holbert, R. L., & Cho, J. (2001). The effects of party- and PAC-sponsored issue advertising and the potential of inoculation to combat its impact on the democratic process. *American Behavioral Scientist, 44*(12), 2379–2397. doi:10.1177/00027640121958384

Pfau, M., Semmler, S. M., Deatrick, L., Mason, A., Nisbett, G., Lane, L., ... Banas, J. (2009). Nuances about the role and impact of affect in inoculation. *Communication Monographs, 76*(1), 73–98. doi:10.1080/03637750802378807

Pfau, M., Szabo, E. A., Anderson, J., Morrill, J., Zubric, J., & Wan, H. (2001). The role and impact of affect in the process of resistance to persuasion. *Human Communication Research, 27*(2), 216–252. doi:10.1111/j.1468-2958.2001.tb00781.x

Pfau, M., Tusing, K. J., Lee, W., Godbold, L. C., Koerner, A., Penaloza, L. J., ... Yang, V. S. (1997). Nuances in inoculation: The role of inoculation approach, ego-involvement, and message processing disposition in resistance. *Communication Quarterly, 45*(4), 461–481. doi:10.1080/01463379709370077

Pfau, M., & Van Bockern, S. (1994). The persistence of inoculation in conferring resistance to smoking initiation among adolescents: The second year. *Human Communication Research, 20*(3), 413–430. doi:10.1111/j.1468-2958.1994.tb00329.x

Pfau, M., & Wan, H.-H. (2006). Persuasion: An intrinsic function of public relations. In C. H. Botan & V. Hazleton (Eds.), *Public relations theory II* (pp. 88–119). Mahwah, NJ: Erlbaum.

Romero, D. M., Meeder, B., & Kleinberg, J. (2011). Differences in the mechanics of information diffusion across topics: Idioms, political hashtags, and complex contagion on Twitter. *Proceedings of the 20th international conference on World Wide Web* (WWW '11) (pp. 695–704). New York: AMC.

Schultheis, E. (2012, January 17). Romney ad preempts Bain attacks in Florida. *Politico* [Web log message]. Retrieved from http://www.politico.com/blogs/burns-haberman/2012/01/romney-ad-preempts-bain-attacks-in-florida-111137.html

Shepard, A. C. (2000, December 1). A late-breaking campaign skeleton (Bush's DUI arrest). *American Journalism Review.* Retrieved from http://www.ajr.org/Article.asp?id=218

Slater, M. D. (2002). Entertainment education and the persuasive impact of narratives. In M. C. Green, J. J. Strange, & T. C. Brock (Eds.), *Narrative impact: Social and cognitive foundations* (pp. 157–181). Mahwah, NJ: Erlbaum.

Southwell, B. G., & Yzer, M. C. (2009). When (and why) interpersonal talk matters for campaigns. *Communication Theory, 19*, 1–8. doi:10.1111/j.1468-2885.2008.01329.x

Stiff, J. B., & Mongeau, P. A. (2003). *Persuasive communication* (2nd ed.). New York, NY: Guilford.

Sutton, C. H. (2011). *Inoculating against jealousy: Attempting to preemptively reduce the jealousy experience and improve jealousy expression* (master's thesis). University of Georgia, Athens.

Szabo, E. A., & Pfau, M. (2002). Nuances in inoculation: Theory and applications. In J. P. Dillard & M. Pfau (Eds.), *The persuasion handbook: Theory and practice* (pp. 233–258). Thousand Oaks, CA: Sage.

Trammell, K. D. (2006). Blog offensive: An exploratory analysis of attacks published on campaign blog posts from a political public relations perspective. *Public Relations Review, 32*(4), 402–406. doi:10.1016/j.pubrev.2006.09.008

Trent, J. S., Friedenberg, R. V., & Denton, R. E. (2011). *Political campaign communication: Principles and practices* (7th ed.). New York, NY: Rowman & Littlefield.

Wan, H. H., & Pfau, M. (2004). The relative effectiveness of inoculation, bolstering, and combined approaches in crisis communication. *Journal of Public Relations Research, 16*(3), 301–328.

Watts, W. A., & Holt, L. E. (1970). Logical relationships among beliefs and timing as factors in persuasion. *Journal of Personality and Social Psychology, 16*(4), 571–582. doi: 10.1037/h0030063

Weinberger, J., & Westen, D. (2008). RATS, we should have used Clinton: Subliminal priming in political campaigns. *Political Psychology, 29*(5), 631–651. doi:10.1111/j.1467-9221.2008.00658.x

Wicks, R. H., Bradley, A., Blackburn, G., & Fields, T. (2011). Tracking the blogs: An evaluation of attacks, acclaims, and rebuttals presented on political blogs during the 2008 presidential election. *American Behavioral Scientist, 55*(6), 651–666. doi:10.1177/0002764211398085

Wigley, S., & Pfau, M. (2010). Communicating before a crisis: An exploration of bolstering, CSR and inoculation practices. In W. T. Coombs & S. J. Halladay (Eds.), *The handbook of crisis communication* (pp. 568–590). Oxford, England: Wiley-Blackwell.

Wlezien, C., & Erikson, R. S. (2002). The timeline of presidential election campaigns. *The Journal of Politics, 64*(4), 969–993. doi:10.1111/1468-2508.00159

Wood, M. L. M. (2007). Rethinking the inoculation analogy: Effects on subjects with differing preexisting attitudes. *Human Communication Research, 33*(3), 357–378. doi:10.1111/j.1468-2958.2007.00303.x

Zhou, L., & Hovy, E. (2006, March). *On the summarization of dynamically introduced information: Online discussions and blogs.* Paper presented at the AAAI Symposium on Computational Approaches to Analysing Weblogs (AAAI-CAAW), Stanford, CA.

Part IV

Reviewing Trends

Scholarship Evaluating Media
Engagement and Exposure Effects

CHAPTER CONTENTS

10 The Effects of Engagement with Entertainment

Riva Tukachinsky

Chapman University

Robert S. Tokunaga

University of Hawai'i at Mānoa

A meta-analysis was employed to evaluate the state of research on the persuasion effects of involvement with entertainment media. The study investigates the effect of homophily, empathic identification, parasocial relationships, and transportation with entertainment media on attitudinal, behavioral and knowledge-related outcomes. The study identifies the specific conditions under which the effects vary. Results from the meta-analysis suggest that media involvement is moderately associated ($r = .27$) with persuasive outcomes. The content of the entertainment message (e.g., health, political), controlling for other study artifacts, significantly moderated the effect of involvement on outcomes. Directions for future research and theory development are suggested.

Popular forms of entertainment media, including novels, movies, soap operas, and television programs, can influence audience's beliefs, knowledge systems, attitudes, and behaviors (Moyer-Gusé, 2008). Such effects can be unintentional if, for example, a message inadvertently promotes risky sexual behaviors and sex role stereotypes. Some media producers and researchers, however, use media's persuasive potential by developing entertainment-education messages that promote healthy behaviors and reinforce prosocial outcomes. For instance, radio soap opera programs aired in South Africa, India, and South America have brought awareness to HIV/AIDS, encouraged adult education, promoted family planning practices, and delegitimized domestic violence (Papa et al., 2000; Singhal & Rogers, 1999). In the United States, non-profit organizations, such as Hollywood, Health & Society, educate media professionals on socially responsible ways to portray health-related issues in storylines of television shows.

In response to the efficacy of entertainment media to produce both socially desirable and undesirable effects on viewers, exploration of the mechanisms underlying narrative persuasion and education entertainment became a growing area of inquiry in mass communication studies. Social cognitive theory (SCT; Bandura, 2001) and theories of narrative persuasion (Moyer-Gusé, 2008; Slater & Rouner, 2002) together suggest that viewers' involvement with narratives and characters plays a key role in motivating these outcomes. Despite being firmly grounded in theory, mixed findings and inconsistent approaches in studying the effects of entertainment media have obscured the relationship between involvement with entertainment media and attitudes, knowledge, and behaviors.

The present study uses meta-analytical procedures to aggregate and synthesize findings from 20 years of research on entertainment media. The principal goal of this project is to determine the cumulative effects of involvement on persuasion outcomes across the body of literature on entertainment media in hopes of bringing clarity to the research. This synthesis may reveal conditions under which the effects of involvement with entertainment media vary. This general objective is particularly important given the large diversity of research on entertainment-education and narrative persuasion in terms of the samples used, media stimuli employed, operationalization of involvement variables, and outcome types (knowledge, attitudes, and overt behaviors) examined.

The contribution of the meta-analytical approach to studying the effects of involvement with entertainment media on outcomes extends well beyond the scope of each individual study. Not only can the cumulative effect of involvement on persuasion outcomes be determined, but this investigation can parse the effects of specific involvement types on persuasion outcomes. Because most involvement studies are rooted in a single theoretical paradigm, they incorporate only one or two involvement variables in their investigation, making direct comparisons between the different modes of involvement impossible. These comparisons, however, can be valuable in understanding the similarities and differences between involvement types and evaluating the assumptions different theories make in discussing the importance of one involvement type or another. This meta-analysis can overcome the narrow focus of previous studies by comparing the effects of several theoretically-derived variables of involvement on persuasion outcomes.

Modes of Involvement with Entertainment Media

The term *involvement* is used to describe remarkably different aspects of media consumption (Wirth, 2006). Involvement has been defined as a set of dispositions toward the media message such that message relevancy and importance are thought to increase the audience's involvement (Johnson & Eagly, 1989; Sherif & Hovland, 1961; Todorov, Chaiken, & Henderson, 2002). Others define involvement as the amount of mental effort a given message demands. Media stimuli can thus be ordered by level of involvement to the extent that television would be considered less involving than print (Salomon, 1984). Involvement in this study refers to the property of message processing that occurs through engagement with the narratives and characters (Moyer-Gusé, 2008; Slater & Rouner, 2002).

In this chapter we investigate the effects of four specific types of involvement with entertainment media: homophily with characters, empathic responses to characters, transportation in narratives, and parasocial interactions and relationships with characters (PSI/PSR). These four variables were selected because they are of major theoretical interest across a number of different perspectives and widely studied in the communication discipline. Although other involvement variables (liking, wishful identification) have been identified in the media involvement literature, the relationships between these variables and persuasion outcomes have not received similar attention from researchers.

Homophily

Homophily is a subjective perception of similarity between oneself and another. In the context of media consumption, audience members see themselves as similar to a media persona (Eyal & Rubin, 2003). Homophily can occur in a specific domain (a trait such as aggression) or may be perceived across multiple dimensions (overall similarity in personality). This type of involvement relies on a process of social comparison; media consumers compare their *actual* self-concept (who viewers think they are) to the perceived attributes of the character and evaluate levels of correspondence. Homophily is conceptually distinct from other forms of social comparison, such as wishful identification where individuals compare characters to their ideal self-concept (Cohen, 2001). According to SCT (Bandura, 2004), homophily with characters can increase self-efficacy and change outcome expectations of the behavior embedded in the entertainment media, which, in turn, influences persuasion outcomes. Perceived similarity to a character can also increase perceptions of vulnerability to a threat presented in the message.

Parasocial Relationships (PSR)

Viewers may engage in parasocial or quasi-social, one-direction interactions (PSI) with media personae (Horton & Wohl, 1956). In parasocial interactions, viewers experience friendliness and companionship with television characters (Levy, 1979; Rubin, Perse, & Powell, 1985). PSR can exist across multiple media encounters and continue outside the media exposure context (Klimmt, Hartmann, & Schramm, 2006). PSR are largely based on the same mental models that organize and manage real-life interpersonal relationships (Tukachinsky, 2011). Some viewers may even experience a sense of loss when a character they formed PSR with goes off air (Eyal & Cohen, 2006). Preexisting PSR increase attention to messages featuring the character with which the relationship is formed (Klimmt et al., 2006) and facilitate cognitive responses to and post-viewing discussion of the message (Papa et al., 2000; Rubin & Perse, 1988).

Empathic Identification

In this study, empathy is conceptualized as a state response to media characters rather than an enduring trait. Empathic responses are comprised of two major components: cognition and affect (Davis, Hull, Young, & Warren, 1987). The cognitive part of empathy relies on theory of mind (ToM). ToM entails recognition of other people's mental states, understanding others' concerns or intentions, and adopting others' perspectives (Blakemore & Decety, 2001; Carruthers & Smith, 1996). The affective component of empathy involves the observer's co-experience of others' emotional states. Although the cognitive and affective components of empathy are theorized as independent processes that rely on distinct neural circuits (Davis et al., 1987; Shamay-Tsoory, Aharon-Peretz, & Perry, 2009), it appears that the processes are deeply intertwined in most circumstances (Langdon, Coltheart, & Ward, 2006).

The simulation theory of empathy explains that cognitive perspective-taking is an important precursor of emotional empathy. Making inference about another's internal state allows the perceiver to represent mentally the emotional responses of others. The perceiver simulates possible alternate selves and imagines being in the position of the other. In the context of media, audience members may temporarily suspend their self-concept and "become the character," sharing the character's emotional states and understanding the events from the character's perspective (Cohen, 2006). Empathy for media characters thus involves the mental simulation of a character's state and a link between one's self-concept and the self-concept of the character.

Transportation

Transportation refers to absorption in narratives to the extent that all mental systems become fixed on the narrative (Green & Brock, 2002). Transportation differs from the involvement types previously discussed because it focuses on involvement with the narrative rather than with characters. When experiencing transportation, media consumers immerse themselves in a storyline and temporarily forget about the actual world. This process involves a shift in attention from the physical environment to the narrative and the experience of narrative-consistent mental imagery. Transportation intensity can be moderated by various factors, such as narrative quality (Green & Brock, 2002), individual differences (Dal Cin, 2005), personal relevance, and prior knowledge (Green, 2004).

Involvement with Entertainment and Media Effects

Several theoretical perspectives explain the different pathways through which involvement with entertainment media can catalyze effects of entertainment media on knowledge acquisition, attitudes, and behaviors.

Observational Learning

SCT suggests that involvement, mainly in the form of empathy, PSR, and homophily, is likely to increase viewers' attention to the behaviors modeled by the characters. The attention to and retention of behaviors elicited by characters in the narrative facilitate observational learning (Bandura, 2004; Brown & Fraser, 2004). Linking the character to one's self-concept (homophily) can facilitate self-efficacy and increase the chances of reenacting the learned behavior.

Counterarguing

Media involvement can produce persuasion by facilitating the generation of message-consistent thoughts and making it difficult to engage in counterarguing. The extended elaboration likelihood model (Slater & Rouner, 2002) explains that individuals become immersed in entertainment media with the intention of having uninterrupted enjoyment and suspension of disbelief. Counterarguing with the message is therefore incompatible with this goal, making individuals less likely to engage in counterargument with persuasive messages. While immersed in story narratives, readers are less likely to note errors and counterfactual details in the story even when explicitly instructed to do so (Green & Brock, 2000; Marsh & Fazio, 2006). Message recipients temporarily suspend their real-life knowledge, compromising their ability to develop counterarguments to a message (Green & Brock, 2000). Involvement types, such as transportation, make individuals less critical of the message and more susceptible to persuasion.

Social Influence and Heuristic Processing

Attraction to and liking of a message source is used as a heuristic that increases audiences' persuasion and compliance (Tedeschi, Schlenker, & Lindskold, 1972/2009). Involvement with characters portrayed in narratives can increase liking of and attraction to the character, which can affect persuasion outcomes of the message. PSR with media figures, for example, can reduce the possibility of viewers experiencing reactance to persuasive messages by eliminating potential perceptions of freedom limitations (Moyer-Gusé, 2008). PSR create hospitable environments for compliance because parasocial engagement strengthens the view that the message source, the character, is credible (Rubin & Step, 2000).

Parasocial Contact

Involvement in the form of empathic identification and PSR can influence outcomes by reducing stereotypes toward out-group members. According to the contact hypothesis, intergroup stereotypes are lessened by having direct positive relationships with a typical out-group member (Pettigrew, 1998). The formation of PSR or empathizing with a media character from an out-group can improve the perceptions of the out-group as a whole (Schiappa, Gregg, & Hewes, 2005). Even observing in-group characters engaged in a positive relationship with an out-group character promotes intergroup relationships by modeling the actions of the in-group characters (Ortiz & Harwood, 2007).

Mental Imagery

Mental imagery is an important constituent of empathic identification and transportation that can foster emotional responses to the persuasive message. Vividness and emotions help to encode, retain, and reactivate learned information, increasing the likelihood of persuasion (Taylor & Thompson, 1982). Mental imagery through specific modes of involvement with entertainment media, such as empathic identification and transportation, therefore increases learning and persuasion.

Theories of narrative persuasion, learning, and cognitive processing provide five theoretically compelling reasons why involvement with entertainment media influences attitudes, knowledge, and behaviors. They discuss how involvement improves the likelihood of persuasion through increased attention, emotional responses, liking of and attraction to characters and the narrative, and decreased stereotyping and counterarguing behaviors. Given the strong foundation for the relationship between involvement with entertainment media and outcomes across a wide range of persuasion theories, the following hypothesis is posited:

> **H1**: Involvement with entertainment media is positively related to post-exposure message-consistent attitudes, knowledge, and behaviors.

Similarities and Differences Between Types of Involvement

The four involvement types are driven by at least one of the following four mental processes: allocation of attention to the message, generation of issue-relevant thoughts (elaboration), elicitation of emotional reactions, and development of links between the message and one's self-concept (MacInnis & Jaworski, 1989; Perse, 1990; Wirth, 2006; Zillmann, 1994). Table 10.1 presents the definition of each mental process and articulates how they contribute to media effects. Dual-processing models of persuasion, for instance, suggest that generating message-consistent cognitions reduces counterarguing and enhances persuasion (ELM; Petty & Cacioppo, 1986). Also, relating a message to one's self-concept by noting similarities between oneself and the character may increase social learning of the modeled behaviors (Bandura, 2001).

Similarities and differences in the mental processes (attention, generation of cognitions) underlying media involvement can help to discriminate among the four involvement types (homophily, empathic identification, PSR, transportation). As illustrated in Table 10.1, a given mode of involvement can encompass more than a single mental process resulting in partial overlap of the involvement types. For instance, transportation involves three mental processes: attention allocation, generation of message-related emotions, and message-related

Table 10.1 Mental Processes Comprising Involvement in the Context of Entertainment Media and Effects

Mental process	Involvement modes that incorporate the process	Theoretical link between mental processes and media effects
Increased attention allocation	• Transportation, Empathy, PSR, Homophily	• Increased learning through attention (SCT)
Generation of message-relevant cognitions (mental imagery and mental simulation of events and mental simulation of the characters' inner world)	• Transportation • Empathy	• Reduced counterarguing (ELM, extended ELM) • Mental simulation as preparation for behavior (retention and production stages of learning, SCT)
Generation of emotional responses to events and/or characters	• Transportation • Empathy • PSR (to a lesser degree)	• Increasing learning (SCT, attention stage) • Increasing liking (heuristic persuasion)
Linking the message to one's self concept through social comparison, self-concept suspension, or perspective taking	• Empathic responses • Homophily	• Reducing counter-arguing (ELM) • Increasing learning (SCT, attention stage)

cognitions. Empathic identification overlaps with transportation in relation to message-related emotions and cognitions but differs from transportation in the link that created between the message and one's self-concept.

Homophily and empathic identification both involve a link between one's self-concept and the media character. Yet, homophily differs from empathic identification in that homophily involves a comparison between oneself and the character, requiring viewers to see themselves as autonomous entities from the character. Empathic identification, in contrast, involves a process of merging between the viewer's and character's identities to the point where viewers temporarily lose their self-concept and "become" the character (Cohen, 2001). Given the role of perspective-taking in empathic responses, homophily may exacerbate empathic responses of media consumers by stressing similarities between them and the character.

Empathic identification differs from PSR in that viewers see characters as friends in PSR but maintain their distinct self-concept (Cohen, 2001; Giles, 2002). Viewers "become" the character in empathic identification. Transportation can be discriminated from PSR in that transportation requires immersion in the narrative to the extent that viewers forget about the mediated context of their experience. Immersion or absorption are not only unnecessary for PSR, but in fact, some factors can increase PSR while at the same time inhibit transportation. One such example is breaking the "fourth wall," which occurs when an actor directly addresses the viewer by talking to the camera. This practice increases PSR because characters interact directly with their audience, promoting the illusion of a friendly exchange between viewers and characters (Auter, 1992). However, breaking the fourth wall is an impediment to transportation and empathic identification because it interrupts the suspension of disbelief by highlighting the line between the media world and the real world (Cohen, 2006).

Transportation and empathic identification are related such that consumers perceive media events and characters as genuine. From absorption in the narrative, viewers develop a better ToM of characters, understand character's inner states, simulate character's emotions, and enact emotional responses. Empathy for characters also transports viewers into the fictional world and enhances their vicarious experience of the narrative's events. Although transportation and empathy are related experiences, it has been argued that they can occur independently (Tal-Or & Cohen, 2010). Viewers can empathize with characters and share perspectives without losing their sense of the physical world. Alternatively, viewers can become absorbed in the narrative without merging their self-concept with the character. These viewers, while transported, may not empathize with any particular character and experience the narrative from their own perspective (Oatley, 1994, 1999). In fact, some story-related facts are often known to the viewer but not to the character. Media consumers may therefore be transported but unable to share the character's perspective (Zillmann, 1994).

Given the distinguishable mental processes that impel the four involvement types described in various theories, homophily, PSR, empathy, and transportation may have differential impact on persuasion outcomes.

>**RQ1**: Are there significant differences in the relationships between persuasion outcomes and homophily, PSR, empathic identification, and transportation?

Type of Outcome

Knowledge acquisition and changes in attitudes and behaviors are the primary outcomes addressed in narrative persuasion and entertainment-education research. There is some reason to think that the media effects of involvement with entertainment media are not uniform across these outcome types. Factual learning, or the process of gaining information about the world, attitudes, and cultural norms (Eisenberg, 1936), can be accomplished with even modest levels of involvement with narratives and characters. This type of learning can occur from mere exposure to entertainment media and is not contingent on becoming involved with characters or narratives, so the relationship between involvement and knowledge acquisition is expected to be relatively weak. Attitudes and behaviors, in contrast, are more persistent and difficult to change. Therefore, changes in attitudes and behaviors require character or narrative involvement to elicit detectable change. Thus, the following hypothesis was developed:

H2: Involvement with entertainment media has a greater effect on attitude and behavioral outcomes than knowledge outcomes.

Contextual Moderators of Involvement

Over the past 20 years, research has examined media involvement in a wide variety of contexts ranging from the impact of short stories on college students' beliefs about gays (Green, 2004) to the impact of soap-opera exposure on Hispanic women's awareness of cancer screening (Murphy, Hether, de Castro Buffington, Baezconde-Garbinati, & Frank, 2011). Another goal of this meta-analysis is to investigate whether the effects of involvement with entertainment media are consistent across wide range of contexts in which media involvement is studied, or whether certain conditions enhance or reduce the effects of involvement on post-exposure outcomes. Several characteristics of studies may moderate the effect size of these relationships. The moderators investigated in this project include the type of sample, operationalization of exposure, type of stimuli, and research topics.

Audience

Many studies that test media involvement theories are conducted on convenience samples of college students. Student samples tend to be relatively homogeneous in social economic status, educational level, and age. Narrative persuasion and education-entertainment learning theories (Bandura, 2004; Moyer-Gusé, 2008) do not explicitly address individual differences of audience members as moderators of the effects of involvement with entertainment media. Although theories of involvement specify conditions under which different individuals may become involved with certain entertainment content (message relevance; Cohen & Ribak, 2003; Green, 2004), these theories only discuss the precursors of involvement, not its outcomes. Theory does not inform predications about whether differences exist in the effects of involvement with entertainment media on post-exposure outcomes between students and non-student populations.

Operationalization of Exposure and Study-Design

There may be theoretical reasons to believe that type of exposure (single exposure, long-term exposure) influences the relationship between involvement and outcomes. Arguments can be made to explain why single exposure or long-term exposures increase effect sizes. Single-exposure experimental studies conducted in a controlled laboratory setting can improve internal validity and eliminate confounding variables, thereby making it more likely to detect stronger correlations between involvement and outcomes. Repeated exposure to narratives, in contrast, promotes greater modeling effects than single-media exposure. However, long-term exposure studies typically employ surveys and

quasi-experimental designs making them more susceptible to external con-
founders than single-exposure experimental studies. This can attenuate the
effects between involvement and outcomes.

Types of Stimuli

Questions persist about whether written narratives or audiovisual stimuli, such
as television and film, more effectively transport viewers into the narrative
world (Green & Brock, 2002). One line of reasoning asserts that written narratives may be more engaging because reading a narrative is a self-paced activity
that requires considerable attention and self-projection. Attention and imagi-
nation dedicated to reading may increase the relationship between involvement
and post-exposure outcomes. The competing claim is that audiovisual media
provide audiences with greater sensory stimulation, making mental simulation
more likely to occur and therefore potentially intensifying media effects.

Topic

Theories of narrative persuasion, learning, and cognitive processing rarely,
if ever, discuss the relative influence of exposure to entertainment messages
due to different content areas (health topics, political and social issues). The
content of the persuasion message, however, may influence the relationship
between involvement and outcomes; yet, not enough information is available
to make a sound hypothesis. In the absence of a sound theoretical rationale
for a directional hypothesis and the exploratory nature of this objective of the
meta-analysis, the following research question is posed:

> **RQ2**: Do audience characteristics (students/non-students), study design
> and exposure operationalization (single lab/repeated exposure), stimuli
> used (written/audiovisual), and content areas (health/social and political)
> moderate the relationship between involvement and persuasion outcomes
> (attitudes, knowledge, behavior)?

Methods

Selection of Studies

Literature Search.   Studies used in the meta-analyses were obtained in two
ways. First, relevant electronic databases (Medline, PsychLIT/Psych Abstracts,
Social Sciences Citation Index, Communication and Mass Media Complete,
and ProQuest) were searched. The search located journal publications,
master's theses, and doctoral dissertations from a wide range of disciplines and
conference papers from the communication discipline. The following terms
(including stems and their derivations, noted by an *) were used to perform

the search: education entertainment, edutainment, and combinations of the terms: absorption, affinity, attraction, empathic identification, engagement, homophily, involvement, identification, modeling, narrative, transportation, parasocial relation*, parasocial interact*, perceived similarity, perspective taking, The aforementioned terms were combined with the terms attitude, character, entertainment, media effect*, and persuasion. Second, review articles (Moyer-Gusé, 2008), book chapters (Cohen, 2006), and literature reviews of relevant empirical studies were consulted for additional references.

Inclusion Criteria.   To be included in the meta-analysis, a study had to meet the following criteria. First, each study had to report a quantitative relationship between homophily, transportation, PSR/PSI, or empathic identification with at least one behavior, behavioral intention, attitude, or knowledge-gain outcome variable. As the purpose of the meta-analysis was to examine effects of involvement on outcomes, studies that did not assess the relationship between involvement types and knowledge, attitudes, and behaviors were not included in the analysis. Three types of studies did not fit this criterion: studies examining precursors of involvement (effect of attachment style and sex on PSI intensity; Cohen, 1999), studies reporting validity and reliability of scales without correlating the scales with outcomes (e.g., Andersen & de Mancillas, 1978), and studies evaluating the effect of an involvement type on other media experience variables rather than attitudes, knowledge and behaviors (e.g., perceived realism; Bilandzic & Busselle, 2011). Moreover, studies that did not employ quantitative measures of involvement and outcomes but instead used unstructured interviews or qualitative analyses of audience's responses were not included in the analysis (e.g., Papa et al., 2000).

Second, the study must have used as its stimulus spectator entertainment media, not media campaigns or video games. Spectator entertainment media include film, television, and literary works (short stories). Because information in entertainment television programming, films, and novels are argued to be processed similarly (Cohen, 2006; Mar, Tackett, & Moore, 2010), studies using these varied stimuli can be included in a single meta-analysis. Non-spectator media (video games) require different types of involvement (interactivity) where message recipients have more control over the type of content viewed than spectator entertainment media (Chaffee & Metzger, 2001). Non-spectator entertainment media falls outside the scope of the present meta-analysis because involvement and information processing happen through theoretically different modes.

Finally, several publications that met the scope criteria outlined above were excluded from the meta-analysis due to measurement incompatibility. Fifteen studies were not included because their measures of involvement or outcomes did not correspond to the involvement variables of interest (transportation, empathic identification, homophily, PSR), or the way constructs were operationalized made it impossible to code them (e.g., Morgan, Movius, & Cody, 2009; Ward, 2004). Cases were also removed if the items they used in the study assessed self-reported media effects (e.g., agreement with a statement, "I made changes in my behavior *because of the program*"). Lastly, three studies were excluded because they examined PSR with media personae were depicted in varied media settings with whom individuals were able to create relationships (e.g., a baseball player and spokesperson; Brown, Basil, & Bocarnea, 2003).

On the basis of the inclusion criteria, 40 publications that reported findings from studies on 50 independent samples were initially considered for the meta-analysis. Twenty-four of the 40 studies did not report information in ways that allowed for the computation of compatible effect sizes. For these cases, corresponding authors were sent a request to provide the missing information. Two-thirds of the authors contacted provided correlation matrices of the missing data. In two instances, missing information in a journal publication was obtained from an earlier dissertation or conference paper in which data were reported more exhaustively. Consequently, 35 research reports that documented results of 45 separate studies were included in the meta-analysis. The total sample size of the studies was 9,836. Table 10.2 presents the summary characteristics of these studies.

Coding of Studies

The studies were coded several ways to address the hypotheses and research questions of this project. The meta-analysis summarized (a) the relationship between overall media involvement and overall outcomes, (b) the relationship between individual involvement types and overall outcomes, and (c) the relationship between overall involvement and independent outcome types. Some studies could be coded for multiple involvement types and/or outcomes. Effect sizes were coded and averaged to appropriately test the hypotheses and RQ1. Additionally, study characteristics, including sample, topic of message, type of stimulus, and information about the research design, were coded for the moderator tests addressed in RQ2.

Operationalization of Involvement Modes.   Coding each study of involvement in a specific involvement type relied on the strict definitions presented in the literature review. To review, homophily was defined as a subjective perception of similarity between the audience member and the character and was found in 13 studies. PSR was defined as a perceived interpersonal relationship between the viewer and the character. Seven studies, all of which used some combination of items from Rubin's PSI scale (Rubin et al., 1985), were relevant to the PSR category. Empathic identification was conceptualized as the feeling of being the character, feeling for the character, or assuming the character's perspective. Thirteen studies, which used all or a subset of items from Cohen's (2001) identification scale or created their own items that captured similar constructs, were put in this category. Finally, transportation was defined as absorption in the storyline and the development of story-related mental imagery. Thirty studies, which primarily employed components of the Green

Table 10.2 Description of Studies Included in the Meta-Analysis

	N	Sample	Topic	Outcome	Stimulus	Design	Total[a]	Homophily[a]	PSR[a]	Empathy[a]	Trans-portation[a]
Appel & Tobias (2010) Study 1	181	Austrian 75% UGS	Social	A	*Murder at the Mall* (story)	LE	.42 (.14)				.42 (.14)
Appel & Tobias (2010) Study 2	133	Austrian adults	Health	A	Story adapted from Kopfman et al., 1998	LE	.34 (.12)				.34
Bae (2008)	1500	Korean adults	Health	A, B	*Open Your Eyes* (reality TV)	CSS/QE	.48 (.04)			.48 (.04)	
Bilandzic & Busselle (2008)	162	U.S. UGS	Social	A	Films (comedy, action, si-fi)	LE	.25 (.11)				.25 (.11)
Brown & Cody (1991)	1170	Indian adults	Social	A	*Hum Log* (TV soap)	LE	.03 (.03)		.03 (.03)		
Busselle & Bilandzic (2009) Study 1	413	U.S. UGS	Social	A	*Rescue Me* (TV drama)	LE	.28 (.08)			.35 (.09)	.22 (.07)
Busselle & Bilandzic (2009) Study 2	211	German UGS	Social	A	*Station agent* (indep. film)	LE	.44 (.10)			.53 (.10)	0.34 (.10)
Busselle et al. (2009) Study 1	152	U.S. UGS	Social	A	*Law & Order* (TV crime)	LE	.45 (.12)				.45 (.12)
Busselle et al. (2009) Study 2	200	U.S. UGS	Social	A	*Third Watch* (crime drama)	LE	.38 (.10)				.38 .10)

(continued)

Table 10.2 Continued

	N	Sample	Topic	Outcome	Stimulus	Design	Total[a]	Homophily[a]	PSR[a]	Empathy[a]	Transportation[a]
Dal Cin (2005)	110	Canada, U.S. UGS	Social	A	Short stories and movie clips	LE	.09 (.18)				.09 (.18)
deGraaf et al. (2009)	152	Netherland UGS	Social	A	Story	LE	.13 (.13)			.10 (.13)	.15 (.13)
deGraaf et al. (2011) Study 1	80	UGS	Social	A	Story	LE	.04 (.17)			.10 (.17)	-.01 (.17)
deGraaf et al. (2011) Study 2	159	UGS	Social	A	Story	LE	.19 (.12)			.24 (.12)	.13 (.13)
deGraaf & Hustinx (2011)	180	UGS	Social	C	Story	LE	.18 (.09)	.21 (.08)		.25 (.09)	.19 (.09)
Eyal (2010)	303	U.S. UGS	Health	B, C	Popular television shows	CSS/QE	.18 (.08)	.18 (.08)			
Green (2004)	152	U.S. UGS	Social	A	Just as I Am (story)	LE	.28 (.13)				.28 (.13)
Green & Brock (2000) Study 1	90	U.S. UGS	Social	A, C	Murder at the Mall (story)	LE	.22 (.09)				.22 (.09)
Green & Brock (2000) Study 2	68	U.S. UGS	Social	A, C	Murder at the Mall (story)	LE	.22 (.22)				.22 (.22)
Green & Brock (2000) Study 3	269	U.S. UGS	Social	A, C	Murder at the Mall (story)	LE	.18 (.11)				.18 (.11)

Study	N	Sample	Topic	Mechanism	Narrative	Design					
Green & Brock (2000) Study 4	222	U.S. UGS	Social	A	*Two were Left* (story)	LE	.30 (.09)				.30 (.09)
Greenwood (2007)	85	U.S. UGS	Social	A	Popular television shows	CSS/QE	-.04 (.14)	-.04 (.14)			
Hoffner & Cohen	144	Fans, U.S.	Social	A	*Monk* (TV)	CSS/QE	.25 (.14)			.25 (.14)	
Igartua et al. (2011)	56	UGS	Social	A	*Opus dei* (movie)	LE	.17 (.22)				
Igartua (2010) Study 3	45	UGS	Social	A	*A day without a Mexican* (movie)	LE	.36 (.23)				
Mazzocco et al. (2010) Study 1	137	UGS	Social	A	Story	LE	.45 (.11)				.45 (.11)
McKinley (2010)	349	U.S. UGS	Health	A, C	*Party of Five* (TV drama)	LE	-.25 (.08)	-.54 (.07)	-.40 (.08)	-.26 (.08)	.19 (.09)
Moyer-Gusé & Nabi (2008)	367	U.S. UGS	Health	B, C	*The OC* (TV drama)	LE	.03 (.09)	-.05 (.09)	.05 (.09)	.08 (.09)	.05 (.11)
Moyer-Gusé (2011)	50	U.S. UGS	Health	A, B	*Law & Order* (TV crime)	LE	.24 (.29)			.24 (.29)	
Moyer-Gusé et al. (2011)	243	U.S. UGS	Health	A, B, C	*Sex and the City* (TV)	LE	.34 (.09)			.34 (.09)	
Murphy et al. (2012a)	173	U.S. adults	Social	A, B, C	*Law & Order* (TV crime)	CSS/QE	.66 (.12)	.66 (.13)			.67

(continued)

Table 10.2 Continued

	N	Sample	Topic	Outcome	Stimulus	Design	Total[a]	Homophily[a]	PSR[a]	Empathy[a]	Trans-portation[a]
Murphy et al. (2011)	502	U.S. adults	Health	A, B, C	Desperate Housewives (TV)	CSS/QE	.71 (.06)				.71 (.06)
Murphy et al. (2012b)	149	Hispanic women in the U.S.	Health	B, C	El Con (Spanish language TV series)	CSS/QE	.17 (.10)	.08 (.11)			.26 (.10)
Ortiz & Harwood (2007)	367	U.S. UGS (not-gay/ Black)	Social	A	Will & Grace (TV comedy)	CSS/QE	.23 (.08)			.23 (.08)	
Ritterfeld & Jin (2006)	165	U.S. UGS	Social	A, C	Angel Baby (movie, drama)	LE	.53 (.13)			.53 (.13)	
Rouner, Long, & Slater (2006)	58	U.S. UGS	Social	A	Law & Order (TV crime)	LE	.26 (.21)				.26 (.21)
Rouner, Long, & Slater (2006)	119	U.S. UGS	Social	A	West Wing (TV drama)	LE	.43 (.15)				.43 (.15)
Schiappa et al. (2005) Study 1	74	U.S. UGS	Social	A	5 Feet Under (TV drama)	CSS/QE	.46 (.15)	.46 (.15)			
Schiappa et al. (2005) Study 2	80	U.S. UGS	Social	A	Queer Eye (Reality TV)	LE	.67 (.13)	.67 (.13)			

Study	N	Sample	Domain	Outcome	Narrative	Design					
Schippa et al. (2005) Study 3	31	U.S. UGS	Social	A	Dress to Kill (Comedy)	LE		1.02 (.22)	1.02 (.22)	.04 (.13)	.17 (.16)
Slater & Rouner (2006)	83	U.S. UGS	Social	B	Law & Order (TV crime)	LE		.13 (.15)	.17 (.15)	.33 (.18)	.58 (.15)
Slater & Rouner (2006)	91	U.S. UGS	Social	B	If These Walls Could Talk (TV drama)	LE		.47 (.15)	.49 (.13)		
Stitt (2008)	129	U.S. UGS	Health	C	Law & Order; Party of 5, Grey's Anatomy (TV drama & crime)	LE		.26 (.16)			.26 (.16)
Tian & Hoffner (2007/2010)	226	Online viewers	Social	B	Lost (TV action)	CSS/QE	.71 (.08)	.96 (.08)	.63 (.08)	.54	
Vaughn et al. (2009)	96	U.S. UGS	Social	A	Two were left (story)	LE		.86 (.24)			.86 (.24)
Zhang & Busselle (2007)	110	U.S. UGS	Social	A	Law & Order (TV crime)	LE	.00 (.15)	.02 (.14)			-0.01 (.15)

Note: UGS = undergraduate students, CSS/QE = cross sectional survey or quasi experiment, LE = lab experiment, A = attitudinal outcomes, B = behavioral intentions/behaviors, C = cognitive outcomes.

[a] Fischer's z_r adjusted for unreliability of measures followed by SE in parentheses.

and Brock's (2000) transportation scale or used equivalent items, were coded for correlation between transportation and outcomes.

Involvement variables were coded into one of the four categories based on the scales and attendant items used in each study regardless of the labels used by the researcher to refer to the variables. This allowed for the consistent coding of variables that had been labeled inconsistently or interchangeably in the studies. In this body of research, it is not uncommon for two studies to use a measure of identification, where one measures homophily and the other measures empathy. Conversely, studies used different labels (experiential involvement or being in the narrative) but assessed these variables using almost identical items that capture the same theoretical construct of transportation.

Outcome Variable Type.   Following Hovland's classic categorization of responses to persuasion (Dillard, 1993), outcome variables were divided into three main types: cognitions, attitudes, and behaviors. Cognitions in this project were defined as factual knowledge and beliefs ($n = 12$). Measures that asked participants to estimate their chances of contracting HIV and their knowledge about the effects of binge drinking would fall into this category. Attitudes refer to affective responses, evaluations, and judgments (Fazio, 1986), and encompass subjective views and values ($n = 38$). Although perceptions of condom effectiveness would be coded as a knowledge outcome, cases that measure favorable evaluations of condom use would be coded as an attitude study. Attitudes also included self-perceptions, such as self-efficacy and self-esteem. Finally, behavior outcomes ($n = 11$) refer to self-reported behaviors or behavioral intentions, such as willingness, agreement, or expressed intention to engage in certain behaviors (Ajzen, 1991). Because some studies measured more than one outcome variable (e.g., attitudes and behaviors), the number of correlations aggregated exceeds the number of studies.

Topic.   The entertainment media used as the stimulus in each study was coded into one of two content types: (a) health topics, such as organ donation and safe sex ($n = 11$), and (b) political and social issues topics, such as capital punishment and ethnic/racial stereotypes ($n = 34$).

Study Design.   Each study was coded for the type of designed used to collect the data. The coding procedure discriminated between two types of designs: single laboratory or multiple exposures. Studies coded into the single laboratory exposure category ($n = 34$) included experiments that exposed participants to the entertainment media stimulus at only one time point and asked them to complete at least one post-test outcome measure. The multiple exposure studies ($\boldsymbol{n} = 11$) included quasi-experiments or designs where a single survey was administered after participants were repeatedly exposed to entertainment media.

Stimulus Type.   The medium of the stimulus (audiovisual/print) was coded since message modality has implications for pace and amount of sensory stimulation (Green & Brock, 2002). Print stimuli, such as an excerpt from a novel, are considered self-paced media with minimal sensory stimulation whereas audiovisual stimuli (TV programs, films, and radio programs) allow less control over pace, and include more opportunity for sensory stimulation than print stimuli. Fourteen cases were coded as print stimuli cases, and 30 cases were put in the audiovisual stimuli category.

Population. Studies were coded by the type of sample they used. The studies were coded into two categories: studies of college student ($n = 37$) or non-student ($n = 8$) samples.

Publication Type. Studies were coded by their source. Published studies included peer-reviewed journal articles ($n = 34$) whereas conference papers and proceedings, dissertations, or other sources not published in peer-reviewed journals at the time of data collection were coded into the unpublished studies category ($n = 11$).

Coding Reliability

Six published reports that included 20 correlations were coded by two independent coders to establish intercoder reliability. Studies used to establish intercoder reliability were selected by dividing the pool of articles into strata to guarantee the sample represented a full range of types of variables and analyses. Cohen's Kappa for coders' agreement rate was above .90 across all coding categories. All disagreements were resolved by the first author.

Analysis

The effect sizes coded from the original studies were transformed into a common metric, Pearson's r correlation. The correlations and their standard errors were adjusted for measurement error, a study artifact that has the potential to attenuate effect sizes. Reliability was estimated using the Spearman-Brown formula for computing single-item alphas when the scale's reliability was not reported.

The results of fixed-effect and random-effects meta-analyses are reported (Anker, Reinhart, & Feeley, 2010; Borenstein, Hedges, Higgins, & Rothstein, 2010; Hedges & Vevea, 1998). In fixed-effect model meta-analyses, a common, "true" effect size that underlies all cases included in the meta-analysis is assumed. In random-effects models, in contrast, each effect size is treated as a unique sample from a population of studies; the effect sizes taken from each study is assumed to vary from other studies (Hedges & Vevea, 1998). Random-effects models therefore do not represent the mean effect size of the cases in the meta-analysis; rather, they estimate a mean effect size of all studies in the population from which the sample of studies in the meta-analysis was drawn. Model choice, however, largely depends on the assumptions made and the generalizations desired (Anker et al., 2010), so both types of meta-analyses were conducted for this project.

Fixed-effect meta-analysis was used to test the homogeneity of effect sizes. Effects were clustered into groups based on the levels of a given moderating variable. A series of Hedges's Q-tests were then used to explore the heterogeneity between and within these groups of studies. First, the total variance (Q_{total}) across the effect sizes is computed along with the variance within each level of the moderating variable (Q_{within}). The difference between the total variance and the variance within each group ($Q_{between}$) can be interpreted as a measure of the variance between the proposed levels of the moderating variable. This $Q_{between}$ test, considered an omnibus test of differences among levels (analogous to the F value in ANOVA), indicates whether differences between groups of effect sizes exist (Card, 2011).

Finally, a meta-regression was performed to examine the unique effect of each moderating variable, controlling for other moderators simultaneously. Meta-regression estimates the effect of one moderator on the relationship between involvement and outcomes while holding constant other potential moderating variables. This procedure is desirable when high intercorrelations between moderator variables exist in the regression model, as is the case with this meta-regression analysis.

Results

H1: Effects of Involvement

The first hypothesis posited that involvement with entertainment media has an effect on outcomes. All correlations between involvement types (homophily, empathic identification, PSR, and transportation) and outcomes (knowledge, attitude, behavior) for each study were averaged to a single effect size; that is, each study only contributed one effect size to the meta-analysis used to test H1. The sample-weighted mean effect size for the relationship between involvement and outcomes, using a fixed-effect model meta-analysis, showed support for H1, $r = .27$, $p < .001$, $SE = 0.01$, 95% CI [.25, .30]. The cumulative effect was moderate to large in magnitude using Cohen's (1988) conventions for interpreting effect sizes. A summary of the random-effects model meta-analysis is provided in Table 10.3.

Hedges's Q test demonstrates that the effect sizes of involvement on outcomes were not homogeneous, $Q(45) = 313.66$, $p < .001$. A significant Q-total statistic indicates substantial variability in the effect sizes beyond what is expected due to sampling error suggesting a possibility of moderating variables (Lipsey & Wilson, 2001). To summarize, H1 was supported by the data, revealing medium to strong effects of involvement on post-viewing outcomes. The effect of involvement, however, is homogeneous, which suggests that this relationship is moderated by third variables. This possibility is explored in RQ1 and H2.

Table 10.3 Fixed and Random Effects of Different Involvement Overall and by Involvement Type

	Fixed effects		Random effects	
	r	*95% CI*	*r*	*95% CI*
Overall	.27***	[.25, .30]	.30***	[.23, .37]
Transportation	.32***	[.28, .36]	.29***	[.22, .36]
Empathy	.32***	[.28, .36]	.26***	[.14, .36]
Homophily	.19***	[.14, .25]	.30***	[.03, .53]
PSR	.07**	[.02, .11]	.12	[-.03, .26]

Note: CI = confidence interval.
** $p < .01$. *** $p < .001$.

RQ1: Comparison between Involvement Types

A total of 67 correlations were meta-analyzed to test Hypothesis 2. A $Q_{between}$ test was conducted to see whether the involvement type moderated the relationship between involvement with entertainment media and outcomes. The $Q_{between}$ test evaluates whether the levels of a moderator variable account for significant variance among effect sizes (Hedges & Olkin, 1985; Lipsey & Wilson, 2001).

First, the average effect of PSR was significantly smaller than the average effects of all other involvement types (PSR vs. homophily: $Q_{between}$ (1, 21) = 11.82, $p < .005$; PSR vs. transportation: $Q_{between}$ (1, 17) = 68.63, $p < .001$; PSR vs. empathic identification: $Q_{between}$ (1, 35) = 227.59, $p < .001$). Second, the average effect size for homophily and outcomes cases differed significantly from studies that assessed the effect of transportation on outcomes, $Q_{between}$ (1, 42) = 12.99, $p < .001$ and empathic identification on outcomes, $Q_{between}$ (1, 28) = 13.22, $p < .001$. Third, the difference between the average effects of transportation and empathic identification on outcomes was non-significant, $Q_{between}$ (1, 46) = .001, *ns*.

Table 10.4 presents the mean effect size and corresponding confidence intervals for each involvement type using fixed-effect and random-effects model meta-analyses. To summarize, types of involvement led to different magnitude of effects. PSR yielded the weakest effects, whereas transportation ($r = .32$, 95% CI [.28, .36], $k = 31$), empathic identification ($r = .32$, 95% CI [.28, .36], $k = 17$), and homophily ($r = .19$, 95% CI [.14, .25], $k = 31$) had moderate to large effects.

H2: Outcome Types

Hypothesis 2 argued that involvement influences attitude and behavior outcomes more strongly than knowledge-based outcomes. To examine this hypothesis, the type of specific outcome measure (attitudes, knowledge, behaviors) used in the study was coded. In total, 61 correlation coefficients were coded.

The Q test revealed that there was considerable variability among the effect sizes of involvement on the three outcome types, $Q(60) = 534.13$, $p < .001$. A $Q_{between}$ test conducted to see whether the type of outcome moderated the relationship between involvement and outcomes revealed significant differences between the types of outcomes. A significant difference was documented between studies that measured behavior/behavioral intention and attitude outcomes, $Q_{between}$ (1, 48) = 83.67, $p < .001$. A significant difference between the effect sizes for studies that measured behaviors/behavioral intentions and knowledge outcomes was also found, $Q_{between}$ (1, 21) = 83.67, $p < .001$. However, no differences were detected between attitude and knowledge outcomes, $Q_{between}$ (1, 47) = 0.53, $p > .05$.

Table 10.4 presents the mean fixed-effect and random-effects effect sizes by outcome type. As predicted in H2, involvement with entertainment media resulted in greatest change in behaviors or behavioral intentions ($r = .41$, $p < .001$, 95% CI [.38, .43], $k = 11$), followed by attitudes ($r = .26$, $p < .001$, 95% CI [.23, .29], $k = 37$) and knowledge ($r = .23$, $p < .001$, 95% CI [.17, .30], $k = 12$).

RQ2: Contextual Moderators

A meta-regression was used to examine whether various study characteristics moderated the relationship between involvement and outcomes. Independent study effect sizes (the criterion variable in meta-regression) were regressed on dummy coded variables that represented the study characteristics (the predictor variables). These moderating variables included sample type (students, non-students), study design (single exposure, multiple exposures), stimulus type (print, audiovisual), and topic area (health, social/political issues). Meta-regression enables multiple predictors to be examined simultaneously; the unique contribution of each moderating variable in the relationship between involvement and outcomes, holding other predictors constant, can be obtained through meta-regression.

Table 10.4 Fixed and Random Effects of Involvement in Different Context

	Fixed effects		Random effects	
	r	95% CI	r	95% CI
Attitudes	.26***	[.23, .29]	.30***	[.23, .36]
Behaviors and behavioral intentions	.41***	[.38, .43]	.37***	[.26, .47]
Knowledge and beliefs	.23***	[.17, .30]	.25*	[.04, .44]

Note: CI = confidence interval.
* $p < .05$. *** $p < .001$.

Table 10.5 Meta Regression Showing Moderating Study Characteristics

	b	SE	z
Constant	.29		
Sample (students vs. non-students)	.04	.07	1.66
Study design and exposure operationalization (multiple exposures vs. single lab exposure)	.03	.07	1.19
Topic (health vs. social)	−.06***	.04	3.80
Stimulus (print vs. audiovisual)	.01	.05	.25

Note: SS $_{regression}$ = 431.00, SS $_{residual}$ = 292.71, MS $_{regression}$ = 86.20, MS $_{residual}$ = 7.51, R^2 = .60.
*** $p < .001$.

The results of the meta-regression are presented in Table 10.5. Of the study characteristics, only study topic area (health, political/social issues) moderated the effects of involvement on outcomes when all characteristics were included in the model ($b = -.06$, $SE = .04$, $p < .001$). Study design, sample type, and stimulus types were not significant predictors in the meta-regression. The regression coefficients of the meta-regression were used to compute the mean effect size for the levels of each moderating variable, again controlling for other study characteristics. As Table 10.6 demonstrates, the average effect size of studies that investigated the influence of involvement on outcomes in health contexts was significantly larger ($r = .34$, $p < .001$, 95% CI [.32, .35]) than the effects of studies in social and political contexts ($r = .23$, $p < .001$, % CI [.22, .25]).

Table 10.6 Effect of Involvement by Study Characteristics Based on a Meta-Regression

	r	95% CI
Population		
Students	.23***	[.22, .27]
Non-students	.31***	[.30, .35]
Study design and exposure operationalization		
Single lab exposure	.31***	[.29, .34]
Multiple or long-term exposures	.26***	[.24, .28]
Topic		
Health-related topics	.34***	[.32, .35]
Social & political topics	.23***	[.22, .25]
Stimulus materials		
Print stimulus	.29***	[.27, .31]
Audiovisual stimulus	.28***	[.26, .30]

Note: CI = confidence interval.
*** $p < .001$.

Publication Bias

Null hypothesis testing based on probability is generally used as the main decision rule for evaluating hypotheses in quantitative social scientific research. A drawback of this significance testing is its sensitivity to sample size. Larger samples have greater statistical power that can detect weak effects whereas studies using smaller sample sizes must have more robust effects to reach statistical significance (Levine, Weber, Park, & Hullett, 2008). The reliance on significance testing in empirical research has led to publication bias as studies with larger sample sizes are more likely to be published because of the increased chance of significance due to greater statistical power (Levine, Asada, & Carpenter, 2009). This bias can be detected in a negative relationship between the effect size a study reports and its attendant sample size (Card, 2011). To test whether publication bias is present in the relationship between involvement and outcomes, a meta-regression analysis was conducted. The individual effect sizes were treated as the criterion variable and sample size was used as the predictor. Results indicate that sample size was not significantly related to the size of the reported effect ($b = -.001$, $S.E. = .001$, $p > .05$), which suggests no evidence of publication bias.

Additionally, a *fail-safe N* was computed to see how many studies reporting null effects would need to be included in the meta-analysis for the observed cumulative effect of involvement on outcomes to become nonsignificant. Using Orwin's (1983) equation, the fail-safe N was calculated with the following criteria: k was 45 studies, $\overline{ES_k} = .27$, and $\overline{ES_c} = .03$. The standard error of the weighted mean effect size was .03. The fail-safe N is 360 studies, which indicates that 360 studies reporting null effects would need to be included in the meta-analysis for the cumulative effect size to become trivial. The large fail-safe N indicates that the results of the meta-analysis are robust and unlikely to be influenced by publication bias.

Discussion

The present investigation examined the influence of involvement with entertainment media on knowledge, attitudes, and behaviors through meta-analysis. The results suggest there is a moderate to large relationship between involvement with entertainment media and post-exposure outcomes. The effects are particularly prominent when the outcomes of interest were behavioral intentions or behaviors; nevertheless, involvement still had a moderate effect on knowledge acquisition and attitude change. These findings support the widely held notion that involvement plays a central role in the effects of entertainment media.

Theories of entertainment and narrative persuasion maintain that there are multiple distinct, albeit related, psychological processes of involvement that lead to media effects through different mechanisms (Moyer-Gusé, 2008). Despite extensive theorizing, relatively little research has examined the extent to which these involvement types are indeed independent and dissimilar. Scale-validation work (Busselle & Bilandzic, 2009) sheds light on the relationships *between* involvement types, but this line of research does not address the ways different involvement types operate in generating media effects. The current study endeavors to understand the differences between the effects that different involvement types have on viewing outcomes. Doing so can indirectly evaluate assumptions underlying theories of involvement and narrative persuasion.

Various theoretical perspectives discuss why different involvement types affect media consumers. To review, transportation results in attitude, knowledge, or behavior outcomes through increased attention, mental simulation, the generation of pro-message cognitions, and the elicitation of emotions. Empathic identification involves the same processes as transportation but also incorporates perspective-taking, which creates a link between messages and the viewers' self-concept. PSR are also said to increase attention, emotions, and cognitions but lack the mental simulation component present in empathic identification and transportation. Finally, homophily is seen as a process of social comparison that links the message to the viewers' self-concept and but lacks the mental simulation and emotional components of empathic responses and transportation.

Given the conceptual overlap and distinctions among the types of involvement, a direct comparison between the effect of empathy, transportation, PSR and homophily on viewing outcomes can assist in identifying the critical mental processes that bring about narrative persuasion and entertainment-education effects. The results of the present study demonstrate that transportation in the narrative and empathic identification with characters having the strongest influence over knowledge, attitude, and behaviors. Homophily has a lesser effect on post-exposure outcomes, and PSR has the smallest impact on viewers. These results indicate that two mental processes—mental simulation and emotional responses—are the most critical components of narrative persuasion and education-entertainment effects. Mental simulation and emotional responses are present in transportation and empathic identification but are mainly discussed in relation to PSR or homophily.

These findings are consistent with narrative persuasion theories, such as extended ELM (Slater & Rouner, 2002), that underscore the importance of absorption (transportation) in producing media effects. At the same time, theoretical approaches that emphasize the role of homophily and PSR (SCT, reactance) appear to account for more secondary mechanisms of education-entertainment and narrative persuasion effects. This is, of course, not to say that media consumers do not engage in social learning or that parasocial interactions with characters do not reduce reactance to the persuasive message. Rather, while these processes occur, they do not appear to be the *primary* mechanisms of effects. The results hint at the possibility that most of the influence of entertainment media effects may be carried by other processes (strong emotions and mental imagery) apart from similarity to and liking of the characters. This tentative conclusion requires further research to substantiate the exact mental processes that mediate the relationship between involvement experiences and persuasion outcomes.

Future Directions

This meta-analysis synthesizes existing literature on the effects of media entertainment, and the results provide a roadmap of where prospective scholarship on entertainment involvement should be directed. Three questions regarding theory, methodology, and application were generated from the findings of this investigation and are discussed in the following section.

What Is the Utility of Differentiating Between Involvement Types with Entertainment Media?

The findings from meta-analysis provide an opportunity to revisit the distinctions between the involvement types. Although not a central focus of this investigation, the meta-analysis reveals very strong relationships between homophily, PSR, empathic identification, and transportation. In the studies located during the literature search, the average correlations between these involvement types ranged from $r = .48$ to $r = .86$. The high correlations between the involvement types puts into question whether these involvement types should be considered discrete variables. These results should be taken with caution, however, as different studies have employed different measures.

An alternative view of involvement types distinguishes between narrative involvement (transportation) and character involvement, which constitutes an "overarching category of concepts related to how viewers interact with characters" (Moyer-Gusé, 2008, p. 409). Recent studies have adopted this conceptual approach and used the transportation scale to measure "narrative involvement" and created a "character involvement scale" that combines items assessing perspective taking (a component of empathic identification), homophily, and PSR (Murphy, Frank, Mora, & Patnoe-Woodley, 2011). However, the meta-analysis places in question the utility of such character/narrative involvement distinctions. The data suggest that empathic identification and transportation are highly correlated, and their effects on viewing outcomes are empirically indistinguishable.

This by no means suggests that all modes of involvement should be assessed together by a single measure for the sake of parsimony. Rather, the results indicate yet another approach to studying sub-components of involvement. There is likely considerable overlap among the four involvement types, which results in the high inter-correlations between them. It may therefore be more fruitful to rethink the way involvement is measured by focusing on the mental processes underlying involvement with entertainment media (emotional responses, mental simulation, self-concept link). Theory on entertainment media effects would benefit from future research that experimentally manipulates these mental processes, rather than the broader involvement types, so the actual modes of information processing can be isolated.

How Can We Improve Measurement?

The coding procedure for the meta-analysis underscored serious methodological shortcomings that pervade media involvement research. It appears that the field of media involvement suffers from the *jingle-jangle fallacy*, which has been a longstanding malady in many social and psychological sciences (Kelley, 1927). The jingle fallacy occurs when a single term is used to reference two or more different psychological processes. This fallacy is represented in media entertainment research by scholars who fail to discern between individual involvement types but instead use the general label of identification. Conversely, the jangle fallacy is used to describe occasions where two or more terms are used to represent the same theoretical construct. Homophily and identification are commonly used to represent the same fundamental construct (perceived similarity). Given that terminological confusion with the meaning of identification, it is problematic when some studies used scales of involvement with items that ask "to what extent do you identify with the character" without providing a concrete definition for the term identification.

Imprecise and inaccurate terminology is not surprising given that media involvement is studied across multiple disciplines, and different research traditions contribute their own unique terminologies. Unfortunately, however, conceptual and methodological inconsistency occurs in the communication discipline as well. This makes it difficult for researchers to interpret results across studies. Therefore, it is imperative for scholars to be more sensitive to questions of construct validity.

How to Plan Narrative Persuasion and Education-Entertainment Studies More Effectively?

The meta-analysis informs researchers' decision-making process in designing future studies. To determine the sample size appropriate for testing research hypotheses, scholars are advised to conduct prospective power analysis (American Psychological Association, 2009). With conventional levels of acceptable power set at .80, the target sample size depends on the anticipatory effect size. Lacking knowledge of the true effect size in the population, scholars may use small, medium, and large effects as generic estimates (O'Keefe, 2011). The results of the present meta-analysis provide researchers with a more precise estimate of the magnitude of the anticipated effect size. Examination of each involvement type separately is particularly important because, as this study showed, a sample sufficiently large to reasonably detect the effects of empathic identification may not be suitable for detecting the considerably smaller effect of PSR, increasing the probability of Type II error.

How to Transfer Education-Entertainment from Laboratory Studies to Real-World Interventions?

Laboratory experiments are often used to develop theories (Shapiro, 2002). Given the persuasive potential of entertainment media in eliciting pro-social outcomes, attempts have been made to apply what has been learned in basic research in crafting media messages created to promote socially favorable outcomes. Special attention should be directed to understanding how laboratory-based studies generalize to other populations, contexts, and stimuli. The findings from the meta-analysis demonstrate that the outcomes of involvement with entertainment media are comparable among college students and non-student populations. The effects of media involvement are not significantly moderated by methodological design (single exposure, repeated exposure). It was, however, not possible to distinguish between the amount of exposure (single exposure/ repeated exposures) and setting (laboratory/naturalistic setting). Attempts should be made in future research to disentangle research design-related issues.

Finally, the results of the meta-analysis demonstrate that involvement with health-related entertainment messages has a greater impact than social and political entertainment content. Because many education-entertainment efforts are directed at promoting health issues, such as organ donation, safe sex practices, and preventative care, a better understanding of what makes health messages more influential than political and social messages may help in designing other types of prosocial campaigns. Building on traditional ELM approaches to persuasion (Petty & Cacioppo, 1986), it may be that people in general are more motivated and able to process messages related to their health than social or political messages. Individuals may have low personal relevance to or prior knowledge of social and political issues, which contribute to less knowledge, attitude, and behavior change despite involvement with media. It is well established that personal relevance and prior knowledge can enhance involvement (empathic identification and transportation; Cohen & Ribak, 2003; Green, 2004), but theory on media entertainment would benefit from examining whether these variables amplify the effects of involvement on outcomes.

Limitations and Conclusions

The current meta-analysis is not without its limitations. The sample size was appropriate for the analyses undertaken in the present investigation but insufficient for examining higher-order interactions, such as the interaction between outcome type (attitudes, behaviors) and involvement types. Most studies measured outcomes immediately after exposure, with only few studies reporting follow-up measures of long-term effects. Although different media involvement types do not radically differ in short-term, differences in the rate of decay of effects may be uncovered with repeated follow-up measures of outcomes.

Despite the limitations of this project, this meta-analysis identifies important effects of exposure and media involvement across various contexts, samples, and outcomes. The meta-analysis endeavored to include studies from diverse methodologies, disciplines, and conceptual traditions. In this systematic synthesis of research on media entertainment, it is possible to take important steps forward to organize the literature, determine theoretical and methodological challenges, and forecast directions for future research.

Acknowledgments

The authors thank the researchers who provided us with information necessary for the meta-analysis: Rick Busselle of Washington State University, Helena Bilandzic of University of Erfurt, William Brown of Regent University, Sonya Dal Cin of University of Michigan, Anneke deGraaf of Radboud University Nijmegen, Keren Eyal, of IDC Herzilya, Peter Gregg of University of Minnesota, Cynthia Hoffner of Georgia State University, Seung-A Annie Jin of Boston College, Emily Moyer- Gusé of The Ohio State University, Sheila Murphy of University of Southern California, Michelle Ortiz of The Ohio State University, Donna Rouner of Colorado State University, Edward Schiappa of University of Minnesota, Michael Slater of The Ohio State University, Qing Tian, Nan Zhao of University of Southern California, Leigh Ann Vaughn of Ithaca College and Lingling Zhang of Towson University. We also would want to thank Noel Card of The University of Arizona for assistance on the early stages of the project and Jonathan Cohen of University of Haifa for commenting on an earlier version of the manuscript.

References

References marked with an asterisk indicate studies included in the meta-analysis.

Ajzen, I. (1991). The theory of planned behavior. *Organizational Behavior and Human Decision Processes, 50*, 179–211. doi:10.1016/0749-5978

American Psychological Association. (2009). *Publication manual of the American psychological association* (6th ed.). Washington, DC: Author.

Andersen, P. A., & de Mancillas, W. R. T. (1978). Scales for the measurement of homophily with public figures. *Southern Journal of Communication, 43*, 169–179.

*Appel, M., & Tobias, R. (2010). Transportation and need for affect in narrative persuasion: A mediated moderation model. *Media Psychology, 13*, 101–135. doi:10.1080/15213261003799847

Auter, P. J. (1992). TV that talks back: An experimental validation of a parasocial interaction scale. *Journal of Broadcasting and Electronic Media, 36*, 173–181. doi: 10.1080/08838159209364165

Anker, A. E., Reinhart, A. M., & Feeley, T. H. (2010). Meta-analysis of meta-analyses in communication research: Comparing fixed-effects and random-effects analysis models. *Communication Quarterly, 58*, 257–278. doi:10.1080/01463373.2010.503 154

*Bae, H. S. (2008). Entertainment-education and recruitment of cornea donors: The role of emotion and issue involvement. *Journal of Health Communication, 13,* 20–36. doi:10.1080/10810730701806953

Bandura, A. (2001). Social cognitive theory of mass communication. *Media Psychology, 3,* 265–266. doi:10.1207/S1532785XMEP0303_03

Bandura, A. (2004). Social cognitive theory for personal and social change by enabling media. In: A. Singhal, M. J. Cody, E. M. Rogers & M. Sabido (Eds.), *Entertainment-education and social change.* NY: Routledge.

*Bilandzic, H., & Busselle, R. (2008). Transportation and transportability in the cultivation of genre-consistent attitudes and estimates. *Journal of Communication, 58,* 508–529. doi:10.1111/j.1460-2466.2008.00397

Blakemore, S. J., & Decety, J. (2001). From the perception of action to the understanding of intention. *Nature Reviews Neuroscience, 2,* 561–567. doi :10.1038/35086023

Borenstein, M., Hedges, L. V., Higgins, J. P. T., & Rothstein, H. R. (2010). A basic introduction to fixed-effect and random-effects models for meta-analysis. *Research Synthesis Methods, 2,* 97–111. doi:10.1002/jrsm.12

Brown, W. J., Basil, M. D., & Bocarnea, M. C. (2003). The influence of famous athletes on health beliefs and practices. *Journal of Health Communication, 8,* 41–57. doi:10.1080/10810730305733

*Brown, W. J., & Cody, M. J. (1991). Effects of a prosocial television soap opera in promoting women's status. *Human Communication Research, 18,* 114–142.

Brown, W. J., & Fraser, B. P. (2004). Celebrity identification in entertainment-education. In A. Singhal, M. J. Cody, E. M. Rogers, & M. Sabido (Eds.), *Entertainment-education and social change: History, research, and practice* (pp. 97–115). Mahwah, NJ: Erlbaum.

Bushman, B., & Anderson, C. (2001). Media violence and the American public. Scientific facts versus media misinformation. *American Psychologist, 56,* 477–489. doi:10.1111/j.1468-2958.1991.tb00531.x

*Busselle, R., & Bilandzic, H. (2009). Measuring narrative engagement. *Media Psychology, 12,* 321–347. doi: 10.1080/15213260903287259

*Busselle, R. W., Bilandzic, H., & Zhou, Y. (2009, May). *The influence of television fiction on real world victim sympathy.* Paper presented at the annual meeting of the International Communication Association, Chicago, IL. Retrieved from http://www.allacademic.com/meta/p300817_index.html

Card, N. A. (2011). *Applied meta-analysis for social science research.* New York, NY: Guilford Press.

Carruthers, P., & Smith, P. K. (1996). *Theories of theories of mind.* Cambridge, MA: Cambridge University Press.

Chaffee, S. H., & Metzger, M. J. (2001). The end of mass communication? *Mass Communication and Society, 4,* 365–379. doi:10.1207/S15327825MCS0404_3

Cohen, J. (1988). *Statistical power analysis for the behavioral sciences* (2nd ed.). Mahwah, NJ: Erlbaum.

Cohen, J. (1999). Favorite characters of teenage viewers of Israeli serials. *Journal of Broadcasting & Electronic Media, 43*(3), 327–345.

Cohen, J. (2001). Defining identification: A theoretical look at the identification of audiences with media characters. *Mass Communication & Society, 4,* 245–264. doi:10.1207/S15327825MCS0403_01

Cohen, J. (2006). Audience identification with media characters. In J. Bryant & P. Vorderer (Eds.), *Psychology of entertainment* (pp. 183–197). Mahwah, NJ: Erlbaum.

Cohen, J., & Ribak, R. (2003). Sex differences in pleasure from television texts: The case of Ally McBeal. *Women's Studies in Communication, 26*, 118–134. doi: 10.1080/07491409.2003.10162454

*Dal Cin, S. (2005). *The use of stories as persuasive tools* (doctoral dissertation). University of Waterloo, Ontario, Canada.

Davis, M., Hull, J., Young, R., & Warren, G. (1987). Emotional reactions to dramatic film stimuli: The influence of cognitive and emotional empathy. *Journal of Personality and Social Psychology, 52*, 126–133. doi:10.1037/0022-3514.52.1.126

*de Graaf, A. Hoeken, H. Sanders, J., & Beentjes, H. (2009). The role of dimensions of narrative engagement in narrative persuasion. *Communications, 34*, 385–405. doi:10.1515/COMM.2009.024

*de Graaf, A., Hoeken, H., Sanders, J., &. Beentjes, J. W. (2011). Identification as a mechanism of narrative persuasion. *Communication Research,* 1–22 doi:10.1177/0093650211408594

*de Graaf, A., & Hustinx, L. (2011, May). *The effect of reader-character similarity on identification and narrative persuasion.* Paper presented at the meeting of the International Communication Association, Boston. Retrieved from http://www.allacademic.com/meta/p489079_index.html

Dillard, J. P. (1993). Persuasion past and present: Attitudes aren't what they used to be. *Communication Monographs, 60,* 90–97. doi:10.1080/03637759309376299

Eisenberg, A. L. (1936). *Children and radio programs.* New York, NY: Columbia University Press.

*Eyal, K. (2009, June). *The role of television characters in explaining audience sexuality.* Paper presented at the meeting of the International Communication Association, Singapore. Retrieved from http://www.allacademic.com/meta/p404423_index.html

Eyal, K., & Cohen, J. (2006). When good friends say goodbye: A parasocial breakup study. *Journal of Broadcasting & Electronic Media, 50*(3), 502–523.

Eyal, K., & Rubin, A. M. (2003). Viewer aggression and homophily, identification, and parasocial relationships with television characters. *Journal of Broadcasting & Electronic Media, 47,* 77–98. doi:10.1207/s15506878jobem4701_5

Fazio, R. (1986). How do attitudes guide behavior? In R. H. Sorrentino & E. T. Higgins (Eds.), *The handbook of motivation and cognition: Foundation of social behavior* (pp. 204–243). New York, NY: Guilford Press.

Giles, D. C. (2002). Parasocial interaction: A review of the literature and a model for future research. *Media Psychology, 4,* 279–305. doi:10.1207/S1532785XMEP0403_04

*Green, M. C. (2004). Transportation into narrative worlds: The role of prior knowledge and perceived realism. *Discourse Processes, 38,* 247–266. doi:10.1207/s15326950dp3802_5

*Green, M. C., & Brock, T. C. (2000). The role of transportation in the persuasiveness of public narratives. *Journal of Personality and Social Psychology, 79,* 701–721. doi:10.1037/0022-3514.79.5.701

Green, M. C., & Brock, T. C. (2002). In the mind's eye: Imagery and transportation into narrative worlds. In M. C. Green, J. J. Strange, & T. C. Brock (Eds.), *Narrative impact: Social and cognitive foundations* (pp. 315–341). Mahwah, NJ: Erlbaum.

*Greenwood, D. N. (2007). Are female action heroes risky role models? Character identification, idealization, and viewer aggression. *Sex Roles, 57,* 725–732. doi:10.1037/0022-3514.79.5.701

Hedges, L. V., & Olkin, I. (1985). *Statistical methods for meta-analysis.* New York, NY: Academic Press.

Hedges, L.V., & Vevea, J. L. (1998). Fixed and random-effects models in meta-analysis. *Psychological Methods, 3*, 486–504. doi:10.1037/1082-989X.3.4.486

Horton, D., & Wohl, R. R. (1956). Mass communication and parasocial interaction. *Psychiatry, 19*, 215–229.

*Igartua, J. J. (2010). Identification with characters and narrative persuasion through fictional feature films. *Communications. The European Journal of Communication Research, 35*, 347–373. doi:10.1515/comm.2010.019

*Igartua, J. J., Barrios, I., & Piñeiro, V. (2011, May). *Persuading people through controversial movies: processes and mechanisms of narrative persuasion.* Paper presented at the annual meeting of the International Communication Association, Boston. Retrieved from from http://www.allacademic.com/meta/p486831_index.html

Johnson, B. T., & Eagly, A. H. (1989). Effects of involvement on persuasion: A meta-analysis. *Psychological Bulletin, 106*, 290–314. doi:10.1037/0033-2909.106.2.290

Kelley, T. L. (1927). *Interpretation of educational measurements.* New York, NY: World Book.

Klimmt, C., Hartmann, T., & Schramm, H. (2006). Parasocial interactions and relationships. In J. Bryant & P. Vorderer (Eds.), *Psychology of entertainment* (pp. 291–313). Mahwah, NJ: Erlbaum.

Langdon, R., Coltheart, M., & Ward, P. B. (2006). Empathetic perspective-taking is impaired in schizophrenia: Evidence from a study of emotion attribution and theory of mind. *Cognitive Neuropsychiatry, 11*, 133–155. doi:10.1080/13546800444000218

Levine, T. R., Asada, K. J., & Carpenter, C. (2009). Sample size and effect size are negatively correlated in meta-analysis: Evidence and implications of a publication bias against non-significant findings. *Communication Monographs, 76*, 286–302. doi:10.1080/03637750903074685

Levine, T. R., Weber, R., Park, H. S., & Hullett, C. (2008). A communication researchers' guide to null hypothesis significance testing and alternatives. *Human Communication Research, 34*, 188–209. doi:10.1111/j.1468-2958.2008.00318.x

Levy, M. R. (1979). Watching TV news as parasocial interaction. *Journal of Broadcasting, 23*, 68–80. doi:10.1080/08838157909363919

Lipsey, M. W., & Wilson, D. B. (2001). *Practical meta-analysis.* Thousand Oaks, CA: Sage.

MacInnis, D. J., & Jaworski, B. J. (1989). Information processing from advertisements: Towards an integrative framework. *Journal of Marketing, 53*, 1–23.

Mar, R. A., Tackett, J. L., & Moore, C. (2010). Exposure to media and theory-of-mind development in preschoolers. *Cognitive Development, 25*, 69–78. doi:10.1016/j.cogdev.2009.11.002

Marsh, E. J., & Fazio, L. K. (2006). Learning errors from fiction: Difficulties in reducing reliance on fictional stories. *Memory and Cognition, 34*, 1140–1149. doi:10.3758/BF03193260

*Mazzocco, P. J., Green, M. C., Sasota, J. A., & Jones, N. (2010). This story is not for everyone: Transportability and narrative persuasion. *Social Psychological and Personality Science, 1*, 361–368. doi:10.1177/1948550610376600

*McKinley, C. (2010). *Examining dimensions of character involvement as contributing factors in television viewers' binge drinking perceptions.* Unpublished dissertation, University of Arizona.

Morgan, S. E., Movius, L., & Cody, M. J. (2009). The power of narratives: The effect of entertainment television organ donation storylines on the attitudes, knowledge, and behaviors of donors and non-donors. *Journal of Communication, 59,* 135–151. doi:10.1111/j.1460-2466.2008.01408.x

Moyer-Gusé, E. (2008). Toward a theory of entertainment persuasion: Explaining the persuasive effects of entertainment-education messages. *Communication Theory, 18,* 407–425. doi:10.1111/j.1468-2885.2008.00328.x

*Moyer-Gusé, E., Chung, A., & Jain, P. (2011). Identification with characters and discussion of taboo topics after exposure to an entertainment narrative about sexual health. *Journal of Communication, 61,* 387–406. doi:0.1111/j.1460-2466.2011.01551.x

*Moyer-Gusé, E., Jain, P., & Chung, A. H. (2011, May). *Reinforcement or reactance: Examining the effect of a explicit persuasive appeal following an entertainment-education narrative.* Paper presented at meeting of the International Communication Association, Boston. Retrieved from http://www.allacademic.com/meta/p490620_index.html

*Moyer-Gusé, E., & Nabi, R. L. (2008, November). *Explaining the persuasive effects of entertainment education programming: an empirical comparison of three theories.* Paper presented at the meeting of the National Communication Association, San Diego, CA. Retrieved from http://www.allacademic.com/meta/p259290_index.html

*Moyer-Gusé, E., & Nabi, R. L. (2010). Explaining the effects of narrative in an entertainment television program: Overcoming resistance to persuasion, *Human Communication Research, 36,* 26–52. doi:10.1111/j.1468-2958.2009.01367.x

*Murphy, S. Hether, S., de Castro Buffington, S., Baezconde-Garbinati, S., & Frank, L. B. (2011). *Preventing cancer in primetime: Using an entertainment education approach to reach underserved Hispanic audiences.* Manuscript submitted for publication.

*Murphy, S., Hether, H., Felt, L. J., & Buffington, S. (2012a). Public diplomacy in prime time: Exploring the potential of entertainment education in international public diplomacy. *American Journal of Media Psychology, 5,* 5–32.

*Murphy, S. T., Frank, L. B., Moran, M., & Woodley, P. (2012b). Involved, transported or emotional? Exploring the determinants of change in knowledge, attitudes, and behavior, in entertainment education. *Journal of Communication 61,* 407–431. doi:10.1111/j.1460-2466.2011.01554.x

Oatley, K. (1994). A taxonomy of the emotions of literary response and a theory of identification in fictional narrative. *Poetics, 23,* 53–74. doi:10.1016/0304-422X(94) P4296-S

Oatley, K. (1999). Why fiction may be twice as true as fact: Fiction as cognitive and emotional simulation. *Review of General Psychology, 3,* 101–117. doi:089-2680/99/S3.00

O'Keefe, D. J. (2011). The asymmetry of predictive and descriptive capabilities in quantitative communication research. *Communication Methods and Measures, 5,* 113–125. doi:10.1080/19312458.2011.568375

*Ortiz, M., & Harwood, J. (2007). A social cognitive approach to intergroup relationships on television. *Journal of Broadcasting and Electronic Media, 51,* 615–631.

Orwin, R. G. (1983). A fail-safe N for effect size in meta-analysis. *Journal of Educational Statistics, 8,* 157–159. doi:*10.2307/1164923*

Papa, M. J., Singhal, A., Law, S., Pant, S., Sood, S., Rogers, E. M., & Shefner-Rogers, C. L. (2000). Entertainment-education and social change. *Journal of Communication, 50,* 31–55.

Perse, E. (1990). Audience selectivity and involvement in the newer media environment. *Communication Research, 17,* 675–697. doi:10.1111/j.1460-2466.2000. tb02862

Pettigrew, T. (1998). Intergroup contact theory. *Annual Review of Psychology, 49,* 65–85. doi:10.1146/annurev.psych.49.1.65

Petty, R. E., & Cacioppo, J. T. (1986). *Communication and Persuasion: Central and Peripheral Routes to Attitude Change.* New York, NY: Springer-Verlag.

*Ritterfeld, U., & Jin, S. A. (2006). Addressing media stigma for people experiencing mental illness using an entertainment-education strategy. *Journal of Health Psychology, 11,* 247–226.

*Rouner, D., Slater, M. D., & Long, M. (2006, June). *Narrative persuasion: Effects of subsequent discussion.* Paper presented at the meeting of the International Communication Association, Dresden, Germany. Retrieved from http://www.allacademic.com/meta/p93146_index.html

Rubin, A.M., Perse, E. M., & Powell, R. A. (1985). Loneliness, parasocial interaction, and local television news viewing. *Human Communication Research, 12,* 155–180.

Rubin, A. M., Perse, E. M., & Taylor, D. S. (1988). A methodological examination of cultivation. *Communication Research, 15*(2), 107–134.

Rubin, A. M., & Step, M. M. (2000). Impact of motivation, attraction, and parasocial interaction. *Journal of Broadcasting & Electronic Media, 44,* 635–654. doi: 10.1207/s15506878jobem4404_7

Salomon, G. (1984). Television is "easy" and print is "tough": The differential investment of mental effort in learning as a function of perceptions and attributions. *Journal of Educational Psychology, 76,* 647–658.

*Schiappa, E., Gregg, P. B., & Hewes, D. E. (2005). The parasocial contact hypothesis. *Communication Monographs, 72,* 92–115. doi:10.1080/0363775052000342544

Shamay-Tsoory, S. G., Aharon-Peretz, J., & Perry, D. (2009). Two systems for empathy: A double dissociation between emotional and cognitive empathy in inferior frontal gyrus versus ventromedial prefrontal lesions *Brain, 132,* 617–627. doi:10.1093/ brain/awn279

Shapiro, M. A. (2002). Generalizability in communication research. *Human Communication Research, 28,* 491–500.

Sherif, M., & Hovland, C. I. (1961). *Social judgment: Assimilation and contrast effects in communication and attitude change.* New Haven, CT: Yale University Press.

Singhal, A., & Rogers, E. M. (1999). *Entertainment-education: A communication strategy for social change.* Mahwah, NJ: Erlbaum.

Slater, M. J., & Rouner, D. (2002). Entertainment-education and elaboration likelihood: Understanding the processing of narrative persuasion. *Communication Theory, 12,* 173–191.

*Slater, M. D., Rouner, D., & Long, M. (2006). Television dramas and support for controversial public policies: Effects and mechanisms. *Journal of Communication, 56,* 235–252.

*Stitt, C. (2008). *Differences in theoretical constructs of processing health information in narrative entertainment television messages* (doctoral dissertation). University of Arizona, Tempe.

Tal Or, N., & Cohen, J. (2010). Understanding audience involvement: Conceptualizing and manipulating identification and transportation. *Poetics, 28,* 402–418. doi:10.1016/j.poetic.2010.05.004

Taylor, S. E., & Thompson, S. C. (1982). Stalking the elusive "vividness" effect. *Psychological Review, 89*, 155–181.

Tedeschi, J. T., Schlenker, B. R., & Lindskold, S. (1972/2009). The exercise of power and influence. In J. T. Tedeschi (Ed.), *The social influence processes* (2nd ed., pp. 287–345). Chicago, IL: Aldine-Atherton.

*Tian, Q., & Hoffner, C. (2007, May). *Parasocial interaction and identification with liked, neutral, and disliked characters*. Paper presented at the ICA convention, San Francisco. Retrieved from http://www.allacademic.com/meta/p172887_index.html

*Tian, Q., & Hoffner, C. (2010). Parasocial interaction with liked, neutral and disliked characters on a popular TV series. *Mass Communication & Society, 13*, 250–269. doi:10.1080/15205430903296051

Todorov, A., Chaiken, S., & Henderson, M. D. (2002). The heuristic-systematic model of social information processing. In J. Dillard & M. Pfau (Eds.), *The persuasion handbook: Developments in theory and practice* (pp. 195–211). Thousand Oaks, CA: Sage.

Tukachinsky, R. H. (2007, November). *Transportation and identification as two modes of involvement with fictional texts*. Paper presented at the meeting of the National Communication Association, Chicago, IL. Retrieved from http://www.allacademic.com/meta/p191506_index.html

*Vaughn, L. A., Hesse, S. J., Petkova, Z., & Trudeau, L. (2009). "This story is right on": The impact of regulatory fit on narrative engagement and persuasion. *European Journal of Social Psychology, 39*, 447–456. doi:10.1002/ejsp.570

Ward, M. L. (2004). Wading through the stereotypes: Positive and negative associations between media use and black adolescents' conceptions of self. *Developmental Psychology, 40*, 284–294. doi:10.1037/0012-1649.40.2.284

Wirth, W. (2006). Involvement. In S. Bryant & P. Vorderer (Eds.), *The psychology of entertainment* (pp. 199–213). Mahwah, NJ: Erlbaum.

*Zhang, L., & Busselle, R. W. (2007, May). *Exploring automatic racial attitudes revealed in thoughts about a television narrative*. Paper presented at the meeting of the International Communication Association, San Francisco. Retrieved from http://www.allacademic.com/meta/p169987_index.html

Zillmann, D. (1994). Mechanisms of emotional involvement with drama. *Poetics, 23*, 33–51. doi:10.1016/0304-422X(94)00020-7

CHAPTER CONTENTS

11 Selective Exposure, Extended Exposure, and Sidetracked Exposure

A Model of Media Exposure on the Internet and Consequential Effects

Xigen Li

City University of Hong Kong

Xudong Liu

Macan University of Science and Technology

This chapter analyzes the process of information access and media exposure on the Internet and the context in which selective exposure occurs. It also discusses how the need for cognitive closure and Internet search self-efficacy affect selective exposure and how extended and sidetracked exposures interact with selective exposure to produce potential persuasion effects. A theoretical model of media exposure on the Internet is proposed with theoretical propositions. The chapter concludes that people may access information beyond their initial intent. The reinforcement effect of selective exposure in online settings will be modified or significantly weakened if multiple media exposures occur.

Research on media use has found that people tend to select the media messages they agree with, and their beliefs and attitudes are reinforced through accessing information consistent with their pre-existing beliefs and attitudes (Garrett, 2009a; Iyengar & Hahn, 2009; Knobloch-Westerwick & Meng, 2009; Kobayashi & Ikeda, 2009; Stroud, 2010). Some of these studies dealt with selective exposure on the Internet and have found evidence of selective exposure online (Garrett, 2009a, 2009b; Johnson, Bichard, & Zhang, 2009). Selective exposure facilitated by the features of online information access raises concerns about whether it leads to fragmented political views (Kobayashi & Ikeda, 2009; Stroud, 2008). Bennett and Iyengar (2008, 2010) brought up the thesis of the reinforcement effect of the media content, and contended that an era of minimal effect may arrive due to audience fragmentation and the easiness to find information consistent with one's beliefs.

In the digital age, media channels proliferate, and people are exposed to information from a broad range of media. Will online exposure still follow a confirmation bias pattern addressed by cognition dissonance theory (Festinger, 1957)? With the increasing amount of information and the increasing complexity of information structure and retrieval, to what degree could the intentional exposure to attitude-consistent information in online settings could achieve its goal, and lead to reinforcement of existing beliefs and attitudes? When people browse information on the Internet and face tremendous amounts of information and different routes to access information, it may not be easier to achieve selective exposure. Instead, they may experience extended and sidetracked exposures. As a result of selective, extended, and sidetracked exposure, the reinforcement effect of media content may decrease in online settings, and media exposure on the Internet may result in significant changes in beliefs and attitudes toward specific issues.

This chapter analyzes the process of information access and media exposure on the Internet and the contexts and situations in which people choose selective exposure. It discusses how several sociological and psychological factors lead to different types of media exposure in online settings. We propose the need for cognitive closure as a new rationale to investigate selective exposure and other information seeking strategies. Internet search self-efficacy is also explored as a predictor of type of media exposure. We further examine how extended and sidetracked exposures interact with selective exposure and produce potential persuasion effects. We eventually build a theoretical model of media exposure on the Internet, and propose theoretical propositions on media exposure in online settings for future research.

Political Predisposition and Selective Exposure

Selective exposure refers to the behavior that "people tend to see and hear communications that are favorable and congenial to their predispositions" (Berelson & Steiner, 1967, pp. 529–530). They prefer to see and hear congenial information than hostile messages (Frey, 1986). In the media realm, selective exposure refers to the phenomenon that media users do not access available media messages equally in terms of choice of content and time spent, but prefer and avoid certain information (Zillmann & Bryant, 1985). Selective exposure often concerns political information (Johnson et al., 2009; Stroud, 2010). Politically motivated selective exposure, "the tendency to craft an information environment that reflects one's political belief" (Garrett, 2009b, p. 677), has inspired many studies that have reached conflicting conclusions (for reviews, see Garrett, 2009b; Stroud, 2008).

As more information is produced and presented on the Internet, and more people access information through the Internet, scholars have raised questions regarding selective exposure patterns in the digital age, and suspect that the Web could invite a return to selective exposure to predominantly attitude-consistent messages (Chaffee, Saphir, Graf, Sandvig, & Hahn, 2001). Prior (2007) argues that increased media channels and differences in access and forms of media significantly affect news exposure, political learning, and consequent political behaviors. As information grows exponentially and more media channels are available, people may not necessarily be exposed to more diversified political information. Increasing media channels, instead, could lead to less political knowledge and less involvement in politics. There are a growing number of websites and services that permit their audience to self-select channels or key-words and filter their exposure to different ideas, such as YouTube, Google News. Sunstein (2001) notes that emerging technologies give people the power to filter what they see. People take the initiatives to personalize the informa-tion they access with a high level of precision. Bennett and Iyengar (2008) con-tend that the increased availability of information implies an important degree of selective exposure to political information, while Iyengar and Hahn (2009) suggest that Internet technology narrows, rather than widens, users' political horizons because people select media sources that they expect to be consistent with their political beliefs (p. 34). The patterns of exposure to information online have been explored to confirm the propositions of selective exposure and the reinforcement effects (Garrett, 2009a; Graf & Aday, 2008; Johnson et al., 2009). Audiences have been found to take advantage of the features of the Internet to access information that confirms their attitudes (Johnson et al., 2009; Kobayashi & Ikeda, 2009; Stroud, 2007; Wojcieszak & Mutz, 2009).

Political predisposition is a main factor that leads to selective exposure. Peo-ple with strong party affiliation and political ideology go to specific media to find information that confirms their beliefs and opinions (Stroud, 2008). Politi-cal orientations positively predict selective exposure to political information (Johnson et al., 2009). When selective exposure happens, information congru-ent with their opinions and beliefs updates their existing opinions and beliefs (Barabas, 2004; Holbert, Garrett, & Gleason, 2010). As a result, people are assured of the validity of their beliefs or attitudes (Kruglanski & Webster, 1996; Pierro & Kruglanski, 2008). The preset beliefs are then intensified through exposure to information that confirms existing opinions. Klapper (1960) asserts that mass communication does not directly influence people, but just reinforces people's predispositions. Predispositions and the related processes of selective exposure play a role as a mediator in persuasive communication.

Political orientation and beliefs also motivate people to avoid the unpleas-ant dissonance that results from incompatibility between political attitudes and messages encountered (Knobloch-Westerwick & Meng, 2009). Festinger's (1957) theory of cognitive dissonance proposes that people are motivated to resolve cognitive conflict and maintain cognitive equilibrium. Selective expo-sure reduces the chances of engaging opinion-incongruent political informa-tion, and therefore could be predicted by intention to reduce dissonance. The meta-analysis of Hart, Eagly, Albarracín, and Brechan (2009) demonstrated that selective exposure as a defense mechanism to avoid or relieve discom-fort has been confirmed in the majority of research concerning information exposure. In the new media context, researchers have also found substantial evidence for Festinger's cognitive dissonance theory (Knobloch-Westerwick & Meng, 2009), although in some cases people are more likely to seek reinforce-ment information than to avoid dissonant information (Garrett, 2009a, 2009b).

On the other hand, Atkin's (1973) theory of informational utility suggests that people opt for specific information when its value is greater than the effort that must be invested to obtain it (Atkin, 1985; Knobloch-Westerwick,

Carpentier, Blumhoff, & Nickel, 2005; Knobloch, Carpentier, & Zillmann, 2003). In other words, people seek information that can reduce uncertainty, regardless of whether the information elicits dissonance. This is in contrast to cognitive dissonance hypothesis that people's information exposure strategy focuses on the avoidance of information that will cause dissonance, as a defense of prior attitude or judgment (Knobloch et al., 2003). Recent research has confirmed that high information utility positively influences selective exposure to both positive and negative news (Knobloch-Westerwick et al., 2005).

Critics of selective-exposure theory argue about whether the underlying psychological motivation to access opinion-congruent information actually exists (Garrett, 2009b). Recent research sometimes runs contrary to the long-standing ideology-motivated selective exposure hypotheses. For example, when checking factual information through news stories, readers don't intentionally abandon the information with which they disagree; when they look at one side of an issue, they check the other side at the same time (Garrett, 2009b; Graf & Aday, 2008; Stroud, 2008). While forms of political involvement predict attention to "attitude-consistent" messages, they also predict counter-attitudinal attention at least as strongly (Chaffee et al., 2001). People with strong party affiliation may intentionally seek counter arguments online (Knobloch-Westerwick & Meng, 2009). These findings suggest that people with political predisposition may start with selective exposure, but they don't necessarily end with selective exposure. They may extend their exposure to a wider range of information than just those items that reinforce their beliefs.

In the online environment, several aspects of information differ from that of the offline world. First, the information availability. The amount of information online is enormous and the information is expanding and updating at any given time. Second, the sources and forms of information. Information from a wide range of sources is accessible to anyone who has access to the Internet, be it from traditional media or the emerging social media. The information is presented in various formats, including text, graphics, audio, and video. A mixture of sources and forms of information brings about a comprehensive and diversified view of the world. Third, the control over information access. One may browse information while online, or download the information for later access. RSS reader allows users to pre-select what to include in their information bracket. With all the above changes, exposure beyond opinion-consistent information may occur more frequently because of easy access to counter arguments and sometimes difficulty in avoiding such information. While people may have some control over what type of information to include in their information bracket through tools such as RSS reader, they may not control what information they will eventually access. The changing scenarios of online information access pose new questions about online media exposure and the effects of media exposure on attitude and behavior changes and call for a closer examination of the factors that influence political information exposure online and the consequent persuasion effects of online media exposure. The information exposure online also requires a new theoretical framework wherein the factors that play important roles in online information access are taken into account.

Need for Cognitive Closure and Extended Exposure

Political information exposure requires individuals to retrieve, screen and eventually decide which items to consume. The investment of such cognitive effort depends on the motivation for undertaking the process (Thompson, Meriac, & Cope, 2002). While communication research has long found that ideology motivates people to look for information consistent with their beliefs, most studies have focused on the effects of political variables on information access and selective exposure but have overlooked the effects of intrinsic variables. Scholars argue that the transmission of social behaviors and political preferences is not purely cultural, and political preferences could be inherited through genes (Hatemi et al., 2001). Studies found that genetic differences account for substantial individual differences in political beliefs, behaviors, and responses to the political environment, and however indirectly—genetics plays a role in the formation of political and social attitudes (Abrahamson, Baker, & Caspi, 2002; Hatemi, Dawes, Frost-Keller, Settle, & Verhulst, 2003; Hatemi et al., 2007). These findings point to the fact that intrinsic variables such as human genome and personality could play a role in the preferences of political information processing. The Need for Cognitive Closure (NFCC), a psychological factor, is found to affect the reactions to political information access and exposure (Holbert & Hansen, 2006).

As a theoretical framework, the NFCC provides insights into how people's inclination to accept an unambiguous and firm solution influences how they process information. The NFCC refers to an individual's desire for a firm answer to a question, as opposed to uncertainty, ambiguity, or confusion (Kruglanski, 1989). It "represents a dimension of stable individual differences as well as a situationally evocable state" (Kruglanski & Webster, 1996, p. 263). As a cognitive motivation, the NFCC produces multiple biased behaviors toward the closure. The bias is first reflected in the extensiveness of the information taken into account before judgment, as the NFCC creates an urgency to seize on closure quickly (Choi, Koo, Choi, & Auh, 2008). Under the pressure of NFCC, the validity of a solution is subordinate to any strategy that can lead to faster closure. The NFCC also instills in the individual a permanent tendency to "freeze" the closure; that is, the individual will be biased toward preserving information that is viewed as useful in attaining and securing the closure. The cost of closure "freeze" is the termination of further information seeking and processing.

People with high NFCC also demonstrate biased processing of specific information; although diverse information is available, only the information that leads to less confusion will be selected and processed to achieve an urgent closure. People with a high NFCC are reluctant to access information incongruent with their own opinions (Kruglanski & Webster, 1996); exposure to incongruent information might benefit a valid judgment, but it could also produce confusion and delay closure (Knobloch-Westerwick & Meng, 2009). People with high NFCC are likely to access attitude-consistent information and avoid information that opposes prior beliefs. Seizing information consistent with prior viewpoints safeguards those viewpoints, reduces information processing difficulties, and facilitates a quick solution. Once the closure is attained, the information processed for the closure is "frozen" along with other relevant information.

The NFCC provides a useful theoretical framework to explain the ways of political information access and different types of media exposure. People with high NFCC, who have a tendency to "seize-and-freeze" in information processing, are more likely to focus on a narrow scope of information, ignore multiple perspectives of the issue, and stick to their initial beliefs without adjustment. Therefore, the tendency to "seize-and-freeze" in information processing and the information processing bias due to high NFCC pave the way for selective exposure. On the other hand, people with low NFCC are not pressed by the need for closure, so they demonstrate less bias in the information seeking process. They want to know the "how" and other aspects of an issue (Kruglanski & Webster, 1996). While they may have preset ideas on what information to seek, they do not limit their information seeking to the preset range. Extended exposure occurs when people with low NFCC suspend judgment in their information seeking until the information they obtain is sufficient to dispel their uncertainty (Kruglanski & Webster, 1996). Some even intentionally process opposing opinions and other relevant information (Lavine, Lodge, & Freitas, 2005).

Extended exposure is the process of accessing information beyond the initial search intent, regardless of whether it is consistent or inconsistent with the predispositions. Chaffee et al. (2001) found that the subjects paid similar attention to attitude-consistent messages and counter-attitude messages. Attention to counter-attitudinal political messages is a common occurrence among those politically involved people. The listeners of ideologically contrary political talk radio do not conform to the ideological and partisan dispositions of those who self-select ideologically similar programming. They seem to be ready to receive rather than resist ideologically counter messages (G. Lee & Cappella, 2001). Counter-attitudinal information might be useful for various reasons such as understanding the whole issue and learning about how the other side articulates on the issue. People may benefit from access to the counter-attitudinal information to make more informed decisions. Chaffee et al. (2001) also noted that people in a media pervasive environment are difficult to avoid counter-attitudinal information because the coverage on political issues by mainstream news media often give each side balanced treatment. Therefore exposure to counter-attitudinal information is unavoidable when watching or reading news. The online settings offer relatively easier access to a broader range of information compared to traditional media such as newspaper and television, and therefore there will be more opportunities for balanced information seeking (Valentino, Banks, Hutchings, & Davis, 2009), a form of extended exposure. While Chaffee et al.'s (2001) study found that political involvement did not make a big difference in producing attention to attitude-consistent and counter-attitudinal messages, for the same politically involved people, it could be expected that the extent to which they access political information could be negatively influenced by NFCC. Extended exposure may occur more often with people with low NFCC.

NFCC differs from intent to reduce cognitive dissonance in its way to influence selective exposure. When seeking political information on the Internet, a person with high NFCC will focus on the information that will reduce uncertainty and provide a firm answer in order to achieve a quick closure. The level of NFCC will predict the extent that information is taken into account before judgment, and it could lead to information-processing bias such as selective exposure. On the other hand, a person with high cognitive dissonance will try to avoid the information that will cause cognitive conflict. The intent to reduce cognitive dissonance predicts what information to avoid, but not necessarily what specific information to focus on. Since the information filter is cognitive dissonance, the information accessed could be much broader than the selective exposure predicted by NFCC. Therefore, NFCC could be a stronger predictor of selective exposure than cognitive dissonance. The potential effect of NFCC on exposure to information challenges the simple assertion on the relationship between political belief and selective exposure, the effect of cognitive dissonance on selective exposure and the minimal media effects thesis. If political predisposition leads to selective exposure, the relationship could be moderated by NFCC.

Sidetracked Exposure in Online Information Seeking

The concern about intensified selective exposure to political information with reinforcement of political beliefs on the Internet and the minimal media effects that ensue is based on the following assumptions: (a) one has some control of what the Internet provides; (b) one has the ability to seek and find the information desired; and (c) selective exposure occurs more often than other types of media exposure. While the Internet offers easy access to political information, and the search engines and various online communities that organize information simplify the process of finding information (Wojcieszak & Mutz, 2009), looking for specific information on the Internet may still not be as simple as the minimal media effects hypothesis assume (Bennett & Iyengar, 2008, 2010). In fact, selective exposure in online settings could be challenged by users' limited control over the information search process and information seeking efficacy. While a motivation toward selective exposure orients readers to obtain information consistent with their beliefs, search engines provide information based on website traffic and the search terms used and often give priority to paid advertisements (Jepsen, 2006). Thus, the information search process is primarily controlled by search engines' retrieval system combined with specific queries, rather than being customized by selective exposure intentions.

Therefore, sidetracked exposure may occur in the process of online information seeking. Sidetracked exposure refers to the process of running into the information that is off the preset scope of information seeking, and the hyperlinked information is accessed by the information seeker accidentally or intentionally. Sidetracked exposure contains two steps: Search results first expose the information seeker to a list of hyperlinks which orient the audience to different websites that may contain information inconsistent with the preset scope of information seeking. Then some of the hyperlinks may be clicked and accessed by the information seeker. When facing a long list of hyperlinks, an information seeker must decide whether to explore or ignore these links (Graf & Aday, 2008). Without sufficient clues about the content of the websites, the information seeker may find it difficult to decide whether the information in the websites is consistent with his or her beliefs. Thus, sidetracked exposure sometimes is difficult to avoid for those using the search engines to find political information on the Internet. People with a clear goal of information seeking may also experience sidetracked exposure. For example, conservative information seekers could go to specific news websites, just as conservative viewers turn to FOX News (Iyengar & Hahn, 2009). But when seeking information and browsing web pages, one may encounter information that goes counter to one's attitudes or beliefs, especially when one is not particularly skilled in setting the parameters of online information search. Inadvertent exposure to information that one would otherwise avoid occurs sometimes online (Brundidge, 2010; Kim, 2008). People who search to learn and investigate may actively take advantage of sidetracked exposure to scrutinize relevant information for making political judgments (Kim, 2008; Maheswaran & Chaiken, 1991). Sidetracked exposure sometimes facilitates access to multiple aspects of political issues and potentially expands the scope of knowledge, which is contrary to the assumption of the minimal media effects.

We illustrate the different types of media exposure and their relationships in Figure 11.1. Media exposure, including selective, extended, sidetracked exposure, falls into two categories: intentional and unintentional exposures. Active information seeking on the Internet usually starts as intentional. But intentional information search could also produce the information beyond the initial search scope. Therefore intentional exposure may be accompanied by unintentional exposure. Distinguishing different types of exposure—selective, extended, sidetracked, and two categories intentional vs. unintentional—is useful because different types of media exposure sometimes overlap, and each type of exposure plays a different role in producing persuasion effects (Figure 11.1).

Selective exposure is an intentional process that engages cognitive effort in screening information (Garrett, 2009a; Graf & Aday, 2008; Zillmann & Bryant, 1985), while extended and sidetracked exposures may be intentional or unintentional. When extended exposure occurs, one may intentionally seek counter-attitudinal information. When sidetracked exposure occurs, the information not originally sought bumps into the process and is eventually accessed by the information seekers. Sidetracked exposure encountered by information seekers with low NFCC could lead to further exploration, and therefore it is intentional exposure to the information beyond what is originally sought;

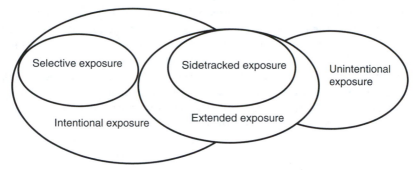

Figure 11.1 Conceptual explication of media exposure.

while sidetracked exposure by information seekers with high NFCC may not raise further interest, but be ignored, and therefore it is unintentional.

Unintentional exposure refers to that information that one does not purposively seek but "accidentally" runs into his/her information searching baskets (probably because of the seeker's search strategy or because of search engine's operation mechanism) and becomes accessible to the information seeker. Unintentional exposure occurs with both extended exposure and sidetracked exposures. A large part of extended exposure is the active and intentional access to information beyond the preset scope. Extended exposure includes sidetracked exposure, which starts from accessing information beyond the preset scope accidentally (unintentional). Sidetracked exposure could be intentional when the information that bumps into the sight attracts seekers' attention and conscious information access beyond the initial search intent follows. While intentional exposure demands deliberate action to retrieve and process information, unintentional exposure typically is an inadvertent cognitive process. The importance of unintentional exposure in political learning is confirmed by findings from passive learning and low-involvement learning. Sometimes people learn about the political issues through incidental exposure to news media coverage of politics (Krugman & Hartley, 1970; Zukin & Snyder, 1984). People who are not interested in politics can be reached and even influenced by information they would not purposefully seek if they are overwhelmed by pervasive and obtrusive information (Petty & Cacioppo, 1996; Schoenbach & Lauf, 2002). Exposure to television news can lead to incidental learning for which attention is not required (Zukin & Snyder, 1984).

Unintentional exposure happens more often with information sought on the Internet than with information sought through other types of media due to that hyperlinks in cyberspace could expand the scope of the information significantly. Although in the case of the traditional media, such as newspaper, one can still encounter extended and sidetracked exposures by just reading the headlines, with a constrained scope of information offered by the traditional media, it is relatively easier to avoid exposure to information not consistent with one's beliefs. But selective avoidance, which suppresses exposure to heterogeneous arguments, is not empirically supported in political web browsing (Kobayashi & Ikeda, 2009). The Internet is interactive in nature, and people take advantage of that interactivity to exchange and share information (Wojcieszak & Mutz, 2009). In the interactive communication exchange, unintentional exposure to information not consistent with one's beliefs occurs frequently (H. Lee, 2005), because a user cannot always detect whether the texts online contain opinion-congruent information (Garrett, 2009a). When information accumulates online, the difficulty of scanning for consistency with one's opinion increases, especially in interactive contexts such as online forums and online newspapers. For example, someone who expects to read news stories online from sources that support his/her opinions on health care reform could be exposed to just as many opinions that disagree with those attitudes. Even in the like-minded political blogs, one still cannot avoid disagreements posted by antagonistic audiences (Johnson et al., 2009). The frequent unintentional exposure suggests that the information that one is exposed to in online settings could be opinion-reinforcing, opinion-countering, or completely irrelevant to what the person initially planned to acquire. It could be the case that a sizable portion of the information retrieved will not confirm existing beliefs.

Internet Search Self-Efficacy

Information on the Internet is open to everyone. Those who know what to look for and maintain their favorite sources of information such as a blog, specific news websites, and social media such as Facebook or Twitter, may go directly to the places to get information. Selective exposure occurs more often with those people. But since information on the Internet is growing rapidly and the structure and content of the Internet change regularly, the information one seeks is not necessarily as accessible as one wishes. The capacity to access the information one wants and to achieve expected outcomes depends on the ability to retrieve and process information. When people are restricted in their abilities to search and find information, they may access only the available information (Fischer, Jonas, Frey, & Schulz-Hardt, 2005). Therefore, whether selective exposure can be achieved in online settings depends on a user's control over the information search process.

According to social cognitive theory, the ability to utilize information technologies successfully in order to achieve desired outcomes is predicted in part by self-efficacy (Rains, 2008). Self-efficacy is an individual's belief in his or her ability to perform a particular task successfully (Bandura, 1997). This perception varies across situations and specific tasks so it cannot be measured by a single scale (Bandura, 1997). The task-specific measures of self-efficacy assess the ability to complete a specific task under certain conditions. Several studies have examined the effects of self-efficacy on acquiring specific information (Thompson et al., 2002; Tsai & Tsai, 2003). Eastin and LaRose (2000) found that Internet self-efficacy has a direct effect on the expectation of finding credible information. Individuals with a weak perception of self-efficacy may get frustrated more easily by obstacles to fulfilling their goals, make less effort on a task, and tend to give up more quickly than those with higher self-efficacy (Compeau & Higgins, 1995). Therefore, self-efficacy could influence the execution of the search strategy and the degree to which the desired information can be retrieved.

When self-efficacy is applied to online information seeking, we term it Internet search self-efficacy. Internet search self-efficacy is defined as the perception of one's ability to obtain desired information when seeking information on the Internet. It differs from Internet self-efficacy (Eastin & LaRose, 2000) in that Internet search self-efficacy only applies to online information seeking but not other Internet related activities. As suggested by the findings of the effects of self-efficacy on various specific tasks, it could also be expected that Internet search self-efficacy would affect the results of online political information seeking. People with high Internet search self-efficacy are more likely to obtain the information they want than are those with low Internet search self-efficacy, who could get lost in the sea of information on the Internet (Caldas, Schroeder, Mesch, & Dutton, 2008). In the case of selective exposure, one with high Internet search self-efficacy might do better in obtaining the information consistent with their beliefs with persistent confidence and efforts. Under the extended exposure situation, a person with high Internet search self-efficacy may be able to locate a broad range of information related to the issues on which he or she is focusing. Those with lower Internet search self-efficacy, on the other hand, could encounter more difficulties in retrieving desired information with decreased confidence and efforts (Compeau & Higgins, 1995). As people's Internet search self-efficacy varies, the types of media exposure could become more diversified in online settings than what the minimal media effects propositions suggest.

However, the degree to which one can fulfill the goals of online information seeking relies on one's ability to control the information seeking process. Internet search self-efficacy, the perception of one's ability to complete a specific task, does not measure the actual information seeking skills. Internet search self-efficacy differs from actual information seeking skills in its level of controlling information seeking process. Therefore, we need to distinguish the two concepts: the Internet search self-efficacy and the information seeking skill. While it is expected that Internet search self-efficacy will partly predict type of media exposure, people who feel efficacious in information seeking may not in fact are skilled and could still experience side-tracked exposure. A high level of Internet search self-efficacy may not actually allow the information seeker to achieve the goals of online information seeking. Therefore, the variable may produce some noise in predicting type of media exposure.

Whether one can retrieve the information from the Internet as one seeks depends on the actual skills of information seeking used on the Internet. Therefore, it will be ideal to measure the actual skills of information seeking through the Internet. However, in the proposed study of the predictors of media exposure in online information seeking, we may not be able to measure the actual information seeking skills due to its technical nature. With the understanding that Internet search self-efficacy may produce some noise in predicting type of media exposure, Internet search self-efficacy could still be considered as a predictor of type of media exposure for the following reasons: (a) self-efficacy is found to be a reliable predictor of goal-oriented actions in previous studies; (b) "Internet search self-efficacy" will be carefully constructed as a comprehensive measure of one's perceived ability of online information seeking; and (c) special considerations will be taken to insure the construct validity when measuring the concept. To reduce the noise of Internet search self-efficacy in predicting the types of media exposure on the Internet, the measure of the variable will include all relevant aspects regarding the perception of one's capacity in the online information search context, including the type of information sought, the knowledge about the information sought, the availability of resources for information search (Afifi & Weiner, 2004), and previous information exposure experience (LaRose & Eastin, 2004). Some of these aspects are directly related to online information seeking experience. To further control the noise of Internet search self-efficacy in predicting type of media exposure, years of Internet use, and the experience of using search engines and other information seeking methods could be used as control variables to offset the inadequacy of Internet search self-efficacy in measuring the actual information seeking skills, and help discern the predicting value of Internet search self-efficacy in the information seeking process.

Diversified Media Exposure and Consequential Media Effects

The effect of media exposure is an issue that perplexed media scholars. Most of the studies take selective exposure as a dependent variable and did not go further to explore the effects of selective exposure. Sears and Freedman (1967) pointed out that many studies of selectivity either ignore the aspects of attitude change, or try to dismiss the possibility (p. 200). Some scholars attempt to elucidate the effects of selective exposure. For example, Adams et al. (1985) found after exposure to the film approving a Democratic candidate, individuals developed more favorable attitudes toward the candidate. Kaid's (1997) study showed that exposure to partisan presidential television advertising made the partisan viewers more positive toward the partisan candidate. Stroud's (2007) study revealed those who viewed the film *Fahrenheit 9/11*, an anti-President George W. Bush documentary, had significantly more negative attitudes toward Bush compared to those who intended to view the film. While these studies showed some effects of exposure, they failed to demonstrate the reinforcement effect of selective exposure. Whether selective exposure to attitude-consistent information reinforces attitudes has hardly ever been studied (see Stroud, 2010).

Bennett and Iyengar (2008) proposed that the minimal media effects thesis in the online context was a result of selective exposure, which leads to reinforcement of political beliefs. However, based on our analysis of online information seeking, selective exposure in online settings may sometimes be difficult to attain. What people actually obtain from the Internet could be decided by their NFCC and Internet search self-efficacy. These factors may change the direction of information seeking and eventually lead to media exposure other than selective exposure. In the process of political information retrieval, extended exposure and sidetracked exposures could take place more often than selective exposure does.

Extended exposure and sidetracked exposure may allow information seekers to encounter information inconsistent with their beliefs. No studies have ever examined the effects of extended and sidetracked exposures. The findings of a few studies of media exposure offer some insights into the effects of exposures other than selective exposure. Political predisposition is a factor considered to play a crucial role in accessing media content. After controlling for political predisposition, exposure to more campaign ads on television did affect viewers' attitudes (Overby & Barth, 2009), Warner's (2009) study attempted to test the fragmentation thesis as a result of preselecting the ideological perspective of the political content that people encountered on the Internet. The results demonstrated that exposure to ideological homogeneity produced attitude extremism in the conservative condition. The moderate condition, which includes media not so ideologically homogeneous, reduced extremism, and the mixed condition, which includes conservative, liberal and moderate media, demonstrated no significant attitude change. Zaller (1996) noted when audiences are exposed to opinion-consistent and opinion opposing messages, each opposing message system could cancel out the real effects of the separate messages if received alone. From the results of the above studies and discussions, we learned that media exposure other than selective exposure does lead to attitude changes. While exposure to attitude-consistent information may produce a stronger attitude, exposure to partisan messages will generate some effects whether the messages are consistent with one's political beliefs or not.

Different types of media exposure may produce different types of effects on attitude at varying levels. As the theory and previous research suggest, selective exposure will produce reinforcement effect, which strengthens pre-existing political beliefs. However, because selective exposure could be accompanied by extended and sidetracked exposures on the Internet, the level of reinforcement effect of selective exposure will be moderated by extended and sidetracked exposures. Those information seekers who do not have a strong political predisposition could experience extended and sidetracked exposures. Selective exposure moderated by extended and sidetracked exposures could lead to weak or even no reinforcement effects. As a result of encountering new information and possibly attitude-incongruent political information with strong arguments, extended and sidetracked exposures could produce other types of persuasion effects such as attitude formation. Attitude formation refers to the process of establishing an attitude which is not present at the time of information access and is gradually shaped through cognitive processing of new or attitude-incongruent information. The more one experiences extended and sidetracked exposures, the more opportunities to access attitude-incongruent information and arguments against the pre-existing beliefs, and the more likely new attitudes could be formed. As more attitude-incongruent information is accessed, and the arguments accepted, even the pre-existing attitudes could be adjusted or discarded, which leads to attitude change. Therefore, depending on the political predisposition, the types of media exposure, and the intrinsic and external factors involved in information seeking on the Internet, persuasion effects such as attitude reinforcement, attitude formation, and attitude change may occur correspondingly.

The potential changes in attitudes and behaviors that result from media exposure are based on cognitive processing of the information obtained from the Internet. The information received does not necessarily align with the intention of or motivation for political information seeking; the ideas and opinions embedded in the information obtained define whether the information is consistent with the political beliefs or not. Thus, people with selective exposure intention could encounter different perspectives of the issues when they access information (Garrett, 2009a; Wojcieszak & Mutz, 2009). The subsequent cognitive activities could result in consequences against the original intention to pursue selective exposure. The information incongruent with beliefs could motivate some people to seek more information from mass media or other sources and/or force them to review their initial opinions or beliefs (Huckfeldt, 2007). In the review process, the information could substitute long-standing dispositions or beliefs in decision making and could eventually persuade the information consumer to revise and even change original attitudes and opinions (Barabas, 2004).

A review of the literature of information seeking on the Internet and the effects of media exposure and the discussion of media exposure on the Internet lead us to conclude that the consequence of accessing political information via the Internet is the composite outcome of selective exposure, extended exposure, and sidetracked exposure. The effects of media messages on the Internet are contributed by all types of media exposure. Information seekers on the Internet have opportunities to access a broad range of information with diverse political views than to access only information consistent with their political beliefs. The influences of selective exposure, extended exposure, and sidetracked exposure interact and offset each other. In sum, the eventual consequences of media exposure could contain the full spectrum of persuasion of media messages: attitude formation, reinforcement, and change (Holbert et al., 2010)—instead of only reinforcement of pre-existing political beliefs.

Information incongruent with initial expectations is often processed more thoroughly than expectancy-confirming information (Maheswaran & Chaiken, 1991) because it provides new messages (Price, Cappella, & Nir, 2002). Therefore, it will draw upon more cognitive resources to decode and could produce a stronger effect than messages without such new stimuli. The exposure to opinion-incongruent information could offset part of the influence of congruent information in the formation of opinions and attitudes. While research on the hostile media effect suggests that incongruent information is both highly salient and interpreted and dismissed as source bias (Gunther & Liebhart, 2006; Gunther & Schmitt, 2004), research on cognitive processing suggests that belief-inconsistent political information could have more power than the information consistent with one's beliefs in predicting media's ability to persuade. In line with this rationale, we expect that, while opinion-congruent information reinforces beliefs, the same amount of incongruent information will negate the reinforcement effect and result in possible changes in attitude.

A Model of Media Exposure and Consequential Effects in Online Settings

To explain the information seeking process and media effects in online settings, we propose a model of media exposure and persuasion effects. The model starts with the factors that influence type of media exposure. Political predisposition is a main factor that motivates people to pursue selective exposure while seeking political information online, but information seeking may not be constrained to selective exposure. People with strong political predispositions may also actively look for additional information and cross-check information from the other side, which results in extended exposure (Figure 11.2).

The model further demonstrates the effect of Need for Cognitive Closure (NFCC) in the information exposure process. NFCC governs the mode of information seeking and determines which type of exposure one will experience when seeking information online. Those with high NFCC are more likely to focus on a narrow scope of information and to avoid diversified information in order to ensure quick closure, so they may experience selective exposure. Those with low NFCC are more likely to prefer variety, uncertainty, and flexibility of thought, and to have a high tolerance for ambiguity (Kruglanski & Webster, 1996). They are expected to choose extended exposure and access more information than what is consistent to their political beliefs. They may even take advantage of sidetracked exposure to peruse the information that is off the preset scope to expand their knowledge.

Internet search self-efficacy is the third factor that predicts type of media exposure. In online settings, selective exposure could be attained by people with a high level of Internet search self-efficacy. Internet search self-efficacy will affect people's ability to use search engines and other information seeking tools to achieve their goals and eventually determines the type of media exposure. High Internet search self-efficacy enables people to access information consistent with their predispositions with confidence and efforts. Low Internet search self-efficacy leads to unintentional exposure and could sidetrack users in the direction of information they did not initially seek. Internet search self-efficacy could also facilitate users to achieve extended exposure.

Based on the discussion of the factors that influence type of media exposure, we propose the following five propositions:

Proposition 1: Selective exposure is positively predicted by political predisposition, NFCC, and Internet search self-efficacy in online settings.

Proposition 2: Extended exposure is positively predicted by political predisposition and Internet search self-efficacy, and negatively predicted by NFCC.

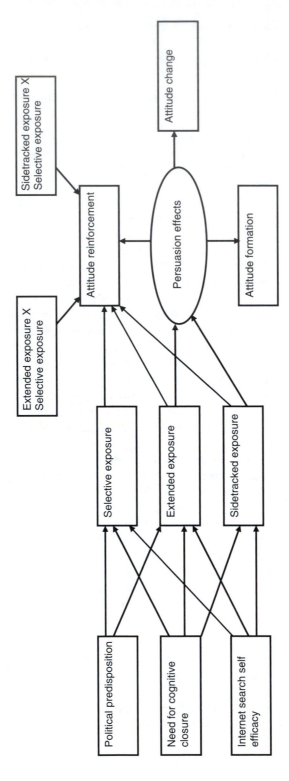

Figure 11.2 A model of media exposure and consequential effects in online settings.

Proposition 3: Sidetracked exposure is negatively predicted by Internet search self-efficacy and NFCC.

Proposition 4: NFCC is a stronger predictor of selective exposure than intent to reduce cognitive dissonance.

Proposition 5: Information seekers in online settings experience more extended exposure and sidetracked exposure than they do selective exposure.

With the understanding that selective exposure could be accompanied by extended exposure and sidetracked exposure, the consequence of accessing political information via the Internet becomes the composite outcome of all types of exposure. The effects of media messages on the Internet may go beyond the reinforcement of pre-existing political beliefs to contain the full spectrum of persuasion of media messages: attitude formation, reinforcement, and change.

The second part of the model illustrates the persuasion effects produced by different types of media exposure. As suggested by previous research, selective exposure will lead to attitude reinforcement. In the process of online information seeking, extended exposure and sidetracked exposure may also affect the level of attitude reinforcement. When extended and sidetracked exposures occur, the reinforcement effect of selective exposure could be moderated by extended and sidetracked exposures. Extended exposure and sidetracked exposure are the main factors in producing persuasion effects. The information accessed through extended and sidetracked exposures may contain the information beyond the initial search intent and preset search scope and that inconsistent with pre-existing beliefs and attitudes. Through the active or passive access to the information beyond the preset scope, extended exposure and sidetracked exposure facilitate learning on different aspects of political issues and may expand political knowledge. Extended and sidetracked exposures are expected to produce effects beyond attitude reinforcement and to affect attitude formation and change positively.

Because more cognitive resources could be devoted to processing opinion-incongruent information and intentional information exposure than are devoted to processing opinion-congruent information and unintentional information exposure, the access to belief-inconsistent information in extended exposure and sidetracked exposure could produce stronger effects than belief-consistent information in selective exposure does. Therefore, extended exposure and sidetracked exposure are expected to exert more influence on attitude formation and change than selective exposure does on attitude reinforcement. Exposure to belief-inconsistent information is also expected to generate stronger persuasion effects than opinion-congruent information in selective exposure does.

Based on the discussion on the influence of different types of media exposure on attitude reinforcement, attitude formation and change, we develop five additional propositions:

Proposition 6: Attitude reinforcement is negatively predicted by extended exposure and sidetracked exposure.

Proposition 7: Attitude reinforcement of selective exposure is moderated by extended exposure and sidetracked exposure.

Proposition 8: Extended exposure and sidetracked exposure positively predict attitude formation and change.

Proposition 9: The effects of media exposure on attitude formation and change decrease as opinion congruency with information sought increases.

Proposition 10: The effects of exposure to opinion-congruent information on attitude reinforcement are weaker than the effects of exposure to opinion-incongruent information on attitude formation and change, holding the amount of information accessed constant.

Discussion and Summary

Selective exposure and the consequential reinforcement effect thesis have been re-examined in the digital age as new media technologies facilitate online information seeking. Although evidence has shown that politically polarized consumers are motivated to be selective when accessing news information, our review of the literature on the online information seeking process and media exposure and our analysis of the factors that influence media exposure in online settings suggest that people use both selective and non-selective strategies to access political information online and that selective exposure is contextual and conditional. In online settings, selective exposure occurs along with extended and sidetracked exposures, and the assumption of the minimal media effects that only information consistent with beliefs is accessed could hardly be satisfied. Selective exposure interacts with other types of media exposure that users encounter when they seek information online, even if their initial goal was to look for information that confirms their pre-existing beliefs.

Given that it is necessary to re-examine the minimal media effects thesis in online settings, the assessment also needs to take into account both intrinsic and extrinsic variables in order to grasp the whole picture of information access on the Internet and to attain a better understanding of persuasion effects in online settings. Based on a literature review and an analysis of the information access process, selective exposure, and other types of media exposure in online settings, we propose a model of media exposure and the consequential effects in online settings and arrive at several propositions regarding media exposure and information access in the digital age. The introduction to and the deliberations about extended exposure and sidetracked exposures and intentional vs. unintentional media exposure offer novel perspectives from which researchers could reexamine information access and media exposure online. Our key points on media exposure in online settings and the consequential effects are summarized here.

First, selective exposure can be difficult to attain in online settings because of regular changes in information structure and content, and information seekers' capacity to search and process information. Therefore, the intent to achieve selective exposure because of political beliefs may not be exercised as a clear-cut objective in online settings. Those individuals who already have strong opinions on a topic and maintain their regular sources of information may go directly to their favorable sources such as a blog and a news website or a social media such as Facebook and Twitter and are less likely to experience extended and sidetracked exposures. Others who don't have strong opinions and are in the stage of initial opinion formation could experience more side-tracked exposure and intentional extended exposure besides selective exposure although such sidetracked and extended exposures could grow progressively less likely as opinion strengthens. With the ever-changing information structure and content of the Internet, even those who maintain their regular sources of information, may still need to find related information through search engines and other means of information identifying. When people seek information online, the degree to which extended and sidetracked exposures occur could be affected by search engines' specific features and Internet search self-efficacy. Media exposure online may extend to information incongruent with one's political beliefs. Because people experience multiple types of media exposure, the reinforcement effect of selective exposure may be offset by other types of exposure such that the effects of media exposure on the Internet may be a composite of the effects of all types of media exposure. The minimal media effects thesis overlooks—or at least underestimates—the effects of non-selective exposure and faces new challenges from the effects caused by side-tracked exposure and other types of online media exposure.

Second, selective exposure could be constrained by Internet search self-efficacy. Search engines provide tools that allow users to find and access information efficiently, but those who seek information vary in their ability to find and sort information that meets their specific goals. Sometimes, information seekers cannot find the specific information they seek. They may check information other than what they initially seek, and experience extended and sidetracked exposures. The ability to achieve selective exposure to a specific topic relies on the user's ability to control the information seeking process. While Internet search self-efficacy is the perception of one's ability to seek information on the Internet and is not a direct measure of one's actual information seeking skills, as a comprehensive measure of one's perceived capacity of achieving a specific goal under the online information seeking context, and a predictor of goal-oriented behavior, it is expected to affect type of media exposure. Since selective exposure could be affected by Internet search self-efficacy, only those who have relatively high Internet search self-efficacy could attain certain level of selective exposure while others may end up with a broader range of media exposure. The reinforcement effect of media exposure in online settings would be modified and significantly weakened if multiple media exposures occur as a result of low Internet search self-efficacy.

Third, selective exposure is contextual and conditional. Online settings are interactive, so what one will get next depends on the action taken in response to the messages received. The content that one accesses on the Internet is dynamic; while people with selective exposure intention may find some information consistent with their beliefs, not all of the information they access will be within a specific political or ideological scope. A click on a hyperlink may lead to a place that contains information beyond one's preset scope, and hyperlinks to desired content that worked at one time may not work later. It is even more difficult to predict what kind of messages one may receive when one participates in interactive discussions. NFCC also serves to define information seeking strategies. Information seekers with low NFCC could go beyond their initial selective exposure intention to explore more extensively across a range of information, so they could experience sidetracked exposure in addition to extended exposure.

Fourth, selective exposure to opinion-congruent information leads to weaker effects than does exposure to opinion-incongruent information. In the online context, the effects that are due to selective exposure could be relatively weak compared to the effects of other types of media exposure because of the nature of the information accessed and cognitive involvement. The opinion-congruent information obtained through selective exposure may not bear much difference from one's initial beliefs, and requires few cognitive resources to decode and analyze so, if there is a reinforcement effect, what is added to the pre-existing beliefs could be relatively limited. On the other hand, exposure to opinion-incongruent information through extended and sidetracked exposures brings with it a significant amount of new and stimulating information to which one must devote significant cognitive resources to decode and analyze. Thus, the effects of extended and sidetracked exposures are based on more active cognitive processing, which may produce attitude formation and change. Therefore, the same amount of extended or sidetracked exposure to opinion-incongruent information could produce a stronger effect than that of selective exposure to opinion-congruent information.

Conclusions

An analysis of information seeking and access in online settings leads us to conclude that selective exposure is only a small part of media exposure and that media exposure in online settings could be a combination of selective exposure and non-selective exposure. People with political predispositions may experience different types of media exposure in addition to selective exposure in online settings due to intrinsic and extrinsic factors. While information seekers may try to control the information search process, they could be exposed to a wide range of diverse information due to NFCC and Internet search self-efficacy. Even if people manage to access information selectively, some of them will experience extended and sidetracked exposures. As extended exposure increases, one retrieves a more complete profile of the subject under scrutiny and learns more about the attendant issues. In the context of political communication, although this conclusion does not support the minimal media effects thesis, it could ease the concerns about the fragmentation of audience and the narrow scope of information that people will access. It is plausible that information consumers are increasing their exposure to diverse information with multiple perspectives on political issues when they seek information on the Internet and that such media exposure expands their knowledge and facilitates sound political learning and decision-making. The concerns over the high level of selectivity of information and, hence, the minimal media effects in the digital age do not seem to reflect the reality of information access and media exposure on the Internet. With multiple types of media exposure in online settings, the full spectrum of persuasion of media messages—attitude formation, reinforcement, and change—is likely to be in play, rather than only reinforcement of pre-existing beliefs and opinions.

The goals of this chapter are to analyze the process of information access and media exposure on the Internet, extend the theoretical understanding of the relationship between selective exposure and the reinforcement effect, and explore the moderating factors in the information access process and the effects of extended and sidetracked exposures. The chapter also suggests theory-based concepts for future studies of media exposure in online settings. Bennett and Iyengar's (2008) thesis concerning the reinforcement effect of media content and the minimal media effects in the digital age was the catalyst for our examination of the information access process and media exposure in online settings. Our thoughts were also inspired by Holbert et al.'s (2010) analysis of selective exposure and reinforcement effect. How selective exposure affects attitudes and opinions is a complicated question, and there is still a dearth of empirical studies on whether selective exposure to attitude-consistent information reinforces attitudes (Stroud, 2010). While some studies have confirmed their positive relationship (Chaffee & Miyo, 1983; Lavine et al., 2005; Stroud, 2010), questions about the effects of selective exposure await additional research.

We integrate the psychological constructs NFCC and Internet search self-efficacy from social cognitive theory into a theoretical model of media exposure and the consequential media effects and develop several propositions regarding information access and the persuasion effects of media exposure in online settings. These propositions could be refined through qualitative deliberations and tested with quantitative research. The propositions and the model of media exposure on the Internet offer a broad perspective of theorizing information access and media exposure on the Internet, and the theoretical framework provides a new direction for future research on the interactive process of information access and media exposure in online settings.

Theory and research on media exposure have a long way to go to solve the puzzles that still perplex media researchers. The discussion and analysis here are just preliminary thoughts with which we hope to stimulate discussion and empirical research. When we try to find answers to some questions, new questions arise. For example, if sidetracked exposure in online settings offsets the effect of selective exposure, to what extent does sidetracked exposure produce persuasion effects that overcome the reinforcement effect? What is the mechanism of media exposure in online settings that produces attitude formation and changes? What are the key differences between the effects produced by selective exposure and non-selective exposure? All these questions leave ample space for scholars to explore through empirical observations that provide clear and confirmative answers about the dynamic state of information access on the Internet.

References

Abrahamson, A. C., Baker, L. A., & Caspi, A. (2002). Rebellious teens? Genetic and environmental influences on the social attitudes of adolescents. *Journal of Personality & Social Psychology, 83*(6), 1392–1408. doi:10.1037//0022-3514.83.6.1392

Adams, W. C., Salzman, A., Vantine, W., Suelter, L., Baker, A., Bonvouloir, L. (1985). The power of the right stuff: A quasi-experimental field test of the docudrama hypothesis. *Public Opinion Quarterly, 49*(3), 330–339. doi:10.1086/268931

Afifi, W. A., & Weiner, J. L. (2004). Toward a theory of motivated information management. *Communication Theory, 14*(2), 167–190. doi:10.1111/j.1468-2885.2004.tb00310.x

Atkin, C. K. (1973). Instrumental utilities and information seeking. In P. Clark (Ed.), *New models of communication research* (pp. 205–242). Newbury Park, CA: Sage.

Atkin, C. K. (1985). Informational utilities and selective exposure to entertainment media. In D. Zillmann & J. Bryant (Eds.), *Selective exposure to communication* (pp. 63–92). Hillsdale, NJ: Erlbaum.

Bandura, A. (1997). *Self-efficacy: The exercise of control.* New York, NY: W. H. Freeman.

Barabas, J. (2004). How deliberation affects policy opinions. *American Political Science Review, 98*(4), 687–701. doi:10.1017/S0003055404041425

Bennett, W. L., & Iyengar, S. (2008). A new era of minimal effects? The changing foundations of political communication. *Journal of Communication, 58*(4), 707–731. doi:10.1111/j.1460-2466.2008.00410.x

Bennett, W. L., & Iyengar, S. (2010). The shifting foundations of political communication: Responding to a defense of the media effects paradigm. *Journal of Communication, 60*(1), 35–39. doi:10.1111/j.1460-2466.2009.01471.x

Berelson, B., & Steiner, G. A. (1967). *Human behavior.* New York, NY: Harcourt.

Brundidge, J. (2010). Encountering 'difference' in the contemporary public sphere: The contribution of the Internet to the heterogeneity of political discussion networks. *Journal of Communication, 60*(4), 680–700. doi:10.1111/j.1460-2466.2010.01509.x

Caldas, A., Schroeder, R., Mesch, G. S., & Dutton, W. H. (2008). Patterns of information search and access on the world wide web: Democratizing expertise or creating new hierarchies? *Journal of Computer-Mediated Communication, 13*(4), 769–793. doi:10.1111/j.1083-6101.2008.00419.x

Chaffee, S. H., & Miyo, Y. (1983). Selective exposure and the reinforcement hypothesis an intergenerational panel study of the 1980 presidential campaign. *Communication Research, 10*(1), 3–36. doi:10.1177/009365083010001001

Chaffee, S. H., Saphir, M. N., Graf, J., Sandvig, C., & Hahn, K. S. (2001). Attention to counter-attitudinal messages in a state election campaign. *Political Communication, 18*(3), 247–272. doi:10.1080/10584600152400338

Choi, J. A., Koo, M., Choi, I., & Auh, S. (2008). Need for cognitive closure and information search strategy. *Psychology & Marketing, 25*(11), 1027–1042. doi:10.1002/mar.20253

Compeau, D. R., & Higgins, C. A. (1995). Computer self-efficacy: Development of a measure and initial test. *MIS Quarterly, 19*(2), 189–211. doi:10.2307/249688

Eastin, M. S., & LaRose, R. (2000). Internet self-efficacy and the psychology of the digital divide. *Journal of Computer-Mediated Communication, 6*(1). doi:10.1111/j.1083-6101.2000.tb00110.x

Festinger, L. (1957). *A theory of cognitive dissonance*. Stanford, CA: Stanford University Press.

Fischer, P., Jonas, E., Frey, D., & Schulz-Hardt, S. (2005). Selective exposure to information: The impact of information limits. *European Journal of Social Psychology, 35*(4), 469–492. doi:10.1002/ejsp.264

Frey, D. (1986). Recent research on selective exposure to information. In L. Berkowitz (Ed.), *Advances in experimental social psychology* (Vol. 19, pp. 41–80). New York. NY: Academic Press.

Garrett, R. K. (2009a). Echo chambers online?: Politically motivated selective exposure among Internet news users. *Journal of Computer-Mediated Communication, 14*(2), 265–285. doi:10.1111/j.1083-6101.2009.01440.x

Garrett, R. K. (2009b). Politically motivated reinforcement seeking: Reframing the selective exposure debate. *Journal of Communication, 59*(4), 676–699. doi:10.1111/j.1460-2466.20

Graf, J., & Aday, S. (2008). Selective attention to online political information. *Journal of Broadcasting & Electronic Media, 52*(1), 86–100. doi:10.1080/08838150701820874

Gunther, A. C., & Liebhart, J. L. (2006). Broad reach or biased source? Decomposing the hostile media effect. *Journal of Communication, 56*(3), 449–466. doi:10.1111/j.1460-2466.2006.00295.x

Gunther, A. C., & Schmitt, K. (2004). Mapping boundaries of the hostile media effect. *Journal of Communication, 54*(1), 55–70. doi:10.1111/j.1460-2466.2004.tb02613.x

Hart, W., Eagly, A. H., Albarracín, D., & Brechan, I. (2009). Feeling validated versus being correct: A meta-analysis of selective exposure to information. *Psychological Bulletin, 135*(4), 555–588. doi:10.1037/a0015701

Hatemi, P. K., Dawes, C. T., Frost-Keller, A., Settle, J. E., & Verhulst, B. (2003). Integrating social science and genetics: News from the political front. *Biodemography & Social Biology, 57*(1), 67–87. doi:10.1080/19485565.2011.568276

Hatemi, P. K., Gillespie, N. A., Eaves, L. J., Maher, B. S., Webb, B. T., Heath, A. C. (2001). A genome-wide analysis of liberal and conservative political attitudes. *Journal of Politics, 73*(1), 271–285. doi:10.1017/S0022381610001015

Hatemi, P. K., Hibbing, J. R., Medland, S. E., Keller, M. C., Alford, J. R., Smith, K. B. (2007). Not by twins alone: Using the extended family design to investigate genetic influence on political beliefs. *American Journal of Political Science, 54*(3), 798–814. doi:10.1111/j.1540-5907.2010.00461.x

Holbert, R. L., Garrett, R. K., & Gleason, L. S. (2010). A new era of minimal effects? A response to Bennett and Iyengar. *Journal of Communication, 60*(1), 15–34. doi:10.1111/j.1460-2466.2009.01470.x

Holbert, R. L., & Hansen, G. J. (2006). Fahrenheit 9-11, need for closure and the priming of affective ambivalence: An assessment of intra-affective structures by party identification. *Human Communication Research, 32*(2), 109–129. doi:10.1111/j.1468-2958.2006.00005.x

Huckfeldt, R. (2007). Unanimity, discord, and the communication of public opinion. *American Journal of Political Science, 51*(4), 978–995. doi 10.1111/j.1540-5907.2007.00292.x

Iyengar, S., & Hahn, K. S. (2009). Red media, blue media: Evidence of ideological selectivity in media use. *Journal of Communication, 59*(1), 19–39. doi:10.1111/j.1460-2466.2008.01402.x

Jepsen, A. L. (2006). Information search in virtual communities: Is it replacing use of off-line communication? *Journal of Marketing Communications, 12*(4), 247–261. doi:10.1080/13527260600694308

Johnson, T. J., Bichard, S. L., & Zhang, W. (2009). Communication communities or "cyberghettos?": A path analysis model examining factors that explain selective exposure to blogs. *Journal of Computer-Mediated Communication, 15*(1), 60–82. doi:10.1111/j.1083-6101.2009.01492.x

Kaid, L. L. (1997). Effects of television spots on images of Dole and Clinton. *American Behavioral Scientist, 40*(8), 1085–1094. doi:10.1177/0002764297040008009

Kim, Y. M. (2008). Where is my issue? The influence of news coverage and personal issue importance on subsequent information selection on the web. *Journal of Broadcasting & Electronic Media, 52*(4), 600–621. doi:10.1080/08838150802437438

Klapper, J. T. (1960). *The effects of mass communication.* Glencoe, IL: Free Press.

Knobloch-Westerwick, S., Carpentier, F. D., Blumhoff, A., & Nickel, N. (2005). Selective exposure effects for positive and negative news: Testing the robustness of the informational utility model. *Journalism & Mass Communication Quarterly, 82*(1), 181–195. doi:10.1177/107769900508200112

Knobloch-Westerwick, S., & Meng, J. (2009). Looking the other way: Selective exposure to attitude-consistent and counterattitudinal political information. *Communication Research, 36*(3), 426–448. doi:10.1177/0093650209333030

Knobloch, S., Carpentier, F. D., & Zillmann, D. (2003). Effects of salience dimensions of informational utility on selective exposure to online news. *Journalism & Mass Communication Quarterly, 80*(1), 91–108. doi:10.1177/107769900308000107

Kobayashi, T., & Ikeda, K. (2009). Selective exposure in political web browsing: Empirical verification of "Cyber-balkanization" in Japan and the USA. *Information, Communication & Society, 12*(6), 929–953. doi:10.1080/13691180802158490

Kruglanski, A. W. (1989). *Lay epistemics and human knowledge: Cognitive and motivational bases.* New York, NY: Plenum.

Kruglanski, A. W., & Webster, D. M. (1996). Motivated closing of the mind: "Seizing" and "Freezing." *Psychological Review, 103*(2), 263–283. doi:10.1037/0033-295X.103.2.263

Krugman, H. E., & Hartley, E. L. (1970). Passive learning from television. *Public Opinion Quarterly, 34*(2), 184–190. doi:10.1086/267788

LaRose, R., & Eastin, M. S. (2004). A social cognitive theory of Internet uses and gratifications: Toward a new model of media attendance. *Journal of Broadcasting & Electronic Media, 48*(3), 358–377. doi:10.1207/s15506878jobem4803_2

Lavine, H., Lodge, M., & Freitas, K. (2005). Threat, authoritarianism, and selective exposure to information. *Political Psychology, 26*(2), 219–244. doi:10.1111/j.1467-9221.2005.00416.x

Lee, G., & Cappella, J. N. (2001). The effects of political talk radio on political attitude formation: Exposure versus knowledge. *Political Communication, 18*(4), 369–394. doi:10.1080/10584600152647092

Lee, H. (2005). Behavioral strategies for dealing with flaming in an online forum. *The Sociological Quarterly, 46*(2), 385–403. doi:10.1111/j.1533-8525.2005.00017.x

Maheswaran, D., & Chaiken, S. (1991). Promoting systematic processing in low-motivation settings: Effect of incongruent information on processing and judgment. *Journal of Personality & Social Psychology, 61*(1), 13–25. doi:10.1037/0022-3514.61.1.13

Overby, L. M., & Barth, J. (2009). The media, the medium, and malaise: Assessing the effects of campaign media exposure with panel data. *Mass Communication & Society, 12*(3), 271–290. doi:10.1080/15205430802461095

Petty, R. E., & Cacioppo, J. T. (1996). *Attitudes and persuasion: Classic and contemporary approaches.* Boulder, CO: Westview Press.

Pierro, A., & Kruglanski, A. (2008). "Seizing and freezing" On a significant-person schema: Need for closure and the transference effect in social judgment. *Personality and Social Psychology Bulletin, 34*(11), 1492–1503. doi:10.1177/0146167208322865

Price, V., Cappella, J. N., & Nir, L. (2002). Does disagreement contribute to more deliberative opinion? *Political Communication, 19*(1), 95–112. doi:10.1080/105846002317246506

Prior, M. (2007). *Post-broadcast democracy: How media choice increases inequality in political involvement and polarizes elections.* New York, NY: Cambridge University Press.

Rains, S. A. (2008). Seeking health information in the information age: The role of Internet self-efficacy. *Western Journal of Communication, 72*(1), 1–18. doi:10.1080/10570310701827612

Schoenbach, K., & Lauf, E. (2002). The "Trap" Effect of television and its competitors. *Communication Research, 29*(5), 564–583. doi:10.1177/009365002236195

Sears, D. O., & Freedman, J. L. (1967). Selective exposure to information: A critical review. *Public Opinion Quarterly, 31*(2), 194–213. doi:10.1080/10584600701641565

Stroud, N. J. (2007). Media effects, selective exposure, and Fahrenheit 9/11. *Political Communication, 24*(4), 415–432. doi:10.1080/10584600701641565

Stroud, N. J. (2008). Media use and political predispositions: Revisiting the concept of selective exposure. *Political Behavior, 30*(3), 341–366. doi:10.1007/s11109-007-9050-9

Stroud, N. J. (2010). Polarization and partisan selective exposure. *Journal of Communication, 60*(3), 556–576. doi:10.1111/j.1460-2466.2010.01497.x

Sunstein, C. R. (2001). *Republic.Com.* Princeton, NJ: Princeton University Press.

Thompson, L. F., Meriac, J. P., & Cope, J. G. (2002). Motivating online performance: The influences of goal setting and Internet self-efficacy. *Social Science Computer Review, 20*(2), 149–160. doi:10.1177/089443930202000205

Tsai, M.-J., & Tsai, C.-C. (2003). Information searching strategies in web-based science learning: The role of Internet self-efficacy. *Innovations in Education & Teaching International, 40*(1), 43–50. doi:10.1080/1355800032000038822

Valentino, N. A., Banks, A. J., Hutchings, V. L., & Davis, A. K. (2009). Selective exposure in the Internet age: The interaction between anxiety and information utility. *Political Psychology, 30*(4), 591–613. doi:10.1111/j.1467-9221.2009.00716.x

Warner, B. R. (2009). Segmenting the electorate: The effects of exposure to political extremism online. *Communication Studies, 61*(4), 430–444. doi:10.1080/10510974.2010.497069

Wojcieszak, M. E., & Mutz, D. C. (2009). Online groups and political discourse: Do online discussion spaces facilitate exposure to political disagreement? *Journal of Communication, 59*(1), 40–56. doi 10.1111/j.1460-2466.2008.01403.x

Zaller, J. (1996). The myth of massive media impact revived. In D. C. Mutz, P. M. Sniderman, & R. A. Brody (Eds.), *Political persuasion and attitude change* (pp. 17–78). Ann Arbor: University of Michigan Press.

Zillmann, D., & Bryant, J. (1985). *Selective exposure to communication.* Hillsdale, NJ: Erlbaum.

Zukin, C., & Snyder, R. (1984). Passive learning: When the media environment is the message. *Public Opinion Quarterly, 48*(3), 629–638. doi:10.1086/268864

CHAPTER CONTENTS

12 Leveling Up

A Review of Emerging Trends and Suggestions for the Next Generation of Communication Research Investigating Video Games' Effects

Anthony M. Limperos

University of Kentucky

Edward Downs

University of Minnesota Duluth

James D. Ivory

Virginia Polytechnic Institute and State University

Nicholas David Bowman

West Virginia University

Research involving the uses and effects of video games has been published for nearly three decades. Despite the medium's rich potential for a broad range of societal applications and effects, the bulk of communication research dealing with video games has focused on a relatively narrow range of conceptual problems. This chapter presents an analysis of the advancement and evolution of four emerging areas of games research: gaming and cognition, gaming and health, alternative responses to anti-social gaming content, and social dimensions of gaming. In addition to reviewing the literature for each of these areas, directions for future research are suggested.

In the early 1980s, the first social-scientific research focusing on the uses and effects of video games began to appear. Despite the unparalleled growth of the video game industry and a voluminous amount of research that has been conducted, it has been a number of years since an article focusing solely on the state of video games research has appeared in *Communication Yearbook* (Wigand, Borstelmann, & Boster, 1986). Indeed, social-scientific research on video game uses and effects has become a major focus of mass media research, including publications in top-rated communication journals and collected volumes of research reports (Vorderer & Bryant, 2006). Yet, the bulk of that research has been focused on a relatively narrow range of conceptual problems, despite the medium's potential for a broad range of societal applications and effects. Research which focuses on the effects of video and electronic games is generally concerned with understanding any type of impact that the game-playing situation and/or experience has on the game player (Vorderer & Bryant, 2006). Historically, most of the research involving the effects of video games has been largely concerned with potential negative impacts (Lee, Peng, & Park, 2009). More recently, though, there have been advances in previously underdeveloped areas of gaming effects research dealing with a broader spectrum of positive and problematic effects, and we envision seeing more of these innovative research trajectories in the near future.

As the critical mass of information related to the effects of games has grown, many scholars have provided pieces that synthesize and reflect upon the entire body of gaming effects research (Lee et al., 2009; Vorderer & Bryant, 2006). There have been many studies and commentaries on the effect of violent video games on aggression and anti-social behavior (Anderson, 2004; Anderson et al., 2010; Ferguson, 2007; Sherry, 2001). While it is true that a majority of the research has focused on the resultant impact of games, other studies have specifically focused on describing the content and types of portrayals that are present in popular video games (Downs & Smith, 2010; Smith, Lachlan, & Tamborini, 2003; Williams, Martins, Consalvo, & Ivory, 2009). Finally, there have also been entire books dedicated to understanding how video games can impact learning, health, and other prosocial outcomes (Gee, 2003; Ritterfeld, Cody, & Vorderer, 2009).

Research on the effects of video games in the field of communication is guided by a variety of theoretical perspectives, and is constantly evolving. This evolution can be observed in new research foci that consider new mechanisms related to gaming and cognition, video games and health, games as experiential spaces for reflection and introspection, and the social aspects of video gaming. This chapter will highlight theory and research in each of these areas, and suggest directions to advance existing scholarship so that we can better understand the effects of video games.

Gaming and Cognition

While previous research focused on video games as either cognitive tasks involving hand-eye coordination and anticipation of motion (e.g., Kuhlman & Beitel, 1991) or media stimuli with rudimentary real-time interaction (e.g., Scott, 1995), recent changes in the way video games are played have dramatic implications for the study of cognitive responses to them. When the Nintendo Wii console was released in 2006, the innovative gyroscopic controller packaged with the Wii console helped Nintendo stand out from its competitors. However, with the later releases of the Microsoft *Kinect* and PlayStation *Move*, one could argue that the defining characteristic of seventh generation consoles was the advent of motion control devices as primary interface mechanisms. The incorporation of kinesthetic, motion-sensing technology added a new element of game play from which gamers had the ability to learn (Downs & Oliver, 2009). On screen motions that were previously conducted through a series of symbolic button pushes were replaced with the physical motions involved with playing sports, marksmanship, driving, yoga, guitar playing, and dancing. In addition to motion controllers, improvements in processing power, data storage, graphic resolution, and audio fidelity all contributed to enhancing the end-user experience by making game play feel more real. Now more than ever, our games have become simulations.

Video Games as Simulators

Conceptually, a simulation is a representation or model of a physical or social system (Heinich, Molenda, Russell, & Smaldino, 1996) that allows a user to engage, change, and observe the system's characteristics in a manner that is consistent with reality (Squire, 2003). In the case of video and computer games, these mediated environments are often algorithm-based, artificial worlds (Lieberman, 2006) that can be categorized into hi-fidelity and low-fidelity environments (Thiagarajan, 1998). Although the line between hi- and low-fidelity environments may admittedly be hazy at times, scholars (Arsenault, 2008; Steuer, 1992) hint that the line may be defined by the *depth* and *breadth* of the simulation. For example, *Guitar Hero* may be able to teach multiple basic music skills like melody, harmony, and rhythm at the surface level (read: breadth), but it may not be hi-fidelity enough for a person to transfer their virtual guitar playing skills into the real world as the guitar interface does not have frets or strings (read: depth) (Arsenault, 2008). However, flight simulators used by military instructors provide enough breadth and depth of simulation so that pilots can train on a hi-fidelity, simulated system and transfer the skills they've learned into a real cockpit.

Although fidelity fluctuates from video game to video game, it is easy to see how everything from *America's Army* (Nieborg, 2004) to *Tiger Woods' Golf* (Downs & Oliver, 2009) has the potential to teach through simulation. With the addition of motion control devices as primary interface agents for many of today's games, cognitive scripting of video game content or simulated material can give way to implicit motor learning or muscle memory (Masters & Maxwell, 2004; Poolton, Masters, & Maxwell, 2007). This means that video game simulation has the potential to cognitively script information, and could possibly change and refine behaviors. It must also be recognized that both cognitive and behavioral learning is situated within a specific, dynamic system that is designed to focus on some skills, but not others. For game researchers, this places an emphasis on examining not only content-driven factors of video games, like the presence of violent, sexual, or antisocial content that could be scripted, but also context-driven factors as well (Gee, 2008a; Squire, 2006). Context factors include such items as how game players are choosing to interact with the game interface, whether they are playing alone, or with others (e.g., Jansz & Martens, 2005), or whether or not game players feel immersed in the game environment. The question becomes how do we theoretically anchor this type of research.

Theories of Learning and Cognition

Few would argue that video games cannot facilitate learning. Many works from scholars chronicle the relationship between video games and various cognitive and behavioral processes (see Egenfeldt-Nielsen, 2006; Gee, 2003, 2006, 2008a, 2008b; Ke, 2008; Kebritchi & Hirumi, 2008; Kirriemuir & McFarlane, 2004; Squire, 2006). However, methodological limitations such as variations in stimulus material, the focus on different types of game players, varied exposure times during experimental sessions, and lack of control groups, impedes our ability to fully understand the processes through which video game simulation influences learning (Egenfeldt-Nielsen, 2006). In the midst of these methodological limitations, the use of theory-guided research becomes a strong asset to our understanding of cognitive processes. In one of the most comprehensive manuscripts to engage this topic, Egenfeldt-Nielsen (2006) outlines many different educational theories to demonstrate how they can be used in a video game/simulation context. Although a full review of Egenfeldt-Nielsen's work is beyond the scope of this chapter, he focused his efforts on many different traditions in educational theory, including behaviorism, cognitivism, and socio-culturalism. This following section will provide a brief overview of how theories from each of these domains can be applied to our understanding of video games and cognition.

Behaviorist Theory.   There is a well-documented behaviorist tradition in the study of video games as learning tools (Kebritchi & Hirumi, 2008; Egenfeldt-Nielsen, 2006; Prensky, 2001). The behaviorist approach to using video games tends to rely on the works of theorists such as Skinner, Thorndike, and Watson (Egenfeldt-Nielsen, 2006) and results in games designed with skill-and-drill functionality (less affectionately known as drill-and-kill; Prensky, 2001). The stimulus-response paradigm in game design operates through the mechanisms of repetition and reward. This type of learning can be beneficial in some domains of learning. For example, those that focus on the learning of facts, or declarative knowledge, like math, spelling, or science; or areas that focus on physical and reflex skills, such as typing, playing a musical instrument, or any repetitive sports simulation (Prensky, 2001). Although there is evidence that these types of mediated simulations can be helpful, scholars question if these types of games are providing enough structure and context for game players to transfer what they've learned into the real world (Egenfeldt-Nielsen, 2006). Research in this area should examine if video games used in this manner are able to effectively teach metacognitive skills such as critical thinking, and whether or not game players reflect on their experiences in meaningful ways (Kiili, 2005).

Social Cognitive Theory (SCT).   Perhaps the most frequently used theory for the study of games and learning is social cognitive theory (Bandura, 2002). Many chapters and empirical reports have examined how game players can learn through modeled behavior (see Buckley & Anderson, 2006; Downs & Smith, 2010; Lee & Peng, 2006; Lieberman, 2006; Weber, Ritterfeld, & Kostygina, 2006, for a review). SCT's strength lies in its ability to explain the processes that govern how people learn modeled behaviors through their interaction with mediated content. However, it is limited in scope because the primary richness of social cognitive theory is in the mechanisms detailing the cognitive scripting of information, and identifying the circumstances under which a modeled behavior is likely to manifest itself. What SCT does not do well is account for subtle changes or refinements in behavioral learning (as opposed to cognitive learning). This limitation can be explained by SCT's focus on content variables with less of an emphasis on contextual variables. When it comes to the cognitive learning of a behavior, SCT works well, but when it comes to explaining how behaviors are modified, or how skills rehearsed from a video game simulation will transfer to real-world environments, SCT falls short. Another theory, situated cognition, could be operating parallel to SCT and may hold additional explanatory power for understanding this type of learning environment.

Situated Cognition.   If games are truly becoming more like simulators, then examining how content to be learned is situated from a contextual standpoint is critical. Advocates of the theory of situated cognition propose that learning occurs best when members of a community have the opportunity to observe and practice a behavior *in situ* (Brown, Collins, & Duguid, 1989). Video games and simulations have the ability to situate learning in a specific context, because they can "put language into the context of dialogue, experience, images, and action" (Gee, 2006, p. 178). In essence, this type of learning environment allows game players the ability to take game content and apply it in a virtual domain or virtual community of practice. Take for example *America's Army*. This simulation allows game players to learn and use terminology and tactics necessary for success in various field operations. The ability to use and rehearse the proper protocols under many different circumstances allows game players the ability to manipulate and rehearse *in situ* the practices they are taught. They also have the opportunity to learn from others who have more experience. Learning rules from the community of practice can facilitate indoctrination into that community (Lave & Wenger, 1991).

   From a situated perspective, video game simulation lets game players think through many possible solutions and gives them opportunities to create mental models of their experiences. From these models, the game player can imagine other scenarios and play them out to determine if a behavior or tactic succeeds or fails. Each of these opportunities, in turn, simulates an experience that will become part of a schema that can be used for action in the real world (Gee, 2008b). With enough experience situated in context, a game player can generate the necessary schema and scaffolding needed to transfer knowledge into other similar domains of practice. For example, learning how to effectively clear an area of enemy soldiers in *America's Army* could be of potential benefit in a number of situations, including: in a *Halo* or *Call of Duty* tournament, a real-life paintball match, or during a live field operation.

Future Research in Gaming and Cognition

Using the theoretical approaches listed previously as well as other theories of learning and cognition will help to extend not only our understanding of cognitive and behavioral learning as media effects, but will serve to inform and refine theories of cognition. At the same time it will also provide practical information for game designers who want to optimize the educational experience (Kriz & Hense, 2006). The different theoretical approaches also serve as a guide to inform researchers on how to delineate between different types of learning. Specifically, researchers should be careful to identify and measure as many types of relevant learning as possible when conducting games research. For example, they should examine whether learning in simulation environments is geared to be primarily cognitive or behavioral; implicit versus explicit; or procedural versus declarative in nature.

Another area ripe for the study of games and cognition is through the examination of how technological affordances facilitate or hinder learning and the transfer of skills. Sundar's MAIN model (2008) provides the theoretical architecture for understanding how the technological affordances of modality, agency, interactivity, and navigability could influence the learning process. For example, modality speaks to the number of sensory channels that a medium appeals to. Televisual media such as video games are considered multimodal as they appeal concurrently to both visual and aural channels with moving images and sound. Although the dual-coding of information through two different modalities is beneficial in learning environments (Paivio, 1991) empirical work (Downs, Boyson, Alley, & Bloom, 2011; Mayer & Moreno, 1998) has found that certain combinations of modalities (ex. visual and aural) are better than others in mediated learning environments. The study of modality in video games can help game designers to understand the conditions under which certain modalities can facilitate the learning process, or create a situation favorable to cognitive overload. Agency (the perceived source of information), interactivity (the ability to input and receive feedback from a medium) and navigability (the ability to understand one's position in virtual space), all have additional implications for learning in video game environments.

In addition, a host of mediating variables could also influence cognition in video game simulation environments. Variables such as presence (Tamborini & Skalski, 2006), natural mapping (Skalski, Tamborini, Shelton, Buncher, & Lindmark, 2011), flow (Kiili, 2005), identification (Downs, 2010; Klimmt, Hefner, & Vorderer, 2009), and customization (Sundar, 2008) could all work within the parameters of the previously detailed theories and provide information for game developers on how to maximize cognitive and behavioral learning. Examining the use of intrinsic versus extrinsic motivation in gaming and cognition studies can also be beneficial (Malone, 1981; Prensky, 2001). Above all, learning is a process that develops over time so game scholars would benefit from conducting more longitudinal studies in lieu of one-shot experiments to document the effectiveness of video game simulations (Ke, 2008). Exploring video games as simulation agents through the lens of learning and cognition can help to unlock the secrets of cognitive processes and provide insight into how both content and context variables improve learning. As cognitive processes do not change for better or worse, continued research in this domain is critical for the understanding of media effects of both prosocial and anti-social games.

Gaming and Health

Although questions and concerns pertaining to the potential negative behavioral impacts of video games have dominated both public and scholarly discourse, there has been a steady rise and sustained interest in understanding how games might impact healthy behaviors (Lee et al., 2009). Shortly after releasing its Wii console, Nintendo introduced the companion Wii Balance Board and began advocating the idea of exercising at home through the use of "exergames." Other game makers such as Microsoft and Sony have followed Nintendo's lead by introducing their own motion-based gaming controls complete with exercise-based applications. Also, there has been a considerable amount of research that has focused on understanding how video games can be used to teach, motivate, and impact healthy life choices and behaviors (see Lieberman, 2006; Ritterfeld et al., 2009; Peng & Liu, 2008). Yet, despite the relatively well-developed research involving video games and health promotion, studies that focus specifically on the effectiveness of commercial health games have only recently begun to emerge. Given the exponential growth of these types of games, it is important for games researchers to continue to investigate which variables might contribute to the overall effectiveness of these types of games.

Previous and Current Research on the Health Benefits of Video Games

Studies focusing on the health benefits of video games have been on the rise since the 1990s. A majority of the studies in this area have focused on clinical and intervention-based applications of serious games. By definition, "serious games" are those which blend aspects of simulation and learning with entertainment (Ritterfeld et al., 2009). Furthermore, those who interact with a serious game often do so to experience some type of benefit that exceeds the sheer entertainment value often associated with *most* types of gaming. Although serious games have received considerably less attention than other areas of gaming, findings from a recent systematic analysis generally support the idea that games designed for intervention and other health-related purposes are an effective channel for influencing individuals toward healthy outcomes and behaviors (Baranowski, Buday, Thompson, & Baranowski, 2008).

In one of the earliest studies to assess the effectiveness of a video game in a health-related context, Brown et al. (1997) designed and tested a juvenile diabetes game (*Packy & Marlon*) and found that adolescents' self-efficacy, attitudes toward their own care, and communication about their disease was improved by a video game that focused on bolstering these outcomes. Other studies have found that video games can be used to increase feelings of efficacy toward safe-sex negotiation (Thomas, Cahill, & Santilli, 1997) and knowledge about sports-related concussion symptoms (Goodman, Bradely, Paras, Williamson, & Bizzochi, 2006). Across these studies, self-efficacy was identified as the primary mechanism for explaining how knowledge and behavior are encouraged as a result of playing certain types of games. Most of the research on the positive effects of video games has been rooted in classic theories of behavior and psychology.

Recently, Peng (2009) constructed (based on social cognitive theory) and implemented a computer-based eating simulation game and found that it was effective at educating college-aged individuals about how to eat healthier. Accordingly, Baranowski et al. (2008) found that almost all (93%) video games designed for health promotion had a positive impact on learning, behavior, and attitude change, underscoring that video games do work well in promoting desired outcomes, especially when they are designed to do so. However, in recent years, many new commercially available health-focused games have found their way into living rooms all over the world, leading many to ask: Are these games effective and do they have an impact similar to games that are designed with specific outcomes in mind? Emergent research suggests that this is the case; however, the scope of research on this topic is still relatively underdeveloped.

Recently, there has been a rise in research related to commercially available games that promote physical activity and exercise. These games are commonly referred to as "off-the-shelf" active video games (Peng, Lin, & Crouse, 2011, p. 681). Though "serious games" is an umbrella term that is often used to describe everything from games that are designed to educate and train to those which encourage exercise, "off-the-shelf" active video games have often been categorized as having a more "casual" than "serious" orientation (Juul, 2009). Casual commercially available active games can encompass anything from dancing (e.g., *Dance-Dance Revolution*) to adventure/sports titles (e.g., *Wii Sports*), whereas those that focus specifically on exercise (e.g., *Wii Fit*, *Biggest Loser*) have a more serious orientation. Despite the fact that there has been much popular press and anecdotal evidence in support of active games in promoting healthy behaviors, initial studies in this area show that effectiveness of active games can be attributable to a number of different factors.

Peng, Lin, and Crouse (2011) found that playing active video games does indeed facilitate light to moderately intense physical activity. Although this study found aggregate evidence that active games do encourage and promote physical activity, there hasn't been much support for the idea that playing them can actually lead to desired outcomes such as weight loss. For example, there have been studies that have focused on understanding if *Dance-Dance Revolution* could promote weight loss/positive outcomes amongst children, and the results have been conflicting (Madsen, Yen, Wlasiuk Newman, & Lustig, 2007; Maloney et al., 2008). While some researchers have tried to understand if playing active games can produce tangible health benefits, others have tried to understand the motivational role that these active gaming technologies might play in everyday life, as well as the psychology of playing active games.

Although evidence shows that active video games can promote and encourage physical activity, the answer of whether or not playing these games is equal to or better than other types of physical activity remains in question. Although some studies have shown correlational evidence to support the idea that playing active games and simulators can actually increase one's general propensity for physical activity, a recent study found that activity levels of children who received and used an active video game for the Wii console were no different than children who had access to a similar game that did not involve physical activity (Baranowski et al., 2012). Even though the results of that study seem to suggest that exergames (and potentially other active games) might not be advantageous when compared with other activities, emerging research seems to suggest that positive outcomes associated with active games is linked with individual psychology and user interactions with game features and technology.

Active games, especially those that focus on exercise, contain many different technological characteristics and message features that should be well suited for promoting healthy behavior and recent studies have begun to disaggregate and understand how user experiences and variations with in-game features impact these gaming experiences. For example, researchers have found that seeing oneself on-screen in exercise games can enhance feeling of efficacy, as long as the player is comfortable with their real body image (Song, Peng, & Lee, 2011). Furthermore, studies have also shown that games, which adjust body image based on real biometric data, might actually have a negative impact on the in-game experiences and future use of exergames (Jin, 2009, 2010). Other studies have highlighted the importance of player performance, feedback, and mapping in cueing positive game experiences and intentions to revisit exergames (Limperos & Oliver, 2012). Peng, Lin, Pfeiffer, and Winn (2012) designed an exergame with different manipulated features and found that motivation and engagement with exergames are related to intrinsic need satisfaction and enjoyment. Together, these studies show that understanding the health benefits and effectiveness of commercially based active video games is a rather complex task that is influenced by the duality of individual and experiential factors, and interactions with gaming interfaces.

Future Directions in Gaming and Health Research

Research concerning the impact of games on various health outcomes will likely continue to be a vibrant area in the future, especially as new gaming technologies emerge. While past and current research into gaming for health (both clinical and commercial) has led to general understanding of why certain games are either effective/ineffective, it will be important for future research to consider a greater diversity of mechanisms related to this gaming context in order to more fully understand the *process* by which these games are influential.

As is the case with any type of media in today's society, understanding the utility, effectiveness, and psychology of active and other types of serious games will require researchers to consider how individual differences, variations in gaming technology, and game content/features interact to shape game player experiences and outcomes. Classic theories of psychology and behavior have already proven to be valuable in helping researchers understand the impact and design of effective serious games (Baranowski et al., 2008; Lieberman, 2006; Peng, 2009; Peng et al., 2012). In addition to some of the classic theories, understanding what contributes to game player enjoyment in serious gaming will likely be a topic of great interest in future serious games studies (Haring, Chakinska, & Ritterfeld, 2011). While it is important to continue to apply classic theories and frameworks in order to explain how serious games motivate and elicit outcomes amongst certain populations, future research must also consider the role that technology itself can play in shaping outcomes of gaming.

Another aspect of serious games research that needs greater specificity involves how the effectiveness of these types of games is conceptualized, measured, and discussed. While some studies have found more naturalistic ways to assess whether or not different types of serious games have longitudinal effects, there is still much debate about short-term experimental studies and what they really tell us about the effects of these games. In most clinical and intervention studies that focus on serious games, the action of playing a game is often what researchers hope will exert influence on some real-world attitude, behavior, or cognition. Researchers often anticipate that such results will be lasting, even in the absence of the game. While assessing behavior intentions, attitudes, and cognition-related outcomes are important, assessing the intentions for future use of a particular serious game is an important aspect often omitted from this type of research. Assessing future use or continued access to a serious game is important for understanding what sustains motivation and ultimately keeps people engaged with certain games. In addition to understanding individual orientation and psychological responses, studies that focus on physiological responses (e.g., heart rate, blood pressure, and weight) to serious games have been and will continue to be crucial for understand the value of active and serious games.

A final consideration of research in the area of health and gaming involves sample populations. Most of the aforementioned research involving games and health involve different populations. Media effects research has shown us that media messages are often not received uniformly and that individual differences can have a meaningful impact on the way that messages are received (Oliver & Krakowiak, 2009). Therefore, it will be important for researchers to consider how effective certain types of health games (commercial or otherwise) are in light of sample populations and individual differences. For example, children, college-aged adults, and more elder individuals may all have different experiences with a particular type of game. Therefore, it is important for researchers to temper conclusions about the utility and effectiveness of certain types of games in light of different sample populations.

Though the bulk of this section of the chapter focuses mostly on future research opportunities involving active games, the broader landscape of serious games research contains studies involving everything from therapeutic uses of games to intervention, education, and behavioral/skill development (see Kato, 2010; Wilkinson, Ang, & Goh, 2008). With the emergence of journals focusing on health benefits of games, funding opportunities, and the continued proliferation of gaming technologies, serious gaming research will likely garner interest for years to come. Generally, we have learned that video games have the ability to motivate and encourage healthy behavior, but future research must do more to understand exactly *why* this is the case.

Alternative Reponses to Anti-Social Content in Gaming

The media effects paradigm has considered the role of anti-social mediated content in explaining observed anti-social influences of its audience—particularly in video games as users are actively engaged in the violation of social morals rather than merely witness to these violations. In particular, research applying the general aggression model to video game content argues that this repeated rehearsal of aggressive scripts in virtual environments creates similarly valenced and readily accessible models of behavior within gamers who, in response to provocation, are significantly more likely to respond aggressively (Anderson & Bushman, 2002). Bandura's (2002) social cognitive theory is often invoked to explain how anti-social virtual content is most likely to stick with video game players as the constant exposure to bad behavior is exacerbated by the game's requirement of user focus and control—games require users to be active perpetrators rather than passive spectators of anti-social action.

At the same time, anecdotal and empirical evidence continues to implicate video games as powerful devices in the teaching of cognitive, behavioral, and affective scripts, for better (understanding complex biological and engineering applications; cf. Mayo, 2007) or for worse (engaging in street racing and unlicensed driving following video game play; Fischer, Kubitzki, Guter, &

Frey, 2007). Research on popular video game content continues to suggest that the presence of anti-social content like violence (Smith, Lachlan, & Tamborini, 2003), sex (Brathwaite, 2006), and profanity (Ivory, Williams, Martins, & Consalvo, 2009), can be somewhat dangerous because it provides anti-social models of behaviors (e.g., the general aggression model, Anderson & Bushman, 2002). The American Psychological Association has adopted the position that there is "converging evidence that exposure to media violence is a significant risk factor for aggressive and violent behavior" (APA, 2003, para. 1). Yet, effect sizes gleaned from this research remain small (Sherry, 2001) and crime statistics—both violent and nonviolent—continue to decline. One way to reconcile this empirical discord is to consider the possibility that anti-social content might lead to no meaningful effects, or in some cases, might actually result in prosocial response. We identify three possible ways in which this effect can be expected: morality, lack of interest, and appreciation.

Morality and Reappraising Game Content

Morality has been a focal point for video game theory and research and emerging studies suggest that a variety of contextual cues related to moral disengagement in gaming have a differential impact on outcomes of the gaming experience (Hartmann & Vorderer, 2010). As interactive spaces, games are thought to be particularly adept at allowing gamers to encounter, learn and even rehearse reactions to a variety of different emotional states, including those concerned with morality (Grodal, 2000; Johnson, 2010). But how does an individual's morality explain their motivation to enact (or not) the models of morally questionable behaviors experienced in video games? Emerging research applying moral foundations theory (Haidt & Joseph, 2004) suggests that innate moral judgments may be key to this process. For example, Tamborini, Eden, Bowman, Grizzard, and Lachlan (2012) report that variance in individual moral intuitions is predictive of how gamers appraise and eventually react to violent media content. Early research has found initial evidence to suggest that moral intuitions are not only predictive of gamers' appraisals of content as moral or immoral, but also of in-game responses to such content. Specifically, Tamborini and colleagues found that when a video game presented gamers with a choice to commit a moral violation, gamers who felt strongly about the particular situation (i.e., inflicting harm on an innocent) avoided the violation. Conversely, gamers who did not have a strong intuitive reaction to the moral presentation made seemingly random decisions to violate or not in an effort to play with different outcome scenarios (Joeckel, Bowman, & Dogruel, 2012). This observed "gut" (moral intuition-based) or "game" (experience-based) reaction is in line with current theorizing on the function of morality in entertainment media, specifically Raney's (2010) notion of moral disengagement—that we actively suspend our moral code in order to maximize media enjoyment. Indeed, the research expands this line of reasoning further to suggest that while we initially suspend morality in favor of enjoyment, there are aspects of our moral codes that are likely non-negotiable.

Appreciation in Reflection of Anti-Social Content

The dominant paradigm in media effects research hinges on the rewards associated with the experience of enjoyment as reinforcing the retention of anti-social models of behavior. Yet, recent theorizing by Oliver and Raney (2011) suggests this to be a myopic view of the entertainment experience that masks an equally prevalent and powerful media effect: appreciation. Understood as introspective behaviors aimed at helping individuals reflect upon truth and purpose in their own life (Oliver & Raney, 2011), such an effect seems plausible in explaining the apparent paradox of experiencing enjoyment from sad or tragic media, such as *Schindler's List* or *Old Yeller* (cf. Oliver, 1993). In short, Oliver argues that a powerful motivation for consuming media is to seek out meaningfulness, and that this experience is orthogonal from the more basal hedonic motivation.

Whether or not video games are capable of invoking feelings of meaningfulness is not known. On the one hand, video game technologies are particularly well-suited at increasing feelings of social presence, a known predictor of narrative processing and feelings of connectedness with game characters (Tamborini & Bowman, 2010) that is likely associated with feelings of meaningfulness. Bowman, Schultheiss, and Schumann (2012) found that increased feelings of responsibility for and control over character actions—both dimensions of character attachment—were predictive of playing games for prosocial motivations, and this line of argumentation might be extended further to suggest that increased prosocial involvement with a virtual narrative might elicit more powerful feelings of meaningfulness. On the other hand, it could be argued that video games as a form of popular entertainment have been long established as simple challenge and competition games (Sherry, Lucas, Greenberg, & Lachlan, 2006) and that the learned expectations associated with their consumption are firmly rooted in the hedonic model. Atkin (1985) argues that learned expectations are a robust indicator of selective exposure, as they guide the types of media we seek as well as the gratifications sought in them. From this, it may simply be the case that gamer audiences do not seek meaningfulness in their gaming experience, thus mitigating any potential for the medium to provide reflection and introspection. Moreover, one might wonder whether or not the gameplay elements of a video game might be counter-productive to the reflection elements of the same, as they might compete for the limited cognitive resources of the gamer (cf. Schneider, Lang, Shin, & Bradley, 2004). For example, the highly regarded first-person shooter *Medal of Honor: Allied Assault* begins by placing gamers on the beaches of Normandy as part of the WWII Allied invasion forces, but the game quickly shifts from its dramatic, panoramic, and retrospective presentation of the invasion to a more narrow, fast-paced, and isolated perspective in order to allow the gamer to concentrate on getting from checkpoint to checkpoint. This shift in perspective also brings with it a focus on murdering your opponent rather than reflecting on the historic gravity of the event itself. Related to this, video game play is known to be significantly more cognitively taxing than other forms of media (Bowman & Tamborini, 2012; Reinecke et al., 2012), and this increased task demand may interfere with our ability to process more introspective narrative elements, as suggested to some extent by Schneider et al. (2004).

Loss of Interest in Anti-Social Content

As entertainment software, we commonly assume that video games are inherently engaging and interesting. Yet, an often-overlooked effect of game content on individuals is that of disinterest; we can become less interested or attracted towards a thought, feeling, or behavior after experiencing its mediated version. Bogost (2011) argued that gaming experiences are not inherently enjoyable, and that we can be both repulsed and engrossed by game content. Notably, this is not a cathartic argument, as catharsis would assume individuals to have some affinity toward the content so as to expunge it in advance of real-world consequences (a concept that has been heavily critiqued in the literature; Bushman, 2002). Rather, disinterest argues that video game portrayals can create or reinforce our negative gut reactions. An example of such disinterest can be found in the browser-based casual game *The Torture Game*, a game that invites players to take turns "tortur[ing] the poor guy using different objects" (ArcadeCabin.com, para. 2). Gameplay is simple, violent, graphic, and is not justified by any narrative element. Reaction to the game was (and continues to be) very intense, with even avid video gamers questioning the role of such content in the general panacea of gaming (Kongregate, 2008). Similar content can be found in more mass-produced and commercially successful video games, such as the crime and murder elements of the popular *Grand Theft Auto* series.

Yet, such repulsion is precisely what Bogost (2011) argues is both (a) a potential media effect and (b) a decidedly prosocial one. In being repulsed, gamers are reminded of their own humanistic limits, and by vicariously experiencing the role of executioner, are left with a feeling of guilt and disgust from bearing witness to their own actions. Moreover, the real-world implications of this process are not trivial. Video games may perhaps play an even more compelling role in other contexts, allowing for the simulation of similar actions and forcing individuals to cope with the consequences of their own actions.

Future Research on Alternative Explanations to Negative Content

The studies and theories cited above suggest that the relationship between anti-social content and individual effect is perhaps more complicated than "bad content leads to bad things." For example, while current research suggests that gamers have a limit as to how much they can suspend their moral intuition in video games, we might suggest that repeated exposure to moral violations might weaken our resolve, particularly if games reward us for committing moral violations. Tamborini (2011) argues that moral intuitions are initially fostered from our non-mediated cultural environment and reinforced or manipulated through long-term exposure to media content. While popular media generally adheres to rather than violates societal-level moral standards (cf. Klapper, 1960), producers will occasionally break these expectations to surprise audiences; this is particularly common in video games where content norms related to what is and is not appropriate are not as well established. Recent data indeed suggest that entertaining media content can result in shifts in moral judgment (Tamborini, Weber, Eden, Bowman, & Grizzard, 2010), and a logical extension of this research may be to examine long-term influences on moral intuition stemming from video game play rewarding anti-social over prosocial behaviors.

In terms of loss of interest, we see the concept as moving beyond the much-maligned notion of catharsis and argue that the learning of anti-social models of cognition, affect, or behavior can result in the internalization and eventual rejection of the same—yet this claim has yet to be tested empirically. Research in this vein might consider disgust or repulsive reactions to media content as integral in the model/script retention process, as work by Tamborini, Weber, Bowman, Eden, & Skalski (in press) reports that audience interpretations of the levels of graphicness, justification, and realism of a violent act are significant determinants of their evaluations of said act.

Finally, research regarding the role of meaningfulness (see Oliver & Raney, 2011) in video games is perhaps the most underdeveloped of the three perspectives highlighted here. As media psychologists continue to focus their attention on the dual outcomes of enjoyment and appreciation, research on meaningfulness should be particularly relevant. While research has explored the role of interactive game play dynamics on enjoyment of video games (e.g., Klimmt, Hartmann, & Frey, 2007; Vorderer, Hartmann, & Klimmt, 2003), meaningful responses to game content should be similarly examined. Player expectations are also integral to this research, as an understanding of what individuals seek from video games likely serves as an indicator of appraisals of how enjoyable or meaningful the experience is (cf. Palmgreen, Wenner, & Rayburn, 1980)— one particularly novel area of player expectations is in the area of vitality and recovery, which argues that video games are a resource-contributing rather than a resource-depleting activity that helps us cope with stressors, such as those in the workplace (cf. Reinecke, 2009; Reinecke, Klatt, & Kramer, 2011).

In addition to understanding these responses to various types of games, it is also important to consider the influence of interactions that people have with one another while playing video games.

Social Dimensions of Gaming

As much of the literature reviewed above indicates, an extensive body of research has examined responses to media that are fundamentally social in nature. The study of actual social dynamics of video game users' interaction, however, has been a relatively recent development. Consequently, the number of studies that have examined video games as a "one-way" medium—effectively as stimuli provoking responses in their users—far outstrips the emerging body of literature investigating video games as a medium through which people interact socially with one another.

Previous and Current Research on Social Dimensions of Video Games

The relative paucity of research on social interaction involving video games over their history is somewhat unusual considering that even the earliest prototypes of video games were designed for two players to use simultaneously. Both *Tennis for Two*, a rudimentary oscilloscope-based analog tennis simulator developed by nuclear scientist William Higinbotham in 1958 as a novelty to entertain visitors to the U. S. Department of Nuclear Energy's Brookhaven National Laboratory in Upton, NY, and *Spacewar!*, a digital rocketship dueling game completed by a group of students at the Massachusetts Institute of Technology in 1962, required two users to play (Consalvo, 2006; Kirriemuir, 2006; Lowood, 2006; Rockwell, 2002). Later commercial video games have tended to follow the example of the seminal 1972 arcade and console hit *Pong* (Lowood, 2006; Rockwell, 2002) by allowing users to play against each other in pairs or alone against a computer-controlled opponent, with typical arcade and home video game consoles designed to allow users to play alone or in pairs (Williams, 2006). The dynamics of social interaction between players of these games, though, tended to be understudied for decades. A few studies conducted during the first couple of decades after video games became a commercially popular medium did examine social interactions between game users, such as Fisher's (1995) survey of young arcade visitors, which found that the primary motivation for users' patronage of arcades was to socialize with others, and Mitchell's (1985) research on families' use of home console video games together. Most research on the medium, though, examined video game users' demographics, use of the medium, and potential effects on individual users rather than on social interaction between users.

To an extent, the limited amount of research on social interactions between video game users during the medium's early years is justified by the predominance of video game use as an individual activity. Indeed, nearly three quarters of respondents to Selnow's (1984) early survey of video game users reported playing video games by themselves, even at arcades, leading him to conclude that "videogame playing is typically a solitary activity" (p. 155). Selnow's survey results also suggested that rather than engaging with other players, heavy game users might engage in a type of "electronic friendship" (p. 155) with the medium itself by engaging in some form of social interaction with video games as a "surrogate companion" (p. 155).

For decades, most video game consoles did not allow users to play games with others who were not present in the same place at the same time. Meanwhile, an array of text-based role-playing MUD (Multi-User Dungeon) games were being played together online by users by the dawn of the 1980s, starting with the development of the original *MUD* game by computer-science students at the University of Essex between 1978 and 1980 (Bartle, 2010; Castronova, 2002). These MUDs and similar text-based variants received some attention from researchers, particularly as a domain for social interaction and self-representation, and community (e.g., Bruckman & Resnick, 1995; Rheingold, 1993; Turkle, 1994). The prominence of MUDs as a focus of research dealing with the social role of commercial video games is limited, however, because of the relatively small audience of the Internet during MUDs' early heyday, the noncommercial nature of most MUDs, and MUDs' lack of graphics or fast-paced play. Instead, MUDs have typically received more attention in literature dealing with online communities (e.g., Rheingold, 1993).

More research on social interaction in video games would follow the advent of Massively Multiplayer Online Role-Playing Games (MMORPGs), an online video-game genre with partial roots in the online text MUDs (Mortensen, 2006). The two brothers who originally developed the 1996-release *Meridian 59*, which was arguably the first commercial three-dimensional MMORPG, while they were students at the Massachusetts Institute of Technology and Virginia Tech were inspired by an early commercial MUD called *Scepter of Goth* (Ludlow & Wallace, 2007). The wildly popular MMORPG *EverQuest*, released in 1999, was the target of one of the first scholarly efforts to document the prevalence and dynamics of social interaction in video games. Castronova (2001) surveyed *EverQuest* users to examine their demographics and social behavior, as well as the economics of "real-life" trade of game items. Among his findings were that one in five respondents considered *EverQuest*'s fictional world of "Norrath" to be the place where they "live," that about the same number reported that they would spend all of their time in Norrath if they could, and that respondents spent an average of more than four hours a day playing the game.

Yee (2006a, 2006b) conducted a series of surveys involving users of *EverQuest* and three other popular MMORPGs to investigate their demographics, motivations, and experiences. Yee's surveys produced a number of results indicating the strong social dynamics in the games. A substantial minority of male respondents and a slight majority of female respondents rated their friendships in the games as comparable or superior to friendships outside of the games, and 15.7% of male respondents and 5.1% of female respondents reported having dated someone they met in a game (Yee, 2006a, 2006b). Substantial numbers of respondents also reported playing the games with a romantic partner or family member, and that they believed playing the games facilitated development of a number of useful interpersonal skills (Yee, 2006a, 2006b).

Subsequent studies of MMORPG users have produced similar results, indicating that many MMORPG users make good friends in the games (Cole & Griffiths, 2007), are primarily drawn to the games for their social dynamics (Griffiths, Davies, & Chappell, 2004), feel that they can be "more themselves" in the games than in real life (Cole & Griffiths, 2007), and tend to take part in game communities that are primarily social in nature (Williams et al., 2006). Further, newer technological features in MMORPGs, such as voice "chat" functionality, have been found to enhance feelings of community among users (Williams, Caplan, & Xiong, 2007). So robust are the social dynamics of virtual environments like those in MMORPGs that users exhibit similar interpersonal behavioral patterns via their online avatars as they do in real life (Yee, Bailenson, Urbanek, Chang, & Merget, 2007). Given the powerful social dynamics of online environments, researchers have suggested that their users' online behavior could be used to model "real-life" phenomena from economic trends (Castronova et al., 2009) to disease epidemics (Balicer, 2007; Lofgren & Fefferman, 2007).

In recent years, much of the research on social dimensions of games has focused on genre leader *World of Warcraft*, which has been a dominant presence in the commercial MMORPG market since its initial 2004 release and boasted as many as 12 million subscribers worldwide by 2011 (Ivory, 2012). Therefore, *World of Warcraft* heavily informed the literature on a vast array of social dimensions of online games, either through studies specifically focused on events in *World of Warcraft* ranging from social dynamics of player groups (e.g., Williams et al., 2006) and modes of interaction (e.g., Williams et al., 2007) to epidemiological implications of the spread of in-game "plagues" of character afflictions (e.g., Balicer, 2007). Additionally, general surveys of MMORPG users, while not targeting *World of Warcraft* specifically, have typically received large portions of their response data from *World of Warcraft* users (e.g., Cole & Griffiths, 2007). Another prominent source of research data about users of online games has been *EverQuest II*, which lacks *World of Warcraft*'s dominant market share but has had a disproportionally high presence in communication research on MMORPGs due to a collaboration between the game's producers (Sony Online Entertainment) and a team of researchers (e.g., Williams, Consalvo, Caplan, & Yee, 2009; Williams, Yee, & Caplan, 2008).

Future Research on Social Dimensions of Gaming

While many social dimensions of video games have been charted extensively in recent years, there is still a need for further investigations of their social dynamics. Even though studies have found evidence that social behaviors in online game environments sometimes mirror offline behaviors, the extent to which the study of game environments can be used to inform an understanding of human behavior will not be fully understood until we have a better understanding of when game behaviors mirror offline behaviors and when they do not. Therefore, a program of research should explore the limits of the "mapping" (Williams, 2010) between online and offline behaviors to better determine when social dynamics of the two settings are similar and when they are not.

Also, just as past research on traditional arcade and console video games appears to have been carried out more or less independently of research dealing with early online MUD-type games, research on social dynamics of MMORPG games appears to be carrying on without much comparison to social interaction on more traditional console games. While we know a lot from existing research about social dimensions of MMORPGs, particularly a few MMORPGs such as *World of Warcraft* and *EverQuest II* that have been the focus of numerous studies, this literature addresses only a fraction of the types of games that exist in which people can interact socially online. In addition to MMORPGs, many other types of games, including the action games that have traditionally comprised video games' most popular genres, are also now often played online. Presently, many popular console games, such as "shooter" games and sports titles, allow friends and strangers to battle it out online in brief contests hosted by services such as Microsoft's Xbox Live network or Sony's Playstation Network. While there has been some effort to examine the group dynamics of online "shooter" games (e.g., Eastin, 2007; Eastin & Griffiths, 2006, 2009), much more work needs to be done to document the nature of interaction in these shorter-term, less community-focused settings and compare them to the well-documented social dynamics of MMORPGs. In fact, given that a multitude of video games now exist, with a vast variety of social interactions and motivations, a comprehensive understanding of social interaction in video games may require a typology of video-game dimensions germane to social interaction (e.g., presence of competition and cooperation; intensity, frequency, and duration of interaction; extent of anonymity/pseudonymity; photorealism of avatars) to guide how research from one game environment can be applied to another. In general, then, we have learned that video games have rich social dimensions, but we must do more to understand how and when those social dimensions vary by comparison to each other and by comparison to our real-world social lives.

General Discussion and Concluding Thoughts

A lot has changed in the last 30 years since the initial research into the effects and societal impact of video games first began to appear. There have been seven generations of game consoles. Motion controllers are slowly replacing single joystick-and-button game controllers. Budgets to fund some popular game franchise releases now eclipse the budgets of some Hollywood films.

Despite these changes, many things have stayed the same. Gamers still spend countless hours devoting themselves to achieving high scores, exploring virtual worlds, and competing for bragging rights. Regardless of video game or game console preference, gamers from all generations still become nostalgic about their all-time favorite games and reminisce with others about their epic wins and defeats. In many ways, games have a way of uniting people across generations and cultures in a virtual world of shared experiences.

The summaries of different areas of gaming effects research that we provided in this chapter were written with those shared experiences in mind. Our explorations into the world of games and cognition, health and gaming, alternative explanations to gaming content, and the social dimensions of video games were not designed to be the definitive road map of where games studies must go; rather, they were written to promote thought and discussion. Our hope is that some scholars will find these ideas provocative, and that others will continue to pursue their own unique lines of inquiry. Regardless, the vision that we have spelled out here was written with the intent to galvanize the community of video game researchers through the shared experience of scholarly inquiry.

While we concede that this chapter is limited to a few specific areas of gaming effects research, we want to acknowledge that other methodological approaches continue to be important in video games research. Strides in our understanding of video games' social roles have been made from the critical and cultural studies perspectives. These explorations examine how game narratives differ from other media forms and how these changes influence perceptions and game play dynamics (see Jenkins, 2004, 2006). In an attempt to engage the discussion about ways of knowing and methodological differences, Williams (2005) explained that critical and empirical scholars must not continue to look past one another and instead should embrace one another's ideas. However, Williams (2005) cautioned that bridging research differences may not be an easy task by stating:" "few humanists are going to learn statistics and few social scientists are going to suddenly try ethnography—realistically, the initial steps simply need to be open-mindedness and connections" (p. 458). Again, while we do not definitively engage literature outside of the effects paradigm in this chapter, we want to recognize that the issues and questions we pose could be engaged from a variety of perspectives.

Video games are complex medium that involve concepts and constructs which describe the relationships and influences between game players, gaming contexts, and game systems. Describing and understanding general game play experiences and the effects of those playing experiences will garner interest for years to come. As gaming has changed over the years, the questions that we have asked and are interested in understanding have also evolved. We now think about video games as teaching tools, potential for forces of good, and simulators for many different facets of life. If video games can indeed be thought of as simulations of real-world events, the possibilities for future research are endless. The ability to leverage our current understanding of many diverse content areas such as those explored here, with customizable and malleable virtual worlds, allows us the ability to explore the many nuanced facets of the human psyche.

References

American Psychological Association. (2003, October). Violent video games: Myths, facts, and unanswered questions. Retrieved from http://www.apa.org/science/about/psa/2003/10/anderson.aspx

Anderson, C. A. (2004). An update on the effects of playing violent video games. *Journal of Adolescence, 27*, 113–122. doi:10.1016/j.adolescence.2003.10.009

Anderson, C. A., & Bushman, B. (2002). Human aggression. *Annual Review of Psychology, 53*, 27–51. doi:10.1146/annurev.psych.53.100901.135231

Anderson, C. A., Shibuya, A., Ihori, N., Swing, E. L., Bushman, B. J., Sakamoto, A., … Saleem, M. (2010). Violent video games effects on aggression, empathy, and prosocial behavior in eastern and western cultures: A meta-analytic review. *Psychological Bulletin, 136*, 151–173. doi:10.1037/a0018251

ArcadeCabin.com (n.d.). The torture game – game details. Retrieved from: http://www.arcadecabin.com/play/the_torture_game.html

Arsenault, D. (2008). Guitar Hero: Not like playing a guitar at all? *Loading …, 2*(2), n.p.

Atkin, C. (1985). Informational utility and selective exposure to entertainment media. In D. Zillmann & J. Bryant (Eds.), *Selective Exposure to Communication* (pp. 63–92). Hillsdale, NJ: Erlbaum.

Balicer, R. D. (2007). Modeling infectious diseases dissemination through online role-playing games. *Epidemiology, 18*, 260–261. doi:10.1097/01.ede.0000254692.80550.60

Bandura, A. (2002). Social cognitive theory of mass communication. In J. Bryant & D. Zillmann (Eds.), *Media effects: Advances in theory and research* (pp. 121–153). Mahwah, NJ: Erlbaum.

Baranowski, T., Adbelsamad, D., Baranowski, J., O' Connor, T., Thompson, D., Barnett, A., … Chen, T-A. (2012). Impact of an active video game on healthy children's physical activity. *Pediatrics, 129*, 636–642. doi:10.1542/peds.2011-2050

Baranowski, T., Buday, R., Thompson, D. I., & Baranowski, J. (2008). Playing for real: Video games and stories for health-related behavior change. *American Journal of Preventative Medicine, 34*, 74–82. doi:10.1016/j.amepre.2007.09.027

Bartle, R. A. (2010). From MUDs to MMORPGs: The history of virtual worlds. In J. Hunsinger, L. Klastrup, & M. Allen (Eds.), *International handbook of Internet research* (pp. 23–39). Dordrecht, The Netherlands: Springer.

Bogost, I. (2011). *How to do things with videogames*. Minneapolis: University of Minnesota Press.

Bowman, N. D., Schultheiss, D., & Schumann, C. (2012). "I'm attached, and I'm a good guy/gal!": How character attachment influences pro- and anti-social motivations to play massively multiplayer online role-playing games. *CyberPsychology, Behavior, and Social Networking, 15*, 169–174. doi:10.1089/cyber.2011.0311

Bowman, N. D., & Tamborini, R. (2012). Task demand and mood repair: The intervention potential of computer games. *New Media & Society, 14*, 1339–1357. doi:10.1177/1461444812450426

Brathwaite, B. (2006). *Sex in video games.* Rockland, MA: Charles River Media, Inc.

Brown, J. S., Collins, A., & Duguid, P. (1989). Situated cognition and the culture of learning. *Educational Researcher, 18,* 32–42. doi:10.2307/1176008

Brown, S. J., Lieberman, D. A., Gemeny, B. A., Fan, Y. C., Wilson, D. M., & Pasta, D. J. (1997). Educational video game for juvenile diabetes: Results of a controlled trial. *Informatics for Health and Social Care, 22,* 77–89. doi:10.3109/14639239709089835

Bruckman, A., & Resnick, M. (1995). The MediaMOO project: Constructionism and professional community. *Convergence, 1,* 94–109. doi:10.1177/135485659500100110

Buckley, K. E., & Anderson, C. A. (2006). A theoretical model of the effects and consequences of playing video games. In P. Vorderer & J. Bryant (Eds.), *Playing video games: Motives, responses, and consequences* (pp. 363–378). Mahwah, NJ: Erlbaum.

Bushman, B. (2002). Does venting anger feed or extinguish the flame? Catharsis, rumination, distraction, anger and aggressive responding. *Personality and Social Psychology Bulletin, 6,* 724–731. doi:10.1177/0146167202289002

Castronova, E. (2001). *Virtual worlds: A first-hand account of market and society on the cyberian frontier.* CESifo Working Paper No. 618. http://ssrn.com/abstract=294828

Castronova, E. (2002). *On virtual economies.* CESifo Working Paper No. 752. http://ssrn.com/abstract=338500

Castronova, E., Williams, D., Shen, C., Ratan, R., Xiong, L., Huang, Y., & Keegan, B. (2009). As real as real? Macroeconomic behavior in a large-scale virtual world. *New Media and Society, 11,* 685–707. doi:10.1177/1461444809105346

Cole, H., & Griffiths, M. D. (2007). Social interactions in massively multiplayer online role-playing gamers. *CyberPsychology and Behavior, 10,* 575–583. doi:10.1089/cpb.2007.9988

Consalvo, M. (2006). Console video games and global corporations: Creating a hybrid culture. *New Media and Society, 8,* 117–137. doi:10.1177/1461444806059921

Downs, E. (2010, June). *Eighteenth century video games: Using the Hegelian dialectic to explain how individuals identify with avatars during game play.* Paper presented at the 60th Annual Meeting of the International Communication Association, Singapore, Malaysia.

Downs, E., Boyson, A. R., Alley, H., & Bloom, N. R. (2011). iPedagogy: Using multimedia learning theory to iDentify best practices for MP3 player use in higher education. *Journal of Applied Communication Research, 39,* 184–200. doi:10.1080/00909882.2011.556137

Downs, E., & Oliver, M. B. (2009, May). *How can Wii learn from video games? Examining relationships between technological affordances and socio-cognitive determinates on affective and behavioral outcomes.* Paper presented at the 59th Annual Meeting of the International Communication Association, Chicago, IL.

Downs, E., &, Smith, S. L. (2010). Keeping abreast of hypersexuality: A video game character content analysis. *Sex Roles, 62,* 721–733. doi:10.1007/s11199-009-9637-1

Eastin, M. S. (2007). The influence of competitive and cooperative group game play on state hostility. *Human Communication Research, 33,* 450–466. doi:10.1111/j.1468-2958.2007.00307.x

Eastin, M. S., & Griffiths, R. P. (2006). Beyond the shooter game: Examining presence and hostile outcomes among male players. *Communication Research, 33,* 448–466. doi: 10.1177/0093650206293249

Eastin, M. S., & Griffiths, R. P. (2009). Unreal: Hostile expectations from social gameplay. *New Media and Society, 11,* 509–531. doi:10.1177/1461444809102958

Egenfeldt-Nielsen, S. (2006). Overview of research on the educational use of video games. *Digital Kompetanse, 1*, 184–213.

Fischer, P., Kubitzki, J., Guter, S., & Frey, D. (2007). Virtual driving and risk-taking: Do racing games increase risk-taking cognitions, affect, and behaviors? *Journal of Experimental Psychology: Applied, 13*, 22-31. doi:10.1037/1076-898X.13.1.22

Fisher, S. (1995). The amusement arcade as a social space for adolescents: An empirical study. *Journal of Adolescence, 18*, 71–86. doi: 10.1006/jado.1995.1006

Ferguson, C. J. (2007). Evidence for publication bias in video game violence effects literature: A meta-analytic review. *Aggression and Violent Behavior, 12*, 470–482. doi: 10.1016/j.avb.2007.01.001

Gee, J. P. (2003). *What video games have to teach us about learning and literacy.* New York, NY: Palgrave/Macmillan.

Gee, J. P. (2006). Are video games good for learning? *Digital Kompetane, 3*, 172–183.

Gee, J. P. (2008a). Video games and embodiment. *Games and Culture, 3*, 253–263. doi:10.1177/1555412008317309

Gee, J. P. (2008b). Learning and games. In K. Salen (Ed.) *The ecology of games: Connecting youth, games, and learning* (pp. 21–40). The John and Catherine T. MacArthur Foundation series on digital media and learning. Cambridge, MA: MIT Press.

Goodman, D., Bradely, N. L., Paras, B., Williamson, I. J., & Bizzochi, J. (2006). Video gaming promotes concussion knowledge acquisition in youth hockey players. *Journal of Adolescence, 29*, 351–360. doi:10.1016/j.adolescence.2005.07.004

Griffiths, M. D., Davies, M. N. O., & Chappell, D. (2004). Demographic factors and playing variables in online computer gaming. *CyberPsychology and Behavior, 7*, 479–487. doi:10.1089/cpb.2004.7.479

Grodal, T. (2000). Video games and the pleasures of control. In D. Zillmann & J. Bryant (Eds.), *Media entertainment: The psychology of its appeal* (pp. 197–213). Mahwah, NJ: Erlbaum.

Haidt, J., & Joseph, C. (2004). Intuitive ethics: How innately prepared intuitions generate culturally variable virtues. *Daedalus, 133*, 55–66. doi:10.1162/0011526042365555

Haring, P., Chakinska, D., & Ritterfeld. U. (2011). Understanding serious games: A psychological perspective. In P. Felicia (Ed.), *Handbook of research on improving learning and motivation through educational games: Multidisciplinary approaches* (pp. 413–430). New York, NY: IGI Global.

Hartmann, T. & Vorderer, P. (2010). It's okay to shoot a character. Moral disengagement in violent video games. *Journal of Communication, 60*, 94–119. doi:10.1111/j.1460-2466.2009.01459.x

Heinich, R., Molenda, M., Russell, J. D., & Smaldino, S. E. (1996). *Instructional media and technologies for learning* (5th ed.). Englewood Cliffs, NJ: Prentice-Hall.

Ivory, J. D. (2012). *Virtual lives: A reference handbook.* Santa Barbara, CA: ABC-CLIO.

Ivory, J. D., Williams, D., Martins, N., & Consalvo, M. (2009). Good clean fun? A content analysis of profanity in video games and its prevalence across game systems and ratings. *CyberPsychology and Behavior, 12*, 457–460. doi:10.1089/cpb.2008.0337

Jansz, J. & Martens, L. (2005). Gaming at a LAN event: The social context of playing video games. *New Media & Society, 7*, 333–335. doi:10.1177/1461444805052280

Jenkins, H. (2004). Game design as narrative architecture. In N. Wardrip-Fruin & P. Harrigan (Eds.), *First person: New media as story, performance, game* (pp. 118–130). Cambridge, MA: MIT Press.

Jenkins, H. (2006). *Convergence culture: Where old and new media collide.* New York: New York University Press.

Jin, S. A. (2009). Avatars mirroring the actual self versus projecting the ideal self: The effects of self-priming on interactivity and immersion in an exergame, *Wii Fit. Cyberpsychology & Behavior, 12,* 761–765. doi:10.1089/cpb.2009.0130

Jin, S. A. (2010). Does imposing a goal always improve exercise intentions in avatar-based exergames? The moderating role of interdependent self-construal on exercise intentions and self-presence. *Cyberpsychology, Behavior, and Social-Networking, 13,* 335–339. doi: 10.1089/cyber.2009.0186

Joeckel, S., Bowman, N. D., & Dogruel, L (2012). Gut or game: The influence of moral intuitions on decisions in virtual environments. *Media Psychology, 15,* 460–485. doi:10.1080/15213269.2012.727218

Johnson, J. L. (2010, September 21). Games are modern morality. *Escapist Magazine.* Retrieved from http://www.escapistmagazine.com/articles/view/issues/issue_272/8130-Games-Are-Modern-Morality-Plays

Juul, J. (2010). *A casual revolution: Reinventing video games and their players.* Cambridge, MA: MIT Press.

Kato, P. M. (2010). Video games in health care: Closing the gap. *Review of General Psychology, 14,* 113–121. doi:10.1037/a0019441

Ke, F. (2008). A qualitative meta-analysis of computer games as learning tools. In R. E. Ferdig (Ed.), *Handbook of research on effective electronic gaming in education* (pp. 1–32). New York, NY: IGI Global. doi:10.4018/978-1-59904-808-6.ch001

Kebritchi, M., & Hirumi, A. (2008). Examining the pedagogical foundations of modern educational computer games. *Computers & Education, 51,* 1729–1743. doi:10.1016/j.compedu.2008.05.004

Kiili, K. (2005). Digital game-based learning: Towards an experiential gaming model. *Internet and Higher Education, 8,* 13–24. doi:10.1016/j.iheduc.2004.12.001

Kirriemuir, J. (2006). A history of digital games. In J. Rutter & J. Bryce (Eds.), *Understanding digital games* (pp. 21–35). London, England: Sage.

Kirriemuir, J., & McFarlane, A. (2004). Literature review in games and learning. *FutureLab.* Retrieved from http://www.futurelab.org.uk/download/pdfs/research/lit_reviews/Games_Review1.pdf

Klapper, J. T. (1960). *The effects of mass communication.* New York, NY: Free Press.

Klimmt, C., Hartmann, T., & Frey, A. (2007). Effectance and control as determinants of video game enjoyment. *CyberPsychology and Behavior, 10,* 845–848. doi:10.1089/cpb.2007.9942

Klimmt, C., Hefner, D., & Vorderer, P. (2009). The video game experience as "true" identification: A theory of enjoyable alterations of players' self-perception. *Communication Theory, 19,* 351–373. doi:10.1111/j.1468-2885.2009.01347.x

Kongregate.com. (2008). The Torture Game 2 debate: Evil or stress-relieving? Retrieved from http://www.kongregate.com/forums/3/topics/26096?page=1

Kriz, W. C., & Hense, J. U. (2006). Theory-oriented evaluation for the design of and research in gaming and simulation. *Simulation & Gaming, 37,* 268–283. doi: 10.1177/1046878106287950

Kuhlman, J. S., & Beitel, P. A. (1991). Video game experience: A possible explanation for differences in anticipation of coincidence. *Perceptual and Motor Skills, 72,* 483–488.

Lave, J., & Wenger, E. (1991). *Situated learning: Legitimate peripheral participation.* New York, NY: Cambridge University Press.

Lee, K. M., & Peng, W. (2006). What do we know about social and psychological effects of computer games? A comprehensive review of the current literature. In P. Vorderer & J. Bryant (Eds.), *Playing video games: Motives, responses, and consequences* (pp. 325–346). Mahwah, NJ: Erlbaum.

Lee, K., Peng, W., & Park, N. (2009). Effects of computer/video games and beyond. In J. Bryant & M. B. Oliver (Eds.), *Media effects: Advances in theory and research* (3rd ed., pp. 551–556). Mahwah, NJ: Erlbaum.

Lewis, M. L., Weber, R., & Bowman, N. D. (2008). "They may be pixels, but they're MY pixels!" Developing a metric of character attachment in role-playing video games. *Cyberpsychology and Behavior, 11,* 515–518. doi:10.1089/cpb.2007.0137

Lieberman, D. (2006). What can we learn from playing interactive games? In P. Vorderer, & J. Bryant (Eds.), *Playing video games: Motives, responses, and consequences* (pp. 379–397). Mahwah, NJ: Erlbaum.

Limperos, A. M., & Oliver, M. B. (2012, May). *Assessing the viability of mediated exercise technologies in motivating future exercise intentions.* Paper presented at the 62nd Annual Meeting of the International Communication Association, Phoenix, AZ.

Lofgren, E. T., & Fefferman, N. H. (2007). The untapped potential of virtual game worlds to shed light on real world epidemics. *Lancet Infectious Diseases, 7,* 625–629. doi:10.1016/S1473-3099(07)70212-8

Lowood, H. E. (2006). A brief biography of computer games. In P. Vorderer & J. Bryant (Eds.), *Playing computer games: Motives, responses, and consequences* (pp. 25–41). Mahwah, NJ: Erlbaum.

Ludlow, P., & Wallace, M. (2007). *The Second Life Herald: The virtual tabloid that witnessed the dawn of the metaverse.* Cambridge, MA: MIT Press.

Madsen, K. A., Yen, S., Wlasiuk, L., Newman, T. B., & Lustig, R. (2007). Feasibility of a dance video game to promote weight loss among overweight children and adolescents. *Archives of Pediatrics and Adolescent Medicine, 161,* 105–107. doi:10.1001/archpedi.161.1.105-c

Malone, T. W. (1981). Towards a theory of intrinsic motivation. *Cognitive Science, 4,* 333–369. doi:10.1016/S0364-0213(81)80017-1

Maloney, A. E., Bethea, T. C., Kelsey, K. S., Marks, J. T., Paez, S., Rosenberg, A. M., ... Sikich, L. (2008). A pilot of a video game (DDR) to promote physical activity and decrease sedentary screen time. *Obesity, 16,* 2074–2080. doi:10.1038/oby.2008.295

Masters, R. S. W., & Maxwell, J. P. (2004). Implicit motor learning, reinvestment and movement disruption: What you don't know won't hurt you? In A. M. Williams & N. J. Hodges (Eds.), *Skill acquisition in sport: Research, theory and practice* (pp. 207–228). London, England: Routledge.

Mayer, R. E., & Moreno, R. (1998). A split-attention effect in multimedia learning: Evidence for dual processing systems in working memory. *Journal of Educational Psychology, 90,* 312–320. doi:10.1037//0022-0663.90.2.312

Mayo, M. J. (2007). Games for science and engineering education. *Communications of the ACM, 50,* 30–35.

Mitchell, E. (1985). The dynamics of family interaction around home video games. *Marriage and Family Review, 8,* 121–135. doi:10.1300/J002v08n01_10

Mortensen, T. E. (2006). WoW is the new MUD: Social gaming from text to video. *Games and Culture, 1,* 397–413. doi:10.1177/1555412006292622

Nieborg, D. B. (2004). America's Army: More than a game? In T. Eberly & W. C. Kriz (Eds.), *Transforming knowledge into action through gaming and simulation* [CD ROM]. Munchen: SAGSAGA.

Oliver, M. B. (1993). Exploring the paradox of the enjoyment of sad films. *Human Communication Research, 19,* 315–342. doi:10.1111/j.1468-2958.1993.tb00304.x

Oliver, M. B., & Krakowiak, K. M. (2009). Individual differences in media effects. In J. Bryant & M. B. Oliver (Eds.), *Media effects: Advances in theory and research* (3rd ed., pp. 517–531). Mahwah, NJ: Erlbaum.

Oliver, M. B., & Raney, A. A. (2011). Entertainment as pleasurable and meaningful: Differentiating hedonic and eudaimonic motivations for entertainment consumption. *Journal of Communication, 64,* 984–1004. doi:10.1111/j.1460-2466.2011.01585.x

Palmgreen, P., Wenner, L. A., & Rayburn, J. D. (1980). Relations between gratifications sought and obtained. *Communication Research, 7,* 161–192. doi:10.1111/j.1468 2958.1993.tb00304.x

Paivio, A. (1991). Dual coding theory: Retrospect and current status. *Canadian Journal of Psychology, 45,* 255–287. doi:10.1037/h0084295

Peng, W. (2009). Design and evaluation of a computer game to promote a healthy diet for young adults. *Health Communication, 24,* 115–127. doi:10.1080/10410230802676490

Peng, W., Lin, J-H., & Crouse, J. (2011). Is playing exergames really exercising? A meta-analysis of energy expenditure in active video games. *CyberPsychology, Behavior, and Social Networking, 14,* 681–688. doi:10.1089/cyber.2010.0578

Peng, W., & Liu, M. (2008). An overview of using electronic games for health purposes. In R. Ferdig (Ed.), *Handbook of research on effective electronic gaming in education* (pp. 388–401). Hershey, PA: IGI Global.

Peng, W., Lin, J-H, Pfeiffer, K. A., & Winn, B. (2012). Need satisfaction supportive game featrues as motivational determinants: An experimental study of a self-determination theory guided exergame. *Media Psychology, 15,* 175–196. doi:10.1020/15 213269.2012.673850

Poolton, J. M., Masters, R. S. J., & Maxwell, J. P. (2007). Passing thoughts on the evolutionary stability of implicit motor behaviour: Performance retention under physiological fatigue. *Consciousness and Cognition, 16,* 456–468. doi:10.1016/j.concog.2006.06.008

Prensky, M. (2001). *Digital game-based learning.* New York, NY: McGraw-Hill.

Raney, A. A. (2010). Media enjoyment as a function of affective dispositions toward and moral judgment of characters. In K. Döveling, C. von Scheve, & E. Konijn (Eds.), *Handbook of emotions and the mass media* (pp. 166–178). London, England: Routledge.

Reinecke, L. (2009). Games at work: The recreational use of computer games during working hours. *CyberPsychology & Behavior, 12,* 461–465. doi:10.1089/cpb.2009.0010

Reinecke, L., Klatt, J., & Kramer, N. C. (2011). Entertaining media use and the satisfaction of recovery needs: Recovery outcomes associated with the use of interactive and noninteractive entertaining media. *Media Psychology, 14,* 192–215. doi:10.108 0/15213269.2011.573466

Reinecke, L., Tamborini, R., Grizzard, M., Lewis, R., Eden, A., & Bowman, N. D. (2012). Characterizing behavioral affinity as needs satisfaction: Predicting selective exposure to video games and resultant mood repair. *Journal of Communication, 62,* 437–453. doi:10.1111/j.1460-2466.2012.01649.x

Rheingold, H. (1993). *The virtual community: Homesteading on the electronic frontier.* Reading, MA: Addison-Wesley.

Ritterfeld, U., Cody, M. J., & Vorderer, P. (2009). *Serious games: Mechanisms and effects.* New York, NY: Routledge.

Rockwell, G. (2002). Gore galore: Literary theory and computer games. *Computers and the Humanities, 36,* 345–358. doi:10.1023/A:1016174116399

Schneider, E. F., Lang, A., Shin, M., & Bradley, S. D. (2004). Death with a story: How story impacts emotional, motivational, and physiological responses to first person shooter video games. *Human Communication Research, 30,* 361–375. doi:10.1111/j.1468-2958.2004.tb00736.x

Scott, D. (1995). The effect of video games on feelings of aggression. *The Journal of Psychology: Interdisciplinary and Applied, 129,* 121–132. doi:10.1080/00223980.1995.9914952

Selnow, G. W. (1984). Playing videogames: The electronic friend. *Journal of Communication, 34,* 148–156. doi: 10.1111/j.1460-2466.1984.tb02166.x

Sherry, J. L. (2001). The effects of violent video games on aggression: A meta-analysis. *Human Communication Research, 27,* 409–431. doi:10.1111/j.1468-2958.2001.tb00787.x

Sherry, J. L., Lucas, K., Greenberg, B. S., & Lachlan, K. (2006). Video game uses and gratifications as predictors of use and game preference. In P. Vorderer & J. Bryant (Eds.), *Playing video games: Motives, responses, and consequences* (pp. 213–224). Mahwah, NJ: Erlbaum.

Smith, S. L., Lachlan, K., & Tamborini, R. (2003). Popular video games: Quantifying the presentation of violence and its context. *Journal of Broadcasting & Electronic Media, 41,* 58–76. doi:10.1207/s15506878jobem4701_4

Skalski, P., Tamborini, R., Shelton, A., Buncher, M., & Lindmark, P. (2011). Mapping the road to fun: Natural video game controllers, presence, and game enjoyment. *New Media & Society, 13,* 224–242. doi:10.1177/1461444810370949

Song, H., Peng, W., & Lee, K. (2011). Promoting exercise self-efficacy with an exergame. *Journal of Health Communication, 16,* 148–162. doi: 10.1080/10810730.2010.535107

Squire, K. (2003). Video games in education. *International Journal of Intelligent Games and Simulation, 2*(1), 49–62.

Squire, K. (2006). From content to context: Videogames as designed experience. *Educational Researcher, 35,* 19–29. doi:10.3102/0013189X035008019

Steuer, J. (1992). Defining virtual reality: Dimensions determining telepresence. *Journal of Communication, 4,* 73–93. doi:10.1111/j.1460-2466.1992.tb00812.x

Sundar, S. S. (2008). The MAIN model: A heuristic approach to understanding technology effects on credibility. In M. J. Metzger & A. J. Flanigan (Eds.), *Digital media, youth, and credibility* (pp. 73–100). Cambridge, MA: MIT Press.

Tamborini, R. (2011). Moral intuition and media entertainment. *Journal of Media Psychology, 23,* 39–45. doi:10.1027/1864-1105/a000031

Tamborini, R., & Bowman, N. D. (2010). Presence in video games. In C. Bracken & P. Skalski (Eds.), *Immersed in media* (pp. 87–111). New York, NY: Routledge.

Tamborini, R., Eden, A., Bowman, N. D., Grizzard, M., & Lachlan, K. A. (2012). The influence of morality subcultures on the acceptance and appeal of violence. *Journal of Communication, 62,* 136–157. doi:10.1111/j.1460-2466.2011.01620.x

Tamborini, R., & Skalski, P. (2006). The role of presence in the experience of electronic games. In P. Vorderer & J. Bryant (Eds.), *Playing video games: Motives, responses, and consequences* (pp. 415–428). Mahwah, NJ: Erlbaum.

Tamborini, R., Weber, R., Eden, A., Bowman, N. D., & Grizzard, M. (2010). Repeated exposure to daytime soap opera and shifts in moral judgment toward social convention. *Journal of Broadcasting & Electronic Media, 54,* 621–640. doi:10.1080/088 38151.2010.519806

Tamborini, R., Weber, R., Bowman, N. D., Eden, A., & Skalski, P. (in press). "Violence is a many-splintered thing": The importance of realism, justification, and graphicness in understanding perceptions of and preferences for violent films and video games. *Projections: The Journal for Movies and Mind.*

Thiagarajan, S. (1998). The myths and realities of simulations in performance technology. *Educational Technology, 38,* 35–41.

Thomas, R., Cahill, J., & Santilli, L. (1997). Using an interactive computer game to increase skill and self-efficacy regarding safer sex negotiation: Field test results. *Health Education and Behavior, 24,* 71–86. doi: 10.1177/109019819702400108

Turkle, S. (1994). Constructions and reconstructions of self in virtual reality: Playing in the MUDs. *Mind, Culture, and Activity, 1,* 158–167. doi: 10.1080/10749039409524667

Vorderer, P., & Bryant, J. (2006). *Playing video games: Motives, responses, and consequences.* Mahwah, NJ: Erlbaum.

Vorderer, P., Hartmann, T., & Klimmt, C. (2003). Explaining the enjoyment of playing video games: The role of competition. In D. Marinelli (Ed.), *Proceedings of the 2nd International Conference on Entertainment Computing (ICEC 2003), Pittsburgh* (pp. 1–8). New York, NY: ACM.

Weber, R., Ritterfeld, U., & Kostygina, A. (2006). Aggression and violence as effects of playing violent video games? In P. Vorderer & J. Bryant (Eds.), *Playing video games: Motives, responses, and consequences* (pp. 347–362). Mahwah, NJ: Erlbaum.

Wigand, R. T., Borstelmann, S. E., & Boster, F. J. (1986). Electronic leisure: Video game usage and the communication climate of video arcades. In M.L. McLaughlin (Ed.), *Communication Yearbook 9* (pp. 275–293). Beverly Hills, CA: Sage.

Wilkinson, N., Ang, R. P, & Goh, D. H. (2008). Online video game therapy for mental health concerns: A summary. *International Journal of Social Psychiatry, 54,* 370–382. doi:10.1177/0020764008091659

Williams, D. (2005). Bridging the methodological divide in games research. *Simulation & Gaming, 36,* 447–463. doi:10.1177/1046878105282275

Williams, D. (2006). A brief social history of game play. In P. Vorderer & J. Bryant (Eds.), *Playing video games: Motives, responses, and consequences* (pp. 197–212). Mahwah, NJ: Erlbaum.

Williams, D. (2010). The mapping principle, and a research framework for virtual worlds. *Communication Theory, 20,* 451–470. doi:10.1111/j.1468–2885.2010.01371.x

Williams, D., Caplan, C., & Xiong, L. (2007). Can you hear me now? The impact of voice in an online gaming community. *Human Communication Research, 33,* 427–449. doi:10.1111/j.1468-2958.2007.00306.x

Williams, D., Consalvo, C., Caplan, S., & Yee, N. (2009). Looking for gender: Gender roles and behaviors among online gamers. *Journal of Communication, 59,* 700–725. doi:10.1111/j.1460-2466.2009.01453.x

Williams, D., Ducheneaut, N., Xiong, L., Zhang, Y., Yee, N., & Nickell, E.. (2006).

From tree house to barracks: The social life of guilds in World of Warcraft. *Games and Culture, 1,* 338–361. doi:10.1177/1555412006292616

Williams, D., Martins, N., Consalvo, M., & Ivory, J. D. (2009). The virtual census: Representations of gender, race, and age in video games. *New Media & Society, 11,* 815–834. doi:10.1177/1461444809105354

Williams, D., Yee, N., & Caplan, S. (2008). Who plays, how much, and why? Debunking the stereotypical gamer profile. *Journal of Computer-Mediated Communication, 13,* 993–1018. doi:10.1111/j.1083-6101.2008.00428.x

Yee, N. (2006a). The demographics, motivations, and derived experiences of users of massively multi-user online graphical environments. *Presence: Teleoperators and Virtual Environments, 15,* 309–329.

Yee, N. (2006b). The psychology of massively multi-user online roleplaying games: Motivations, emotional investment, relationships and problematic usage. In R. Schroeder & A. S. Axelsson (Eds.), *Avatars at work and play: Collaboration and interaction in virtual shared environments* (pp. 187–208). London, England: Springer.

Yee, N., Bailenson, J. M., Urbanek, M., Chang, F., & Merget, D. (2007). The unbearable likeness of being digital: The persistence of nonverbal social norms in online virtual environments. *CyberPsychology and Behavior, 10,* 115–121. doi:10.1089/cpb.2006.9984

CHAPTER CONTENTS

13 Theoretical Underpinnings of Reducing the Media's Negative Effect on Children

Person-Centered, Negatively-Valenced Evaluative Mediation within a Persuasion Framework

Eric Rasmussen

Texas Tech University

While the extant research in the field of parental mediation provides ample evidence that parent-child conversations influence children's reactions to the media, little research provides theoretical explanations for the ability of these conversations to benefit children. In response to this paucity of theory-based explanation, this chapter situates active mediation within a framework of individual-differences persuasion, develops the conceptualization of active mediation to reflect its persuasive purpose, and shows how such a persuasive framework for active mediation can elucidate the processes at work when parent-child conversations are aimed at thwarting the potentially negative influence of media exposure on children.

Since the widespread adoption of television, scholars, governments, and parents have sought to illuminate ways to prevent children from experiencing the negative effects of mass media exposure (Buijzen & Valkenburg, 2005; Chakroff & Nathanson, 2008). Because most of a child's media exposure occurs in his or her own home, parents are in the best position to influence a child's perceptions and use of the media (Browne, 1999; Hogan, 2001). Research shows that the various forms of parental "active" mediation, especially negatively-valenced evaluative mediation, have consistently been shown to be among the most effective ways to reduce the media's negative effect on children (Austin, Hust, & Kistler, 2009; Nathanson, 2001a).

Parental mediation research has largely been conducted to determine "what" parents can do to counteract negative media effects. Unfortunately, relatively less research in the field places mediation strategies within theoretical frameworks capable of explaining "why" or "how" parental mediation efforts work. However, upon deeper scrutiny, it is apparent that within the extant active mediation research is embedded evidence indicating how existing theories of persuasion may play an important role in helping us understand how certain forms of active mediation operate to curb negative media effects.

Apart from parental mediation research, a vast body of research has resulted in the development of several theories of persuasion that explain how human communication can influence attitudes, opinions, values, beliefs, and behaviors. Although negatively-valenced evaluative mediation essentially constitutes parental efforts to influence children's reactions to media exposure, persuasion theories have never been employed as explanatory mechanisms for the role of such mediation.

The purpose of this chapter is to demonstrate how the field of children and media would benefit from approaching the study of active mediation within a framework of individualized persuasion. Specifically, this chapter reviews past and current conceptualizations of active mediation, proposes an updated conceptualization of active mediation based on its persuasive intent, identifies theories of persuasion through which negatively-valenced evaluative mediation can be understood, establishes the potential benefits that an individual-differences, persuasive conceptualization of negatively-valenced evaluative mediation could have, and concludes with a call for research using such a conceptualization. It is hoped that the propositions herein will advance theoretical arguments and predictions regarding active mediation, and thus, allow scholars to provide parents with increasingly effective tools for helping their children cope with potentially negative media effects.

Active Mediation

Active mediation has been defined as "conversations that parents have with children about television" (Nathanson, 2001a, p. 120). One form of active mediation has been referred to as "factual" mediation. Factual mediation is intended to inform or educate children about technical aspects of programming (Nathanson, 2010) or about literary devises such as plots and settings (Singer & Singer, 1998). Factual mediation constitutes a parent's attempt to improve children's critical viewing skills (Dorr, Graves, & Phelps, 1980). In contrast, "evaluative" mediation refers to parents' provision of opinions about television content (Nathanson, 2004). Evaluative mediation often comes in the form of statements by the parents about their approval or disapproval of characters' behaviors (Nathanson, 2010), or in other words, positive or negative evaluations about television content (Nathanson, 2004).

Evaluative mediation is consistently more effective than factual mediation at influencing children's attitudes and behaviors (Cantor & Wilson, 2003; Corder-Bolz, 1980; Doolittle, 1980; Horton & Santogrossi, 1978; Nathanson, 2004; Nathanson, 2010; Nathanson & Cantor, 2000; Nathanson & Yang, 2003; Watkins, Sprafkin, & Gadow, 1988). Children are either more likely to resist potentially negative media content or to accept potentially positive media content when parents offer value judgments related to the content.

The valence of evaluative mediation is important when attempting to reduce negative media effects. "Positive" mediation refers to a parent's active endorsement or praise of media content (Austin, Bolls, Fujioka, & Engelbertson, 1999;

Nathanson, 2001a), while "negative" mediation refers to a parent's condemna-
tion or refutation of media content (Austin et al., 1999; Nathanson, 2001a).
Negative mediation is identified with intentional or purposeful discussion
by parents who are strongly concerned with the media's influence on their
child (Fujioka & Austin, 2002), and appears to be the most appropriate form
of mediation for use by parents seeking to thwart negative media effects. A
combination of negative and evaluative mediation is often related to positive
outcomes and "is an especially important form of parental influence" (Austin,
Hust, & Kistler, 2009, p. 233).

The extant research tells us much about what types of active mediation
are effective at reducing negative media effects, but tells us less about why
and how the various forms of active mediation function. Nathanson (2003)
lamented:

> Most previous work on mediation has not helped us understand why
> certain strategies are effective and others are not. This limitation is the
> inevitable result of research that does not derive mediation strategies from
> theories which suggest that the strategies will be effective. As a result,
> when mediation succeeds or fails, we have no available explanatory
> framework that can account for the results. (p. 3)

Negatively-Valenced Evaluative Mediation as Persuasion

Fortunately, mediation research has made first steps at deriving theoretically-
based mediation strategies, though most of these explanations are offered only
as post hoc explanations for descriptive findings (Nathanson, 1999). Taken
together, however, these explanations suggest that active mediation likely
works by altering children's attitudes about television and television content.
Table 13.1 summarizes some of the explanations given for the effects of active
mediation in several studies. Despite these explanations, mediation scholars
lament the generally descriptive nature of mediation research (Chakroff &
Nathanson, 2008). Post-hoc explanations for descriptive findings are undoubtedly insightful, but by their nature they are no more than educated connections
made between research results and researchers' knowledge of other processes.
To truly understand how and why mediation efforts function, the field of media
and children could benefit from offering more than post-hoc connections to
evidence from information processing and social influence phenomena. The
field would benefit more by empirically testing the explanatory power of social
influence theories. By doing so, the field as a whole could move beyond investigating what mediation strategies work toward a better understanding of why
and how parents can alter their children's experiences with media exposure.

Recognizing the need for mediation research to be better informed by
empirical investigations of social influence theories, Chakroff and Nathanson
(2008) hearkened back to Schramm, Lyle, and Parkers' (1961) argument that
parents should serve as a counterbalancing effect to adult television content:

Table 13.1 Theoretical Explanations for How Active Mediation Functions

Study/Author	Age Range	Main Findings	Explanation for Findings
Fisher et al. (2009)	12–16	Active mediation moderated the effect of sexual content exposure on the likelihood of and intent to engage in sexual behaviors, and sex expectancies.	Active mediation can "cultivate skepticism, reduce perceived desirability and similarity of portrayals" (p. 122), and signal to the child the value parents place on certain TV messages and the amount of attention the child should give to those messages.
Hicks (1968)	5–8	Children's behaviors towards toys and a Bobo doll were more likely to match the valence of the mediation when they were accompanied by the adult who made the comments than when they played alone.	Hicks' (1968) explanation of these effects was decidedly descriptive, but it is possible that children's behavior was impacted more in the presence of the confederate because the prescriptive norm (the confederate's stated position towards the behavior) was more salient and accessible while in the confederate's presence than outside of their presence (Rhodes, Roskos-Ewoldsen, Edison, & Bradford, 2008).
Lwin, Stanaland, & Miyazaki (2008)	10–12	Children who reported receiving high levels of active mediation were less likely to disclose personal information online.	Active mediation allows the child to "attend to salient and pertinent stimuli" in their environment (p. 207), and to "create schemas for interpreting experiences" (p. 207). Active mediation can direct a child's attention to information the parent deems important at the expense of less important information, and can help integrate attitudes into the child's existing schema related to an object.
Nathanson (1999)	2nd–6th graders	Active mediation worked first by influencing children's perceptions of the importance of violent content and how much attention they gave the content. Children's perceived importance and attention were associated with aggressive tendencies.	When children perceive media content to be important, they are motivated to learn from the content, elaborate more on the content, and are thus more likely to be affected by the content. And vice versa, when children hear parents' criticism of media content, they do not perceive the content to be important, and thus do not learn the mediated material.

Study/Author	Age Range	Main Findings	Explanation for Findings
Nathanson, Eveland, Park, & Paul (2002)	Care- givers of 2nd–8th graders	Active mediation of sexual content is predicted by threat perceptions on one's own and on other kids. Self-efficacy and response-efficacy were positively related to active mediation.	Protection Motivation Theory: One's appraisal of a threat can increase one's desire to protect themselves—or their children—which increases protection behaviors, such as active mediation. One's self-efficacy beliefs also influence protection behaviors.

"It seems that the goal for any mediation message would be to counter the features of the media content that are likely to cause harmful effects" (Chakroff and Nathanson, 2008, p. 557). If at their most basic level negatively-valenced evaluative mediation messages constitute parents strategic efforts to change or maintain their child's attitudes, beliefs, or behaviors in the face of undesirable media content, the function of these messages essentially constitute a definition of social influence.

Social influence, or persuasion, has been defined as an attempt by one party to change or maintain another party's opinion or behavior (Dillard, 2010). Although the conceptualization of negatively-valenced evaluative mediation is akin to the definition of persuasion, it has only rarely, if ever, been theoretically employed as such. In a parental mediation context, researchers have tested counterbalancing strategies and have determined that they work, but have provided little empirical evidence of how or why the counterbalancing works. One must look to theories of persuasion to make that distinction.

Resistance to persuasion has been defined as "the antithesis of persuasion" (Knowles & Linn, 2004). It is a psychological reaction against perceived pressure for change (Knowles & Linn, 2004; Moyer-Gusé, 2008). Thus, media messages have the power to persuade a child if the message can overcome the child's resistance to that message. Therefore, the primary aim of negatively-valenced evaluative mediation messages is to create greater resistance in the child to media messages.

Persuasion Can Clarify Conceptualization of Active Mediation

Considering active mediation within a persuasion framework would provide at least three main benefits to the field of media and children. First, it would allow mediation scholars to resolve a lack of consensus that exists in the conceptualization of active mediation. Second, it would allow scholars to more fully explain why and how active mediation functions. Lastly, it would orient scholars to approaching mediation research from an individual-differences approach.

The diverse language used to define active mediation illustrates the lack of consensus that prevails among parental mediation scholars regarding the construct. Active mediation has been referred to as "guidance" (Bybee, Robinson,

& Turow, 1982), "evaluative guidance" (van der Voort, Nikken, & van Lil, 1992), "explanation" (Livingstone & Helsper, 2008), "instructive" mediation (Barkin et al., 2006; Valkenburg, Krcmar, Peeters, & Marseille, 1999), "interpretive" mediation (Eastin, Greenberg, & Hofshire, 2006), "active co-use" (Livingstone & Helsper, 2008), "evaluative" mediation (Mesch, 2009), "pre-arming" (Padilla-Walker & Coyne, 2011), "television cohesion" (Rothschild & Morgan, 1987), "promotive" mediation (Lwin, Stanaland, & Miyazaki, 2008), and "discussion" (Warren, 2001).

More important than the difference in labels of active mediation, however, are the different interpretations of active mediation represented by each label. For example, Warren (2001) defined active mediation as "purposeful interpretation of content in terms children can understand" (p. 212). This definition is akin to the definition of factual mediation. On the other hand, Valkenburg et al. (1999) defined instructive mediation as "parents' explanation of things that happen on TV, that certain shows are unrealistic, or that good or bad things are done by characters" (p. 54). The three separate clauses in the latter definition appear to include factual, evaluative, positive, and negative mediation. Thus, it is impossible to accurately compare studies using each of these two conceptualizations simply because the definitions are qualitatively different.

In order to reconcile these inconsistencies, as well as to increase scholars' understanding of why and how active mediation functions, mediation research could benefit from a conceptualization of active mediation that reflects the fundamental persuasive motivation behind the various forms of active mediation. Therefore, I submit the following conceptual definition of active mediation: *parent-child discussion of the media or media content that is intended to impact how and the extent to which children are influenced by media exposure.*

It is apparent from the active mediation literature that the conceptual definition of the construct should reflect parents' motivations for engaging in active mediation. For example, much of the mediation research can be classified into two major categories: research investigating the (a) effects of mediation or (b) the predictors of mediation (Valkenburg et al., 1999), categories that speak directly to parents' motivations for engaging in discussions with their children about the media. For example, the effects-based research shows that active mediation is effective at reducing unwanted media effects, and at increasing media's prosocial effects. Perhaps the only reason we would be interested to know that active mediation does not change the media's effect is to establish boundary conditions.

Much of the research focusing on predictors of active mediation has found that parental concern about negative TV effects is the strongest determinant of active mediation efforts (Austin, Knaus, & Meneguelli, 1997; Austin & Pinkleton, 2001; Bocking & Bocking, 2009; Brown & Linne, 1976; Nathanson, 2001b; Warren, 2001). It is also logical to suggest that parents would not engage in active mediation if they were not concerned about the media's effect on their children. This conclusion assumes that any discussions with children

about the media that are not intended to impact the influence of media exposure on children should not be included under the umbrella of active mediation, but should be considered some other type of parent-child communication,
even if that communication is about or occurs in the presence of media.

Including parents' persuasive motives in active mediation's conceptual definition will provide clarity to our efforts to describe *what* types of active mediation function to what effect. One category of parental mediation research
attempts to tap the occurrence of mediation (Valkenburg et al., 1999). Using a
conceptual definition of active mediation that does not reflect parents' motives
for the mediation would undoubtedly tap into parent-child communication in
the presence of the media or about the media that is not intended to influence
the child in any way. For example, Austin, Roberts, and Nass' (1990) measure of active mediation asked about the frequency of parent-child discussions
about things they see and hear on TV. An example will prove instructive as to
how this item does not necessarily measure a parent's attempt to impact how
their child is influenced by TV. Imagine a parent and their adolescent watching
American Idol together. It is illogical to suggest that a parent's comment about
the pitchiness of a contestant's voice necessarily reflects the parent's efforts to
influence how their child is affected by *American Idol*, yet this type of communication is presumably measured by items such as that from the Austin et
al. (1990) example. Instead, measures of the frequency of active mediation
should reflect parents' intentions, such as those used by Padilla-Walker and
Coyne (2011). Instead of asking how often parents talk to their children about
what they see on television or the Internet, they asked "how often do you talk
to your child about what they see on television or the Internet in an attempt to
avoid negative influences before they occur?" Questions that reflect parents'
persuasive intentions will presumably preclude the measurement of parent-
child communication about the media that really does not reflect the persuasive purpose of the parent-child discussion.

Including parents' motives in active mediation's conceptual definition may
also help scholars further explicate the more important questions of *why* and
how active mediation efforts work to impact media's exposure's influence
on children. Several scholars have lamented the atheoretical nature of active
mediation research. Nathanson and Yang (2003) argued: "A substantial proportion of the experimental work on mediation has not addressed the theoretical significance of the messages it has produced and tested. As a result,
the mediation literature includes research that is difficult to synthesize" (p.
112). Cantor and Wilson (2003) proposed that tying mediation efforts to theory
would "help untangle the causal mechanisms involved" with mediation efforts
(p. 396). By changing the focus of the conceptual definition from what active
mediation is to also include why it is performed, it is hoped that the focus
of mediation scholars will also change to the reasons why and how parents'
efforts to impact the influence of media on children function the way they do,
instead of investigating what works and offering post-hoc arguments about
why certain results were obtained.

Persuasion Can Help Explain Why and How Active Mediation Works

Research shows that several theories of persuasion may be ripe for consideration in the context of active mediation. This section briefly describes several robust theories of persuasion in order to establish their potential usefulness as frameworks through which to understand the functionality of negatively-valenced evaluative mediation. These descriptions are not meant to be an in-depth review of the theories, but are meant to provide sufficient evidence that the theories are appropriate for investigation in a parental mediation context.

Inoculation Theory.   Nathanson (2001a) argued that active mediation "can take place before, during, or after" the child's media exposure (p. 117), suggesting that active mediation can occur in an effort to prevent a child from experiencing the effects of future encounters with media content. Such prevention hearkens to Inoculation theory. Presented as a medical analogy, McGuire (1961) suggested that just as exposing a person to a weakened form of a virus in order to stimulate resistance to the full-strength virus, resistance to persuasive messages can be developed by pre-exposing a person to either a weakened form of the persuasion or to some other belief-threatening material. Similarly, Fujioka and Austin (2002) alluded to the power of active mediation to confer immunity on children by helping them develop skeptical or critical thinking skills about the persuasive intent of television, though parental mediation and such inoculation have never been jointly studied.

A parent employing an inoculation-based mediation message might warn the child that an important value held by the child will be threatened by television messages that try to persuade the child to believe or act contrary to that value. This threat from the parent to the child would be followed by an explanation by the parent of why the television message is wrong, thus giving the child a defense against the persuasive media attack on his or her beliefs or attitudes.

The majority of the studies investigating the effectiveness of inoculation-theory based messages at conferring resistance to counter-attitudinal messages used college student participants, but a handful of inoculation studies revealed that children as young as elementary-school age can also be influenced by inoculation messages. For example, Pfau, Van Bocken, and King (1992) found that inoculation messages produced less positive attitudes about smoking and a greater intention to resist peer pressure to smoke among sixth and seventh graders. Szabo (2000) found similar results for children as young as fifth graders.

It is possible that positive effects of active mediation in the extant literature are a result of the threat and defenses to threat transmitted through the mediation message. Without empirical investigation within a framework of inoculation theory, we can only make an educated supposition that this is the case. Systematic study of mediation within a framework of inoculation theory could provide valuable insight into the potential mechanisms through which mediation works.

Extended Parallel-Processing Model (EPPM).   EPPM suggests that parental persuasion to the child will be effective if three conditions are present: (a) the message contains a level of threat, in the form of severity of and susceptibility to the danger; (b) the child considers him or herself capable of dealing with the threat; and (c) a belief by the child that the recommended response to the threat can eliminate the threat (Witte, 1994). Depending on the level of these components in the parents' persuasive message, the child will have a fear control response or a danger control response. A fear control response means the child will focus on eliminating the threat, and a danger control response means the child will focus on how to eliminate the threat, or in other words, will accept the parents' recommendation in the face of the unwanted media message. In EPPM, fear-control and efficacy determine one's resistance to unwanted, persuasive media messages. Messages in this model are essentially fear appeals.

For example, if a parent does not want a child to be persuaded by a media portrayal to believe that dishonesty is acceptable, the parent would talk to the child about the potential severity of the dangers of dishonesty and the child's susceptibility to those dangers. The child, in turn, would need to feel capable of avoiding dishonesty. EPPM suggests that the parent should express confidence in the child's ability to avoid dishonesty. In this case, EPPM maintains that the child would develop resistance to media messages portraying dishonesty in a good light either through increased accessibility of counterarguments or via the avoidance of material depicting dishonesty in a good light (Roskos-Ewoldsen, Arpan-Ralstin, & St. Pierre, 2002).

Recent studies show that the EPPM has proven successful at positively influencing the attitudes of 10th graders (Roberto et al., 2007a, 2007b), teenage mothers ages 15–19 (Witte, 1997), and sexually active black or Latina girls ages 15–21 (Roye, Silverman, & Krauss, 2007). Theories such as EPPM could better inform our understanding of how active mediation impacts adolescents and children when scholars test a priori hypotheses that emanate from the theories themselves.

Elaboration Likelihood Model (ELM).   According to Petty and Cacioppo's (1986a) elaboration likelihood model, a parent wanting to persuade their child to reject or avoid potentially negative media messages should send a message to the child that coincides with issues in which the child claims a personal stake. ELM argues that persuasion occurs via either the central or peripheral processing route (Petty & Cacioppo, 1986a, 1986b; Petty & Wegener, 1999). Messages that are processed by the central processing route are both relevant to the receiver's attitudes and contain arguments of sufficient strength to produce elaboration, or issue-relevant thinking. When arguments are strong, and when the receiver has the motivation and ability to elaborate on the message, long-lasting persuasion should occur (Cacioppo & Petty, 1989; Harkins & Petty, 1981; Petty, Cacioppo, & Goldman, 1981; Petty, Cacioppo, & Heesacker, 1981). Messages that are processed peripherally do not contain strong arguments about the issue, and tend to rely on heuristics unrelated to the objectives of the message (Booth-Butterfield & Welbourne, 2002).

In order to be processed centrally by children (or adolescents), the active mediation message must contain issue-relevant arguments, and must be presented when the child is both able and motivated to attend to the message. With the right kind of message and under the right set of conditions, ELM maintains that a child can be persuaded to ignore, avoid, contend with, or overcome media messages that have the potential to persuade the child to adopt attitudes, beliefs, and behaviors contrary to those which the parent hopes the child will adopt. Once persuaded, according to ELM, this change in position can "persist over time, resist counterpersuasion, and predict future behavior— the 'triple crown' of interpersonal influence" (Griffin, 2009, p. 197; see also Petty & Cacioppo, 1986b).

Although most of the research investigating the predictive validity of the ELM involves college-aged adolescents, recent research provides evidence that the ELM can be applied towards children's processing of messages. For example, 84 children ages 3–5 watched one of four TV ads for a new cereal (Bargh, McAlister, & Cornwell, 2011). Results showed that, consistent with ELM, high-involvement children were more likely to respond positively towards the ad than low involvement children. Similarly, the ELM predicted young adolescent girls' (ages 12–13) responses to a brief eating disorder prevention video (Withers, Twigg, Wertheim, & Paxton, 2002). Specifically, highly involved girls had reduced drive for thinness, reduced body dissatisfaction, and reduced intention to diet after watching the intervention video.

Nathanson (1999) concluded that children are more likely to be affected by messages when they elaborate on the content of the messages. While it is logical to suggest that active mediation messages have the potential to increase children's elaboration of media messages, some research suggests that active mediation can re-interpret, or bias, a child's elaboration of media messages (Nathanson & Cantor, 2000). Active mediation, then, could reduce the influence of media messages on children if it reduces children's elaboration of the media messages or if it can re-interpret children's thinking about media messages. Investigations within an ELM framework would provide greater illumination of the process of active mediation as it potentially alters children's experiences with media exposure.

Protection Motivation Theory.   For the purposes of parental mediation research, Rogers' (1983) protection motivation theory suggests that children would be motivated to protect themselves from potentially negative media messages when they (a) understand the severity of the risk, (b) understand their vulnerability to the risk, (c) believe that the recommended behavior has the ability to reduce the risk, and (d) believe they have the ability to perform the recommended behavior. The theory posits that children can be persuaded, in this case by parents, to avoid health, social, or interpersonal risks (Rogers, 1983).

If a parent wanted to counteract, or help a child build resistance to, glamorized portrayals of drinking alcohol found in beer commercials, protection motivation theory suggests that a parent's negatively-valenced evaluative mediation message should contain four parts that address (a) the severity of the risk of alcohol consumption, (b) the child's vulnerability to believing that drinking beer is a glamorous activity, (c) strategies for overcoming the persuasion to drink beer and evidence that those strategies will work, and (d) evidence for and confidence in the child's ability to perform those strategies.

Initial research by mediation scholars shows that protection motivation theory is a potentially valuable theoretical framework within which parental mediation can be understood. Primary caregivers of 265 second to eighth graders were surveyed about their perceptions of threat to their own child, perceptions of threat to other children, self-efficacy, response efficacy, TV exposure, and mediation behaviors (Nathanson, Eveland, Park, & Paul, 2002). Results showed that active mediation of sexual content is predicted by threat perceptions (on one's own and on other kids). Self-efficacy and response-efficacy also were positively related to active mediation. Scholars' understanding of the ways in which active mediation functions can be greatly enhanced when, as in Nathanson et al. (2002), active mediation is informed by and investigated within a framework of a robust persuasion theory.

Narrative Persuasion. A narrative is defined as a story that is interpreted by the audience in the context of their individual histories (Norrick, 1997; Ochs, Smith, & Taylor, 1989; Schiffrin, 1984). Narratives are stories we tell others about ourselves, events, or cultural values (Zander, 2007). The practice of storytelling in daily interactions between parent and child is an important part of how children develop an understanding of their social world (Cristofaro & Tamis-LeMonda, 2008), and is an essential part of the parent-child relationship (Nelson & Fivush, 2004; Newcombe & Reese, 2004; Reese & Fivush, 1993).

Like active mediation, narratives can be factual, evaluative (Haden, Haine & Fivush, 1997), positive, or negative (Miller & Sperry, 1988). Parents in some populations often use narratives for the purpose of teaching their children about the importance of family, about gender roles, and about education (Cristofaro & Tamis-LeMonda, 2008). Parents' relating of narratives to children has been shown to have positive developmental effects (language, cognitive, social, emotional, and cultural) (Reese & Farrant, 2003; Reese & Fivush, 1993; Reese, Haden, & Fivush, 1993).

"Referential" narratives, like factual mediation, inform or educate children by providing objective, factual information about objects (Nathanson, 2010). Evaluative narratives, like their parental mediation counterparts, provide qualitative statements about media content (Nathanson, 2004) and are more effective than the simple provision of information (factual mediation and referential narrative) at achieving the desired result.

While the similarities between active mediation and narratives are striking, no research investigates the efficacy of narratives used as a parental mediation strategy. Current theorizing about how narratives function to influence children suggests that narratives may be an effective form of active mediation. In her review of the use of narratives in entertainment-education, Moyer-Gusé (2008) argued that narratives encourage children's involvement with the message. Narratives can then become a form of persuasion that goes unnoticed by the child as an overt attempt to persuade the child against adopting an attitude or behavior propagated by media content. Children may also be less likely to counterargue with a message when it is embedded within a narrative, and may be more likely to be influenced by that message (Moyer-Gusé, 2008).

Just as evaluative mediation is more effective than factual mediation, narratives require a certain amount of sophistication if they are to command the child's involvement in the story being told. The story must be interesting to the child, and the narrative must be of sufficient quality so that the persuasive content and intent is not obvious (Slater & Rouner, 2002). The drama that unfolds in a narrative must be sufficient to overtake the child's awareness of the persuasive intent of the narrative (Slater & Rouner, 2002). Furthermore, Slater and Rouner (2002) suggest that narratives require less audience involvement than other forms of persuasion, such that a compelling story that maintains the child's interest may have enough staying power to at least temporarily influence the child's acceptance of values and beliefs espoused by the narrative's message. If entertainment-education can employ narratives to effective, persuasive outcomes for children, scholars may also be able to inform parental mediation research by testing the viability of similar narrative strategies.

Persuasion Orients Active Mediation to an Individual-Differences Approach

It is true that the use of such persuasive frameworks reiterates what the active mediation literature already acknowledges, that individual differences will in part determine how children respond to active mediation efforts. The empirical employment of persuasion theories to active mediation, however, could allow scholars to go beyond determining what individual differences are important considerations, to explaining why those differences have an effect. Likewise, it is possible that active mediation research has been accused of being generally atheoretical in nature (Nathanson, 2003) because of its focus on relationships between variables, and not on explaining the reasons for those relationships. On the other hand, persuasion research's focus on social influence processes goes beyond describing what individual characteristics are important to consider, to informing scholars why those characteristics make a difference.

Parental mediation research has largely approached the study of the effectiveness of mediation strategies from a variable-centered perspective, which is different than a person-centered, or individual-differences approach. A variable-centered approach studies phenomena with the assumption that the population of interest is a homogenous, interchangeable group, and with the intent of describing relationships between variables (Laursen & Hoff, 2006) external of individual characteristics. On the other hand, an individual-differences approach to research assumes that the population is heterogeneous and focuses on considering how variables are related to each other because of differences in individuals (Laursen & Hoff, 2006). Research approaching the study of active mediation from an individual-differences perspective proffers hypotheses based on research that explains why certain children should be expected to respond in a specific way to a given mediation message. Such an approach would lead researchers away from a tendency to only offer post-hoc explanations for their findings, thus leading to a theoretically-grounded understanding of the active mediation process. For example, a variable-centered approach to parental mediation research might ask whether or not a certain mediation message impacts children's aggressive tendencies. This approach focuses on the relationship between the message variable and children's reactions to the message. On the other hand, an individual-differences approach might investigate the way in which children's personalities impact the effectiveness of the mediation strategy. The individual-differences approach focuses on the moderating impact of individual characteristics on the relationship between the independent and dependent variables, and emanates naturally from persuasion theories that are focused on the processes of social influence. An individual-differences approach to the study of active mediation could do more to explain why certain children respond in particular ways to specific mediation messages than research employing a variable-centered approach that seeks only to describe relationships between mediation messages and homogenous groups of children.

While an exhaustive review of common individual differences in childhood personality and identity characteristics and their predictive patterns is not the purpose of this chapter, a handful of common child characteristics is sufficient to demonstrate the need for research on active mediation that is persuasion-based, negatively-valenced, evaluative, and tailored to individual children.

Cognitive Development. Research on the media's effect on children provides substantial evidence that children at different levels of cognitive development respond differently to media exposure (Dorr et al., 1980; Valkenburg, 2004; Vandewater et al., 2005; Wilson & Drogos, 2009). The parental mediation literature is also beginning to investigate children's cognitive development as a predictor and moderator of the effectiveness of active mediation strategies. Table 13.2 presents detailed information on five of these facets of cognitive development shown by active mediation research to have a significant effect on mediation's effectiveness. It should also be noted that for the most part, the various explanations offered for how cognitive development impacts the effectiveness of active mediation are offered as post-hoc explanations. Much less research appears to empirically test a priori hypotheses associated with these explanations.

This work is beginning to paint a picture of what types of mediation messages are best for children of different levels of cognitive development in its

Table 13.2 Cognitive Development and Mediation's Effectiveness

Facet of Cognitive Development	Explanation	Active Mediation Evidence	Cognitive Developmental Explanation
		Buijzen (2007)	
Memory	One's ability to store information in and retrieve information from memory increases with age (Roedder, 1981).	Children ages 7–10 responded more positively to active mediation than children ages 5–6.	Older children are better able to retrieve and apply knowledge and skepticism towards commercials. They have the ability to use information they have stored in memory to influence their evaluations of TV content.
		Buijzen & Mens (2007)	
		Factual mediation was ineffective among children ages 5–10, while evaluative mediation was effective for children ages 9–10, effective for 7- to 8-year-olds only when combined with factual mediation, and not effective for children ages 5–6.	Evaluative mediation messages are easier to understand and process. With age also comes an increased ability to retrieve and apply information from memory.
		Buijzen, van der Molen, and Sondij (2007)	
Perceptual boundedness	The extent to which children pay attention to and understand the perceptually salient features of the media and its messages (Strasburger, Wilson, & Jordan, 2009). A shift from perceptual to conceptual boundedness occurs around age 8 (Cantor, 2009; Valkenburg, 2004; Wilson & Drogos, 2009).	Active mediation reduced negative emotional responses of younger children (among children ages 8–12) who viewed high amounts of scary news coverage, but not for the older children in the group.	Younger kids are more afraid of explicit portrayals of violence, while older children exhibit greater fear of abstract political and societal issues (beyond perceptual cues).
		Nathanson (2010)	
		Mediation statements are more effective for kindergartners and first graders, and mediation questions are more effective for fifth and sixth graders.	Older children have an increased ability to pay attention to content features that are not as perceptually salient. Questions encourage thinking in conceptual terms rather than in perceptual terms.

Cognitive capacity	Children's ability to hold information in working memory and efficiently process information. With increased cognitive capacity, children can process multiple messages simultaneously (Fisch, 2000; Strasburger et al, 2009).	Nathanson (2004) Evaluative mediation was generally more effective than factual mediation at reducing aggressive tendencies and positive evaluations of violence, especially among children ages 5–7 when compared to children ages 10–12.	Nathanson (2004) Young children do not have the cognitive capacity to think about factual mediation and the TV violence concurrently. For older children, factual mediation may backfire since they have more cognitive capacity to devote attention to things such as violence without negative evaluations present to bias the processing.
		Wilson & Cantor (1987) Pre-viewing active mediation helped reduce fear of snakes for second and third graders, but increased fear of snakes for kindergartners and first graders.	The demands of dual-task situations such as thinking about the mediation and its implications for subsequent media exposure exceed the processing capacities of young children (Cantor & Wilson, 1988).
Prior existing knowledge and real-world experience	The more one knows about or has experience with an object, the greater the likelihood that future encounters with the object will be biased (Salomon, 1984). Prior real-world experience and knowledge naturally increase with age (Fisch, 2000).	Nathanson (2004) Among children ages 10–12, factual and evaluative mediation were more effective for those considered heavy viewers of television violence, while neither form of mediation was effective for those considered light viewers of TV violence.	Nathanson (2004) Prior experience with television violence reduced the demands on children's processing capabilities.

(continued)

Table 13.2 Continued

Facet of Cognitive Development	Explanation	Active Mediation Evidence	Cognitive Developmental Explanation
		Nathanson & Yang (2003)	
		Children considered heavy viewers of TV violence had the least positive orientation toward a violent TV program when they received a mediation message comparing the character's actions to how people act in real-life, while the same message produced the most positive attitudes toward the violent program among light-viewers of television violence.	Children with high amounts of past experiences with violent content may perceive the content as more socially realistic than children with low amounts of past exposure to violent content.
		Cantor & Wilson (1984)	
Metacognition	The ability to think about one's own thought processes (Cantor & Wilson, 1984).	Children ages 9–11, and not children ages 3–5, were affected by active mediation of scary content when they were told to keep thinking that the scary content was not real.	Older children have the ability to think about their own thoughts when instructed to do so, and thus control their thoughts better than younger children.

various facets. Active mediation messages are more effective when tailored to the child's individual needs. Unfortunately, little research appears to make a priori predictions about how children will react to certain forms of active mediation messages based on children's level of a specific aspect of cognitive development. More work is needed assessing the effectiveness of negative-evaluative, persuasive mediation within a cognitive development theoretical framework. Such future research would help scholars deliver more effective, developmentally-appropriate strategies to parents.

A discussion about developmentally appropriate active mediation messages would not be complete without a statement or two about potential starting points for hypothesis testing for some of the categorical qualitative shifts in cognitive development summarized by Strasburger et al. (2009). For example, older children have the ability to reason hypothetically, instead of based simply on what they see happening in the media. Parents could take advantage of this cognitive ability by crafting mediation messages that are also hypothetical in nature. Such messages, Nathanson and Yang (2003) found, may function best in the form of statements for younger children (ages 5–8) and in the form of questions for older children (ages 9–12). Future research directed by a priori hypothesizing from such cognitive development perspectives could help scholars better understand why certain forms of mediation work for some children and not for others.

Autonomy. Mediation research could also benefit by the empirical consideration of aspects of children's social development, such as autonomy. As a child's level of perceived autonomy changes during his or her development, parental mediation messages could be improved by reflecting the child's current level of autonomy in order to increase the likelihood that the message will be attended to by the child.

A normal step in children's development includes their ability to identify actions over which they own control. In other words, children reach a certain level of identity development at which they realize they have the power to choose for themselves (Nucci, 1996; Smetana, 2002). These steps in autonomy development often occur at or around adolescence. Adolescents spend more time with socialization agents outside the home, such as with peers and media, than pre-adolescents and children (Padilla-Walker, 2007), reflecting their need for increased autonomy. Adolescents are more critical of the appropriateness of their parents' reactions to prosocial behaviors than younger children (Wyatt & Carlo, 2002), and their conformity to the values and expectations of their peers rises during the transition to adolescence (Padilla-Walker & Carlo, 2007).

Just as with other facets of identity, a child's proper sense of autonomy at various stages of development, and a parent's support of the child's autonomy, are essential for healthy personal and social development (Grolnick & Ryan, 1989; Joussemet, Koestner, Lekes, & Landry, 2005; Ratelle, Larose, Guay, & Senecal, 2005; Ratelle, Guay, Larose, & Senecal, 2004). This "autonomy-support" includes appropriate encouragement of a child's initiative, offering of choices, responses to a child's needs, provision of rationale for rules and acknowledgement of the child's perspective, especially at points in a child's life in which greater autonomy is desired by the child (Lekes, Gingras, Philippe, Koestner, & Fang, 2010).

Autonomy-supportive parent-child communication seems to be corroborated by parental mediation research, and may explain how differing levels of autonomy predict why children of different ages do not react the same way to an identical persuasive mediation message. For example, work by Wilson and Cantor (1987) and Hoffner, Cantor, and Badzinski (1990) suggests that a child's age must be considered in the development of active mediation messages, especially for adolescents, since they begin to develop their own identity (Arnett, 1995) and they begin to create peer group identities (Buhrmester & Furman, 1987; Bukowski, Hoza, & Boivin, 1993; Hartup, 1993).

Active, persuasive mediation for children at different levels of social development, then, must look different. As a field, parental mediation scholars can test autonomously-appropriate persuasive messages for children within varying demographics. Appropriate types of persuasive messages can then be identified that may be generalizable to children at different ages.

Cognition/Factual Mediation and Affect/Evaluative Mediation. One set of individual personality differences that influences people's interactions with their environment is one's affective or cognitive orientation and attitudes (for a review, see Mayer & Tormala, 2010). For example, research with adolescents has found that Need for Cognition plays a part in whether or not they can be persuaded by certain messages. For example, high school students high in Need for Cognition were more likely to engage in condom use when they received a safe-sex message in written format, while their counterparts who were low in Need for Cognition responded better to the same message in cartoon format (Bakker, 1999). Another study provided evidence that children (ages 4–15) are less likely to engage in cognitive effort when processing messages than adults (Te'eni-Harari, Lampert, & Lehman-Wilzig, 2007).

Children and media scholars have generally found that cognitive mediation approaches attempting to change attitudes have failed to do so (Dorr et al., 1980; Watkins et al., 1988), and have actually increased negative television effects due to increased salience of the medium's features or content (Doolittle, 1980; Huesmann, Eron, Klein, Brice, & Fischer, 1983). Nathanson (2003) exposed children ages 5–12 to a five-minute episode of a violent children's television show. One of the experimental conditions included cognitive mediation. Results showed that cognitive mediation had either no effect on children's subsequent evaluations and reactions to violent TV, or it had the effect of making the children more vulnerable to the televised violence.

Additionally, several parental mediation studies have employed affective mediation approaches to influence children's emotional responses to violence on television. Affective mediation emphasizes feelings and emotions, in contrast to the detached and technical viewpoint taken by cognitive mediation

(Nathanson, 2003). Studies investigating the effectiveness of affective approaches to mediation generally show that such emotion-based input has the potential to override negative media effects (see, for example, Corder-Bolz, 1980; Nathanson & Cantor, 2000; Voojis & van der Voort, 1993). In fact, affective mediation is considered more effective than cognitive mediation because children's desire to be accepted by their peers and society can overpower their cognitive, rational judgments about violence they see on television (Austin, Pinkleton, & Fujioka, 2000). In order to improve the predictability of active mediation efforts, it may be less important to know that affective messages are more effective than cognitive messages than it is to know what types of children are consistently predisposed to be affected by different message types.

Although each of these studies explored the effectiveness of cognitively- or affectively-oriented messages, they did not account for the cognitive or affective orientation of the child participants. The next step for parental mediation scholars is to determine, from an individual-differences approach, if the cognitive- or affective-orientation of children can explain previous results in this line of research, and if such an orientation has other implications for parental mediation strategies. By investigating the predisposition of children to process certain messages in certain ways, parental mediation scholars will be better able to predict which types of messages are bested suited for persuading children with similar personality features.

Gender. "Gender is a quintessential element of human identity" (Egan & Perry, 2001, p. 451), and has been identified by parental mediation scholars as an important predictor of mediation's success. Boys and girls often respond differently to the same parental mediation effort. An individual-differences approach would allow us to identify specific ways of talking to each gender that are relevant and likely to be attended to by each child. More specifically, certain aspects of the identity of each gender already provide a wealth of information about what types of persuasive mediation messages would be most effective for each.

For example, boys and girls differ in terms of their concept of aggression. Aggression is arguably the media effect that has received the most scholarly attention, including among parental mediation researchers. Active mediation of violent television has proven successful at reducing aggressive behavior (Hicks, 1968), tolerance for aggression (Horton & Santogrossi, 1978), and aggressive attitudes (Corder-Bolz, 1980). Nathanson and Cantor (2000) found that girls were not as susceptible as boys to experiencing an increase in post-exposure aggression, and suggested that girls may be less vulnerable to physical violence and more vulnerable to interpersonal hostility. These arguments suggest that there is something inherent in boys and girls that influences the way they are each affected by television violence and related mediation.

Other research also points to differences in boys and girls relative to the media. Men and boys tend to watch horror, action and adventure, and sports movies, violence and vigorous action, and content related to performance and achievement, while women and girls prefer romantic content, tragedies, soap operas, dramas, medical serials, and content related to social and interpersonal issues (Hansen & Hansen, 2000; Haynes & Richgels, 1992; Knobloch, Callison, Chen, Fritzsche, & Zillmann, 2005; Knobloch-Westerwick & Alter, 2007; Oliver, 1993, 2000; Potts, Dedmon, & Halford, 1996; Preston & Clair, 1994; Valkenburg & Janssen, 1999).

A parent, then, cannot necessarily expect persuasive active mediation to work the same way for a daughter as it does for a son. These differences may also be explained by the different self-construals boys and girls have of themselves. Cross and Madson (1997) argue that men and boys in America generally have independent self-construals. They orient their lives around an individualistic perspective, have a desire for autonomy, and act in a way that makes them stand alone. On the other hand, women and girls in Western societies have interdependent self-construals. They view relationships with others as an integral part of their being, and whose thoughts and actions are understood relative to the thoughts and actions of others.

Active mediation messages aimed at persuading girls to not adopt values portrayed by the media could be more effective if they relate to girls' interdependent self-construal, while those aimed at boys might be more effective when they emphasize boys' independent self-construal. For example, in opposition to glamorized portrayals of smoking, boys may respond better to messages telling them how smoking affects them as individuals, such as their machismo, while girls may respond better to messages telling them how smoking will affect their interpersonal relationships.

Messages that take into account individual differences, whether tailored to a specific personality trait or level of cognitive or social development, would answer the call for messages to be relevant to the child in order to be cognitively attended to by the child (Petty & Cacioppo, 1986b). Such relevant and specific messages are more likely to create positive feelings about the message, even if the message includes potentially aversive components, such as the threat (Slater, 2006) necessary in several of the aforementioned persuasion theories. Burnkrant and Unnava (1989) argued that personalized language increases one's motivation to elaborate on persuasive messages. Persuasive, negatively-valenced evaluative mediation messages founded upon what we know about children's individual differences can be used to combat the media's socialization effect. The study of such specifically tailored messages can provide additional insight into the predictability of the effectiveness of active mediation messages (Nathanson, 2010).

Conclusion

Scholars are interested in learning how parents can prevent children from experiencing potentially negative media effects. In addition to the research that describes what types of active mediation work to that end, parental mediation research could benefit by the examination of negatively-valenced evaluative mediation within theoretical frameworks that have the capacity to elucidate why and how the mediation operates to benefit children.

To that end, this chapter demonstrated how the field of children and media would benefit from the conceptualization of negatively-valenced evaluative mediation as persuasion tailored to individual differences. This chapter proposed an updated conceptualization of active mediation based on its persuasive intent, identified theories of persuasion through which negatively-valenced evaluative mediation can be understood, and established the potential benefits that a persuasive conceptualization of negatively-valenced evaluative mediation focusing on children's individual differences could have. This chapter argues that approaching the study of active mediation from such an individual-differences, persuasive perspective encourages researchers to create a priori hypotheses that emanate from the literature that explains why children with certain characteristics should be expected to respond in a specific way to a given mediation message.

Further, this chapter identified specific aspects of development and personality worthy of consideration as individual differences in the development of these mediation messages. Admittedly, the seemingly endless number of individual characteristics that could affect active mediation's ability to alter children's experiences with media exposure makes it appear that no single active mediation message can be applied to more than one child. Fortunately, we can identify groups of individuals who are similar enough that they share similar characteristics (Laursen & Hoff, 2006), so that an individual-differences approach to mediation research is a viable possibility. A valuable comparison for the constant refining of the most appropriate mediation messages for children with certain characteristics may be the research that has been conducted over the years that has directly influenced the production of children's educational television programs by the Children's Television Workshop (CTW). Since 1970, CTW has conducted or commissioned research by scholars with the intent to identify how to best use television to educate a broad range of children (Sammur, 1990). Over time, this research has promoted refinements in CTW programming content in order to improve the educational power of CTW programs. Similarly, mediation research may need to undergo a similar refinement process in order to increase our understanding of what mediation messages work best for different children.

This does not mean that scholars' efforts in the meantime to provide parents with information for their applied mediation activities are in vain and unproductive. Just as it is illogical to withhold beneficial treatment for a terminally ill patient simply because a cure is not available, it does not make sense to withhold active mediation just because we are still learning about how it works. It is hoped that the propositions herein will advance theoretical arguments and predictions regarding active mediation, and thus, provide scholars with information that will allow them to supply parents with effective tools for helping their children cope with potentially negative media effects.

References

Arnett, J. (1995). Adolescents' uses of media for self-socialization. *Journal of Youth and Adolescence, 24*, 519–533.

Austin, E. W., Bolls, P., Fujioka, Y., & Engelbertson, J. (1999). How and why parents take on the tube. *Journal of Broadcasting and Electronic Media, 43*, 175–192.

Austin, E. W., Hust, S. J. T., & Kistler, M. E. (2009). Powerful media tools: Arming parents with strategies to affect children's interactions with commercial interests. In T. J. Socha & G. H. Stamp (Eds.), *Parents and children communicating with society: Managing relationships outside of home* (pp. 215–240). New York, NY: Routledge.

Austin, E. W., Knaus, C., & Meneguelli, A. (1997). Who talks how to their kids about TV: A clarification of demographic correlates of parental mediation patterns. *Communication Research Reports, 14*, 418–430.

Austin, E. W., & Pinkleton, B. E. (2001). The role of parental mediation in the political socialization process. *Journal of Broadcasting & Electronic Media, 45*, 221–240.

Austin, E. W., Pinkleton, B., & Fujioka, Y. (2000). The role of interpretation processes and parental discussion in the media's effects on adolescents' use of alcohol. *Pediatrics, 105*, 343–349.

Austin, E. W., Roberts, D. F., & Nass, C. I. (1990). Influences of family communication on children's television-interpretation processes. *Communication Research, 17*, 545–564.

Bakker, A. B. (1999). Persuasive communication about AIDS prevention: Need for Cognition determines the impact of message format. *AIDS education and prevention: Official publication of the International Society for AIDS Education, 11*, 150–162.

Bargh, D., McAlister, A., & Cornwell, T. B. (2011). Information processing by preschool children: A test of the elaboration likelihood model. *AMA Winter Educators' Conference Proceedings, 22*, 230–231.

Barkin, S., Ip, E., Richardson, I., Klinepeter, S., Finch, S., Slora, E., & Krcmar, M. (2006). Parental media mediation styles for children aged 2 to 11 years. *Archives of Pediatric & Adolescent Medicine, 160*, 393–401.

Bocking, S., & Bocking, T. (2009). Parental mediation of television: Test of a German-speaking scale and findings on the impact of parental attitudes, sociodemographic and family factors in German-speaking Switzerland. *Journal of Children and Media, 3*, 286–302.

Booth-Butterfield, S., & Welbourne, J. (2002). The elaboration likelihood model: Its impact of persuasion theory and research. In J. Dillard & M. Pfau (Eds.), *The persuasion handbook: Developments in theory and practice* (pp. 155–173). Thousand Oaks, CA: Sage.

Brown, J. R., & Linne, O. (1976). The family as mediator of television's effects. In R. Brown (Ed.), *Children and television* (pp. 184–198). Beverly Hills, CA: Sage.

Browne, N. (1999). *Young children's literacy development and the role of televisual texts*. New York, NY: Falmer Press.

Buhrmester, D., & Furman, W. (1987). The development of companionship and intimacy. *Child Development, 58*, 1101–1113.

Buijzen, M. (2007). Reducing children's susceptibility to commercials: Mechanisms of factual and evaluative advertising interventions. *Media Psychology, 9*, 411–430.

Buijzen, M., & Mens, C. (2007). Adult mediation of television advertising effects: A comparison of factual, evaluative and combined strategies. *Journal of Children and Media, 1*, 177–191.

Buijzen, M., van der Molen, J. H. W., & Sondij, P. (2007). Parental mediation of children's emotional responses to a violent news event. *Communication Research, 34,* 212–230.

Buijzen, M., & Valkenburg, P. (2005). Parental mediation of undesired advertising effects. *Journal of Broadcasting & Electronic Media, 49,* 153–165.

Bukowski, W., Hoza, B., & Boivin, M. (1993). Popularity, friendship, and emotional adjustment during early adolescence. In B. Laursen (Ed.), *Close friendships in adolescence* (pp. 23–38). San Francisco, CA: Jossey-Bass.

Burnkrant, R., & Unnava, H. (1989). Self-referencing: A strategy for increasing processing of message content. *Personality and Social Psychology Bulletin, 15,* 628–638.

Bybee, C., Robinson, D., & Turow, J. (1982). Determinants of parental guidance of children's television viewing for a special subgroup: Mass media scholars. *Journal of Broadcasting, 26,* 697–710.

Cacioppo, J., & Petty, R. (1989). Effects of message repetition on argument processing, recall, and persuasion. *Basic and Applied Social Psychology, 10,* 3–12.

Cantor, J. (2009). Fright reactions to mass media. In J. Bryant & M. B. Oliver (Eds.), *Media effects: Advances in theory and research* (pp. 287–303). New York, NY: Routledge.

Cantor, J., & Wilson, B. (1984). Modifying fear responses to mass media in preschool and elementary school children. *Journal of Broadcasting, 28,* 431–443.

Cantor, J., & Wilson, B. (1988). Helping children cope with frightening media presentations. *Current Psychology: Research & Reviews, 7,* 58–75.

Cantor, J., & Wilson, B. (2003). Media and violence: Intervention strategies for reducing aggression. *Media Psychology, 5,* 363–403.

Chakroff, J., & Nathanson, A. (2008). Parent and school interventions: Mediation and media literacy. In S. L. Calvert & B. J. Wilson (Eds.), *The handbook of children, media, and development* (pp. 552–576). West Sussex, England: Blackwell.

Corder-Bolz, C. (1980). Mediation: The role of significant others. *Journal of Communication, 30,* 106–118.

Cristofaro, T. N. & Tamis-LeMonda, C. S. (2008). Lessons in mother-child and father-child personal narratives in Latino families. In A. McCabe, A. L. Bailey, & G. Melzi (Eds.), *Spanish-language narration and literacy: Culture, cognition, and emotion* (pp. 54–91). New York, NY: Cambridge University Press.

Cross, S., & Madson, L. (1997). Models of the self: Self-construals and gender. *Psychological Bulletin, 122,* 5–37.

Dillard, J. (2010). Persuasion. In C. Berger & M. R.-E. Roloff (Eds.), *The handbook of communication science* (2nd ed., pp. 203–218). Thousand Oaks, CA: Sage.

Doolittle, J. (1980). Immunizing children against possible antisocial effects of viewing television violence: A curricular intervention. *Perceptual and Motor Skills, 51,* 498.

Dorr, A., Graves, S., & Phelps, E. (1980). Television literacy for young children. *Journal of Communication, 30,* 71–83.

Eastin, M. S., Greenberg, B., & Hofshire, L. (2006). Parenting the Internet. *Journal of Communication, 56,* 486–504.

Egan, S., & Perry, D. (2001). Gender identity: A multidimensional analysis with implications for psychosocial adjustment. *Developmental Psychology, 37,* 451–463.

Fisch, S. M. (2000). A capacity model of children's comprehension of educational content on television. *Media Psychology, 2,* 63–91.

Fisher, D. A., Hill, D. L., Grube, J. W., Bersamin, M. M., Walker, S., & Gruber, E. L. (2009). Televised sexual content and parental mediation: Influences on adolescent sexuality. *Media Psychology, 12,* 121–147.

Fujioka, Y., & Austin, E. W. (2002). The relationship of family communication patterns to parental mediation styles. *Communication Research, 29,* 642–665.

Griffin, E. (2009). *A first look at communication theory* (7th ed.). New York, NY: McGraw-Hill.

Grolnick, W., & Ryan, R. (1989). Parent styles associated with children's self-regulation and competence in school. *Journal of Educational Psychology, 81,* 143–154.

Haden, C. A., Haine, R. A., & Fivush, R. (1997). Developing narrative structure in parent-child reminiscing across the preschool years. *Developmental Psychology, 33,* 295–307.

Hansen, C., & Hansen, R. (2000). Music and music videos. In D. Zillmann & P. Vorderer (Eds.), *Media entertainment: The psychology of its appeal* (pp. 175–196). Mahwah, NJ: Erlbaum.

Harkins, S., & Petty, R. (1981). Effects of source magnification of cognitive effort on attitudes: An information processing view. *Journal of Personality and Social Psychology, 40,* 401–413.

Hartup, W. (1993). Adolescents and their friends. In B. Laursen (Ed.), *Close friendships in adolescence* (pp. 3–22). San Francisco, CA: Jossey-Bass.

Haynes, C., & Richgels, D. (1992). Fourth graders' literature preferences. *Journal of Educational Research, 85,* 208–219.

Hicks, D. (1968). Effects of co-observer's sanctions and adult presence on imitative aggression. *Child Development, 39,* 303–309.

Hoffner, C., Cantor, J., & Badzinski, D. (1990). Children's understanding of adverbs denoting degree of likelihood. *Journal of Child Language, 17,* 217–231.

Hogan, M. (2001). Parents and other adults: Models and monitors of healthy media habits. In D. G. Singer & J. L. Singer (Eds.), *Handbook of children and the media* (pp. 663–680). Thousand Oaks, CA: Sage.

Horton, R., & Santogrossi, D. (1978). The effect of adult commentary on reducing the influence of televised violence. *Personality and Social Psychology Bulletin, 4,* 337–340.

Huesmann, L., Eron, L., Klein, R., Brice, P., & Fischer, P. (1983). Mitigating the imitation of aggressive behaviors by changing children's atttudes about media violence. *Journal of Personality and Social Psychology, 44,* 899–910.

Joussemet, M., Koestner, R., Lekes, N., & Landry, R. (2005). A longitudinal study of the relationship of maternal autonomy support to children's adjustment and achievement in school. *Journal of Personality, 73,* 1215–1236.

Knobloch, S., Callison, C., Chen, L., Fritzsche, A., & Zillman, D. (2005). Children's sex-stereotyped self-socialization through selective exposure to entertainment fare: Cross-cultural experiments in Germany, China, and the United States. *Journal of Communication, 55,* 122–138.

Knobloch-Westerwick, S., & Alter, S. (2007). The gender news use divide: Americans' sex-typed selective exposure to online news topics. *Journal of Communication, 57,* 739–758.

Knowles, E., & Linn, J. (2004). The importance of resistance to persuasion. In E. Knowle & J. Linn (Eds.), *Resistance and persuasion* (pp. 3–11). Mahwah, NJ: Erlbaum.

Laursen, B., & Hoff, E. (2006). Person-centered and variable-centered approaches to longitudinal data. *Merrill-Palmer Quarterly, 52,* 377–389.

Lekes, N., Gingras, I., Philippe, F., Koestner, R., & Fang, J. (2010). Parental autonomy-support, intrinsic life goals, and well-being among adolescents in China and North America. *Journal of Youth and Adolescence, 39,* 858–869.

Livingstone, S., & Helsper, E. (2008). Parental mediation of children's internet use. *Journal of Broadcasting & Electronic Media, 52*, 581–599.

Lwin, M. O., Stanaland, A. J. S., & Miyazaki, A. D. (2008). Protecting children's privacy online: How parental mediation strategies affect website safeguard effectiveness. *Journal of Retailing, 84*, 205–217.

Mayer, N., & Tormala, Z. (2010). "Think" versus "feel" framing effects in persuasion. *Personality and Social Psychology Bulletin, 36*, 443–454.

McGuire, W. (1961). The effectiveness of supportive and refutational defenses in immunizing and restoring beliefs against persuasion. *Sociometry, 24*, 184–197.

Mesch, G. (2009). Parental mediation, online activities, and cyberbullying. *Cyberpsychology & Behavior, 12*, 387–393.

Miller, P. J. & Sperry, L. L. (1988). Early talk about the past: The origins of conversational stories of personal experience. *Journal of Child Language, 15,* 293–315.

Moyer-Gusé, E. (2008). Toward a theory of entertainment persuasion: Explaining the persuasive effects of entertainment-education messages. *Communication Theory, 18*, 407–425.

Nathanson, A. I. (1999). Identifying and explaining the relationship between parental mediation and children's aggression. *Communication Research, 26*, 124–143.

Nathanson, A. I. (2001a). Mediation of children's television viewing: Working toward conceptual clarity and common understanding. In W. Gudykunst (Ed.), *Communication Yearbook* (Vol. 25, pp. 115–151). Mahwah, NJ: Erlbaum.

Nathanson, A. I. (2001b). Parent and child perspectives on the presence and meaning of parental television mediation. *Journal of Broadcasting & Electronic Media, 45*, 201–220.

Nathanson, A. I. (2003, May). *The effects of mediation content on children's responses to violent television: Comparing cognitive and affective approaches.* Paper presented at the annual meeting of the International Communication Association, San Diego, CA.

Nathanson, A. I. (2004). Factual and evaluative approaches to modifying children's responses to violent television. *Journal of Communication, 54*, 321–336.

Nathanson, A. I. (2010). Using television mediation to stimulate nontraditional gender roles among caucasian and African American children in the US. *Journal of Children and Media, 4*, 174–190.

Nathanson, A. I., & Cantor, J. (2000). Reducing the aggression-promoting effect of violent cartoons by increasing children's fictional involvement with the victim: A study of active mediation. *Journal of Broadcasting and Electronic Media, 44*, 125–142.

Nathanson, A. I., Eveland, W. P., Park, H. S., & Paul, B. (2002). Perceived media influence and efficacy as predictors of caregivers' protective behaviors. *Journal of Broadcasting and Electronic Media, 46*, 385–411.

Nathanson, A. I., & Yang, M. (2003). The effects of mediation content and form on children's responses to violent television. *Human Communication Research, 29*, 111–134.

Nelson, K., & Fivush, R. (2004). The emergence of autobiographical memory: A social-cultural developmental theory. *Psychology Review, 111*, 486–511.

Newcombe, R., & Reese, E. (2004). Evaluations and orientations in mother-child narratives as a function of attachment security: A longitudinal investigation. *International Journal of Behavioral Development, 28*, 230–245.

Norrick, N. (1997). Collaborative narration of familiar stories. *Language in Society, 26,* 199–220.

Nucci, L. (1996). Morality and personal freedom. In E. Reed, E. Turiel, & T. Brown (Eds.), *Values and knowledge* (pp. 41–60). Mahwah, NJ: Erlbaum.

Ochs, E., Smith, R., & Taylor, C. (1989). Detective stories, at dinner time: Problem solving through co-narration. *Cultural Dynamics, 2,* 238–257.

Oliver, M. B. (1993). Exploring the paradox of the enjoyment of sad films. *Human Communication Research, 19,* 315–342.

Oliver, M. B. (2000). The respondent gender gap. In D. Zillmann & P. Vorderer (Eds.), *Media entertainment: The psychology of its appeal* (pp. 215–234). Mahwah, NJ: Erlbaum.

Padilla-Walker, L. (2007). Characteristics of mother-child interactions related to adolescents' positive values and behaviors. *Journal of Marriage and Family, 69,* 675–686.

Padilla-Walker, L., & Carlo, G. (2007). Personal values as a mediator between parent and peer expectations and adolescent behaviors. *Journal of Family Psychology, 21,* 538–541.

Padilla-Walker, L. M., & Coyne, S. M. (2011). "Turn that thing off!" Parent and adolescent predictors of proactive media monitoring. *Journal of Adolescence, 34,* 705–715.

Petty, R., & Cacioppo, J. (1986a). *Communication and persuasion: Central and peripheral routes to attitude change.* New York, NY: Springer-Verlag.

Petty, R., & Cacioppo, J. (1986b). The elaboration likelihood model of persuasion. In L. Berkowitz (Ed.), *Advances in experimental social psychology* (Vol. 19, pp. 123–205). San Diego, CA: Academic Press.

Petty, R., & Wegener, D. (1999). The elaboration likelihood model: Current status and controversies. In S. Chaiken & Y. Trope (Eds.), *Dual process theories in social psychology* (pp. 37–72). New York, NY: Guilford.

Petty, R., Cacioppo, J., & Goldman, R. (1981). Personal involvement as a determinant of argument-based persuasion. *Journal of Personality and Social Psychology, 41,* 847–855.

Petty, R., Cacioppo, J., & Heesacker, M. (1981). The effects of rhetorical questions on persuasion: A cognitive response analysis. *Journal of Personality and Social Psychology, 40,* 432–440.

Pfau, M., Van Bockern, S., & King, J. G. (1992). Use of inoculation to promote resistance to smoking initiation among adolescents. *Communication Monographs, 59,* 213–230.

Potts, R., Dedmon, A., & Halford, J. (1996). Sensation seeking, television viewing motives, and home television viewing patterns. *Personality and Individual Differences, 21,* 1081–84.

Preston, J. M., & Clair, S. A. (1994). Selective viewing: Cognition, personality and television genres. *British Journal of Social Psychology, 33,* 273–288.

Ratelle, C., Guay, F., Larose, S., & Senecal, C. (2004). Family correlates of trajectories of academic motivation during a school transition: A semiparametric group-based approach. *Journal of Educational Psychology, 96,* 743–754.

Ratelle, C., Larose, S., Guay, F., & Senecal, C. (2005). Perceptions of parental involvement and support as predictors of college students' persistence in a science curriculum. *Journal of Family Psychology, 19,* 286–293.

Reese, E., & Farrant, K. (2003). Social origins of reminiscing. In R. Fivush & C. A. Haden (Eds.), *Autobiographical memory and the construction of a narrative self* (pp. 29–48). Mahwah, NJ: Erlbaum.

Reese, E., & Fivush, R. (1993). Parental styles of talking about the past. *Developmental Psychology, 29,* 596–606.

Reese, E., Haden, C. A., & Fivush, R. (1993). Mother-child conversations about the past: Relationships of style and memory over time. *Cognitive Development, 8*, 403–430.

Rhodes, N., Roskos-Ewoldsen, D., Edison, A., & Bradford, M. B. (2008). Attitude and norm accessibility affect processing of anti-smoking messages. *Health Psychology, 27*, S224–S232.

Roberto, A. J., Zimmerman, R. S., Carlyle, K. E., & Abner, E.L. (2007a). A computer-based approach to preventing pregnancy, STD, and HIV in rural adolescents. *Journal of Health Communication, 12*, 53–76.

Roberto, A.J., Zimmerman, R. S., Carlyle, K. E., Abner, E. L., Cupp. P. K., & Hansen, G. L. (2007b). The effects of a computer-based pregnancy, STD, and HIV prevention intervention: A nine-school trial." *Health Communication, 21*, 115–124.

Roedder, D. L. (1981). Age differences in children's responses to television advertising: An information-processing approach. *Journal of Consumer Research, 8*, 144–153.

Rogers, R. (1983). Cognitive and physiological process in fear appeals and attitude change: A revised theory of protection motivation. In J. Cacioppo & R. Petty (Eds.), *Social ssychophysiology: A source book* (pp. 153–176). New York, NY: Guilford Press.

Roskos-Ewoldsen, D., Arpan-Ralstin, L., & St. Pierre, J. (2002). Attitude accessibility and persuasion: The quick and the strong. In J. Dillard & M. Pfau (Eds.), *The persuasion handbook: Developments in theory and practice* (pp. 39–61). Thousand Oaks, CA: Sage.

Rothschild, N., & Morgan, M. (1987). Cohesion and control: Adolescents' relationships with parents as mediators of television. *The Journal of Early Adolescence, 7*, 299–314.

Roye, C., Silverman, P. P., & Krauss, B. (2007). A brief, low-cost, theory-based intervention to promote dual method use by black and Latina female adolescents: A randomized clinical trial. *Heath Education & Behavior, 34*, 608–621.

Salomon, G. (1984). Television is "easy" and print is "tough": The differential investment of mental effort as a function of perceptions and attributions. *Journal of Educational Psychology, 76*, 647–658.

Sammur, G. B. (1990). Selected bibliography of research on programming at the Children's Television Workshop." *Educational Technology, Research and Development, 38*, 81–92.

Schiffrin, D. (1984). How a story says what it means and does. *Text, 4*, 313–346.

Schramm, W., Lyle, J., & Parker, E. (1961). *Television and the lives of our children*. Stanford, CA: Stanford University Press.

Singer, D. G., & Singer, J. L. (1998). Developing critical viewing skills and media literacy in children. *Annals of the American Academcy of Political and Social Science, 557*, 164–179.

Slater, M. (2006). Specification and misspecification of theoretical foundations and logic models for health communication campaigns. *Health Communication, 20*, 149–157.

Slater, M. D., & Rouner, D. (2002). Entertainment-education and elaboration likelihood: Understanding the processing of narrative persuasion. *Communication Theory, 12*, 173–191.

Smetana, J. (2002). Culture, autonomy, and personal jurisdiction in adolescent-parent relationships. In R. Kail & H. Reese (Eds.), *Advances in child development and behavior* (Vol. 29, pp. 51–87). San Diego, CA: Academic Press.

Strasburger, V. C., Wilson, B. J., & Jordan, A. B. (2009). *Children, adolescents, and the media* (2nd ed.). Thousand Oaks, CA: Sage.

Szabo, E. A. (2000). *Inoculation, normative appeals, and emotion as strategies to promote resistance to adolescent smoking* (doctoral dissertation). University of Wisconsin-Madison.

Te'eni-Harari, T., Lampert, S. I., & Lehman-Wilzig, S. (2007). Information processing of advertising among young people: The elaboration likelihood model as applied to youth. *Journal of Advertising Research, 47*, 326–340.

Valkenburg, P. M. (2004). *Children's responses to the screen: A media psychological approach*. Mahwah, NJ: Erlbaum.

Valkenburg, P. M., Krcmar, M., Peeters, A. L., & Marseille, N. M. (1999). Developing a scale to assess three styles of television mediation: "Instructive mediation," "restrictive mediation," and "social coviewing." *Journal of Broadcasting & Electronic Media, 43*, 52–66.

Valkenburg, P., & Janssen, S. C. (1999). What do children value in entertainment programs? A cross-cultural investigation. *Journal of Communication, 49*, 3–21.

Vandewater, E. A., Bickham, D. S., Lee, J. H., Cummings, H. E., Wartella, E. A., & Rideout, V. J. (2005). When the television is always on: Heavy television exposure and young children's development. *American Behavioral Scientist, 48*, 562–577.

van der Voort, T., Nikken, P., & van Lil, J. (1992). Determinants of parental guidance of children's television viewing: A Dutch replication study. *Journal of Broadcasting and Electronic Media, 36*, 61–74.

Voojis, M. W., & van der Voort, T. H. A. (1993). Learning about television violence: The impact of a critical viewing curriculum on children's attitudinal judgments of crime series. *Journal of Research and Development in Education, 26*, 133–142.

Warren, R. (2001). In words and deeds: Parental involvement and mediation of children's television viewing. *The Journal of Family Communication, 1*, 211–231.

Watkins, L., Sprafkin, J., & Gadow, K. (1988). Effects of a critical viewing skills curriculum on elementary school children's knowledge and attitudes about television. *Journal of Educational Research, 81*, 165–170.

Wilson, B., & Cantor, J. (1987). Reducing children's fear reactions to mass media: Effects of visual exposure and verbal explanation. In M. McLaughlin (Ed.), *Communication Yearbook 10* (pp. 553–573). Newbury Park, CA: Sage.

Wilson, B. J., & Drogos, K. L. (2009). Children and adolescents: Distinctive audiences of media content. In R. L. Nabi & M. B. Oliver (Eds.), *The Sage handbook of media processes and effects* (pp. 469–485). Thousand Oaks, CA: Sage.

Withers, G. F., Twigg, K., Wertheim, E. H., & Paxton, S. J. (2002). A controlled evaluation of an eating disorders primary prevention videotape using the elaboration likelihood model of persuasion. *Journal of Psychosomatic Research, 53*, 1021–1027.

Witte, K. (1994). Fear control and danger control: A test of the extended parallel process model (EPPM). *Communication Monographs, 61*, 113–164.

Witte, K. (1997). Preventing teen pregnancy through persuasive communications: Realities, myths, and the hard-fact truths. *Journal of Community Health, 22*, 137–154.

Wyatt, J., & Carlo, G. (2002). What will my parents think? Relations among adolescents' expected parental reactions, prosocial moral reasoning, and prosocial and antisocial behaviors. *Journal of Adolescent Research, 17*, 646–666.

Zander, M. J. (2007). Tell me a story: The power of narrative in the practice of teaching art. *Studies in Art Education: A Journal of Issues and Research, 48*, 189–203.

About the Editor

Elisia L. Cohen earned her Ph.D. in Communication from the University of Southern California and is an Associate Professor of Communication and Associate Member of the Markey Cancer Center at the University of Kentucky. Today, she is the Director of the Health Communication Research Collaborative at the University of Kentucky. Her research has been supported by the Centers for Disease Control and Prevention, National Institutes of Health, Merck pharmaceuticals, and an unrestricted gift from GlaxoSmithKline. She is an investigator with the Rural Cancer Prevention Center, St. Louis Center for Excellence in Cancer Communication Research, and past media coordinator for the Cervical Cancer-free Kentucky initiative. Her research on public communication, public opinion, and public health has appeared in such journals as: *Health Communication, Health Education and Behavior, Journal of Applied Communication Research, Journal of Broadcasting and Electronic Media, Journal of Communication, Journal of Health Communication, Qualitative Health Research,* and *Prometheus.* She is married and has one daughter, Addison Lydia.

About the Contributors

Yannick C. Atouba is a doctoral candidate in organizational communication and organizational studies in Department of Communication at the University of Illinois at Urbana-Champaign. His research focuses on the formation, the evolution, and the outcomes of interorganizational networks among nongovernmental organizations.

Brenda L. Berkelaar is an Assistant Professor at The University of Texas at Austin where she studies work and careers. She is curious about why we do the work we do and how new technologies alter work and careers. Using qualitative and quantitative approaches, her current research projects address processes, ethics, and literacies associated with personnel selection and online screening (i.e., cybervetting); organizational socialization; the meanings of work; the presentation and interpretation(s) of self and information online; and career development. Dr. Berkelaar's work has appeared in *Communication Monographs*, *Management Communication Quarterly*, and *China Media Research*, as well as a number of edited books.

Nicholas David Bowman is an Assistant Professor of Communication Studies at West Virginia University where he teaches and conducts research on issues related to communication technology and media psychology. In general, his work examines how interactive media channels have altered the way in which individuals create, share, and make meaning of messages—specifically, he focuses on social media applications and entertainment media devices. Primary areas of research include the role of implicit morality in making meaning of entertainment content, the influence of cognitive task demand on both video game play and social media usage, and the relationship between character attachment and virtual behaviors in digital environments. He has published work in *Computers and Human Behavior*, *CyberPsychology, Behavior and Social Networking*, *Journal of Communication*, and *Media Psychology* and serves on the editorial boards of *Communication Research Reports* and *Journal of Media Psychology*.

Patrice M. Buzzanell is Professor in the Brian Lamb School of Communication at Purdue University. She has published 3 books and more than 130 articles and chapters in areas such as career, leadership, work-family, resilience, and feminist communication theory and practice. ICA Fellow (2011) and NCA Carroll C. Arnold Distinguished Lecturer (2010), she has delivered keynote addresses around the globe. She has served as President and on the Executive Boards for ICA (2006–2012), Council of Communication Associations (CCA, 2007–2012), and the Organization for the Study of Communication, Language & Gender (OSCLG, 1998–2002). Her research, teaching, mentoring, and service have earned multiple awards and honors from her professional associations, universities, and local community. She currently works with the Purdue NSF ADVANCE Diversity Catalysts and her fourth engineering team in the Engineering Projects in Community Service (EPICS) at Purdue, focusing on women's empowerment in Ghana.

Josh Compton is a Senior Lecturer in Speech in the Institute for Writing and Rhetoric at Dartmouth College. His scholarship of inoculation theory, political humor, and speech pedagogy has appeared in Human Communication Research, Journal of Applied Communication Research, Health Communication, Communication Theory, Arts and Humanities in Higher Education, and other journals. His political humor analyses have been included in several books, including Routledge's Laughing Matters (2008) and Lexington's The Daily Show and Rhetoric (2011). He was a recipient of the National Speakers Association's Outstanding Professor Award, and his teaching has been recognized by the International Communication Association and Pi Kappa Delta National Honorary. He also maintains an active public speaking schedule, presenting interactive workshops on such topics as public speaking and inoculation theory.

Katherine R. Cooper is a doctoral student in the Department of Communication at the University of Illinois, Urbana-Champaign. She studies organizational communication, and her main research interests include interorganizational collaboration and nonprofit organizations.

Edward Downs is an Assistant Professor and co-director of the Media Lab in the Department of Communication at University of Minnesota, Duluth. His research may be broadly defined under the rubric of media effects, technology, and cognition. Recent trajectories examine how affective, cognitive, and behavioral processes are influenced by video game simulation, as well as examining best practices for the integration of various classroom technologies.

Flaviu A. Hodis received his Ph.D. in Educational Psychology (Statistics and Measurement) from Southern Illinois University Carbondale in August 2008. He is currently a Senior Lecturer in the School of Educational Psychology and Pedagogy at Victoria University of Wellington, New Zealand. Flaviu's substantive research program focuses on understanding how chronic self-regulatory preferences shape people's motivation to select and pursue specific goals related to academic achievement and interpersonal communication. His methodological interests relate to advanced methods for analyzing change in multiple processes that unfold over time and interact with one another (latent growth modeling, multivariate latent change modeling, growth mixture modeling, and autoregressive latent trajectory modeling). Flaviu has co-authored a number of articles, which were published in journals such as the *Journal of Educational Psychology, Journal of Applied Communication Research, Basic Communication Course Annual, Journal of Statistical Software,* and *Applied Mathematical Sciences.*

Georgeta M. Hodis obtained her Ph.D. in Intercultural Communication from Southern Illinois University Carbondale in 2009. She is a Lecturer in the School of Communication, Journalism, and Marketing at Massey University. Georgeta's research interests center on communication instruction and cultural identity. Currently, she is investigating the role that students' strategic pursuit of value, control, and truth effectiveness underlies their willingness to communicate, communicative self-efficacy, communication apprehension, and their communication with teachers. One of the articles that Georgeta co-authored was awarded the Top Published Journal Article of 2010 by the Communication Apprehension and Competence Division of the National Communication Association (NCA). Her research has been published in the *Journal of Applied Communication Research, International Journal of Communication,* and the *Basic Communication Course Annual.*

Bobi Ivanov is an Associate Professor in the School of Journalism & Telecommunications at the University of Kentucky. His research interests concern the influence of mass media communication, message processing, and resistance to influence, particularly the uses of inoculation. His scholarship has appeared in book and journal publications such as *Communication Monographs, Communication Reports, Communication Research, Human Communication Research, Journal of Communication, The International Journal of the Image, Health Communication, Central Business Review, Communication Research Reports,* and *The International Journal of the Arts in Society.* He has received a "Distinguished Article Award" for a publication appearing in *Communication Monographs.*

James D. Ivory is an Associate Professor in the Department of Communication at Virginia Tech, where he has worked since 2005. His primary research interests deal with social and psychological dimensions of new media and communication technologies, particularly the content and effects of video games, virtual environments, and simulations. He has served as head of the Association for Education in Journalism and Mass Communication's Communication

Technology division and is currently vice chair of the International Communication Association's Game Studies interest group.

Jinseok Kim is a Ph.D. student at Graduate School of Library and Information Science at University of Illinois at Urbana-Champaign. His main research area is to find out hidden social networks of people without asking them about their relationship. For this, he looks into the formation and evolution of people's interpersonal relationships through exponential random graph (p*) modeling. He completed his M.A. in communication (2012) at University of Illinois at Urbana-Champaign and his B.A. in English Language and Literature (2001) at Yonsei University. Prior to coming to the M.A. program in 2010, he had worked as a South Korean government official for ten years in public administration and security. Also, he was an assistant secretary to the President of Korea. He had helped the President to communicate with the public through social media from 2008 to 2009.

Xigen Li is an Associate Professor in the Department of Media and Communication, City University of Hong Kong. Dr Li's research focuses on the impact of communication technology on mass communication, media use and communication behavior on the Internet, and social influence on media content. Dr. Li has been conducting research on media and Internet communication since 1995. His study of news media on the Internet published in 1998 proposed a new communication model evolved from the interactive nature of the Internet newspapers and demonstrated that Internet media are altering the traditional mass communication model from that of communication of one-to-many to communication of many-to-many. More recently, Dr. Li has been examining online communication behaviors from various theoretical perspectives. His publications have appeared in *Journalism and Mass Communication Quarterly*, *Journal of Communication*, *Journal of Broadcasting and Electronic Media*, *Journal of Computer-mediated Communication*, and *New Media and Society*.

Anthony M. Limperos is an Assistant Professor in the School of Journalism and Telecommunications and the Division of Instructional Communication at the University of Kentucky. Broadly, his research focuses on media uses and effects with a particular interest in media psychology. Specifically, he is concerned with understanding the psychological and behavioral impacts of video games and new communication technologies in health, instructional, and entertainment contexts.

Xudong Liu is an Assistant Professor in the Faculty of Humanities and Arts at Macau University of Science and Technology, where he teaches undergraduate and graduate courses in online journalism, online marketing, and new media. His primary research interests center on online psychology and behaviors. Recently Dr. Liu has been investigating the influence of social media usage on journalism quality, people's perception of media credibility, and media exposure. He has published articles in *Howard Journal of Communications* and other academic journals.

Kristen Lucas is an Assistant Professor in the Management Department at the University of Louisville, where she directs the business communication initiative for the College of Business. Her research and teaching interests focus on workplace dignity and how the achievement of dignity at work is impacted by communication and social class differences. Her research has been published in the *Journal of Business Ethics*, *Communication Monographs*, *Management Communication Quarterly*, and the *Journal of Applied Communication Research*.

Pieter Maeseele is a Research Professor at the Faculty of Political and Social Sciences of the University of Antwerp (Belgium). As a media sociologist, his research agenda broadly focuses on social and political issues relating to science, technology, and the environment in the media. His work has been published in *International Communication Gazette*, *Environmental Communication: A Journal of Nature and Culture*, *Javnost – The Public*, *Science Communication*, *Journal of Science Communication*, and other journals and edited books. He explicitly wishes to thank Professor Hans Verstraeten (Ghent University) as well as two anonymous reviewers and the editor for their very helpful and constructive comments in helping him to clarify his arguments.

Peter Monge is a Professor of Communication at the Annenberg School for Communication and Journalism and Professor of Management and Organization at the Marshall School of Business, University of Southern California. He is also the Director of the Annenberg Networks Network, a research center focused on communication network theory and research. He has published five books, the most recent of which is *Theories of Communication Networks* (with Noshir Contractor). He has published theoretical and research articles on organizational communication networks, evolutionary and ecological theory, collaborative information systems, globalization, and research methods. He is an elected Fellow and a former president of the International Communication Association (ICA, 1997–1998). He has received the ICA Steven H. Chaffee Career Productivity Award and the B. Aubrey Fisher Mentorship Award, where eight of his doctoral advisees have won dissertation awards. He is a Distinguished Scholar of the National Communication Association. From 1986 to 1993, he served as editor of *Communication Research*.

Daniel J. O'Keefe is the Owen L. Coon Professor in the Department of Communication Studies at Northwestern University. He has been a faculty member at the University of Michigan, Pennsylvania State University, and the University of Illinois at Urbana-Champaign. His research focuses on persuasion and argumentation. He has received the National Communication Association's

Charles Woolbert Research Award, its Golden Anniversary Monograph Award, its Rhetorical and Communication Theory Division Distinguished Scholar Award, and its Health Communication Division Article of the Year Award, the International Communication Association's Best Article Award and its Division 1 John E. Hunter Meta-Analysis Award, the American Forensic Association's Daniel Rohrer Memorial Research Award, the International Society for the Study of Argumentation's Distinguished Research Award, and teaching awards from Northwestern University, the University of Illinois, and the Central States Communication Association.

Katherine Ognyanova is a doctoral candidate and Annenberg Fellow at the University of Southern California, Annenberg School for Communication and Journalism. She does research with a broad focus on transformations of the media system and social implications of technology. Her doctoral thesis explores applications of network theory and methodology in the area of media studies. As a member of the Annenberg Networks Network (ANN), Katherine works on projects studying the dynamics of scientific collaboration and virtual team formation. She is also part of the Metamorphosis group, conducting research on the impact of new media on civic engagement and intergroup dialogue in local communities. In addition to her work at USC, in 2010 Katherine participated in the Oxford Internet Institute Summer Doctoral Program. In 2012, she was awarded a Fellowship with the Consortium on Media Policy Studies at the Federal Communications Commission.

Macarena Peña-y-Lillo is a doctoral student in Communication at the University of Illinois at Urbana-Champaign. She obtained her master's degree in Communication from the same school under a Fulbright fellowship in 2012. Her bachelor's degree is in Communication and Journalism from the University of Chile. Her main research interest is health promotion through organizational channels.

Andrew Pilny is a Ph.D. student in the Department of Communication at the University of Illinois Urbana-Champaign. He earned a bachelor's degree in political science in 2008 and master's degree in communication in 2010 from the same university. He grew up in Oak Lawn, Illinois, and graduated Oak Lawn Community High School in 2004. His main area of research is organizational communication with a focus on social movement organizations and inter-organizational networks. He is mostly interested in the factors that influence and are influenced by different social movement networks. He likes to use many different research methods but specializes in social network analysis. He is also interested in communication and behavior in virtual worlds.

Oliver Quiring is a full Professor at the Department of Communication of the Johannes Gutenberg-University of Mainz. He studied social sciences with a focus on communication science in Nuremberg, Germany. His doctoral dissertation (Nuremberg/Germany) deals with the impact of economic news on voting preferences. His second dissertation (in German "Habilitation," Munich/Germany) focused on the concept of interactivity. His research interests include political and economic communication as well as research into digital and interactive media.

Eric Rasmussen is an Assistant Professor in the Department of Public Relations at Texas Tech University. His research focuses on the interaction between children, parents, and media. He is especially interested in how and why parental mediation influences the ways children respond to media exposure. More specifically, he seeks to understand the combination of the ubiquity of electronic media, individual differences among children and adolescents, and the ability of both mediated and parental messages to persuade children. His research is often in the context of parental mediation's ability to alter the media's effect on children's self-esteem and aggression. His current research examines how parent-to-child persuasion impacts children's cognitive processing of media messages. His research program has been recognized by his colleagues. He was nominated by The Ohio State University School of Communication in 2012 for the prestigious presidential fellowship, and he was awarded the School's Walter B. Emery Junior Researcher of the Year Award in 2011.

Ariann Sahagun is a recently graduated Master's student in Communication from the University of Illinois at Urbana-Champaign. Her main project is piloting a social network in Costa Rica as a participatory action research project that involves members of the network in the development of the project. Her work and interests center on building nonprofit networks that support collective impact.

Michelle Shumate is an Associate Professor in the Department of Communication Studies at Northwestern University. She is the director of the Network for Nonprofit and Social Impact. Michelle investigates the dynamics of interorganizational networks designed to impact large social issues, developing and testing theories to visualize, understand, and enable effective interorganizational networks in a variety of contexts including nongovernmental organization (NGO)-corporate partnerships, development and disease NGOs, expert-NGO partnerships in sustainable development, and interorganizational networks for healthy communities. She was awarded a National Science Foundation CAREER award and a Beckman Fellowship at the Center for Advanced Study at the University of Illinois.

Robert S. Tokunaga is an Assistant Professor in the Department of Communicology at the University of Hawai'i at Mānoa. His research examines the social and psychological impact of electronic and digital technology use. He has published papers in the past on cyberbullying victimization, lateral surveillance, and the deficient self-regulation of Internet use.

Riva Tukachinsky is an Assistant Professor at the Department of Communication Studies at Chapman University. Her research interests include cognitive and affective processes underlying media effects. Specifically, she is interested in involvement with characters and narratives and mental representation of media messages as they pertain to learning, persuasion, and emotion regulation. Her research has been published in journals such as *Journal of Communication* and *Mass Communication and Society*.

Sijia Yang is a Ph.D student in the Annenberg School for Communication at University of Pennsylvania. He completed his master's in communication from the Department of Communication at University of Illinois at Urbana-Champaign. He also holds a B.A. in English literature from Renmin University of China. Sijia studies how personal influences—including both interpersonal discussions and social network attributes—affect collective opinion, attitude, and behavior in the new media environment, especially about issues pertaining to environmental protection and public health. In the past, he has written and presented papers in academic conferences on public opinion and political discussion in China's cyberspace under the government's censorship policy. He argued for a trifold framework: normative reflections bridging western democratic theories and Chinese sociopolitical philosophies, empirical designs linking normative ideals with actual online political communication processes, and methodological innovations suitable for analyzing large-size and linkage-rich data online.

Marc Ziegele is a research assistant at the Department of Communication of the Johannes Gutenberg-University of Mainz. He studied media management in Germany and currently works on his doctoral thesis on the discussion value of online news. He is fascinated by the idea that public online user discussions in the direct context of news items can modify subsequent users' perception and the effects of traditional media content. Besides analyzing structurally integrated mass communication and interpersonal communication, his research interests concern a broad spectrum of online communication including participation research, research on online privacy behavior, analyses of electronic-word-of-mouth and new business models for media companies, and theory development within interactive online environments.

Author Index

Subject Index

Page locators in *italics* indicate figures and tables.